WEBSTER'S
WINE PRICE GUIDE

1985
EDITION

WEBSTER'S WINE PRICE GUIDE

Consumer and Professional Handbook

Edited by Oz Clarke

Deputy Editor: Rosemary George MW

1985
EDITION

WEBSTER'S/MITCHELL BEAZLEY

LONDON

Webster's Wine Price Guide is an independent publication. Whilst we would like to express our gratitude for all the help, information and encouragement we have received from the wine trade, we would like to make it clear that we have received neither samples nor subsidies and that responsibility for content is editors' and publishers' alone.

By the time the guide is printed, distributed and bought, there will be instances where wines have shifted price category. This happens in any publication dealing with the inconstant factor of price. The information contained in the guide was correct to the best of our knowledge when we went to press, and the important point is that the impression of *relative price* and *relative value* is almost certainly still accurate even if a particular price has changed.

Webster's is planned as an annual publication: we welcome any suggestions you may have for the 1986 edition.

Although every care has been taken in the preparation of the guide, neither the publishers nor the editors can accept any liability for any consequences arising from the use of information contained herein.

Created and designed by
Webster's Wine Price Guide Limited,
5 Praed Street, London W2 1NJ;
in association with Mitchell Beazley
International Limited, Artists House,
14/15 Manette Street, London W1V 5LB

ISBN 0 85533 548 3

Typeset by Modern Word Processing, Hull
Printed and bound in the UK by
William Clowes Ltd, Beccles
Data processing by Meditext

Managing Editor Alexandra Boyle
Art Director Mel Petersen
Copy Editor Naomi Good
Designer Mark Richards
Research and Editorial Assistant Jean Gordon

FOREWORD

The great world of wine has room for experts of all styles and degrees. By my polling methods, though, there is one area where everyone is a perpetual student: the subject of prices.

A cliché is not necessarily true for being stale. Wine's own hoary catch-phrase would be much nearer the truth if it went '. . . but I know what I can afford'. Price, after all, is where we all get our first grip on the whole slithery subject. Even the most practised eye flickers rapidly to the right-hand column.

This is the raison d'être of *Webster's Wine Price Guide.* There are guides, guides and more guides to the châteaux of Bordeaux or the vineyards of Burgundy – and come to that to off-licences from Dover to Cape Wrath (no, not a South African bush port).

Webster's is the one that tells you how much you will have to pay, for what, to whom – and hence how you can get the most (of wine, of quality, of rarity – whatever you are looking for) for least.

It does much more. By analyzing the structure of the wine trade it shows you the inside track. It recommends values and vintages, suggests schemes for starting to collect, spells out the pros and cons of the multifarious ways in which the modern wine trade beguiles its clientèle.

These are all useful and sterling virtues. It would be hard *not* to use such a book even if it were just a dry compendium.

But *Webster's* has another vital ingredient: a sense of humour. Oz Clarke and Rosemary George have a feel for the fun of the thing which constantly lifts the guide to the level of entertainment. You will find yourself forgetting what price it was you wanted as you start to read – and can't stop.

HUGH JOHNSON JULY 1984

Contents

How to use the Price Guides

To get the most out of the lists in the following pages, please remember that *Webster's Wine Price Guide* is a price GUIDE, not a price LIST. An invaluable reference whenever you are ordering or buying wine, it is not meant to replace up-to-date merchants' lists.

What it *does* do, however, is give you a unique opportunity to compare prices; to develop a sense of what you can reasonably expect to pay for any given wine; to spot a bargain; to work out exactly what you can afford – *and to find it.*

Wines are listed by vintage (and as non-vintage). Vintages run from the most recent to the oldest you are likely to find. Within these categories wines are banded by price.

Prices are per bottle, including VAT, unless otherwise specified. Remember that price may be affected if you buy a case or more.

Stockists are listed in brackets after each entry in ascending order of price. Wines will, naturally, fall into the price band of the lowest price we know of; where there are likely to be wide variations in price we have tried to give some indications of the reasons for this – but if you find that a wine you are considering falls right outside the listed range, draw your own conclusions and act accordingly!

***Best value for money buys**
Stars denote wines that one or more of the suppliers listed consider particularly good value for money *in their class.* We have made every effort to include all the merchants' own recommendations that we received.

How the wines have been selected
Our aim, in this guide, has been to present a selection of the wines available in this country that is as comprehensive, wide-ranging, varied and interesting as possible. It reflects the known preferences and changing tastes of today's wine drinkers, the enterprise and enthusiasm of British merchants, the incredible variety that is on offer to the consumer here, and, inevitably, the tastes and opinions of the *Webster's Wine Price Guide* Editors themselves. We hope that no firm favourites have been omitted – but if yours isn't in, please write and tell us about it for next year's edition; equally, we have tried to include some rarities and less-well-known wines to encourage the adventurous.

How the lists were compiled
First, we informed the wine trade of our plans and invited merchants to send us their lists and to select for us their own 'best value for money' wines. Their response was magnificent and we have listed wines from nearly a hundred merchants' lists – ranging from specialist mail-order suppliers to supermarkets.

Then we selected wines for inclusion in our price guides along the lines indicated above. These we fed into a database (of some 15,000 entries) in order to group them, as they appear in the book, by region, type, wine, vintage and price.

Further information
If you would like to find out more about a particular merchant, consult the Directory at the back of the book; if you are looking for a local supplier consult the regional lists at the end of the Directory.

**All prices, unless otherwise stated, are* per bottle inclusive of VAT. *Where merchants only sell by the case we have divided by twelve the VAT inclusive price of a* single case.

**When clubs have both member and non-member prices (e.g. LADV) we have used the* non-member *prices.*

**When a wine is obviously widely available – e.g. a well-known brand – we have not listed all stockists, but chosen one or more to create a price-point.*

Merchant Codes

The following list of abbreviations enables you to identify the merchant(s) from whose list(s) the wines mentioned in the regional *price guides* were selected.

For merchants' full addresses and descriptions of their specialities, see the Merchant Directory at the end of the book. There is also a regional directory to help you find the merchants in your part of the country.

A&K Arriba Kettle & Co
ADN Adnams
ASHE T. F. Ashe & Nephew
AV Avery's
BAL Balls Brothers
BBR Berry Bros & Rudd
BIB Bibendum
BOW Bow Wine Vaults
BWC Berkmann Wine Vaults
BYR D. Byrne & Co
C&B Corney & Barrow
CB Cynthia Bacon
CDM Caves de la Madeleine
CHAP Chaplin & Son
COL Henry C. Collison
CPW Cape Province Wine
CUL W. H. Cullen
CV Chesterford Vintners
DAV J. T. Davies & Sons
DDIR Domaine Direct
DOL Dolamore
ECD Ebury Chatham & Dover
EHR Ehrmanns
ESV Ellis Son & Vidler
FFW Farthinghoe Fine Wine & Food
FINT Findlater Mackie Todd
GH Gerard Harris
H&B Hedges & Butler
H&D Hicks & Don
HBV High Breck Vintners
HHC Haynes Hanson & Clark
HT Henry Townsend
HUN The Hungerford Wine Co
HW House of Wilkins
IMB Imbibers Wines
J&B Justerini & Brooks
JH John Harvey & Sons
JMW J. Moreno Wines
L&S Laymont & Shaw
L&W Lay & Wheeler
LADV Les Amis du Vin
LHV Lorne House Vintners
M&S Marks & Spencer
MACK Mackie & Co
MAL Malmaison Wine Club
MART Wine Cellars (The Market)
MWS Manor Wine Shop
ODD Oddbins
OWL O. W. Loeb & Co
P&C Peatling & Cawdron
PD Peter Dominic
PG Peter Green
PIP Christopher Piper Wines
QR Quellyn Roberts
RACK Arthur Rackham's Wine Shops
REID Reid Wines
RGA Richard Granger
RGHR Roger Harris Wines
RH Richard Harvey Wines
RSV La Réserve
SAIN Sainsbury's
SF Stapylton Fletcher
SR Seymour Ramsay
STON Stonehaven Wines
STUD The Wine Studio
STWC Sunday Times Wine Club
SW Sherston Wine Co
T&W T&W Wines
TAN Tanners of Shrewsbury
TES Tesco's
THRE Threshers
UNW Unwins
VICT Victoria Wine Co
VIGN La Vigneronne
WAIT Waitrose
WGA Wine Growers Association
WHIT Whitesides
WILL Willoughby's
WNRY The Winery
WSOC The Wine Society
WW Windrush Wines
YAPP Yapp Bros
YFW Yorkshire Fine Wines

Preface

Everyone likes to get a bargain, but - even more important - no one likes to pay over the odds. Value for money is not something that comes only with low prices: what the French call *rélation prix-qualité* determines how good a deal you are getting in any price bracket. Wine is no exception. A classed growth wine at £20 can be infinitely better value *in its class* than a table wine at £2.

So this is the purpose of *Webster's Wine Price Guide*: to enable our readers, whatever their incomes, to get the best value for money within a given budget. A simple list of wine prices cannot achieve this, any more than a list of hotels or restaurants in price order will tell you exactly what you are going to get for your money. A real *guide* organises the basic price information in context and provides enough background and guidance for the reader to make his or her own assessment.

The idea for this guide first arose some years ago when I realised (and found that many friends felt the same) that whilst I felt at home buying certain kinds of wine - claret for example - and was prepared to push the boat out from time to time for wines of whose quality I was confident, I was inhibited when it came to others I did not know so well, such as burgundy. Some of the wines seemed so expensive that I was unsure, not so much whether I wanted to spend the money, which *was* a consideration, but whether I would be paying a fair price. I took the easy way out and bought the wine I knew at prices I felt able to judge. Yet I knew that I would sometimes be prepared to splash out for the occasional less familiar bottle, if only I could be sure that I was not paying over the odds. I needed a comprehensive and objective wine price guide.

Webster's aims to give people the confidence to make buying decisions at every price level, for every occasion and purpose. Confidence comes not from learning price lists by rote but from understanding what a wine is likely to cost and why. We have tried, therefore, to present the prices of this most fashionable and enjoyable of consumer goods in a way that promotes *understanding* not just *knowing*.

As the guide's Editor stresses, there is a huge range of wine available to us in the UK. But I fear that wine is yet another commodity where the more money (in total) you can set aside for buying, the better value you can command. Not many of us can buy in the sort of quantities that attract better than modest discounts, but even a small move in the direction of supposedly recherché habits like 'laying down' wines, or even simply searching out the go-ahead (including some supermarkets) or specialist merchant can quickly yield excellent and money-saving results to supplement *ad hoc* buying. It is not a matter of snobbery, nor even connoisseurship, but plain economics and pleasure, and we hope that *Webster's* will give some would-be wine fanatics the courage to come 'out of the cellar'.

If collectively as wine lovers – and our numbers rise sharply every year – we become more adventurous in our buying, the overall quality of wine sold in Britain will improve further as merchants are encouraged to sell more 'individual' wines and fewer branded wines that are sold on price alone.

A list of those people who have so generously helped us in many different ways with the preparation of *Webster's* appears below, but I would like to say a few personal words of thanks: first to James Mitchell, who gave me my first case of classed growth claret and paid my wages at Mitchell Beazley long enough for me to recycle a good deal of them in the UK wine trade; to Hugh Johnson for years of creative friendship and inspiration – not to mention his unique contribution to wine literature, most recently with the incomparable *Wine Companion*; to my step-father, Michael Parry-Crooke, for introducing me to a decent wine merchant; and, of course, to the editors of *Webster's* – Oz Clarke who has written the main text and introductions and whose book this really is – his formidable wit, palate, memory and sheer enthusiasm have made him an ideal work companion; and Rosemary George who ran the research and compiled the lists with unflappable aplomb, and whose tremendous knowledge and love of her subject have been the backbone of the guide.

ADRIAN WEBSTER

INTRODUCTION

We're fortunate in Britain. We may not have much luck with growing wine, but when it comes to buying it we have a better chance of a good bottle than any Frenchman, Spaniard, Italian or German who has vines growing on his very doorstep. And *Webster's* objective is to help everybody make the best of this good fortune.

We call ourselves a wine price guide, and we intend to interpret 'guide' in as open and friendly a way as possible. We're not scouring the country trying to pinpoint every town's fleeting and profit-strangling 'best-buy'; we're not interested in once-off 'special offers' which are sold out a week after we go to print. No, what we want to do is to give everyone the confidence to know what a given wine *should* cost; to say that just because it's cheaper doesn't mean that it's necessarily a better bargain, and to point out the areas which seem to us to be particularly good or bad value. With the tremendous range of wines available we have no need to buy bad wine. Every shop will have a better wine at the same price – or less – if we know which one to ask for. It's our job to try to make that choice easier.

France, as always, is bursting with quality, although not always in the places you might expect. We now get a higher standard of the much-maligned Beaujolais Nouveau than the French themselves, while the year-round standard of High Street Beaujolais still leaves a lot to be desired. Red burgundy is going through a very sticky patch but whites, and in particular Chablis, are booming. Across the country, *red* Bordeaux is on the up and up, while white seems quite unable to cash in on the world-wide thirst for light white styles. Southern France has taken the hint from the torrid vineyards of the New World, and is at last producing really good basic reds. Next stop, fresh, fruity whites.

Italy has taken something of a hammering recently. Her overworked famous names – Valpolicella, Chianti, Soave, Frascati deserve all they get. But there is a feast of high quality, well priced wine from places like Friuli, Trentino, and the Südtirol. If Germany can rid herself of the curse of the EEC Tafelwein stigma, the 1983 vintage has fortuitously provided loads of good wine at all price levels. Neither should Spain be considered simply as a plonk producer. She's *far* better than that.

Australia, New Zealand, the USA – have we tried even *one* of their wines? We must. They're now leading the world in the exciting developments which are pushing back the frontiers of plonk, and will soon have the oxidized, the dirty, the acid and the foul screaming for mercy in the face of their efforts.

Yes, we *are* lucky. There probably aren't enough days in the year to try them all, but here are *Webster's* resolutions for 1985.

* I will never again say 'I don't know much about wine, but I know what I like.' Instead I shall say 'I want to know more about wine, and there's only one way to do that – try something different!'
* I will *not* blindly order my usual Soave or Valpolicella in an Italian restaurant, but I will try a name I haven't heard of.
* I *will* try a sweet wine this year. I may swear I don't like sweet things, but I shall be honest with myself, and ask whether I have ever tried a *good* sweet wine. So, single

vineyard Sauternes and Barsacs, Italian Moscato Naturales, Austrian Beerenauslese or Australian Muscats, watch out here I come!

* I will, every month, order at least one bottle of something which is still too young. And I'll put it under the stairs for a year. Just to see what happens.

* If I can't pronounce a wine's name, instead of just avoiding it I'll enlist the help of someone who *can* pronounce it. And if I have a go, and make a hash of it, I'll have a good laugh – and try the wine just the same!

* I will try a southern hemisphere wine. New Zealand, Chile, South Africa, Australia . . . I'll keep on making jokes about the Australians – but that won't stop me trying their wine.

* If I'm having any celebrations this year, I'll buy my champagne *now,* and store it cool and dark. With all the fresh green wine around, it'll improve no end with the storage – and I'll have *much* happier guests.

* I shall always try a Vin de Pays instead of a brand name, anonymous 'house' red or white. The price will be about the same, and I'll be buying something positive and identifiable, with an individual's name and vineyard on the label.

* I'll give rosé one last chance. I'll get it as young as possible, from Rioja, Catalonia, northern Italy, Alsace or southern France. As I said, one last chance.

* I will *not* buy an EEC Tafelwein. Either I shall buy an honest Liebfraumilch, or I'll be brave and try an unfamiliarly named hock instead; even one with a vineyard name! Otherwise it's like sticking to baby food when you've got a full head of teeth.

* I will try an English wine. They say 1983 was our best vintage ever. How will I know if I don't try it?

* I will stop *not* drinking sherry. And I shall drink it in a large glass. If it's dry, I'll cool it down, and I may even put a lump of ice in it – who says I can't?

* And finally, I will have fun. There's no point in wine if it doesn't give me fun. If it doesn't make my eyes shine and my heart happy. At £2 or £20 a bottle, that's the only objective a true wine maker has had, since man first tripped over the grape basket and started it all fermenting. Pleasure – that's what a wine maker's aiming at when he sets his vats in motion. Pleasure – that's all we're after when we slap down the readies at the off-licence counter. And to make sure we all know where to find it, and what we should pay – *that's* why *Webster's* is here.

OZ CLARKE

ACKNOWLEDGEMENTS

We could not, of course, have produced the guide at all were it not for the enormous assistance and co-operation we have received from the wine trade throughout the world, particularly in the UK. Almost without exception every member of the UK wine trade whom we approached (sometimes for extremely sensitive information) bent over backwards to help us, often without even knowing quite what we were going to do with the information they gave us. As an independent publication we may, by the nature of things, put a nose or two out of joint by what we have said or what we have omitted, but we are confident that the attitude of the trade in the UK clearly indicates that all good suppliers consider knowledge of wine and its enjoyment as greater causes than their own immediate self interest in any particular wine.

Our thanks especially go to the following (members of the trade and others) who have generously put information and expertise at the disposal of the guide: Burton Anderson; Australian High Commission; David Bedford MW, Victoria Wine Co; Nick Belfrage MW, Wine Cellars; Joy Bell, UG Closure & Plastics Ltd; Joseph Berkmann, Berkmann Wine Cellars; Liz Berry MW, La Vigneronne; Mark Bingley MW, H. Parrot & Co; David Bird MW, Stowells of Chelsea; Neil Braithwaite, Geoffrey Roberts Associates; Julian Brind MW, Waitrose; John Burton, Wine & Spirit Association; David Carr Taylor, Carr Taylor Vineyards; Allan Cheesman, Sainsbury's; Comité Interprofessionnelle des Vins de Bourgogne; Comité Interprofessionnelle des Vins d'Alsace; Comité Interprofessionnelle des Vins de Bordeaux; Nick Clarke MW, Collison & Sons Ltd; Tim Clarke, Deinhard & Co Ltd; John Clevely MW, H. Parrot & Co; Clive Coates MW, Les Amis du Vin; Mr Cook, Hatch Mansfield & Co Ltd; David Cossart MW, Ellis Son & Vidler; Jean Pierre Couderc, Les Salins du Midi; Robin Don MW, Hicks & Don; Robert Drouhin, Joseph Drouhin; Georges Duboeuf, Georges Duboeuf; Jorge Dias, Atkinson Baldwin; John Dunkley, Riecine; Enoteca di Chianti Classico (Greve); Charles Eve MW, IDV Peter Dominic; Brooks Firestone, Firestone Vineyards Ltd; Food & Wine from France; Chris Foulkes, Mitchell Beazley; Geoffrey Frankcom, Chianto Classico Consorzio; Robin Frost, John Harvey & Son; Derek Gannaway, IEC Wine Society; Geoffrey Godbert, German Wine Information Centre; Richard Goodman, Cooks New Zealand Wine Co; Amy Henderson, Torres Wines; Don Hewitson, Cork & Bottle; Ronnie Hicks MW, Hicks & Don; Jack Hill, H. Sichel & Sons Ltd; Rich Hinkle; Anthony Hogg; Johnny Hugel, Hugel & Fils; David Hunter, H. Sichel & Sons Ltd; Andrew Hyatt; Italian Trade Centre; Gérard Jaboulet, Paul Jaboulet Ainé; Ian Jamieson MW, Deinhard & Co Ltd; Brian Jordan, Bowlish House Restaurant; Robert Joseph, What Wine; Jacquie Keay, Le Nez Rouge Wine Club; Tony Laithwaite, The Wine Club; Nick Lander, L'Escargot Restaurant; Adrian Lane, Tesco's; Max Laurie, Consultant for Wine & Spirit Association; David Lemmon, Chianti Putto Consorzio; Rob Lilley, Ehrmanns Ltd; Simon Loftus, Adnams & Co; Comte A. de Lur Saluces, Château d'Yquem; Duncan McEuen, Christie's; Malcolm McIntyre, Champagne Bureau; Jean-François Mau; Charles Metcalfe; David Molyneux-Berry MW, Sotheby's; J. Moreno Wines; Christian Moueix; Angela Muir MW, Grants of St James; Hamilton Narby, Château Guiraud; New Zealand High Commission; Andrew Nunn, Lawlers Ltd; Richard Nurick, Hawkins & Nurick; Lou Pack, Dreyfus & Ashby; Alison Pendree, Champagne Bureau; David Peppercorn MW; Alistair Peebles, Berry Bros; Protuguese Trade Centre; Katherine Powell, Chantovent UK; Freddie Price, Dolamore Ltd; Henri Quancard; Mike Rayment, Château Musar; René Renou; Geofrey Roberts; Christopher Rowe, Findlater Mackie & Todd; David Rutherford, Martini & Rossi Ltd; Mark Savage MW, Windrush Wines; Robin Scott-Martin, John Harvey & Sons; Seagrams; Carol Shave, Stonehaven Wines; Gabrielle Shaw, Corney & Barrow; Tony Stebbings, Yvon Mau UK; Alistair Stevens, Stevens Garnier Ltd; Nick Strahan, Mentzendorff & Co; Michael Symington; Arnold Tasker MW, Saccone & Speed; Helen Thompson, O. W. Loeb & Co Ltd; Renato Trestini, Alivini Co Ltd; Richard Tanner, Tanners of Shrewsbury; Peter Vinding-Diers, Château Rahoul; Vinos de Españа; Anne-Marie Vivier, Louis Eschenauer SA; M. Vuillier, Château Rieussec; Bill Warre MW, J. E. Fells; Richard Wheeler, Lay & Wheeler; Peter Whiting, Stonehaven Wines; Denis Williams MW, H. Sichel & Sons Ltd; Tony Willis, Bulgarian Vintners; Parry de Winton, Dreyfus Ashby & Co Ltd; Robin Woodhouse; Robin Yapp, Yapp Bros.

We do have one request of the wine trade. There are enormous discrepancies in the descriptions of the same wines in different merchants' lists – so much so that it has sometimes been a task of Sherlock Holmesian complexity to establish whether we were comparing like with like.

If all merchants could describe their wines with the same accuracy and detail as we found in the best compiled lists, we are sure that it would be very much in customers' interests – and it would reduce the level of our computer's (and editors') indigestion!

For those obscurities, duplications, or plain errors that, despite all our efforts, we have failed to iron out, we ask our readers' indulgence.

Planning for Pleasure

I have an article in front of me which suggests that the basic requirement for starting a cellar is 62 dozen bottles of wine. Which is 744 bottles. It's a wonderful concept, but fantasy is the more likely description for most of us. We have an average annual wine consumption of 14 bottles per head. Which means that our average British drinker would take about 53 years to get through that lot. We would have to hope that, wine being what it is, his thirst would dramatically increase, otherwise we can't see much reason for the 'statistically normal' drinker having a cellar at all; better to get the exercise trotting round to the off licence every 26.107 days.

But there is some reason behind trying to plan your cellar requirements, and one of the most important is the pleasure of the whole thing. If there's a collector lurking in the heart of most wine drinkers, part of the excitement of wine is being missed if we simply buy wine on the hoof. Every time we buy more wine than we actually need, we're giving ourselves the chance to leave it a bit, see if it improves, maybe realise it simply tails off. And we're also giving ourselves the chance to have the wine in far better condition than if it's just ripped off the shop shelf as we dash for the train home. If we're giving a dinner party, or celebrating some happy event – or, even better, anticipating one – that can make a very important difference, which could dramatically improve the chances of success for the whole shebang.

And some experiences simply have to be laid down for. Although there are a few merchants who make a speciality of offering mature wines, they are all well aware of their value, and most unlikely to sell them for less. Most merchants will be able to offer you an eight- or nine-year old claret, but a major château won't be anything like its best after eight or nine years. Most merchants can offer you three-year old burgundy or Rhône. But when the wine's properly made, three years may hardly be enough to soften the acids and tannins. And though merchants will offer you two-year old white Burgundy, the flavours which *make* the expense worthwhile hardly ever show themselves before five or six years. You may like your champagne with the greenness gone off it, but a merchant simply rolls over his stock as it becomes available. There's lots of good champagne around, but very little of it is halfway mature. And you may like to finish off a meal with the rich, rare, red flavours of vintage port. With high interest rates and declining consumption, it's years since most merchants could offer mature vintage port, let alone prepare it properly. Only the most specialised merchants can hope to help out with a mature vintage requirement. Mature Sauternes then? Again, almost unavailable – but at least you can drink it young.

For all these – you gotta plan – or you gotta substitute. For your mature red wines you *can* buy fully-aged Rioja, Dão or Bairrada straight off the shelf. For your white Burgundy experience, you *can* buy Australian or American Chardonnay with no forethought. For your mature fizz, the more 'sunny' wines of Spain's cava, or Australian and Californian fizz will get you close-ish. For your vintage port you could take the thin-blooded way out and buy 'late bottled' or you could branch out to the rich, exciting, but sedimentless pastures of Australian liqueur muscats, old brown sherries, Malagas or madeiras. Otherwise you must look at what you want your wine drinking and entertaining to achieve and plan accordingly. And by beginning to plan now you'll be saving money by the end of the year, and giving yourself and your friends priceless pleasure by the end of the decade.

Look at the amount of money you spend on wine now. Look at your probable consumption each week. Look at how many dinner parties you normally give each year. Look at how you normally cater for Christmas, New Year, Easter, birthdays, anniversaries. Look at the number of times that you've muttered 'Damn, run out', at a crucial or unexpected social moment. Think of those dinner parties when you made do with Beaujolais when you could have afforded claret. When the wine was a little edgey or tough – or just plain dull, because it was unsettled and unready. And did that anniversary celebration turn sour because of the sour youthfulness of the fizz? If you're answering yes to these questions, it's time to do a little planning.

Firstly – decide for yourself what kind of wine *you* like best. If it's claret or vintage port, you should get going on a long-term plan right away. You should start to buy claret 'en primeur', that is, the year following the vintage – and port as young as possible. And you should do this systematically every year. Buy claret as good as you can afford, since it will take longer to mature, but fill in with the lighter lesser growths. Over a few years you'll begin to build up a pattern which will allow you, literally, the claret or port for every occasion. And, as a cheaper mature claret fill-in, five-year old Australian or American Cabernet Sauvignon, six-year old Rioja Reserva, three-year old Alto Adige or Friuli Cabernet, or Carmignano. As port fill-ins crusted ports are very good, and even a proper ruby, laid down for a year, will make a decent drink. Red burgundy is now very difficult to buy, but good examples still benefit from a few years and good vintages need about six years maturity. Buy grower burgundy, and only from a burgundy specialist. Burgundy is almost impossible to duplicate. Old Rioja sometimes gets near it. Otherwise Alto Adige Pinot Noir, and some Californian and New Zealand Pinots are good and soon ready. Beaujolais Crus just might do – they don't taste like Burgundy, but can feel like it. Rhône wine is easier to buy, and the big wines may need ten years. Côte Rôtie and Hermitage should be bought and treated like claret. As fill-ins, Châteauneuf-du-Pape from a good grower is fine wine and underpriced, and the village wines of Vacqueyras and Cairanne as well as Lirac, Saint Joseph and Crozes Hermitage will do while you wait for the big ones.

White burgundy not only has good substitutes, but sometimes these wines – Australian, New Zealand and New York State Chardonnays – can match Côte d'Or flavours at only two years old. North Italian and Pacific Northwest and Southern French can match the Mâconnais. Do buy a case of real white burgundy from a single vineyard, and leave it for a while; those other Chardonnays will painlessly fill the gaps. And champagne? Don't buy more expensive vintage champagne too young. Buy good quality non-vintage. Six to nine months will dramatically improve most of them. There *is* no substitute, but the champagne method is making fine wine all over the world. You can try them all out, while you start planning your next ten years' drinking requirements.

THE IDEAL CELLAR

It was Allan Cheesman, the Wine Director of Sainsbury's, who brought the exercise down to earth. 'The major difficulty', he said, 'is the fact that our prices are quite keen, even for fine wine, and you can end up with a lot of wine for £1,000.' He then proceeded to prove his point admirably, producing a total of 17 cases of wine, ranging from Vin de Pays to Grand Cru white burgundy. That's 204 bottles. Yes,it does seem an awful lot of wine, but while we're panicking about where on earth to put it all - and, if we start at Sainsbury, how we're going to get it into the car with the groceries - isn't it a quietly exciting prospect? Surely it arouses the 'collector' latent in so many of us. As soon as we start to talk in terms of 'laying down' wine, or 'buying for investment', we start thinking in terms of 'owning', and the pleasure of ownership and the drawn-out anticipation involved in wine collecting is very much part of the thrill.

Wine collecting is unique, because all your anticipation and pride in a bottle is directed towards that moment when you pull the cork and pour out the wine. This doesn't make it a less exciting hobby; in many ways it becomes more exciting. Every time you take a bottle out of the rack, read the label yet again, hold it to the light to see how the colour is developing, and gently return it to its cubbyhole to rest for just a little longer, you're building up to the final pleasure. The fact that each bottle has a finite life gives an intensity to the pleasure of collecting it, because the pleasure has three clearly defined phases.

First comes the purchase and anticipation immediately engendered by the knowledge of possession. Next the decision to drink it; the preparation, the occasion, the friends you share it with and, of course, the flavour of the wine - as good as, better, or maybe worse, than you expected. And then the memory of the wine, the chat and discussion, the store of experience it adds to, and the smile that comes to your lips as you stumble across the browning label you soaked off and left in a drawer. Ah yes, the friends, the food, maybe the jokes and laughter of an evening long gone are still held in the flowing script on the label.

People who deride the power of wine to move and warm the thoughts have no romance in their souls. To get the best out of wine collecting, give in to the romantic urge just a little, loosen your collar and tie, and forget the financial burdens or benefits in the face of the timeless pleasure your wines will always give you.

Indeed we reckon that our experts are all romantics at heart. None of them was keen on the idea of investing in wine purely for monetary gain. We asked them to note in their selections whether some of the wines might later be sold to finance another purchase. We got several well-deserved fleas in our ear, because, although there is no doubt that good wine can increase enormously in value, and as such can become a considerable item to trade or barter - and although no-one minds the barter or trade-in of occasional, inevitable overstocks - few merchants are happy to view wine in such a cold-blooded way.

Finc wine is a work of art, made by men of passion and commitment to be drunk, not to be shuffled round the balance sheets like a tanker full of crude oil. Most private customers who buy with the intention of re-selling eventually ask the merchant concerned to re-purchase it from them, which is almost as though the private customer was acting as a bank for the merchant! What they should do (unless they have a non-VATable swap in mind) is to contact Christie's or Sotheby's direct, but although we aren't quite so determinedly against investment as David Bedford of Victoria Wine ('I am very, very anti wines being used as stocks and shares and will have nothing to do with it.') yet we do agree the purpose in wine 'investment' should be to have the chance of drinking an expensive wine at a later date which was bought for a much lower price earlier on.

Alastair Peebles of Berry Brothers probably has more experience of wine 'investment' than most, and is equipped to help customers to roll over their stocks. He states categorically that 'Pure investment involves buying vintage claret or vintage port from top châteaux and shippers respectively. The vintage itself must be highly regarded. The investment should be viewed strictly over the long term, five years or more. Laying down for drinking, on the other hand, involves choosing wine which will develop well over however long is required. Lesser châteaux in Bordeaux and most wines from Burgundy, Rhône and the Loire fall into the second category. Rarely, however, will they prove to be a sound investment in terms of *money*.' Exactly. Once you've got your hands on some wine, paid for it, got back on to speaking terms with the bank manager, it somehow seems a bit clinical to sell it to finance the purchase of a lawn mower or a sun roof for the Ford Fiesta.

Our experts have chosen a fascinating array of wines, and their cellars are wonderfully idiosyncratic. Tony Laithwaite of The Sunday Times Wine Club is certainly one of the few people who would lay down Bulgarian wine! But that's exactly what we like to see. Wine *is* about personal prejudice. It's about *your* taste buds, *your* idea of a good time, *your* idea of a perfect partnership with food. If one of our experts had come up with a cellar entirely stocked with Beaujolais Nouveau and Vinho Verde, and said that's what he liked, we'd have said 'Publish and be damned!' with a broad grin.

In fact, all the cellars are good, balanced reflections of the chief interests of the merchants involved. They are understandably biased towards red wine, since – as Messrs Hicks and Don specifically point out in their introduction – much white wine can be bought on the hoof and doesn't need laying down, and they are biased towards the classics. We applaud Tony Laithwaite's determination to seek out the less well-known wines, as do, in their different ways, Victoria Wine and Les Amis du Vin.

But we would voice some general concerns: why so little from Spain or Italy? has no one thought of Chile? The passing references to South Africa, New Zealand and Australia are welcome, but shouldn't there be more? having said that, the selections show the marvellous range of wines in the UK marketplace. No country in the world is luckier than we are, both in the variety of wines available, and in the quality of the wine merchants choosing, shipping, and selling them to us.

These "ideal cellars" are planned as an annual Webster's *event. Next year we will be looking again at this year's selections to see how their prices moved and their quality held up. Our current experts and others will select new cellars for 1986.*

Les Amis du Vin *Clive Coates MW*

Assuming that most people have finite amounts of money and space, it is my belief that one should concentrate all one's resources into red wine. Although something like a fine Puligny will improve in bottle and appreciate in value, even these sort of wines can be bought off the peg without much difficulty. Red wines, many of them needing ten years to mature, are a different matter. Hence I have concentrated exclusively on red wines.

Believing that most people are fairly traditional, particularly when it comes to buying 12 bottles, I have initially concentrated on Bordeaux and Burgundy, in the ratio of about 2 to 1, with later additions from the Rhône, and Bandol, Cahors and Chinon, les Amis specialities.

On the assumption that our customer does not, at present, have a cellar full of wines I have taken wines which, for the most part, are for drinking during the period 1985–90 rather than post-1990. I have therefore concentrated on relatively recent vintages, leaving the 83s until next year.

Prices are based on members' prices (i.e. 5% or so off full retail). Quantity discounts are not taken into account, but would apply.

£100 Cellar

Château Lariveau, Côtes Canon Fronsac, 1982. *Voluptuous, rich, fruity wine from the best*

vintage for many years. Drink 1986–1992.
12 for £37.28

Savigny-les-Beaune, cuvée Maillard, 1982. *Elegant, fragrant wine with all the fruit of the Pinot Noir grape, from a small but well-respected grower. Drink 1985–1990.* 12 for £00.00

£500 Cellar

The above two wines, plus:

Le Sarget de Gruaud Larose, St-Julien 1981. *The second wine of Château Gruaud Larose, a full, long-lasting wine from a very good vintage. Drink 1986–1994.* 12 for £68.96

Château Caronne Ste Gemme St-Laurent, 1979. *An excellent Cru Bourgeois Supérieur big, firm, rich. Drink from 1985–1992.* 12 for £52.85

Château Feytit Clinet, Pomerol 1978. *A small property with a high reputation. A found, fleshy, full, ripe, wine with plenty of style. Drink 1985–1995.* 12 for £88.40

Gevrey Chambertin, 1981 George Lignier. *Very fine wine from one of the best domaines. Full, oaky and rich, long on the palate. Drink 1985–1992.* 12 for £96.45

Gigondas, Domaine de Pradas, 1982. *A splendid wine from the best village in the Rhône outside Châteauneuf. Full but round, bags of extract and depth. A lot of class. Drink 1985–1990.*
12 for £45.60

£1,000 Cellar

The above seven wines plus:

Château de Marbuzet, St-Estèphe 1978. *The second wine Cos D'Estournel. Depth and finesse, from an excellent vintage. Drink 1986–1994.*
12 for £95.00

Château Trois Moulins, St-Emilion 1978. *One of the best Grand Cru Classś. Full, meaty, complex and full of fruit. Drink 1985–1993.*
12 for £104.40

Nuits St-Georges, 1981 Dupasquier. *Excellent wine from a small domaine. Round beautifully balanced, on the delicate side. Drink 1985–1990.*
12 for £89.10

Châteauneuf-du-Pape, Château de Beaucastel, 1979. *Probably the best estate in Châteauneuf, and therefore a very fine wine. Just about ready, great complexity and concentration of flavour: quite marvellous. Drink 1985–1993.* 12 for £71.02

Chinon, la Chapellerie, 1982 M. Olek. *Quite extraordinary: very full (but not hard) rich, plummy almost chocolaty in flavour. Marvellous vintage. Drink 1986–1994.* 12 for £47.85

Bandol, Domaine de la Bastide Blanche, 1979 M. Bronzo. *Using an unusually high (70 per cent). proportion of the Mourvedre grape, M. Bronzo, one of the best growers in Bandol makes a wine which, though a bit hard at the outset, is very complex, warm and richly fruity after half a dozen years or so. Drink 1986–1996.* 12 for £48.11

Cahors, Domaine de Meriguet, 1981. *An excellent year. This is solid, meaty and ripe but still needs a year or two to show is best. Drink 1986–1994.* 12 for £34.62

Berry Bros & Rudd *A.R.T. Peebles.*

Laying down wine, along with do-it-yourself and hang gliding, must rank amongst the world's most rewarding pastimes. Below are three different cellars, assembled subjectively, with arbitrary sums of money.

Pure investment involves buying vintage claret or vintage port form top châteaux and shippers respectively. The vintage itself must be highly regarded. This investment should be viewed strictly over the long term, five years or more. Laying down for drinking involves choosing wines which will develop well over however long is required. Lesser châteaux in Bordeaux, and most wines from Burgundy, Rhône and the Loire, fall into the second category, and will seldom prove to be a sound financial investment. The three cellars below are a mixture of these two constituents, investment and drinking.

Once one has embarked on one's cellar, it is well worth considering just adding a few bottles each year to build it up into something worthwhile, a 'library' for the future.

£100 Cellar

*In my view £100 is too small an amount to make a broad impact. I have therefore concentrated mainly on one area and I have not included burgundy because of the expense. I have used a three bottle minimum because (a) it is better for dinner parties and (b) where one is drinking it on ones own, it always seems a shame when you have had one nice bottle that you cannot repeat the experience. The Symbol * indicates a wine that could be used as an investment and resold.*

Ch. Houissant, St-Estèphe 1978. *Good quality Cru Bourgeois for drinking from 1985 on.*
3 for £17.25

Ch. Fombrauge, St-Emilion 1979. *Well made wine from a property that has continued to improve over the last few years. Drink from 1985.*
3 for £17.25

*Ch. Haut-Bages Libéral, Pauillac, Fifth Growth 1981. *Full bodied. Drinking from 1988.* 3 for £17.85

*Ch. Labégorce-Zédé, Margaux 1982. *A fine Margaux for drinking from 1992.* 3 for £15.00

Ch. Doisy-Védrines, Barsac 1979. *Delicious with the strawberries.* 3 half-bottles for £12.00

Côte Rôtie 1978. *One of the finest Rhône wines available. This fine vintage will start to be ready in 1985.* 3 for £21.00

£500 Cellar

*Fonseca 1970. *A very good vintage and shipper. Drinking from 1985.* 3 for £38.85

*Graham 1977. *the best vintage of the decade. Drinking from 1994.* 3 for £36.45

Ch. Peyrelongue, St-Emilion 1975. *Good Cru Bourgeois for drinking now and over the next three or four years.* 6 for £27.90

*Ch. Batailley, Pauillac, Fifth Growth 1975. *Top quality château from a very fine vintage. Drinking from 1985.* 6 for £72.00

Ch. Roquegrave, Médoc 1978. *Well made Cru Bourgeois of consistent quality. Drinking from 1986.* 6 for £24.90

*Ch. Kirwan, Margaux, Third Growth 1978. *Fine wine from a very reputable château. Drinking from 1988.* 6 for £49.80

*Ch. Malartic-Lagravière, Graves 1981. *Robust, lighter weight claret. Small production. Drinking from 1988.* 6 for £36.00

Ch. de Malle, Sauternes, Deuxième Cru Classé 1979. *Very good dessert wine. Will improve over the next few years.* 3 for £17.85

Beaune, Clos du Roi 1978. *Fine burgundy from a great vintage. Drinking from 1985.* 6 for £57.90

Gevrey-Chambertin 1976. *Amongst the heaviest wines of Burgundy. Another successful year for drinking now.* 6 for £54.00

Meursault Charmes, Prosper Maufoux 1981. *Top quality white burgundy that will reach its peak in 1985.* 6 for £69.60

£1,000 Cellar

*Warre 1977. *The best vintage of the decade. Drinking from 1994.* 6 for £72.90

*Dow 1970. *A very good vintage and shipper. Drinking from 1985.* 3 for £38.85

*Quinta do Noval 1966. *A delicious, fully mature vintage port.* 3 for £54.00

Ch. Gazin, Pomerol 1970. *A top quality Pomerol for drinking now.* 2 magnums for £45.00

Ch. Trottevieille, St-Emilion 1971. *Small property in a successful year. Drinking now.* 3 for £36.00

*Ch. Langoa-Barton, St-Julien, Third Growth 1975. *A fine château in a very successful year. Drinking from 1985.* 3 for £42.00

*Ch. Cos d'Estournel, St-Estèphe 1978. *Amongst the best châteaux in Bordeaux today. Drinking from 1990.* 6 for £87.00

*Ch. d'Angludet, Margaux Cru Bourgeois Supérieur Exceptionnel 1979. *A property producing wines well above its station. Drinking from 1988.* 6 for £32.40

*Ch. Cantemerle, Haut-Médoc, Fifth Growth 1981. *Greatly improved property. Drinking from 1990.* 6 for £40.50

*Ch. Pichon Longueville Baron, Pauillac, Second Growth 1982. *Top château in a very successful year. Drinking from 1994.* 6 for £60.00

Ch. Coutet, Barsac, Premier Cru Classé 1975. *One of the two great properties of Barsac. For drinking now.* 3 for £33.00

Vosne-Romanée 1978. *Long lasting burgundy. Drinking from 1985.* 6 for £64.20

Le Corton 1978. *Fine, full-bodied wine for drinking from 1985 on.* 6 for £74.20

Nuits St-Georges, Clos Moillard des Grands Vignes 1976. *Mature burgundy for drinking over the next year or two.* 3 for £39.00

Chassagne-Montrachet, Les Perrières, Prosper Maufoux 1981. *Amongst the best white wines in the world today. Can be drunk now but will improve.* 6 for £76.50

Chablis, Vaudésir, Grand Cru, J. Moreau 1981. *From the best vineyards of the area. Can be drunk now but will improve.* 6 for £46.80

Côte Rôtie 1978. *One of the finest Rhône wines available. This fine vintage will start to be ready for drinking in 1985.* 6 for £42.00

Pouilly Fumé de Ladoucette, Château du

Nozet 1983. *One of the best Blanc Fumés available which improves with two to three years ageing.* 6 for £46.80

Berry Bros. United Kingdom Cuvée Champagne, Shipped by Binet Fils & Cie., Reims. *Impossible to leave out of any larger cellar. For drinking now.* 6 for £54.00

Peter Dominic *Charles Eve MW*
I have assumed for all three selections that I am starting a cellar from scratch. Thus some of the wines that I have chosen will be ready (depending on one's taste) very soon. However I have been careful to find wines which will develop well, if left.

The lists very much reflect my tastes and I have naturally selected the best value for money that suit my palate and perhaps my way of life, or at least the one I strive for! I find claret, white burgundy, Rhône and sweet Bordeaux the most satisfying of wines. Moselle and Rhine wines, port and red burgundy have a place but not so important in my cellars.

£100 Cellar
Rather than have a lot of different bottles, I would like to have fewer wines, and more of each.

Château Patache d'Aux CB 1982 Cru Bourgeois, Médoc. *Deep colour, firm fruit and a solid structure – some one will have to split the case with me. Drinking in 1990.* 6 for £24.00

Chablis, 1er Cru la Fourchaume 1982, Bouchard Père et Fils. *Silky and full of promise, this needs time to develop. I will enjoy this in 1986.* 6 for £29.70

Châteauneuf-du-Pape, Domaine de Cabrières 1980. *A very traditional wine from a well sited property, and that needs time. Put down until 1985.* 3 for £15.90

Château Musar 1977, Lebanon. *I am a great admirer of the skill, wine and courage of Gaston Hochar. Excellent drinking at any tme over the next decade.* 3 for £14.07

Château Giscours 1979, 3ème Cru, Margaux. *A very great wine which the Château believes is its best ever. It will keep for another 10 years.* 3 for £23.25

£500 Cellar
I have aimed at having a few whole cases to keep for sale or because I think the wines are particularly good and will last. Some repetition of wines from the £100 cellar.

Château Chasse Spleen, 1983 Cru Exceptionnel, Moulis. *An excellent example of this vintage which will be a very important part of a cellar.* 12 for £75.00 (est)

Château Duhart-Milon-Rothschild 1982 4ème Cru Pauillac. *An excellent 1982, that will reward keeping for eight to ten years.* 12 for £88.00

Château Giscours 1979. *See comment above.* 12 for £93.00

Meursault Charmes 1982 French bottled Bouchard Père et Fils. *This has the weight and concentration to lay down and develop the exquisite Chardonnay fruit over the next six to eight years.* 12 for £75.00

Château Forcas Dupré, 1978, Cru Bourgeois Supérieur Médoc. *A good solid wine that has a character that I enjoy, but must await until 1988.* 6 for £29.70

Brunello di Montalcino 1978, Altesino. *Although drinkable now, I sense it has a good future. I look forward to a bottle every other year to see how long it will last.* 6 for £40.74

Zeltinger Sonnenuhr Riesling Auslese 1982, Fruhmesse Stiftung. *Though 1982 was not a good year, I await the 1983s and need some Ausleses to keep a balance of stock.* 3 for £18.90

Château Filhot 1975, Sauternes. *Delicious already, but I do like my sweet (very) old.* 3 for £25.05

Delaforce 1977 Vintage Port. *A great vintage which should be in any good cellar. A few bottles are sufficient, and not approachable until 1992.* 6 for £60.00

Châteaneuf-du-Pape, Domaine de Cabrières 1980. *See comment above.* 6 for £31.80

£1,000 Cellar
Château Pichon Longueville Lalande 1983 2ème Cru Pauillac. *One of the best 1983s tasted by our buyers.* 12 for £130.00 (est)

Château Giscours 1982, 3ème Cru Margaux. *Enormous wine with great potential. To put away until 1992.* 12 for £122.00

Château Canon 1981 Premier Grand Cru Classé, St-Emilion. *Delicious, attractive and well balanced. I will consider this in 1989.* 12 for £95.00

Les Echezeaux 1979, Bouchard Père et Fils. *A great wine, with depth and length. Enjoyable from 1986.* 12 for £165.60

Corton Charlemagne 1982, Bouchard Père et Fils. *Needs a few years to show its individual, powerful character.* 12 for £171.60

Delaforce 1977 Vintage Port. *See comment above.* 12 for £120.00

Kreuznacher Hofgarten Wurzer Spätlese 1981, Estate bottled, von Plettenberg. 12 for £49.08

Châteauneuf-du-Pape, Domaine de Cabrières 1980. *See above.* 12 for £63.60

Château Suduiraut 1979, Sauternes. *Expensive but an excellent vintage of this delicate and superb sweet wine. Keep for five years.* 6 for £72.00

Gewürztraminer Réserve Personnelle 1979 Hugel. *A tremendous vintage giving a wine of concentration and vigour. Ideal to linger over on a summer evening.* 12 for £68.28

Findlater Mackie Todd *Christopher Rowe*
Recent indulgence in post-prandial reverie placed me in the delightful situation of being instructed by a geneous uncle to acquire, at his expense, a cellar for £100. I was more than overjoyed, however, when a further schooner of vintage port increased the sum available to £500 and by the time the decanter contents had gone the way of all good wine a £1,000 cellar had been discussed!

My uncle is of a somewhat unpredictable disposition and, being acutely aware that sober reflection might curtail my purchasing ability, I decided to play it safe and draw up separate plans for each of the possible levels of expenditure. Obviously my selections are based on the stocks I know best and they may be somewhat traditional – but so is my uncle! When I come to replenish I will be more adventurous and look further to the future.

£100 Cellar
Findlater's Dry Fly Sherry Amontillado. *Useful for a casual visitor. Medium appeals to a wide audience.* 2 for £6.64

La Luna Manzanilla. *Light and dry, this sherry makes one of the best aperitifs when gently chilled.* 1 for £3.23

Findlater's Vintage Character Port. *An inducement to post-prandial reveries. A fine old ruby with no sediment.* 1 for £5.00

Anjou Rosé. *Enjoyable with most dishes and just the wine for picnics.* 6 for £12.48

Côtes du Rhône Blanc 1983 bottled by J. Moreau. *Quaffable dryish white.* 6 for £16.02

Bereich Niersteiner 1983 Dr. Itschner. *A medium hock, attractive as an aperitif or with fish.* 6 for £14.46

Ch. Roubaud Rouge 1983. VDQS from Costières du Gard. *Reasonably full-bodied wine which can accompany most red meat.* 6 for £14.82

Ch. Combes des Dames 1981 AC Bordeaux. *Ready to drink but will keep well for three years.* 6 for £20.16

Duc de Marne NV Champagne. *Fairly dry. Shipped by Findlater's since 1876. Just in case my uncle decides to give me the £500 cellar as well.* 1 for £7.90

£500 Cellar
Findlater's Dry Fly Amontillado Sherry. *See above.* 6 for £19.92

Findlater's Dry Sercial Madeira. *An alternative to sherry and as a partner to soups.* 3 for £15.48

La Luna Manzanilla. *See above.* 6 for £19.38

Taylor's LB Vintage Port 1978. *For serving after lunch or dinner. No sediment.* 3 for £19.62

Findlater's Bual Madeira. *An alternative to port.* 3 for £15.48

Findlater's Anjou Rosé. *See above.* 6 for £12.48

Rüdesheimer Rosengarten 1982, Dr. Itschner. *Good medium hock from Nahe Valley – Splendid for general entertaining of a more formal nature.* 12 for £34.20

Muscadet de Sèvre et Maine 1983, Domaine des Pierres Noires 'sur lie'. *Lovely fresh Muscadet for first course fish dishes.* 9 for £28.71

Mâcon Lugny les Charmes 1982. *To accompany main course fish and white meat dishes.* 12 for £46.20

Meursault les Tillets 1980 FB. *A fine white burgundy for special occasions.* 6 for £47.34

Ch. Roubaud Rouge 1983. VDQS from Costières du Gard. *See above.* 12 for £29.64

Beaujolais Villages 1983, Ch. des Vergers. *Showing delightful, ripe fruity and lively Gamay.* 9 for £32.13

Ch. Roc-Saint-Bernard 1978, Fronsac. *Drinks very well with roast lamb.* 12 for £49.56

Ch. de Beaucastel 1980. *A fine Châteauneuf. Marvellous with the heavier red meat dishes.* 6 for £38.22

Ch. Louvières 1978, Graves. *A château bottled claret for special occasions. Can be kept for some years.* 6 for £43.62

Duc de Marne NV Champagne. *For celebrations and special parties.* 6 for £47.40

£1,000 Cellar

Dry Fly Amontillado. 12 for £39.84

Findlater's Dry Sercial Madeira. 6 for £30.96

La Luna Manzanilla. 12 for £38.76

Taylor's LB Vintage Port 1978. 6 for £39.24

Fonseca Vintage Port 1970. *For special occasions.* 6 for £90.30

Findlater's Bual Madeira. 6 for £30.96

Ch. Filhot 1976 Sauternes. *To serve with strawberries.* 3 for £24.30

Niersteiner Gutes Domthal 1983, Dr. Itschner. *For general entertaining.* 12 for £30.48

Rüdesheimer Rosengarten 1982, Nahe, Dr. Itschner. *For aperitifs and slightly more formal entertaining.* 12 for £34.20

Ch. Thieuley 1983. *Unusual and delightful Bordeaux Clairet – dryish rosé. Serve lightly chilled.* 12 for £34.80

Côtes du Marmandais Blanc VDQS. *Quaffable and elegant white for everyday drinking.* 12 for £30.60

Côtes du Rhône Blanc. *Very useful for a not too expensive supper party.* 12 for £32.04

Pouilly Blanc Fumé 1981, Les Champs de la Croix. *Excellent dry white Loire for more formal occasions.* 12 for £61.32

Meursault les Tillets 1979. *A white burgundy with which to spoil oneself – a real treat.* 12 for £102.84

Côtes de Ventoux 1983, Domaine de Troussel. *Generous red wine from southern Rhône.* 12 for £32.40

Faustino V Reserva 1978 Rioja. *Marvellous value with rich but elegant flavour and oaky overtones.* 12 for £34.68

Ch. de la Rivière 1979, Fronsac. *Most attractive style and will keep for some years yet.* 12 for £59.40

Ch. Nenin 1978, Pomerol. *For special entertaining.* 12 for £139.92

Duc de Marne NV Champagne. *See above.* 6 for £47.40

Krug Grande Cuvée. *A fine champagne with which to toast uncle's generosity.* 3 for £66.21

Hicks & Don *Ronnie Hicks MW & Robin Don MW*

Few people are able to plan their ideal cellar without some financial constraints. Once these are applied, the selection becomes a matter of competing priorities.

In the £100 cellar we have gone for variety in small quantities at reasonable prices. Except where sherry and port are concerned, Hicks & Don normally supply by the case, so find two friends to share your order, which is based on four-bottle units.

The £500 cellar allows us to recommend a few cases for laying down, while the £1,000 cellar brings us to the point where we can give our usual advice that most white and inexpensive red wines should be bought from hand to mouth. Laying down is best concentrated on claret, burgundy, Rhône wines, and top quality Rhine and Moselle of outstanding vintages only.

£100 Cellar

Popina Bianco. *A good sound white wine.* 4 litres for £10.23

Blanc de Blancs, Laforet. *Just the kind of crisp dry white wine they drink in Brittany with anything that comes out of the sea.* 4 for £10.72

Bereich Bernkastel 1983. *Gloriously grapey fresh medium dry Moselle.* 4 for £9.80

Popina Rosso. *Well balanced, fruity and of medium body.* 4 litres for £10.23

Hicks & Don Vin de Table Rouge No. 2. *A good honest red wine with 12° of alcohol and a touch of class.* 4 for £9.89

Costières du Gard, Domaine de St-Benezet 1982. *Fairly light yet very fruity, for drinking 1984/85.* 4 for £9.44

Château l'Hermitage Bordeaux 1981. *Very good light claret for drinking over next three years.* 4 for £12.68

Private Cuvée, Méthode Champenoise, Brut.

Sparkling Cava from the Penedès, pleasantly dry and not too acid. Ideal for parties. 4 for £15.72

Manzanilla de Sanlucar. *Pale sherry, dry and delicious with a fresh and fragrant nose and the soft salty tang of a true manzanilla.* 1 for £3.26

Amontillado de Sanlucar. *Superbly smooth medium-dry.* 1 for £3.26

Shooting Port. *Full bodied ruby. Drink with the Stilton.* 1 for £4.73

After Dinner Madeira. *Intriguingly rich, tempered by dryness on the finish. A really fine dessert madeira.* 1 for £5.16

£500 Cellar
The same selection as for the £100 cellar but 3 bottles each of the amontillado, port and madeira, and 12 bottles each of the rest, making a total expenditure of £312.36. Plus the following wines for laying down (estimated duty paid delivered price).

Coteaux du Tricastin 'Domaine du Vieux Micocoulier' 1981 Delaunay. *For drinking between 1985 and 1988.* 12 for £33.50

Lirac 1983 Sabon. *For drinking between 1986 and 1990.* 12 for £39.00

Château la Falotte, Côtes de Bourg 1981. 12 for £34.04

Château Haut-Blaignan, Médoc 1982. 12 for £36.66

A 1983 Claret (to be chosen). 12 for £36.00

£1,000 Cellar
The selection so far, plus £25 to up-grade port to crusting/vintage quality. Plus one case each of the following better quality wines for laying down.

Wehlener Sonnenuhr Riesling Auslese 1983. *Deserves to be kept for 3–4 years to develop full powers.* 12 for £48.30

Johannisberger Ernterbringer Riesling Spätlese 1983. *By 1988 this wine should be showing its paces.* 12 for £45.08

Gigondas or Vacqueyras 1983. *Probably a keeper, say 1989–1995.* 12 for £48.30

Givry Les Celliers aux Moines 1982. *Drink 1987–1991.* 12 for £53.76

Côte Rôtie 1982. *Try in 1989. Will keep for six or more years thereafter.* 12 for £79.91

Château Grand-Pey-Lescours, St-Emilion 1982. *At its best 1990–1998.* 12 for £52.84

Château Beychevelle, St-Julien 1982. *Memorable bottle in time for the turn of the century! Will keep for many years.* 12 for £142.60

Lay & Wheeler *Richard Wheeler*
In making our selection we have chosen wines that we believe represent quality, individuality and value for money and which include a variety of exciting styles.

The wines we have recommended all come from the most highly reputed growers; some small and little known, others, of course, now very famous but who in our opinion all produce classical, well-made wines which show the true distinctive and traditional characteristics of their particular region.

Most of these growers have been personally known by us for many years and we do regard the close relationship that we have with them as a very important part of our work. It plays an important contribution in ensuring that we can purchase the finest wines from the world's most serious and dedicated vignerons.

£100 Cellar
1982 Lacoste Borie, Pauillac. *The second wine of Grand Puy Lacoste. Good structure with well-balanced fruit and acidity.* 4 for £20.68

1982 Crozes Hermitage, de Vallouit. *Delicious, rich and spicey from the better, steep slopes.* 4 for £13.12

1983 Château Montalivet Graves, Pierre Coste. *Beautifully made, fully flavoured.* 4 for £13.28

1983 Schloss Vollrads, Kabinett, Blue Capsule. *Light, delicate, delightful Riesling. Extremely elegant – medium dry.* 4 for £19.08

1982 Mâcon Villages Blanc, Les Donzelles, Cave Co-operative de Vire. *Delightfully fresh and full of character.* 4 for £15.64

1983 Côte de Brouilly, Bocuse. *Lively, grapey and distinctive. A really delicious wine, particularly attractive at cellar temperature.* 4 for £14.64

£500 Cellar
1982 Château Ducluzeau, Listrac. *Owned by Madame Borie, wife of the proprietor of Ducru Beaucaillou. Depth, richness and a firm positive style.* 12 for £48.93

1981 Château Chasse Spleen, Moulis. *One of the most consistent Bourgeois properties in the Médoc. Will develop elegance and finesse with maturity.* 6 for £37.98

1982 Réserve de la Comtesse, Pauillac. *The second wine of Pichon Lalande. Deep purple colour, immense fruit and richness. Needs time but will be excellent.* 12 for £84.12

1980 Morey St-Denis, Dujac. *Extremely elegant, classic Burgundy from a serious and highly respected grower.* 6 for £56.88

1981 Chablis Grand Cru, Blanchot, Albert Pic. *A splendid vintage in Chablis and a fine example of rich, distinctive Chardonnay.* 12 for £85.56

1981 Gewürztraminer, Fleur de Guebwiller, Schlumberger. *Full, pungent, spicey from one of the region's leading producers.* 6 for £27.24

1982 Savennières, Château de Chamboureau. *A fine estate and Yves Soulez makes a Chenin wine which develops great elegance and style.* 12 for £47.64

1982 Côte Rôtie les Jumelles, Paul Jaboulet Ainé. *Powerful, rich Syrah from a fine vintage which requires keeping.* 6 for £39.66

1981 Ruppertsberger Geisbohl, Riesling, Kabinett, Dr Burklin Wolf. *Stylish, grapey, medium dry hock from the Palatinate. Well-made.* 12 for £53.88

1979 Rully Blanc, Pierre Cogny. *In our opinion Pierre Cogny produces the finest Rully. This Chalonnaise wine has weight, power and breeding.* 6 for £35.52

£1,000 Cellar
1983 Château Labégorce-Zédé, Margaux. *Delicious ripe fruit, tannin and acidity. Full of charm and elegance. An outstanding 1983.* 12 for £59.00

1982 Château Prunerie, Lalande Pomerol, J. P. Moueix. *Has weight, richness and length. Most appealing, chewy, luscious Pomerol style.* 12 for £46.00

1982 Château Haut-Bailly Graves. *A property now producing first-class wine. Elegant, opulent and distinguished.* 12 for £100.68

1981 Château Belair, 1er Grand Cru Classé, St-Emilion. *Made by the brilliant Pascal Delbeck. Lovely, ripe, juicy.* 12 for £106.92

1981 Chassagne-Montrachet, Etienne Sauzet. *Beautifully balanced, finely scented. Has depth and length. Should be kept.* 6 for £54.84

1982 Rully Blanc, Pierre Cogny. *See above.* 12 for £71.04

1982 St-Joseph, Le Grand Pompée, Jaboulet Ainé. *An underrated appellation of the Rhône. this wine has depth, power and rich spiciness.* 12 for £44.88

1980 Châteauneuf-du-Pape, Domaine de Vieux Télégraphe. *Rich and full bodied, an outstanding wine from a fine estate. Will be approaching its peak in three years. Splendid quality.* 12 for £60.72

1982 Maximin Grunhauser Abtsberg Riesling, Spätlese. *Beautifully fresh and delicate. Class and fine balance.* 12 for £79.32

1979 Tignanello, DOC, Antinori. *The legendary wine from Antinori. Powerful and elegant.* 6 for £47.28

1981 Riesling, Réserve Speciale, Schlumberger. *Classic, clean, fresh, fully-flavoured.* 12 for £49.68

1980 Chorey les Beaune, Tollot Beaut. *Very stylish Pinot Noir from a Domaine we much admire.* 12 for £68.28

1983 Château Montalivet, Graves, Pierre Coste. *Beautifully made, fully flavoured.* 12 for £39.84

1981 Château Lamothe Guignard, 2ème Cru, Sauternes. *A property which has recently changed hands and which is producing really exciting wine.* 12 for £35.04

1976 Bollinger. *Wonderful Champagne!* 12 for £170.40

O. W. Loeb *Helen Thompson*
Some selections from our lists to assure yourself some satisfying drinking in the future.

£100 Cellar
A case of:
1982 Hermitage La Chapelle, Paul Jaboulet Ainé.

In the 1982 the star regions were Bordeaux and the northern Rhône. This wine is outstanding.

£500 Cellar
A case each of:
1982 Hermitage La Chapelle, Paul Jaboulet Ainé.
1982 Cornas, Paul Jaboulet Ainé.
1982 Château Potensac, Médoc.
1982 Château L'Enclos, Pomerol.
1979 Châteauneuf-du-Pape Pignan, J. Reynaud.

1982 Riesling Schlossberg Grand Cru, Faller Frères.
1981 Chablis Grand Cru Les Clos Estate bottled Louis Michel.

In the Cornas we have an up-and-coming challenger to Hermitage, even less forward. The two clarets are fine examples of their areas in a fine year; not yet shipped so we have to keep a little money in hand to pay the duty and VAT. The Pignan is almost as distinguished as Reynaud's celebrated Château Rayas. The Schlossberg is a Riesling site par excellence and the 1982 from the Domaine Weinbach has a great elegance. The 1981 vintage in Chablis is still closed in but this Grand Cru has a fine future.

£1,000 Cellar
You could, of course, buy two cases of each of the seven wines above and then sell one of them to finance future drinking. But we prefer to add a few more wines.

A case each of:
1980 Nuits St-Georges Les Vaucrains Domaine Henri Gouges.
1980 Corton Bressandes, Tollot-Beaut.
1981 Château Carbonnieux Léognan, Graves.
1976 Vouvray Clos Naudin moelleux, A. Foreau.

The two red Burgundies are from one of the most promising recent vintages; each has real Pinot Noir character. Don't let 1981 be overlooked in all the enthusiasm for 1982 clarets: the earlier vintage produced some classic wines. A sweet wine with great keeping qualities and enormous potential for development from the finest grower in Vouvray.

You may wonder where the German wines are. Still in Germany is the answer. Next year I shall look forward to selecting one or two top quality wines, probably from the Saar and Ruwer and from the Nahe in the very promising 1983 vintage.

Sainsbury's *Allan Cheesman, Director of Off-Licence Buying*
The major difficulty in selecting cellars was the fact that our prices are quite keen even for 'fine wines' and you can end up with a lot of wine for £1,000. All the wines are either the straight JS label or Vintage Selection and as far as possible I have estimated vintage availability – prices are naturally estimates.

£100 Cellar
Château Barreyres 1981 Haut Médoc. 3 for £10.05

Château de Gourgazaud 1982 Minervois. 3 magnums for £13.80

Domaine Andre Brunel 1980 Châteauneuf-du-Pape. 3 for £14.25

Sainsbury's Muscadet de Sèvre et Maine. 6 for £11.70

Sainsbury's Wiltinger Scharzberg Kabinett 1982. 6 for £15.00

Clos St-Georges 1981. 6 for £16.80

Sainsbury's Extra Dry Champagne. 3 for £17.85

£500 Cellar
Château Barreyres 1981 Haut Médoc. 24 for £80.40

Château Grand Puy Ducasse 1979 Pauillac. 6 for £43.50

Les Forts de Latour 1977 Pauillac. 6 for £38.70

Beaune Premier Cru 1979 Chanson. 12 for £75.00

Meursault 1980 Moillard. 12 for £81.00

Riesling Réserve Personelle 1979 Hugel. 12 for £71.40

Sainsbury's Wiltinger Scharzberg Kabinett 1982. 12 for £30.00

Clos St-Georges 1981. 6 for £16.80

Domaine de la Soucherie Layon 1982. 6 for £16.80

Sainsbury's Extra Dry Champagne. 12 for £71.40

£1,000 Cellar
Château Barreyres 1981 Haut Médoc. 24 for £80.40

Château Cissac 1973. 12 for £83.40

Gevrey Chambertin 1979 Chanson. 12 for £105.00

Quinta da Bacalhoa 1981. 12 for £41.40

Château de Gourgazaud 1982 Minervois. 12 magnums for £55.20

Corton Charlemagne 1982 Chanson. 12 for £167.40

Chablis Premier Cru 1982/83. 12 for £49.80

Château de la Dimerie Muscadet de Sèvre et Maine sur lie 1983. 24 for £61.20

Kiedricher Heiligenstock Kabinett 1982/83
Dr Weil. 12 for £47.88

Kreuznacher Narrenkappe Auslese 1976
Nahe. 12 for £59.40

Clos St-Georges 1981. 12 for £33.60

Moulin Touchais 1964. 12 for £66.60

Sainsbury's Extra Dry Champagne.
24 for £141.80

Tanners Wines *A.R. Tanner*
With these sums available I would spend the money on table wine. At the £100 level, only red wines have been included, my recommendation being that the customer should puchase white wines as and when needed. It seemed imperative that one New World wine should be included – Australia seemed to offer the best value for money.

Bordeaux and the Rhône offer excellent value for money, while satisfactory red burgundy is expensive; both the £100 and £500 dozens reflect this. A carton of fine white burgundy and Sauternes is included in the £500 selection.

Despite there being 18 bottles from 5 non-European countries in the £500 selection, we do believe that we are fortunate in our geographical location and that Europe offers us excellent value for money.

The £1,000 cellar offers far greater scope for a more interesting, more balanced selection. We are currently enjoying a point in time where, after a succession of good vintages in Europe, there are some wonderful wines available. In this selection it has been possible to include some very fine bottles.

We seem to have laid down no Italian or Spanish wines. Excellent inexpensive red wines can be had from both countries. Together with inexpensive French reds they will help make the cellars last longer.

£100 Cellar
Château L'Etoile Graves 1979. *A generous 'gamey' wine with classic finesse.* 3 for £10.29

Château La Rose Perrière, Lussac St-Emilion 1979. *A generous soft wine.* 3 for £10.62

Château Lalande de Borie, St-Julien 1979. *Lovely fruit. Year after year this second wine of Ducru-Beaucaillou is particularly good.* 3 for £13.32

Rully Rouge, Pierre Cogny 1978. *A delicious light Pinot of an excellent year.* 3 for £17.55

Château du Grand Moulas, Côtes du Rhône, M. Ryckwaert, 1982. *Full, rich with depth and fruitiness, this wine is the best inexpensive Rhône wine we know.* 3 for £8.49

Vacqueyras Réserve de Paradis, 'La Fourmone' Roger Combe, 1978. *Great concentration of flavour, offered by an excellent grower in a very good year.* 3 for £11.31

Châteauneuf-du-Pape, Domaine du Vieux Télégraphe H. Brunier et Fils, 1980. *Strong in body and alcohol yet soft and generous, an excellent alternative to now expensive burgundy.* 3 for £14.19

Wynns Coonawarra Estate Cabernet Sauvignon 1979. *Delicious Australian Cabernet without being too powerful.* 3 for £16.35

£500 Cellar
Château Macquin St-Georges, St-Emilion 1981. *Fruity and with very good colour, a useful early developing wine.* 6 for £22.02

Château Chicane, Graves 1981. *Delicious flavour, elegant. Fruit and length.* 6 for £23.04

Château Lalande de Borie St-Julien 1981. *Has lively juice and fruit combined with great charm and length.* 6 for £34.80

Château Chasse Spleen, Moulas 1981. *Big, rich, strong, concentrated oaky wine.* 6 for £36.72

Châteauneuf-du-Pape, Domaine du Vieux Télégraphe H. Brunier et Fils, 1980.
See above. 6 for £28.38

Gigondas, L'Ousteau Fauquet 1979. *Generous mouthful of concentrated Grenache from a dedicated grower. Worth keeping.* 6 for £22.98

Hermitage 'La Chapelle', Paul Jaboulet Ainé 1980. *Classic, magnificent rich Syrah wine of an outstanding vintage.* 6 for £42.12

Côte Rôtie E. Guigal, 1979. *Rich Syrah with that delicious elegance that only Guigal seems to achieve.* 6 for £47.10

Rully Rouge, Pierre Cogny 1978.
See above. 4 for £23.40

Beaune Bressandes Domaine Henri Germain 1980. *Rich Côte d'Or Pinot coupled with elegance and lightness from a talented wine maker.*
2 for £14.58

Te Kauwhata Cabernet Sauvignon Cooks 1981 (New Zealand). *Classic Cabernet for early drinking.* 2 for £7.52

Chardonnay, Joseph Phelps, 1978 (California). *Rich buttery Chardonnay. A big wine from one of California's best wineries.* 2 for £18.86

Château Musar Rouge 1977 (Lebanon). *A remarkable full generous Cabernet of excellent quality from an unusual source.* 2 for £9.20

Cabernet Sauvignon, Trefethen, 1978. *Very generous, a powerful wine from California.* 4 for £35.80

Wynns Coonawarra Estate Cabernet Sauvignon 1979. *Attractive, generous. One of Australia's best wines.* 4 for £21.80

Nederberg Vintage Cabernet Sauvignon 1979. *A full firm South African red that will benefit from keeping.* 4 for £15.44

Chablis Grand Cru les Clos René Dauvissat 1981. *Delicious Chardonnay from one of the few Chablis producers still maturing wine in barriques.* 3 for £20.01

Puligny Montrachet 'Les Referts' Domaine Etienne Sauzet 1981. *Rich buttery Côte d'Or Chardonnay from one of the best estates.* 3 for £32.04

Château Guiteronde, Sauternes 1981. *Classic rich dessert wine. Superb fruit and length.* 3 for £11.55

Château Doisy-Daëne 2me Cru Sauternes 1981. *Dry, fragrant, light but with great length, this wine is unusual.* 3 for £18.36

£1,000 Cellar

Château Macquin St-Georges, St-Emilion (J. P. Moueix) 1979. *See above.* 12 for £45.00

Château Chicane. Graves 1981. *See above.* 12 for £46.08

Château Lalande de Borie St-Julien 1981. *See above.* 9 for £52.20

Château Chasse Spleen Moulas C.B. 1981. *See above.* 9 for £55.08

Château Brane Cantenac 2me Cru Margaux 1979. *Well balanced and with plenty of fruit, developing well.* 6 for £54.90

Château Léoville Poyferré 2me Cru St-Julien 1979. *Round generous Cabernet. Very elegant. Good after-taste.* 6 for £62.58

Château Guiteronde Sauternes 1981. *See above.* 3 for £11.55

Château Doisy-Daëne. 2me Cru Sauternes 1981. *See above.* 3 for £18.36

Rully Rouge, Pierre Cogny 1978. *See above.* 6 for £35.10

Beaune Bressandes. Domaine Henri Germain 1980. *See above.* 6 for £43.74

Chambolle Musigny, Domaine Georges Roumier 1980. *A superbly made elegant wine from one of the Côte de Nuits greatest growers. An underrated year.* 3 for £28.20

Bonnes Mares Domaine Georges Roumier 1980. *A very big reserved wine that will show superbly in about four years time.* 3 for £49.62

Chablis Premier Cru Vaillons René Dauvissat 1981. *Classic, generous in Chardonnay fruit and length of flavour.* 6 for £31.80

Chablis Grand Cru les Clos René Dauvissat 1981. *See above.* 6 for £31.80

Puligny Montrachet, Domaine Leflaive 1981. *Bearing a simple commune appellation but made by a superb producer. This is a delicious wine.* 2 for £17.22

Puligny Montrachet 'Combettes' Domaine Etienne Sauzet 1981. *Rich buttery Chardonnay from an excellent estate.* 2 for £22.54

Bienvenues Bâtard Montrachet. Domaine Leflaive 1981. *Huge and delicious, fine bouquet, fruit and flavour.* 2 for £25.88

Château du Grand Moulas, Côtes du Rhône 1982. *See above.* 12 for £33.96

Châteauneuf-du-Pape, Domaine du Vieux Télégraphe H. Brunier et Fils, 1980. *See above.* 8 for £37.84

Hermitage La Chapelle Paul Jaboulet Ainé 1980. *See above.* 8 for £56.16

Côte Rôtie E. Guigal, 1979. *See above.* 8 for £62.80

Cabernet Sauvignon, Trefethen, 1978. *See above.* 4 for £35.80

Wynns Coonawarra Estate Cabernet Sauvignon 1979. *See above.* 4 for £21.80

Nederberg Vintage Cabernet Sauvignon 1979. *See above.* 4 for £15.44

Te Kauwhata Cabernet Sauvignon Cooks 1981. *See above.* 4 for £15.04

Chardonnay, Joseph Phelps 1978 (California). *See above.* 4 for £37.72

Château Musar Rouge 1977 (Lebanon). *See above.* 4 for £18.40

Victoria Wines *David Bedford MW*
One of the jobs I dislike most is trying to suggest a cellar for someone I don't know. It's hard enough for a great friend, but for the 'unknown' taste and likes are so personal that it's a veritable minefield. Accepting defeat before I start, I hereby give warning that what follows is *my* choice for *my* cellar under the various financial constraints placed upon me. I will keep my fingers crossed that there are some people who like the things that I like. As your safety factor, it has always been my Company's policy to take unopened bottles back and change them for other goods to the same value – assuming they are bought from us in the first place and are still in good condition.

£100 Cellar
I have assumed this £100 is for the special occasions, so I have gone for a good claret and a good burgundy.

Ch. Lamothe Cissac 1978. *A superb Médoc from a great vintage – no need to worry if you don't drink it all this year.* 4 for £27.00

Pernand Ile de Vergelesses 1973. *A lovely full soft flavour. Drink now.* 4 for £30.40

And to make up the money:

Ch. de la Cassemichère, Muscadet 1982. *Fresh, light, but well-flavoured. A number one on our Dry to Sweet (1–9) Selector Scale.* 4 for £12.76

Binger Scharlachberg Riesling Kabinett 1979. *A delicate grapey Nahe wine, a number three.* 4 for £16.40

Ruster Beerenauslese 1981. *A sweet Austrian wine to go with the raspberries and cream. A number eight, and incredibly beautifully balanced.* 3 for £14.85

£500 Cellar
Multiply the above by five is the easy answer! Actually I think the easiest way to solve the £500 and £1,000 cellar is to list the starters in various categories and show the case price for each wine so that you can then juggle between reds and whites, champagne and port as your fancy takes you. You can also have less than case lots, because the total is going to qualify you for the 5 per cent discount which you should remember to subtract.

Starters for £500 and £1,000 Cellars
Vins de Pays de L'Uzège. *Fruity and ideal for the large party occasion.* 12 for £23.88

St-Emilion, Grants of St James. *Soft, medium and a much under-rated claret.* 12 for £45.48

Ch. Haut Sociondo 1978. *A super petit château of class. Will keep.* 12 for £41.88

Ch. Lamothe Cissac 1978. *See above.* 12 for £81.60

Ch. Pavie 1976. *Soft, big, powerful and very well made. Will keep.* 12 for £102.00

Ch. Ducru Beaucaillou 1976. *Classic! Will keep and improve.* 12 for £153.60

Burgogne Rouge, Jadot 1982. *A little young but already good. Will improve.* 12 for £46.68

Pernand Ile des Vergelesses 1973. *See above.* 12 for £91.20

Vosne Romanée Les Malconsorts 1979. *Classic! Will keep and improve.* 12 for £140.40

Caramany, Côtes du Roussillon Villages 1982. *One of the best of Roussillons.* 12 for £28.68

Crozes Hermitage, Dom. de Thalabert 1982. *Big, fruity and well made. Will improve.* 12 for £55.20

Châteauneuf-du-Pape, Dom. de Beaurenard 1979. *Classic of the area.* 12 for £66.00

Wynns Coonawarra Estate Cabernet Sauvignon 1979. *A top Australian. Big, powerful.* 12 for £69.60

Beringer Cabernet Sauvignon 1980. *A top Californian. Again, big and powerful.* 12 for £68.40

Barolo Brunate 1979. *A very fine example of this Italian wine.* 12 for £81.60

Tignanello 1977/79. *A deservedly famous Italian.* 12 for £80.40

Raimat Special Selection 1978. *Relatively unknown Spanish but jolly good.* 12 for £37.80

Marqués de Riscal Rioja 1978. *A claret style Rioja.* 12 for £45.48

Vins de Pays du Jardin de la France. *Good, dry white for large parties (1).* 12 for £23.88

Ch. de la Cassemichère 1982, Muscadet. *See above (1).* 12 for £38.28

Chablis Grants of St James 1982. *Extremely good example of a classic area (1).* 12 for £50.28

Sancerre Dom. Des Trois Noyers 1982. *Sancerre at its best (1).* 12 for £55.20

Meursault 1982, Jadot. *Top class and classic (2).* 12 for £105.60

Chassagne Montrachet La Romanée 1980. *Expensive, but great (2).* 12 for £126.00

Gewürztraminer 1981. *Beautiful, spicey and elegant (3).* 12 for £51.48

Ch. Doisy-Védrines 1978. *Middle priced Sauternes and jolly good too (9).* 12 for £114.00

Deidesheimer Hofstuck Kabinett 1982. *Well made and not too expensive hock (3).* 12 for £35.88

Binger Scharlachberg Riesling Kabinett 1979. *See above (3).* 12 for £49.20

Wiltinger Scharzberg Riesling 1982. *Not too expensive grapey Mosel (4).* 12 for £35.88

Wachenheimer Luginsland Riesling Spätlese 1981. *A very nice Spätlese (4).* 12 for £69.60

Forster Ungeheuer Scheurebe Auslese 1979. *A lovely grapey and honey flavoured Auslese (7).* 12 for £72.60

Rosemount Estate Show Chardonnay 1982. *A top class show winning Australian (3).* 12 for £66.00

Ruster Beerenauslese 1981. *See above (8).* 12 for £59.40

Blanc Foussy, Vin Vif de Touraine. *A super champagne substitute (1).* 12 for £51.48

Mercier NV Brut Reserve. *My favourite NV champagne (1).* 12 for £94.20

Dom Ruinart Blanc de Blancs 1973. *The very special occasion champagne (1).* 12 for £180.00

Harveys Directors' Bin. *In my view the best old tawny port there is.* 12 for £92.40

Graham Malvedos, Single Quinta 1968. *Jolly close to the best vintage ports.* 12 for £119.40

Warre or Dow 1970. *Classic vintage, still a bit young but top class.* 12 for £168.00

The Wine Club *Tony Laithwaite*

I have chosen wines that will taste more interesting if kept a while they are not wines that will appreciate in retail value, however – unusual names and appellations do not fare well at auctions. So re-selling to finance new purchases is not part of my scheme. The wines of Château du Trignon are vinified by carbonic maceration. This does not mean that they do not age well, it means they age *rapidly*. We ship the wine after one year's bottle ageing. Two further years usually take the wine to its peak. Well worth those two years. Trignon has a unique style unlike any other Rhône estate, and I think he has more medals to his credit than any other grower in the Valley.

Our Morgon I treat as always more like Burgundy than Beaujolais and I know that an extra two years always pays off well.

£100 Cellar

Ch. du Trignon Sablet Côtes du Rhône AOC. *Already with 2 years' bottle age. Given 2 years more this maceration carbonique wine seems to age 20 years. Remarkable effect.* 12 for £46.40

Louis Genillon 1982 Morgon AOC. *Really marvellous and substantial Cru Beaujolais, just getting into its stride. Does an amazing mimic of good Pinot Noir.* 12 for £52.99

£500 Cellar

Riesling 'Schlossberg' 1981 Paul Blanck et Ses Fils. *Only just losing its muted style. Will really flower in 3 years' time.* 24 for £145.98

Pavlikeni Estate 1979 Bulgarian Cabernet 'Balkan Vine'. *You tried it at the Festival. It ages Brilliantly. (3–4 years). Bulgarian! To lay down! Man's an imposter! Probably a Commie, too! No, comrades, but just you try it – our Pavlikeni resembles no other Iron Curtain Cabernet.* 24 for £51.58

Col Sandago Est. 1980 'Costa delle Pergole'. *An oak-aged Italian Cabernet. (2 years).* 24 for £83.20

Ch. du Trignon Sablet Côtes du Rhône AOC. *See above.* 24 for £92.80

Louis Genillon 1982 Morgon AOC. *See above.* 24 for £105.98

£1,000 Cellar

Riesling 'Schlossberg' 1981 Paul Blanck et Ses Fils. *See above.* 48 for £291.96

Pavlikeni Estate 1979 Bulgarian Cabernet 'Balkan Vine'. *See above.* 60 for £128.95

Col Sandago Est. 1980 'Costa delle Pergole'. *See above.* 48 for £166.40

Ch. du Trignon Sablet Côtes du Rhône AOC. *See above.* 48 for £185.60

Louis Genillon 1982 Morgon AOC. *See above.* 48 for £211.96

Deputy Editor's Cellar *Rosemary George MW*
My choices were dictated purely by personal preferences. I have included some which I know that I would like to have in my cellar in a year or ten years. They are wines which are worth laying down because they will improve in bottle over the months or over the years and also will not be readily available when they are ready to drink. I also aimed for a selection of the unusual as well as the traditional, and for wines that I will enjoy sharing with discerning and appreciative friends.

£100 Cellar
Sainsbury's Champagne. *The best value-for-money champagne around. Worth giving it a few months.* 4 for £25.80

1982 Chablis 1er Cru Vaillons, François Raveneau. *From Chablis' best wine maker. Not a great vintage, but a wine made in the traditional way and designed to age for a few years.* 4 for £20.66

1975 Torres Gran Coronas. *From Spain's most talented winemaker: full, rich flavour.* 4 for £15.96

1980 Crozes Hermitage, Domaine de Thalabert. *Full bodied and spicey Syrah fruit; will develop well over the next few years.* 4 for £21.52

1981 Sauvignon de St-Bris, Robert Defrance. *Fresh and crisp.* 4 for £15.00

£500 Cellar
1982 Château Chasse Spleen. *Excellent wine making from a great year.* 12 for £95.45

1982 Chablis 1er Cru Vaillons, François Raveneau. *See above.* 12 for £61.70

1970 Reserva 904, La Rioja Alta. *Where else can one find mature wine at such a price? Lovely, rich and fruity.* 12 for £59.64

1979 Bernkasteler Bratenhöfchen Riesling Spätlese, Lauerburg. *A light, elegant Moselle; delicious for summer drinking.* 12 for £68.04

1981 Hermitage, Gerard Chave. *The best grower in this part of the Rhône Valley has produced a wine that needs to be forgotten about for several years.* 12 for £99.60

1982 Riesling Réserve Personnelle, Faller Frères. *A delicious wine, with delightful Alsace character. Needs time to develop.* 12 for £74.16

Sainsbury's Champagne. *No cellar is complete without a few celebratory bottles.* 6 for £38.70

£1,000 Cellar
It was tempting just to double up the £500 cellar. However, in the interests of variety . . .

1981 Irancy, Leon Bienvenu. *A little known red Burgundy from the Chablis region.* 12 for £53.40

1976 Torres Gran Coronas Black Label. *A really stylish Spanish wine, from the country's greatest wine maker.* 12 for £119.52

1982 Cablis 1er Cru Chapelot, François Raveneau. *A little known vineyard, from a great wine maker.* 12 for £61.70

1981 Côte Rôtie la Chevalière d'Ampuis, Robert Jasmin. *A rich peppery wine, with lots of body and length.* 12 for £87.00

1982 Domaine de Chevalier. *One of my favourite châteaux that has made a great wine in a great vintage.* 12 for £151.00

Ghiaie della Furba 1979, Tenuta de Capezzana. *One of the best wines to come out of Tuscany; following the trend for Cabernet Sauvignon based wines in Italy.* 12 for £46.20

1971 Niedermenninger Herrenberg Riesling Auslese, von Kesselstatt. *Incredibly cheap for the vintage and the estate.* 12 for £59.40

1970 Fonseca. *A vintage port that will not demand too much patience.* 12 for £132.48

1978 Château Grand Puy Lacoste. *Another favourite château and an excellent vintage.* 12 for £100.80

1976 Gewürztraminer, Cuvée Christine Schlumberger. *Lovely, rich spicey. A great year.* 12 for £106.20

1973 Alfred Gratien Crémant. *A glass of Alfred Gratien champagne lured me into the wine trade. For celebrations.* 6 for £79.80

Editor's Alternative Cellar *Oz Clarke*

£100 Cellar
I'm not going to hang about. Straight to the off-licence and the supermarket and blow the lot on good straight drinking wine to make me feel bubbly rather than reflective.

I'm an optimist, and this cellar reflects the fact that with £100 to spend, I'm convinced that sooner or later I'll have £500, so I'll just spend my £100 on 'now' wines.

Viña Faustina 1982/3. *Big sturdy nouveau-style Rioja. Tremendous now, and just as good next year.* 6 for £17.00

Bordeaux Jeune. *The Bordeaux equivalent of new Beaujolais, but really claretty and distinctive.* 6 for £15.00

Côtes du Rhône Beaumes de Venise. *The best of the mdoern fruity Rhône styles.* 6 for £15.00

Lamberti Novello. *Italy's fighting back against Nouveau, too!* 6 for £15.00

Vin de Pays de Gascogne. *Biting, fresh white country wine.* 6 for £14.52

Ch. de Juges Bordeaux. *Nettly, sharp, tangy white Bordeaux.* 6 for £14.10

Clos St-Georges 1981. *England's best value sweet wine - bar none.* 1 for £2.80

Waitrose Champagne. *Fresh, bright, fling-it-down - fizz.* 1 for £5.95

Clairette de Die Tradition. *Sparkling Muscat with a kick - and pretty dry too.* 1 for £4.75

£500 Cellar

This is much more like it. I can start to indulge, *but I am still sublimely confident that it's not a long term venture, just enough to keep me going while I save for the £1,000 Cellar, so I'm looking for wines to have fun with over the next 12 months, and I'll start right away by upping my order of those single bottles to half a dozen.*

Clos St-Georges 1981. 6 for £16.80

Waitrose Champagne. 6 for £35.70

Clairette de Die Tradition. 6 for £28.50

Since I'm on the fizz and sweeties, I'll stay there for a bit.

Ch. Guiteronde 1980. *Unfashionable, but high quality,. 'real' Sauternes.* 6 for £22.50

Moscato Naturale Vietti. *Sensational, slightly frizzante Muscat. Possibly Italy's best dessert wine.* 6 for £20.82

Alfred Gratien NV. *The best, the most traditional mature full champagne style.* 6 for £45.00

Duc d'Orfin Anjou Méthode Champenoise. *Sharp-fruited, delicious fresh fizz, for when I can't cope with the Gratien.* 6 for £21.30

Pommerer Sonnenuhr Riesling Kabinett 1983. *Marvellous, apple-fresh Mosel from a good year.* 6 for £15.00

Chardonnay Vino da Tavola Tiefenbrunner Südtirol. *Light, creamy Chardonnay; soft, but ultra fresh.* 6 for £15.00

St-Véran 1982 Caves de Prissé. 6 for £23.00

St-Véran 1983 Duboeuf. 6 for £24.00

Two superb examples of an undervalued Mâconnais appellation.

I'm still not going to have any real long distance runners, because I'm sure that by the time I've done some damage to this little lot, I'll have saved £1,000 for the Major League.

1983 was a wonderful year for the good Beaujolais growers. These are three of the best. Janodet is outstanding, as yet only available ex cellars. Won't some enterprising merchant import his wine?

Beaujolais Villages Cuvée Grange Chartron 1983 Jacques Mathiot. 6 for £18.00

St-Amour Domaine du Breuil 1983. 6 for £20.00

Morgon Domaine Janodet 1983. 6 for £22.00

Domaine des Anges Côtes du Ventoux. *Rich, peppery southern Rhône, made by an Englishman.* 6 for £21.90

Raimat Abadia. 6 for £13.50

Lancorta Rioja Reserva 1976. 6 for £13.50

Spanish wines showing lots of fruit and also that lovely creamy oak softness.

Wynns Ovens Valley Shiraz. 3 for £12.51

Rosemount Coonawarra Cabernet Sauvignon. 3 for £12.87

Cousinho Macul 1976 Cabernet Sauvignon. 3 for £11.25

Cooks Cabernet Sauvignon 1983. 3 for £9.60

New World reds at their best.

I'll keep the rest of the £100 cellar and that looks like £500 or so.

£1,000 Cellar

At last! A few of those long distance runners and a few of the rare, unique bottles you dream about and rarely buy.

I have to start with claret. I've been pining to lay some down and now I will.

Ch. Kirwan Margaux 1981. 6 for £39.10

Domaine de Chevalier Graves 1981.
6 for £60.00

Two of the best from an underrated, but classic vintage.

Lafon Rochet St-Estèphe 1982.
La Tour Carnet St-Laurent 1982.
Léoville Barton St-Julien 1982. 18 for £120.00

Grand Puy Lacoste 1983.
Pichon-Longueville Lalande 1983.
12 for £100.00 EC

Wonderful wines from two tremendous vintages.

There's not much left after that bash, but there are other bottles I just must have. These will keep.

St-Joseph la Grande Pompée 1982.
6 for £24.30

Hemitage La Chapelle 1982. 3 for £24.36

Châteauneuf-du-Pape Les Arnevels 1981.
3 for £10.77

How much have I got left? Only £140. I must get some more Chardonnay, and Chablis is the best value for that this year.

Chablis 1er Cru Vaillons Dauvissat 1983.
3 for £14.28

Chablis Grand Cru Les Clos Dauvissat 1983.
3 for £17.22

The Cote D'Or is so expensive but:

Auxey Duresses Duc de Magenta. 3 for £14.45

And the New World Chardonnays to balance the dozen.

Orlando Chardonnay (Aus) 3 for £13.20

£80 left. Some special bottles and some oddballs to shock my friends.

Billecart-Salmon Blanc de Blancs 1979.
2 for £20.50

Capezzana Carmignano 1981. 2 for £6.58

Hargrave New York State Chardonnay.
2 for £15.00

St-Helena Pinot Noir New Zealand.
2 for £10.00

Bailey's Australian Liqueur Muscat.
2 for £15.00

And finally a few bottles of real Burgundy:

Volnay Santenots 1979 Lafon. 1 for £8.98

Clos de la Roche 1980 Ponsot. 1 for £9.50

Vosne Romanée 1979 Rion. 1 for £8.50

I never could add up, but (with the £500 cellar) this looks like £1,000, and I feel I've only just begun. Give me another £1,000 and I'll start all over again.

Storing Wine

Even if you dash into the off-licence on the way home, snatch up the nearest bottle, and have got the cork between your teeth before you can fit the key into the Yale, there are a few things you can do to give the poor suffering wine some chance of tasting half-decent.

But maybe you are one of the growing band of wine buyers who pores over lists, comparing prices, fingers darting restlessly over calculator keys to see whose discounts are matched by whose credit terms, or which collection bonus is possibly outweighted by an invitation to a tasting. For you, buying wine is a hobby and a pleasure streaked with seriousness. You want to make sure that your wine arrives in good condition, that it rests in the right place, at the right temperature, for the right length of time, and can then be shown at its best, like a girl being prepared for her first teenage party. It may sound an awful palaver, but to a wine enthusiast, it's no more trouble than tying flies for an angler, or cleaning spikes for an athlete.

Probably you're somewhere in between, prepared from time to time to give a wine a bit of reverence, but more likely to regard the first principle of wine-drinking as being the fun one. Since the first, chance fermentation of a bunch of grapes, wine has been made with one purpose – to give pleasure. So my aim is simply to suggest a few ways to make sure that the pounds you spend bring you the pleasure you've earned.

I'm not going into details of buying here – the rest of the book is supposed to be doing that – I'll just state the obvious. Think before you buy. The worst way to buy any wine is that dash to the off-licence for a frantic scanning of the shelves, resulting in a hasty purchase which may not taste as you expect, may not be suitable with the food you are eating, and may have cost you more than you intended to spend.

It's much better to buy ahead. Give yourself an extra five minutes in the supermarket or wine merchants to browse, to get the pleasure of making a decision. Try to think about the rest of the week. Should you be buying several bottles at once? One thing's for sure: even the most basic wine tastes better if you get it home and let it rest for a while. This means you will start storing a few bottles at home, and if you're subject to human nature you'll begin to find you're buying the odd bottle more than you need, and pretty soon you'll find there's a dozen bottles lying around the kitchen, the study, or the garage. You're teetering on the brink of becoming a bit of a wine collector. So, we'd better get it stored and preserved as well as possible, because storage conditions really do affect the eventual condition of a wine.

Where to store?

If you've got an underground cellar, you're laughing. You can store all your wines down there and they'll be in near perfect conditions. If you don't have such a cellar, let's improvise. Firstly, fine expensive wines are too precious to leave hanging around. They appreciate in value and get so much better if they're stored carefully – don't take chances. Leave them with a friend who's got a cellar, or else hire storage at a wine merchant's – that'll cost £2-£3 a year per case, but will be worth it.

Back at home, this is what to aim for. A reasonably stable temperature. Gradual rises and falls don't matter too much, but ideally it should stick at around 12°C. That's quite a bit cooler than most families would stand for, so just settle for keeping the wine away from radiators and hot pipes. Even so, wine is fairly sturdy stuff. I was down in the white wine cellar in one of London's leading hotels surrounded by top Chablis and Meursaults, and the sweat was breaking out on my brow. 'Why so warm?' I gasped. 'Oh', they replied, 'we cool them down

before the customer gets them; we never get complaints.' I headed for the fresh air, banging my head on a central heating pipe next to the Chassagne-Morgeot 1979.

Bright lights and vibrations and loud noise and strong smells are all supposed to affect wine. Bright lights are certainly bad, and I can see that a relentless diet of Heavy Metal and Reggae might seriously affect a wine's sang-froid. But I'm not convinced that the kitchen smells are really going to penetrate the capsule and the cork and reduce a Beaujolais Villages to a medley of oxtail soup, cauliflower and chicken biryani.

Vibration? Well, it depends on what that means. Half of London's most famous cellars are under the arches near railway terminals and must suffer dreadfully every weekday at rush hour. My first 'cellar' was half a dozen bottles under my bed at Oxford. Yes, well, let's move on . . .

All these precautions will be to no avail if the cork dries out. So always store wine bottles on their sides. If the wine stays in contact with the cork, it won't shrink and shrivel, and the air won't get in. If you can also keep the atmosphere slightly humid, the cork is even less likely to dry out.

To keep wines on their sides, the best thing is to invest in some wine racks, and put them somewhere quiet and out of the way – under the stairs, in an old fireplace, in a broom cupboard, even in the garage or potting shed, although you may have to go out at dead of night to stop your neighbours taking too close an interest in your to-ings and fro-ings.

I keep mine in the loft. Yes, the worst place in the house. But I've packed them in firm cardboard whisky boxes and a few wooden claret cases, stacked on their sides and wrapped in finest Irish wool blankets to insulate them against changes in temperature. My mother came up to see the flat and looked in the loft. 'Lord', she said, 'what are you doing with all the best blankets? You'll catch your death of cold.' I told her I wasn't concerned about getting too cold so long as my wines didn't get too hot. Ever since, she's thought I was a little bit odd.

Summary

* Let wine rest as long as you can (if you can) after buying. The longer the journey and the better the wine, the longer it should rest. Drink the supermarket Blanc de Blancs the same day without fear, but keep a mature claret or burgundy quiet for at least two to four weeks.

* Keep all wine – except boxes and cans – on its side: to keep the cork wet.

* The darker your store the better and for champagne that's essential – light hurts it.

* The less vibration the better.

* Cold is preferable to heat – but stability is really the most important thing. Avoid proximity to radiators and cooking at all costs.

* Ideas for location: under stairs, in cupboards, unused fireplaces, in racks high on unused corridor wallspace, against outside walls.

The Condition and Care of Wine

Kick a dog, leave a plant without water in the hottest part of the kitchen, lock a child out of doors in the winter cold, and you'd expect some reaction. The dog might be distinctly unfriendly, the plant would probably die, and the child would be so cold that sulky looks and chattering teeth would be the only visible signs of life. One way or another, if you are expecting to get any pleasure out of these objects of affection, a mixture of abuse and neglect is pretty certain to put the mockers on it. Because these are all living things, including that plant. Abuse a living thing – it reacts. But *cosset* a living thing, and there's every chance it'll not only do what you want, but do it even better than you expect.

Wine is just the same. It's a natural product, made from fresh grapes. It's composed of living organisms, gradually inter-reacting, sometimes under-reacting, sometimes over-reacting, going from a fresh, headstrong youth, through a balanced maturity (with luck), and then fading into a tired decline as the various elements begin to lose vigour and strength. During that period, the wine will react to what you do to it, just like a human, a rubber plant or a dachshund would.

This can often explain the times when a wine seems to be 'out of condition'. It may merely be bruised, and will return to health, given a little time to rest and recover its wits. Or we may simply be pulling the cork when it's too young or too old. One thing is certain – it's almost impossible to be certain!

The unique taste sensation of wine is the result of fermentation and subsequent maturing; which turn perfectly simple grapes of no great personality into an astonishing spectrum of flavours requiring tasting terms to be borrowed from other experiences. We also need to borrow a vocabulary for the condition of wine. Let's look at a few terms and take the curse off them.

Dumb: Yes, a young wine is often dumb, especially when it's just been bottled and the winemaker intended it to age a bit. It's probably merely trying to sort out its component parts.

Sick: Of course a wine can be sick – why not? Most commonly this is 'bottle sickness' and manifests itself by no smell when you expect one, or a slightly ugly pong; be gentle with the wine and it'll pass.

Troubled: *Troublé* in French, this is quite a common fault in light, young whites, and some reds. It means the wine tastes as though the fermentation has begun to work again, and there may be a tiny fizz. There's more than a shred of truth to the old belief that wine is sympathetic to the rising of the sap in the spring, and the stripping of the vine in the autumn. Just wait till it's had its little tantrum. However, if the wine is also cloudy and turbid, the trouble is less likely to go away.

Tired: Lifeless, dull, and often too old. As with humans, age is irreversible, and must simply be enjoyed for its frailer qualities.

Corked: The big one! This *doesn't* mean that there are little bits of cork floating round in the wine. That's usually just over-enthusiastic corkscrewing. Corked means the wine has become contaminated by some uncleanness in the cork, making the wine smell of damp old lumps of wood and mildew. A totally corked wine may be quite rare, but a slightly tainted wine is surprisingly common, and there does seem to be a general problem with cork quality just now, as wine producers try to make little economies to save a few ha'pence. They also whisper that the fashion for high cork platform heels on ladies' shoes created quite a shortage. A poor cork, and careless storage, may also lead to weeping corks, and a rather large gap between wine and cork. It needn't be fatal, but it's never a good sign, and is sure to have quickened the ageing of the wine.

COSTS IN WINE PRODUCTION

So many things influence the cost of a bottle of wine that it would take more than a four-page article to get to the bottom of it all. Some of these factors are relatively constant, but others show fluctuations which help to explain the enormous price variations between the different products. We have chosen a few of these features, and we start with a man who decided to create his own vineyard from scratch.

1984 is the 10th anniversary of the Firestone Vineyard in California's Santa Ynez Valley. Nowadays Brooks Firestone reckons to sell three million dollars worth of wine in an average year, which gives him income of $43,802 dollars for his pains. Even my maths can work that out at about 1.5 per cent of his sales, and before you say 'the guy must be crazy!', let him explain. Brooks and Kate Firestone didn't establish the vineyard, ten years ago, as a bright-eyed attempt to make a mint out of the wine boom. Firstly, Brooks already had a successful business career - Firestone Tyres being the family business which would have earned him all the money he wanted. Secondly, he decided to establish Firestone at precisely the time when the first busts were hitting the floor after people had streamed into California convinced that wine was the new gold rush. Brooks Firestone had no such illusions. Indeed, when he first asked André Tchelistcheff, California's most famous wine guru, to be his adviser, Tchelistcheff looked him up and down, and with something approaching a snort said 'So, you want to start a winery! How much money can you afford to lose?'

Brooks replied coolly that he could afford to lose some, but he was blowed if he was going to lose much. Indeed he was able to produce a 20-year Master Plan, and says now that if he hadn't already worked out the daunting odds, he could never have kept going. In July 1976, for instance, Firestone sold $9,000 worth of wine, while paying out capital and expense items and a whopping interest charge amounting to $300,000. He started to spend money in 1974, and his first projected profit was in 1981.

Out of the $3 million from sales, it will cost the vineyard a grand annual total of $1,713,000 in salaries, discounts, expenses and the numerous taxes the simple job of making and selling wine is subjected to. Of 15 employees on the winemaking side, one spends *all* his time looking after the endless government and state regulations, documentations and demands. The more general winery costs will come to $337,000, 11.9 per cent of the $3 million, and interest charges are a staggering 28.9 per cent at $876,000. Add all that together and you're left with $63,000. Tax that and you have $43,802. In fact, the total winery tax bill is $118,903, which means that from this $3 million turnover business, the government gets 3.96 per cent, while the Firestones get just 1.5 per cent.

It was Brooks Firestone's belief in his own business acumen that made him realise that he *wouldn't* laugh all the way to the bank. Even with all his credentials, he had the utmost difficulty finding business partners to finance the venture, and when you see that the interest on finance eats up 28.9 per cent of generated income against his own 1.5 per cent, it does leave a sour taste in the mouth. But his business sense allowed him to weigh up every argument and decide that he could afford to create a lifetime's dream, while being realistically aware that he couldn't make any proper money out of it. As he himself says, "Anyone who considers a new winery venture had better love vineyards and wine, because there will be precious little time for anything else . . . Kate and I love the growing vineyards, the developing vines, the continual excitement and challenge of the farming and craftsmanship." As for selling the stuff, when Tchelistcheff asked

"How do you know you can sell the wine?", Brooks answered "André, for 12 years I have been selling something round and black that nobody wants to buy in a cut-throat market. If I can do that, I can sell something that everybody loves."

That word love comes round time and again. The love, the passion, the intertwining dependence of a wine maker and his land, his vines, his wine. How else can one explain the wine makers of Bonnezeaux and Quarts de Chaume, of Sauternes, of Barolo, Burgundy and Bernkastel? For many of them it is scarcely possible to make money, yet their produce is so fine that it keeps them at the wheel in the belief that sooner or later the wind of fashion will change and let them reap the rewards. And in the knowledge that if they don't cling to their birthright, few others would invest the sweat and the tears for a return measured in pride rather than pounds.

Yet they at least have some choice. Their land is valuable. They could swallow that pride, sell up and go and work in the town. Few do. But what about the grower in Spain's Valdepeñas, in France's Midi, or in Italy's Puglia? He is bound to his land not by love but by poverty. His produce is poor, his vines are relatively valueless, yet such regions offer no other means of scraping a living. He *has* to continue to work his vines. It might be as well to ponder what kind of factors they are which affect our tastebuds so crucially that we begrudge £2.00 for a bottle of Chianti, yet feel £20 is cheap for Château Latour.

To get an immediate reference point let's go straight to the heart of the argument – Bordeaux, and its great red wines. The most basic cost anywhere is that of planting a vineyard, and for a straight AC Bordeaux this has risen from an average of 13,028 francs a hectare of vines in 1960 to 101,049 francs in 1982. Most of that rise has occurred since 1979, when the cost was only 59,379 francs. As we get out of our inflationary spiral, it's as well to remember that France is in the thick of hers. Production costs for one hectare of the slightly superior Côtes de Bordeaux have risen steeply from 3,320 francs in 1960, to 17,746 francs in 1979 and 25,914 francs in 1982.

The Bordeaux authorities go so far as to produce a leaflet showing the growers how they must cost their affairs. On a 20 hectare AC Bordeaux vineyard, yielding 50 hectolitres per hectare (hls/ha), they estimate the total cost of the production and sale of that crop at 466,354 francs. Which means a grower needs to get 4,200 francs for 900-litre *tonneau* to cover his costs. The authorities this year announced a price for basic red Bordeaux of 4,300–4,700 francs a *tonneaux.* Anyone who's paying out money to treat his vines, replace his barrels, or get his grape must analysed is going to be in the red before he's even started.

Most of Bordeaux red is ordinary drinking stuff; the fabled red wines are only the tip of the iceberg, but it may be reassuring to know that they do indeed cost a lot more to make, often over three times as much for even the most measly classed growth. Bordeaux production costs in 1982 were reckoned to be 20,213 francs per hectare, while Médoc classed growth costs were 61,852 francs. Most costings were relatively similar, but costs of vinification and depreciation of vineyard were reckoned to be lower for the classed growth, while labour and 'general' expenses were each 35 per cent higher. Labour = care. 'General' expenses = new oak barrels, new winery equipment, etc. The finest classed growths incur far higher costs, due to newer and better quality winery equipment, more new oak barrels, severe pruning in the vineyard, rigid selecting-out of substandard vats, retaining an expensive adviser, costs of advertising and salesmen and longer financing of stock before sale.

So, if the production costs can be radically different inside a single area, obviously they'll differ enormously around the world. But first, let's take a look at that most basic commodity of all – land. This may not be relevant if you've inherited holdings passed from father to son since the Great Flood. But if you have to buy land, it's going to have a considerable bearing on the final cost of the wine. In the Napa or Sonoma Valleys in California, top-dog hectares can cost as much as $60,000 each, while in the high quality but less fashionable Santa Ynez Valley, land is between $4,500 and $11,000 a hectares. To finance that difference, the grower is straightway asking for $2–$3 more per bottle.

In Italy, top Frascati land, with a thirsty market on its doorstep, heads up at 130 million lire a hectare. But then it is quite close to Rome, and those slopes would do just nicely for weekend villas. Sicily, still building a reputation for itself, asks for 40 million lire per hectare. Still sounds a lot to me. But spare a thought. Chianti's famous vineyards can be bought for 25–30 million lire/ha. Cruel shifts in fashion can slash the value of a family's holdings, just as it can increase their value. A good vineyard on the German Rheinhesse at the moment cost around £40,000 for one hectare, with the wine much in demand. The Chianti vineyards, with demand in decline, can cost less than a third.

France shows even starker differences. In Champagne, where a vigneron can earn a fair living easier than anywhere else in France, this is reflected by a land price of between £35,000 and £70,000 per hectare. In Hermitage, the south's top red area, the cost of a hectare is only £5,700. Further south, in the *vin de pays* areas round the Mediterranean, good vineyards cost less than £2,000 a hectare. If you're buying a vineyard the finance needed for that purchase is going to differ dramatically, and affect accordingly the price you need to achieve for your wine.

If you have to replant, with modern nursery methods of grafting and cloning, the plantation costs are relatively similar. It'll cost between £7,000 and £10,000 a hectare in California, and between £7,000 and £8,500 in Nierstein. But the differences can be more marked: a hectare replanted for £5,000 in the South of France will yield in three years. A hectare in a first growth Sauternes vineyard will cost more like £8,500, and there'll be no usable yield for five years.

And that yield will make a big difference when the grapes are finally harvested. Germany is notorious for big yields, and even the good parts of Nierstein were producing as much as 220 hls/ha in 1983 from their Müller-Thurgau grapes. The lower yielding Riesling produced less, yet even that was up at 110 hls/ha. Which would bring a wry smile to the lips of the Hermitage grower who managed about 35 hls/ha in 1983. The *vin de pays* producer with 80 hls/ha wouldn't feel so hard done by, but if he were in a little-known southern *appellation contrôlée* he'd only be getting 50 hls/ha, enjoying neither the price Hermitage commands nor the yields Nierstein produces.

Even so, at least his yields will be fairly stable. Not everyone is so lucky. In 1983 a decent yield in southern England was a positively Germanic 160 hls/ha. It was a pretty good year in 1982, yet most production was under 50 hls/ha. The yields in 1981 and 1980 were closer to Sauternes levels. But Sauternes never gets very high either, yet can plunge lower than anyone. A classed growth Sauternes château is allowed 25 hls/ha, but a more realistic average figure would be nearer 16 hls/ha.

Yet pickers must still be employed. It will cost a Sauternes vineyard, with its laborious methods of vintageing, about 10,000 francs a hectare to pick its 16 hls. Yet when machine picking is used, French costs can drop to as little as 1,600 francs per hectare. You can't machine pick in Sauternes. You can do what you like in California, and the difference between hand and mechanical picking there is about £220 a hectare.

Most wines don't need oak barrels to age in, but those that do immediately add to the cost. A good French oak barrel costs around £150. It will hold 300 bottles of wine, though some will be lost through evaporation. On a top estate, though the apparent cost is 50p a bottle, the true cost is about £1 for every year of maturing before release.

The price of a basic bottle, label, cork and capsule is about 1.60–1.80 francs.

The price of a top quality set is nearer 3.60 francs, with the best corks particularly costing more. The packing carton can be as little as 3.60 francs, or as much as 30 francs and so it goes on. There are many other variables, but we hope this chapter serves to show that there *is* a reason behind the cost of that bottle: it's not just fashion, or greed, or someone pushing the market to its limits. Maybe it is just that the finest quality – however one defines that – does cost a bit more to produce. And, if you're better at your sums than I am, you can also work out that you won't necessarily be making a better living out of expensive wine than you will out of cheap.

BUYING WINE ABROAD

I have a sneaking feeling that the per capita figures for our annual wine consumption may be erring on the conservative side. They say that there are 25 million wine drinkers in the UK, and that on average they drink about nine litres of wine each. I wonder if that figure isn't about a bottle too low, because as well as tearing down to the supermarket or wine bar, Britons have discovered the thrills and spills of buying wine abroad. And because of that, hazarding a guess, we reckon an extra 25 million bottles of wine may have been imported this year in the boot of the car.

This figure is based on common sense rather than Customs and Excise statistics, which don't take into account the contents of car boots, since their concern is with container trucks and the bottles of wine on which we *do* pay duty. But what makes it likely is that we Brits made 5.1 million visits to France last year, regardless of trips to the rest of Europe. Over four million of these visits were by cross-channel ferry; that includes people going on holiday, businessmen, daytrippers hellbent on getting boozed up to the nines – all with one thing in common. Because of the taxation system on wines and spirits, they're all determined either to beat the system, or at least squeeze every bit out of it they can.

Our drinking habits put us in the middle of the field in volume terms: we're 14th in Western European wine consumption – only ahead of Finland, Sweden and Norway – and even in beer consumption we're only seventh, but our enthusiasm is far greater than that paltry showing implies.

In actual money terms we have no rivals. Great Britain accounts for over 30 per cent of the entire Western European alcohol market in money terms! So, if we're only 14th in wine consumption, and seventh in beer . . . Yes, the Chancellor of the Exchequer is doing terribly well out of the poor old drinker. Which goes some way to explain the passionate desire of the most law-abiding Anglo Saxon to outwit the law when it comes to liquor and wine.

There's a non-taxable allowance of 10 bottles of wine per person when we return home from wherever we've been in the EEC. That's for wine bought *in* the EEC – not in a duty free shop. The Customs men see the duty free shop as public enemy No. 1; your whole allowance is brought down to the minimum if you have so much as a tooth mug of left-over Duty Free gin. On those French visit figures alone, if we suggested that only 2.5 million of those 5.1 million French trips were made by drinking adults, from France alone we might be looking at an extra 25 millon bottles fighting it out in the back with the lilo and the suntan lotion. It *could* be twice that figure. But it looks as if the 25 million British wine drinkers are polishing off a bottle more each than the figures show!

We would certainly agree with the

Customs men about one thing. Don't buy your wine in a British Duty Free. The limited choice is generally between commercial brands which have had the gumption to get themselves listed, and which you could get in any high street shop back home. Yes, you save money, but that's all. You get no thrill of discovery, of something personal and exciting, which must surely be the reason for buying wine abroad. Of course we'd expect the French to do it better; when you have the chance, just compare the airport shop at Charles de Gaulle in Paris with any British equivalent. Top wines, low prices. A real merchant's selection. But that's something we've got loads of over here, and the French hardly have any. Even Paris has only a handful – and one is owned by an Englishman, and another is run by an Englishwoman!

No, what buying wine abroad should mean for us is buying wine in its region of production, from the people who made it. Most parts of France and much of the rest of Europe have 'promotional' wine cellars. Visit them. Taste the wine. *Don't* buy. Instead, take note of what you tasted, then head for the person who made the wine. Personal introductions from English merchants are very helpful, but otherwise the 'Vente Direct', or 'direct sales' signs sprout from every roadside. Stop. Taste. Enjoy the excitement of being within a handshake of he man who made the wine *but* don't be pressured. All wine makers will naturally tell you that their wine is best. Since they can't all be right, take your time, visit several cellars, decide which *you* like best. A decent wine grower will appreciate a serious approach, and you'll often end up with a bottle costing only a few francs more than the local trade would have had to pay even in the best areas, and only a few centimes in the hot South. One thing to remember: you should obtain a form on which you state when you're leaving the country, which will excuse you foreign VAT (but remember to give this to the Customs at your point of exit).

Sure, there *are* risks. The wine may quite simply not taste the same back home. But it *will* save you money, and it will be *your* wine, *your* choice. That's worth a few fond memories months later in the gloaming as the holiday pics begin to curl at the edges.

Wine and the Cost of Living

If you think you've noticed an inexorable rise in the cost of a bottle of wine, year by year becoming more expensive – think again. Certainly, it has become more expensive, but at the same time, hasn't it actually become less painful in terms of the squeals your wallet makes as you draw out the folding ones? Haven't you found yourself thinking that in fact it's a fairly affordable way to put a touch of luxury and romance into your life? And doesn't the cost of other items in your weekly budget make you wince rather more than your wine bottle does?

Well, that makes sense, because if we take the classic Whitehall figures of a Civil Service executive officer's salary, and see whether he would have found wine more or less affordable in 1983 than in 1961, it's clear that he should be finding it a lot easier to buy the occasional bottle nowadays. The basic age 18 salary in 1961 was £458 p.a. It makes you rub your eyes, doesn't it! When you think that basic unemployment benefit alone is roughly £1,000 a year now, this poor chap was putting in a 40-hour week to take home less than a tenner. It doesn't seem very likely that he hoarded the pennies to buy wine – more likely he needed them to get his shoes mended. But if he *did* decide to splash out, this is what Findlaters of Wigmore Street would have charged him in their shop: house claret, 7*s* 6*d* (37½p). (Just writing shillings and pence makes everything feel cheap!) Mâcon Blanc, 7*s* 6*d* (37½p); Valpolicella, 8*s* (40p); Niersteiner Domtal, 11*s* (55p); house champagne, 21*s* (£1.05).

The surprise on that list is the cost of Niersteiner Domtal. Nowadays one of the cheapest wines on a merchant's list, in the 1961 list it is outpricing the claret and the white burgundy, and is over half as expensive as the champagne. Valpolicella is a pretty cheap wine now too, and here it is topping the claret and the white burgundy. So our executive officer would need to spend about 4% of his weekly salary to get a bottle of claret.

By 1970/71 our 18-year-old civil servant had managed to up his pay to £741 p.a., an increase of over 60 per cent. Since they invented the system in 1962, the Retail Price Index (RPI) had risen from 100 to 147 (1971), so our chap was better off, his salary moving comfortably ahead of prices. The only trouble was, although inflation was running at such a low level, wine prices had virtually doubled. The claret was now 75p; the Mâcon 90p; the Niersteiner had leapt to £1.00, and Valpolicella had gone crazy – up from 40p to £1.05. It might almost have been worth drinking the house champagne at £1.95. So, while he was generally better off, his bottle of claret would now consume over 5% of his weekly salary.

The next decade was the one where inflation really got dug in. The RPI had already jumped 11.5% in 1971. By 1975 it was rising 38 points in the year, and in 1980 alone it rose 73 points. It had taken from 1962 to 1973 for it to move from 100 to 171.3. By 1983 the pace was slowing down again, while the executive officer was now bringing in £4,546 p.a., almost 10 times as much as in 1961. The RPI was standing at 625.1, so prices were more than six times higher than in 1962. Good for him. His salary had kept comfortably ahead. But will he have begun to drink any more wine? Well, house claret was now £2.62, Niersteiner was £2.43, Mâcon Blanc was a startling £4.27, Valpolicella, after its big hike, was settled at £2.04, and the house champagne was £7.55. Claret was up seven times, while Niersteiner was up just over four times. Mâcon had gone through the roof, and was now nearly twelve times as expensive, while Valpolicella was only five times pricier. Champagne? Seven times more expensive than in 1961.

Since he is now earning just over £90 a week, he needs to spend just under 3% of his weekly salary to get his bottle of claret.

However, if he switches to Valpolicella, he will only be spending just over 2%.

It is interesting to note that while the two most traditional British wines (claret and champagne) have fairly closely followed the general price rise pattern, the two newcomers (Valpolicella and Niersteiner) have had to keep their prices very competitive to break into the bottom end of the market. And Mâcon Blanc has been swept along on the craze for white burgundy, making huge demands on a limited area. So it *is* true; the kind of wine most of us buy is rising less than the rate of inflation, and on an average wage the percentage of a weekly salary needed to buy a bottle has virtually halved since 1961.

The cost of living: 1960-1983

How inflation and the rise in the cost of living over the past 20 years or so has affected our wine purchasing power: this table sets out price rises since 1960 for various wines, and other foods and drinks, in relation to a young civil servant's average salary.

	1961	1971	1983**
18-year-old civil servant's entry salary	£458	£741*	£4,546
Wines: house claret	7*s* 6*d* (£0.37½)	£0.75	£2.62
Niersteiner Domtal	11*s* (£0.55)	£1.00	£2.43
Mâcon Blanc	7*s* 6*d* (£0.37½)	£0.90	£4.27
Valpolicella	8*s* (£0.40)	£1.05	£2.04
house champagne NV	21*s* (£1.05)	£1.95	£7.55
Beer (pint)	1*s* 2*d* (£0.06)	£0.09½	£0.70
Tea (¼ lb)	1*s* 9*d* (£0.09)	£0.09	£0.35½
Beef (1 lb, braising)	2*s* 9½*d* (£0.14)	£0.21	£1.50
Bread (2 lb loaf)	1*s* 9*d* (£0.09)	£0.09½	£0.37

* Salary scale dates from April, 1970.
** Prices are Ex VAT.

Retail Price Index was established at 100 in January 1962. Subsequent increases were: 1965 - 109.5; 1971 - 147; 1975 - 230; 1980 - 470.5; 1981 - 531.9; 1983 - 625.1.

The Wine Business in the UK

When you think that in numerous parts of the civilized Western World, you can only buy wine from stores controlled by government monopolies. When you think that the idea of a 'wine merchant', offering a selection of the world's wines, was almost unheard of in France until a young Englishman decided that Paris should have at least one proper shop. When you think that if you're in Piedmont or Tuscany there's little chance of being able to buy anything but Piemontese or Tuscan wines. When you think of such things, you begin to realise how lucky we are in Great Britain. Not only do we have the widest choice of wines offered anywhere in the world, but we have the greatest freedom in deciding how we will purchase them.

This all stems from the fact that we have never been major wine producers, and consquently London, and perhaps Bristol, have become the great trading centres of all the world's wines. But successive chancellors have seen wines as an iniquitous luxury import and tax it accordingly and relentlessly. Until this year. Who ever would have thought that any ruling from Strasbourg could benefit the British consumer! Although wine prices may still seem high to us, they are cheap in global terms.

Until about 20 years ago the retail wine trade was largely divided between two different operations: the traditional wine merchant of pinstriped and old-school-tie memory, and the licensed grocer. Since they pursued their trade with little competition in a period of low inflation and slight public awareness, the fact that they were often the fourth or fifth in a line of profit-taking middlemen between grower and consumer did not materially affect their businesses.

The '60's changed all that. Brewery and distillery groups, by dint of a headlong series of mergers and takeovers, became the dominant figures in the UK drinks business – which led to the birth of the High Street chains of today's household names.

At the same time the supermarkets began to sell wine, initially in a fairly uninspiring way, but throughout the '70s they improved their product, so that by 1984 they have achieved not only the dominant position in wine retailing, but also a quality/price ratio which is frequently the best available on an ever-expanding range of wines. Those four or five middlemen have now shrunk to one or two – the broker who advises the supermarket buyer on direct purchases from the wine-maker, and sometimes an agent in this country.

With the traditional wine merchant now a rarity, a new breed of 1980s specialists has appeared who have taken over the time-honoured job of friendly neighbourhood wine adviser. Sometimes they sell from a shop, sometimes they sell only by the case, sometimes they operate as wine warehouses, but in these days of high interest rates, and endemic impatience, they no longer keep extensive stocks of well-matured clarets and burgundies. They'll either offer the majority of these wines very young for the customer to invest in, or they'll steer him on to the 'modern' wine areas where a wine is ready to drink as soon as it hits the shelves. The 'mature classics' market has in itself become a speciality for a very few merchants, who can charge high prices for rare bottles.

Let me explain what I mean by 'traditional' and 'modern' specialists.

In my view a traditional wine merchant is someone who stocks and offers a wide range of mature vintage wines. Now, it would be fairly uncontentious to put Berry Bros in this category, but I'm not sure how to place companies like Lay and Wheeler or Adnams. Neither would be happy, I dare say, to be thought unduly traditional, although in many ways they fit the description, and Lay and Wheeler is doing well against its stated aim of trying to produce the best wine list in the country.

A company like Hicks and Don would certainly claim to be specialists in 'opening' offers – particularly of claret – and in sherry; Yapp Bros specialise in the Loire and the Rhône; and so on. But these and similar companies also offer some of the things that could lead one to describe them as traditional in the best sense. What? Advice, planning, storage, first-hand knowledge of what they are offering and in general a willingness to be guide, philosopher and friend to the wine enthusiast. If you're not a wine expert, despite the fact that you not only have Webster's to show you the way but a plethora of excellent wine books on the market, I feel on balance that I'd suggest you try to find such an ally.

What I can't tell you is exactly where to find him or her; they exist in the most august old-school-tie companies, and amongst the modern specialists, and it's possible that the person behind the counter at Oddbins (in particular) – although in this kind of shop probably not for the long haul – may be a mine of information.

Remember also that price is not in and of itself the answer – quality of service and advice across the board is essential to successful wine buying. This means horses for courses; don't bring out a case of the 1978 Aloxe-Corton (specially reserved for you by Loeb) for the office party – buy a case of supermarket champagne.

I've been trying to avoid making the kind of definitions that this chapter demands, but – bearing in mind the caveats I've given – here goes.

Traditionalists
Plus points: personal service and advice. Credit. Storage. Delivery. Ability to return wines not to your liking – even if perfectly OK. Wide range.
Drawbacks: not usually cheap. Not so many 'new discovery' wines. Not many special offers. Aren't many anyway and often hard to find.

Specialists
The new enthusiasts of the wine trade. They usually run both retail and wholesale operations, often with a particularly strong point like Italian, Spanish, or 'French country wines'.
Plus points: enthusiasm. Good discounts for cases and larger orders. Tastings. Some exclusivity in many of the wines they offer, so you feel you've got something a bit different. Imaginative opening offers of young wines; at the lower end of the market these fellows can sell you a case of wine which works out at a couple of quid for a bottle that might cost £3.50 even in a supermarket. Usually storage. Usually credit – but not if you want the discounts.
Drawbacks: they simply cannot afford to keep huge stocks of mature wines (although they will probably find them for you) – maybe soon no one will be able to. Sometimes you have to pay extra for delivery. Often 12 bottles is a minimum order.

Wine warehouses
Usually located outside city centres.
Plus points: keen prices. Pre-purchase tastings. Wide range of cheaper wines. Fair advice. Some delivery.
Drawbacks: one case minimum. No sophistication. No storage. Few opening offers.

Licensed grocers
A few, like Cullens, operate as serious and competitively-priced wine merchants. Otherwise you get delicatessens which often have a cheap range of their particular country's basic wines, and urban corner shops carrying cheap wines – often very cheap and tasting like it. Anything classic fairly expensive.

High Street chains
These dominate the city centres now. They should offer competitive prices and a wide range. In fact only their bigger branches do. But Victoria Wine and Peter Dominic both have extensive ranges stored centrally which can be ordered.
Plus points: usually good for 'new wave' wines. Some have credit schemes. Some case discounts. Some delivery. Also some clubs and tastings.
Drawbacks: expensive for classics. Little personal advice. Some overloading with own brands and brewery-owned lines.

Supermarkets
Some are simply cheap and dull. The best, i.e. Sainsbury, Tesco, Waitrose, offer some of the best value in the UK.
Plus points: price. Self-service. Highly efficient quality control at cheaper end.
Drawbacks: no delivery. No credit. Little advice. No discounts. No returns. Only the bigger stores carry the fine wine range.
See also *Supermarkets*.

Mail Order and Wine Clubs
Here again, definitions are difficult. Many traditional merchants and modernists alike sell by mail. Some run specialist wine clubs for defined interest groups.

Some are exclusively mail order like Les Amis du Vin, The Wine Society and The Sunday Times Wine Club. In fact wine clubs seem to be the common factor in many a marketing man's perception of where the upwardly mobile Brit is at today; no self-respecting charge or credit card company can be without one, and they've certainly got the spenders on their books.

The best of these clubs and societies offer high-quality wines at fair prices, and often a real chance to learn about wine with tours, lectures, tastings and even

hot-lines for problem-solving.
Plus points: delivery (obviously). Fun frills. You can choose from a list at leisure with your reference books to hand.
Drawbacks: the need to maintain quantity supplies means that not many 'wonderful little properties' can really be followed except as special offers. Prices are, frankly, not the lowest – but most members prize convenience and the relationship (albeit that of correspondents) most highly. Usually a case or mixed case minimum.

Cash and Carry Discount Stores
Augustus Barnett and Oddbins started this craze, but only Oddbins has gone from strength to strength, now offering some of the cheapest cash prices and most knowledgeable staff anywhere.
Plus points: price. Range. Special offers.
Drawbacks: some cheap wines are really cheap-tasting. Little personal advice (except Oddbins). No laying down/storage. No credit. No delivery.

It is also worth looking out for the one-off operations like Del Monico or Milroys in London's Soho or Hoggs in Edinburgh – strictly cash businesses with erratic stock lines (in some cases), but often offering (as in the case of Del Monico) astonishing value for money in everything from Portuguese reds at well under £2.00 per bottle up to classed growth clarets back to 1970. If you can find a wine you like to drink regularly at a good price in such a store, not even your best regular wine merchant friend will be able to compete.

Auction
See *Buying Wine at Auction.*

Conclusion
Shop around, of course. But remember your spending-power and the worth of a good relationship with an expert you can trust. I wouldn't buy an unknown *petit château* for laying down from anyone who had not actually tasted that wine. That sort of experience is something you can't really price.

For a detailed description of individual wine suppliers see the *Directory* (p. 400).

Wine Consumption in the UK

In 1983 Britons spent £1,750 million on 750 million bottles of wine – that's a 10% increase on 1982, and shows that the 25 million British wine drinkers put back about 30 bottles a year each. And it's not just company directors and High Court judges doing all the drinking – the C2, D and E social groups like skilled industrial workers, taxi drivers and labourers, have shown a 20% increase in wine consumption in the past four years, while the 'top people' grouping has grown by 11%. This confirms the view that wine is regarded as a relatively cheap and highly effective symbol of upward mobility. Since 1975, when there were 18,766,000 wine drinkers in the UK, the consumption per capita has risen steadily from 5.21 litres in 1975 to 7.85 litres in 1982, with 1983 likely to show a further 9.2% rise. As the table below shows, France is our leading supplier of table wines, in 1983 up 12.11% in volume on 1982, with Germany second, up 23.43%, and Spain third, up 8.82%. Italy, in fourth place, is down 7.10%. However, look at the value of the wines. France is up 25.18% in value, with *appellation contrôlée* particularly strong. West Germany is only up 15.03%, since volume increase is in cheap blends. Spain, up 13.73%, shows the decline in Spanish plonk, and its replacement with quality Rioja and Penedès wine, while Italy, down in volume but way up 49.15% in value, shows the switch away from big bottle cheapos to designated quality wines.

Wine Imports into the UK 1983

Country	Litres	% change	Value £	% change
France	151,156,000	+ 12.11	168,138,000	+ 25.18
W. Germany	96,452,000	+ 23.43	74,592,000	+ 15.03
Spain	84,197,000	+ 8.82	51,982,000	+ 13.73
Italy	53,121,000	– 7.10	35,084,000	+ 49.15
Yugoslavia	18,826,000	+ 27.87	4,759,000	+ 26.90
Cyprus	11,278,000	+ 4.91	4,735,000	+ 20.48
Portugal	11,037,000	– 7.90	15,714,000	– 0.67
USA	3,959,000	– 16.91	5,057,000	+ 1.01
Netherlands	1,419,000	– 55.50	1,789,000	– 38,73
Others	13,777,000	+ 51.16	9,127,000	+ 66.45

Wine Consumers in the UK 1970-83

Year	Consumers
1970	13,840,000
1971	13,827,000
1974	19,324,000
1975	18,766,000
1977	21,151,000
1980	23,949,000
1983	25,000,000

Source: Target Group Index

Growth of Wine Consumption in the UK 1970-83

Year	Litres
1970	95,300,000
1971	116,700,000
1974	186,900,000
1977	187,200,000
1980	276,500,000
1983	373,000,000

Source: British Customs and Excise

Buying Wine at Auction

The first time I went to a wine auction I missed the four lots I was after because I was too frightened to raise my finger. My heartbeat doubled every time I came within a fiver of my limit. The trouble is, the wines were going incredibly cheaply, and it wasn't until right at the end of the sale that I managed to struggle to my feet, and wave the catalogue frantically in the air. Since I was earning somewhere in the region of £20 a week – this *was* 10 years ago! – I would still have ducked out, but a charming no-nonsense lady with a blackbelt in karate was at my side in seconds, making me fill in my name and address. Then I went to Australia.

But before I headed Down Under I did leave a cheque behind, thus confirming my ownership, and it was one of the best things I ever did. This is what I bought: Château Branaire-Ducru 1966, £11 a case; Château Pichon-Lalande 1970, £13.50 a case; Château Ducru-Beaucaillou 1970, £14.50 a case. And here are the average prices they were fetching per case earlier this year: Château Branaire-Ducru 1966, £200; Château Pichon-Lalande 1970, £250; Château Ducru-Beaucaillou 1970, £300.

Unwittingly I had followed the one golden rule of wine investment: only invest in the top properties and only in classic vintages. 1966 and 1970 were classics – when the trade and the press are united in praising the quality. These three properties are three of the best, and most popular, in the Médoc.

When I got back from Down Under, flushed with success, I went to a trade clearance sale of a company which had also gone under while I was checking out the facilities at Bondi Beach. There was a large range of unlabelled wines set out at a pre-sale tasting. A lot of the wine was poor, but one batch of white was superb. I inquired from the Christie's auctioneer who told me the wine came from a Burgundian merchant in Chambolle-Musigny. The auction started. My lot came up. No one bid. My heart raced. Up went the finger. Bang. Lot 100 to Mr Clarke for £1.50 a case. I bought ten cases. I wish I'd bought a hundred, because the wine was a Meursault which did not have the proper documentation, and it is the only time I've ever had the fridge crammed with white burgundy just in case the vicar called.

This shows two extremes of auction house activity, and both can be of great use to us as private individuals. But let's just survey exactly what these auction houses are, with their pros and cons.

The UK has two very important houses, Sotheby's and Christie's, both based in London, and holding regular sales, as well as other companies, usually provincial, which hold occasional sales. All you need is the sale catalogue, available on request, and a cheque book. There are *no* special conditions. However, what you must have is some knowledge of the wines concerned, or some impartial advice as to their probable quality. Pre-sale tastings will usually only show wines whose quality is unproven: classic clarets and ports you will be expected to take on trust. Do *not* walk into an auction without knowing what you want, and the price you are prepared to pay. Remember the auctioneer acts for the vendor, who pays a commission. The buyer doesn't.

Christie's and Sotheby's have a wider experience of an enormous range of wines than almost any wine merchant could manage, and their advice is sought by trade and public alike. This advice is free. Use it, and note it in your catalogue, which will also contain useful information.

Points to note if buying at auction

1 You will be bidding against the trade, but since the trade will wish to re-sell, you can get the wine, in effect, at trade price less the merchant's margin. For this reason, check the price you would nor-

mally pay for a particular wine.
2 Remember to check if the stock is subject to VAT. Much stock is from private sources, and is only liable for VAT if the vendor is registered – that's 15% saved. Stocks liable for VAT are marked by a dagger. How apt.
3 You can buy in bond. If you are resident abroad, or feel you know something about the Budget others don't, this can be a bonus. However, if the wine is offered 'duty paid but available in bond', remember that if you decide to take it duty paid it will immediately become liable to VAT.
4 Digest the information given in the catalogue about where the wine is lying and what delivery charges will apply to the lots you are interested in. Neglecting to calculate these (and to include VAT where applicable) could make the total of your invoice surprisingly large.
5 There *are* some super bargains, but not in the endlessly traded classic ports and clarets from mature vintages, where the vendors are finally taking their big profits. Earlier this year you could buy a dozen magnums of Chablis Les Preuses 1978 – an astonishing, exciting, deep-flavoured wine – for £42 a dozen at Sotheby's. If you wanted some mature claret, Château Siaurac 1970, a fine, big wine from the little known area of Lalande-de-Pomerol, was £38 a dozen. Such wines would be quite unobtainable through normal channels. But of course, you'd be buying at least a dozen bottles.

Other bargain areas are good German wines from the 1971 and 1976 vintages; burgundy, except from the top half dozen estates, is very cheap, often as little as half of a merchant's price. The reason is that burgundy has shown it cannot be trusted. If you know the wine, or taste it first, it is one of the few ways left to buy mature burgundy; for example, in 1984 you could buy 1952 Gevrey-Chambertin for £75 a dozen. But there was no tasting of the wine. Even so, the risk was almost worth it. Unfashionable claret vintages lag a long way behind the trail-blazers – 1967, 1969, 1973, 1974, 1977 and 1980 are all vintages where the price remains low and relatively static.

Some cautionary words
1 There is no guarantee that your bid will be successful.
2 If you don't like the wine, you can't take it back. Once the vendor has been paid, unless there is a blatant fault, you're lumbered.
3 Although the auctioneer will give you what information he has, there is no guarantee the wine has been well stored, which may materially affect the quality of an older wine.
4 You can easily get stampeded into buying more than you want. Wine is often sold in 'parcels'. The buyer of the first lot in a group of wines under one description will immediately be offered the other lots in that group at the same price. The buyer can decide to take none, some or all of them. Always stick to your limits, and, when possible, form a group of friends to bid. Large lots are always relatively cheaper.

Selling
If you, as a private individual, have wine you want to sell, you will need a licence. The auction house provides that licence, and can also advise on whether the bottles in Aunt Agatha's last will and testament contain anything worth more than the price of a packet of fags.

And those wines I bought 10 years ago? Will I sell! Not a chance!

Some Auction House Addresses

London
Christie, Manson & Woods, 8 King Street, St. James's, London SW1, sales twice monthly.
Christie's South Kensington, 85 Old Brompton Road, London SW7, monthly sales.
Sotheby's, 34-35 New Bond Street, London W1, twenty-four sales annually.

Outside London
Edwards, Bigwood & Bewlay, The Old School, Tiddington, Stratford-upon-Avon, sales held quarterly.
Charles Hawkins & Sons, Lynn Road, Downham Market, Norfolk, sales May and November.
Phillips, Oxford, 39 Park End Street, Oxford, sales twice annually.
Lithgow & Sons, Station Road, Stokesely, Middlesbrough, Cleveland, two sales annually.

Some Recent London Auction Prices
The following list of recent auction prices gives you an idea of the vast range of quality and price that buying in this way affords. The very brave could have picked up a case of *vino da tavola bianco* for £14.00, while the connoisseur who wanted his '45 Mouton in its original case had to pay £7,200. Prices are per case of 12 bottles unless otherwise indicated, and are all quoted ex-VAT.

Bordeaux

NV	Château La Croix de Saint Louis, Bordeaux Rouge	£20
1981	Château Toumilon, Graves (white)	£32
1979	Château Les Sables Peytreau, Bordeaux Blanc	£20
1977	Château Bonnet, Bordeaux Rouge	£25
1976	Château Belle Croix, Bordeaux Supérieur, shipped and bottled by the IEC Wine Society	£33
1976	Château Terrasse, Bordeaux Supérieur	£30
1975	Château La Grâce Dieu (London bottled), Grand Cru St-Emilion	£40
1975	Château Patache d'Aux (London bottled) Grand Cru Bourgeois, Médoc	£40
1971	Château Gigault, Côtes de Blaye	£31
1970	Château Gruaud-Larose 2eme Cru Classé St-Julien (for six bottles)	£220
1970	Château La Lagune 3eme Cru Classé, Haut-Médoc	£220
1970	Château Léoville-Las Cases 2eme Cru Classé, St-Julien	£290
1970	Château La Mission-Haut-Brion Cru Classé de Graves	£380–£580
1970	Château Mouton-Rothschild 1er Cru Classé, Pauillac	£400–£720
1970	Château Pape-Clément Cru Classé de Graves	£200
1970	Château Pavie 1er Grand Cru Classé, St-Emilion	£180
1970	Château de Pez Cru Bourgeois, St-Estèphe	£175
1966	Château Latour 1er Cru Classé, Pauillac	£760
1966	Château Lynch-Bages 5eme Cru Classé, Pauillac	£300
1966	Château Mouton-Rothschild 1er Cru Classé, Pauillac	£880
1966	Château Haut-Brion 1er Cru Classé, Graves	£740
1961	Château Calon-Ségur 3eme Cru Classé, St-Estèphe	£370
1961	Château Léoville-Las Cases 2eme Cru Classé, St-Julien	£600
1961	Château Palmer 3eme Cru Classé, Margaux	£1,700
1961	Château Palmer 3eme Cru Classé Margaux (magnums)	£2,500
1961	Château Rauzan-Gassies 2eme Cru Classé, Margaux	£290
1945	Château Mouton-Rothschild 1er Cru Classé, Pauillac	£5,000
1945	Château Mouton-Rothschild: in the same sale	
	in original cases	£7,200
	six bottle lot with cachet of wooden case	£1,800

Burgundy

NV	Beaujolais-Villages, Lucien Père & Fils	£28
1979	Chablis	£40
1979	Chablis, Fourchaume	£50
1978	Bonnes Mares, Clair Daü	£190
1978	Corton, Bonneau de Martray	£170
1978	Corton-Charlemagne, Comtes de Grancey, Louis Latour	£400
1978	Echézeaux	£160
1977	Morey St-Denis, Bouchard Père	£40
1976	Gevrey-Chambertin, Clos St. Jacques, Clair Daü	£150
1976	Givry	£48
1976	Pouilly-Vinzelles	£30
1973	Meursault, Cuvée de Loppin, Hospices de Beaune	£150
1972	Meursault les Casses-Têtes, Jean Germain	£69
1971	Corton les Maréchaudes, Doudet-Naudin	£105
1967	Clos Vougeot, Chanson	£60
1966	Aloxe-Corton les Boutières (Berry Bros)	£85
1959	Echézeaux, Domaine de la Romanée-Conti (for one bottle)	£60
1953	Chambertin, Averys selection (for six bottles)	£660

Port

1977	Warre	£96
1975	Fonseca (for six bottles)	£82
1975	Warre	£74
1970	Croft	£120
1966	Fonseca	£180
1966	Taylor	£180
1963	Fonseca	£260
1960	Cockburn	£185
1960	Croft	£185
1960	Graham	£190
1945	Taylor	£1,050
1935	Taylor	£950

Rhône

1979	Côte Rôtie, Brune et Blonde, Guigal	£80
1978	Châteauneuf-du-Pape	£48
1978	Châteauneuf-du-Pape, Domaine de Beaucastel	£100
1976	Châteauneuf-du-Pape	£38

Sauternes

1976	Château d'Yquem (for 24 halves)	£480
1970	Château Filhot	£140
1967	Château Suduiraut	£300

Germany

1978	Scharzhofberger Kabinett	£29
1976	Niersteiner Findling Auslese	£58
1976	Oppenheimer Kreuz Riesling Beerenauslese	£92
1971	Erbacher Honigberg Spätlese	£62
1971	Trittenheimer Apotheke Auslese	£62

Other

NV	Vino da Tavola (bianco)	£14
NV	Asti Spumante, Bosca	£18
NV	Coteaux Varois 'Bellestelle' red/white/rosé	£16
1979	Dolcetto d'Alba, La Spinona	£30
1977	Cabernet d'Anjou Rosé, Château du Breuil	£18
1977	Westbury Muller Thurgau and Reichensteiner	£30

Stop Press: Sotheby's introduced a buyer's premium of 10 per cent on 1 June 1984. This has enabled them to reduce vendor's premium on larger sales.

WINE BARS AND RESTAURANTS

I've just walked out on the wine bar round the corner. Walked out *on,* not walked out *of.* The reason? We wanted to celebrate. Champagne, we thought, what else? Just a straight affordable bottle of fizz after a hard day's slog. Within moments of scanning the flimsy wine list, my spontaneous enthusiasm was taking a karate chop across the knuckles. They offered only one champagne - and it was £13.50 a bottle. For a top quality wine, one might have swallowed hard and dived deep into the old wallet. But this was one of the cheapest brands on the market, and within 150 yards it was available in a shop for £5.79. A little bit of vinous sleuthing revealed that the trade price was £4.85. That wine bar was putting on about 175%, because they knew full well that there will always be people who must drink champagne, for a variety of celebratory or romantic reasons, and who will therefore pay the price.

'So', I hear you cry, 'what happened to your celebration?' Oh, I had it all right. We spent five minutes on the tube (40p each), and emerged at Leicester Square, where the Cork & Bottle wine bar offered me a Grande Marque champagne, in perfect condition, for just £10.50.

One would have thought that Leicester Square would be one of the most expensive places in London in terms of rates, rent and those city centre overheads which can cripple a business. But Don Hewitson, the owner of the Cork & Bottle has his economics far more under control than the half-empty, over-priced wine bar down the Fulham Road. He doesn't see any point in sitting on stocks of wine that no one wants in the hope of a double profit margin when it finally does sell.

The wine bar business is booming. As UK wine drinkers top the 25 million mark for the first time, one of the places they are most likely to spread their wings a bit is in a wine bar. It's young people, it's fast-talking, fast-thinking people for whom wine is providing that shot of sophistication that the glossy media advertisements tell them they need. And it's price-conscious people too. As the choice of leisure time pursuits grows even wider, no one can catch a share of those weekly paypackets by standing still and overcharging the public. The Hewitson philosophy is to pack people into his wine bars, persuading them by a mixture of enthusiasm, knowledge and gossipy good humour to drink more - and more adventurously - and to keep mark-ups low enough to achieve that end. Since overheads are the same if there are 10 or 100 people in the space, the only things that are going to wreck the sums are donations to the St John Ambulance Brigade to help supply first aid to exhausted cork-pullers and glass-washers.

I suppose you could say it's a high risk philosophy, but is it? Reduced margins, increased turnover: whether or not it's the good business it sounds to me, it clearly gives the customer good value for money.

By putting themselves forward as meeting places, usually with some attempt to provide an attractive ambience, the wine bars offer a direct alternative to the traditional pub, with the crucial difference that while pubs where women on their own feel entirely at ease are probably a minority; the wine bar, right from the start, has seemed to have more of an air of gentility and sophistication to lure in the increasingly powerful female lobby. Any business wishing to profit out of alcohol now ignores women's wishes at its peril. The traditional male dominance of the decision-making in alcohol purchase is on the way out, as is reflected in the fact that over half the take-home wine bought last year was from a supermarket or grocery - and over 70% of those purchases are reckoned to be by women.

An important area where Hewitson feels the wine bar must succeed to be profitable is food. A wine bar now has to calculate its covers like a restaurant, and a key to success is to provide 'nearly' restaurant food at 'not nearly' restaurant prices. The food also allows more flexibility in the profit margins than the wine, since it is more difficult for a customer to compare the price of a created dish, than that of a wine whose name is familiar from the off-licence shelves. That profit flexibility, of 60-100 per cent, is very important, as the fixed costs of running any establishment escalate. In 1973, his quarterly electricity bill was £300. Today it's £2,600. Almost nine times more. In that time his house wine has gone from £1.45 to £4.00 – less than three times. Which could explain why he's unwilling to praise his house red and white; as he points out, house wine is the worst value in the place. For 70p a bottle more than the house white you could get a first rate Sauvignon. Hewitson gives the advice that in a wine bar the real bargains are the special offers and unfamiliar names. Look for wines on sale which you *don't* recognize from the supermarket shelves – estate German wines, Riojas, wines from Portugal, Australia and New Zealand. The wine bar gives you the opportunity to be adventurous without tears. Take it!

Restaurants

The strengths of a restaurant are usually of a more serious and committed kind than those of a wine bar where, although the owner may *want* you to snatch up a plate of the chicken liver paté, wolf down a portion of microwave Lasagna, and have a slice of gateau with your coffee and (he hopes) port, the simple fact is – you don't *have* to. If you insist, you can sit for an hour at your table with that glass of house wine, looking doleful and putting all the other customers off their drink, and there's not a great deal the proprietor can do about it except give you black looks and spill oxtail soup over your shoes without apologizing.

But even the mere decision to go to a restaurant is now a major one; I mean, you have to eat there, don't you? Restaurants sell food, like clothes shops sell trousers, and the whole process of buying, preparing and serving food is an increasingly expensive one. Before you even start to drink, you can reckon on £10 a head for food at a reasonable restaurant. See what I mean? It's not the same as popping down to the wine bar for a quick bottle of Sauvignon at £4.95.

And restaurants sell a lot more than just food. They sell you the surroundings in which to indulge. Don Hewitson's calculation that fixed running costs are up by 900 per cent over a ten-year period is going to have even more of an effect on the restaurant owner, because although in a wine bar you can squeeze 20 or 30 drinkers standing at the bar into a space which they'd write to their MP about if it was during rush hour on the Bakerloo Line, that enforced *bonhomie* isn't the reason people go to restaurants. If you were simply hungry and had to eat something, you could eat at home; you could have a hamburger, or a kebab, or a take-away. No, restaurants have to give you 'effect' with your food – and that costs. Décor, furnishings, quality staff, a wide choice of foods which may go unordered and to waste at the end of the night, and a long, unhurried time in which to allow you to relish it all.

Which brings us to the wine. Somehow those expenses have to be covered, and the emphasis differs radically from a wine bar. Basically you go to a wine bar to drink, and maybe eat. You go to a restaurant to eat, and maybe drink. So, while in a wine bar the cost of wine is the thing to which a customer will be most sensitive, in a restaurant, his warning light is going to flash on because of the cost of the food. There's no great ignominy in a restaurant in ordering the house red or white, much less than if you took someone into a wine bar for a drink and a bite and said 'Oh, we'll just have the cheese and biscuits.' So, more and more, wine *has* to be a regular profit maker, and the mark of an outstanding restaurateur (from the wine drinker's point of view) is that he doesn't just get a printed list from a central supplier, slap on 100-300 per cent, and use the money he makes to subsidize his inefficiency or greed elsewhere. He regards wine as an integral part of the meal – just as exciting as the food – and attempts to offer the customer a wide choice and good value.

Brian Jordan of Bowlish House in Shepton Mallet (winner of the 'Wine List of the Year' award in 1980 and 1982) puts it pretty bluntly. Food must stand on its own two feet he says simply, and so must wine. If wine is forced to provide profit which is lacking from the food side of things, he sees the customer being offered a less than honest deal, and he is even prepared to leave out his overheads in calculating his wine price – which is, of course, easier in deepest Somerset than in London's West End. While he'll put 66 per cent on the food, and calculate that as one-third overheads, one-third profit, he reckons to put a 50 per cent mark up on the average buying price of his wine, and that allows him to have a section on his list of 15 wines priced at £3.50 a bottle, including VAT. And not just plonk. What about a 1978 cru Beaujolais, or a 10 year old Dão?

Obviously one can't demand that every restaurateur has Brian Jordan's massive enthusiasm for his wine list, but his opinion that one of the problems with restaurant wine prices and quality is simple laziness is hard to refute. It's so *easy* to be lazy with wine and get away with it. But food, even with microwaves, frozen pre-preparations and the rest, is much more difficult, because the customer is likely to feel more confident in being critical. In a restaurant, there is often social pressure to seem knowledgeable about wine, and to avoid loss of face many customers will plump for a familiar, pronounceable name, and not carp at the price. And since one market rule says charge what the buying public will stand, the lazy restaurateur can always justify himself.

However, Jordan thinks that the days of such an attitude are numbered. Historically, wine was a mark of privilege, and the privileged were not supposed to squeal if you whacked up the profit margin. Not any more. We may be getting better off as a nation, but we're working harder for what we earn, and want to make sure we spend it effectively. Wine is one of the growth areas across all levels of society, and its increased popularity will force restaurant prices down. As the public becomes more exposed to wine prices, particularly nowadays through the enormous influence of supermarkets on buying patterns, it'll be a dwindling number of us who tolerate exorbitant wine prices.

The Bowlish House list is so large, one would expect there to be an enormous profit-devouring stock held. But only the top 20 sellers are stocked even by the case, and his absolute maximum purchase is five cases. Otherwise the stock is as little as two to six bottles. A look at his sales pattern shows the sense of this. In January this year, his 194 customers drank 43 bottles of house wines at £3.50, but, from his enormous list – and he has 225 wines under £10 – only six particular wines were ordered three times or more, and only nine were ordered twice. A stock of two to six bottles per wine thus seems quite enough.

February obviously brought an influx of customers sensing an early end to winter, because his 287 customers bought 55 bottles of house wines, and 10 bottles of Beaujolais Nouveau. There were 11 wines ordered more than three times, but only three of them – a Sancerre, an Alsace Riesling, and a Côtes du Rhône, were the same as in January. In fact the greatest consistency was shown by the fact that 18 per cent of his customers each month ordered dessert wine by the glass.

Nick Lander owns and runs L'Escargot in London's Soho, and although the pace of life here is considerably more hectic, he also does not allow a blind profit motive to dominate his policy. He puts something on his list if he thinks it should be there. Trimbach's Clos Ste-Hune Riesling is one of the most exciting wines Alsace produces – that's why he lists it. He's rather pleased if he sells a bottle a week. He lists the award-winning (Australian) Mount Helen Chardonnay for the same reason. While he's been selling two bottles of these, he'll have sold 876 house whites and 430 house reds in a fortnight. Like most good restaurateurs he'd like to sell less house wine, since although he goes to some lengths to select a good one, he also has to take a lower gross profit to keep it below the magic £5 figure.

His philosophy is to subsidize the special and rare wines by maintaining his margins on the 'expense account' favourites. So the Sancerre, of which he sells about 90 bottles a week, and buys in considerable quantity at a very good price, sells at £8.50, because he reckons that's a fair price for that wine. Château Canon 1971 he bought for "not a great deal less than £20", but he sells it at £25 inc VAT. Croizet-Bages he bought for £9.17 and was selling for £18.50, Pernand-Vergelesses 1973 white was £12.50 from a £5 purchase price. Again, fair prices, because these sorts of wine are not generally available (and as this chapter goes to press both sold out and irreplaceable – which is why I said 'was'), and he is fulfilling one of the restaurateur's traditional rôles – seen less and less – that of providing the purchase, storage and serving of special bottles for, presumably, special occasions. In general, though, he will buy from a wholesale wine merchant a case at a time; and with a list which makes a point of attractive layout and blurb, he rarely uses the auction houses, simply because he doesn't want to spend a lot of cash, and then mess up the list when the wine's run out because he can't re-purchase it.

One thing all restaurateurs seem agreed on. If you want a bargain, don't go for the obvious. The lesser-known areas are rarely sold, and even the Rhône is under-rated. Italian reds, for them as like 'em, are often the *only* reasonably priced wines in posh restaurants, since francophilia has invaded the system to such an extent. And if they were dining out in an expensive London restaurant, there seemed to be one golden rule. *Beware* the classed growth claret. It's the lazy restaurateur's easiest way to pretend he has a classy list, and he's sure to beef up the margins accordingly.

Supermarkets

'Why do I buy wine in a supermarket?' said Jill with an air of incredulity just polite enough to allow me a moment to consider whether my question was quite as stupid as she thought. I mean, I hadn't said: why do you breathe, why do you eat? there are lots of other ways of buying wine after all. 'Yes', I said, 'why?' 'Because everything goes on one cheque!'

Simple as that. In these days of working mothers and endless rush, to be able to do the entire week's shopping in one place, and dispose of the lot with one cheque is an advantage not to be overlooked. And not only the ease of paying with one cheque. The ease of putting all your purchases into one bag. The ease of only having to find one parking space, and only having to load the car once. It all began to sound a little *too* idyllic. 'Ah', I remembered, 'what about Waitrose?' – they have off-licence departments where you have to pay separately – 'You'll need two cheques there at least.' 'Oh no', Jill said, 'not at my Waitrose. The girl at the groceries till cashes my cheque for whatever I ask, and I hand over the cash in the off-licence department.'

Another blow to preconceptions about the impersonal nature of supermarkets and their inflexibility. But I thought I saw a chink. 'Well, I suppose *you* know what you want', I continued, 'so the fact that there's no expert advice doesn't bother you'. Again, Jill was way ahead. At her Waitrose, she said, the manager was tremendously knowledgeable, and, whenever she needed advice, it wasn't just of the 'ah, well, yes, the liebfraumilch is very nice today, goes very well with curry. Oh. I see, red, yes, well, you'll be wanting the, er . . . Beaujolais. Very French, Beaujolais, very French, and you know what they say about the French' variety. No, this manager goes to wine courses, does his homework, and so far hasn't once given her bad advice.

I'd expected a balanced discussion about the pros and cons of supermarket wine-buying with someone who seemed to be a very typical consumer, and here she was, getting so enthusiastic that any one of half a dozen big chains could have hired her on the spot to do their PR. And Jill wasn't finished yet. 'If I go to Tesco or Sainsburys, I get all information I need from the label on the shelf, and the labels on the wine. And if I can't pronounce it, I don't get embarassed having to ask for it and getting my tongue in a twist. I just shove it in a basket along with the cornflakes and the pound and a half of Danish.'

One of the biggest criticisms of supermarkets has been that while a traditional wine merchant is always able to give you excellent advice, a supermarket can't. But where do you find this beleaguered band, the traditional wine merchant? Go into the majority of high street wine shops and you will be extremely lucky to find knowledgeable staff. Find a traditional wine merchant, and you will probably find a very traditionalist viewpoint. You may find this reassuring, and you may be in accordance with his views on the old favourites of claret, burgundy, hock and port. But the world of wine has suddenly become modern and fast-moving, fresh, young-tasting and uncomplicated. I hate to say it, but might you not be happier browsing down the line of bottles with their explanatory tags, with no one trying to make your mind up for you, and no one pressuring you, and quite enough basic information given on the label?

I picked out two bottles at random to see if the labels would give me the help I needed. The first was Sainsbury's white Rioja Seco Vina Castil 1982. A long name, but Rioja Seco was printed in the biggest letters, and just under that it said bluntly 'Spanish Dry White Wine'. The label had rather a nice picture, and gave the alcoholic strength as 11 degrees – very useful and rarely done. I turned the bottle round and the back label gave me all the info that most wine merchants would

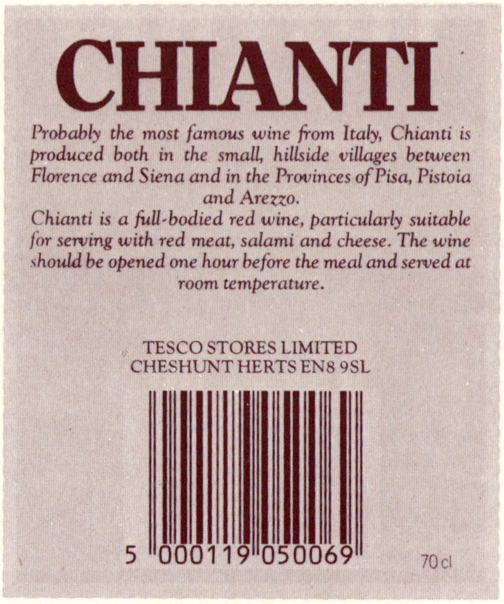

have been able to give me. It said 'A dry white wine from the Rioja wine-growing region 150 miles northeast of Madrid. The blend of Viura and Garnacha Blanco grapes produce a dry, crisp, white wine of distinctive character. Serve lightly chilled with hors d'oeuvres, white meat or fish dishes'. And finally a sweetness indicator of two, which means on a scale of one to nine it's just about bone dry. With information like that, simple, friendly, and quite technical enough for the wine snob to witter on about Garnacha Blanco while he pulls the cork, all I need to do is buy it and make up my own mind if I like it.

The label on the Tesco Mâcon Blanc Villages 1982 was similarly helpful: 'Medium Dry White Wine' was accurate for the 1982 style, and again the producer and the strength were indicated. The back label stated: 'This wine is made from Chardonnay grapes grown on the limestone soil of the area. It has a very clean bouquet with a crisp, dry palate. It is ideal with fish or white meats. Serve chilled'. That's enough for me, and *I'm* inquisitive to the point of rudeness.

What about choice? Aren't supermarkets traditionally rather poor on choice? 'Good God', said Jill, 'I don't *want* too much choice. I just want to know that the wines that are there will be good for what they say they are.' It's easy to forget that an enormous range of wines poorly presented will merely confuse. A smaller range, carefully presented, will help even the most finicky buyer in making his own decisions. A quick check on Sainsbury's list showed that all the big stores carry 34 different French white wines. You can get an *appellation contrôlée* Saumur for £1.69 a bottle, a white Bordeaux for £1.90, or, if that doesn't satisfy you, perhaps a 1980 French-bottled Meursault for £6.75, or a 1964 – yes, a 1964 Moulin Touchais sweet Anjou for £5.55. Claret going back to 1971, Mosel Auslese back to 1975 or 1976. The choice looked very carefully defined; they do not stock 20 old clarets, just a couple, the same with hocks, the Rhône wines, Beaujolais. Enough to satisfy, not enough to accumulate dust.

Seeing that 1971 Château Cissac brought me up with a jolt, because I'd thought that even if the choice was good in the basics, surely it wouldn't be any good for the 'specials'. That too has changed. Waitrose have always led the way in providing high quality wines in their stores, but then they've led the way in foodstuffs too. Now the others are following Waitrose's lead. Sainsbury have brought out their 'Vintage Selection', confident in their market leader position and their reputation as every suburban housewife's favourite multiple.

Tesco, under new leadership, are turning the market upside-down, with a string of first-class, cheap wines, innovative labelling and packaging, and now the first evidence of the eagerly awaited move up-market with the beginnings of château-bottled claret, domaine-bottled Châteauneuf-du-Pape, and some of the most honest Italian wines on sale anywhere. It wasn't like my first visit to Tesco . . .

In 1977 I was working down at Chichester for the summer, and discovered they did rather a good Spanish sparkler for £1.59, which kept us all chirpy after rehearsals. To my intense surprise, at the back of the little kiosk, I saw a bottle of Château de Camensac 1969, a classed growth Médoc, looking very out of it indeed, and probably distinctly embarassed by its price tag – £1.50! My money was on the counter before the assistant could wipe the dust off the label.

That night supper was graced with classed growth claret, thanks to Tesco. Next night too, and at the end of the week, with stocks running low, the bewildered manager ordered a whole case. Back it came in its stencilled wooden box, and I handed over 18 crisp green ones. We had some wonderful parties after the show, and a few weeks later I was back in for another case. The manager gave me a distinctly old-fashioned look, and said that when Head Office saw that his branch had managed to sell two cases of classed growth claret, they had smelt something fishy. They doubted the motives for my purchases, they said, and they were very sorry, but I couldn't have any more! I pleaded that all I was trying to do was to improve the cash flow of the branch. But yes, the wine was lovely, and, well, cheap. I suppose I should be grateful for the two cases we did drink, but that's the trouble with wine people; our lives are filled with the bargain we just missed, or the wine we didn't quite buy enough of.

How things have changed! But in 1977 the supermarkets were just flexing their muscles, preparing to become a major force in wine. Since then, however, the wine-drinking boom has gathered its full head of steam, and the supermarkets have benefited more than any other group. It is reckoned that 54 per cent of the take-home wine trade is through licensed grocers, and the lion's share is the supermarkets'. Indeed, independent analysts reckon that Sainsburys alone sell perhaps 15 per cent of all the off-trade wine in Britain. Luckily, with this power has come responsibility. Prices are low and quality increasingly good across the board.

The new breed of supermarket wine buyers includes many of the brightest, most original thinkers in the wine-buying world. This eagerness to prove their right to hold a commanding position in retailing is certainly best illustrated by their own label brands. Simple liebfraumilch, simple vin de table, simple Bardolino: any wine that needs to be young and fresh should be bought from a supermarket, where the turn-round of stock can be as quick as six weeks. Many basic wines have no ability to age at all. A good supermarket, buying direct, involving its own quality control at every point of the operation, and achieving low-margin, high-turnover sales won't give a liebfraumilch the chance to age anyway – and thank goodness for that.

Jill was off to do her shopping. I wanted a bottle of champagne – interviews are tiring. But I hadn't got any food in the house, and I'd run out of washing up liquid and toothpaste and – yes, of course I did. I went to the supermarket for the lot.

A chart showing a selection of the wines being sold by supermarkets in May 1984 (and their prices) is overleaf.

Supermarket Wines

		Waitrose	Sainsbury's
France	1982 Beaujolais	£2.69	£2.69
	Bordeaux Rouge	£2.25	£2.95 St-Emilion
	Vin de Pays	£1.89 Hérault, Dom. de St Macaire	£1.98 Hérault
	Mâcon Blanc	£3.15 1982 Mignot	
	Bordeaux Blanc	£2.15 Entre-Deux-Mers	£2.18
	Muscadet	£2.15	£2.15
	Sauternes	£3.45	£3.60
	Sparkling, Veuve de Vernay	£3.35	£3.35
	House Champagne NV	£5.95	£6.45
	Rosé Anjou	£1.99	£1.89
Germany	Liebfraumilch	£1.99	£2.08
	Piesporter	£2.29	£2.25
Italy	Chianti Classico	£2.25	£2.25
	Valpolicella	£1.95	£1.99
	Lambrusco	£2.15	£2.10
	Soave	£1.95	£1.99
	Asti Spumante	£3.75	£3.29
Spain	Rioja	£2.29 1980 Olarra	£2.45 1979 Viña Alberdi
	Table Wine	£1.89	£1.79
	Sherry Sweet/Medium/Dry	£2.25	£2.45
Portugal	Vinho Verde	£2.19 Verdegar	£2.19
	Port	£3.49 Ruby	£3.55
Wine boxes	French Red (3 litres)	£7.85	£7.95
	French White (3 litres)	£7.75	£9.95 Muscadet
	German White (3 litres)	£9.15 Liebfraumilch	£8.95 Bereich Zell

Fine wines available in May 1984 from supermarkets include **Bordeaux red:** *1977 Château Léoville-Poyferré, St-Julien £6.65, and 1977 Château Lynch Bages, Pauillac £6.95 from Waitrose; 1979 Château Grand Puy Ducasse, Pauillac £7.45, Château Giscours, Margaux £7.50, 1971 Château Cissac, Médoc £8.99 from Sainsbury.* **Bordeaux white:** *1980 Château Lafaurie-Peyraguey, Sauternes £6.95, 1976 Château Filhot, Sauternes (sweet) £8.55 from Waitrose.* **Burgundy red:** *1982 Beaujolais Château de Poncié, Fleurie £4.35 and 1979 Gevrey-Chambertin, Chanson £8.95 (Sainsbury); 1979 Gevrey-Chambertin, Boisset £7.95 and 1974*

Supermarket Wines

Tesco	**Marks & Spencer's**	**Safeway**
£2.49	£2.75	£2.47
£2.75 Médoc	£2.25	£2.29
£1.95 Côtes du Ventoux	£1.99 French Country	£1.71 de Vaucluse
£2.99	£3.49	£3.51 1982
£2.05	—	—
£2.19	£1.99	£2.09
£3.29	—	£3.57 Château du Pick
£3.35	—	£3.75
£5.99	£6.99	£6.09 Pol Albert
£1.99	£2.69 litre	£1.89
£1.99	£1.99	£1.75
£2.25	£2.49	£2.19 Michelsberg
£2.19	£1.99	£1.75
£1.99	—	£1.99
£1.99	£1.89	£1.81
£1.99	£1.89	£1.81
£2.99	£3.59	£3.49
£2.15 Viña Lagran	£2.99 Marques de Pomerol	£1.97 Bodegas Campo Blanco £2.69 1976 Domecq Domain
£1.79 Penedès	—	£1.97 Bodegas Viña Montebro
£2.89	£2.69	£2.46
£2.19	£2.15	£1.81
£4.25	£3.49	£4.09 Cockburn's Ruby
£7.99 Vin de Pays du Gard	—	£7.69 Vin de Pays du Tarn
£7.99 Vin de Pays du Gard	£8.50 Vin de Pays	£7.69 Vin de Pays du Gard
£9.21 Liebfraumilch	—	—

Nuits St-Georges, Deschamps £8.95 from Waitrose. **Burgundy white:** *1980 Meursault, Moillard £6.95, 1981 Puligny-Montrachet, Clos de la Mouchère £8.45 (Sainsbury) 1981 Pouilly Fuissé, Barolet £4.95 (Waitrose).* **Loire white:** *1964 Moulin Touchais, Anjou £5.75 (Sainsbury).* **German white:** *1976 Erdener Treppchen Auslese Eiswein £5.45 (Sainsbury).* **Champagne:** *Non-vintage Veuve Clicquot £9.55 (Waitrose, Sainsbury) non-vintage Bollinger £10.29 and 1976 Veuve Clicquot £11.95 (Waitrose).* **Port:** *1972 Taylor's Vargellas £8.75, 1965 Fonseca Guimaraens £8.95, 1970 Taylor's £11.55 (all from Waitrose).*

Wine Boxes

Most wine in boxes is horrid. Sorry, but it is! I've been sniffing and gurgling away at these wines ever since the furore over the quality of their contents in 1982. Yet the public seems to love them. In 1983 wine boxes notched up a 30 per cent increase in sales while the general light table wine market moved ahead by an equally impressive 13 per cent. The projection for 1984 is that wine boxes will move ahead by another 21 per cent, while overall light table wine will increase by 12 per cent. The brand leaders in the wine box game are Stowells of Chelsea, and they think that their branded boxes will increase sales by 48 per cent in 1984! All these figures mean that £100 million a year is now being spent on wine boxes, and these cardboard cartons with their foil bags inside now account for 11 per cent of all take-home wine sold in Britain. And they were only introduced a little over three years ago! By 1990 it is predicted that boxed wine will hold a market share of 20 per cent.

The reason given for their success is their convenience. It can't be their price. Sainsbury's claret costs £1.90 for a 70cl bottle. The three-litre box of Stowells' claret costs £9.15 on the Sainsbury shelf – which makes a bottle-equivalent price of £2.13. Stowells' Muscadet is also £9.15 for three litres, while Sainsbury's Muscadet works out nearly 20p a bottle cheaper at £1.95.

As for quality, comparative blind tastings between identical wines from bottle and box have always shown the boxed wines to be in a far poorer state; that six-month shelf-life guarantee is debatable. Any cheap white bottle (and three-quarters of the market is in cheap white) which you don't finish in one go will keep perfectly well re-corked in the fridge. After a week it will still be better than the boxed equivalent.

At the moment, since wine drinking is supposed to be to do with the pleasures of taste, we have to give a thumbs down to boxes. However, the box chaps are aware of the problems, and both Colmans and Stowells are striving to increase the quality of their boxed wines. Fingers crossed; there's a long way to go.

A Selection of 3-litre wine boxes

Red

Côtes du Rhône (SAIN)	8.95
Vin de Pays de l'Ardèche, Maison du Rouret (RACK)	8.49
Berri Estates Shiraz (RACK)	7.69
Sainsbury's Coteaux d'Aix en Provence	7.95
Tesco's Valpolicella	8.25
Tesco's Chianti	8.25
Thresher Chianti	7.69
Victoria Wine French Full Red	8.25
Vin de Pays des Pyrenées Orientales (VICT)	9.29
Waitrose French Dry Red Wine	7.75
Colman's French Red Wine (WAIT)	7.85
Stowell's Claret (SAIN)	9.95

White

Stowell's Muscadet de Sèvre et Maine (SAIN)	9.95
Muscadet de Sèvre et Maine, Sautejeau (THRE)	9.99
Vin de Pays de l'Ardèche, Maison du Rouret (RACK)	8.49
Berri Estates Riesling (RACK)	7.69
Sainsbury's Gaillac Medium Dry	7.95
Sainsbury's Entre Deux Mers	8.95
Sainsbury's Bereich Zell	8.95
Tesco's Soave	8.25
Californian Chenin Blanc (TES)	9.77
Colman's Liebfraumilch (THRE)	9.59
Thresher Soave	7.69
Victoria Wine French Dry White	8.25
Waitrose French Dry White	7.75
Colman's French White (WAIT)	7.85
Tesco Austrian White	8.39
Cloberg Yugoslav Laski Riesling (TAN)	10.41
Sainsbury's Hungarian Olasz Riesling	7.95
Tesco Austrian White	8.39

Foreign Exchange Rates

Because we are, with all due respect to English growers, basically talking about a foreign commodity, exchange rates are an extremely important factor in the cost of the wine we drink. The most recent example of the role exchange rates play was the boom in California wine sales as the pound strengthened against the dollar in 1979, 1980 and 1981 - only to level off since the pound's slide in 1982.

But just look at the lira exchange rate for the years 1970 to 1978 and try to work out how much you would be paying for a basic bottle of Chianti at an exchange rate of 1,500 lira to £1. The difference between that rate and today's increases the cost of the basic wine by 60 per cent (although not, thank goodness the whole bottle price since we pay our duty and VAT in pounds). Or think what burgundy would cost at the 1975 to 1978 exchange rate for the French franc; and a quick look at the chart will tell you why branded German wines are so price sensitive - there are only a *third* as many Deutschmarks to be had for your pound as there were in 1966! Most Spanish table wine prices would look pretty sick at the 1977 exchange rate; and, although our chart does not stretch to the Swiss franc, that legendary currency's ascendancy (even over the mark) is a major reason why Swiss wines are so rare here. Of course, we are a good deal poorer than most of our European counterparts these days and deserve the break we are getting in France, Spain and Italy at least - but it can't be denied that this should be a good time for anyone wanting to take advantage of the rates and lay down some decent wines in case we collapse against these currencies too.

Exchange Rates at mid-June 1961–1984

Year	French francs	German marks	Italian lire	Spanish pesetas	US dollars
1961	13.70	11.10	1,734	167.00	2.80
1966	13.68	11.22	1,743	167.00	2.79
1970	13.23	8.71	1,508	166.95	2.39
1971	13.37	8.48	1,511	168.27	2.41
1972	13.03	8.22	1,509	167.52	2.59
1973	10.94	6.61	1,557	149.72	2.58
1974	11.75	6.01	1,559	136.90	2.39
1975	9.07	5.30	1,420	126.70	2.27
1976	8.42	4.57	1,541	120.60	1.77
1977	8.50	4.05	1,522	119.00	1.71
1978	8.43	3.83	1,577	143.45	1.83
1979	9.22	3.98	1,784	139.07	2.10
1980	10.67	4.61	2,194	187.07	2.35
1981	11.21	4.69	2,346	188.50	2.00
1982	11.91	4.79	2,395	193.70	1.73
1983	11.74	3.92	2,310	212.75	1.54
1984 (July)	11.53	3.79	2,305	212.80	1.32

FRANCE

We don't appreciate our good fortune in having France so close. The *entente* may not always be as *cordiale* as it should be, but when the romance of Europe is only two hours away on a boat, and you can get a day return for £7.50, it's often cheaper to go to France for lunch than to book a table in the King's Road. And as wine drinking in the UK has at last broken through the social barriers and become regarded as one of the most affordable and dependable pleasures of life, to have France as our nearest and even, on a clear day, visible neighbour is to have the greatest wine nation in the world on our doorstep.

Far back in history, France's start in wine was made by the Romans, and many of her greatest vineyard areas - the Rhône, Burgundy, Champagne, the Loire, Bordeaux - were established by them. France has more vineyard areas perfectly balanced between the excesses of too much and too little heat, too much and too little rain, than any other part of the world. She stretches her ripening periods as long as she can, to catch that spark of genius in the fruit which will always distinguish the great classic French wines. And, maybe because the temperate climate had already put its own process of natural selection to work, the vines planted and propagated by the Romans were largely the local vines, found in the river valleys and on warm hillsides where the first 'professional' vineyards were established. With a few extra additions from Germany in the north, and Spain in the south, these vines - now so familiar as Cabernet Sauvignon, Merlot, Pinot Noir, Chenin, and many others - can produce in France what are regarded world-wide as their definitive types of wine. In the course of two thousand years you pick up a few tips, and, with the exceptions of the sweet riesling wines of Germany, and the fortified wines of Spain and Portugal, it is the classic French styles by which the whole world of wine making has set its standards.

Frequently we hear the cry go up from California, from Australia, from Italy maybe, that they have 'beaten' the French; that a series of blind tastings has proven California Cabernets to be better than Bordeaux classed growths, Australian Chardonnays more exciting than their white burgundy equivalents, or Italian sparkling wine superior to champagne. No, No, No! What *is* all this talk of 'beating' or 'better than'? A few devoted, passionate wine makers, aiming at the heights of French tradition, can frequently achieve small quantities of great, heart-stopping wines. But France produces superlative bottles by the million from her top areas, and, until the baying at her doors gets too insistent, she is wise enough to take this sincerest form of flattery in her stride. Soon the adolescent phase of 'my dad's bigger than your dad' will pass, and the new wine makers will no longer be content to copy. Their own unique styles of wine will then become apparent over 20–30 years. Well, that's quite some rush! France ambled through 2,000 years defining and refining her best products. Interestingly, she has also opened her eyes to the fact that these avid imitators must have something in their favour too, and so the latest phase of her centuries-long process of re-definition and improvement is under way.

Notice has been taken of the lessons learnt in trying to reproduce the great, cool-climate reds and whites in hot, steaming areas like California, South Africa and Australia. The majority of France's wine production is in her southern belt, spreading in an endless carpet of vines from the Alps to the Pyrenees. Hot, dirty, disorganised vineland, difficult to control, and all too easily prey to the evils of overproduction and faulty vinification. Almost by way of returning the compliment, southern France, led by the go-ahead and knowledge-thirsty graduates from the Montpelier Oenology School, is now taking advantage of the efforts of so many New Worlders to mimic France's best wines, by using their techniques to improve her worst wines. Not only has France historically proved her ability to produce the world's finest, but the days of the awful coarse heady reds, and dull, flat whites may be numbered. France could have reacted to the considerable challenges to her position as the world's Number One by standing on her dignity. Luckily she didn't, and the future is unremittingly bright if the improvements and awareness which are beginning to change the problem areas like Anjou, the Languedoc and Burgundy can be carried through.

Britain is the amenable target of much of this marketeering. Not only is French quality frequently the best, but French promotions, often brilliantly orchestrated from the Piccadilly headquarters of Food and Wine from France, seem to head off all challengers before they can even get their running spikes on. She has only lost out in the 'light fruity' styles, allowing Germany to streak ahead, and it looks as though Italy may be allowed to steal a march in the semi-sparkling, semi-alcoholic nursery world of the red and white Lambrusco styles, although one has the feeling that any self-respecting Frenchman wouldn't be seen dead drinking stuff like that in the first place. Elsewhere it's almost as though France likes nothing better than a challenge. It's only with the enthusiastic entry into the promotional arena of Spain's *Vinos de España,* that she's had a real rival, but they have an awful lot of catching up to do.

French wines are booming. In 1983 we imported 481 million litres of all sorts of wine, an increase of 9.3 per cent over 1982, and of that the French share was a massive 149 million litres, an increase of nearly 14 per cent over the same period. This is the overall figure for wines, but it is the sparkling and still table wines which France does best, and which show her dominance of the market. The UK held her top position in the champagne export stakes with a consumption up by 28 per cent and *appellation contrôlée* sparklers – in other words champagne-method substitutes – pushed ahead 52 per cent.

In the 'light wine' sector, which basically means still, unfortified wines, France has a very firm 38 per cent grip on the market, and once again 1983 proved to be a bumper year. Much of the growth can be attributed to an advertising campaign which played on the gut feeling of the consumer that French is best – even in the plonk division – and then assured them that best could also be cheap. French white plonk, or *vin de table,* whose quality is frequently less exciting than that of other countries, was up 25 per cent, and the increase in French white *appellation contrôlée* wines was way ahead of the market at 33.6 per cent.

If red was getting left behind, it was still doing very well, showing an increase of 11.7 per cent, pretty good going in a market shifting towards white at an alarming rate. Interestingly it was wines such as the traditional light reds of Bordeaux, and the newly-trendy light reds of Beaujolais which led the field. With the 1983 vintage being good and big right across France, and with Budget reductions to boot, goodness knows what 'les Frogs' may achieve in 1984!

BORDEAUX

Claret is our wine. We trust it. We own it. Before you start rushing for your atlases to see if Bordeaux has suddenly shifted north and tacked itself onto the Scilly Isles, I'll repeat that. We *do* own it. We own the taste, the style, the fame. Bordeaux's land, of course we don't own, although we did for a couple of hundred years up to 1453. But it is the British who made claret into the greatest red wine in the world. We should be proud of our achievement, and not indulge in our customary national self-denigration. It was British merchants, both in Bordeaux and over here, who encouraged and shaped the style of the wine which is called claret. And if the Americans are beginning to make more noise about it, it's nice to know that we started it all those centuries ago.

We created a rather British sort of wine, famous for its reserve, and its cool dry flavours, and rarely given to the pudgy overblown richness we might admire in a red Rhône or burgundy. Its fame is based on the Cabernet Sauvignon grape, grown on gravel soil, and its pleasure is ensured by the soft backup offered by the Merlot grape. It is this pair, helped by Cabernet Franc and Petit Verdot, which has made 'claret' the taste that every new-wave vintner of the New World wants to imitate. Yet, just as Burgundy keeps the secret of the Pinot Noir to itself, few people anywhere outside Bordeaux have managed to re-create claret.

Claret has the most tantalising and unlikely combinations of flavour of any red wine. There's the blast of pure fragrant blackcurrant essence as the basic fruit, and then the exotic dry perfumes of lead pencil shavings, fresh wrapped cigars and the intense piney smell of cedar tree resin to weave an endlessly fascinating balance of sweet and dry tastes. Increasingly nowadays this is also blended with the buttersweet overlay of fresh oak barrels, all of it adding up to one of the most complete and absorbing tastes of any sort that the world possesses.

That's the flavour everyone is doing their damnedest to reproduce, but they can't pin down its magic any more than my words can. But then, that's the flavour most of Bordeaux would like to achieve as well, because the properties which make this kind of wine represent perhaps two per cent of the entire production of what is the most varied and most important single wine area in the world.

However that two per cent can't always achieve those flavours, because vintage variations are considerable in Bordeaux! In fact the relatively temperate seaside air is a tremendous factor. In all but the very hottest years the sunshine is tempered by cool breezes off the Atlantic. If the year nevertheless gets too hot, as in 1959 and 1976, and in some cases 1982 and 1983, the flavour will be rich and strong and burnt, and it will be more like the Californian or Italian attempts at claret, using the Cabernet or Merlot grapes. If the summer rains and autumn gales roll in off the Bay of Biscay, and the grapes can't ripen, then the taste will be thin and green and rather raw, resembling the Cabernets of the Loire valley or New Zealand. Only in the years of balance, like 1966, 1970, 1978, 1979, do those astonishing sweet and dry, ripe and raw flavours mix together.

Our special relationship with claret further expresses itself in the way that we judge every vintage, every wine, on its own merits. We don't accord that privilege to other wine areas, but in Bordeaux, as we drink a 1980 and find it a little green and light, we say: 'Yes, well, it wasn't that good a year, they had a lot of trouble bringing in the vintage . . .' – and in brackets one can almost hear the whisper 'poor fellows, what a pity about that rain, but they did their best for us'. If a 1976 seems rather chocolatey and sweet, out come the excuses again: 'Ah, yes, of course they had a lot of problems with drought in 1976, and then there was that rain just before the vintage . . .'. Again, the 'poor fellows' is almost audible in a claret drinker's voice. Because here, we're probably talking about disappointing bottles of wine. But you'd never know it. There is no other wine to which we so endlessly give the benefit of the doubt as claret.

If we drink a Barolo we have an image of what Barolo should taste like. If the wine doesn't match up to *that* image, then we say it's a poor Barolo. The Barolo producer may say: 'Hey, I had the same trouble with the spring frosts as the claret producer did, I got those wretched summer storms too, and just as I was giving my grape pickers their vintage breakfast and telling them to look sharp, the heavens opened here as well and spoilt my wine. Give me a break!' And so says the Hermitage man, the Rioja man, the California man, the Australian and the South African.

But only the claret man gets our devoted sympathy. Those other tastes are either met or missed. And only in claret (although we have some kind of ideal of what we would like all claret to be — an endless 1961 first growth Pauillac decanted for two hours and just at its peak) do we find a thousand pleasures in the occasion when the wine doesn't measure up to our ideals. And this is simply because the British are more familiar with claret than any other wine. Whenever arguments flare as to the relative merits of different wines, claret has a start of many generations. And whenever importers try to dent claret's traditional hold on our market, saying: 'These wines, from Italy/Spain/other parts of France are as good, as classic as claret, and should be as highly regarded', they are up against the same brick wall of contented prejudice. Claret has the familiarity of centuries to rely upon. With the possible exception of the small vintage port market, no other wine does.

But familiarity can breed contempt. The one thing the UK has based much of its love affair on is the good ratio of quality to price. On the whole this has held, and usually to our advantage rather than the wine grower's. In fact British buyers of classed growth claret would traditionally expect a financial gain on selling part of their mature stock, gain which would be sufficient to cover costs of replacement *and* allow them to drink the rest for free. The Bordeaux growers only began to claw back some of the profit in the 1960s. By the 1970s, the world economic situation, exacerbated by American intervention, caused growers to bump up prices in an orgy of profit-taking. And the first people to stop buying? The British. One could almost feel the pain as British buyers pulled out, but pull out they did, and the Bordeaux market went into a period of shock and slump from which it has only recently emerged. Nowadays the message is clear: if the quality is high, we'll pay the price. As we did for 1982. But if the quality isn't right, don't try to pull a fast one on price.

Prices. Those high prices are for the classed growths, the investment wines from the Médoc communes, Graves, St-Emilion, Pomerol, not the everyday stuff. It's that two per cent – the Grands Crus. It seems a tiny percentage, given their fame, but it may drop even further; only five years ago they represented five per cent of total sales. Certainly their export markets are stronger, in particular in the USA and northern Europe, where connoisseurs continue the tradition, begun by the British nearly 300 years ago, of seeking out the particular rather than the average. In export terms they account for seven per cent of sales, but even that is a drop from 11 per cent only five years ago. Yet in 1983 Bordeaux exported more than ever before. Sales from the top grands crus properties were up eight per cent on 1982, and sales from the basic properties were up by nearly 15 per cent – putting the basic generic wines 45 per cent up on five years ago. That's how their five per cent share of the market has turned into two per cent for the posh wines. Everyone is selling more, but the basic wines are selling the most.

This is crucially important, because while a major château can prune heavily to reduce yield, declassify part of the crop, use new oak barrels to improve flavour and fix its own price, none of these expedients is available to the peasant farmer with a few acres. He has to sell his wine at whatever bulk price the market is offering. It is only by dint of three big vintages in the last five years that he has managed to make any money at all, because prices have remained worryingly stagnant, rising only a few hundred francs a barrel in five years.

The base price for a 900-litre tonneau of claret was 4,100 francs in 1982 - about 3.12 francs a bottle. In 1983 it rose by the princely sum of 200 francs to 4,300 francs - about 3.17 francs a bottle. The brilliance of a vintage doesn't affect the basic grower's price, whereas it can make the fortune of a big property. If the producer of basic claret was the kind of chap who liked to buy imported equipment, or go on foreign holidays, he just couldn't afford it, the franc is now so weak against the dollar and the pound.

Château Gloria is a well known, but not classified property in St-Julien. Gloria sold its 1981 for 29 francs a bottle, and followed this with a price of 33 francs for the 1982. So the owner was raking in about 10 times the mount of the basic producer. Granted his costs were a lot higher, and granted his wines were a lot better, but then so is his profit margin. The difference caused by crossing the line into the classed growths is shown by the fifth growth Château Lynch-Bages. Its 1981 started at 44 francs a bottle, while its 1982 put on 11 francs to start at 55 francs. The wine at Lynch-Bages is better than at Gloria, but the costs aren't all that different, yet he takes home an extra 22 francs a bottle. But if you're a Premier Cru Classé, the top wine of the region, then the profit possible per bottle is enough to make a basic Bordeaux producer turn to drink. Château Lafite 1981 started at 100 francs a bottle, but 1982, on a wave of excitement about its quality, opened at 170 francs a bottle.

I repeat, the difference in quality is massive, the costs in a top classed growth are enormously higher, but there is a dangerous gap, always large, between the top and the bottom in Bordeaux. Ideally the top prices should drop and the bottom prices should rise. In reality the only way to get the bottom prices to rise is to increase demand, and yet, whenever prices have risen following an increase in demand, the vital domestic market has simply switched to Côtes du Rhône and Beaujolais. Whenever *their* prices have risen and Bordeaux has eased, the consumer switches back. With declining domestic consumption, and a switch to white which Bordeaux alone seems unable to exploit, there's not enough money chasing too much wine at the bottom end of the market. Up with the major classed growths, there's too much money chasing not enough wine.

It might be worth our while just to unravel briefly these various areas of Bordeaux, with their vastly differing abilities to earn a fair return.

The Médoc

The prestigious part of the Médoc is the Haut-Médoc - itself an appellation - but the really juicy business gets done in the four main commune appellations.

Margaux. This is the one nearest to Bordeaux and covers various villages producing wines which at one extreme can be rather sludgy and solid, and at the other, the most fragrant, perfumed red wines France has yet dreamed up. The great Margaux wines come from the village of Margaux itself. They're not hefty, but they do take a long time to set your pulse racing - at least 10 years ageing in a good vintage. Then they're quite light, stunningly perfumed, and absurdly delicious. People pay high prices for them and still get a bargain.

St-Julien. This is perhaps the best village of all for catching a glimpse of the most perfect clarets. There are two main styles. One is almost honeyed; a rather soft, round, terribly attractive, gentle wine. The other is the glorious cedar cigar-box austerity mixed with enough fruit to fatten out these austere perfumes. Textbook claret occurs more often in this village than any other. And people pay.

Pauillac. The most famous – it has three of the world's greatest red wines sitting inside its boundaries. This is where the blackcurrant really comes into its own. The best wines are almost painfully intense, a mixture of blackcurrant and the lead pencil sharpenings which sends experts leaping for their cheque books. Me? I just find I can remember this taste better than any other. Which is a good thing, since I don't often drink Pauillacs – they're the most expensive of all.

St-Estèphe. This is regarded as a rather more everyday village. That's not entirely fair, because in their slightly harder, chunkier way St-Estèphes provide some of Bordeaux's sturdiest and most satisfying clarets. There aren't many famous names, since the area was established too recently to get full benefit from the 1855 classification, and most of the wines are relatively cheap for what they are.

Haut-Médoc. There are two separate appellations, Moulis and Listrac, but the general feeling is that if you're not in one of the frontline villages, you're Haut-Médoc. There are a few classed growths, and one superb one – Château La Lagune – but there are lots of smaller château, often slightly less ripe, but always fairly cheap.

Médoc. The less fashionable bit. Lots of good wine, often marked by a big earthy fresh fruit, which makes them some of the best Bordeaux to knock back and yet feel you've had a real mouthful.

Graves

It built its reputation as a white wine area. Trouble is, it was a bad reputation! Though the whites are now back on form, it's the reds which are more important. The top three or four châteaux are very good and as expensive as any Médoc. But the less well known châteaux are cheapish, and mostly make very good, rather old-fashioned wines.

St-Emilion

It's such a well known name, yet there are very few famous châteaux. It has its own 'classification', but its's so sprawling that it has never really done the cause of St-Emilion much good, and is now being changed to try to give it some oomph. It has two of Bordeaux's best châteaux – Cheval Blanc and Ausone – and a dozen others of top quality, but below that level it's slightly hit and miss, with the classification not helping to identify which are exceptional and which are time-servers. There are also numerous areas annexing the name St-Emilion, like St-Georges or Puisseguin-St-Emilion. They're often OK, if sometimes a little solid, and would be better value if they didn't trade on the St-Emilion handle.

Pomerol

It gives one hope, Pomerol does. Fifty years ago, no one seemed to know it existed. Even 20 years ago Britain was largely oblivious of this small area harbouring perhaps the world's greatest red wine – Chateau Pétrus – and a string of others keen to mount a challenge. It has no classification, but any vineyard which has been picked out by the local house of Jean-Pierre Moueix can be regarded as being of good classed growth standard. It has a satellite area, Lalande de Pomerol, which is usually pretty good.

Fronsac, Bourg and Blaye

Fronsac has been promoted for at least 10 years as Bordeaux's next rising star. Well, maybe they didn't shout loud enough, because it's certainly not got there yet. But the wines are very good, having some of Pomerol's roundness, and a real bite too. They're worth buying and keeping for a bit. Bourg and Blaye also have high hopes, but as yet Bourg is the more attractive proposition.

The rest

Best of the rest is the Côtes de Castillon, on the road out of St-Emilion. Prices are reasonable, quality is excellent. The Entre-Deux-Mers has a surprising amount of good red but sadly, we are now in the low-priced world of the anonymous and the forgettable. Some châteaux are starting to bottle their own wine, and they are worth seeking out, probably under a Bordeaux Supérieur label.

Now it's up to you to decide. If you like the sound of any of these – go out and try them. No fine words are going to be a substitute for the real thing.

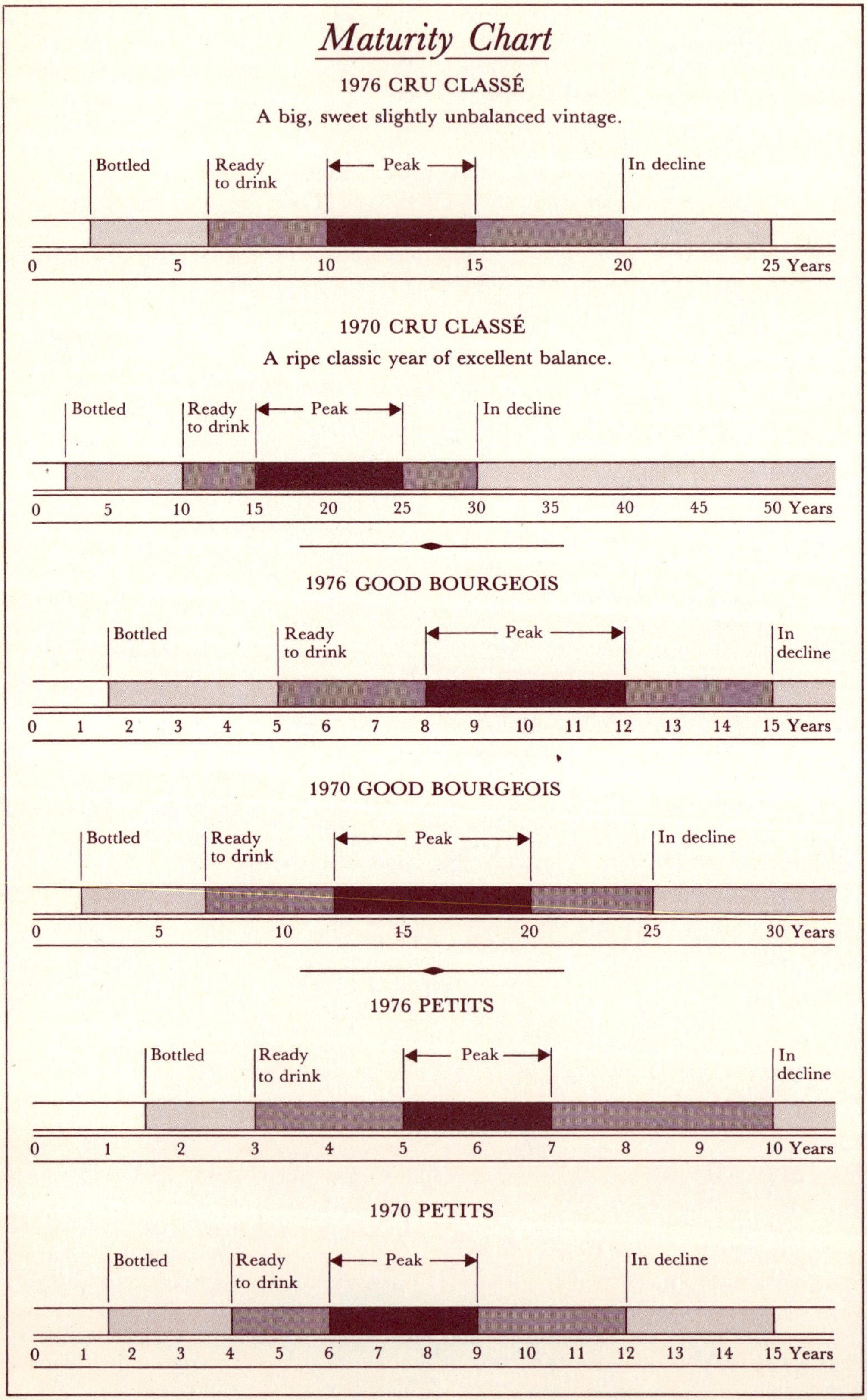
Maturity Chart
1976 CRU CLASSÉ
A big, sweet slightly unbalanced vintage.
Bottled
Ready to drink
Peak
In decline
0 5 10 15 20 25 Years
1970 CRU CLASSÉ
A ripe classic year of excellent balance.
Bottled
Ready to drink
Peak
In decline
0 5 10 15 20 25 30 35 40 45 50 Years
1976 GOOD BOURGEOIS
Bottled
Ready to drink
Peak
In decline
0 1 2 3 4 5 6 7 8 9 10 11 12 13 14 15 Years
1970 GOOD BOURGEOIS
Bottled
Ready to drink
Peak
In decline
0 5 10 15 20 25 30 Years
1976 PETITS
Bottled
Ready to drink
Peak
In decline
0 1 2 3 4 5 6 7 8 9 10 Years
1970 PETITS
Bottled
Ready to drink
Peak
In decline
0 1 2 3 4 5 6 7 8 9 10 11 12 13 14 15 Years

Vintage Table

Claret vintages are accorded more importance than those of any other wine. So much so that good wine from a less popular vintage can get swamped under all the brouhaha. We have a positive parade of 'Vintages of the Century', although the noise and fuss more often start in Bordeaux or on the volatile American market than in the UK's more cautious quarters.

Vintage is crucial because wines do age at different rates according to what vintage they come from; wines may get more delicious or less delicious as they mature; some wines will be better to drink before they are fully mature, because at least they've got a good splash of young fruit and their final balance may not be terribly impressive. Wines also mature differently according to the quality level of the property.

This is often expressed in Bordeaux by a 'classification', with Premier Grand Cru Classé at the top, followed by Grand Cru Classé, followed by various forms of 'Bourgeois', and then simply the property's name – the petit château. After this is the generic appellation – like 'Bordeaux Supérieur' which rarely needs any ageing. So a 1978, for instance, from a Premier Cru, might take 20 years to be at its best, a good Bourgeois might take 10, and a petit château might take five years.

The grape variety is also important. Wines based on the Cabernet (many of the Médocs and the Graves) will mature more slowly than wines based on the Merlot (most Pomerols and St-Emilions).

A = Quality B = Value for money C = Drink now D = Lay down

1983
AD
It *looks* as though it's going to be very good. Even the tiniest château won't be over here till later this year, and no major wine will be seen for some time. There's lots of good Cabernet, and the wines are very ripe, so we *may* have a classic, long-keeping vintage on our hands. Watch this space.

1982
AD
Astonishing vintage. The grapes came in at unheard-of ripeness levels, and right from the start the wines were so sweet and juicy that people wondered if they would last. They will. The top wines will be a sensation. 'But', as one Bordeaux expert said, 'will they be claret?' Buy to keep, but don't drink any except the 'smallest' for at least five years, probably 10.

1981
BD
The Cinderella. So much fuss has been made of 1982 and 1983, that this excellent vintage has been largely forgotten. 1981s lack the flesh and weight of 1982, but have all the quiet elegant flavours of true claret. Dry, cedary, still young, these need keeping, but the potential is all there, and they're not too expensive.

1980
BC
And *no one's* remembered this vintage! It isn't all that ripe, but the wines are very attractive in a dry, slightly green sort of way. They still have some tannin, but this is a vintage to drink now, because the maturity may not be all that interesting.

Vintage Table

1979 ABD No one's quite made up their mind about this one yet. It started out with people saying it was big and soft, for drinking early while you waited for the bigger boys. But it's *much* better than that. The balance, colour and fruit of the top wines is excellent, and if they just lack a spark of brilliance, they'll nonetheless be very fine classic claret in 6–10 years. The smaller wines are mostly ready and *are* soft and easy-going, and at their peak now. Also they're not too pricey, and quite plentiful.

1978 AD Another enigma. They started out big and sweet, and yet are now positively dry, with a green raw blackcurrant streak of flavour. They're also quite hard, and the bigger wines have all the makings of something really special. The St-Emilions and Pomerols aren't always quite so good, and the lesser wines are at their extremely attractive peak now.

1977 BC This is the nearest thing Bordeaux has had to a bad vintage in the last 10 years. The wines are dry, rather sharp-edged and raw, but many of them have a good biting Cabernet fruit, and the use of new oak barrels has softened some of them too. They shouldn't be expensive, and if you like dry claret, try a 1977 Médoc. But *don't* pay too much for it!

1976 C A tricky vintage, marked by a taste of over-ripeness in the wines. Even the top wines have a slight raisin sweetness to them, which makes them just a tiny but dull. Even so, if you like fuller, blowsier claret, there are some good wines, especially from Pomerol, which will last a fair while yet. Little wines are no longer at their best, and taste too sweet and flabby to give much excitement to a claret lover.

1975 D This is the kind of vintage claret buffs love, because it keeps everyone arguing furiously for years. Is it too hard? Will the fruit hold out? Will it blossom, will it go mean and lifeless? Oh bliss for a thousand dinner parties! This was initially hailed as the best since 1961. Few would still claim that status for it, but many traditionalists still rate it as a highly successful old-fashioned vintage. Our view is that the tannin has hardly budged yet, that in all but the best wines the colour is beginning to brown, and the fruit has got a compressed raisiny taste which makes some of the wines taste more like Barolo than claret. Some small châteaux are quite good in a dry sort of way. Unless you like tannin, avoid these 1975s, and if you've got some in your cellar, you'll have to leave them another five years to see what happens, because they're not much fun right now.

1974 BC If ever there was an unloved vintage this is it. But following the dictum that 'men don't make passes at girls who wear glasses' – yet behind those lenses may be a shy but very attractive proposition – we offer 1974 as a 'good bet'. The wines aren't all that ripe, but they have good colour and the tannin has largely softened. The rather mean acidity which made the lips pucker to start with has also become quite genteel. Although the green, almost gooseberry edge remains a marker for the

Vintage Table

1974 *contd* vintage, they're true claret in their dry, slightly gauche way. Also, it was a *big* vintage. Since we don't know anyone who admits to buying or drinking 1974, there must be an awful lot hanging around, and we say don't pay much, but don't dismiss 1974.

1973 C With a year like 1973 one sometimes thinks, if you like wine of this sort, why drink claret? They are mostly marked by their softness, which has often now turned to a flabby sugary dullness. There are some successes - Pomerol was better than most - but the wines lack any of the Cabernet bite, and the gentle honeyed Merlot fruit which might have done five years ago is usually now submerged in the light, browning goo. Unless you like very soft, light wines, on the downhill straight, avoid these.

1972 And avoid these, for completely different reasons. One reason is emotional. This is the worst, most overpriced vintage that Bordeaux has ever tried to force on the market and a lot of poor dumbos were caught with glazed eyes by the wines. We *hope* we'd have said: if it tastes thin and sour, if there's no ripe fruit to beat the acid and tannin, if it's the most expensive ever, and it's always going to taste of cold tea and gooseberries, don't buy the damn thing. Well, it wasn't that easy in the madcap days of 1973. So, despite the odd survivor, give these a miss. If you want to 'drink dry', search out a 1974 or a 1977.

1971 C One of the great 'might have beens'. A small crop. A ripe one. (I should know. I singlehandedly harvested about two per cent of Château d'Angludet, and didn't get wet once). And yet, and yet. It was vaunted as lean and long-term, a good stayer versus the fatter 1970. Not by me, it wasn't. There was I, willing my vintage to succeed, but every tasting I did failed to change my mind - they just don't match up to 1970 at all. They're light, mostly rather soft and raisiny, with some of the Pomerols and St-Emilions showing the richness needed to balance the softness, and just a few of the gutsier Médocs and Graves showing the dry claret edge most of them lack. They're not cheap, so if you have a choice between 1970 and 1971 at a similar price, always choose the 1970.

1970 AB CD These are the wines which they said in 1973 were sweet, flattering, for quick succulent quaffing. I'm told they said the same about 1953, 1929 and 1900. All I can say is that my first sampling was in 1972, and I went batty about them, they were so rich and ripe. I haven't changed my mind yet. They went through a tough patch - thank goodness, or everyone would have drunk them - and they're still not ready, but they have a rare rich fruit, combined with those marks of great claret - the cedar, the mint, the blackcurrant - which marks them out as a truly super vintage. Yes, you can drink even the top wines now, and the lesser wines *should* be drunk. But the fruit is so good, there's no rush.

Vintage Table

1966 AC — This seemed like the perfect claret vintage. Quite a lot of wine, immediately showing all the hallmarks: high tannin, quite high acid, good stern fruit and colour – it all looked like textbook stuff. It may yet prove so, but they've been going through rather a long 'dumb' period and, rather than flowering gloriously at the end of the tunnel, some of them are showing brown and age before they ever completed their articles. It will be a great shame if the 1966s don't deliver the goods, because they *have* promised a great deal and often still do. They have become very expensive, and we wouldn't recommend buying now, but if you or your friends possess some, do try them. Look for that cedary dry perfume, and a point of blackcurrant fruit in the heart of the wine. Find those, and you're OK. Otherwise it could be an expensive disappoinment.

1961 ABC — Expensive, yes – fiendishly! Disappointing, hardly ever. It's difficult to believe there could be a better vintage than this. There wasn't much of it, and the fruit seemed so concentrated and intense, it was almost too much of a good thing to start with. Their development has been slow, reliable and expensive. If you really want to push the boat out, a good classed growth 1961 offers you a better chance of a truly astonishing wine experience than any other wine category in the world. But don't tell the bank manager – or he'll ask why he wasn't invited.

A = Quality B = Value for money C = Drink now D = Lay down

Most other vintages of the 1960s will now be risks; 1969 and 1967 are probably drying out, 1964 can still be good, rather big solid wines, and 1962, one of the most gorgeous fragrant vintages since the war, is just beginning to show the ladders in its stockings. If your godfather's treating you, and offers 1959, 1955 or 1953, accept with enthusiasm. If he offers you 1949, 1947 or 1945, get it in writing before he changes his mind.

BORDEAUX WINE MERCHANTS

The Bordeaux wine merchant is traditionally referred to as the 'négociant'. This implies a rather traditional burgher, respected for his skills of choosing, blending and storing wines, and finally for being able to satisfy the needs of his markets, year by year, vintage by vintage. But take the term 'le négoce'. This is the overall term for the trade they ply. Suddenly it's not quite so flattering. It has overtones of callous bargaining from a position of strength, uninfluenced by the needs of the growers themselves. And 'le négoce' adds something rather more sinister to the blending, maturing, and need-fulfilling role; it's the kind of title which could be accompanied by a derisory spit into the gravel outside a grower's cellar. Often it was. Often it is. Because the history of Bordeaux is a seemingly endless battle between grower and merchant.

Bordeaux has had many crises and disasters, booms and busts in its history, and usually it is the growers who have come off worst. Yet Bordeaux, more than most other wine areas, should have a strong growers' lobby, because most of the important properties are of a reasonable size, and selling one basic product: Château This or Château That red wine. By comparison, champagne, sherry or port are almost industrial products; they're changed so much from their basic state, that they demand heavy involvement from merchants to create the product. Burgundy is so small that it was virtually impossible for a wine to use the name without being blended in with the produce of a dozen tiny properties just to get a saleable quantity. Yet Bordeaux, with its multitude of fair-sized properties, has always offered a tradeable amount of a simple agricultural product; if the grapes are picked ripe, and the wine is made cleanly, it will even mature by itself.

Bordeaux has always been a trading town, an import-export town, and the wine was merely one of many items which interested traders who set up business there. After the capitulation of La Rochelle in 1230, Bordeaux remained stoutly English till 1453, and a formidable trade in wine was built up by the Dutchmen, Englishmen and Irishmen who had settled there. Northern Europe provided ready markets, and as trade increased they began to push back the frontiers of wine-growing round the town. The traditional area of the Graves was eventually unable to cope with the demands of the expanding market, but the draining of the Médoc marshes made available an enormous area, ripe for large-scale cultivation. It may have been the Dutch who drained it, but it wasn't the foreign merchants to set up the estates; it was primarily the *parlementaires,* the predominantly French, wealthy professional classes intent upon achieving the status of landed gentry.

With the development of the Médoc, spreading away from the town, a third category of Bordeaux wine man established himself – the broker or courtier. The traditional merchants had neither the time nor the inclination to slog round the country lanes looking for their best buys each year, so a local man did it for them, and quickly established himself as an invaluable link.

The gulf that now appeared was based on more than casual dislike. Most of the merchants were foreigners, many had never even been naturalised, and their names had a solid Anglo-Saxon ring to them – Barton, Lawton, Johnston, Skinner, Foster – or else Schröder, Schyler, Beyermann, Geissler, Toebarts, from across the North Sea. They established the prices they were prepared to pay for various properties. These properties were largely owned by families of French descent. Those prices were low.

There is no more basic resentment then the feeling that one is being taken advantage of by a foreigner on one's own soil. And these properties, or 'Crus' as they came to be known, had begun making special wine by the costly expedients of planting only the best land, reducing yields, taking care to vinify, age, and clarify the wine, and ruthlessly 'selecting out' below-standard barrels when they came to assemble the final wine. With a large estate, these costs could be borne, but French inheritance laws ensured that properties were split and split again. What they needed was a good price for the wine. They didn't get it.

Interestingly, it was those courtiers who often ensured that they didn't. Since the selling of Bordeaux's fine wines was basically an export operation, the growers needed the merchants rather more than the merchants needed the growers. The merchants traded both ways, bringing in enormous quantities of imports. One leading shipper was importing 40 different sorts of sugar in the nineteenth century, but only listing six basic wines for export. Another famous name was making more money out of olive oil than wine until the First World War. Thus the courtiers assumed positions of immense importance, since their tasting decisions on the young wines would be taken as gospel by the merchants, and a Cru unable to please a courtier faced immediate ruin.

By the nineteenth century that ruin was given a helping hand by nature. After a brief period of prosperity, which was the result of an artificial shortage created by fungal disease in the vineyards, Bordeaux was ravaged by phylloxera, which weakened, then killed virtually all of France's vines. For the last 20 years of the century there was hardly a good vintage, and when the 1899 and 1900 vintages ended the dearth with a blaze of quality, the cult of claret had been supplanted by other wines. The 1900s, great classic wines, were only welcomed by the merchants because the crop was big and they'd be able to screw down the prices.

This state of affairs lasted, amazingly, till the 1960s. But the crisis bit deepest between the wars. Many châteaux changed hands, some of them being bought by the merchants themselves. More recently, some have gone to American and foreign interests. But during the 1930s the fourth important part of the Bordeaux wine trade had struggled into existence – the growers' co-operatives. These had long been present in other parts of France, but had been fiercely resisted by the merchants, who understandably preferred to keep the grower in as weak a position as possible. But they flourished as the smaller growers became desperate to find an escape from the thrall of the merchants. Within 20 years there were 60 co-ops controlling 60 per cent of the Gironde wine production. They became, and remain, strongest in the lesser areas, where properties are smaller and have no renown. Yet two of the most famous are at St-Estèphe, and at Pauillac which produces over one million bottles a year in a village with three first growths.

The uneasy alliance between the four parties concerned – grower, merchant, courtier and co-operative – might have continued, and indeed a reasonable balance looked likely during the 1960s, but external events were not going to let things rest. American interest in claret began to flare in the 1960s. In the early 1970s with the world heading towards economic crisis, for one mad shining moment claret looked like a rock-sure investment. America and other traditional buyers, like ourselves, seized upon claret as the perfect hedge against inflation. The growers must have felt that a whole century of depression was giving way to the Golden Days. They doubled prices. They doubled them again. The merchants sucked up what they could, then with the small 1971s and the horrid 1972s they literally ran out of wine as the prices teetered in the sky.

It all ended with a terrible thump. The 1973 vintage produced masses of light, simply adequate claret. The house of Cruse, one of Bordeaux's most ancient and respected merchants, was brought to trial for falsifying wines. All of Bordeaux fell under suspicion, and the market lurched from shortage to glut as the world stopped buying.

As things stand now, it does look as though equilibrium has returned. Many of those merchants who lorded it over the growers are out of business, and their role of purchasing, maturing and bottling wines is largely superseded by the co-operatives and the châteaux doing their own bottling and selling. Several merchants saw the trend and have begun to expand into the Midi. Others, like Sichel, Mau and Coste, have forged a modern, saleable style of wine in an old-fashioned town.

Foreign buyers are less and less keen to pay a full middleman's fee, and want direct contact with the property. Which leaves us with the courtier, now acting as a kind of commission agent. He owns no stock, he pays no interest charges, and when a popular vintage like 1978 or 1982 comes up, all he needs is some friends at the châteaux, a telex machine, and a list of phone numbers in his chief export markets.

Brand Name Clarets

Brands have a purpose; to provide you with consistency and reliability. As well as giving you complete confidence in quality, there's an underlying implication of well-bred sophistication guiding you through the tricky shallows of wine choice. For this they make you pay. And pay. Well, think of all those hoardings telling you how good you'll feel, those TV ads with dinner party guests being dazzlingly appreciative of your perfect dinner party wine, those full-page, misty-eyed ads in the glossies. Who else is going to pay for them?

Although you may find individual wine-makers who are more concerned with quality than the size of their profit margin, brands aren't made by winemakers. They're made by advertising men, image builders, and at the top of their list of priorities comes the desire to make money. And rather far down that list comes the quality factor which may help or hinder their efforts - depending, of course, on the brand. After all, the brand is taking advantage of the average consumer's nervousness faced with wine choice. So the very most the majority of brands are going to aim at is bland acceptability.

It was significant, and depressing, that a French wine company, desperate to find the style of red wine which would please the US consumer of the 1980s, put on a comprehensive market research exercise and came up with the startling news that red Blue Nun would be just perfect. How did they know? Well, they poured a glass of Blue Nun Liebfraumilch, then they took this little phial of cochineal . . . Hmmm. It *is* depressing, isn't it?

If that's the case, isn't Bordeaux going to be singularly ill-suited to the needs of a brand in the mass market? Bordeaux's red wine is traditionally rather harsh when young, and it has a reputation for dramatic changes in quality vintage by vintage. Indeed Bordeaux's most famous wine brand - Mouton Cadet - was founded on the back of three vintages (1930/31/32) which Baron Philippe de Rothschild considered unsaleable as Mouton-Rothschild. However, advances in the last 10 years, both in vineyard control and in vinification, mean that, barring some dreadful unforeseen catastrophe, we shall *never* see the like of those appalling vintages again.

THE COST OF A BOTTLE

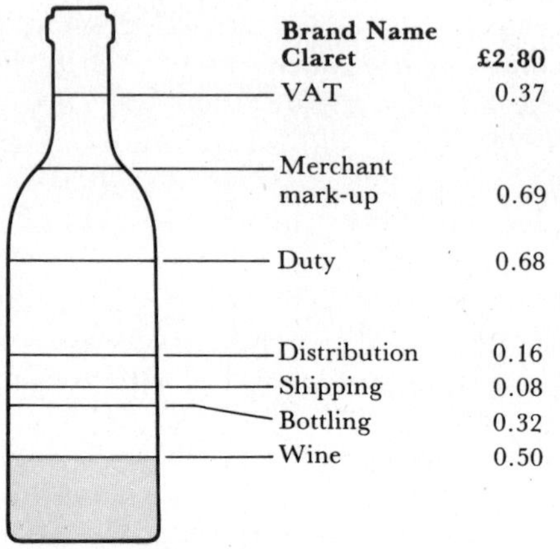

As anti-rot sprays evolve, parasite control is improved, and experiments continue along such astonishing lines as artificially quickening the ripening of the vine (it's true; they've evolved a spray which can advance ripening by up to two weeks!), the standard of basic Bordeaux can now be virtually guaranteed. Ally that to methods of 'whole grape' vinification which cut down the tannin and squeeze out the fruit from even the most menial grapes, and surely it implies that brands *can* be successfully created here?

Perhaps it does. Yet these modern methods of vinification, which may be a strength in the Midi, are a definite drawback in Bordeaux. They tend to make all wines, from whatever region of France and type of grape, taste remarkably similar, like variants on a theme of Beaujolais. In the Midi, with the dullish Carignan grape, there's every reason to try to taste like Beaujolais. But Bordeaux has got far more of its own character than Beaujolais has ever had. Why should it even consider tasting like Beaujolais?

It must be said that the major brands – Mouton Cadet, Cordier Claret, Sandeman's Claret, Harveys No. 1 – have no intention of aping Beaujolais, and attempt to stick to a flavour which is recognisably Bordelais. They are promoting a claret brand rather than just a red wine brand. And they certainly vary with the vintage, though with their price consciousness and their quantity demands, not always beneficially. But there's a new form of brand nowadays, the supermarket 'own label'. It may not mind if its claret tastes like Beaujolais so long as the price is right; it knows no traditional restraints, and is ideally placed to take advantage of Bordeaux's increasing modernity and efficiency *and* the relative weakness of wine brands in the UK.

Market research showed last year that despite all the promotional money spent, only 10 per cent of the interviewees could name even two brand names for wine of any sort. This means that the one fundamental strength looked for by any brand owner, that of consumer loyalty which refuses to switch brand allegiance despite price differentials and the usual blandishments, doesn't exist in England. Good! And bad. It is not a good thing in wine for brands to dominate the market. Uniformity is a thing to which wine in general, and Bordeaux wine in particular, is temperamentally unsuited. Yet it is a bad thing for the wine market to become too price conscious. If prices are forced down by ruthless 'own label' competition, it will result in the uniformity of bottom-of-the-barrel junk, bought and sold by parties too concerned with increasing profit margins to register the hopelessly poor quality, not of any particular vintage, but of the biggest obstacle to any quality image – the ever-present lazy and unambitious producer. Too much of that, and after reading those glossy wine brand ads, rather than risk the enamel on our teeth we'll pay the extra for the brand. Just to be on the safe side.

Some brand-name clarets

Belair Claret (HT, RGA, ASHE)	c. £2.85
Berry's Own Selection, Good Ordinary Claret	c. £2.95
Bin Claret, A. Mouiex (BOW)	£3.10
Bordeaux Rouge Club Claret (MWS)	£3.50
Bordeaux Rouge, Cordier (RACK)	£2.75
Bordeaux Rouge, J. P. Mouiex (ADN)	£3.05
Chaplins House Claret	£2.63
★Claret, Yvon Mau (ODD)	£2.29
Davies House Claret	£2.39
Dolamore Selection Médoc	£2.99
Dolamore Selection St-Emilion	£3.65
Findlater's Club Claret	£3.01
★Harveys Bordeaux Rouge	£2.88
Harveys No. 1 Claret (VICT, UNW)	£3.85
Hedges & Butler Claret	£2.90
★Hedges & Butler Médoc	£3.30
Hedges & Butler St-Emilion	£3.65
Hicks & Dons Claret	£3.08
Justerini's House Claret	£3.20
Le Berger Baron (H&B, UNW)	c. £3.26
Les Amis du Vin Claret	£2.99
Médoc, Cordier (P&C)	£3.05
Médoc, Delamere (WILL)	£2.81
Médoc, Delaunay Frères (THRE)	£3.39
Médoc, M. Preller (QR)	£2.29
Médoc, Morgon Fruze (PD)	£3.25
Médoc, Cruze (MWS)	£4.15
Médoc, Nathaniel Johnston (CHAP)	£3.03
Merchant Vintners Claret (ADN, L&W)	c. £2.65
Montagne St-Emilion (WAIT)	£2.85
Mouton Cadet (widely available)	£3.75–£4.50
Peatlings Claret	£2.59
Peter Dominic Claret	£2.55
Sainsbury's St-Emilion	£2.95
Sainsbury's Claret	£2.09
Sandemans Claret (THRE)	£3.59
St Michael Claret	£2.25
St-Emilion, Cordier (P&C, GH, MWS)	c. £3.39
St-Emilion, M. Preller (QR)	£3.45
St-Emilion, J. P. Moueix (BAL, ADN)	£3.75
St-Emilion, Nathaniel Johnston (CHAP)	£3.26
Stapylton Fletcher Claret	£2.70
Tanners Claret	£3.24
★Tesco Claret	£1.99
Tesco Médoc Claret	£2.75
Threshers Claret	£2.79
Troisgros Rouge (CV)	£3.20
Victoria Wine Claret	£2.49
★Waitrose Claret	£2.25
Willoughby's Daily Claret	£2.69
The Wine Society's Claret	£2.65
The Wine Society's St-Emilion	£3.95
Yorkshire Fine Wine House Claret, Henri Rodier	£3.17

Clarets out of their Class

Make up a classification for something, and in no time you'll be deluged with cries of 'not fair!' People will dredge up a sackful of candidates who should have been included, and they'll whisper and jeer at numerous inclusions of which they don't approve . . . Nowhere is this more true than in Bordeaux.

It's virtually a regional pastime trying to rearrange the classifications of 1855 which put a ranking – by price, actually – of first to fifth growth on 61 red Bordeaux properties, or 'châteaux' as they're called, and 24 sweet white Sauternes and Barsacs. With the reds, it effectually condemned as second best any Médoc château which wasn't on that list, and even so the list includes many examples of wines at fifth growth level which people say should be second or third, and there are some at second or third which people feel should be fourth or fifth.

The going gets really sticky when suggestions are made that châteaux should be declassified altogether, and that other unclassified châteaux should be admitted to the inner sanctum in their place. This can make or break the reputation and fortune of a proprietor, because, on the current tide of enthusiasm for good claret, any owner of a classed growth Médoc is probably sitting on assets worth a million pounds.

One of the most exciting things for a claret devotee to attempt is to catch a château at the beginning of a revival in its fortunes, or to be the first to find a château which no one knew was making great wine. Because while a reputation is being built or re-built, the quality will always keep ahead of the cost, and you can get fine wine at a bargain price, simply because fashion hasn't yet given that particular wine the nod. However, in the competitive claret market, quality does tell, and the price will rise.

Webster's puts forward a list – by no means exhaustive – of wines that we consider are performing 'out of their class'. Since Bordeaux classifications are mostly rigid (although this year's re-think of the St-Emilion classification allows a welcome degree of flexibility), wines that have long been thought of as 'out of their class' may now be obtaining far higher prices than the rating would imply, but that rating stays firm. Châteaux Palmer, Grand-Puy-Lacoste and Lynch-Bages are cases in point. Only Mouton-Rothschild, after 50 years of struggle, has managed to dent the 1855 classification by moving from second to first growth in 1973. Otherwise, this list, based on the average prices merchants had been paying for the various châteaux's wines in the earlier part of the nineteenth century, holds good.

Graves has its own small classification, containing a very wide quality range. St-Emilion is even more unpredictable, and will remain so until the new tasting-orientated judgements begin to take effect in the next few years.

Pomerol, despite its superstar, Château Pétrus, has no classification at all, while Sauternes sticks uncritically with its own 1855 version.

For red wines, it's that classification which counts, and it has made more châteaux famous than the rest of Bordeaux put together. Here goes . . .

Médoc

Minor châteaux performing like top Bourgeois wines

Andron-Blanquet
Lamothe
Malescasse
Maucamp
Patache d'Aux
Potensac
Ramage La Batisse
Sociando-Mallet
La Tour de By
La Tour Pibran
La Tour St-Joseph
Victoria

Top Bourgeois performing like classed growths
d'Angludet
Beau-Site-Haut-Vignoble
Chasse-Spleen
Cissac
Colombier Monpelou
Haut-Bages-Averous
Hortevie
Labégorce-Zédé
Lanessan
Meyney
Ormes-de-Pez
de Pez
Siran
La Tour de Mons
Villegeorge

Classed growths outperforming their reputation
Camensac
Dauzac
d'Issan
Lafon-Rochet
Langoa-Barton
La Tour-Carnet
St-Pierre
Tertre

Graves
outperformers
Carbonnieux (white)
Couhins (white)
Fieuzal (red and white)
Malartic-Lagravière (red and white)
La Tour-Martillac (red)

Pomerol
outperformers
Clos René
Feytit-Clinet
La Grave Trigant de Boisset
Siaurac (Lalande de Pomerol)
Les Templiers (Lalande de Pomerol)
La Tour à Pomerol

St-Emilion
outperformers
Balestard-La-Tonnelle
Berliquet
Cadet-Piola
Dassault
La Dominique
Fombrauge
Monbousquet
St-Georges
La Serre

Sauternes
outperformers non-classed
Bastor-Lamontagne
Chartreuse
Guiteronde
Liot
St-Amand

Sauternes
outperformers Classed growths
Doisy-Daëne
Doisy-Védrines
de Malle
Nairac
Suau

Two areas which are under-rated and usually offer good bargains are Fronsac, including Canon-Fronsac, whose wines have much in common with Pomerol, and Côtes de Castillon, an area of straight Bordeaux Supérieur near St-Emilion, whose wines have far more class than that title implies.

SECOND WINES

'Second Wine' sounds a bit cheap, doesn't it? Like 'seconds' when you're buying china in the January sales, or second class when you're buying a train ticket. But how often have you said, as you lovingly pick up your set of Wedgwood plates which cost you half of the 'perfect' price, 'You can't tell the difference, and look at the money I've saved!'? How often have you wondered whether you should buy a first-class train ticket and then thought 'I'm blowed if I'll pay the extra just to sit in a carriage all by myself'?

Well, there's a bit of both in this second wine business. Although you will be able to tell the difference side by side between, say, Château Léoville-Las Cases and its second label, Clos du Marquis, have a bottle of the Clos du Marquis by itself and you might well think that you were drinking Léoville. At half the price. And as the prices of top clarets get more and more scarey, maybe the slightly less concentrated, less exciting taste of the second wine is perfectly satisfying in itself. At half the price.

The second wines from the major Bordeaux châteaux can be defined, approximately, as being wines from the same vineyard as the château label itself, which, for various reasons, have been 'selected out' of the top wine. Legally they could be included, but to maintain the quality of the Grand Vin, certain barrels are put apart when the final selection is made. These may be the produce of particularly young vines, since the wine from the young vines won't have the concentration and staying power that is demanded from an expensive classed growth. They may be from sections of the vineyard which, due to the vagaries of the weather, didn't produce quite the right style, or which are just traditionally less good. Or they may include first class wine from mature vines and good parts of the vineyard which just doesn't fit into this particular vintage of the Grand Vin style. For example, if Merlot grape produces an enormous crop and the tougher Cabernet falls a bit short on quantity, then a wine maker may decide to use less Merlot, so as to preserve the balance he wants. In which case he'll beef up his second wine with wine of first wine quality.

There is another form of second wine. Sometimes a major château buys up a lesser property nearby, and begins to use its label for its second wine. Since it is in the same appellation this is perfectly legal. Cos d'Estournel uses the seven-hectare vineyard of Château Marbuzet like this, and Lynch-Bages uses the tiny three-hectare vineyard of Haut-Bages-Averous in the same way.

There are some wines which people think of as second wines but which are in fact quite separate. Château Lalande Borie is thought of as Ducru-Beaucaillou's second wine, but in fact it is made from vines which M. Borie bought from the third growth Château Lagrange, and it is made in the old cellars of the fourth growth Château St-Pierre.

Maintenance of the standards in the château's top wine is the reason for these second labels. And as the price of the best claret increases to sky-high levels, we should be grateful that proprietors are taking their responsibilities seriously by excluding any wine which would compromise the quality of the Grand Vin. When you do taste first and second wines of the same vintage together, there's no question of not being able to tell them apart. The second wine almost always lack a little of the drive, a little of the lingering, tantalizing flavour of the Grand Vin. The flavours which shout at you in the Grand Vin are more likely to whisper in the second wine. But they'll be ready to drink much more quickly, and that is often their chief virtue. They give you a suggestion, within four or five years of the vintage, of the glorious flavours the Grand Vin may take 20 years to achieve. Indeed for some châteaux making lighter wine, five or six years may be more than the second wine wants.

These second wines have been around a fair while. Château Margaux produced its first Pavillon du Château Margaux in 1908, Léoville-Las Cases, its first Clos du Marquis in 1904, and Brane-Cantenac swear they've been producing a second wine since the eighteenth century. But their present importance is a very recent development. In the last 10 years vineyard and vinification methods have improved dramatically. More and more grapes are being harvested, yet higher and higher prices are being asked as château owners become aware of the investment potential of their wines. So the wine maker has a duty to ensure the highest possible standard for the Grand Vin. Which is good news all round. More reliable Grand Vin, and some very tasty first cousins at about half the price. But remember, they are *second* wines. In a top year the best effort of a lesser château is likely to have a spark of brilliance that the finest second wine will rarely have.

Cordier really got the UK market going only three or four years ago, with the launch of the 1979 vintage of second wines from Gruaud-Larose, Talbot and Meyney. These wines are still among the best and others *Webster's* would particularly recommend are La Parde de Haut-Bailly, Clos du Marquis (Léoville-Las Cases), Lalande Borie (Ducru-Beaucaillou), Marbuzet (Cos d'Estournel), Haut-Bages-Averous (Lynch-Bages), Réserve de la Comtesse (Pichon Lalande) and, best of all, Moulin des Carruades (Château Lafite).

Some recommended Second Wines of Bordeaux

Château	Second Wine
Brane-Cantenac	Domaine de Fontarney
Gruaud-Larose	Sarget de Gruaud-Larose
Haut-Bailly	La Parde de Haut-Bailly
Haut-Brion	Château Bahans Haut-Brion
Lafite-Rothschild	Moulin des Carruades
Latour	Les Forts de Latour
Léoville-Las-Cases	Clos du Marquis
Margaux	Pavillon Rouge du Château Margaux
Meyney	Prieur de Meyney
Pichon-Longueville Lalande	Réserve de la Comtesse
Prieuré-Lichine	Château de Clairfont
Talbot	Connétable Talbot

CONFUSING CHÂTEAUX

'Psst. Got a lovely bottle of Château La Tour here, only £2.50 to you. Or how about this? Château Lafitte 1978 for £2.95? I'm robbing meself. And look at this little beauty. Château Eyquem 1979, special price for you, guv, £2.30! I'm giving it away!'

He's not really. He's charging a perfectly fair market price. Château La Tour should be about £2.50. What? A first growth Pauillac for £2.50? Aye, there's the rub. Is it Château Latour or Château La Tour? See the difference? For Château Latour in Pauillac you'd probably have to pay £2.50 for a very small glass of it. But our Château La Tour comes from the village of Ste-Foy-le-Grande. And it's made by the local co-op. Come to think of it, perhaps £2.50 is a bit steep.

So, Château Lafitte 1978 for £2.95? another first growth Pauillac going for a song? 'Fraid not. This is Château Lafitte, with two 't's. Miles from Pauillac, out in the backwoods of Premières Côtes de Bordeaux, which may sound grand, but isn't. Lafite (one t) 1978 is far too young to drink. Lafitte (two t's) 1978 is rather wishing it was drunk in its prime about 18 months ago.

Well, at least that Château Eyquem will go down a treat with the pudding. I've always been partial to a really good sweet white wine. Excuse me, they don't make sweet white wine at Château Eyquem. They don't make white wine at all. Heresy, you cry, but it's true. Château Eyquem makes 600 barrels a year – of red wine. And it's nowhere near Sauternes. It's in the Côtes de Bourg, about as far away from Sauternes as you can get in Bordeaux.

These three little 'deceptions' aren't as absurd as you might think. There are a lot of La Tours around, quite a few Lafittes, and don't put it past a greedy restaurateur to add a pound or two to the price and carefully forget to say 'Of course, this isn't the famous Château Latour', when you order the wine. After all, Pauillac's Château Latour is named after a tower in the grounds. There are lots of towers all around Bordeaux, and each one can rightfully name a vineyard. I'm afraid you have to be careful, and, as we've said before, there are very few too spread out bargains in restaurant or shop prices for fine claret, and the one thing which is certain *not* to be underpriced is classed growth claret.

Here is *Websters'* Top Ten of some of the more famous 'real things' versus 'hoaxers'. Some of these sound-alikes are perfectly good wines. Just so long as they don't pretend to be what they're not.

The Real Thing	**'Not' the Real Thing**
Château Gazin, Pomerol	Château Gazin, Graves Château du Gazin, Canon-Fronsac
Château Beauséjour, St-Emilion 1er Grand Cru Classé *and* Château Beau Séjour, St-Emilion 1er Grand Cru Classé	Château Beauséjour, Puisseguin-St-Emilion Château Beauséjour, Montagne-St-Emilion Château Beauséjour, St-Estèphe
Château Belair, St-Emilion 1er Grand Cru Classé	Château de Bel-Air, Lalande-de-Pomerol Château Bel-Air, Pomerol Château Bel-Air, Puisseguin-St Emilion Château Bel-Air, Ste-Croix-du-Mont Château Bel-Air, Lussac-St-Emilion Château Belair, Premières Côtes de Blaye
Château Canon, St-Emilion 1er Grand Cru Classé	Château Canon, Canon-Fronsac Château Canon de Brem, Canon-Fronsac
Château La Croix, Pomerol	Château La Croix, Fronsac
Château Lagrange, St Julien 3ème Cru Château Lagrange, Pomerol	Château Lagrange, Lussac-St-Emilion
Château St-Pierre (-Sevaistre) 4ème Cru	Château St-Pierre, Graves
Château Latour 1er Grand Cru	Château Latour à Pomerol Château La Tour de By, Medoc Château La Tour de Roc Château La Tour-Blanche

CLARET IN RESTAURANTS

It does the heart good to find a restaurant wine list where the Château Margaux 1928 is a good 20p cheaper than the Asti Spumante, and the Château Talbot 1933 weighs in at the same price as the Rüdesheimer. You wouldn't have caught me drinking Rüdesheimer or Asti Spumante in 1938.

And you wouldn't find that price comparison in 1984. It's Bertorelli's 1938 wine list which offers these rare treats and gives you the choice of the Margaux at 10/- or the Asti at 14/-. We tried to find a restaurant which keeps its wine list prices as low as possible without the danger of landing its owner in the funny farm. One which gave us a reasonable comparison was the Bell Inn at Aston Clinton. They were charging what seems a fairly typical £7.50 for their Asti and an unexorbitant £45.00 for the Haut-Brion 1971, one of Margaux's fellow first growths. So the first growth claret, instead of being slightly cheaper than the Asti is now nearly eight times as expensive.

The Bell's claret list is excellent, and fairly priced, but it does show that you can't expect mainstream claret bargains in a restaurant over here any more. If you're prepared to take the plunge, the Rhône, Burgundy(!), south-west France, White Bordeaux and Italy all give you a much better chance of a bargain. If you want something resembling a claret bargain, it might be better to hop over to France.

France is often held up as the prime exponent of the art of overcharging on wine lists. At the three star Michelin level, almost certainly, but at the level of 'good average' not at all. La Coupole in Paris will offer you Château Grand-Puy-Lacoste 1966 for £18, way below English wholesale price, and the Pomerol Château L'Enclos 1970 at £12. In France they like to drink their top clarets much younger than we do, and so new young clarets are normally expensive. We are more aware of the value of old wines over here and have to pay accordingly. But they don't like them old, and frequently older wines just never get ordered and are relatively forgotten – which gives us the chance to sneak in and drink fine and cheap.

WINE LIST

Cocktail Bertorelli 1/2

Royal Tokay (Hungarian) 6/0

BORDEAUX (Red)

		Bot.	½-Bot.
Table Claret	Glass 5d	2/9	1/6
Médoc	Glass 6d	3/3	1/9
St. Emilion		4/3	2/4
St. Julien		4/3	2/4
Château Tetre Dugay ...		6/0	3/3
„ Margaux, 1928 ...		10/0	5/6
„ Hautrive... ...		6/0	3/3
„ Talbot, 1933 ...		6/6	3/6

BORDEAUX (White)

		Bot.	½-Bot.
Sauternes ...	Glass 6d	3/3	1/9
Sauternes, Superior		4/0	2/3
Haut Sauternes		6/0	3/3
Barsac		4/0	2/3
Graves (Sec.) ...	Glass 6d	3/3	1/9
Graves, Superior		4/0	2/3
Special Haut Sauterne ...		7/0	3/9

BOURGOGNE (Red)

	Bot.	½-Bot.
Bourgogne	3/6	2/0
Pommard	5/6	3/0
Beaune	5/0	2/9
Chambertin	6/6	3/6
Macon	4/0	2/3
Beaujolais	4/0	2/3
Chateauneuf du Pape ...	5/0	2/9
Volnay	5/0	2/9
Nuits Porets 1926	6/6	3/6

BOURGOGNE (White)

	Bot.	½-Bot.
Chablis	3/9	2/0
Chablis Superieur	5/0	2/9
Pouilly	6/0	3/3

MOSELLE & RHINE WINES

	Bot.	½-Bot.
Still Moselle	5/6	3/0
Niersteiner	5/6	3/0
Liebfraumilch	5/6	3/0
Zeltinger Berg	5/6	3/0
Rüdesheimer	6/0	3/3

ITALIAN WINES (Red)

		Bot.	½-Bot.
Barolo		5/0	2/9
Lambrusco		5/0	2/9
Barbera		4/6	2/6
Chianti (no label)	Baby 1/4	4/9	2/6
Chianti Brolio	Baby 1/6	6/6	3/3
„ Spaletti		6/0	3/3
„ Gancia (Radda in Chianti)		6/0	3/3
„ Ruffino		6/0	3/3
„ Aldobrandini ...		6/0	3/3
„ „	Baby 1/5		
Barbera Zoppa		4/6	2/6
Freisa		4/0	2/3
Nebiolo		5/0	2/9

ITALIAN WINES (White)

	Bot.	½-Bot.
Corvo	4/6	2/6
Capri	5/0	2/9
Orvieto, Dry or Abboccato ...	5/6	3/0
Chianti (no label) Baby 1/5	5/0	2/9
Lacrima Christi	5/6	3/0
Castelli Romani	4/6	2/6

EMPIRE WINES

	Bot.	½-Bot.
Sauterne Type	4/6	2/6
Burgundy „	4/6	2/6
Hock „	4/6	2/6

SPARKLING

	Bot.	½-Bot.
Moscato	5/6	3/0
Asti Spumante Sweet ...	12/0	6/6
Asti Spumante Extra Dry	14/0	7/6
Asti Spumante (Red) ...	11/0	6/0
Burgundy (Red)	12/0	6/6

"BIG TREE" WINES

	Bot.	½-Bot.
"Big Tree" Claret	4/0	2/3
„ Burgundy ...	4/6	2/6
„ Chablis ...	4/6	2/6
„ Hock	5/6	2/9
„ Sparkling Muscatel	12/0	6/6

CHAMPAGNES

	Bot.	½-Bot.
Heidsieck, Dry Monopole N.V.	17/0	9/0
Bollinger N.V.	17/0	9/0
Vve. Clicquot Extra Dry 1928	21/0	11/6

SUNDRIES

	Glass	Bot.	½-Bot.
Old Cockburn Port	1/0		
Ruby Port	1/0		
Tawny Port ...	8d	6/3	3/3
Vermouth French ...	7d		
„ Italian ...	7d		
„ Gancia ...	8d	7/6	3/9
Marsala	8d	5/6	3/0
Aperitifs Rossi ...	8d		
Dubonnet, Original ...	10d		
Passito	8d		
Old Brown Sherry ...	10d	8/6	4/0
Pale Dry Sherry ...	8d	6/6	3/3

CYDER

	Glass
Gaymer	6d

MINERALS

Tonic Water 5d Baby Tonic 4d		
Dry Ginger Ale ...	4d	
Lemonade	4d	
Grape Fruit Squash	4d	
Ginger Beer	4d	
Lemon & Orange Squash	4d	
Vichy Celestin ...		1/2

SPIRITS

Gin and It	11d
Martini Manhattan / Bronx Americano } Cocktails	1/0
Whisky (single)	9d
Antiquary (12 year old)	9d
Jamaica Rum	8d
Gin (single)	8d
Holland Gin	9d
Cognac (single)	1/1
Cognac Liqueur	1/4
Cognac Napolean	2/6
Armagnac	1/4
Grappa	1/4

LIQUEURS.

Absinthe Pernot			2/6
Chartreuse (Green)			1/9
„ (Yellow)			1/6
Benedictine	1/4	Grand Marnier	1/4
Advocat	1/4	Cointreau	1/4
Fernet Branca	1/4	Strega	1/4
Maraschino			1/1
Curacao (Orange)			1/1
Kummel	1/3	Anisette	1/1
Kirsch	1/4	Drambuie	1/4
Bitter Campari			1/1
Crême de Menthe			1/0
Cherry Brandy			1/0
San Silvestro			1/4

1983 Opening Offers

At the beginning of September 1983 only the worst could happen. The vineyards were damp and soggy, the vines drooped with unripe, rotting grapes. Many growers were prepared to admit defeat and, with the record 1982 crop still producing happy reverberations in their bank accounts, write off the crop. So what happened? Well, much the same as has happened five years out of the last six: the sun came out and stayed out, climbing daily higher in the sky. The rot was shrivelled off the vines, the grapes ripened superbly, and another big crop of potentially superb wines was in the vat.

Potentially superb is the watchword here. That rot could still taint the wine if it had taken too much of a hold in a particular vineyard, and although the careful estates have made wonderful wine, not all the estates were careful. The best wines lack the remarkable soft richness of 1982 but have something else just as exciting. Something leaner, tauter: the fruit doesn't tumble out of the bottle in quite the same way but the dry dark flavours give tremendous cause for optimism about its eventual development.

There has been some talk that it is not worth buying the 83s since they are opening at prices similar to, or higher than, the 82s. Well, maybe everyone is a little exhausted by the hurly burly of the 1982 campaign, but otherwise there is no reason not to buy the *good* 83 classed growths. Since 1978 there has been a succession of vintages none of which, even 1980, is showing anything but a rise in value. 1983 is probably better than any of these except 1982. Buy quality, pay a proper price, and the long term prospects can only be good.

A number of merchants have been kind enough to send us their 1983 *en primeur* offers in time for our press dates, in several cases before they have gone to press themselves. The whole 'opening offer' business really seems to have taken off – shippers report huge sales to merchants of the 83s, which is surprising given the amazing amount spent on the 82s. This bull market at merchant/shipper level must mean that more and more individuals and institutions are buying in this way. Some say that a bumper vintage in 1984 would kill off the game. We do not think so; this is a growth market for the foreseeable future.

We've excerpted some comments from two of the major specialists' offers:

Simon Loftus of Adnams writes:

'Looking at the overall figures one might indeed imagine 1983 to be truly remarkable. . . . There are certainly some great wines but this is by no means a great year.

The red wines have good natural levels of alcohol but do not, in general, show the residual sugar, the richness at the finish that is so marked a characteristic of the 82s. They seem more tannic, but only because the tannins are less ripe (the index of tannin is actually lower than the previous year). Acidity is rather low. One region . . . clearly did better than the rest and that is Margaux.

1983 is a good claret vintage which has yet to show its true character. There have been suggestions that it is more classic, more typical of Bordeaux than 1982. I find the implied criticism of 1982 quite ludicrous and the acclaim for 1983 premature.'

Richard Wheeler of Lay & Wheeler writes:

'The intense fruit, immediate appeal, and voluptuous style of the 82s is not present. This year more than ever we emphasise the importance of being selective. Growers who failed to combat vine disease in August, who were unable to control temperature during fermentation, or who have over-produced, have not made good wine. There are undoubtedly some really classic wines. Our tastings indicate that the estates who were most successful in 1979 have produced the finest 1983s.'

ADNAMS
£18–£25: Clos du Sabatey, Brondeau, Font Guilhem, Cuvée Pierre Coste; **£25–£40:** La Tour de Grenet, Beaurang, Chicane, Domaine de Gaillat, Montalivet, Ruat-Petit-Poujeaux, Les Templiers, Lacoste-Borie, Potensac; **£40–£70:** Labégorce-Zédé, Puyblanquet, d'Angludet, Chasse-Spleen, Feytit-Clinet, du Tertre, La Fleut Gazin, Vraye-Croix-de-Gay, Haut-Batailley: **£70–£100:** La Lagune, L'Eglise-Clinet, Léoville-Barton, Cos d'Estournel; **£130:** Palmer; **£300 + :** Margaux, Lafite; Prices on application: Cissac, La Tour du Mirail, Bel Air, Haut-Bailly, Pichon-Lalande, Léoville-Las Cases, Ducru-Beaucaillou, Ausone

BIBENDUM
£24–£35: Potensac, Clos du Marquis, Cissac; **£40–£55:** Chasse-Spleen, Cantemerle, Talbot; **£60–£80:** Gruaud-Larose, Cos d'Estournel; **£260–£270:** Haut-Brion, Mouton-Rothschild

CHRISTOPHER
£20–£25: Patache d'Aux, Caronne-Ste-Gemme, La Tour de By; **£30–£50:** Potensac, Marquis d'Alesme; **£70–£80:** La Lagune, Pichon-Baron, Branaire-Ducru; **£100–£135:** Cos d'Estournel, Palmer; **£300 + :** Haut-Brion, Latour, Margaux, Mouton-Rothschild

DOLAMORE
£10–£20: Domaine de Brion, Bel Air, Brondeau, Haut Sociando, du Cartillon; **£20–£40:** Patache d'Aux, Potensac, Haut Grand Faurie, Grand Pey Lescours, Beau-Site, Haut Bages Monpelou, Yon-Figeac; **£40–£60:** Batailley, Clos du Clocher, Larrivet-Haut-Brion, Larmande, d'Angludet, Fonroque, Grand-Puy-Ducasse, Marquis-de-Terme, Feytit-Clinet; **£60–£75:** Cantemerle, Branaire-Ducru, Gruaud-Larose, Langoa-Barton; **£75–£100:** d'Issan, Léoville-Barton, Léoville-Poyferré; **£120 + :** Palmer

HAYNES HANSON & CLARK
£35–£50: Labégorce-Zédé, Clos du Marquis; **£55–£85:** Cantemerle, Talbot, Gruaud-Larose, La Lagune, Léoville-Poyferré, Cos d'Estournel; **£275–£300:** Latour, Margaux, Mouton-Rothschild

HICKS & DON
£15–£25: Meine-Pelgris, Font-Guilhem, Haut Terrey, Tourteau-Chollet, Haut-Poitou, St-Bonnet; **£25–£40:** Laborde, Les Templiers, Beaumont, Tronquoy-Lalande, Lalande, Grand Pey Lescours, Colombier Monpelou, Cissac; **£45–£60:** Belgrave, Maucaillou, Clos du Marquis, Larrivet-Haut-Brion, Larmande, Siran, La Pointe*,L'Enclos, de Pez; **£65–£80:** Malescot St-Exupéry, Haut-Batailley, l'Arrosée, La Lagune, L'Eglise-Clinet, Grand-Puy-Lacoste; **£100–£120:** Cos d'Estournel, Canon; **£120–£135:** Palmer*, Pichon-Lalande*, Ducru-Beaucaillou*, Léoville-Las Cases*; **£160:** Figeac*; **£275–£330:** Margaux, Mouton-Rothschild, Cheval Blanc, Latour, Ausone*

JUSTERINI & BROOKS
£14–£20: Blanchereau, Trinité-Valrose, les Moines, de Portets, de Pitray; **£25–£30:** Plaisance, La Cardonne, Malescasse, de Méaume, Beaumont; **£30–£40:** Potensac, Le Pape, Montalivet, Les Templiers, Cissac; **£40–£75:** Labérgorce-Zédé, Larmande, Clos du Clocher, de Pez, Chasse-Spleen, La Dominique, Haut-Batailley; **£75–£100:** La Lagune, Langoa-Barton, L'Eglise-Clinet, Grand-Puy-Lacoste, Léoville-Barton, Giscours, Haut-Bailly*, Duhart-Milon-Rothschild*; **£100–£150:** Cos d'Estournel, Canon, Palmer, Montrose*, Domaine de Chevalier*, Pichon-Lalande*, Ducru-Beaucaillou*, Léoville-Las Cases*, Figeac*; **£275–£300:** Haut-Brion, Laotur, Margaux, Mouton-Rothschild, Lafite, Ausone*

LAY & WHEELER
£15–£25: Clos du Sabatey, Brondeau, Gasquerie, Gaussens, Cuvée Pierre Coste, La Tour de Grenet, Bellevue, Semonlon; **£25–£40:** Domaine de Gaillat, Ruat-Petit-Poujeaux, Potensac, Cissac, Labégorce-Zédé; **£40–55:** Clos du Marquis, d'Angludet, Chasse-Spleen; **£60–£100:** La Fleur Gazin, Gruaud-Larose, La Lagune, Haut-Bailly*, Grand-Puy-Lacoste*, Belair*, Léoville-Barton, Cos d'Estournel; **£100–£125:** Pichon-Lalande*, Léoville-Las Cases*, Ducru-Beaucaillou*, Palmer: **£270–£300:** Ausone*, Lafite, Latour

LAYTONS
£40–£70: de Marbuzet, Grand-Puy-Ducasse, Ferrière, Lascombes; **£70–£100:** Branaire-Ducru, Haut-Batailley, La Lagune, Petit-Village, Léoville-Poyferré, Cos d'Estournel; **£280–£320:** Haut-Brion, Margaux, Mouton-Rothschild, Lafite

LES AMIS DU VIN
£24–£30: Caronne-Ste-Gemme, Patache d'Aux, Ruat-Petit-Poujeaux, La Tour de Pez, Potensac; **£30–£50:** La Tour Pibran, Lalande, Labégorce-Zédé, Larrivet-Haut-Brion, d'Angludet, Chasse-Spleen; **£50–£70:** Fonroque, Cantemerle, Lagrange, Malescot, d'Issan, La Lagune; **£70–£90:** Gruaud-Larose, Prieuré-Lichine, L'Eglise-Clinet, Haut-Bailly, Léoville-Poyferré, Grand-Puy-Lacoste, Léoville-Barton; **£90–£120:** Cos d'Estournel, Lynch-Bages*, Belair, Canon*, Lafleur*; **£130–£160:** Pichon-Lalande*, Léoville-Las Cases*, Ducru-Beaucaillou*, Domaine de Chevalier*, Palmer*; **£220–£320:** La Mission-Haut-Brion*, Margaux, Ausone*, Latour, Mouton-Rothschild

MACKIE
£20–£40: Beaumont, La Fleur Figeac, La Croix Bellevue, Toulifaut; **£45–£50:** Beauregard, Meyney, Moulinet, Taillefer, Fonplégade, La Tour-du-Pin-Figeac Moueix; **£60–£75:** Cantemerle, Talbot, Gruaud-Larose

TOWNSEND
£35–£50: Cissac, Clos du Marquis, d'Angludet, Chasse-Spleen, Clos-René; **£50–£65:** de Fieuzal, Vraye-Croix-de-Gay, Talbot, Malescot St-Exupéry, Haut-Batailley, Gruaud-Larose; **£65–£75:** La Lagune, Clos l'Eglise, Haut-Bailly, Grand-Puy-Lacoste, Léoville-Poyferré; **£75–£100:** Pavie, Cos d'Estournel; **£120:** Palmer; **£265–£300:** Cheval Blanc, Haut-Brion, Mouton-Rothschild, Margaux, Latour, Lafite-Rothschild; Prices on application: Les-Ormes-de-Pez, Larcis-Ducasse, Lynch-Bages, Beychevelle, Vieux Château Certan, Pichon-Lalande, Léoville-Las Cases, Ducru-Beaucaillou, Figeac, La Mission-Haut-Brion

Prices are per case, ex-cellars Bordeaux.
**Means prices to be confirmed.*

Investing in Clarets

Of course one can make money out of buying young claret. Many people do, and some merchants do little else, but just look back to the cautionary words of Alastair Peebles of Berry Brothers in our 'Ideal Cellars' section. You see, once a product such as fine wine, produced according to the vagaries of the weather, the wine maker and the soil, becomes a simple investment vehicle without regard for the reasons behind its quality and its value, and once it is bought and sold with no notice being taken of the purpose of its existence in the first place – to provide precious high-quality drinking when it has matured into its own balanced beauty of flavours – then the natural restraints on overheating the market no longer apply, and the possibility of a boom-bust as occurred in the mid 1970s can result in everyone losing a lot of money.

Leaving the ethics out of it, it is certainly tremendously profitable to buy claret 'en primeur', as long as the property is of a high standard and renowned, and as long as the vintage is a classic. These wines are expensive to start with, but are nonetheless the most likely to increase in value. If you try to save money on wine investment by buying lesser years or lesser châteaux, you will certainly reduce your chances of making a decent profit and, since there are rogues in the wine business as in any other field, you may end up losing money. When you decide you want to realize your investment – and if you do not want to 'swap' your wine through a merchant – you will have to do it through an auction house, commission and all, and although such re-sale is not liable to tax if done on a moderate basis, don't think the Inland Revenue wouldn't take an interest if they thought you were making a habit of it.

The two best places to measure the health of the wine investment market are Bordeaux itself, and the auction rooms. Here are a few examples from each. The Bordeaux opening prices are normally quoted ex-château in francs per bottle. These prices are not available to private individuals, but convert them to pounds and they make interesting reading, as well as showing how the Bordeaux market moves. Note how the classic properties and classic vintages always perform best. Years like 1975 and 1982 are proclaimed classics. Good years like 1976 and 1979 are not.

Château Latour – 1st Growth

	Price per bottle in fancs		
	Opening	**1979**	**Present**
1982	170		300
1976	44.50	110	270
1975	40.50	200	500

Château Léoville-Las Cases, a fashionable second growth

1982	70		120
1976	17	45	115
1975	14.50	70	200

Château Léoville-Poyferré, less fashionable part of Léoville

1982	45		60
1976	16.50	38	75
1975	15.50	65	125

Fashion in the property and class are the chief determining factors, but it must be admitted that in the present climate most top Médocs, Graves, Pomerols and St-Emilions, from most years except 1977 and 1980, will show a profit to a greater or lesser degree.

London

In the London salerooms the pendulum of fashion can also be seen very clearly. In 1973, at the height of the boom, 1970 Château Latour was first offered at auction for £125 a case. Within a year it could be had for £60, and it wasn't till 1978 that it regularly achieved more than

£125, averaging between £140 and £200. The 1983 price is between £390 and £720! That 1975 Latour, after an opening price of 40.50 francs per bottle, was reaching £540 a case in London in 1983.

Château Léoville-Las Cases 1975, after starting in France at 174 francs a case, was reaching £260 a case in London in 1983, while Léoville-Poyferré 1975, having actually opened higher in France at 186 francs a case, was only fetching £120 a case in London in 1983. The fashionable château, the classic vintage – that way you'll make money. Drinking pleasure? Go for the good underrated or 'on the way up' château in the classic vintage, or the first class château in a generally disregarded year.

PRICE GUIDE

We have tried to make the use of the claret price guide as simple as possible by listing all châteaux alphabetically, regardless of class. The range of merchants' prices shown is compiled from the latest list prices known to us at the date of going to press and the merchants who sell each wine are listed in alphabetical order.

When a wine is quoted EC or IB – normally the 1982s and 1981s – this means that the wine is offered on an en primeur basis (in Bordeaux or at the château) or in bond (in the UK). All EC and IB prices are per dozen. The EC price simply includes the price of the wine in the bottle and excludes shipping, duties and taxes including VAT. The EC price is usually payable when the wine is offered in the summer following the vintage. The other costs (including VAT on both invoices) becomes payable when the wine is shipped. The crus classés and better bourgeois are shipped two years later, and the petits châteaux and the lesser bourgeois after a year. You should check the exact terms of sale with your merchant who will give you a projection of the final 'duty paid delivered' price at current rates of shipping, duty and VAT. Recent auction prices per dozen excluding VAT are included to show what one could expect to pay by this method. Buying at auction can often save you money but see Buying at Auction *for an appraisal of the caveats as well as the advantages.*

All châteaux are listed alphabetically regardless of class.

Andron-Blanquet
cru bourgeois St-Estèphe

1979	4.89–5.19
1978	4.30

Sold by: BYR, GH, P&C, PIP, WNRY

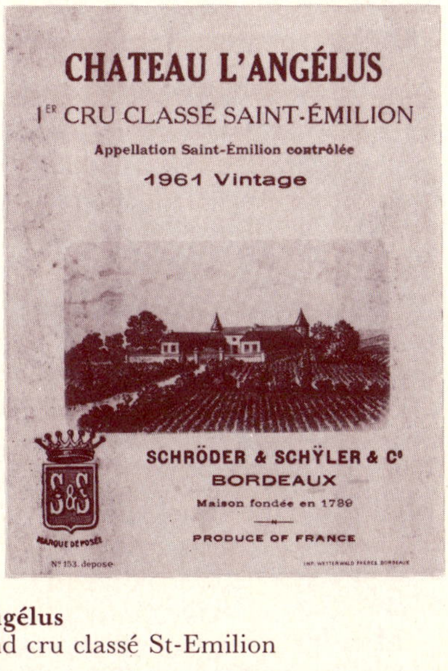

l'Angélus
grand cru classé St-Emilion

This wine is sufficiently well known for one to presume it is a first growth St-Emilion. In fact it is merely one of the biggest and best known Grand Cru Classé. They have a lot of Cabernet in the vineyard, which makes it reasonably gutsy, although the taste is rich and soft. Since 1979, new barrels have improved the wine.

1979	8.85–9.20
1978	9.05–11.20
1976	8.81

Sold by: BWC, H&B, HT, JH, MAL, PIP, WSOC

Recent auction prices

1966	150.00
1970	110.00
1979	52.00

d'Angludet
cru bourgeois exceptionnel Margaux

One of the best known of all the Bourgeois growths, and one of the finest, easily attaining classed growth standards. Owned by an Englishman, Peter Allan Sichel, the wine has much of the perfume of good Margaux without ever going through the traditional tough, lean period. Fairly priced. Good value.

1982* EC IB	50.00-57.96
1982 magnum	9.03
1981	6.27-6.50
1981 magnum	12.82
1980	5.46-6.56
1979	6.73-7.30
1979 magnum	13.97
1978	5.79-9.60
1978 magnum	15.24
1977	5.00
1976	7.50-9.65
1975	8.25
1975 magnum	16.28

Sold by: ADN, BBR, BWC, C&B, CV, GH, HT, JH, L&W, QR, RH, SR, SW, TAN, VIGN, WILL

Recent auction prices

1964	80.00
1966	95.00
1970	125.00—130.00
1975	86.00
1976	94.00
1978	80.00

Ausone
ler grand cru classé St-Emilion

The phoenix rises from the ashes. For many years, people have been referring to Ausone as they would to a slightly mad and distinctly embarrassing maiden aunt. Who then marries the most popular boy in town. The boy in question is Pascal Delbeck, who has been at the château since 1976 and has returned Ausone to its proper position as one of St-Emilion's two first growths. Fine wine and expensive.

1982 EC	354.00
1981 IB	305.00
1981	27.31-28.75
1980	18.10-24.40
1979	26.45-38.32
1978	43.99
1977	13.34
1976	32.80-41.82
1974	11.89
1973	16.50
1952	49.95
1952 magnum	48.00

Sold by: WAIT, ADN, BYR, C&B, HT, HUN, J&B, L&W, MAL, RACK, REID, RSV, VIGN, WILL, WW

Recent auction prices

1961	880.00
1962	340.00
1964	300.00
1966	390.00
1970	330.00-410.00
1976	210.00-250.00
1978	330.00

Bahans-Haut-Brion
Graves

1979*	11.50
1978*	13.80
1977	9.78
1976*	13.80

Sold by: C&B

de Barbe
Côtes de Bourg

1982 EC	22.00
1981*	3.91
1979	4.37
1978	4.60
1977*	3.15

sold by: C&B, DAV, J&B

Recent auction prices

1970	48.00
1971	47.00

Baret
Graves

1982	4.22
1981	4.31
1979*	4.55
1978	4.89
1975	6.05

Sold by: BBR, HBV, SR

Recent auction prices

1961	110.00-140.00
1962	80.00

1970	72.00–80.00
1971	46.00–66.00

Barreyres
cru bourgeois Haut-Médoc

1979	3.55

Sold by: SAIN

Batailley
5eme cru classé Pauillac

Batailley's reputation has been of the squat, solid sort rather than elegant and refined, but recently the wines have performed that extremely difficult Pauillac magician's trick—they've been getting a great deal better, and the price has remained low. The proprietor thinks his 1982 is his best wine for a generation; thank goodness he forgot to put the price up.

1982 EC IB	51.40–61.00
1981 EC	47.04
1982*	6.90
1981*	5.75
1980	5.39–6.13
1979*	3.12–8.91
1978	7.40–10.00
1977	6.50–6.75
1976	7.49–13.00
1976 magnum	18.65
1975	9.72–12.00
1975 magnum	21.99–25.30
1974	6.40
1971	9.80
1970	13.80–14.72
1961	41.00
1959	13.95–15.95

Sold by: AV, BBR, C&B, DAV, ESV, FINT, GH, HBV, HHC, J&B, L&W, MACK, MAL, MART, QR, THRE, TW, UNW, VIGN, WSOC

Recent auction prices

1961	230.00–300.00
1962	170.00
1966	200.00
1969	46.00
1970	110.00–150.00
1973	70.00–78.00
1974	36.00–37.00
1975	80.00–105.00
1976	72.00–74.00

de Beaurgegard
Bordeaux

1981	2.83
1979	2.89

Sold by: CHAP, WILL

Recent auction prices

1966	120.00–125.00
1970	90.00–94.00

Beau Rivage
Premières Côtes de Bordeaux

1961	12.00

Sold by: J&B

Beauséjour
Côtes de Castillon

1976	4.37

Sold by: C&B

Recent auction prices

1970	94.00–100.00

Beauséjour
1er grand cru classé St-Emilion

1970 magnum	24.15
1947 magnum	135.00

sold by: L&W, VIGN

Recent auction prices

1961	290.00
1962	140.00
1964	150.00

Beauséjour
cru bourgeois St Estèphe

1978	7.14

Sold by: OWL

Beauséjour-Bécot
1er grand cru classé St-Emilion

1975 double magnum	48.00
1972 double magnum	37.00

Sold by: VIGN

Recent auction prices

1969	62.00–75.00
1970	130.00
1974	46.00–52.00
1975	86.00–92.00
1976	72.00
1978	65.00–80.00

Beau Site
Médoc

1961	18.50

Sold by: RSV

Beau-Site
cru bourgeois St-Estèphe

Another of the wines which give St-Estèphe a deserved name for good, easy-drinking claret without any particular specialness. Beau-Site is made to be quick-

maturing, and the price paid for the lack of tannin and toughness is a loss of complexity. But it does its job, and at a fair price.

1982	5.18
1981	4.60
1978*	5.20–5.95
1976	4.85
1975	6.38–6.40
1973	6.73
1971	6.50–8.45

Sold by: ADN, BBR, DAV, HBV, MACK, REID, WSOC

Beau-Site-Haut-Vignoble
cru bourgeois St-Estèphe

1975	5.20–8.31
1972	3.95
1970	9.20

Sold by: BBR, FINT, MWS, REID

Recent auction prices

1966	78.00–80.00
1970	150.00

la Bécade
cru bourgeois Listrac

1979	3.73–3.85
1973	4.65

Sold by: LADV, P&C, WILL

Bel Air
Bordeaux Supérieur

1981	3.19
1978	3.45
1976	3.75
1966	8.63

Sold by: C&B, QR, THRE

Bel-Air
Lalande-de-Pomerol

1978	7.55

Sold by: ESV

Recent auction prices

1974	28.00-40.00

Bel Air
Pomerol

1979	6.28–9.60
1978*	5.20–8.30

Sold by: BBR, DAV, HT, TW

Belair
1er grand cru classé St-Emilion

The arrival of Pascal Delback at Ausone had a dramatic effect on Belair too, since it's under the same ownership. Delbeck now lives in Château Belair, and since 1976 his modern methods and scrupulous wine making have dramatically improved the wine. It now stands well up the St-Emilion rankings as a finely balanced, stylish wine.

1982 EC IB	72.50–95.00
1981	8.91
1979*	8.63
1978	8.65–9.17
1961	46.70
1955	23.00
1929	39.50

Sold by: AV, C&B, HHC, L&W, MAL, MWS, REID, RSV, VIGN

Bel-Air-Marquis d'Aligre
cru bourgeois supérieur exceptionnel Margaux

1959	28.50

Sold by: RSV

Belgrave
5eme cru classé Margaux

1980	5.12–5.38
1978	7.90–7.99
1970	9.15
1966	8.58–12.50

Sold by: FINT, HT, PD, TW, WHIT, WILL

Recent auction prices

1973	28.00–29.00

Bel-Orme-Tronquoy-de-Lalande
cru bourgeois Haut-Médoc

1979	4.85
1978	4.60–5.28
1976	3.50–7.50
1966	8.75–10.35
1953	16.95

Sold by: DAV, GH, J&B, MAL, PIP, QR, RSV, SW, WGA

Bertin
Montagne-St-Emilion

1981*	3.45
1979*	4.14

Sold by: C&B

Beychevelle
4eme cru classé St-Julien

Certainly the most expensive fourth growth, but deservedly so since no one ever thinks of this as fourth growth, simply as Beychevelle, and its traditional quality puts it alongside the top seconds. It takes time to mature but does so to an intensely delicious scented blackcurranty, beautifully balanced – and expensive – wine.

1982 EC	94.00–140.00
1981 EC IB	76.00–90.00
1981	9.14–10.35
1979	9.55–10.50

1978	11.50–18.31
1977	7.49
1976	10.75–15.56
1976 double magnum	86.25
1975	14.03–18.40
1975 magnum	27.60
1973	11.55–18.00
1973 magnum	20.00
1972	7.95
1971	17.75–17.83
1971 magnum	34.75
1970	18.53–32.50
1970 magnum	56.00
1966	37.50–46.18
1952	22.95

Sold by: ADN, BBR, BIB, BWC, BYR, C&B, ESV, GH, H&B, HHC, HT, HUN, J&B, JH, LADV, L&W, MAL, OWL, PIP, REID, RH, RSV, SF, SR, TAN, UNW, VICT, VIGN, WGA, WHIT, WILL, YFW

Recent auction prices

1961	480.00–560.00
1962	170.00
1964	165.00–250.00
1966	210.00–380.00
1967	100.00
1969	66.00
1970	220.00–340.00
1971	135.00–170.00
1973	115.00
1975	160.00–165.00
1976	98.00–135.00
1978	115.00–130.00
1979	95.00

Blaignan
cru bourgeois Médoc

1978*	3.65

Sold by: CUL

Bonnet
Bordeaux

1981	3.37
1978	3.12–3.20

Sold by: ECD, WHIT, WILL

Bourgneuf (-Vayron)
Pomerol

1981	6.84
1976*	7.45–9.14
1970*	9.95

Sold by: L&W, PG, VIGN

du Bousquet
Côtes de Bourg

1981	3.20–3.75

Sold by: IMB, SAIN, WILL

Boyd-Cantenac
3eme cru classé Margaux

This is a rarely encountered château which can produce very fragrant sweet-fruited Margaux, but which doesn't always quite get there. Things are set to change, it seems, with the 1983 vintage. Up till

1982, any bottles of Château Pouget will be the same wine, but from 1983 it will be a similar, but different product from neighbouring vineyards.

1980	6.44
1976	10.00
1972	5.85

Sold by: BBR, WSOC, WW

Recent auction prices

1961	300.00
1966	115.00
1970	110.00–130.00
1973	70.00
1975	80.00–95.00
1976	72.00–75.00

Branaire-Ducru
4eme cru classé St-Julien

This château spends most of its life as one of the softest, smoothest St-Juliens, with a flavour of plums and chocolate. Given maturity it's as though this sweetness is eaten up, and the end result is pure, classic cedary St-Julien. At all times in its development it is exciting and enjoyable.

1982 EC	67.00
1981 IB	85.00
1982	7.19
1981	7.64
1979	9.05
1978	9.35–10.65
1976	8.22–11.42
1975	11.79–13.43
1970	11.50–16.95
1967	11.53

1966	17.25–20.80
1961	45.00–45.99

Sold by: ADN, BYR, C&B, GH, J&B, L&W, MAL, PD, RSV, TAN, TW, WHIT, WILL, YFW

Recent auction prices

1964	120.00
1966	180.00–220.00
1967	84.00
1970	130.00–145.00
1971	90.00–94.00
1975	98.00–155.00
1976	70.00–105.00
1978	80.00

Brane-Cantenac
2eme cru classé Margaux

This is a big property, widely sold round the world. Sometimes one wonders if the production is a bit high, because the top years do not always produce the concentration which would back up the obvious perfume and fruit in the wines. Good, but not great just yet.

1982 EC IB	95.00–103.00
1979	7.55–8.85
1978	8.75–11.25
1978 magnum	25.30
1977	6.70
1976	10.35–13.00
1976 magnum	18.98
1975	13.00–14.79
1974	11.00
1973	7.50–10.35
1972	6.12
1971	14.30–18.92
1970	18.00–20.10
1966	21.00–30.65
1964	14.89
1962	20.11

Sold by: ADN, AV, BBR, BIB, BWC, BYR, C&B, ESV, GH, H&B, HUN, J&B, L&W, MART, PIP, REID, SR, TAN, TW, UNW, VICT, WGA, WHIT, WILL, YFW

Recent auction prices

1961	370.00
1964	140.00
1966	185.00–250.00
1967	78.00–80.00
1969	54.00–60.00
1970	140.00
1971	115.00–160.00
1973	78.00
1975	96.00–120.00
1976	70.00–90.00

Calon-Ségur
3eme cru classé St-Estèphe

The château with the heart on its label. This is because the former owner, Marquis de Ségur, though he owned such estates as Lafite and Latour, declared 'my heart belongs to Calon'. It's often been said that Calon-Ségur is reliable rather than memorable, and on present showing, it's certainly good, but seems to lack a spark.

1981	8.28
1979	6.95–10.29
1978	10.80
1976	9.00–13.45
1975	16.00
1973	8.25
1972	6.55
1971	14.26–19.00
1970	14.38
1966*	11.25–18.95
1962	17.25
1961	24.50–42.00
1957	8.50
1955	34.50

Sold by: BAL, BBR, BIB, BYR, DAV, GH, H&B, J&B, L&W, REID, TW, VICT, VIGN, WGA

Recent auction prices

1961	220.00–370.00
1962	140.00
1964	92.00
1966	220.00–260.00
1970	130.00–200.00
1971	110.00–130.00
1973	92.00
1978	72.00

de Camensac
5eme cru classé Haut-Médoc

This wine should be more popular, because the owner puts a great deal of money and effort into the quality of the wine without charging an inflated price. He is

proud of being Grand Cru, and the wine is always good, even in poor vintages like 1969 and 1972, but the top vintages still aspire to rather than reach the true heights.

1982 EC IB	39.50–49.82
1978	3.40–6.71
1975	10.80
1971	6.99
1970 magnum	22.43

Sold by: BWC, DAV, L&W, MWS, PD, PIP, TAN, VIGN

Canon
Canon-Fronsac

1982 EC	31.50

sold by: HHC

Canon
1er grand cru classé St-Emilion

A blind taster would like to be offered Canon as his St-Emilion, because it seems to reek of the soft, buttery Merlot grape as only a top St-Emilion can. It's delicious quite young, and probably should be drunk then, because the youthful flavour is difficult to improve upon.

1982 EC	98.50–150.00

sold by: HUN, J&B

Recent auction prices

1970	120.00–185.00
1975	100.00

Canon-la-Gaffelière
grand cru classé St-Emilion

1979	7.75
1978	8.90
1975	6.87
1973	8.57
1966	15.95
1959	16.95

Sold by: JH, MWS, PG, REID, VIGN

Recent auction prices

1961	210.00–220.00
1966	130.00
1970	100.00
1971	85.00–88.00
1973	62.00–64.00

Cantemerle
5eme cru classé Margaux

Last of the classed growths, though not usually rising so high above this position as many people infer. The property has recently changed hands, and the wines immediately show much more weight and colour, but as yet they still finish a bit short as they did in the 60s and 70s.

1981 EC	57.00
1980*	7.65
1979	7.69–7.95
1978	10.29–11.00
1976	7.99–11.44
1975	11.15–16.96
1974	6.85
1973	9.95–10.35
1970	10.70–21.03
1967	10.95–14.17
1966	16.20–25.29
1962	23.00
1961	22.85
1954 magnum	42.50

Sold by: AV, BBR, BIB, ESV, FINT, GH, HT, L&W, MAL, ODD, OWL, PD, PG, RACK, RSV, TAN, TW, VIGN, WHIT, WSOC

Recent auction prices

1961	220.00–310.00
1964	140.00–165.00
1966	165.00–190.00

1970	96.00-155.00
1971	105.00
1973	70.00
1974	45.00
1975	80.00-115.00
1976	82.00-85.00

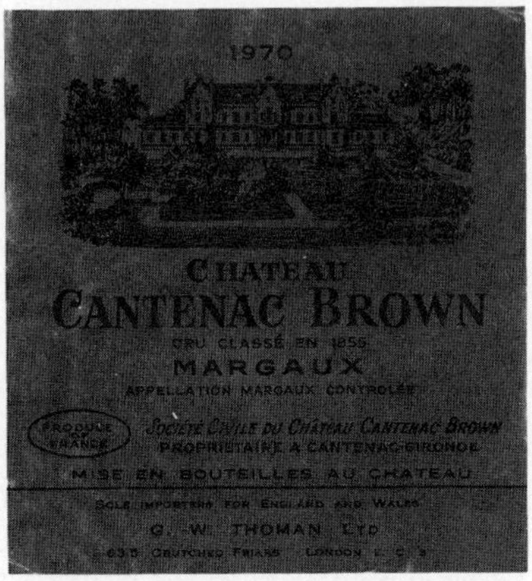

Cantenac-Brown
3eme cru classé Margaux

This is a difficult wine to judge because it takes so long to mature. The 1970 is still miles away from fragrant Margaux, yet the 1924 last year was absolutely superb. So it's worth buying to hold on to as long as any Médoc, but the impatient should try something else.

1979	7.80-7.90
1978	7.32-9.59
1977	6.80
1976	7.50
1975	8.25
1970	14.75-17.97
1953	32.37

Sold by: BYR, FINT, HHC, ODD, PG, QR, REID, TAN, VIGN, WHIT, WILL

Recent auction prices

1961	270.00
1966	175.00-180.00
1970	105.00-130.00
1971	80.00-100.00
1975	72.00-76.00
1976	88.00

Carbonnieux
cru classé Graves

This is a large estate, half red, half white. The red is good, lightish, just missing the top class in the Graves, while the white improves every year, and as a 'modern' wine has a lot of style mixing good fresh fruit with a tiny bit of oak.

1982 EC	51.00
1981	7.88
1979	6.33-6.75
1976	7.65-8.38
1975	7.30-9.95
1974	6.30

Sold by: BBR, C&B, J&B, L&W, MACK, MAL, OWL, PG, QR, SR, VIGN, WHIT, WILL

Recent auction prices

1970	88.00
1975	64.00-80.00

la Cardonne
cru grand bourgeois Médoc

1982 EC IB	34.50-38.00
1981 IB	36.00
1980	4.60
1979	4.69-5.45
1978	5.25-6.29

Sold by: HHC, HT, HUN, J&B, JH, ODD, RACK, VIGN

Caronne-Ste-Gemme
cru bourgeois supérieur Haut-Médoc

1979	4.09-5.12
1978	4.35-4.92
1975	6.10-7.21

Sold by: BYR, CV, FFW, GH, IMB, PIP, WAIT, WILL

Recent auction prices

1970	66.00
1975	60.00
1978	35.00-38.00

Castéra
cru bourgeois Médoc

1976	4.98
1975	4.35

Sold by: MACK, MAL

Chaigneau
Lalande-de-Pomerol

1970	6.09

Sold by: PD

*Please remember that **Webster's** is a price GUIDE and not a price LIST. It is not meant to replace up-to-date merchants' lists.*

Chasse-Spleen
cru grand bourgeois exceptionnel Moulis

A tremendously consistent wine, at the top of the Bourgeois tree, and a prime candidate for elevation in any new classification. The wine is always dark, strong, with a lot of oak and sweet fruit, lacking only a little perfume. It's not cheap, but worth it.

1982 EC IB	48.00-65.00
1981 EC IB	47.00-51.15
1981	6.06-7.26
1981 magnum	12.93
1980	4.99
1979*	5.65-9.50
1978	6.50-9.95
1977	5.90-6.85
1976	7.48-8.61
1975	9.75
1971	19.00

Sold by: ADN, BAL, BBR, BIB, BWC, BYR, C&B, GH, HHC, HUN, J&B, JH, L&W, MAL, MWS, PD, PG, PIP, RSV, SF, TAN, VIGN, WILL, WW

Recent auction prices

1961	220.00
1976	58.00-60.00
1978	66.00-80.00

Cheval Blanc
ler grand cru classé St-Emilion

While Ausone languished, Cheval Blanc has made the very best of its position as a first growth. It stands right next to Pomerol, and seems to share some of the sturdy richness of its neighbours, but adds so much extra spice and fruit flavour that it stands on its own for quality in St-Emilion and (excepting Pétrus) Pomerol. Good years are succulently good. Lesser years, like 1980, can be great successes too.

1982 EC	299.00-410.00
1981	27.89-29.43
1980	20.95
1979	24.73-27.00
1979 magnum	42.55
1978	31.26-43.00
1978 magnum	66.00
1977	14.95-21.10
1976	22.14—29.00
1975	50.00
1975 magnum	108.00-120.00
1974	15.00
1973	20.75-29.35
1972	17.88
1971	28.98-35.00
1970	52.79-60.00
1967	21.00
1966	42.55-75.20
1964	36.50-45.00
1962	44.00-50.00
1955	56.29

Sold by: ADN, BBR, BIB, BYR, DAV, FFW, FINT, HHC, HUN, HT, J&B, L&W, MAL, OWL, PD, QR, REID, TAN, TW, VICT, VIGN, WHIT, WILL

Recent auction prices

1961	1000.00-1400.00
1962	300.00-460.00
1964	320.00-440.00
1966	500.00-725-00
1967	180.00-240.00
1969	150.00
1970	380.00-525.00
1971	300.00-380.00
1975	390.00-540.00
1976	170.00-220.00
1978	290.00-420.00

Chicane
Graves

1982 EC	30.60-32.84
1981	3.97
1981 magnum	8.05
1979	3.51
1978* magnum	9.14

Sold by: ADN, L&W, TAN

Cissac
cru grand bourgeois exceptionnel Haut-Médoc

Traditionalist's delight! This is one of the best known Bourgeois growths due to the increasing efforts of its owner, Louis Vialard, to promote it over here. It deserves its success, and the wine is dark and dry, with lots of oak, perhaps lacking a little fruit to match the oak.

1982 EC	40.00
1982*	5.18
1981*	4.69-4.95
1980	4.22-5.06
1979	4.66-5.98
1979 magnum	11.44
1978	5.90-6.82
1978 magnum	13.52
1977	5.99
1977 magnum	12.05
1976*	6.20-8.19
1975*	6.39-7.65
1974	7.61
1973	6.64-8.95

1973* magnum	17.89
1972	6.15
1971	8.99
1970 magnum	22.43

Sold by: ADN, BAL, BIB, BWC, C&B, HBV, HHC, HUN, J&B, JH, L&W, ODD, PG, PIP, RH, SAIN, SW, TAN, WW, YFW

Recent auction prices

1961	190.00
1969	36.00
1970	86.00–90.00
1971	64.00
1975	80.00–84.00
1978	62.00

Citran
cru grand bourgeois exceptionnel Haut-Médoc

This property is seen a fair amount – not surprisingly, because it covers over 200 acres. On the whole, the wines are good without being startling, and seem to be drinkable fairly young, though holding on to their fruit for a fair while.

1979	4.99–5.35
1970	10.87
1966	11.50

Sold by: PG, REID, VIGN, WHIT, WILL

Recent auction prices

1970	86.00
1971	60.00
1973	50.00–58.00

La Clare
cru bourgeois Médoc

1978	3.82
1976	4.70

Sold by: H&D, PG

Clerc-Milon
5eme cru classé Pauillac

1979	8.15–8.21
1978*	8.58–9.40
1977	6.85
1976	11.10–15.62

Sold by: H&B, WILL, YFW

All châteaux are listed alphabetically regardless of class.

Clos l'Eglise
Pomerol

1979	8.56
1978	8.95

Sold by: HT, SF

Clos des Jacobins
grand cru classé St-Emilion

1980	5.80
1979	5.94–7.36
1978	6.22–6.45
1977	4.93–5.25
1973	6.19
1970	16.90
1964	9.75

Sold by: BWC, GH, P&C, QR, WHIT, WILL

Clos du Clocher
Pomerol

1980	5.94
1979	6.39–7.40
1978	8.76
1977	6.90

Sold by: EHR, FINT, MAL, PG, WW

Recent auction prices

1967	70.00
1976	66.00

Clos du Marquis
St-Julien

1982* EC IB	45.30–70.00
1981 EC	49.45
1981*	7.94
1980	6.49
1979	6.85–6.95
1978	6.99

Sold by: C&B, HHC, HUN, J&B, P&C, UNW, WSOC

Clos Fourtet
1er grand cru classé St-Emilion

For a long time, this has seemed the exact opposite of what one would expect a St-Emilion to be: big, hard, and not appearing to soften much with age. However, the omnipresent Professor Peynaud has been called in and a softer, more charming wine looks likely.

1979	9.60–10.43
1978	11.25
1976	9.13–9.75
1973	8.94
1970 magnum	22.90
1953	32.95
1945	59.95
1934	34.95

Sold by: BBR, BWC, DOL, FINT, MWS, PIP, RSV

Clos René
Pomerol

This is one of the most delicious of all Pomerols. It is so sweet and exciting when very young that it often seems pointless to wait. However, the wine does usually have the backbone to age, and that ripe sweetness of fruit can be just as good mature as young.

1981 EC	50.40
1980	5.85
1979	7.28–8.21
1978	7.19–9.70
1976	9.80
1955	24.50

Sold by: BBR, BOW, FFW, HBV, HT, L&W, OWL, RSV, SF, VICT

la Clotte
grand cru classé St-Emilion

1980	5.29
1979	8.63
1978	7.82

Sold by: C&B

Recent auction prices

1970	80.00
1978	72.00

Connétable Talbot
St-Julien

1980*	4.75–4.99
1979	4.51–5.29

Sold by: CHAP, L&W,RACK, WILL

la Conseillante
Pomerol

The Nicolas family own this property. No, not *the 'Vieux Ceps' Nicolases. This M. Nicolas has no contracts to sell to anyone, concerning himself solely with making the wine. It's good stuff, a little less juicy than some, elegant rather than plummy, and one of Pomerol's best.*

1982 EC	117.00–180.00
1979	11.48
1978	14.09–16.00
1976	11.00
1966	25.00

Sold by: ADN, HT, HUN, J&B, WSOC

Recent auction prices

1966	360.00
1970	280.00
1971	160.00–165.00

la Controlerie
Lalande de Pomerol

1978	4.95
1975	4.75

Sold by: BBR

Corbin-Michotte
grand cru St-Emilion

1961	20.00

Sold by: J&B

Recent auction prices

1966	98.00

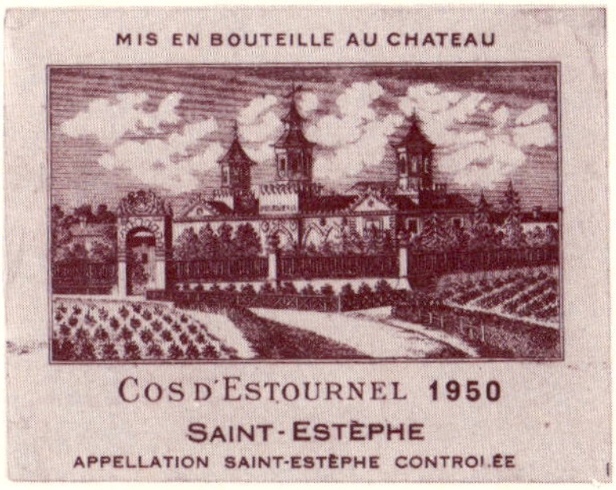

Cos d'Estournel
2eme cru classé St-Estèphe

Now the undoubted leader of St-Estèphe in quality terms, this property is beginning to acquire some of the fame of the top Pauillacs just down the road. The wines are dark, tannic, oaky, classically made for long ageing. They are one of the most expensive second growths. Second label Ch. Marbuzet is good.

1982-EC	117.00–150.00
1981 EC	84.96–90.35
1981	9.62–12.50
1980	7.20–8.75
1979	10.95–11.50
1978	11.07–16.50
1976	10.70–14.25
1975	13.50–27.50
1973	9.70
1971	14.89–24.20
1971 imperial	207.00
1970	15.38–26.50
1966	25.00–33.00
1961	30.00
1955	33.95
1949	29.95

Sold by: AV, BBR, BIB, BYR, C&B, DAV, FINT, GH, HHC, HT, HUN, J&B, JH, L&W, MAL, MWS, QR, REID, RSV, UNW, WGA, WHIT, WILL

Recent auction prices

1962	180.00
1966	220.00–330.00
1967	105.00
1969	52.00–68.00
1970	160.00–220.00
1971	115.00–150.00
1975	130.00–160.00
1976	92.00–105.00

Cos Labory
5eme cru classé St-Estèphe

This is often quoted as being a rather quick-maturing wine, but apart from a vintage like the 1976, the wines usually err on the tough and solid side. Although quite widely solid in the UK and USA, this is still relatively obscure, and should always be fairly cheap.

1982* EC	43.08–60.00
1979	5.99–7.54
1978	7.46
1977	6.18
1975	8.63
1973	7.76
1973 magnum	16.75
1971	9.95
1970	11.10–18.00
1966*	8.65

Sold by: BAL, BBR, BYR, FFW, GH, HUN, L&W, PIP, MWS, TW, UNW

Recent auction prices

1970	86.00–90.00
1978	56.00–58.00

> ***Webster's*** *is an annual publication. We welcome suggestions for next year's edition.*

Coufran
cru grand bourgeois Haut-Médoc

In a Cabernet Sauvignon stronghold like the top of the Haut-Médoc, it's strange to stumble across a château with more Merlot than most St-Emilions – 85 per cent! This has the effect of giving the wine a gentle rather fruit pastille taste, but only rarely does it manage richness or depth.

1981	4.52
1980	4.55
1979	4.38–4.55
1978	5.80
1977	3.45
1976	7.54
1975	6.55
1974	3.91
1970 magnum	16.50

Sold by: BIB, C&B, CUL, J&B, OWL, RH, WAIT, WILL, WW, WSOC, YFW

Recent auction prices

1973	56.00

Crabitey
Graves

1981 EC	19.56
1979	3.68
1976	2.75

Sold by: ESV, P&C

la Croix
Pomerol

1976	7.20–9.30
1970	9.20

Sold by: BIB, BOW, GH, SR, VIGN

la Croix de Gay
Pomerol

1979	9.03
1978	9.30
1975	15.95
1970	11.39

Sold by: J&B, REID, RSV

Recent auction prices

1970	110.00

la Croix de Millorit
Côtes de Bourg

1979	3.85–4.35
1978	3.73–4.89

Sold by: JH, P&C, SF, TW

Croizet-Bages
5eme cru classé Pauillac

This used to be seen quite a lot in the UK and was usually marked by its fairly accessible price and its fairly accessible taste. Round, plummy, not very concentrated, perhaps due to an unusually low percentage of Cabernet Sauvignon; it is still merely good, not special.

1979	5.93–6.04
1978	6.45–14.00
1977	6.05
1976	8.35
1975	7.95–13.15
1970	9.75–12.75

1970 magnum	25.88
1967	10.50
1966	14.00
1961	28.18–41.50

Sold by: AV, BBR, HT, J&B, L&W, MAL, MWS, PIP, REID, RGA, RSV, SF, UNW, VIGN, WHIT

Recent auction prices

1966	140.00
1967	82.00
1970	98.00–125.00
1971	74.00–90.00
1973	60.00
1975	94.00

Croque-Michotte
grand cru St-Emilion

1981 IB	58.00
1975	8.15

Sold by: MAL

Curé-Bon-la-Madeline
grand cru classé St-Emilion

1982	7.53
1976	8.55

Sold by: AV, TW

Dassault
grand cru classé St-Emilion

1979	7.22

Sold by: HT

Recent auction prices

1961	260.00

Dauzac
5eme cru classé Margaux

One of the Médoc's rising stars. In the 1960s and 1970s, it was mostly a bit feeble, but a new owner in 1978 has brought the whole place back to life, and the difficult 1980 vintage was one of the best wines in Margaux. Not too expensive, one to catch before the bandwagon rolls.

1979*	7.05
1978	8.28
1970 magnum	22.43

Sold by: C&B, L&W, RACK

Recent auction prices

1978	62.00

Domaine de Chay
Côtes de Blaye

1981	2.89
1978	3.12

Sold by: DOL, WHIT

Domaine de Cheval Blanc
Bordeaux

1982*	2.77
1978	3.48

Sold by: HBV, YFW

Domaine de Chevalier
cru classé Graves

Stuck in a clearing in a forest is one of Bordeaux's greatest wines, made by one of its nicest men. The red and white are equally brilliant, with the red possessing a superb balance of fruit and oak, and the white being one of France's great white wines. You have to book ahead even to see a bottle of the white, but you might find some red. Buy it. It's expensive and worth every penny.

1982 EC	117.00–190.00
1981 EC	98.40
1980	9.45
1979 magnum	13.51
1978	13.00–14.50
1976	13.70–14.66
1975	10.18–17.83
1970	17.70–18.75
1969	7.50
1967	12.50
1966	22.50
1961	50.00

Sold by: ADN, BYR, DAV, DOL, HT, HUN, J&B, MAL, TW, VIGN

Domaine de Fontarney
Margaux

1982 IB	49.50–50.00
1979	6.05–6.90
1978	6.90
1976	6.15

Sold by: C&B, MAL, SF

Domaine de Gaillat
Graves

1982 EC	30.60-32.84
1981	3.97-4.65
1979	3.51-4.27
1978	4.02-4.96
1978 magnum	9.14
1976 magnum	8.91
1975	4.60

Sold by: ADN, BAL, BWC, BYR, C&B, HT, L&W, OWL, PIP, TAN

Domaine de l'Eglise
Pomerol

1981 EC	50.52
1982	6.90
1981	6.04
1980	6.13
1979	6.61
1978	7.19-10.29
1976	8.83
1975	7.95
1972	5.60
1971	11.00

Sold by: AV, BBR, ESV, HBV, SR, TW

la Dominique
grand cru classé St-Emilion

1982 EC	89.00
1982	8.05
1979	8.83
1978	7.99-9.50
1976	8.97
1975	8.40-9.29
1973	7.98-8.75
1970 magnum	20.59

Sold by: BYR, GH, HBV, HUN, MACK, MAL, P&C, QR, VICT

la Duchesse
Fronsac

1979	3.73
1976	3.45

Sold by: HHC, P&C

Ducluzeau
cru bourgeois Listrac

1982 magnum	5.65

Sold by: L&W

Ducru-Beaucaillou
2eme cru classé St-Julien

One of the glories of the Médoc, and one of the châteaux which has been leading the charge towards superlative quality since the 1960s. It has now distanced itself from most other second growths in price and quality, yet the flavour is so deep and warm, and the balance so good, it's worth the money every time.

1982 EC	134.40-200.00
1981 EC	112.95
1981	11.10-14.38
1981 magnum	26.45
1979	8.75-14.95
1979 magnum	25.30
1978*	7.50-15.00
1978 magnum	27.60
1977	8.63-8.70
1976	11.66-16.26
1975	19.00-21.67
1974	11.27
1973 magnum	23.00
1972	6.75
1971	16.99
1970	25.00-38.73
1970 magnum	55.49
1969	9.60
1967	15.25
1966*	19.70-47.50
1964	28.50
1961	70.00-80.30

Sold by: ADN, AV, BAL, BBR, BIB, BWC, C&B, CHAP, FINT, GH, H&B, HHC, HT, HUN, J&B, JH, L&W, PG, PIP, RSV, SF, SR, VICT, VIGN, WGA, WHIT, WILL, WNRY, YFW

Recent auction prices

1961	420.00-760.00
1966	260.00-500.00
1967	105.00-125.00
1969	60.00-72.00
1970	200.00-330.00
1971	125.00-190.00
1973	84.00-108.00
1974	70.00
1975	160.00-220.00
1976	125.00-160.00
1978	135.00-160.00

EC (ex-cellar) price per dozen, excl shipping, duty and VAT. IB (in bond) price per dozen, excl duty and VAT. Auction prices, per dozen, excl VAT. All other prices, per bottle incl VAT.

Duhart-Milon-Rothschild
4eme cru classé Pauillac

1982 EC	68.50
1979	9.00
1978	8.97-9.32
1976	10.75
1975	8.63
1971	21.81

Sold by: ADN, BWC, GH, J&B, L&W, OWL, PD

Recent auction prices

1970	98.00–125.00
1973	80.00

Duplessis
cru bourgeois Moulis

1979	4.50
1975	5.24

Sold by: GH, ODD

Recent auction prices

1974	23.00

Durfort-Vivens
2eme cru classé Margaux

1970	9.40–19.84

Sold by: L&W, REID, TAN, WSOC

Recent auction prices

1966	150.00–180.00
1970	105.00–135.00

Dutruch-Grand-Poujeaux
cru grand bourgeois exceptionnel Moulis

1979	6.00
1978*	5.49–5.70
1977	3.90

Sold by: ESV, MWS, VIGN, WILL

l'Eglise-Clinet
Pomerol

1982 EC	76.20
1982 magnum	12.95
1981	7.71

Sold by: ADN, L&W

l'Enclos
Pomerol

1970	14.00

Sold by: HT

l'Escadre
Côtes de Blaye

1982 EC	20.50
1981*	3.66
1979*	3.95
1978	4.20

Sold by: J&B, PD

l'Evangile
Pomerol

This property borders on Château Pétrus, and claims some of its style. Nothing can achieve Pétrus' style, but nonetheless this is first class Pomerol, lacking the intensity of big brother Pétrus, but perfumed and rich – and expensive. Output isn't excessive, demand is.

1976	11.00–12.46
1955	31.63

Sold by: HT, REID, WSOC

Ferrande
Graves

1981	3.70–4.99
1980	3.99
1979	4.37
1971	6.70

Sold by: BWC, PIP, WILL

de Ferrasses
Côtes de Castillon

1979	3.49
1978	3.25–3.65

Sold by: BIB, CDM, DOL, WILL, WW

Feytit-Clinet
Pomerol

1981	6.33
1979	6.38
1978	8.63

Sold by: ADN, L&W

de Fieuzal
cru classé Graves

The Graves' rising star. The property is not big, but the winery is ultra-modern, though with, of course, the obligatory lines of new oak barrels. The red is sweet and buttery, but also shows Graves' earthiness and cedar perfume. The white, though unclassified, is scented and exciting. One to watch.

1982 EC	49.20–57.75
1977	6.09

Sold by: FFW, HT, PD

Figeac
1er grand cru classé St-Emilion

Figeac shares many of the qualities of Cheval Blanc and sometims makes an even better wine, but is always ranked as the star of the second team. A pity, because the wine has a beauty and a blackcurranty, minty fragrance not common in St-Emilion. High quality. High price.

1982 EC IB	129.00–157.20
1981 IB	118.00
1980	8.95–9.55
1979	10.16–12.36
1978	12.95–16.10

1977	9.15
1976	11.95–15.53
1975	15.00–21.67
1971	20.07
1970	28.00
1960	13.95

Sold by: AV, BBR, BYR, FFW, HT, J&B, L&W, MAL, ODD, OWL, REID, RSV, TW, VICT, VIGN

Recent auction prices

1961	420.00–480.00
1962	175.00–270.00
1964	180.00–240.00
1966	250.00–380.00
1967	105.00–110.00
1970	230.00
1971	155.00
1976	92.00
1978	120.00
1979	110.00

la Fleur-Gazin
Pomerol

1982 EC IB	59.40–70.00
1981	7.02
1978	8.50

Sold by: J&B, L&W, MAL

la Fleur-Milon
cru grand bourgeois Pauillac

1975	6.10

Sold by: GH

All châteaux are listed alphabetically regardless of class.

la Fleur-Pétrus
Pomerol

This even claims the Pétrus name, but since it is a neighbour and is vinified by the same company (J-P Moueix) it does have some justification. The wine is in the top flight, having some of the mineral roughness of much Pomerol, but also tremendous perfume and length. Real class.

1981	12.65
1980	8.05
1976	13.50
1972	9.20
1971	16.96–33.53

1970	15.28
1967	25.00
1942	38.32

Sold by: AV, BWC, C&B, MAL, UNW

Recent auction prices

1970	180.00–220.00
1971	210.00–280.00
1969	100.00
1977	70.00

Fombrauge
grand cru St-Emilion

This is a big property, quite rightly seen a fair amount in the UK. Its production is bigger than any of the Grand Cru Classés, and, except for Pavie, bigger than any Premier Cru. Usually its wines quickly show a soft, creamy Merlot style, but recent vintages have shown a slightly tougher side. Good quality, good value.

1981	5.01
1980*	4.17
1979	5.02–7.26
1978	5.60–7.70
1976	6.50–6.95
1976 magnum	13.51
1975	8.45
1975 magnum	15.95
1971	8.20
1970 magnum	19.75–20.50

Sold by: BBR, BIB, C&B, CHAP, GH, H&B, JH, L&W, MAL, PIP, QR, VIGN, WNRY, YFW

Recent auction prices

1975	68.00–72.00
1973	50.00–72.00
1970	96.00

Fonbadet
cru bourgeois supérieur Pauillac

This is a little-known Pauillac château which has been producing consistently high quality wine for as long as anyone remembers. It is the type of Cru Bourgeois which really does knock on the door of the 1855 classification, and yet is never too highly priced.

1981	8.60
1980	6.88

Sold by: OWL

Recent auction prices

1966	105.00

Fongalan
Côtes de Bourg

1981★	3.41
1979	3.55

Sold by: AV, HHC

Fonpiqueyre
cru grand bourgeois Haut-Médoc

1976	4.93

Sold by: P&C

Recent auction prices

1976	42.00

Fonplégade
grand cru classé St-Emilion

1982 EC	49.95
1981	6.66
1979	6.66
1978	5.48
1977	4.95
1976	8.10
1967	9.95
1964	12.49

Sold by: CUL, EHR, FFW, MAL, WILL

Fonréaud
cru bourgeois supérieur Listrac

1979	4.92–5.52
1977	4.55
1974	4.25

Sold by: BBR, C&B, J&B

Recent auction prices

1966	82.00

Stars (★) indicate wines selected by the merchants themselves as particularly good value in their class.

Fonroque
grand cru classé St-Emilion

1982 EC IB	45.00–62.00
1979	6.37
1978	6.95

Sold by: AV, C&B, HT, J&B, MAL

les Forts de Latour
Pauillac

1977	8.25
1976	11.80–15.56
1973	10.00
1971	18.50
1970	16.68–20.00
1967	17.50

Sold by: ADN, BWC, BYR, CDM, HT, LADV, L&W, PIP, VIGN

Recent auction prices

1971	115.00

Fourcas-Dupré
cru grand bourgeois exceptionnel Listrac

1981	5.02
1979	4.38
1978	4.99–5.50
1977	4.50
1975	5.80–5.89
1974	4.35
1970	9.50

Sold by: BBR, BYR, J&B, MAL, P&C, PD

Fourcas-Hosten
cru grand bourgeois exceptionnel Listrac

Listrac wines are often thought of as rather harsh, but Fourcas-Hosten, a well known Bourgeois, shows much of the cedary elegance and blackcurrant fruit of a good classed growth, at a much lower price.

1982 EC	30.00
1982	4.98
1980	4.45
1979	5.10–5.75
1978	5.60–6.96
1977	5.45
1976★	7.40–8.48
1966	8.40–16.76

Sold by: BWC, CV, HBV, HT, MAL, PIP, SF, WNRY

Recent auction prices

1970	70.00
1967	60.00
1961	155.00–180.00

Franc-Borie
St-Emilion

1978 magnum	9.78

Sold by: L&W

La Gaffelière
1er grand cru classé St-Emilion

Famous, and traditional. The wine, while not being hard, is nonetheless deep and slightly stubborn, slowly flowering into a good, traditional fairly sweet wine, but usually just missing out at last gasp on the top quality.

1975	10.00–15.00
1970	36.00

Sold by: HUN, MAL, UNW, VICT

Recent auction prices

1970	120.00–155.00

la Garde
Graves

1979	4.75

Sold by: ASHE

le Gardera
Premières Côtes de Bordeaux

1981*	3.89
1980	3.55
1979	3.95
1976	4.14
1975	3.95

Sold by: ADN, BBR, RACK, WHIT

le Gay
Pomerol

1966	14.00–29.95
1961	42.00

Sold by: BBR, RSV

Recent auction prices

1961	165.00–220.00
1962	88.00
1970	82.00–120.00

Gazin
Pomerol

This can produce the extra sweetness and perfume that Nenin usually lacks. Although fairly common on the English market, this is no longer quite as good as it was. It used to be textbook Pomerol. Now it's more notepad Pomerol.

1982 EC	78.00
1981	7.13
1979	8.45
1978	8.28–15.00
1976	8.50–10.24
1975	12.50
1972	6.35–7.50
1970 magnum	22.50
1934	47.95

Sold by: BBR, FINT, GH, HT, HUN, J&B, JH, MAL, OWL, RSV, TW, UNW, VICT, VIGN, WILL, WW

Recent auction prices

1961	185.00–260.00
1962	135.00
1964	130.00
1970	115.00–185.00
1976	70.00–90.00

Giscours
3eme cru classé Margaux

This property used to make particularly hefty, un-Margauxish Margaux, and in a year like 1976 it still does. But in general the wine is now much lighter, much more perfumed and fruity, yet still retaining a strong structure to age the wine. From being less good than its classification, it's now better.

1982 EC IB	95.00–120.00
1981	9.18
1979	7.50–10.35
1978	9.74–12.65
1977*	7.35–8.61
1976	8.29–11.50
1976 magnum	21.45
1975	9.47—14.05
1975 magnum	27.77
1971	14.26
1970	14.38–18.40
1966	17.95–24.00
1964	20.00
1937	30.95
1934	45.95

Sold by: ADN, C&B, CHAP, ESV, GH, HT, J&B, L&W, PD, REID, RSV, SAIN, SF, SR, TAN, THRE, UNW, VIGN, WHIT, WILL, YFW

Recent auction prices

1962	135.00
1966	185.00–230.00
1967	90.00
1970	140.00–170.00

In younger clarets it is always worth shopping around to get the best bargain because, in a highly competitive market, merchants will have bought their stock at different times, from different sources, at different prices.
If you are buying claret of any age in quantity you should compare several merchants' lists, because, as our listings show, the differences in price are often dramatic.

1973	85.00
1975	84.00–145.00
1976	80.00–94.00
1977	46.00
1978	85.00

du Glana
cru grand bourgeois exceptionnel St-Julien

1982 EC	36.30–55.00
1978	5.29
1970*	11.00

Sold by: HHC, HUN, RH, WILL

Recent auction prices

1975	41.00–62.00

Gloria
cru bourgeois St-Julien

Of all the château owners (excepting Baron Philippe de Rothschild) who have tried to nudge themselves up a rung in the 1855 Classification, Henri Martin of this leading Bourgeois growth has the highest profile. Gloria has become expensive and renowned. The quality of the wine has not always been faithful to the quality of the rhetoric.

1982 EC IB	54.00–54.50
1981 IB	55.00
1979	8.10–8.83
1978	7.60–9.69
1978 magnum	16.16
1977	7.90
1976	8.34–8.91
1975	9.55–13.80
1973*	7.25–9.32

Sold by: ADN, BBR, BWC, CHAP, CV, GH, HBV, J&B, JH, L&W, PIP, QR, REID, RH, SF, VICT, VIGN, WHIT

Recent auction prices

1966	200.00
1967	80.00
1970	130.00–200.00
1971	92.00
1973	74.00–80.00
1978	70.00

Gobinaud
Listrac

1975	4.65
1973	5.15

Sold by: BBR

Grand-Barrail-Lamarzelle-Figeac
grand cru classé St-Emilion

1979	7.95–8.00
1976	6.80
1975	7.50

Sold by: MAL, OWL, SR

Grand-Mazerolles
Premières Côtes de Blaye

1978	3.39
1975	3.76

Sold by: WILL

Grand-Pontet
grand cru classé St-Emilion

1961	18.98

Sold by: REID

Recent auction prices

1961	140.00

Grand-Puy-Ducasse
5eme cru classé Pauillac

This was rather overshadowed by Grand-Puy-Lacoste till the last 10 years, but is now asserting itself and making increasingly good wine. Every recent vintage has been a success, and, with a price which is not excessive, its slightly gentle but deep Pauillac style is one to buy.

1980*	5.90
1979	7.45
1978	6.25–10.15
1977	6.20–6.90
1976	6.49–6.90
1976 magnum	16.96
1975	9.49
1973	8.05
1973 magnum	18.80
1959	26.95

Sold by: BBR, BOW, BYR, C&B, L&W, ODD, PG, QR, REID, RSV, SAIN

Recent auction prices

1961	280.00–350.00
1973	60.00
1975	85.00

Grand-Puy-Lacoste
5eme cru classé Pauillac

This wine manages to combine perfume with power in a way which is top Pauillac at its brilliant best. Few châteaux achieve this so consistently as Grand-Puy-Lacoste. The blackcurrant and the cigar-box perfume are rarely in better harmony than here. Not cheap but worth it for a classic.

1982 EC	79.80–99.00
1981 EC IB	66.00–66.72
1981	8.09–9.40

1979	9.00
1978*	7.95–10.64
1978 magnum	21.56
1977	6.75
1976	8.65–17.00
1976 magnum	23.00
1975	9.75–12.36
1974 magnum	15.00
1970*	15.81–15.99
1970 magnum	34.21
1966	24.00
1961	32.20–35.00

Sold by: AV, BBR, BIB, BYR, GH, HT, HUN, J&B, JH, LADV, L&W, MWS, PD, PG, REID, TAN, UNW, VIGN, WILL, WSOC

Recent auction prices

1961	330.00–370.00
1966	180.00
1967	90.00
1969	40.00
1970	115.00–165.00
1971	125.00
1976	68.00–98.00

de la Grange
Premières Côtes de Blaye

1981	3.57

Sold by: C&B

la Grave Trigant-de-Boisset
Pomerol

1980*	6.44
1978	10.35
1977	5.41–5.85
1975	16.10

Sold by: BYR, C&B

Gressier-Grand-Poujeaux
cru bourgeois supérieur Moulis

1966	8.75–14.55

Sold by: MAL, MWS

Recent auction prices

1970	66.00
1971	52.00

Please don't blame ***Webster's*** *or the merchants listed if a wine is sold out or if the vintage you want is no longer available. Wine is a living entity and a limited commodity – continuity of supply cannot, alas, be guaranteed.*

Gruaud-Larose
2eme cru classé St-Julien

Another St-Julien which often starts rich, buttery and sweet but will achieve the full cedary glory if given time, while still retaining a lovely sweet centre. Since this wine is always offered at a fair price, it is a prime candidate for laying down.

1982 EC	79.80
1981 EC	78.00
1982	8.80
1981	10.47
1980	5.99
1979	8.34–8.63
1979 magnum	20.70
1978	7.78–13.25
1978 magnum	17.83–22.14
1977	7.30–7.95
1976	8.19–12.90
1976 magnum	18.57–18.80
1975	11.50–15.95
1975 magnum	28.00
1974	7.25–8.65
1973	6.29–12.34
1972	6.10–7.30
1971	11.63–14.26
1971 magnum	26.35
1970	15.55–23.00
1970 magnum	39.85
1969	10.95
1968	6.33
1967	10.09
1966	14.90–30.48
1966 magnum	63.25
1966 double magnum	172.50
1962	25.24
1961	55.00–60.00
1959	19.85
1947	57.50
1937	36.40
1934	45.95

Sold by: ADN, AV, BAL, BBR, BIB, BYR, C&B, FINT, GH, HHC, HT, J&B, LADV, L&W, MACK, MWS, P&C, QR, REID, RSV, TAN, TW, VIGN, WGA, WHIT, WILL

Recent auction prices

1961	400.00–500.00
1962	220.00–260.00
1964	120.00–160.00
1966	210.00–270.00
1967	92.00–110.00
1970	120.00–230.00
1971	120.00–135.00
1973	84.00–100.00
1974	54.00
1975	120.00–125.00
1976	70.00–86.00
1978	68.00–80.00

Guillemin-La Gaffelière
St-Emilion

1970	4.95

Sold by: WILL

la Gurgue
cru bourgeois supérieur Margaux

1979	5.70
1978	6.75
1961	24.50

Sold by: PIP, RSV, SF

Recent auction prices

1961	145.00

Haut-Bages-Libéral
5eme cru classé Pauillac

1978	8.43–8.90
1977	5.50–5.61
1975	7.85
1975 magnum	21.50
1971 magnum	25.30

Sold by: AV, BBR, ESV, OWL

Recent auction prices

1978	52.00

Haut-Bages-Monpelou
cru bourgeois Pauillac

1982	4.92
1979	7.25
1976	5.45

Sold by: BBR, HBV, DOL

Recent auction prices

1970	92.00

Haut-Bailly
cru classé Graves

If Graves wines are supposed to be severe and earthy when young, Haut-Bailly is the antithesis. Its fruit is sweet and rich from the first moment, and the high percentage of new oak adds to this even further. But the wines do age well, and, though expensive, are of a high class.

1982 EC	65.00–99.00
1981 EC	66.72
1981	8.05
1980	6.93
1979	7.42–8.97
1978	8.83–13.50
1977	7.34–8.15
1976	8.25–13.00
1975	10.64–12.00
1971	11.67
1970 magnum	31.42
1966	20.00

Sold by: ADN, AV, BYR, ESV, GH, HT, HUN, J&B, L&W, MAL, PIP, REID, RH, WNRY, WSOC

Recent auction prices

1966	195.00–210.00
1971	98.00

Haut-Batailley
5eme cru classé Pauillac

There was a time when no one would question Haut-Batailley's superiority over Batailley, yet despite the management of M. Borie of Ducru-Beaucaillou, Haut-Batailley, once dark, plummy and slow to sweeten, is now a much lighter, more charming wine, very attractive, yet not quite so gutsy as before. But then M. Borie is a St-Julien man and that is the style he prefers.

1982 EC IB	64.03–75.00
1979	7.25–9.90
1978	7.50–11.60
1976	8.16–21.00
1975	11.50–15.00
1972	5.85
1970	13.92–14.49
1966	18.21–25.13

Sold by: BBR, BIB, BYR, CHAP, GH, HT, HUN, J&B, L&W, MAL, MWS, ODD, PD, TAN, TW, WHIT, WILL, WNRY, WSOC, YFW

Recent auction prices

1964	100.00
1966	180.00
1967	74.00–76.00
1969	44.00–75.00
1971	110.00–115.00
1973	70.00
1975	64.00–96.00

EC (ex-cellar) price per dozen, excl shipping, duty and VAT. IB (in bond) price per dozen, excl duty and VAT. Auction prices, per dozen, excl VAT. All other prices, per bottle incl VAT.

In younger clarets it is always worth shopping around to get the best bargain because, in a highly competitive market, merchants will have bought their stock at different times, from different sources, at different prices.
If you are buying claret of any age in quantity you should compare several merchants' lists, because, as our listings show, the differences in price are often dramatic.

Haut-Brion
1er cru classé Graves

The only non-Médoc red to be classified in 1855, this is a first growth which has undergone a fair amount of criticism, but there is no doubt as to its quality now. The wines are not big, but are almost creamy in their gorgeous ripe taste, quite unique, but slightly resembling the great Medocs, if anything.

1982 EC IB	330.00-405.00
1981 EC	285.00
1981	30.67-36.89
1980	17.50
1979	19.49-22.43
1978	30.00-43.12
1977	14.35
1976	22.83-42.26
1975	50.00-59.00
1975 jeroboam	517.50
1974	15.60-17.95
1973	20.90
1972	16.95
1971	31.50-39.75
1970	31.54-60.00
1969	16.95
1967	21.00-31.25
1966	51.75-82.67
1964	31.00-43.00
1962	51.75
1961	130.00-172.00
1959	95.00-103.50
1957	30.95
1940	42.00

Sold by: AV, BBR, BIB, BYR, C&B, CHAP, DAV, DOL, FINT, GH, HT, HUN, J&B, L&W, LADV, MAL, PD, QR, REID, RSV, TW, UNW, VIGN, WGA, WHIT, WILL, YFW

Recent auction prices

1961	1050.00-1600.00
1962	400.00-440.00
1964	280.00-350.00
1966	470.00-760.00
1967	220.00
1969	100.00-125.00
1970	380.00-600.00
1971	250.00-260.00
1975	310.00-540.00
1976	220.00-260.00
1978	290.00

Haut-Marbuzet
cru grand bourgeois exceptionnel St-Estèphe

1978	6.99
1972 magnum	18.50
1970	15.99

Sold by: BYR, PG, VICT

Haut-Plaisance
Montagne St-Emilion

1978*	4.54

Sold by: TW

Haut Sociondo
Premières Côtes de Blaye

1978	3.69

Sold by: VICT

Hortevie
cru bourgeois St-Julien

1981	4.00
1978	5.95-8.35
1977	4.04
1976	3.80
1975	4.40-7.13
1973	6.91-7.23

Sold by: BIB, DOL, ESV, H&D, MAL, P&C, VICT, WSOC

Houissant
cru bourgeois supérieur St-Estèphe

1979	5.25
1978	4.70-5.75

Sold by: BBR, HT, MAL, WGA

d'Issan
3eme cru classé Margaux

This is one of the loveliest properties in the Médoc, and it makes one of the truest Margaux wines, hard when young, but perfumed and deep-flavoured after 10-12 years. Rarely seen because of limited distribution, d'Issan will now be more widely available and is worth buying.

1982 EC	57.00-85.00
1982	8.05
1979	9.25
1978	8.50-11.30

1976	8.50
1970	13.15
1962	20.00
1934	43.70

Sold by: BBR, BYR, HBV, HUN, J&B, MAL, OWL, REID, SF, WSOC

Recent auction prices

1961	370.00
1966	200.00
1970	92.00
1973	70.00

Jean Bernard
leres Côtes de Bordeaux

1981	2.82–3.22

Sold by: L&W, WILL

Kirwan
3eme cru classé Margaux

1979	8.14–9.22
1978	6.59–9.64
1977	7.35
1976	7.87–9.60
1975	8.50
1962	12.95

Sold by: BBR, HHC, MWS, OWL, PG, RGA, RSV, WHIT, WILL

Recent auction prices

1961	225.00
1971	84.00
1975	64.00–72.00
1978	78.00

All châteaux are listed alphabetically regardless of class.

Labégorce
cru bourgeois supérieur Margaux

1979	5.29
1978	5.30–5.55
1976	5.13–7.35

Sold by: BAL, BYR, WHIT

Labégorce-Zédé
cru bourgeois supérieur Margaux

1982 EC	42.60–59.00
1981 EC	41.04
1979	6.17
1975	8.45

Sold by: ADN, ESV, HUN, L&W, OWL

Lafite-Rothschild
1er cru classé Pauillac

The greatest wine of the Médoc? Probably. Yet one of the most difficult to get to know and understand. It doesn't stand for power like Latour, or overwhelming perfume like Mouton. No, it stands for balance, for the elegant restrained balance which is the perfection of great claret, and yet, till its day comes, Lafite can seem curiously unsatisfying. Not many of us ever see that 'day'. Those who do simply pray to repeat the experience, or pay and *repeat the experience.*

1982 EC	320.00–500.00
1981	26.16–39.28
1980	20.70–22.50
1979	19.99–43.12
1978	35.00–50.00
1977	16.05–19.60
1976	31.00–45.00
1975	55.00–64.00
1975 magnum	110.00
1974	25.00
1973	21.08–25.00
1973 magnum	58.75
1972	13.50
1971	32.00–42.26
1970	62.10–79.00
1967	25.40
1966	45.00–105.00
1964	28.75
1962	48.00
1961	253.00
1959	95.00
1950	37.50
1948	92.25
1943	59.95

Sold by: AV, BBR, BIB, BWC, BYR, C&B, DAV, FFW, FINT, GH, HT, HUN, J&B, L&W, MACK, MWS, ODD, OWL, PD, QR, RSV, TW, UNW, VICT, VIGN, WGA, WHIT, WILL, WW, YFW

Recent auction prices

1961	1400.00–2300.00
1962	420.00–500.00
1964	350.00–370.00
1966	920.00–1150.00
1967	210.00–270.00
1969	120.00–135.00
1970	640.00–740.00
1971	250.00–360.00
1975	480.00–600.00
1976	290.00–350.00
1977	105.00–125.00
1978	360.00–620.00
1979	195.00–220.00

Lafleur
Pomerol

This tiny property is regarded by Jean-Pierre Moueix as the only Pomerol with the potential to be as great as Pétrus. So far, they couldn't be further apart in style, and Lafleur is marked out by an astonishing austere concentration of dark fruit and an intense tobacco spice perfume. It's already very expensive, and Moueix hasn't picked a loser yet.

1976	33.54
1974	10.93

Sold by: C&B

Lafon-Rochet
4eme cru classé St-Estèphe

This estate has the Médoc's only brand-new purpose-built château. But the vineyard is an old one, bought by Cognac merchant Guy Tesseron in 1960, and has since proved an increasingly good St-Estèphe, having as much body, but a little more perfume than most of them. It's a good bargain buy, given its quality.

1982 EC	39.00
1978	6.55–8.22
1977	5.65
1975	8.95
1970	12.36

Sold by: BBR, BYR, CUL, HT, J&B, REID, TW

Recent auction prices

1975	76.00–88.00
1976	62.00

Lagrange
Pomerol

1982 EC	59.40
1979	9.78
1978	9.17
1974	8.25

Sold by: AV, DOL, L&W, TW

Lagrange
3eme cru classé St-Julien

Much berated for its quality and recently bought by the Japanese Suntory whisky group, this château has been described by Bruno Prats, one of the Médoc's most committed winemakers, as having the best vineyard of all of these still sub-par châteaux. Although I have normally liked the wine, it has lacked a little real class, but this should all change in the next few years, and the price should stay reasonable for a while.

1982 EC	51.00
1982	6.04
1979	6.65–8.00
1978	7.71–9.65
1976	7.95–12.00
1975	9.75–12.90
1970	9.38–12.36
1967	9.95
1966	18.00
1955	16.50

Sold by: ADN, BAL, FINT, GH, HBV, J&B, JH, L&W, PD, RSV, SF, SR, UNW, VIGN, WGA, WHIT, WILL

Recent auction prices

1961	270.00
1966	140.00–175.00
1967	76.00
1969	40.00
1970	96.00–135.00
1973	49.00
1975	62.00–92.00
1976	56.00–62.00

la Lagune
3eme cru classé Margaux

One of the rising stars, this third growth is certainly making second growth wine. Until 1983 it always opened its price conspicuously reasonably, and rewarded early buyers both with the rich, soft intensity of the wine, and a rapidly increasing investment. Gets better and better.

1982 EC	90.00
1981 EC	75.00
1981	10.35
1980	6.25–7.80
1979	8.99–10.25
1978	8.91–14.50
1976	8.25–14.35
1975	10.24–16.61
1975 magnum	24.44–28.00
1975 double magnum	69.00
1975 jeroboam	172.50
1974	8.25–12.00
1973	12.68
1972	6.80
1971	11.25–18.40
1970	16.51–18.65
1966	19.00–35.88
1962	16.50
1961	45.00
1947	37.50

Sold by: ADN, AV, BAL, BBR, BIB, BYR, C&B, CDM, CHAP, DAV, ESV, FINT, GH, HBV, HT, HUN, J&B, LADV, L&W, MAL, MWS, OWL, PG, PIP, QR, REID, RSV, TAN, TW, UNW, VICT, VIGN, WGA, WHIT, WILL, WNRY, WSOC, YFW

Recent auction prices

1961	340.00–390.00
1964	140.00
1966	200.00–230.00
1969	58.00–62.00
1970	130.00–190.00
1971	110.00–150.00
1973	115.00
1975	105.00–145.00
1976	86.00–96.00

Lalande Borie
cru bourgeois supérieur St-Julien

1982* EC IB	45.84–55.75
1982 magnum	7.89
1981*	5.18–6.89
1981 magnum	10.63
1979	5.29–5.32

Sold by: C&B, HUN, L&W, QR, TAN

Lamothe Cissac
cru grand bourgeois Haut-Médoc

1979	4.54
1978	5.59–6.95
1978 magnum	10.47

Sold by: BYR, L&W, VICT

Recent auction prices

1976	58.00

Lanessan
cru bourgeois supérieur Haut-Médoc

Grand Cru Hors Classé is how Lanessan describes itself. This could be a timeless reminder of the fact that a previous owner felt it unnecessary to submit samples for the 1855 classification, and so its traditional ranking as a fourth growth was never ratified. Nowadays, the wine is of classed growth standard, always being incredibly correct, if sometimes slightly lacking in personality.

1982 EC	41.00
1982	5.55
1980	5.53
1978	6.10
1975	6.95–9.50

Sold by: GH, HBV, J&B, MAL, MWS, PD, YFW

Recent auction prices

1973	56.00

All châteaux are listed alphabetically regardless of class.

In younger clarets it is always worth shopping around to get the best bargain because, in a highly competitive market, merchants will have bought their stock at different times, from different sources, at different prices.
If you are buying claret of any age in quantity you should compare several merchants' lists, because, as our listings show, the differences in price are often dramatic.

Langoa-Barton
3eme cru classé St-Julien

This wine is very *good, and considering its Anglo-Saxon Barton connections (the owner frequently sports an Old Etonian tie) we should see more of it. It is in the dry, cedary style, and although sometimes regarded as a lesser version of Léoville-Barton, this is patently unfair since the wine has exceptional character and style, and is always reasonably priced.*

1982 EC IB	73.00–78.00
1981 EC IB	66.00–69.00
1981	7.79
1980*	6.99
1979	8.25
1978	8.25–10.64
1978 magnum	21.79
1977	6.65
1976	7.99–11.50
1975	10.50–14.00
1971	13.50
1966	19.18–23.00
1961	27.50
1952	22.50–30.00
1945	100.00

Sold by: BBR, BIB, BYR, C&B, CHAP, CV, ESV, FFW, GH, HUN, J&B, MAL, PG, QR, REID, RH, RSV, SR, STWC, TAN, TW, VIGN

Recent auction prices

1961	260.00

1966	145.00
1970	150.00
1975	82.00–135.00
1976	78.00–94.00
1978	94.00–105.00

Laroze
grand cru St-Emilion

1982 EC	43.20
1970 magnum	18.65

Sold by: BBR, HT

Larrivet-Haut-Brion
Graves

1982 EC	49.20–55.00
1980	6.61
1975	12.08

Sold by: HUN, L&W, TW

Lascombes
2eme cru classé Margaux

We should see more of this wine since it is British owned, but it made its reputation in America, and that's where it still likes to be drunk. Lascombes is very attractive early on, but the wine gains flesh and character as it ages for a considerable time.

1982 EC	95.00
1982	7.82
1980	7.40
1978	8.10–9.80
1977*	7.75
1976	10.60
1970	19.92

Sold by: BYR, GH, H&B, HUN, SF, TW, WHIT

Recent auction prices

1961	330.00–420.00
1964	125.00

Latour
1er cru classé Pauillac

This is the easiest of all the first growths to understand. You may not like it, but you understand it because it is a massive, dark, hard brute when young, calming down when it ages and eventually spreading out to a superb big blackcurrant and cedar flavour. It used to take absolutely ages, but recent vintages have seemed a little softer and lighter, yet retaining their tremendous core of fruit. Wonderfully consistent, it's no cheaper than the others, but its relative lack of brouhaha sometimes makes it seem so.

1982 EC IB	342.00–450.00
1981 EC	275.04
1981	30.67
1980	17.05–20.05
1979	33.93–40.25
1978	35.00–40.00
1978 magnum	79.64
1977	16.05–17.50
1976	26.66–47.92
1976 double magnum	138.00
1975	50.00
1975 magnum	115.00
1975 jeroboam	552.00
1975 imperial	747.50
1973	19.99–43.00
1972	17.80–21.40
1971	26.50–45.00
1970	39.95–70.00
1970 magnum	119.89
1970 jeroboam	632.50
1969	38.33
1968	10.50
1967	25.00–40.02
1966	55.00–78.78
1965	15.50
1964	38.50–53.53
1964 magnum	107.05
1962	48.30–70.44
1961	150.00–180.00
1959	90.00
1953	80.00
1952	75.04
1937	59.50
1920	75.00

Sold by: AV, BBR, BIB, BWC, BYR, C&B, CHAP, CUL, DAV, FINT, GH, HHC, HT, HUN, J&B, JH, L&W, MAL, MWS, PD, PG, PIP, QR, REID, RGA, RSV, THRE, TW, UNW, VICT, VIGN, WGA, WHIT, WILL, WSOC, YFW

Recent auction prices

1961	1150.00–1850.00
1962	400.00–520.00
1964	340.00–540.00
1966	480.00–760.00
1967	170.00–310.00
1969	125.00–135.00
1970	390.00–720.00
1971	250.00–320.00
1973	220.00
1975	440.00–540.00

Latour à Pomerol
Pomerol

1980	7.13–7.55
1979	9.78–10.59
1978	11.50
1977 magnum	14.95
1974	9.20
1973	11.50–13.37
1972	6.75–7.59
1971	17.25–18.50

Sold by: BYR, C&B, QR, VIGN, YFW

Recent auction prices

1970	230.00
1971	170.00–230.00
1974	46.00–50.00

Léoville-Barton
2eme cru classé St-Julien

The traditionalist's dream. Whoever described claret as a cedary, dry, demanding wine must have been thinking of Léoville-Barton. Despite all the new fashions and trends in Bordeaux, Ronald Barton simply goes on making superlative old-fashioned wine for long ageing, and resolutely charging a non-inflated price for it.

1982 EC IB	80.00–97.00
1981	8.73
1980	6.70–6.79
1979	6.50–10.29
1978	8.86–11.79
1978 magnum	23.86
1978 double magnum	46.00
1978 jeroboam	86.25
1977	7.07–8.30
1976	9.25–12.00
1976 magnum	25.30
1975*	12.00–18.40
1974	7.39–7.80
1971	13.28–13.94
1971 magnum	31.50
1970	16.50
1967	8.70
1966	20.00–28.75
1964	17.08
1952	13.95
1945	39.00

Sold by: ADN, AV, BBR, BIB, BYR, C&B, FINT, HT, J&B, L&W, MAL, MWS, ODD, PD, PG, QR, REID, RGA, RH, SF, TAN, THRE, TW, VIGN, WHIT, WILL, WNRY, WSOC

Recent auction prices

1961	360.00
1962	120.00
1964	110.00–115.00
1966	210.00–270.00
1967	86.00
1970	140.00
1971	140.00
1975	125.00–150.00
1976	84.00
1978	92.00
1979	76.00

EC (ex-cellar) price per dozen, excl shipping, duty and VAT. IB (in bond) price per dozen, excl duty and VAT. Auction prices, per dozen, excl VAT. All other prices, per bottle incl VAT.

Léoville-Las-Cases
2eme cru classé St-Julien

With Ducru-Beaucaillou, this is the most brilliant of the St-Juliens, combining all the sweet honeyed St-Julien ripeness with strong, dry, cedary perfume. The wine is justly famous, and despite a very large production the whole crop is snapped up at some of the Médoc's highest prices. Deservedly so. Quality this high, you pay for.

1982 EC	120.80–200.00
1981 EC	98.40–107.00
1981	10.87–15.00
1980	7.45–9.99
1979	10.29–13.80
1978	14.66–15.50
1978 jeroboam	138.00
1977*	7.20–9.43
1976	10.95–15.53
1975	25.00
1974	6.50–10.00
1974 magnum	14.10
1973	7.91–14.00
1973 magnum	22.55
1972	7.20
1971	16.50–18.98
1970	19.80
1970 magnum	30.00–64.00
1969	9.20

1967	14.00–15.00
1966	35.00
1964	13.95–25.29
1962	26.17–35.00
1961	50.00–67.28
1960	14.38
1948	28.50

Sold by: ADN, BBR, BIB, BWC, BYR, C&B, CHAP, CV, FFW, GH, HHC, HT, HUN, J&B, JH, L&W, LADV, PIP, REID, RSV, SR, TAN, UNW, VICT, VIGN, WHIT, WSOC, YFW

Recent auction prices

1961	380.00–625.00
1962	210.00–280.00
1964	120.00–180.00
1966	290.00–390.00
1967	96.00–145.00
1969	66.00–80.00
1970	175.00–260.00
1971	125.00–175.00
1973	110.00
1975	175.00–260.00
1976	115.00–130.00
1978	165.00
1979	82.00

Léoville-Poyferré
2eme cru classé St-Julien

The Léoville which has got left behind, not only in its unfashionable reputation, but also in the quality of the wine, which always has a dull indistinct flavour compared with other top St-Juliens. For once fashion was an honest critic. However, things are now looking up with new investment and new commitment, and the future could be exciting.

1982 EC	67.20–95.00
1981	9.40
1979	9.75–11.75
1978	8.92–11.50
1978 double magnum	48.30
1977	6.65–7.66
1976	7.48–12.90
1975	12.65–14.95
1973	6.93–7.50
1972	7.50
1970	13.70–26.19
1970 magnum	31.00
1967	9.97–13.94
1966	21.50–27.65
1966 magnum	52.00
1966 double magnum	138.00
1965	8.95
1961	56.34

1959	13.75
1948	46.50
1934	39.95

Sold by: BBR, BIB, FINT, GH, HHC, HT, HUN, J&B, MAL, MWS, PG, QR, RACK, REID, RGA, RSV, TAN, UNW, WAIT, WGA, WHIT, WILL, YFW

Recent auction prices

1961	300.00–310.00
1962	110.00–170.00
1964	125.00
1966	160.00–200.00
1967	90.00
1970	125.00–170.00
1971	94.00–110.00
1973	64.00–94.00
1974	44.00
1975	96.00–120.00
1976	76.00–84.00

Liversan
cru bourgeois supérieur Haut-Médoc

1979*	4.31–4.92
1978	4.19

Sold by: ASHE, BYR, CHAP, CV, MACK, PD

Loudenne
cru grand bourgeois Médoc

An English outpost in the Médoc – and a pink one too, since Loudenne is famous for its rose château. The château is owned by Gilbey's and the wine is seen a lot in such chains as Peter Dominic. The red always seems pleasant, but a little too soft to lay down, and could do with a touch more backbone. The white is straight and fresh.

1981	4.45
1979	4.60–5.45

Sold by: BYR, J&B, PD, SR

la Louvière
Graves

1977	4.70
1975	9.80

Sold by: PD

Lynch-Bages
5eme cru classé Pauillac

This château is so well known that familiarity can breed contempt, and its considerable quality be underestimated. For a Cabernet Sauvignon-dominated wine it is astonishingly soft and drinkable when very young, and yet it ages brilliantly, and has one of the most beautiful scents of minty blackcurrant in all Bordeaux. Reasonably expensive, it is producing fine wine almost every year – and lots of it!

1982 EC	98.50–130.00
1981	8.28
1980	6.45
1979	7.90–10.98
1978	10.30–12.08
1978 magnum	31.97
1977	6.95–8.43
1976	10.93–18.99
1975	15.60–18.50
1975 magnum	38.00
1975 jeroboam	230.00
1973	7.25
1972	7.96
1970	17.50–28.00
1967	13.80–13.95
1966	15.95–36.00
1962	23.00
1961	28.50–63.00
1959	15.95–18.95
1955	45.61

Sold by: BBR, BIB, C&B, CHAP, CV, DAV, FINT, HUN, J&B, JH, L&W, MACK, MWS, QR, RACK, RSV, SAIN, THRE, TW, VICT, VIGN, WAIT, WGA, WHIT, WILL, WNRY, WSOC, YFW

Recent auction prices

1961	300.00–560.00
1962	195.00–320.00
1964	84.00–180.00
1966	260.00–270.00
1967	96.00–110.00
1969	62.00–70.00
1970	200.00–240.00
1973	78.00–92.00
1975	130.00–160.00
1976	82.00–115.00
1978	92.00–125.00

Lynch-Moussas
5eme cru clasé Pauillac

1981 EC	45.00
1979	6.84–7.25
1979 magnum	13.09
1978	7.50–9.14
1976 magnum	15.18
1972	5.00
1971	12.65
1970	9.85–14.75

Sold by: AV, BBR, EHR, ESV, FINT, J&B, REID, TW, VIGN

Recent auction prices

1961	240.00
1970	110.00–125.00
1971	98.00–150.00
1976	76.00

Macquin-St-Georges
St-Georges-St-Emilion

1982 EC IB	26.64–29.00
1981	4.10–4.45
1980	3.91
1979*	3.99–4.53
1977	3.10
1976	4.63

Sold by: BAL, C&B, DAV, HT, L&W, TAN

Magdelaine
1er grand cru St-Emilion

A great St-Emilion, combining the soft richness of Merlot with the sturdiness needed to age. It picks very late to maximise ripeness, and is made with the usual care by J-P Moueix of Libourne. Expensive, but one of the best.

1982 EC	111.00
1981	11.50
1980*	7.13
1979	13.80
1978	12.65
1977	8.05
1976	11.50

Sold by: C&B, L&W

Recent auction prices

1966	220.00–250.00
1967	100.00–125.00
1970	160.00
1971	210.00
1977	46.00

Malartic-Lagravière
cru classé Graves

While its near neighbour, Domaine de Chevalier, hardly ever produces its allowed crop, this property frequently has to de-classify its excess. Even so, the

quality is good, sometimes excellent, and while the white is very attractive young, the red is dry and herby, and capable of long ageing. Usually good value.

1982 EC	49.00
1982	6.90
1976	7.99
1967	9.85
1947	20.00
1934	29.95

Sold by: BBR, HBV, PG, RSV, SF, VIGN

Malescot-St-Exupéry
3eme cru classé Margaux

This château is often held up as a quintessential Margaux. It is quite hard, rather light and lean when young, and rarely shows well to start with. But give it 10 years and the perfume and delicate fruit it displays is topped only by such growths as Margaux and Palmer. Not expensive for its quality.

1982 EC	60.00
1979	7.60
1978*	7.49–11.35
1977	5.75–8.59
1976	7.48–13.50
1976 magnum	21.50–25.36
1975	9.20–11.75
1975 magnum	19.50–29.83
1971	12.59
1970	13.00–16.39
1967	10.45
1966	15.00–21.00

Sold by: ADN, AV, BIB, BYR, CUL, GH, HT, J&B, L&W, MACK, MWS, PG, QR, REID, RH, SR, UNW, VIGN, WHIT, YFW

Recent auction prices

1961	310.00–360.00
1962	145.00
1966	150.00–170.00
1970	120.00–140.00
1975	82.00
1976	80.00

Margaux
1er cru classé Margaux

This troubled first growth seems finally to be back on the rails. Despite continuing ownership uncertainties, the wines since 1978 have replaced Margaux on the pedestal of fragrance, refinement and sheer, ravishing perfume which it had slipped off a dozen or so years before. Many vintages of the 70s are not that special, but the new Margaux is weightier than before, yet with all its beauty intact.

1982 EC IB	286.00–450.00
1981 EC IB	279.00–290.00
1981	30.67–36.89
1980	18.10
1979*	19.49–27.50
1978	31.00–40.00
1976	23.69–41.82
1975	43.12–59.00
1973	16.50–22.80
1972	12.00
1971	24.00–33.75
1971 magnum	75.00
1970	42.55
1970 magnum	110.00
1969	21.08
1967	19.99–24.05
1966	42.50–51.75
1964	29.90–42.55
1962	36.80–50.00
1961	125.00
1960	23.00
1959	69.50
1957	26.95
1952	59.95
1950	36.95
1908	65.00

Sold by: AV, BBR, BYR, C&B, FINT, GH, HHC, HT, HUN, J&B, L&W, LADV, MACK, MAL, OWL, PG, QR, REID, RGA, RSV, SF, TW, UNW, VICT, VIGN, WHIT, WILL, WW

Recent auction prices

1961	1120.00–1850.00
1962	330.00–440.00
1964	220.00–380.00
1966	520.00–700.00
1967	185.00–210.00
1969	125.00–165.00
1970	360.00–620.00
1971	240.00–300.00
1973	145.00–195.00
1974	120.00
1975	340.00–390.00
1976	180.00–210.00
1978	280.00–340.00

Marquis d'Alesme-Becker
3eme cru classé Margaux

1977	5.31–6.23
1970	9.58–12.50
1966	15.00

Sold by: GH, H&D, HT, WILL

Recent auction prices

1969	60.00
1966	110.00
1970	125.00

Marquis-de-Terme
4eme cru classé Margaux

1979	7.99
1978	7.99–8.75
1976	8.75
1964	11.33
1929	45.00

Sold by: CDM, HUN, PG, REID, VIGN

Maucaillou
cru bourgeois Moulis

1979	5.25–6.18
1978	5.30–6.50
1976	7.20

Sold by: AV, BAL, BYR, HHC, HUN, L&W, WHIT

Recent auction prices

1970	64.00

Meaume
Bordeaux

1982 EC	29.00
1981*	3.20
1979	3.45

Sold by: GH, HUN

Meyney
cru grand bourgeois exceptionnel St-Estèphe

This epitomises the 'reliable' style of St-Estèphe, yet is better than that. The wine is big, meaty, and strong, but never harsh. If anything it lacks a little personality, and, with the exception of years like

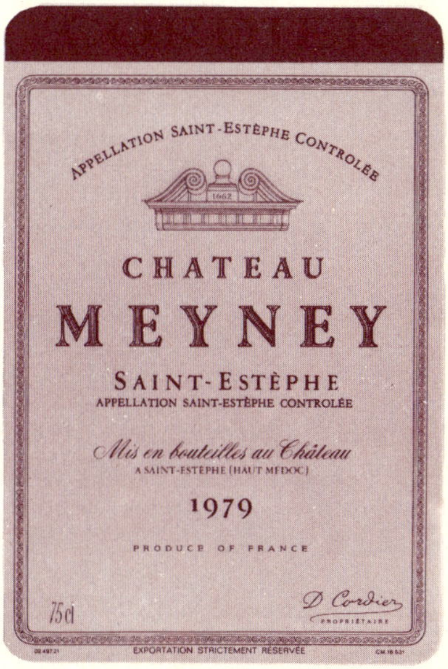

1962, never quite develops the quality of maturity one might expect. Even so, good value. Good second wine – Le Prieur de Meyney.

1980	4.17
1979*	3.35–5.98
1978	5.73–7.59
1977	4.09–5.99
1976	6.69
1975	7.00–7.99
1975 magnum	18.11
1974	4.93–5.45
1972	5.46–7.07
1970	7.47–12.26
1967	8.90
1966 double magnum	69.00
1961	71.83

Sold by: BBR, BIB, DAV, GH, HT, L&W, MAL, P&C, QR, RACK, RSV, TW, WAIT, WGA, WHIT, WILL

Recent auction prices

1962	90.00
1964	68.00
1966	130.00
1970	72.00–92.00
1971	58.00
1976	46.00–66.00

la Mission-Haut-Brion
cru classé Graves

La Mission is in a class apart, between Haut-Brion and the rest. Yet one often feels this 'hors classé' position relies more on weight and massive dark fruit and oak flavours than on any great subleties. For those, you go up to Haut-Brion, or down to Domaine de Chevalier.

1982 EC	294.00
1981 EC IB	175.00–230.15
1981	18.60–19.55
1980	14.85

1979	15.03-19.82
1978	11.74-34.70
1977	9.95-14.95
1976	15.50-25.00
1975	39.00
1975 magnum	98.00
1974	13.55
1973	18.65
1971	21.85-34.36
1970	35.65-50.00
1969	14.95
1967	16.00-25.30
1966	67.00
1964	28.15
1963	12.65
1962	36.50-44.85
1961	107.08
1959	64.48
1957	46.00
1955	50.60
1953	59.80
1949	109.25
1948	75.90

Sold by: ADN, BBR, C&B, DAV, FINT, GH, HHC, HT, J&B, L&W, MAL, VIGN, WW, YFW

Recent auction prices

1961	1440.00
1962	370.00-400.00
1964	350.00-370.00
1966	420.00-540.00
1967	175.00-210.00
1969	100.00
1970	380.00-580.00
1971	260.00-330.00
1976	200.00-240.00
1979	165.00

Montalivet
Graves

1981	3.75-4.27
1979	3.51-4.40
1978*	3.97-4.63
1978 magnum	9.03
1976*	3.99

Sold by: ADN, BAL, CHAP, DAV, ESV, HT, J&B, L&W, TAN

Montrose
2eme cru classé St-Estèphe

This château is often the leanest and toughest of all the St-Estèphes, famous for its dark, tannic character, and its slow, ponderous march to maturity. As such, it used to be the most famous, but despite a recent award as the top St-Estèphe, its recent vintages have seemed lighter and faintly hollow for so sturdy a wine.

1982 EC IB	101.00-105.00
1981	9.78
1979	8.19-10.25
1978	9.75-18.50
1976	9.20-17.50
1975	13.25-16.00
1975 double magnum	92.00
1974	7.55
1973	10.90
1972	7.00
1971	15.53-15.90
1970	18.40-23.35
1970 magnum	40.54
1966	19.00
1962	26.00
1961	35.00-55.00

Sold by: AV, BAL, BBR, BIB, BYR, C&B, FINT, GH, M&B, HT, HUN, J&B, L&W, MAL, MART, MWS, PG, RACK, REID, RSV, TAN, UNW, VICT, VIGN, WGA, WHIT, WNRY, WILL, WW

Recent auction prices

1961	300.00-460.00
1962	165.00
1964	100.00-210.00
1966	180.00-250.00
1967	90.00-105.00
1969	68.00
1970	140.00-220.00
1971	136.00
1974	64.00
1975	130.00-160.00
1976	82.00-96.00
1978	94.00-110.00

Moulin des Carruades
Pauillac

1979	9.95

Sold by: ODD

la Mouline
cru bourgeois Moulis

1979	2.95–3.85

Sold by: ECD, WILL, YFW

Moulinet
Pomerol

1982 IB	64.00
1979	6.24–7.60
1978	4.75–9.70
1976	8.95
1970	10.00
1961	17.75

Sold by: BOW, BYR, GH, H&B, MACK, MWS, RSV, WILL

Mouton-Baronne-Philippe
5eme cru classé Pauillac

Although Baron Philippe's second-best wine, it is nonetheless a separate and classy wine in its own right and dedicated to his late wife's memory. It is softer nowadays than it used to be, but the balance is very good for a fifth growth, with the perfume particularly marked, and it obviously benefits from its association with Mouton-Rothschild.

1982	9.83
1979	7.95–8.50
1978	8.76–9.75
1977	7.70–11.79
1976	11.50
1975	10.06–11.35
1970	13.92–16.50
1961	40.00

Sold by: BYR, H&B, HT, L&W, MACK, RACK, TW, VIGN, WILL

Recent auction prices

1961	420.00
1966	175.00
1970	160.00
1973	78.00
1975	110.00–120.00
1976	76.00

Mouton-Rothschild
1er cru classé Pauillac

The wine that came in from the cold. After 50 years of well-orchestrated lobbying, Baron Philippe de Rothschild managed to raise Mouton to first growth status in 1973, just two years after he had asked (and received) 20,000 francs a tonneau more for his Mouton than Lafite received. Of course it should be a first growth. But then several fifths should probably be seconds. The wine which caused the rumpus does have an astonishing flavour, piling an intense cigar-box and lead-pencil perfume onto the rich blackcurrant fruit, and one can't complain too much at the prices its top wines command.

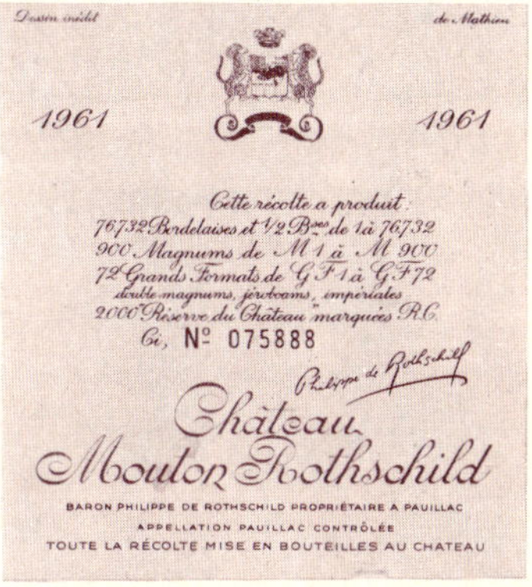

1982 EC IB	310.00–460.00
1982	40.25
1981	31.23–33.00
1980	17.60–24.75
1979	26.00–38.32
1978	32.00–43.00
1977	15.65–22.43
1976	23.63–36.95
1976 magnum	55.34
1976 double magnum	138.00
1975	44.99–50.00
1975 double magnum	276.00
1975 jeroboam	552.00
1974	24.00
1973	30.68
1973 magnum	44.00
1972	14.75
1971	29.50–48.28
1971 magnum	70.00
1970	40.25–70.00
1970 magnum	120.00
1967	25.00–39.68
1966	69.00–75.20
1961	125.00–200.00
1957	39.50
1937	65.00

Sold by: AV, BBR, BIB, BYR, C&B, DAV, FFW, FINT, GH, H&B, HT, HUN, J&B, L&W, MAL, MWS, PG, QR, REID, RSV, TAN, TW, UNW, VICT, VIGN, WGA, WHIT, WILL, WW, YFW

Recent auction prices

1961	1147.00–2000.00
1962	420.00–600.00
1964	300.00–420.00
1966	560.00–850.00
1967	195.00–260.00
1969	120.00
1970	400.00–720.00
1971	240.00–270.00
1973	230.00–260.00
1975	390.00–480.00
1976	230.00–270.00
1977	125.00
1978	310.00–350.00
1979	190.00

Nenin
Pomerol

A thoroughly old-fashioned wine, which quite rightly pleases the Royal Family who order rather a lot of it. But in fact it is rather chunky and solid – a bit

Arran sweaters and land Rover-ish, and has quite a tough core for a Pomerol, which doesn't always disperse into mellow fruitfulness.

1978	8.95–12.94
1977	8.70
1976	8.00–8.39
1973	10.95
1972	5.95
1971	14.72
1970	14.00–18.50
1961	19.95–42.00

Sold by: BBR, FINT, GH, HT, JH, MAL, RSV, TW, VIGN

Recent auction prices

1961	115.00–160.00
1966	195.00
1970	150.00
1971	110.00
1973	66.00–75.00

les Ormes-de-Pez
cru grand bourgeois St-Estèphe

This property should not be confused with Château de Pez, because the styles are quite different. The fruit here is often rather dry, but the oak casks give the wine a softness which is very attractive. Good years, like 1970, will age very well.

1982 EC	43.20–51.00
1980	5.65
1979	6.50–7.40
1978	5.50–12.00
1972	5.95
1970	11.20

Sold by: BWC, BYR, CHAP, GH, HT, MAL, MWS, PIP, RSV, SF, SW, UNW

Recent auction prices

1961	270.00
1970	92.00

In younger clarets it is always worth shopping around to get the best bargain because, in a highly competitive market, merchants will have bought their stock at different times, from different sources, at different prices.
If you are buying claret of any age in quantity you should compare several merchants' lists, because, as our listings show, the differences in price are often dramatic.

Palmer
3eme cru classé Margaux

"Most expensive of the third growths?" asks one of Palmer's owners. "No. Cheapest of the firsts." The way things are going, there's a lot of truth in that. Palmer often out-Margauxs Margaux, for sheer beauty and perfume. And it frequently out-performs most of the first growths in tastings. So, yes, it is very underclassed, but only in the books. The market price is high and shows that Palmer is appreciated where it matters – in how much people are prepared to pay.

1982 EC	115.00–180.00
1981	13.80–14.95
1980	8.89–10.00
1979	12.65–16.68
1979 magnum	33.64
1978	16.96–24.50
1978 magnum	46.06
1977	9.50
1976	19.75–38.32
1975	35.18–40.25
1974	8.60
1973	14.49
1972	8.50
1971	20.00–22.50
1971 magnum	59.00
1970	45.71–50.00
1970 magnum	91.71
1966	56.92
1964	24.90
1960	14.50
1952	30.95
1904	49.95

Sold by: ADN, AV, BBR, BIB, BYR, C&B, CV, FFW, GH, HT, HUN, J&B, L&W, OWL, QR, RSV, SR, UNW, VIGN, WHIT

Recent auction prices

1961	1100.00–1450.00
1962	440.00
1964	180.00
1966	440.00–620.00
1967	155.00
1969	100.00–130.00
1970	350.00–540.00
1971	175.00–220.00
1974	84.00
1975	260.00–400.00
1976	155.00–220.00
1978	220.00–290.00
1979	140.00–150.00

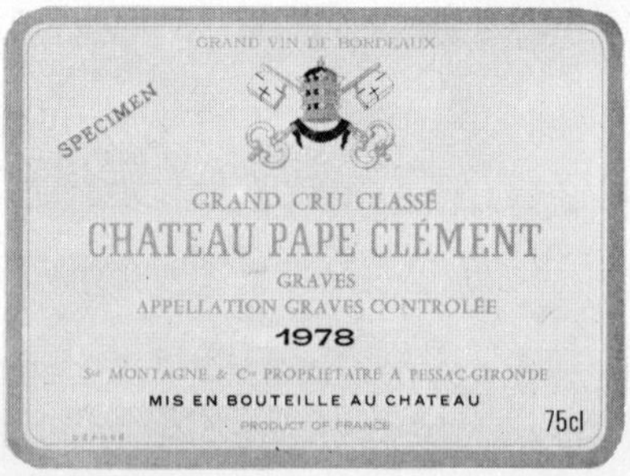

Pape-Clément
cru classé Graves

One of the top Graves, capable of mixing a considerable sweetness from ripe fruit and new oak, with a good deal of tough structure. The big years age remarkably well, while the lesser years still have very good balance for a fair while.

1982 EC	120.00–130.00
1976	9.45–12.48
1975	21.56

1973	8.75
1970	17.50–27.43
1961	50.00
1955	24.50

Sold by: AV, BBR, HT, HUN, J&B, L&W, MACK, MAL, RSV, TAN, TW

Recent auction prices

1961	460.00–550.00
1966	240.00–320.00
1967	100.00–105.00
1970	170.00–220.00
1971	110.00

la Parde de Haut Bailly
Graves

1980	4.75–4.92
1979	4.65

Sold by: CV, RACK, WILL

Patache d'Aux
cru grand bourgeois Médoc

1982* EC	24.60–29.00
1981	4.07–4.85
1979*	4.19–4.69
1978	4.06–5.95
1977	4.09
1976	4.99–6.33
1974	5.30

Sold by: ASHE, BIB, BYR, DOL, FFW, J&B, JH, LADV, MWS, ODD, OWL, P&C, PD, PG, PIP, QR, SW, TW, YFW

Pavie
1er grand cru St-Emilion

Not only is this the biggest major property in St-Emilion, but the yields are fairly high, so the amount of wine made is important to say the least. Perhaps inevitably, the wine is good without being wonderful, stylish without being grand, but it does have the true gentle flavours of good St-Emilion.

1982 EC	82.80–93.00
1981 EC IB	76.00–79.20
1978	10.29–12.30
1978 magnum	21.00
1977	7.25–8.65
1976	8.60–16.19
1975	12.03–15.00
1971	13.23–15.50
1970 dougle magnum	74.75
1959	19.95

Sold by: AV, BIB, BWC, DAV, ESV, HHC, HT, J&B, MAL, PIP, REID, RSV, VICT, VIGN, YFW

Recent auction prices

1962	150.00
1970	170.00
1971	140.00
1976	98.00–100.00

Pavillon Rouge du Château Margaux
Margaux

1976	10.55

Sold by: DOL

Pédesclaux
5eme cru classé Pauillac

1979	6.20
1978	8.45
1976	7.87

Sold by: TW, WILL

Petit-Village
Pomerol

A fairly pricey Pomerol, chiefly because it has been astutely promoted by Bruno Prats, who also owns Cos d'Estournel. It is not one of the soft, plummy Pomerols, and until recently there was a fair amount of Cabernet giving backbone. The wine is worth laying down but the price is always high.

1982 EC	95.00
1979	9.50
1977	8.20
1975	9.99

Sold by: FFW, J&B, MAL

Pétrus
Pomerol

The world's most expensive red wine, and frequently the world's greatest. Astonishingly, its reputation, though surfacing briefly in 1878, has been made since World War II, and in particular since 1962, when the firm of J-P Moueix took a half-share in the property. The firm has given the kiss of life to many Pomerol properties, turning potential into achievement, and with Pétrus it has a supreme creation. Christian Moueix says his intention is to ensure no bottle of Pétrus ever disappoints. It doesn't.

1980	28.75–47.90
1979	51.75–71.87
1978	74.75
1978 magnum	149.79
1976	54.63–95.83
1975 double magnum	598.00
1974	31.50
1971 magnum	250.00
1970	172.50–191.67
1966	180.00

Sold by: BIB, C&B, HT, HUN, J&B, L&W, MAL, WGA, YFW

Recent auction prices

1964	760.00–920.00
1966	1250.00–2200.00
1967	560.00–780.00
1969	280.00–330.00
1970	1080.00–2100.00
1971	740.00–940.00
1975	1000.00–1150.00
1976	500.00–640.00
1978	850.00

de Pez
cru bourgeois supérieur St-Estèphe

De Pez is one of the most famous Bourgeois château of Bordeaux. High quality wine making and a distribution agreement with Gilbey's have helped to project the wine. It's no longer cheap, but the wine is almost always of classed growth standard, big, rather plummy and not too harsh.

1982* EC IB	65.00–79.00
1979	7.28–8.20
1978	7.40–9.10
1975	10.00–10.35

Sold by: BOW, C&B, J&B, PG, SF, SR

Recent auction prices

1961	195.00
1967	86.00
1970	95.00–170.00
1971	88.00–92.00
1975	66.00–84.00

Phélan-Ségur
cru grand bourgeois exceptionnel St-Estèphe

This wine, with its bright yellow label, is always one of the softer St-Estèphes. Although not a lot of new oak is used, the flavour of oak and the soft mellow finish often dominate the wine, which makes it very enjoyable at an early stage.

1978	5.85–7.85
1976	9.15
1975	7.00–10.00
1973	5.50–7.76
1962	16.39

Sold by: HT, MAL, MWS, REID, VICT, WILL

Recent auction prices

1961	175.00
1966	130.00
1970	90.00–105.00
1971	88.00–100.00
1973	48.00–70.00

Pichon Baron
2eme cru classé Pauillac

Often called more masculine than its 'sister', Pichon Lalande, and rightly so, because this is tremendously correct Pauillac only gradually realising its potential. Dryer and lighter than Lalande, it is also less immediately impressive, yet the 1982 was one of the best wines in all of Pauillac. Not cheap but increasingly good.

1982 EC	78.00
1981	11.20
1980	6.95
1979	8.95–9.62
1978	13.50
1977	6.95
1976	10.18
1973	9.49–10.50
1972	7.45–7.80
1971	11.07–12.07
1970	15.55–22.50
1961	56.93
1950	24.00

Sold by: AV, BBR, BYR, CUL, FFW, GH, HUN, J&B, REID, RSV, WHIT

Recent auction prices

1961	400.00–520.00
1962	155.00
1966	185.00–220.00
1967	90.00
1970	160.00–200.00
1973	72.00–92.00
1975	125.00
1976	76.00–105.00
1979	70.00

Pichon Lalande
2eme cru classé Pauillac

Pauillac's newest star announced its intentions with a stunning 1970, and since then has been making a rich, oaky, concentrated wine which was almost too much of a good thing in 1982. Its price has climbed inexorably and it wishes to be seen as the equal partner of St-Julien's leading pair, Léoville-las-Cases and Ducru-Beaucaillou, though whether they want Lalande to join their grouping is another matter.

1982 EC	116.45–160.00
1981 EC IB	82.00–108.00
1981	10.87–13.70
1980	6.70–8.05
1978	13.50–14.40
1977*	6.85–8.77
1976*	10.93–21.39
1976 magnum	26.27
1975	15.00–19.50
1974	9.43
1970	25.00–25.88
1970 jeroboam	316.25
1970 imperial	414.00
1967	10.35–15.50
1966	33.00
1949	39.50
1929	55.00

Sold by: ADN, BBR, BIB, BYR, C&B, CUL, CV, DOL, ESV, GH, HBV, HHC, HT, HUN, J&B, LADV, L&W, PD, RACK, RSV, SR, VICT, VIGN, WGA, WNRY, WSOC, WW, YFW

Recent auction prices

1961	390.00–600.00
1964	145.00–170.00
1966	195.00–300.00
1967	94.00–140.00
1969	66.00–86.00
1970	170.00–230.00
1971	130.00
1975	120.00–170.00
1976	98.00–110.00
1978	105.00–150.00
1979	110.00

EC (ex-cellar) price per dozen, excl shipping, duty and VAT. IB (in bond) price per dozen, excl duty and VAT. Auction prices, per dozen, excl VAT. All other prices, per bottle incl VAT.

Pitray
Côtes de Castillon

1978	3.55–3.74
1975	4.11–6.22
1974	3.55

Sold by: ESV, MAL, P&C, REID, WILL

Plagnac
cru bourgeois Médoc

1980	2.96
1979	2.99–3.85
1975	4.95–6.20

Sold by: MWS, P&C, WILL

la Pointe
Pomerol

1979	7.80
1978	7.82–8.97
1978 magnum	20.54
1976	9.15
1970	16.95

Sold by: BIB, CHAP, L&W, QR, RSV, SF, VIGN, WSOC

Recent auction prices

1974	110.00
1966	175.00
1970	125.00
1973	105.00

Pontet-Canet
5eme cru classé Pauillac

Pontet-Canet seems to swing backwards and forwards from a heavy style to a light style, and it hasn't quite sorted itself out. Although owned by M. Tesseron of Lafon-Rochet since 1975, it hasn't reacted so quickly to his touch. The 1982 wasn't thrilling, but it is a fine property and should improve.

1980*	4.55–5.23
1979	7.75–8.20
1978	7.70–10.50
1977	7.70
1976	8.80
1975	11.90–15.30
1973 magnum	17.50
1970	9.95–14.26
1964	10.95
1953	23.50
1952	13.50
1934	29.95

Sold by: BBR, BYR, ESV, H&B, HHC, J&B, ODD, OWL, PD, PG, REID, RSV, SR, SW, VIGN, WGA, WHIT, WW, YFW

Recent auction prices

1961	300.00
1966	165.00–190.00
1975	90.00–105.00

du Port
Bordeaux

1970	5.37

Sold by: PIP

Potensac
cru grand bourgeois Médoc

Arguably the most exciting of the Bas-Médoc properties, since it is owned by M. Delon of Léoville-Las-Cases, and a broadly similar style of wine making is pursued. This gives wines which have a delicious simple blackcurrant fruit, greatly improved by a strong taste of oak. Not expensive for the quality.

1982 EC	29.90–66.00
1980	4.85–6.49
1979*	5.28
1978	5.25–7.70
1977	6.62
1975	6.51–8.50
1970	8.20–8.95

Sold by: AV, BIB, BYR, CHAP, GH, HHC, HT, HUN, J&B, LADV, MAL, OWL, RH, RSV, SR, VICT, WW, YFW

Recent auction prices

1970	54.00
1973	54.00
1975	56.00
1976	54.00

de Pressac
St-Emilion

1967	8.65
1962	10.05

Sold by: FINT, MAL

Prieur de Meyney
St-Estèphe

1980*	4.29–5.55

Sold by: MWS, RACK

le Prieuré
grand cru classé St-Emilion

1982 EC	58.68
1982 magnum	9.83

Sold by: L&W

Prieuré-Lichine
4eme cru classé Margaux

This is not always one of the most impressive Margaux wines, but it is always one of the most reliable, and in years like 1970, 1971 and 1975 it did excel. Even so, it's fairly priced and although not that perfumed, is a good sound Margaux.

1982 EC	82.00–90.00
1981	8.17
1975	10.73

Sold by: C&B, HUN, WHIT

Recent auction prices

1974	52.00
1975	105.00

Puy-Blanquet
grand cru St-Emilion

1982 EC	43.20
1978	5.91–6.20
1976	6.45–6.84
1976 magnum	10.06

Sold by: BAL, BBR, HT, L&W, TW

Recent auction prices

1973	38.00–46.00

Rahoul
Graves

1979	4.75–5.55

Sold by: BYR, HUN, PIP, WNRY, YFW

Ramage-la Bâtisse
cru bourgeois Haut-Médoc

1980*	4.00–4.95
1979*	4.25–5.72
1976	14.00

Sold by: BYR, CDM, EHR, HUN, MART, SR

Recent auction prices

1975	47.00–72.00

Rausan-Ségla
2eme cru classé Margaux

This is the top second growth in the Médoc. The very top. It should be only an arm's length away from Mouton-Rothschild in quality. In fact, they have been in different worlds. Mouton's quality and reputation was built on devotion and obsessive hard work. Rausan's reputation had declined through disinterest and lack of commitment. But 1983 saw a new oenologist and a triumphant return to quality.

1979	9.45
1978	7.76–7.78
1976	9.03
1975	9.50–17.32
1973	6.93–9.35
1971	11.90
1970	18.50–26.36
1966	18.95–23.69
1964	12.70
1962	19.49
1960	10.60–12.90
1937	32.00

Sold by: ASHE, AV, L&W, MWS, PG, REID, RSV, TAN, VIGN, WHIT, WILL, YFW

Recent auction prices

1961	330.00
1964	125.00
1966	180.00
1967	80.00
1970	125.00–140.00
1971	92.00–100.00

Rauzan-Gassies
2eme cru classé Margaux

Right behind Rausan-Ségla, this should only be an arm and a leg removed from Mouton. But it's the same old story. The style is quite different to Ségla, being harder, dryer, meaner even, but there just isn't the top quality evidence. The soil is as good as ever, so one hopes each year for signs of a change.

1978	9.65
1976	8.45–11.30
1973	9.03
1970	13.23–17.25
1967	9.66
1966	23.00–24.52
1961	30.00–41.98
1959	18.95
1957	12.95

Sold by FINT, J&B, L&W, PG, REID, RSV, TW, VICT, WGA, WHIT

Recent auction prices

1961	230.00–330.00
1962	130.00
1964	125.00
1966	145.00–175.00
1967	88.00
1970	110.00–120.00
1971	84.00–96.00

1973 56.00-70.00
1976 60.00-82.00

Réserve de la Comtesse
Pauillac

1979 6.45
Sold by: WSOC

Richotey
Fronsac

1982* IB 24.00
1980 3.45
1979 3.68
1978 4.14-4.73
1976 4.03
Sold by: C&B, LADV

la Rivière
Fronsac

1979 4.99-5.85
1978 5.34-5.90
1975 5.38
1971 3.90
Sold by: BOW, FINT, JH, WHIT

du Rocher
St-Emilion

1979* 4.70-5.14
Sold by: LADV, LHV, RH

La Rose-Capbern
St-Estèphe

1959 9.50
Sold by: VIGN

> ***Webster's** has been compiled from the latest merchants' catalogues available at the time of going to press but neither we nor the merchants listed can guarantee that all the wines mentioned will be available by the time you read the book. Equally, other wines and new vintages will become available.*

la Rose du Pin
Bordeaux

1982* 2.99
Sold by: ODD

la Rose Pauillac
Pauillac

1976 4.20
Sold by: DAV

la Rose-Trintaudon
cru grand bourgeois Haut-Médoc

1979 5.10-5.71
1978 4.85
1976 6.14
1975 6.19
Sold by: BWC, PG, PIP, VIGN

Rougemont
Graves

1982 2.95
1979 4.11
Sold by: EHR, TAN

Rouget
Pomerol

1976 9.49
1964 13.50-15.95
1962 15.95-16.10
Sold by: HUN, REID, RSV, YFW

Recent auction prices
1961 145.00
1962 110.00
1964 110.00

St-Bonnet
cru bourgeois Médoc

1982 EC 21.85
1979 5.12
1978 4.67
Sold by: HHC, JH

St-Pierre
Lalande de Pomerol

1982 IB 32.00
1978 5.00
1978 magnum 11.04
Sold by: ADN, BAL, C&B, L&W

St-Pierre
St-Emilion

1981 3.57
Sold by: J&B

St-Pierre-Sevaistre
4eme cru classé St-Julien

St-Pierre has been the undiscovered jewel of St-Julien for years, making deep, honeyed wines which none but the faithful ever took much notice of. Those who bought got some of the Médoc's best bargains. The château has now been 'acquired' by Henri Martin, and its fame is sure to be trumpeted. Whether its quiet unhurried quality will cope is another matter.

1982 EC 79.20
1978* 8.05-8.64
1977 6.19
1970 12.00-12.99
Sold by: ADN, HT, HUN, L&W, TAN, WILL

Recent auction prices
1970 135.00

de Sales
Pomerol

An enormous estate, the biggest in Pomerol by a street. This vastness may show a little in a wine which, though always enjoyable, is rarely outstanding, and though it is good, round claret, it doesn't often excite.

1979	8.10
1978	6.49–8.94
1976	10.25
1975	8.61–11.50
1971	11.50
1970	10.35–11.19

Sold by: AV, BWC, BYR, C&B, ESV, FINT, GH, HHC, HUN, J&B, L&W, PG, PIP, WGA

Recent auction prices

1970	120.00–125.00

Sarget de Gruaud-Larose
St-Julien

1981*	5.18
1980*	4.99
1979	4.87–5.58

Sold by: L&W, RACK, WILL

Sauman
Côtes de Bourg

1978	4.05
1976	4.04

Sold by: H&D, QR

Ségur
cru bourgeois supérieur Haut-Médoc

1975	4.51
1973	5.25

Sold by: HT, WILL

Recent auction prices

1969	35.00

Sénéjac
cru bourgeois supérieur Haut-Médoc

1945	34.50

Sold by: ADN

Sicard
St-Emilion

1978	3.54
1976	4.66
1975	4.54

Sold by: P&C

Siran
cru bourgeois supérieur Margaux

Frequently mistaken for a classed growth in blind tastings, this property is in fact mostly made up from the land of Dauzac and Giscours, and the owner doesn't let you forget it. He needn't worry, since everyone agrees with him, and in the meantime this château remains a bargain, given its quality.

1979	8.18
1978	8.92–8.97
1976	7.14
1975	8.10–9.68
1975 magnum	16.10

Sold by: GH, PIP, TAN, WILL

Recent auction prices

1966	86.00

Smith-Haut-Lafitte
cru classé Graves

1978*	6.16–8.45
1976	7.99–8.62
1975	8.50–11.24
1973	7.95
1972	5.50
1971	9.92
1970	11.50

Sold by: ASHE, PG, TW, WHIT, WILL

Recent auction prices

1961	185.00
1970	80.00–98.00
1971	82.00–84.00
1976	48.00–66.00
1978	64.00–66.00

Sociando-Mallet
cru grand bourgeois Haut-Médoc

1979	5.15

Sold by: MWS

Taillefer
Pomerol

1982 EC IB	49.95–67.00
1979	7.02

1978	5.70
1974	4.21
1972	5.30
1962 magnum	25.00

Sold by: C&B, EHR, FFW, GH, J&B, WILL

Talbot
4eme cru classé St-Julien

Because the production is so big, and the price so reasonable, Château Talbot is not always given the credit it deserves. A pity, because Talbot is one of the most carefully made and reliable of the fleshier St-Juliens, only suffering slightly in comparison with its sister Château Gruaud-Larose, and always offering first-class value for money. Maybe the name Talbot just lacks the right ring?

1981 EC IB	59.00–69.15
1981	7.25–9.20
1980	5.68–6.84
1979	6.59–8.90
1979 magnum	18.40
1978	7.41–11.37
1978 magnum	17.25–18.46
1977*	7.04–7.88
1976	7.87–15.49
1976 magnum	17.53–18.00
1975	11.75–18.31
1975 magnum	26.65
1974	5.65–8.80
1973	6.93–9.86
1972	6.10–7.42

In younger clarets it is always worth shopping around to get the best bargain because, in a highly competitive market, merchants will have bought their stock at different times, from different sources, at different prices.
If you are buying claret of any age in quantity you should compare several merchants' lists, because, as our listings show, the differences in price are often dramatic.

1971*	10.95
1971 magnum	26.90
1970	15.00–25.32
1970 magnum	38.00
1969	7.55
1966	19.05–20.00
1966 magnum	26.00–55.20
1966 double magnum	126.50
1962	19.50
1961	33.15–47.61
1959	21.16
1957	11.50
1949	53.00
1947	53.00
1928	37.50

Sold by: ADN, BAL, BBR, BIB, BYR, C&B, CHAP, DAV, GH, HHC, HT, J&B, L&W, MACK, MWS, P&C, PG, QR, RACK, RSV, SR, TAN, TW, VIGN, WGA, WHIT, WILL, YFW

Recent auction prices

1961	280.00–420.00
1962	180.00
1964	105.00–150.00
1966	155.00–240.00
1970	115.00–185.00
1971	125.00–130.00
1973	74.00–96.00
1975	105.00–140.00
1976	86.00–88.00
1978	62.00–90.00

les Templiers
Lalande de Pomerol

1982 EC	24.50
1980*	3.94–4.00
1979	4.26–4.60
1978	5.00
1976	5.54

Sold by: ADN, BYR, H&D, J&B, SR, WW

Terre Rouge
Médoc

1981	3.85–4.29
1981 magnum	8.05

Sold by: ADN, L&W, TAN

Du Tertre
5eme cru classé Margaux

Although classified, few people have heard of this, or could find it up the windy Margaux lanes. But it's worth seeking out, because the wine is unusually good with a lot of body for a Margaux, but that weight is all ripe, strong fruit and the flavour is direct and pure. Funnily enough, not cheap for a relatively unknown, but not expensive for the quality.

1981 EC	60.48
1979	3.01–8.25
1978	7.39–9.20
1976	6.90

Sold by: ADN, ESV, HBV, HT, J&B, L&W, WW

Recent auction prices

1970	90.00–100.00
1973	54.00

Thieuley
Bordeaux

1981*	2.95–3.49

Sold by: HHC, HT, RH, SR, WW

la Tonnelle
Premières Côtes de Blaye

1979	3.40
1978	3.20
1975	3.85

Sold by: BOW, PIP, VICT

Recent auction prices

1971	34.00–37.00

la Tour-Beauregard
St-Emilion

1978	4.70
1976	4.45

Sold by: BBR, WSOC

la Tour-Bicheau
Graves

1981	4.17
1978	5.15–5.71

Sold by: BWC, J&B, PIP

Recent auction prices

1975	40.00–48.00
1976	34.00–42.00
1978	28.00–35.00

la Tour Camillac
Côtes de Bordeaux

1981*	3.89

Sold by: THRE

la Tour-Carnet
4eme cru classé Haut-Médoc

Frequently dismissed as being unworthy of its classed growth position, this lovely estate has begun making wines well worth its fourth growth status. Even so the wine is still comparatively obscure, but the old light and fragrant style is being replaced by something sturdier for decent ageing. It is almost always fairly priced.

1978	7.69
1976	6.59–7.98
1975	9.95
1974	5.65
1949	29.95

Sold by: DOL, J&B, PD, RSV

Recent auction prices

1967	58.00

EC (ex-cellar) price per dozen, excl shipping, duty and VAT. IB (in bond) price per dozen, excl duty and VAT. Auction prices, per dozen, excl VAT. All other prices, per bottle incl VAT.

la Tour-de-By
cru grand bourgeois Médoc

Sometimes this seems like the most perfect drinking claret, and is an outstanding example of the early-drinkable style of Bas-Médoc wines, combined here with a really good dry blackcurrant fruit and a cedary perfume from the barrels. Good value, high quality claret.

1982 EC	27.00–40.00
1981	3.69–5.50
1979	4.60–5.00
1978	4.47–5.37
1977	3.95–4.75
1976	6.30
1970	7.30

Sold by: BAL, BBR, C&B, ESV, HUN, J&B, P&C, SF, THRE, WILL, WSOC

Recent auction prices

1978	45.00–46.00

la Tour-de-Mons
cru bourgeois supérieur Margaux

1980	5.75
1979	5.19–6.99
1978	5.89–6.94
1970	11.50
1924	32.00

Sold by: BYR, CDM, DOL, ODD, REID, VIGN

Recent auction prices

1970	98.00
1971	72.00–82.00
1975	85.00

la Tour-du-Pin-Figeac
grand cru St-Emilion

1980	5.89–6.05
1979	6.40
1978	5.90–6.93
1974	4.36
1971	13.50
1970	10.06

Sold by: BIB, DOL, MACK, REID, RSV, WGA, WILL

Recent auction prices

1970	92.00-98.00
1971	80.00

la Tour-Figeac
grand cru St-Emilion

1982	6.90
1970	10.00-12.47

Sold by: AV, HBV, HT

Recent auction prices

1964	130.00
1970	70.00

Tour-Granins
cru bourgeois Moulis

1976	4.15

Sold by: WSOC

la Tour-Haut-Brion
cru classé Graves

1982 EC	98.40
1981 EC	103.00
1981	9.66
1979	9.22-13.20
1978	10.45-13.83
1976	15.50
1975	14.88-16.96
1970	16.96

Sold by: ADN, FINT, HHC, HT, J&B, VIGN, WW

Recent auction prices

1970	130.00-160.00
1973	62.00

la Tour-Martillac
cru classé Graves

1984 marks the hundredth birthday of some of this property's white vines. Many of the red wine vines date from 1925–28. This sense of classical austerity pervades the wines, making them some of the most satisfying Graves to mature. Fine, old-fashioned wines.

1966	18.50
1961	21.50

Sold by: RSV, VIGN

Recent auction prices

1970	90.00

*Please don't blame **Webster's** or the merchants listed if a wine is sold out or if the vintage you want is no longer available. Wine is a living entity and a limited commodity – continuity of supply cannot, alas, be guaranteed.*

la Tour Peyreau
St-Emilion

1970	6.98

Sold by: MACK

la Tour-Puymirand
Bordeaux

1977	2.65
1976	2.75-4.03
1975	3.45

Sold by: P&C, WILL

la Tour St-Bonnet
cru bourgeois Médoc

1981	4.49-4.52
1979	2.99-5.45
1978*	3.40-4.80
1978 magnum	9.20
1977	5.75
1976	5.18
1975	6.65
1975 magnum	13.50
1971	7.19

Sold by: BAL, BYR, C&B, DAV, FINT, J&B, MWS, PG, PIP, QR, REID, VIGN

Recent auction prices

1973	36.00-40.00
1975	70.00-78.00
1978	45.00-48.00
1979	37.00-39.00

la Tour-Védrines
Bordeaux

1979	3.29
1978	3.35-3.54
1976	3.15
1975	3.35

Sold by: BYR, WHIT, WILL

Tourteau-Chollet
Graves

1980	3.60
1979	3.79

Sold by: CUL, SAIN

Toutigeac
Bordeaux

1981	2.59-3.19

Sold by: ASHE, EHR, MART, TES, VIGN

Tronquoy-Lalande
cru grand bourgeois St-Estèphe

1979	5.29

1978	5.30-5.98
1978 magnum	12.25
1975 magnum	12.08

Sold by: ADN, L&W, WHIT

Troplong-Mondot
grand cru St-Emilion

1982 EC	75.00
1981	7.88
1979	7.70-8.85
1978	7.75
1976 magnum	15.18
1975	9.30

Sold by: AV, BBR, HUN, MWS, PG

Recent auction prices

1966	120.00
1970	100.00

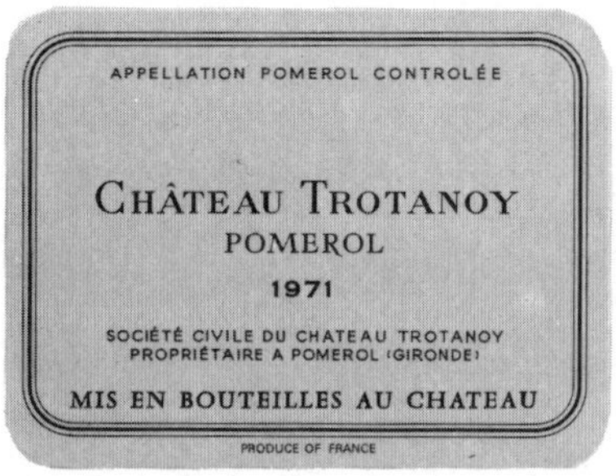

Trotanoy
Pomerol

If you didn't know Château Pétrus existed, you'd say this had to be the perfect Pomerol – rich, plummy, chocolatey fruit, some mineral hardness, and tremendous fat perfume. It's very, very good, and makes Pétrus achievement in eclipsing it (in a friendly way!) all the more amazing.

1981	13.80
1980	9.78-10.35
1979	33.53
1978	19.95
1976	43.12
1976 jeroboam	316.25
1975	43.12
1972 magnum	20.70
1971	52.70
1970	47.90

Sold by: BIB, BYR, C&B, VIGN

Recent auction prices

1970	290.00-440.00
1971	340.00-400.00
1973	88.00
1974	84.00
1976	225.00
1977	64.00

Trottevieille
1er grand cru St-Emilion

1981	6.90
1980	6.62
1978	9.97
1972	5.17
1971	12.00

Sold by: BBR, ESV, HBV

Recent auction prices

1975	125.00
1978	105.00

Verdignan
cru grand bourgeois Haut-Médoc

1978	4.37-5.41
1976	5.50
1975	5.35-6.58

Sold by: ADN, BYR, C&B, PIP, WSOC

Recent auction prices

1973	37.00-38.00
1978	35.00-36.00

Vieux Château Certan
Pomerol

1982 EC	96.00-165.00
1981 IB	96.00
1979	10.40
1978	10.25-14.00
1976	10.25-13.05
1970	20.00

Sold by: ADN, GH, HHC, HT, HUN, J&B, MAL, OWL, RH, RSV, SW

Recent auction prices

1964	280.00
1966	260.00

Vieux-Château-Landon
cru bourgeois Médoc

1981*	4.52

Sold by: STWC

Vraye Croix de Gay
Pomerol

1982 EC	63.00
1978	7.88
1976	9.53

Sold by: HHC, L&W

The editor's notes on these lists are overleaf.

Price Guide – Notes

If you think that the red Bordeaux entry looks a bit top-heavy, you should see the piles of wines that we couldn't include, not only for reasons of space but for fear that the guide would become 'Webster's Claret Price Guide' and a few others! And then take a look at any merchant's list, and you'll find the same thing. Unless the merchant is a specialist in some non-claret field his claret lists will outweigh every other area. (We originally chose and encoded some 5,000 claret entries alone for our data-base.) While German wines may be the bigger growth area in the UK market, apart from his Liebfraumilch and Niersteiner, the presence of Rhines and Mosels will be token. While white wines in general are increasingly taking over from reds as the Great British (wine-drinking) Public's preferred tipple, it's obvious that the merchants' hearts still lie in the red wine fields of Bordeaux.

It is a matter of upbringing – partly because the influential side of our wine-drinking population has been brought up on the Englishman's wine, claret, and partly because the majority of wine merchants will have come from that kind of background. But there's more to it than that. Whenever wine tasters and wine buffs get together, claret is the wine around which most conversation revolves, because it is the most complex and fascinating of all the world's wines. It is based on the Cabernet grape, which has shown itself time and again to be the most exciting and adaptable red wine grape world wide and when grown in Bordeaux, it has shown itself to be the most suitable for gradual ageing and rounding out in bottle, which means that, at the moment, we have a good supply of wines going back 25 years, and an enormous amount of wine, at all levels, going back 15 years. If you really need a wine for the First World War, the General Strike, the Coronation or when England last beat the West Indies, Britain is the place to do it, either through the two great auction houses, or specialists in old vintages such as La Vigneronne or Reid Wines.

We have, quite simply, the most astonishing range of claret here of anywhere in the world. Better than in America, better than France, better than Bordeaux itself. We've spent hundreds of years developing our claret expertise, and we hope that Webster's will help everyone to make the best of what there is.

And, to go along with the wonderful array, ageing potential and the perennial obsession with quality of a number of proprietors has meant that an extra 'Collector's Value' has been added to inherent value in many wines.

Since many of the merchants we list either have multiple outlets, or will willingly sell by mail order, it is more than ever worth shopping around to get the best price. When sees that, with wine after wine, a saving of £2 per bottle or more can be made – and sometimes the difference is as high as £4–£5 or more a bottle – we can only say: use the guide, make a few phone calls, and in a few bottles' (or a bottle's!) time, you'll have saved the price of the guide, and be well on your way to better, cheaper drinking.

EVEN BRIGHTER PROSPECTS?

In 1983 one of New York's leading wine merchants published an opening offer of 1982 classed growth clarets at fairly steep prices. Nothing wrong with that; it was a good vintage. But there was one small problem. None of the châteaux concerned had yet said what their prices were going to be. That list gave them a pretty good idea.

There had been a lot of talk among the growers about starting their offers at prices perhaps 10–15 per cent up on 1981. Although the quality did deserve a price increase, the record crop should in fact have brought a reduction in prices. Any such restraint went out of the window within 48 hours of that greedy, preemptive New York bid. There was a photocopy of that offer on every grower's desk inside two days.

And two things stood out. The US importer had established his own pecking order of quality by assuming different prices for various equally-ranked wines. Bordeaux proprietors, often the most reasonable of men, are obsessed with bettering their neighbours, and the most visible way is by obtaining a higher price for their wines. Anyone who felt that their image had been sullied by the projected price would quickly put that right when he decided on his real price.

Secondly, they could see the massive profits the importers intended to make out of their wines. But overnight they held the whip hand. The frantic excitement being caused by the vintage was obvious, and they decided that, for once, they'd be the people to profit. Most châteaux opened at 50 per cent above their 1981 price. First growths opened 70 per cent up. End of story? No. by the end of the week, the Bordeaux market was furiously trading the more popular châteaux at double the opening price.

Volatility is the middle name of the Bordeaux market when prices for a good vintage are declared, but, in a curious way, it spread the profit round rather more than usual. The growers, who gained a lot of extra money they hadn't expected, had a handsome windfall. The Bordeaux trade certainly made massive sudden-death profits, but so will ordinary consumers who bought early through the various 'primeur' schemes which are now offered to the public by wine merchants. Most of the popular châteaux are already worth 60–70 per cent more than the purchase price after only a year and a half, and the less trendy properties have still gained 30–40 per cent. Private individuals who bought 1982s early will not lose.

However, the chief reason for all this pressure was the USA market. The dollar had become absurdly strong against the franc. Meanwhile the price of many of the leading Californian wines had become overweeningly high, and it became apparent in 1982 that it was time to dash back and disrupt the French market with the open cheque book. Burgundy and Bordeaux lapped up the free flow of dollars.

But whereas in the UK the feeling is that all those 1982s have been sold on to the consumers, in the USA they are still being hoarded by the trade, who haven't yet sold on their stocks of older wines. The dollar *may* remain at its present level, in which case the US *may* buy heavily again, but experts feel that Bordeaux should take the massive bonus of 1982 prices as a once-off, and ensure that the more reliable traditional markets are not alienated. There has not been the hoped-for reduction in 1983 prices, but quality is good, and if the market is sluggish, they can afford to sit on the wine a while longer so long as their cellars are big enough.

That is, the big châteaux can. Lower down the scale it's not the same story at all, and overproduction is becoming something of a problem. As growers in the basic AC Bordeaux areas have given up trying to make money out of white and have re-planted to red, the harvests of red have increased dramatically. In the last few years an extra 70 million litres of red Bordeaux has appeared on the market. That's not easy to deal with; it's like the entire AC Beaujolais harvest being added to AC Bordeaux - and then having to be sold. Because marketing efforts resulted in an increase of sales by 14.5 per cent in 1983, equilibrium is just about being maintained, but there is still the equivalent of 27 months' stock waiting to be sold. So these big, good harvests are a mixed blessing. World demand is drifting away from basic red wine, and ingenuity will be needed to avoid a crisis if the next couple of harvests are a good size.

This is increasingly likely. Rotten vintages are now rare, because the great improvements in pesticides and anti-rot treatments over the last 10 years have ensured that grapes which would have been lost due to bad summer or autumn weather are now preserved in a relatively healthy state. Pesticides will kill the insects which penetrate the grapes and give botrytis rot the 'entrée' to infect the fruit. One grower said with satisfaction that 1973 was the last time that he had been able to slap a bunch of grapes on the vine and see a gaggle of worms tumble out on to the ground. Even so, the new anti-botrytis rot sprays are not an unqualified success. The botrytis fungus quickly becomes resistant to new methods of fighting it, like any self-respecting flu virus would, and some of the new sprays are so fungicidal that they create serious problems in the vinification, because yeast is a living organism which is killed by fungicide, and without healthy yeast the fermentation can't start, resulting in vatsful of rapidly souring grape juice.

Improved vineyard techniques have to be accompanied by improved wine-making techniques. The most noticeable changes recently in basic reds have been the cooler fermentations used, and the 'whole grape' carbonic maceration system, both of which are producing very fresh, straight fruity reds. Claret traditonally needs at least two to three years to mature. If your prices are so low that British supermarkets can offer claret at £1.70 a bottle, you can't afford to mature wine at all. It must be made to be sold immediately, and only these low tannin, high fruit styles will give you a decent drink so young. The starkest examples are the Bordeaux Nouveau wines which are appearing. Well, November 15th is pushing it a bit, but the 'Jeune Bordeaux' styles of, say, six months old can be excellent - fresh, fruity, and still tasting like claret - while people like Pierre Coste in Graves make delicious clarets which have lost none of their personality but all of their rough edge.

The taste of the top clarets is changing too. Look down any list of top properties and one could add in brackets to most of them - Vinification Adviser: Professor Emile Peynaud. The influence of this retired professor is now so widespread that there is a feeling that much of the best claret is now recognisable as 'Vin Peynaud' rather than Château This or Château That! Undeniably he has dramatically improved the quality of many wines which were peforming below their best, an obvious recent example being the revitalised Château Margaux.

He has done this through rigid selecting-out of substandard vats and carefully controlled fermentation temperatures, but his hand is most evident in the use of clean new oak barrels for ageing the wine. Though few châteaux use entirely new oak, most now use a good deal, and there is a feeling that the individuality of many châteaux is now less distinct than it was. There is even some uncertainty as to how the Peynaud wines will age, since it is literally in the last 10 years that his influence has become so all-pervading.

Yet not everyone bows to his influence. Château Cissac remains resolutely independent. Recently a visiting wine merchant took an unlabelled bottle of wine along there, and asked the cellar master to say what it was. He sniffed, gurgled, spat, pondered, then said just one thing 'In this wine do I detect Professor Peynaud?' The wine was Greek. Château Carras. Peynaud is their consultant.

White Bordeaux

There was a time when you could see why Spanish Graves and Spanish Sauternes were such a laughing stock; you only had to taste the real thing to realize what slavish imitations of a poor product they were. White Bordeaux had a terrible reputation and deserved it. Entre-Deux-Mers, Graves, Bordeaux Blanc – they seemed to offer a sad parade of dowdy, dull, sulphured has-beens.

Things have changed. Entre-Deux-Mers and Graves are now names to be sought out enthusiastically, and the sweetish sulphury Bordeaux white is the exception rather than the rule. What has transformed the area is the introduction of cool fermentation methods and the increasing demand for Sauvignon-style whites.

There are two main grapes used in white Bordeaux, the Sémillon and the Sauvignon, and without doubt the Sauvignon is the one everyone wants. Except the growers. A few years ago, everyone was swept along on the rush to Sauvignon, with particularly heavy demand from the USA and northern European markets. The name Sauvignon came to epitomize wine which was bright and sharp, tangy with the taste of green fruit, and dry as a bone. Of course, what they were all after was another Sancerre, preferably at half the price. Sauvignon already grew in Bordeaux as well as the Loire, so it looked like an ideal chance to bolster the lack-lustre sales performance of white Bordeaux. Fair enough, but the majority of the Bordeaux white vineyards were planted to Sémillon, a grape which traditionally has given the body and character to Bordeaux whites. There was a rather impetuous dismissal of Sémillon which the growers quickly came to regret.

Sauvignon by itself isn't the saviour of white Bordeaux. It's very difficult to vinify separately unless the temperature is rigidly controlled, and the must is carefully cleaned up. Sauvignon must has a rather high level of solids, and it's far too easy to make dull, muddy-tasting wine from it. A lot of the Bordeaux Sauvignon reaching the market cries out for blending with some Sémillon, but the USA wants only varietal Sauvignons (i.e. 100%), so the quality considerations come second. The more serious producers who are sticking to white wine are all increasingly in favour of Sémillon; it gives staying power, has lots of fruit, and while the Sauvignon is briefly aromatic then fades, the Sémillon binds that fresh fruit with something fuller and more honeyed – and holds it, too.

Even so, one might have expected the Sauvignon Blanc boom to have helped Bordeaux Blanc prices, but nothing seems to help them. They have tried to react to the market, but the market resolutely refuses to react to their efforts. Indeed the promotional budget last year, which put much emphasis on the qualities of dry white Bordeaux, only resulted in stagnant dry sales, but an increase in the sales of sweet wines!

Yet there is a gap in the market which Bordeaux is brilliantly suited to attack; the 'off dry' white. Bordeaux with a little sugar left in it and fermented cool to keep it light, has a rather neutral, gentle appeal which one might have thought could

THE COST OF A BOTTLE

Bordeaux Blanc Sec	**£2.25**
VAT	0.30
Merchant mark-up	0.50
Duty	0.68
Distribution	0.08
Shipping	0.15
Bottling	0.34
Wine	0.20

Vintage Table

Using cool fermentation, and a greater percentage of Sauvignon, many white Bordeaux are not now being made to age, but all Graves should have at least two to three years, and the best 10 to 20 years.

***1983** Very good. Bordeaux Blanc should be drunk now, Entre-Deux-Mers could age a bit, and most Graves need more time; they have loads of fruit and style.

1982 The Graves are excellent, and can be drunk though most will hold a while, especially those with some wood ageing. Ordinary white Bordeaux tends to be a little flabby.

1981 A small crop, and so, although they are quite soft, they are also quite concentrated. At their best now.

1979 A lovely year. Soft, gentle wines. Ordinary Bordeaux will be too old, but the Graves should be at their peak.

wean the Liebfraumilch drinkers on to French wine. But no, it still doesn't sell, and one can buy 100 cases of Bordeaux Blanc for as little as 5,500 francs. That's about £5 a case, and it's hardly changed in five years of high inflation and general price rises. No wonder there has been an accelerating switch of white vineyards to red, against world trends.

Bordeaux is one of the few regions whose reds are gaining strength at the expense of her whites. Comparing the 1982 vintage with 1962, red AC production increased by 144 per cent while white has decreased by 55 per cent. In the big 1983 vintage, white production dropped from 1.5 million hls in 1982 to 930,000 hls. Equally disturbing is the amount of white wine not being declared for appellation; in 1982 there were 730,000 hls of non-declared wine. Quite simply, it's more profitable for the grower to produce as much as he can, regardless of quality, and just take the base market rate for plonk.

One might think that Graves would be exempt, with its greater renown and tradition of quality, but excepting the remarkable success of speciality wines, like Domaine de Chevalier and white Haut-Brion, Graves has an increasingly 'red' identity. In 1970 there were far more white vineyards than red, 1,500 hectares (ha) to 875 ha. By 1983 white had fallen to 1,417 ha, while red had climbed to 1,904 ha. The only people who seem to be turning to dry white wine are the Sauternais, which is more a measure of their desperate plight as sweet-wine producers than any great belief in the dull but straight dry whites they produce. Yet one *still* feels that Graves, Entre-Deux-Mers and the hinterland of Bordeaux should be able to create a world-pleasing product. Maybe their image has been that of 'bulk blenders' for too long. Six years ago, 30 per cent of all white sales went straight to the blending vats of Germany. By 1983 this had dropped to five per cent as the cheap Italian producers offered better rates. Holland still takes large amounts of 'warming' sweetish wine, but Britain, despite being Bordeaux's most traditional trading partner, hasn't increased her Bordeaux Blanc consumption in six years, despite rocketing sales of whites in general. One would have thought it would be easy to market so simple a concept as Bordeaux Blanc, but maybe it's the very lack of glamour, and lack of charismatic big estates which still condemn Bordeaux Blanc to a breadline image.

PRICE GUIDE

Non-vintage
£2.00–£2.50
Bordeaux Sec, Yvon Mau (ODD)
Bordeaux Sauvignon, Yvon Mau (ODD)
Bordeaux Blanc de Blancs (VICT)
⋆Sauvignon de Bordeaux, Jean Paul Bartier (ASHE)
Bordeaux Blanc, De Maré (BAL)
£2.50–£3.00
Graves, Nathaniel Johnston (CHAP)
⋆du Bourdac (TES)
Belair Sauvignon Sec (RGA)
Mouton Cadet (PG, H&B, RACK, ASHE, UNW, MWS, QR)
Sauvignon Trois Moulins (WHIT, YFW)
The Society's Sauvignon (WSOC)
c. £4.80
Loudenne Blanc (H&D)

1983
£3.00–£5.25
⋆Thieuley (RH)
⋆Domaine la Grave (STWC)

1982
£2.50–£3.00
⋆du Juge (Bordeaux) (WAIT, CUL, HHC)
⋆Les Grenous (ODD)
Tertre du Moulin (SAIN)
⋆Moulin de Launay (L&W, ADN, BAL, TAN)
Reynon (L&W, ESV, C&B, CDM, TAN)
du Bourdac (ODD)
⋆Tertre de Launay (HHC)
Cordier Blanc (RACK)
£3.00–£3.50
⋆Thieuley (L&W, HT)

La Cour Pavillon (J&B)
des Tourtes (TW)
⋆Montalivet (L&W, HHC, CDM)
Archambeau (SF, BWC)
£3.50–£4.50
⋆Grand Vin Sec du Château Doisy-Daëne (L&W, TAN, DOL)
⋆Coutet Sec (Graves) (H&B)
Cantegrive (WSOC)
⋆Loudenne Blanc (PD, SR)
c. £6.50
Carbonnieux (C&B, TW)

1981
£3.25–£5.00
Grand Vin Sec du Château Doisy-Daëne (ADN, HT, C&B, WSOC)

Lasalle (WHIT)
⋆Bellevue (Graves de Vayres) (JH)
La Cour Pavillon (RACK)
⋆Baret (SR)
Montalivet (J&B)
Loudenne (J&B)
Grand R (Dry Rieussec) (MACK, VIGN)
£6.00–£8.00
⋆Olivier (ASHE)
La Louvière (HT)
⋆Malartic-Lagravière (HHC)
c. £13.80
Domaine de Chevalier (C&B)
c. £18.25
Laville-Haut-Brion (L&W)

1980
£2.75–£3.75
Reynon (ADN)
⋆Larrouquey (PG)
£6.25–£7.25
Olivier (WHIT, TAN)
Carbonnieux (MAL)
c. £12.00
Ygrec (L&W, MAL)
c. £16.00
Laville-Haut-Brion (FINT, C&B)

1979
£3.00–£3.50
du Juge (Bordeaux) (BYR)
Padouen Sec (WNRY)
£5.00–£6.50
⋆de Menota (SR)
£5.25–£6.50
Caillou Blanc du Château Talbot (HT, GH)
Carbonnieux (QR, BBR)
c. £10.75
Ygrec (H&D, VIGN)
c. £15.00
Domaine de Chevalier (C&B)
c. £25.00
Laville-Haut-Brion (J&B)

1978
£5.50–£6.25
Caillou Blanc du Château Talbot (MAL, QR)
de Fieuzal (HT)
c. £19.25
Laville-Haut-Brion (HT, MAL)

1977
£10.00–£13.00
Laville-Haut-Brion (WHIT)
Ygrec (FINT)
c. £18.50
Haut-Brion (C&B, MAL)

Merchants stocking each wine are listed after each entry in ascending order of price or in alphabetical order if they offer the wine at the same price. However, prices do fluctuate (there are special offers and discounts as well as price increases) so remember to use ***Webster's*** *as a price GUIDE not a price LIST.*

1976
c. £7.25
La Louvière (MAL)

1975
c. £25.00
Laville-Haut-Brion (VIGN)

1971
c. £5.75
Baret (OWL)

1962
c. £23.00
Laville-Haut-Brion (FINT)

1959
c. £34.50
Laville-Haut-Brion (FINT)

Price Guide – Notes

Everyone does have a simple 'Bordeaux Blanc' and it is usually at the bottom end of the price levels and anonymous to the point of disappearing. Relatively few merchants have a single-domaine wine, but they are worth seeking out, paying special attention to the newly revitalized Entre Deux Mers, but avoiding the more expensive Graves – except for the top growths.

Keep on Trying

Luckily they haven't all given up in Bordeaux Blanc. Although the acreage of white has shrunk, and the price has stayed ominously low, there are enough determined proprietors who are finding ways to please the increasingly critical UK market. They are realising that those who concentrate on quality can command a much higher price than that ludicrous £5 a case quoted earlier.

Peter Sichel of Caves Belair and Pierre Coste of Langon have been the two most influential people in developing the modern style of white Bordeaux, and although Pierre Coste is not entirely convinced that fermentation should be too cool, and he certainly doesn't agree with those who try to pick early to catch an artificial green bite in their wines, his slightly fuller white styles are clean, ultra-fresh, and increasingly popular on the export market.

Yvon Mau amply demonstrates the dilemma of operating in an excessively cost-conscious market, when he shows a basic Bordeaux which is, well, dull, to say the least, and for just a franc or so more he offers a first class wine from a superior vat. No prizes for guessing which he'll sell more of.

In the Graves, Peter Vinding-Diers of Château Rahoul epitomizes the revival of quality-first white Bordeaux wine-making. He uses only Sémillon, gives it a little wood, and feels that one problem is that the Bordelais in the main don't understand that white Bordeaux can't be made in the same way as red. It's more expensive to make white, it needs very careful fermentation, and it is 100 per cent technology. Red, he says, needs a little heart, but there's no room for that in the whites. Maybe it's just that touch of heart that white Bordeaux *does* need to get us buying it.

SAUTERNES

Imagine an agricultural product where the whole objective is to make sure that the fruit looks foul and as rotted as can be, when every morning you peek through the curtains and chortle at the damp dawn mists spreading disease through the vineyards, and after every litle shower of rain you're on your knees praying for a blast of blistering sun, just to make sure the fungus is given a head start in attacking the grape skins.

Well, that's how you have to look at things if you're going to make one of the world's greatest and least-appreciated wines – Sauternes. Because what is happening as the autumn days slide into the chill of winter is that a mutation of ordinary fungus, aptly named 'noble rot' (botytris to the botanists amongst you), is being encouraged to infect the vineyards. This friendly fungus has the scarcely believable quirk of preferring to feed on water rather than on the sugary juice of the grape. So it weakens the grape skin, and sets to siphoning off the H_2O, thus leaving the sugars and the acids to get more and more concentrated, and the resultant gunge can reach incredibly high sugar levels. Which, of course, is the whole point.

Any fool can make an ordinary sweet wine with a mixture of grapes, a bagful of sugar, and a cylinder full of sulphur. It'll be soggy-sweet, thick in the mouth, and a damn sight thicker in the head the next morning. Sadly, such a wine may still be sold here with the proud name of Sauternes on the label, though rather less often since we joined the EEC. Before then, about 70 per cent of all our so-called Sauternes were Spanish! however, great sweet wine can only be made by using grapes infected by noble rot, and of all the areas of France, Bordeaux is easily the most important for these wines.

THE COST OF A BOTTLE

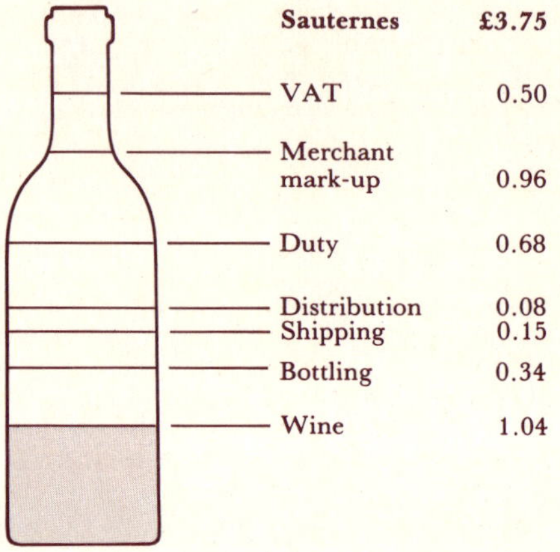

The areas of Loupiac, Cadillac, Ste-Croix-du-Mont and Cérons all use noble rot grapes when they can, but it is Sauternes and Barsac which have traditionally made the finest wines. The grapes are the same as for dry Bordeaux – Sémillon and Sauvignon – but there is also a little Muscadelle, which has the useful habit of giving a false taste of noble rot to the wine. The Sémillon is far more important than the Sauvignon because it is much more susceptible to noble rot, and provides the lanolin-y, almost oily-

Maturity Chart

1983 CLASSED GROWTH SAUTERNES

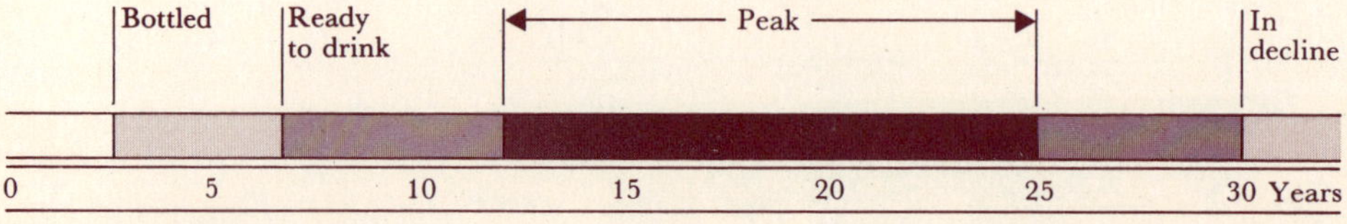

Vintage Table

What Sauternes needs is a bit of luck. While red Bordeaux has been basking in an astonishing run of Indian Summer vintages, with only 1977 out of the last nine rating a poor one – and even that's debatable – the late autumn weather hasn't been so kind to Sauternes. In 1978 and 1981 the botrytis just didn't quite develop, in 1982 the rains came at exactly the wrong time. But 1983 looks as though it is making amends. It's worth remembering that Sauternes can be drunk very young or very old, depending entirely on whether you like the startling sweet shock of young wine or the deep nutty golden honey of older wines. Good Sauternes can last a very long time.

***1983** Not available yet, but everyone's very excited, saying it's the best since 1976.

1982 High hopes killed by rain. Some light, sweetish wines, but lacking concentration.

1981 Not bad, but not terribly exciting. They're coming on to the market now, but we say wait for 1983 and drink 1980s now.

***1980** Underrated and excellent. Quite light, sometimes not even all that luscious, but marvellous high-acid noble rot flavours. Drink or keep.

1979 Highly rated but just slightly lacking in oomph. They're fairly sweet, but have softness where the 1980s have attack.

***1976** Fat, sometimes almost gross, but good heavy wines, really showing the 'lanolin' oiliness of super-ripe Sauternes.

1975 Sometimes thought of as better than 1976, but even when their balance is better they just lack the rich, over-the-top personality of 1976. I'll stick with 1976.

1971 Highly rated, but lacking a bit of drive. The good châteaux made quite light wines, though genuinely sweet. Sometimes slightly one-dimensional.

***1970** Less well thought of than 1971, but in fact more enjoyable for that big, rich sweet taste of over-ripe grapes.

***1969** Hardly rated at all, but superb. Light, with loads of botrytis taste, sweet, but high in acid. If you see one, buy it, because 1969's bad reputation for reds seems to have affected Sauternes, unjustly.

***1967** Simply wonderful. Mature now, with the honey turning to toffee-gold, a good 1967 is as perfect a Sauternes as you'll find.

honeyed depth to the wine, while the Sauvignon helps out with freshness and perfume.

Vintage years are by no means the same as for red Bordeaux, because ripeness and quality of crop are measured in a completely different way. While the objective with red and dry white is to get the crop picked in one fell swoop as soon as it's ripe, and free of rot, in Sauternes they won't normally *start* to pick till mid October, by which time the others will have finished.

The top properties will then make several trips or 'tries' right through the vineyards, picking off the ugly, rot-infected grapes, often one by one, sometimes bunch by bunch. This may go on till mid November, after which the wine is slowly fermented, then stored for two or three years before bottling. It's a long expensive process, and if you're one of those people who says gaily 'Oh, I don't like sweet wine', go out and buy a classed growth Sauternes from 1975/76/79/80. A single taste will tell you that Sauternes isn't just sweet wine it's a most remarkable mixture of honey, and acidity, and golden richness which *must* change your mind about 'real' sweet wine.

Sauternes: Inside the Châteaux

'The honesty of our quality selection policy is the single most expensive factor'. Hamilton Narby of Château Guiraud, a first-growth Sauternes, puts it in a nutshell. Sauternes' quality stands or falls by the ruthless selection of grapes in the vineyards, only picking ones that are affected by noble rot; and then by a cold-blooded selection of those vats and barrels of wine which show enough of the noble rot character to merit the château label. At very least, it's a cripplingly expensive task, but at worst, it puts the owner in a terrible moral dilemma as he faces up to his vats in the cold winter light. With the casual stroke of chalk on a stave he can slash the value of a vat of wine by up to 80 per cent.

But Sauternes will only regain its position on the world market through a pursuit of quality, and that means ruthless selection to avoid the faintest possibility of disappointing the customer. In 1982 the vintage began incredibly early, at the end of September. The weather couldn't have been better. They made two or three 'tries' (i.e. picking sorties) through the vineyards, optimism abounded – and then the heavens opened, and it rained until the grapes were just a sludge on their slimey stalks. Rieussec lost 70 per cent, Guiraud, Nairac, Yquem much the same, and yet the cost of producing that remaining 30 per cent is hardly less than producing 100 per cent.

In 1964, the vintage also began in perfect weather, yet again, down came the rain. Yquem made 11 'tries' in the vineyard, and after all that, made *not one single bottle* of Yquem 1964.

In red wines and dry whites, even though rain may spoil your quality, you still have a recognisable product. Not so in Sauternes. Here, you're always relying on fate's good humours. Firstly, straightforward hot weather isn't enough to cause noble rot; for that you need the special mixture of fog, a bit of rain, and lots of hot, humid sun. Then, if the rain does pelt down, all that patient water-sucking by the fungus is rendered pointless, because the grapes simply dilute again, and all the concentrated sugar is lost.

The level of concentration needed shows in Yquem's figures. Each hectare of vineyard will normally produce about 1,125 bottles – that's in a good year! Ordinary white wine producers would probably get 6,250–7,500 bottles from that same hectare. Each vine at Yquem produces about one glass of wine – about one-sixth of normal production. But they don't save money by only collecting a single glassful's worth of each vine – it costs more to pick less.

It's a skilled job to pick only the grapes which are properly rotted, and any kind of cost-cutting mechanical harvesting is not only impractical, but forbidden. The

1983 harvest at Château Guiraud cost 10,000 francs per hectare to harvest. Just over the river, a dry-white grower, using a mechanical harvester, could pick his grapes for 1,600 francs a hectare, and have his whole crop safely gathered in a couple of days. At Château Yquem, 40 pickers may bring enough grapes for just one barrel in a day. That's about 11 bottles a picker per day. When I did the red wine vintage at Margaux, I reckon I was picking about a bottle's worth every two minutes, and I was *not* their star picker, not by a long way.

The dry-white chap can also get his wine fermented and into bottle in a matter of months. He can have sold his crop in six to 12 months and have the money in the bank. Not so the Sauternes producer. Any self-respecting classed-growth château will age the wine for two to three years, and, although some châteaux have stopped using oak, sometimes pleading modernity, but more honestly pleading that they're damn near broke and can't afford the investment, they should use traditional Bordelais oak barrels. And they're not cheap. New ones holding 225 litres (300 bottles) cost about 1,700 francs each, and a château must have enough barrels to hold three crops. Château Guiraud buys 500 new barrels every year, and renews the entire barrel stock every five years.

One might hope that this labour intensive, caring wine-making process would yield immediate sales and profit, but sales of Sauternes differ from red wines. There is no tradition of *en primeur* buying (when a customer pays the ex-cellars price while the wine is still in barrels), so each vintage may have to be financed for two or three years. And there's no certainty of sale. One famous first growth offered *Webster's* wines stretching back to 1966, with prices ranging from 65 to 130 francs. Their excellent 1969 can be had for just 68 francs. Another top second growth offered six different vintages at between 30 and 32 francs a bottle.

Any comparison with a Médoc classed growth is ludicrous. Their yields are higher, their costs lower, and their stock is long since sold and paid for. And at far higher prices, because the investment fad which has gripped red Bordeaux has so far left Sauternes, which could do with a bit of investment razzamatazz, out in the cold.

Only Châteaux d'Yquem has, through the years, maintained and promoted its 'Super first class' image, and if the rest of Sauternes is sold too cheaply, few would level that criticism at Yquem. Its price can appear at four or five times the level of another first growth, but perhaps a better comparison would be to take the current 1976 vintage and compare Sauternes and Médoc prices on a typical list.

Yquem 1976 is £41.50 a bottle (!!), while first growths Climens and Coutet are at £12.50 and £12 respectively. In reds, Château Latour is £28.75, and Lafite is £33.25, while Ducru-Beaucaillou is £13.50, and Pichon Lalande is £12.50. So Yquem is considerably dearer in relative terms than the top Sauternes just beneath her in classification, and those Sauternes are cheaper than their Médoc equivalents. If we drop to second growth Sauternes and fifth growth Pauillac or Margaux, the differences are even greater, and, while everyone expects to be making money in the Médoc nowadays, Sauternes at best is only managing to tread water.

Hamilton Narby offers "hope and despair, euphoria and chagrin, but above all passion", as the constant companions in a Sauternes château owner's life. And, we might add, a healthy bank balance from another walk of life, because he'd be the first to admit that if he was simply in the Sauternes game for the money, the men in white coats would have carted him off long ago.

Price Guide

Non-vintage
£2.25–£3.00
Premières Côtes de Bordeaux, Nathaniel Johnston (CHAP)
Marquis de la Rose (PG)
Lagrange (Premières Côtes de Bordeaux) (VICT)
La Flora Blanche (WILL, BYR, WAIT, ASHE, YFW, QR, UNW, MWS)
£3.50–£3.75
⋆Sauternes (WAIT, THRE)
Barsac, Nathaniel Johnston (CHAP)
Sauternes, Nathaniel Johnston (CHAP)
Haut Claverie (UNW)
Sauternes, De Maré (BAL)

1982
£4.00–£4.50
des Arrieux (IMB)
Archambeau (PIP)

1981
£3.00–£4.00
Clos St-Georges (SAIN)
Rouquette (AV)
£7.00–£8.50
Rayne-Vigneau (C&B)
Doisey-Daëne (TAN)
Rieussec (C&B, MACK)
Coutet (Barsac) (WSOC)

1980
£2.75–£5.00
⋆Les Courtines (ODD)
du Juge (Cadillac) (TAN)
Fayau (VIGN, PG, BYR)
Cantegril (WSOC)
⋆du Mayne (ASHE)
£5.50–£6.75
⋆Doisy-Védrines (JH)
⋆La Chartreuse (TAN, VICT)
Bastor-Lamontagne (J&B)
Rieussec (ADN, J&B)
Filhot (WHIT)

1979
£3.75–£5.00
du Juge (Cadillac) (L&W)
Haura (C&B)
de Malle (BIB, BYR)
Terfort (GH)
⋆St-Amand (PG)
⋆Guiteronde (H&D)
⋆Menota (PG, MWS)
£7.00–£8.75
Rieussec (AV, L&W)
Filhot (SF)
Doisy-Védrines (DOL)
Broustet (AV)
Lafaurie-Peyraguey (QR)
⋆Coutet (Barsac) (MWS, BYR, H&B)
Guiraud (DOL, J&B)
c. £19.50
de Fargues (C&B)
c. £37.00
d'Yquem (MAL, HHC, C&B)

1978
£5.75–£7.25
⋆Bastor la Montagne (SR)
Cantegril (OWL)
Doisy-Daëne (ADN, SF)
Filhot (WSOC, CHAP, FINT)
Lafaurie-Peyraguey (ADN, WILL, MWS)
Rieussec (ADN, MAL, UNW, DAV, H&D, QR, SR, L&W)
£9.75–£12.25
Doisy-Védrines (VICT)
Suduiraut (TAN, VICT)

1977
c. £5.50
Doisy-Védrines (WHIT)
c. £34.50
d'Yquem (WHIT, MWS)

1976
£3.00–£4.50
★Sahuc-Latour ½ bottle (BAL)
Fayau (WHIT)
£6.75–£8.50
Filhot (FINT, MAL, GH, ODD, WNRY, HHC, CUL, RSV)
Doisy-Daëne (WSOC, HT)
Rayne-Vigneau (ADN)
Coutet (Barsac) (BIB, WNRY, C&B, L&W)
£9.25–£12.75
Padouen (VIGN)
Nairac (TAN)
Climens (MAL, H&D, L&W)
Guiraud (DOL)
Rieussec (TAN)
c. £35.50
d'Yquem (JH, CUL, MAL, WILL, C&B, HHC, VICT, GH, QR *& others*)

1975
£5.25–£6.00
Padouen (RH, YFW)
Liot (WNRY, VIGN, ESV, HUN)
La Chartreuse (ADN)
Guiraud ½ bottle (CHAP)
Guiteronde (JH)
£6.50–£7.50
Menota (OWL)
Doisy-Védrines (HUN, HT)
Coutet (Barsac) (GH, BIB, BBR)
Sigalas-Rabaud (GH)
£8.50–£9.00
Filhot (HT, TAN)
Rieussec (PG, MACK)
Lafaurie-Peyraguey (AV, QR)

Stars (★) indicate wines selected by the merchants themselves as particularly good value in their class.

£11.25–£12.50
Nairac (TAN)
Rabaud-Promis (OWL)
c. £33.00
d'Yquem (UNW, AV, GH, J&B, L&W, HT, BIB, BBR, PG, QR *& others*)

1974
c. £6.50
Rieussec (J&B)

1973
£6.50–£7.00
Doisy-Dubroca (VIGN)
Filhot (MAL, CUL)
£8.00–£9.50
Coutet (Barsac) (HUN)
Nairac (TAN, TW)
c. £27.00
d'Yquem (WILL, GH, HUN, VIGN, QR)

Please don't blame ***Webster's*** *or the merchants listed if a wine is sold out or if the vintage you want is no longer available. Wine is a living entity and a limited commodity – continuity of supply cannot, alas, be guaranteed.*

1972
c. £4.25
de Malle (HHC)

1971
c. £8.50
★Guiraud (MAL, GH, PIP, TAN, SR)
£9.25–£10.00
Coutet (Barsac) (ADN, GH, QR, C&B, PIP)
Suduiraut (ADN)
c. £42.50
d'Yquem (FINT, WNRY)

1970
£9.00–£10.00
Doisy-Védrines (ODD, VIGN, BIB, RSV)
Filhot (GH)
Guiraud (VIGN, HT)
c. £13.00
de Malle (RSV)
c. £15.00
Lafaurie-Peyraguey (RSV)
Suduiraut (HT, RSV)
c. £27.00
d'Yquem (UNW)

1969
c. £9.50
Climens (VIGN, TAN)
c. £26.50
d'Yquem (UNW, VIGN, YFW)

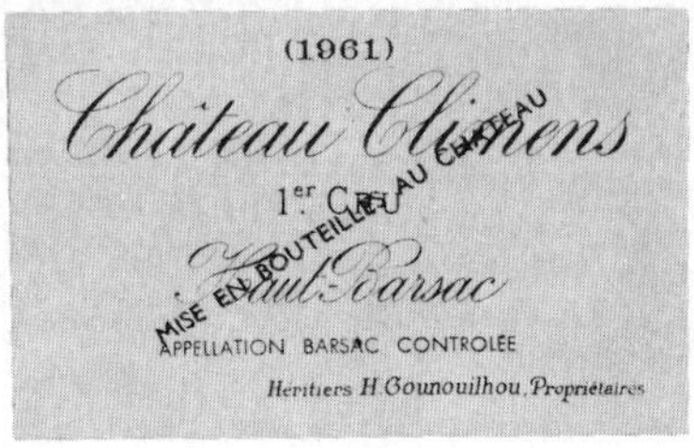

1967
c. £15.50
Guiraud (GH)
Coutet (Barsac) (ADN)

1966
c. £12.00
La Tour Blanche (BIB)
c. £15.00
de Malle (RSV)

1965
c. £23.00
d'Yquem (WILL)

1964
c. £10.00
Guiraud (VIGN)

1961
c. £18.50
Coutet (Barsac) (VIGN)
c. £60.00
d'Yquem (BIB)

1959
c. £27.50
Rieussec (MACK, RSV)

1955
c. £15.50
Gilette (BOW, MAL)
c. £19.30
Coutet (Barsac) (VIGN)

1953
c. £25.00
Gilette, Crème de Tête (MAL)

1950
c. £29.00
Gilette (BOW)

1948
£34.50–£36.00
Rabaud-Promis (RSV)
Coutet (Barsac) (RSV)

1934
c. £55.00
Coutet (Barsac) (RSV)

Quality First

'I can only be optimistic about the future. Things couldn't really get much worse, and a renaissance is virtually certain. The question is, when? And have I chosen the right century?' That's Hamilton Narby of Château Guiraud looking into the future. He is saying what all honest Sauternes proprietors say, what all honest wine merchants in England say, what wine writers say, what drinkers say – what everybody says – that Sauternes must concentrate solely on the quality of the product, that prices *will* rise, and that at last it will be possible for a proprietor to feed and clothe his wife and children once again.

That's the scenario for a perfect world. But there's one problem. We still don't look as though we're willing to pay the price. For a wine which ranks as one of the world's most expensive to produce properly, we won't pay what we'd gladly offer for (even) a fifth growth Pauillac or a Nuits St-Georges. Narby is absolutely right when he states that mediocrity won't sell and that quality is the only saviour. How to achieve it though, when current price levels don't justify the expense and the investment?

Many producers have disappeared or have given up making sweet wine, and more will do so. Which should, of course, lead to a natural concentration of demand on fewer properties, and at length the laws of supply and demand might come into play. History does usually repeat itself, and a hundred years ago, Sauternes was so popular Tsars would buy up almost entire vintages of Yquem. But there's no doubt that this sweet powerful wine goes against the present wine trends.

We don't help in the UK by sticking Sauternes resolutely at the end of the evening with the desserts. The first thing we should do is to realise that it's a brilliant drink on its own, at any time of the day or night; the French usually drink it *before* a meal, and Californians just drink it whenever they can lay their hands on a bottle. Then the second thing we should do is realise that we *must* pay more heavily for the privilege.

Burgundy

"Well, of course, you have to make allowances for burgundy". We had just left a big tasting earlier this year. The burgundies had been desperately disappointing, and we were distressed, because we liked the people who shipped the wines, and up till now this company's wines had always been good to excellent. Well, perhaps things had slipped a bit since the 1979 vintage, but . . . Suddenly that remark from my merchant friend made me see red.

WHY should we make allowances for burgundy? Why should we pat one of the great glories of wine achievement on the head as though it were an errant schoolboy who ought to try harder at his maths? It's almost as if burgundy is a skeleton in the family's cupboard, that bachelor uncle disgracing the family, 'something nasty in the woodshed' we don't care to talk about. But Burgundy is a leader, a region which has given the world many of the greatest wines ever tasted by man, and has never made any bones about selling them dear.

Or has it? How many great bottles of burgundy are still made, or were ever made? How often has an expensive bottle with the right village name, the right vineyard site, the right vintage, blazoned across the label, been nothing but a costly flop? Why should we stand for it? Isn't it time we said *No.* I will *not* pay hard-earned money for mediocre wines trading for too long on a fame and reputation that most of us are too young ever to have put to the test. And my anger made me feel a lot better. It flushed out the growing resentment I felt against burgundy. And I am not alone. People in Britain are questioning the right of the Burgundian merchants to decide the kind of burgundy we want, or, more likely, their right to see how wide they can stretch the contours of a wine's famous name, and how firmly they can maintain the price before the consumer takes his courage in both hands and says: "I've had enough."

Looking back over this paragraph, it does seem a bit passionate, and there's a simple reason. I love burgundy. I care. From the frail strawberry-scented wines of Volnay to the smokey fragrance of Corton and the deep grumbling monsters of Gevrey, I love it. From the apple-sharp whites of St-Aubin to the nutty cream and butter of Meursault and the savoury brilliance of Puligny, I love it. That is why I get so irate at the way that so many of its greatest names are so disregarded by too many of those who choose to make and sell it. And that is why I will make *no* allowances for anything bar the timeless balances between the good and bad fortunes of the weather and the relative skills of an honest wine maker in his given patch of vines.

So what is this place whose inhabitants are getting me so worked up? Well, it wouldn't be too far-fetched to say it is the heart of France, and as such the heart of the world of wine. It manages to encompass the frail cool-climate vineyards of the north, the tantalising checks and balances of the moderate centre, and the strong sunny south all under one general name – that of burgundy. Chablis in the north produces one of the world's driest light whites, and her neighbours produce some careful, subdued versions of good Pinot Noir. The centre begins with the Côte d'Or, just south of Dijon. The Pinot Noir grape in the Côte de Nuits produces many of Burgundy's most famous red wines. It continues into the Côte de Beaune where great Pinot reds and Chardonnay whites are made. It then slides further south into the Chalonnais, producing good, lesser versions of Côte de Beaune reds and whites – and the Mâconnais, where the Chardonnay produces the whole gamut from excellent to execrable, and on to Beaujolais, where the Gamay grape produces Nouveau and . . . hang on! The Gamay grape? Wasn't that banned from Burgundy as long ago as 1395? Well, yes, but things change, you know. Burgundy, if you stick to the core of the Côte de Nuits and Côte de Beaune, really isn't big enough to supply the demand for her wines. It wasn't in 1395; it isn't now. So, the Gamay wines of Beaujolais get lumped in with 'Burgundy'.

Fair enough. That's Central Burgundy. Southern Burgundy starts south of Lyons, and is centred on Châteauneuf du Pape. No, not Pinot, not Gamay. Bigger, sturdier wines from Grenache and Syrah. It does no end of good to the pale Côte d'Or wines. The area continues southwards to Alicante in Spain. Spanish 'burgundy' is cheaper than French burgundy. Worse. But cheaper. And then it extends to Morocco and Algeria. It's not so easy, now that they're not part of France, to call the wines burgundy, but my case of Algerian 'burgundy' is coming along very nicely. Deep red, quite a heavy sediment, and a big red colour. Lovely. Tastes like chocolate. I did have some 1967 French burgundy, but it was never up to much. Until I mixed it with the Algerian. Now *that* was excellent. My uncle said it was exactly what burgundy ought to be.

But Southern Burgundy doesn't stop at North Africa. South Africa does a nice line in 'burgundy'. Australia has loads of it. Not, admittedly, from the Pinot Noir, but the hot country big-croppers of Grenache, Mataro and Syrah make a better 'burgundy'; big, ferruginous stuff to keep out the cold in Poulton-le-Fylde. California, too. 'Burgundy' is one of California's biggest sellers. Pinot Noir? No, they don't use that, it's too expensive. They use Pinot Noir to make varietal Pinot Noir.

Oh dear, has Burgundy come to this pretty pass? An embattled plot of land in the centre of France to which the tentacles of the rest of the world have attached their suckers with the objective of reproducing her style? The trouble is that the style they were mimicking had nothing to with real burgundy in the first place.

True burgundy is from the red Pinot and the white Chardonnay, with a little, distinctly déclassé help from the Gamay and the Aligoté. But Burgundy is so tiny, its fabled wines so small in production yet so ringing in fame, that people have been abusing her name for as long as records have been kept. From 1395 onwards, the authorities have been battling to preserve burgundy's purity because its heart, its core, what has given it worldwide fame, is a thin sliver of land, 30 miles long, and often less than a mile wide, running from Dijon to Chagny, just off the Saône valley, and the grapes which have produced these wines are as different as chalk and cheese.

The white Chardonnay is sweetness and light. Even in the decidedly dicky Burgundian climate it produces a fair to considerable amount of good to excellent wine almost every year, so long as the vines are tended with a modicum of care, picked at a sensible ripeness, and an eye kept on the fermentation temperature. In Chablis, the wine business has adapted itself to the 80s so well that this small northern area is one of France's biggest success stories. In the 1960s the Chablis area was producing perhaps 25,000 hls a year. In 1983 it produced 142,000 hls. And this wasn't simply a lucky vintage, it was the result of considerable investment and vineyard expansion. This was highly controversial, and has changed Chablis from being a flint-dry, austere green wine, not exactly full of mass appeal, but revered by the oyster brigade, into one of the most affordable high quality French whites. Still very dry, but far less biting than before, certainly a few tears are shed for the old style. But nowadays the growers can pay their bills again, and for us the wine is still cheap – currently about half the price of a proper Pouilly Fuissé.

In the Côte d'Or too, things are looking bright for the whites. The 1982 avalanche of ripe Chardonnay grapes came at exactly the right moment. Chardonnay was becoming the buzz word in white wine, the Côte d'Or was the most famous area for Chardonnay, and it had a bumper crop of decent wine. The world can't get enough of good white burgundy, and overall increases of sales in 1983 are impressive. The USA was up 60 per cent, the UK up 63 per cent, Holland up 72 per cent, Japan and Canada up 119 per cent and West Germany up 156 per cent!! The important figures there are the American ones – they took 42 per cent of the total exports – and West Germany's, whose new found infatuation with dry white wine is likely to unsettle any price stability we may have been hoping for.

The Côte d'Or leads the pack in fame, but in fact only produces 16 per cent of Burgundy's white. Chablis and the Mâconnais are the chief white producers, with the Côte Chalonnaise chipping in a bit, and it is encouraging to see how much advantage Chablis is taking of the new-found vogue for its wine style; it is equally distressing to see how little the Mâconnais is achieving.

Pinot Noir is the red grape. It is the sulkiest, trickiest, most tempestuous fine wine grape in the world. It is the prima donna who misses a first night because she has a headache, the debutante who won't come to her own party because her horoscope isn't favourable enough. It is the despair of fine wine lovers. There is no wine which is more assiduously craved or more tirelessly sought than good red burgundy. There is no wine which is more difficult to track down. but when it is good, *it is good,* beyond description. A wine writer once said that all the best wines he had drunk were clarets, but the greatest wines he had drunk were burgundies. One of my most enduring memories is of two Domaine de la Romanée Conti 1955s. Startling, exciting, passionate, the most unique sensation red wine has to offer. On the same occasion, we also drank some first growth 1952 and 1953 clarets. I can't remember the tastes; I can barely remember the names.

That's the dilemma. The Pinot Noir is one of the most savage, primitive grapes still growing in France. It needs a more delicate balance of spring, summer and autumn climate than any other to achieve greatness, and one Burgundian maxim is that you must have unripe grapes, ripe grapes and rotten grapes in equal quantities to achieve that astonishing part-rotted, part-perfumed, part-masculine, part-ethereal flavour which makes great burgundy.

Understandably the fame of Burgundy's greatest bottles has spread far and wide. Understandably, men of power and influence have returned with fistsful of gold to purchase these wines. Understandably, the local growers and merchants, aware that great burgundy may only be produced from one vineyard in five, by one wine maker in five, one year in five, have cast about to satisfy the demands of the world. Since wealth and power and good taste rarely go hand in hand, it isn't long before a new 'created' taste, being but a lumpish facsimile of Burgundy's true worth, is paraded as the real thing, bought as the real thing, and even valued as such.

But it is a mark of the new age of wine – epitomised by the re-emergence of the great estates in Bordeaux, the rise of California and Australia, and the re-thinking of tradition in Italy – that taste, flavour, is becoming more important than reputation. Most of Bungundy's growers and merchants have yet to realise this. We *will* pay money to buy flavour. Not labels. The new age of wine is increasingly aware that true burgundy is a rare experience. The new generation are prepared to pay high prices for such high quality, but have no interest any more in a label for a label's sake.

The view of one merchant is that Burgundy has become too democratised, and that it should return to producing more expensive wine for fewer people. There is some truth in that. Burgundy proper is a tiny area, already overstretching its very limited production. In a wine world where the demand for something special is on the increase, Burgundy does have a unique part to play and the great vineyards must accept their rôle, or Burgundy will eventually end up with no one but itself to sell its wine to.

Laying Down Burgundy

A merchant friend of mine has just (May 1984) got back from Burgundy, where he deals exclusively with a small number of growers who bottle their own wine. 'They've offered me their basic 1982s for 12 francs a bottle – and I don't have to pay for it till I've sold it.'

That's the state of things in Burgundy. The price has dropped six francs in a year. Well, you might say, basic burgundy, hardly surprising. OK, let's take a look at my friend's retail list. He's offering single domaine Gevrey-Chambertin 1982 for £4.75 inc VAT. That's £2 a bottle less than last year. (It's not a Mickey Mouse producer – I've tasted it). His Gevrey-Chambertin Premier Cru is £5.65, £3.80 less than in November '83, and his Charmes-Chambertin is £7.15, again £3.80 less.

This doesn't show how wise we'd all be to purchase at these low opening prices. They're not opening prices. Those were last year. It shows how the prices in Burgundy are dropping, even for good wine. If we'd bought at opening prices, we'd have got good wine, since he's a careful merchant who knows his growers. But burgundy is in a state of crisis, with so many deals being offered, just to shift stock, that there's no point in buying in a big way just at the moment. Except in the case of a very few top estates, where you are reserving a limited edition of wine which you might otherwise not be able to buy, there is no great benefit in committing much money to 'primeur' buying at present.

Firstly, most burgundies just don't appreciate that much in investment terms. Secondly, the last four vintages have produced more of a ragbag of the good, the bad, and the ugggh than even Burgundy normally manages. And thirdly because, like my friend, any commited burgundy merchant is going to be able to make some very keen purchses of 'distressed' stock. Hold on to your money initially, but keep your eyes open for special offers of 1982s and 1983s, and *never* buy risky burgundy without tasting it first. It's too costly a mistake.

Burgundy in restaurants

The world of red burgundy in 1984 has shown itself to be a shifty place, but it does mean there can be bargains for the brave on restaurant lists. Demand for new burgundy vintages is weak, and we've been warned so often about the inability of modern burgundy to age, that, with the exception of the very top properties like Romanée-Conti, De Vogüé and Dujac, mature burgundies have relatively little worth. The sad thing, for a great wine region, is that this low esteem is mostly justified, because there's nothing more seductive on a wine list than a mature burgundy, and no more cruel disappointment than when the wine fails the test. Visions of marvellous rich chocolatey wine swim up from the pages – and that's usually about it. But not always.

A few years ago, at a two star eatery in Paris, I was faced with a first growth claret – five years old and £60 a bottle – or a Charmes-Chambertin 1937 for just £7. At this price it was hardly even a gamble, but for once the wine was super. Yet it *was* a risk. The vast array of treatments that the produce of any patch of vines in Burgundy may be subjected to by a legion of more or less good-hearted men, makes burgundy in restaurants as much a game of blindfold as it is anywhere, except that if you didn't chance your arm on old burgundy in a restaurant, the only other place you'd be likely to find it is in an auction room, where you couldn't order it by the bottle, or send it back if it was duff.

Red or white, young burgundy is expensive on any restaurant list, and the only constructive approach is to choose an obscure name – St-Romain, Ladoix-Serrigny, St-Aubin are three to start off with – or view the whole thing like a day at the races. I see the Tate Gallery restaurant have the Corton-Vergennes 1970 at £8.75. Sure, it may be too old, but any wine man with red blood in his veins will weigh up the odds – and then hand over the folding ones to the bookie behind the bar.

Basic Burgundy

That sounds like a contradiction in terms. Burgundy's expensive, isn't it? Overpriced even; famous, rare, only for the rich? Well, what do you suppose your average Burgundian drinks with his bread and cheese? Claret? Champagne? Hirondelle?? No, every wine region produces its own 'drinking wine', as well as its top names, and Burgundy is no exception. The only problem with Burgundy is that the area is so small, and so much of it is concentrated in the great wines, that the more ordinary ones *are* in short supply, even in Burgundy. Not only that but they're not cheap for your average lunchtime flask of red or white. The most basic burgundy appellation of something like Passe-tout-grains (a mixture of Gamay and Pinot) will cost the Burgundian drinker twice as much as a basic Bordeaux rouge would cost the Bordelais. So some of the townsfolk *will* drink the French equivalent of Hirondelle on weekdays, but they'll still drink burgundy on Sunday.

Sadly, the casual disregard for quality which has hit many of the more famous wines has filtered down to the bottom end too. And while we can get reasonable Bordeaux rouge over here for as little as £1.79, most utterly basic burgundies are hovering round the £4.00 mark. That's a helluva lot to pay for *anything* basic, and our advice in general is - don't. Yet at three recent tastings of major Burgundy houses, the AC Bourgognes, and particularly the Passe-tout-grains, were patently better wines than famous names at four times the price. So, to have the best chance of a taste of the elusive Pinot Noir in its basic form, here are a few tips.

Don't go for Bourgogne Grand Ordinaire. Très Ordinaire. Pas Très Grand. Passe-tout-grains is often excellent. In a year like 1982 it may well be mostly Pinot, instead of the two-thirds Gamay, one-third Pinot norm. Firms like Leroy make it superbly, Chanson makes it well, but, as always, the growers make it best, particularly in the less famous Côte d'Or and Hautes Côtes villages. Try Rion in the prestigious Nuits St-Georges, Thomas in the forgotten St-Aubin, Chaley or Cornu in the Hautes Côtes, and many others like them.

The Hautes Côtes are a happy hunting ground, and a lot of fairly good light Pinot and dry Chardonnay is made there for a decent price. And in whites, the Aligoté grape is often used to produce a dry, sharpish wine, which doesn't much resemble Meursault, but then nor does the price.

Bourgogne Rouge and Bourgogne Blanc are best when they are the products of a grower's less favoured vineyards, usually in the plain. The Bourgogne Rouge of Parent, Pousse d'Or, or Rion, and the Bourgogne Blanc of Millot-Battault or Coche-Dury show what can be achieved by care and good wine making. The basic Bourgognes of firms like Jadot, Latour and Chanson are usually OK, but unfamiliar Bourgogne is generally to be avoided.

As, nowadays, are most Côte de Beaune and Côte de Nuits Villages. These used to be the quite tasty mixture of excess production and less well known villages. The best of these now stand alone, in particular St-Aubin, St-Romain, Santenay, Monthélie, Ladoix-Serrigny, Chorey-lès-Beaune, and Fixin.

Otherwise, in the hunt for basic burgundy at the north end, don't forget that straight Chablis is good and cheap, as is its red neighbour of Irancy. And the nearby Caves Bailly produces one of France's best non-champagne fizzes. In the south, the Côte Chalonnaise does have some good wine but the prices are hardly basic anymore. Rully offers pretty good value. And further south St-Véran and Mâcon-Prissé and -Viré can give good Chardonnay at an easy price.

Price Guide

Red

Non-vintage
£3.50–£4.50
The Society's Red Burgundy (WSOC)
★Bourgogne Rouge Tasteviné, Bichot (UNW)
Bourgogne Rouge Marcilly (SR)

1982
£4.00–£4.50
Bourgogne Rouge, Caves de Vignerons de Buxy (IMB)
Bourgogne Rouge, Robert Chevillon (WW)
Bourgogne Rouge, Louis Jadot (VICT)

1981
c. £3.75
Bourgogne Rouge, Pierre Olivier (ASHE)
c. £5.50
★Bourgogne la Digoine, Aubert de Villaine (ADN)

1980
£3.75–£4.75
Bourgogne Rouge, Chantal Lescure (LHV)
Bourgogne Rouge la Digoine, Aubert de Villaine (MAL)

1979
£3.75–£5.00
Bourgogne Passetoutgrain, Guy Roulot (DDIR)
Bourgogne Rodet (CHAP)
★Bourgogne, Domaine Boisset-Deschamps (HBV)
Bourgogne Rouge Pinot Noir, Domaine Parent (BWC, H&D)
Bourgogne Rouge, Cuvée Latour (RACK)
Bourgogne Marcilly Reserve (BIB)
1976
c. £5.75
Bourgogne Marcilly Reserve (WILL, CDM)
1973
c. £5.50
Bourgogne Marcilly Reserve (BIB, VIGN)

White

Non-vintage
£3.75–£4.75
The Society's White Burgundy, Dépagneux (WSOC)
★Bourgogne, Cuvée Voltaire, Chanson (BAL, TAN)
★The Wine Club's White Burgundy (STWC)
Bourgogne Blanc, Louis Jadot (VICT)

1982
c. £3.50
Bourgogne Aligoté, Bernollin (DDIR)
£4.15–£5.00
Bourgogne Aligoté, M. Rollin (BIB)
★Bourgogne Aligoté, Raymond Ballot-Millot (CV)
Bourgogne Blanc Chardonnay, Clair Daü (HT, DOL)
Bourgogne Blanc, Cuvée Latour (CUL)

1981
£3.75–£5.00
Bourgogne Aligoté, Georges Verret (BOW)
Bourgogne Blanc, Pierre Olivier (ASHE)
★Bourgogne Aligoté, Joseph et Pierre Matrot (C&B)
Bourgogne Blanc, Cuvée Latour (CV)

1980
c. £3.00
★Bourgogne Blanc, Reynier (PG)
£4.00–£4.75
Bourgogne Aligoté, Bichot (UNW)
Bourgogne Aligoté, A & P de Villaine (P&C)

1979
£4.00–£4.25
Bourgogne Rodet (CHAP)
Bourgogne Chardonnay, Guy Roulot (DDIR)
£5.00–£6.25
Bourgogne Blanc, Cuvée Latour (RACK)
Bourgogne Blanc, Tollot-Beaut (MART)
★Bourgogne Aligoté, Vieilles Vignes, Pierre Cogny (TAN)

1978
£4.00–£4.75
★Bourgogne Pinot Blanc, Meulien Pigneret (J&B)
Bourgogne Aligoté, Leroy (BWC)

Sparkling

Non-vintage
£5.40–£5.70
Crémant de Bourgogne Brut, Cave de Viré (HHC)
Crémant de Bourgogne, Henri Gregoire (DDIR)
Sparkling Red Burgundy, A de Condé (FINT)
Sparkling Red Burgundy, Chanson (L&W, TAN)

CHABLIS

THE COST OF A BOTTLE

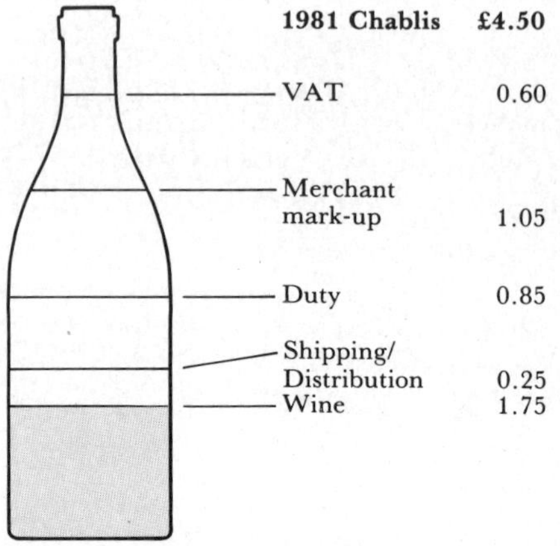

The name Chablis has an international cachet. The trouble is, it's also an international cliché. It has been borrowed all over the world, mainly in California and Australia, but also in Britain (before we joined the EEC), to describe any dry white wine of uncertain provenance. The real thing, made from the Chardonnay grape like all fine white Burgundy, comes from a very small area in northern France, where the vineyards are subject to climatic vagaries that one year can give a record harvest and the next decimate the crop with frost damage.

Britain is one of the largest importers of Chablis, but these sales are dominated by a few producers. Although Chablis is physically closer to the vineyards of Champagne, historically and commercially it has always been linked with those of Burgundy. Consequently more than half the production of Chablis is sold under the names of Beaune négociants, only two of whom actually own vineyards in Chablis - Robert Drouhin and Albert Bichot.

The largest producer in Chablis itself, whose wines are most commonly found in this country is Moreau. However he is a "white wine" expert, rather than a Chablis specialist and his range includes a major brand, Moreau Blanc, as well as wines from all over France. Next comes Henri Laroche, who deals exclusively in the wines of the region, under the domaine labels of Laroche and Jouchère, and also Bacheroy Josselin. The co-operative in Chablis, La Chablisienne, accounts for nerly a third of the area's production. Most of its wine is sold in bulk, though some finds its way over here in bottle, confusingly labelled as though it was the product of a single grower. Another famous Chablis name is that of Albert Pic, now incorporated into the négociant company of Regnard.

Amongst the small growers, some of the best hardly export their wines at all, or only in miniscule quantities. Names to look out for include François Raveneau, René Dauvissat, Louis Michel, William Fèvre, Jean Durup, and Vocoret. These wines will never be inexpensive, as they are made in a way that defies the economies of scale. But, given the quality, they are by no means over-priced. Cheaper and quaffable Chablis can be found in most supermarkets, and as straight, classy dry white, it's hard to beat.

To say that there is a choice in the style of Chablis, is to disguise the fact that Chablis has dramatically changed in style in recent years. Vineyard expansion and political wrangles have created an eminently marketable, but somewhat 'samey' dry Chardonnay. The steely, lip-pursing dryness of old-style Chablis is rarely seen any more. Even so, there are traditional growers who believe in the value of ageing wine in oak barrels for several months; while the 'modernist' school of thought believes that wood damages the intrinsic fruit in the wine and that white wine should be kept away from any contact with oxygen. And within Chablis there is a choice of appellation. Petit Chablis from less favourable slopes is a name that sounds petty rather than petit and is likely to

Vintage Table

***1983** Large vintage; better quality than 1982. Prices going up with supply shortage caused by huge US demand for authentic Chablis. Buy Premiers and Grands Crus for drinking 1987 onwards.

***1982** Largest vintage ever, producing easy-to-drink wines, with little staying power. 1982 provided Chablis at its cheapest for several years. Buy and drink now.

***1981** A small but superlative vintage. Wines to keep or drink, but now increasingly hard to find! Initially not expensive.

1980 A maligned vintage throughout France, though Chablis made classic wines of sound quality. Although fairly acid they're still good drinking.

1979 A record-breaking vintage, that came as the bubble burst in the US market. Sharp fall in prices. Wines drinking well now.

1978 One of the best but also one of the smallest vintages of the decade with a remarkable rich buttery ripeness. Prices rose dramatically. Wines still improving. Buy if you can find them.

1976 The very hot summer made wines high in alcohol and low in acidity. Many are now fading. The beginning of the sharp price rise, with the small crop.

1975 A very fine but small vintage. Now virtually impossible to find.

Maturity Chart

1981 CHABLIS LES CLOS

83's will develop and fade more quickly, and 82's even faster.

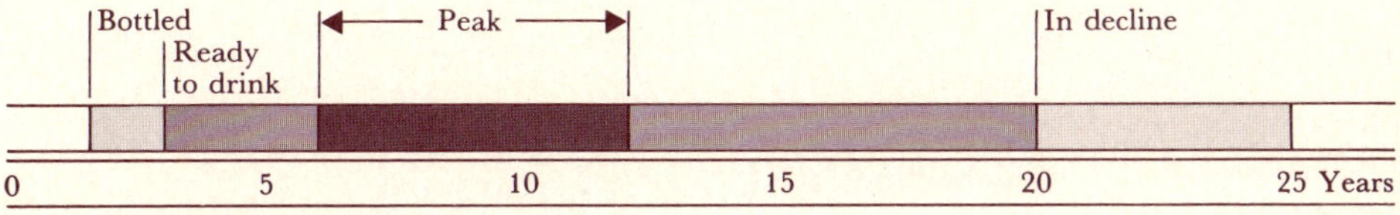

disappear; *simple* Chablis covers the widest area of the appellation. The range of Premiers Crus Chablis includes some twenty-seven names which have been rationalised into twelve main vineyards, and finally there are seven Grands Crus, from a very small patch of land just outside the town of Chablis itself. These are the great wines of the region, that develop, when mature, the traditional *goût de pierre à fusil,* (gunflint) that characterises fine Chablis. They will always be more expensive than *simple* Chablis and the Premiers Crus for their production is so tiny. But pay the price, because they're some of the great wines of France.

HISTORICAL SURVEY

Chablis, perhaps more than any other vineyard, is subject to the laws of supply and demand, and the market forces seem to dictate that there is never an equilibrium but always an extreme of glut or famine. The supply is inevitably determined by the weather. The crucial periods are in May, with the danger of spring frosts, and in June at the flowering. The wrong weather at either time can drastically reduce the crop potential. A small crop causes a heavy demand for Chablis and the inevitable price rises.

At the beginning of the 1970s a commission of Chablis growers and négociants maintained a reasonable price stability. The self-imposed discipline of the commission began to disintegrate when prices fell with the recession of 1974, and the protective insularity of Chablis was finally ruptured in 1976 when prices doubled in six months. Prices rose still further with the 1977 vintage, and with the 1978 vintage (fortunately a great one, though tiny) Chablis went mad. There was an increase in the price for a *feuillette* (132 litres) from 2,200 francs to 3,500 francs. This price was paid by the négociants in Beaune who were anxious to secure their requirements, but prices inevitably fell when the consumer, in America particularly, refused to accept such increases. The 1979 Chablis was much cheaper than the 1978s and the large vintage reversed the situation to one of glut with a stagnant market. The market continued to be sluggish with the 1980 vintage and prices fell still further.

The 1981 vintage was tiny, as a result of the unusually severe frost damage. It was also of excellent quality and prices rose a little with a renewed interest in the market. The 1982 vintage was Chablis' largest hitherto, not a propitious moment for an excessive crop. And once again the growers and négociants met to attempt some organisation of the market. All surplus wine above the basic yield of 50 hectolitres per hectare was blocked, and a price bracket fixed of 1,500 to 1,700 francs per *feuillette,* a measure designed to prevent a further fall in prices. It worked, and Chablis was cheaper than it had been for many years, but not disastrously so, and the customers lost with the high prices of the 1978 vintage returned to Chablis once again.

PRICE GUIDE

White

1983
c. £5.45
Chablis 1er Cru Fourchaume, la Chablisienne (IMB)

1982
£3.25–£4.00
⋆Sauvignon de St Bris, Georges Verret (BOW)
Chablis, Jean Paul Bartier (ASHE)
Sauvignon de St Bris, Domaine Brocard (SF)
Chablis Moreau (QR)
Sauvignon de St Bris, Albert Pic (HUN)
Chablis Domaine 1e Verger, A Geoffroy (SR, CV)
Chablis, Servant (WAIT)
Chablis (PD)
£4.00–£4.50
Chablis, Albert Pic (L&W, C&B)
Chablis, Château de Maligny, Jean Durup (BWC)
Chablis, Domaine de Biéville (ESV)
⋆Petit Chablis, Bacheroy Josselin (YFW)
Chablis 1er Cru, Louis Latour (TW)
Chablis, Philippe Testut (WNRY)
£4.50–£5.00
⋆Chablis, Alain Pautre (HBV)
⋆Chablis, Justerini & Brooks, Special

Selection Bacheroy Josselin (J&B)
★Chablis, la Chablisienne (FFW)
Chablis 1er Cru Vaillons, Domaine Servin (SF)
Chablis 1er Cru Montmains, Domaine Tour Vaubourg (LHV, YFW)
★Chablis 1er Cru Beauroy, Alain Geoffroy (CV)
Chablis 1er Cru Fourchaume, Domaine de l'Eglantière, J. Durup (ASHE)

£5.00–£5.50

Chablis 1er Cru Mont de Milieu, Albert Pic (L&W)
Chablis 1er Cru Vaillons, J. Moreau (J&B)
Chablis 1er Cru Vaillons, Droin (DAV)
Chablis 1er Cru Montée de Tonnerre, Louis Michel (L&W, WSOC, OWL)
Chablis 1er Cru Mont de Milieu, A. Regnard et Fils (JH)
Chablis, Louis Michel (OWL)
★Chablis Beauroy, Georges Verret (BOW)
Chablis 1er Cru Fourchaume, Domaine Pascal Bouchard (MAL)
Chablis 1er Cru Montée de Tonnerre, Albert Pic (BBR)
Chablis Grand Cru Preuses, Domaine Servin (SF)

£5.50–£6.00

Chablis 1er Cru Fourchaume, Bacheroy Josselin (J&B)
Chablis 1er Cru Fourchaume, Domaine de Valéry, Jean Durup (TAN)
Chablis 1er Cru Montmains, Louis Michel (OWL)

£6.00–£6.75

Chablis 1er Cru Fourchaume, Louis Michel (OWL)
Chablis Grand Cru Bougros, Albert Pic (L&W, MAL)
Chablis Grand Cru Vaudésir, Domaine Droin (CHAP)
Chablis Grand Cru Grenouilles, Albert Pic (L&W)
Chablis Grand Cru Grenouilles, Domaine de Château Grenouille (C&B)
★Chablis Grand Cru Vaudésir, Rémon (PG)

£6.75–£7.00

Chablis 1er Cru Vaillons, Domaine de Laroche (H&B)

Chablis 1er Cru Fourchaume, Vieilles Vignes, Henri Laroche (BYR, PIP)
Chablis Grand Cru Blanchot, Henri Laroche (BYR)
Chablis Grand Cru les Clos, Michel Rémon (BAL)
Chablis, Grand Cru les Clos, J. Moreau (J&B)

£7.50–£8.50

Chablis, Grand Cru Vaudésir, Albert Pic (MAL)
Chablis, Grand Cru Blanchot, Vieilles Vignes, Bacheroy Josselin (J&B)
★Chablis Grand Cru Valmur, Rémon (PG)
Chablis Grand Cru Vaudésir (UNW)

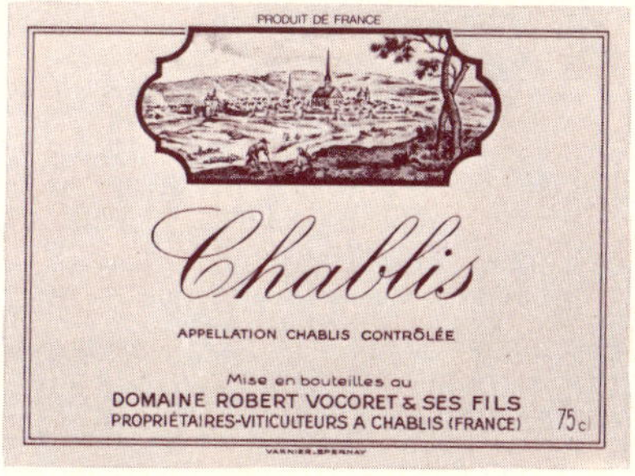

1981

£3.50–£4.50

Sauvignon de St Bris, Sorin-Defrance (DOL)
★Sauvignon de St Bris, R Defrance (VIGN)
Chablis, Jean Durup (DDIR)
Chablis, Roger Seguinot (DDIR)
Chablis, Robert Vocoret (DDIR)

£4.75–£5.00

Chablis 1er Cru Montée de Tonnerre, Jean Durup (DDIR)
Chablis 1er Cru Sechet, René Dauvissat (DDIR)
Chablis 1er Cru la Forêt, René Dauvissat (DDIR)
Chablis 1er Cru Vaillons, René Dauvissat (DDIR, TAN)
Chablis 1er Cru Montmains, Philippe Testut (WNRY, GH)

£5.25–£5.50

Chablis 1er Cru Montée de Tonnerre, A. Regnard et Fils (JH)

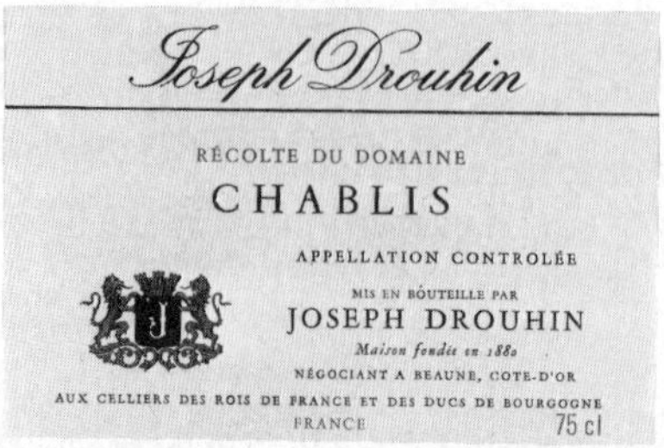

Chablis 1er Cru Fourchaume, Bouchard Père (PD)
Chablis 1er Cru Beauroy, Bacheroy Josselin (J&B)
Chablis 1er Cru Montée de Tonnerre, Michel Rémon (WW)
£5.50–£6.00
Chablis 1er Cru Montmains, Albert Pic (HUN)
★Chablis 1er Cru Monts de Milieu, Albert Pic (L&W)
Chablis Grand Cru Bougros, Domaine Servin (DDIR)
★Chablis 1er Cru Beauroy (RACK)
★Chablis 1er Cru Fourchaume, Rémon (PG)
★Chablis 1er Cru Montée de Tonnerre, Rémon (PG)
£6.00–£6.25
Chablis 1er Cru Montmains, Simmonet-Fèbvre (PD)
Chablis 1er Cru Montée de Tonnerre, Louis Michel (ODD, OWL)
Chablis Grand Cru les Preuses, René Dauvissat (DDIR)
★Chablis Grand Cru les Clos, René Dauvissat (DDIR, TAN)
Chablis, Joseph Drouhin (H&D, MWS)
Chablis 1er Cru Montée de Tonnerre, Domaine de la Tour Vaubourg (TAN)
★Chablis 1er Cru Montmains, Louis Michel (HT)
£6.50–£7.50
Chablis 1er Cru Sechets, Louis Michel (OWL)
Chablis Grand Cru les Preuses, A. Regnard et Fils (JH)
Chablis 1er Cru Montée de Tonnerre (SR)
Chablis Grand Cru Blanchot, Albert Pic (L&W)
Chablis 1er Cru Les Beugnons, Long-Depaquit (MAL)
Chablis Grand Cru Vaudésir, Louis Michel (HT)
Chablis Grand Cru les Clos, Louis Michel (HT, OWL, BIB)
£7.75–£8.75
Chablis Valmur, Moreau (WGA)
Chablis 1er Cru Fourchaume, Albert Pic (VICT)
Chablis Grand Cru les Preuses (CDM)
Chablis Grand Cru Grenouilles, Louis Michel (OWL)
Chablis Grand Cru Blanchots, Bacheroy Josselin (FINT)
Chablis Grand Cru les Clos, Moreau (FINT)
c. £9.20
Chablis Grand Cru Clos des Hospices, Moreau (QR)
c. £10.00
Chablis Moutonne (UNW)
c. £12.80
★Puligny Montrachet les Folatières, Louis Latour (YFW)

1980
£3.50–£4.00
Petit Chablis, Domaine des Courtis (SF)
Sauvignon de St Bris, Domaine Brocard (H&D)
Chablis, Long-Dépaquit (LHV)
£4.50–£5.50
Chablis 1er Cru Vaillons, René Dauvissat (DDIR)
Chablis 1er Cru Montée de Tonnerre, Robert Vocoret (DDIR)
Chablis Domaine la Jouchère (RACK)
Chablis 1er Cru Montée de Tonnerre, Domaine de la Maladière (BYR)
£5.50–£6.00
Chablis Grand Cru les Blanchots, Robert Vocoret (DDIR)
Chablis Grand Cru les Clos, Robert Vocoret (DDIR)
★Chablis 1er Cru Côte de Lechet, Bacheroy Josselin (STWC)
£6.50–£7.50
Chablis 1er Cru, Drouhin (WILL)
Chablis Grand Cru les Preuses, Domaine de la Maladière (BYR, MAL)
Chablis Grand Cru les Clos, Domaine de la Maladière (BYR)
★Chablis Grand Cru Grenouilles, Philippe Testut (WNRY, HT)
Chablis 1er Cru Vaulorent, Domaine de la Maladière (TAN)

c. £8.00

Chablis Grand Cru Blanchots (PIP)

Chablis Grand Cru Vaudésir, Louis Michel (OWL)

1979

£3.50–£4.00

★Sauvignon de St Bris, Sichel (PG)

Pouilly Vinzelles Château de Vinzelles (HUN)

£6.00–£7.00

Chablis 1er Cru les Lys, Bacheroy Josselin (P&C)

Chablis 1er Cru Montée de Tonnerre, Bacheroy Josselin (P&C)

Chablis 1er Cru Mont de Milieu, Bacheroy Josselin (ADN)

Chablis Grand Cru Vaudésir, Albert Pic (L&W)

£7.50–£8.50

Chablis Grand Cru Blanchots, Bacheroy Josselin (YFW)

Chablis Grand Cru les Clos, Louis Michel (OWL, BIB)

Chablis Grand Cru Vaudésir, Louis Michel (OWL, GH)

Chablis Grand Cru Grenouilles, Louis Michel (OWL, SR, BIB)

c. £10.75

Chablis Grand Cru les Clos, Joseph Drouhin (H&D)

1978

£6.00–£7.00

Chablis, Bacheroy Josselin (J&B)

Chablis 1er Cru Vaillons, Bouchard Père (PD)

Chablis 1er Cru Fourchaume, Henri Laroche (BYR, RSV)

£7.50–£8.50

Chablis 1er Cru Vaillons, Albert Pic (L&W)

Chablis Grand Cru Preuses, La Chablisienne (LADV)

Chablis 1er Cru Vaulorent, Domaine de la Maladière (L&W)

£8.00–£8.50

Chablis Grand Cru Blanchot, Domaine Laroche (SR, WILL)

Chablis Grand Cru Valmur, Domaine Maurice Fèvre (L&W)

£9.00–£10.00

Chablis Grand Cru les Clos, Moreau (WSOC, SR)

Chablis Grand Cru les Clos, Louis Michel (FFW)

Chablis Grand Cru Clos des Hospices, Moreau (TW)

1976

c. £11.70

Chablis Grand Cru les Clos, Moreau (REID)

Red

1981

c. £3.90

Bourgogne Irancy, Léon Bienvenu (DDIR)

Coulanges-la-Vineuse, Jean Deligny (PD)

1980

c. £4.00

Bourgogne Irancy, André Melou (DDIR)

1979

c. £3.70

Bourgogne Rouge, Vin des Coteaux de St Bris, Sorin-Defrance (DOL)

1978

c. £3.60

Bourgogne Coulanges-la-Vineuse, Bacheroy-Josselin (WHIT)

Webster's is an annual publication. We welcome suggestions for next year's edition.

Effort Rewarded

The future depends entirely on the size of the 1984 vintage. For the 1983 vintage, which yielded a record 140,000 hectolitres of wine, prices were fixed at a higher bracket; between 1,800–2,000 francs and the crop in excess of 50 hectolitres per hectare was blocked again. With two consecutive record-breaking vintages it would be reasonable to suppose there is plenty of Chablis to be had. But no – all the available wine has been sold. People are keen to buy Chablis again, and are waiting eagerly for the release of the blocked wine. The price of *simple* Chablis has been legally fixed, so the inevitable price rises of a shortage of supply are illustrated in the escalation of the Premiers Crus prices, from 2,000 francs in 1982 to 3,500 francs for a *feuillette* in 1983.

For the moment the situation is stable, but only as long as there is the possibility of a large crop in 1984. If frost or rain at the flowering decimates the crop, as in 1978, there will be no hold on the inevitable price rises, and in the words of one grower – the catastrophe of 1978 will repeat itself.

CÔTE D'OR

The Côte d'Or is the famous bit. The bit with all the household names, the ones which you often wish you could afford. And it's the one we've been seeing less and less of lately. With good reason. It's 10 years now since we began to taste the first offerings of post-EEC burgundy on the British market. Our first reaction was – no thanks, we don't drink rosé. Can we have a glass of Pommard or Nuits St-Georges, please, something nice and chunky, something to put hairs on the chest. 'But this *is* a Pommard or Nuits St-Georges', would come the reply. 'This is the real McCoy, the echt, yer actual.'

For a few years we thought the French would get over it, and start producing the nice thick grape soup again. But they couldn't, not really. The appellation controlée boys had wanted to plug that non-EEC, 'excess production', wink-and-a-nudge loophole for years. So they started to explain that these new wines were 'modern-style' Burgundy, that true Pinot was light and pale and for instant drinking. Yet for that special name – Beaune, Volnay, Chambolle-Musigny, one would have to pay. And pay. After all, it is the 'real thing'.

Well, the Great British Public got fed up. They don't take kindly to paying silk purse prices for sow's ears, and the merchant who now stocks a Nuits St-Georges or a Pommard is the exception rather than the rule. The old style 'burgundy' had nothing to do with actual burgundy grapes and vineyards, and the modern styles offered to us *were* mostly pallid, half-hearted creatures.

THE COST OF A BOTTLE

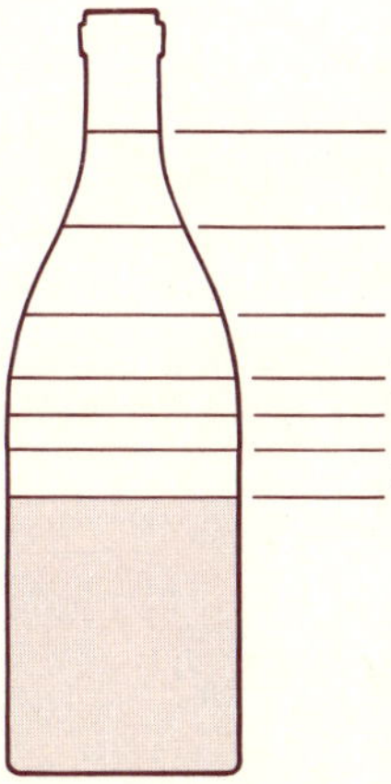

1981 Nuits St-Georges	**£9.15**
VAT	1.19
Merchant mark-up	1.59
Duty	0.68
Distribution	0.16
Shipping	0.08
Bottling	0.30
Wine	5.15

The tide of callously overpriced mediocrity which threatened to destroy the common-sense British burgundy market is on the turn. A few adventurous British merchants have got over there, got their boots dirty, and sought out the embattled breed of growers who do care, and are still making the good stuff. Many of them are bang in the middle of the Côte d'Or, and slowly but surely we can begin to see the kind of character the wines of these different communes should have.

The Côte de Nuits *should* have the biggest wines. Frequently it doesn't, but even so, here's what to expect. The villages of Fixin and Gevrey-Chambertin should produce the biggest, darkest burgundy reds. Deep, plummy, tough, hard when young, but marvellously

Maturity Chart

1978 COTE DE NUITS GRAND CRU

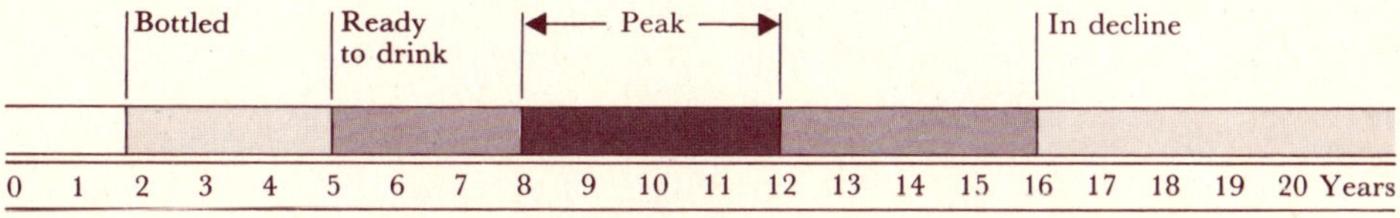

mellow with age. Such wines are slowly re-appearing after a decade when the wines seemed simply unfocussed and hefty. Morey St-Denis isn't well known, but it is no longer cheap either, since it harbours in Messrs Seysse, Ponsot and Bryczek some of the best wine and reputation-makers of the region. These growers and others make good, deep, but fragrant, wine. Many more make famous-name wine half-way to rosé.

Chambolle-Musigny, with its wonderful vineyard names of Les Charmes and Les Amoureuses, can be a light, intensely perfumed 'beautiful' burgundy, but most commercial Chambolle will be too sweet to retain much perfume. The same sweetness is a problem with Clos de Vougeot, famous name, at its best plummy and broad, yet more likely sweet and sullen. Vosne Romanée contains the exotic and fabulously priced Domaine de la Romanée Conti. At their best, Vosne wines catch all the strawberry sweetness of Pinot as well as adding a marvellous meaty savouriness. Nuits St-Georges, when it's good, has a piercing rotty taste on top of a light sweet fruit which is quite gorgeous, whatever it sounds like.

The Côte de Beaune begins in traditionally beefy style with Aloxe-Corton. Ten years ago it was one of the best of all buys for full-flavoured, balanced burgundy. May those days soon return. Most recent Corton and Aloxe-Corton has been pale stuff indeed. Aloxe-Corton also produces the white Grand Cru Corton-Charlemagne which is usually strong and good without quite reaching the standard of the other great whites. From here southwards, reds and whites are often found in the same vineyards, and Pernand-Vergelesses and Savigny-Les-Beaune produce both, not renowned, but pretty reliable.

Beaune is very renowned indeed and, thank goodness, it is one of the few reliable commune wines. It never used to be. The English wine trade gag was of the old-style wine merchant teaching an apprentice. "There are two sorts of burgundy. Beaune. And the rest. We sell Beaune." Until the coming of EEC regulations, Beaune could be virtually anything. Now it is usually quite light, with a soft 'red' fruit and a flicker of something metallic to smarten it up.

Pommard is big braw wine at its best, but it is also the village which is most tugged at by the demands of the market. Growers like Mussey, Pousse d'Or and Parent show what it is really capable of. Pousse d'Or will also show you Volnay at its best, though not in its famous light fragrant 'semi-red' style. D'Angerville gives the most perfumed example of that. Monthélie makes good, but little sought-after red, while Meursault is the first of the three world famous white wine villages. Even commune Meursault should be soft and nutty, but pressure on supplies means that it's well worth going to single vineyard level. There are many good growers and many wines are offered under vineyard name.

Three backwoods villages, all offering excellent value – Auxey-Duresses, St-Romain and St-Aubin – divide Meursault from Chassagne-Montrachet and Puligny-Montrachet, which, in the various Montrachet Grand Crus, provide the peak of great white pleasure. The flavours are strong, the prices are stunning but, with few exceptions, it is worth saving your money for one fine single domaine rather than buying two blended bottles. Chassagne and Santenay also make some rough and ready red.

That list encompasses the great names of Burgundy. The less lucky villages often find their wines lumped into Côte de Nuits- or Côte de Beaune-Villages, at one time the best value Côte d'Or drinking. Best value now is either in the lesser villages in the eddies away from the mainstream, or in the villages of the Hautes Côtes. They are the vineyards hidden in the twisting, twining valleys behind the main slope. A lot of investment in planting Pinot Noir and Chardonnay has led to a fair amount of good, dry light wine being made. It used to be said – oh, they'll only manage one good vintage in five. Not true. With less commercial pressure, growers are producing good affordable wine *every* year.

Vintage Table

WHITE

White burgundy is far less prone to vintage fluctuation than red, and in most years can produce a fair amount of pretty good wine. As the demand for the region's wines increases, the grower becomes less eager to sell to a merchant. Except when the merchant owns vineyards, the standard of his commune and single vineyard wines may not always be worth the price.

1983 Some wonderful wine, from the growers who picked early enough and vinified carefully, but also some disasters. Those who picked late frequently found the wines far too alcoholic and difficult to vinify. Add rot problems in many areas, and many of the white wines will taste more like Côtes du Rhône.

1982 Hailed as a great year, now seen as a good year. There's loads of wine and it's fairly full and ripe, but rarely has a lot of concentration of taste. However, some wine makers couldn't control fermentation in the hot autumn, and basic village wines tend to be fairly bland.

1981 They tried hard, but had precious little raw material to work with. Though experts say the wines will come round, their style is mostly so dry and skinny and fruitless it's difficult to see it. A few good Pulignys and Chassagnes.

1980 Less good than the reds, but still quite a lot of good, high acid, bone dry wine. But there was a rot problem, and many wines from Meursault and some from Chassagne are already falling apart.

1979 These can be extremely good. Although the vintage was big, and the wines haven't got masses of deep, memorable nuances, the fruit is now soft and fully mature, and the oak maturing has left us a buttery gentle burgundy to drink now.

1978 As with the reds, this vintage hit the nation with a fanfare of trumpets. It seemed as though it was going to be an absolute corker. Yet, as the wines reach maturity, there's something rather hefty and solid about a lot of them, almost sweet in a toffeeish way. Hopefully it'll pass, but I think I'd drink mine now for the big though edgey pleasures they offer at the moment.

1976 No one ever claimed that the whites were as great as the reds, but funnily enough they've probably given more pleasure. They've always been a bit fat and oily, but, though they're mostly getting a bit tired, that sticky, ripe taste leaves me with many fond memories.

***1973** This excellent vintage nearly slipped away unnoticed in the rush. It wasn't immediately appreciated, and it's only recently that people have been saying – 'Good God, best white vintage of the decade.' It's fading now, but has been the epitome of the luscious yet savoury flavours of good oak-burned Chardonnay.

Vintage Table

RED

The last decade has been a very difficult one for the Côte d'Or, and the region has been unable to find a genuine price/quality/value balance. These notes are by necessity generalizations, but based on typical wines of reliable producers.

1983 Some wonderful wine, but a horrendously difficult year. There was a great deal of rot in the vineyards, whatever people say, and only the good hillside sites succeeded. The successes, however, are marvellous, with all the weight and strength of 1976 but far more fruit.

1982 A sad vintage. Massive overproduction, with uniformly healthy but unexciting grapes being culled in record quantities, and even those who pruned severely made light wines. Those who didn't made rosé, and many top Côte de Nuits sites are the worst offenders.

1981 A skinny, desperate vintage. Very little wine, and most have a hard charmless rasp from trying to salvage a reasonable quantity from very few grapes. Few successes because they just lack fruit.

1980 The good guys made excellent wine. Though initially dismissed as poor, this vintage has produced a lot of dry, well-coloured burgundy, particularly in the Côte de Nuits, and they can still age. Unfashionable. Buy it.

1979 The perfect commercial vintage, they called it. Hmmm. Lots of wine, certainly, and some very attractive mid-weight stuff from good estates, but some blended wines are already too old, even from Grand Cru vineyards.

1978 Potentially superb. Wonderful balance of fruit and acidity and tannin. They're mostly a bit unyielding at the moment but the fruit is all there. The problems of generalising appear when you put two Grand Cru Chambertins from next-door vineyards but different wine makers up against each other. One is brown and sweet, delicious, but fading at six years old, the other is dark and purple and needs 10 years. So, what do you say?

1977 Pretty feeble. A few first class growers like Tollot-Beaut, Chevalier of Ladoix, Gouges of Nuits St-Georges made good light wine. But don't take the risk.

1976 Hailed as a sensation, it's suffering from the same problems as 1975 claret. The fruit is drying and the tannin still grabs you by the tonsils. It *may* turn out big and classic in a few years, but I wouldn't bank on it.

1972 Another vintage which suffered because of Bordeaux's bad reputation. The wines were very hard to start with. But now they're good.

Vintage Table
RED

1972 *cont* Sturdy. Dry, strong-tasting Pinot Noir, not smooth and sweet, but the real thing.

1971 This *may* be one of the best recent vintages. As always there's this infuriating inability to say for sure. The good wines are beautifully balanced, with that lovely mixture of strawberry fruit with the rather more surprising 'impolite' elements of really good burgundy. Even the best are ready now.

Stable prices from Louis Jadot
What becomes most apparent looking at the comparative list of Louis Jadot Burgundy prices is that no one could complain of this company pursuing a policy of ruthless price increases. Since prices rocketed for the exciting 1978 vintage, they have in general been drifting back downwards. But since these are, even in 1984, very much in the realms of expensive to very expensive wine styles, it does bring back the shock of those first 1978 prices, and how expensive they seemed in the cheaper world of 1980 when they were first offered. It is also encouraging to note that the less good vintages are offered at a reasonable discount, even though demand for such famous names as Corton and Beaune Clos des Ursules might tempt producers to raise the price regardless every year. The 1984 prices show further falls, which are due partly to the big 1982 vintage coming on stream, but also to the fact that Burgundy is losing her customers for the more expensive wines, and as she struggles to realign her quality objectives, prices will have to fall to keep stock moving.

On Sale	Bourgogne Rouge	Bourgogne Blanc	Beaune Clos des Ursules	Corton
1970			£2.29 (1966)	£2.41 (1964)
1971			£2.29 (1967)	£2.68 (1967)
1972			£2.62 (1967)	£2.93 (1967)
1973	£1.68 (1970)	£1.68 (1971)		£4.38 (1967)
1974	£1.66 (1970)	£1.77 (1971)	£3.65 (1971)	£4.32 (1971)
1975	£2.79 (1970)	£2.79 (1971/2)	£3.65 (1971)	£4.32 (1971)
1976	£2.01 (1971)	£2.02 (1972)	£4.32 (1971)	£4.65 (1971)
1977	£2.51 (1972)	£2.51 (1973)	£5.87 (1972/3)	£7.98 (1972)
1978	£3.88 (1972/3)	£3.88 (1976/7)	£7.09 (1974)	£9.31 (1972/3)
1979	£4.77 (1977/8)	£5.36 (1978)	£10.38 (1974/6)	£12.83 (1972/3)
1980	£6.17 (1978) £4.34 (1977)	£5.16 (1978)	£9.14 (1977) £9.80 (1974/6)	£14.80 (1978) £10.38 (1976) £12.35 (1972/3)
1981	£5.09 (1978) £4.48 (1977)	£5.31 (1978)	£10.93 (1979) £11.81 (1978)	£13.08 (1972/3)
1982	£4.96 (NV)	£5.23 (NV)	£11.05 (1979)	£13.20 (1972/3)
1983	£3.93 (NV)	£4.61 (NV)	£10.42 (1980) £11.12 (1979)	£12.42 (1982) £12.36 (1980)

Source: Hatch Mansfield
These figures are based on whosesale prices plus 25% mark-up and VAT.

Hospices de Beaune

The Hospices de Beaune is a beautiful building. It is one of the best hospitals in France. It has also been bequeathed vineyard domaines that make up the most important holding in Burgundy. In November it holds a sale of the new wines. The TV cameras whirr as the bids are made, the newspapers report the prices and speculate on what they mean for the Burgundy market in general. They mean nothing.

The Hospices de Beaune sales in November are pure theatre. Without doubt, they raise a lot of money for the hospital, but to pretend that they have the same relevance to the market as the opening prices for the classed growth Bordeaux châteaux is absurd. Since the bidding is entirely in the hands of the local négociants, it is not difficult for the prices to reflect the Burgundian position as they would like to see it. Price rises at the sale are a useful prelude to the 'need' to charge higher prices for their own ranges of wines. Of course, that sword has two edges. The growers will also see the prices notched up and calculate their chances accordingly.

This whole performance is a pity for two reasons. Firstly, it is yet another excuse for Burgundian growers and merchants to avoid establishing a fair price which fits the quality of the product. And secondly the Hospices makes some first-class wines, under the supervision of Bernard Porcheret, a bearded giant who is one of Burgundy's most talented wine makers. Taste his wines in the barrel, and you'll taste some of the best wines in the Côte de Beaune. But however well he does, the wines are *all* removed to local négociants' cellars for 'raising' – see *Burgundy introduction.* Sadly, the only wine bottled by the Hospices itself goes to the patients and guests at Hospice dinners. Last year a prominent French magazine ran a blind tasting of Hospices wines 'raised' by different négociants. Their relationship to each other was about as constant as that of two mayflies in a typhoon. As one Burgundian remarked last year, what *is* the point of the Hospices making first class wine, when the négociants are allowed to mess it up?

Historical Price Survey of Hospices de Beaune: red and white

Average price of 225 litres* in French francs

1947	*old francs*	70,206	1965	1,496
1948		79,069	1966	3,052
1949		116,304	1967	2,451
1950		65,475	1969	5,583
1951		73,964	1970	3,805
1952		115,144	1971	8,590
1953		111,274	1972	9,966
1954		69,274	1973	9,158
1955		124,463	1974	6,874
1957		180,387	1975	7,203
1958		99,625	1976	9,832
1959		234,761	1977	11,087
1960	*new francs*	1,777	1978	16,810
1961		3,983	1979	13,891
1962		3,407	1980	11,524
1963		2,349	1981	15,499
1964		2,732	1982	17,164

Source: Joseph Drouhin

*the amount of a Burgundian pièce, a traditional unit of sale

NÉGOCIANT AND GROWER

The general name for a wine merchant in French is *'négociant-éleveur'*. Négociant is the word used over here, it has a businessman's ring to it. It smacks of commerce, haggling and making deals. But for the Burgundy trade in particular the word *éleveur* has great importance. An *éleveur* in French is literally one who raises, as in raising a child. Children are born possessing certain genetic traits, but some of their characteristics will be conditioned, a result of their upbringing and environment - of their raising. They may develop as shy or gregarious children, smiling or sullen. So it is with wine.

Once the grapes are stripped from the vine and thrown into the vat, the process of 'raising' has begun. Usually it is started by the grower, after which the responsibility is frequently passed on to the *négociant-éleveur* (who may incidentally also be a grower himself to some degree). At the time, whatever the base wine was like, he has the chance to coax the wine into the shape he eventually wishes to commercialise.

He can do this by careful ageing in oak barrels, by blending different growers' wines from the same vineyard to achieve a balanced style, or by blending wines from the same general appellation to satisfy a need for a consistent 'village' wine. Or he can play with the AC laws in such a way that wines which have no connection with the vineyard or village names on the label are added, surreptitiously, to help the poor feeble natural wine the consumer would otherwise have been expected to appreciate. So the *négociant-éleveur* is a businessman concerned with market share, turnover and profit margins, and he is also creator of the finished product he deals in.

If the grower were just that, a grower of grapes, the world of burgundy would be much simplified. However, he is traditionally supposed to be the wine maker too. The skills of vine tending and wine making are very different. Judging by the yields often produced, there are many expert vine tenders in Burgundy, but judging by the eventual flavour of the wines, there are not many growers who really know how to turn their notoriously tricky Pinot Noir grapes into good wine. There are many *négociant-éleveurs* who have made it their lifetime's work to ease the strain. The result is that over the years it is not so much the vineyard or vintage which has determined the quality and style of a burgundy; it is the extent to which the natural wine has been 'raised' into the shape the market seems to prefer.

These two groups are the main actors in Burgundy's performance. But there is a third group: the people who drink it. It is Burgundy's misfortune that such a tiny area should have shown itself so adept at producing great wine. Word gets around. Demand grows, then outstrips supply. Especially with a climate like Burgundy's, so far north for a red wine area that in times gone by they were hard put to make good wine more than one year in three. Sunless summers still alternate with waterless summers, hail is frequent, and rot is usually panting to take hold on the vines.

But those rare good years were so sought after by the likes of us that it is hadly surprising that ways were found to provide them more frequently. Demand was relentless, and relentless demand is at the heart of both Burgundy's prosperity and her present crisis. For have no doubt, Burgundy *is* in crisis. For too long that demand has been satisfied by less than scrupulous means. Either the *négociant-éleveur* has had to find ways to create the necessary wine out of non-Burgundian sources, or the grower has fertilised heavily, pruned lightly, and resorted to planting high-cropping new varieties of vines.

After the war a variety of Pinot Noir called the 'Pinot droit' (straight Pinot) was promoted by the nurserymen. The wine wasn't great, but the yield was big and regular. By 1970 the nurseries had almost forgotten what the old, gnarled true Pinot was. By 1984 the mood had swung against the 'Pinot droit', but it will take another 20 years of replanting programmes for the balance in the vineyards to tip back to the true Pinot Noir. Of course the direct result of this high yielding, low personality vine has been large amounts of light insipid wine (the white Chardonnay is much more gutsy, but it too has been over-stretched by demand). In an effort to give their wines some of that old-time bezazz, the growers have resorted to the sugar sack with gay abandon, producing masses of dull, thick, sweet burgundy.

For years there has been a profitable merry-go-round of uncritical négociants buying lazy growers' produce, and slapping on the profit margin. Yet the writing is at last on the wall for this dual conspiracy - and 1982 wrote it large. The massive price hikes for the 1978 vintage triggered off an overdue alarm response in the consumer. With a lot of 1979 to sell into a falling market, things were still fairly healthy, but with the advent of an unpopular 1980 and an uninteresting 1981, négociants stopped buying, and growers' cellars were left bulging with precisely the vintages they didn't want. There was so much wine in 1982 that (for the last time) the négociant could smile contentedly as he thumbed through the desperate offers the growers were making just to clear their cellars. Some négociants made merciless use of the 1982 glut, forcing prices down by as much as 50 per cent for the 1982s and by a good deal more for the 1980s and 1981s.

It will be proved a pyrrhic victory. Despite the demand for white being high, and the vintage quality good, the standard of négociants' 1982 reds and whites leaves much to be desired, and the UK burgundy market has finally grown sick of it all and will no longer meekly accept what is offered. In 1984, when the négociants go back to offer terms, yet another group of the braver growers will slam the door in their faces, and ring up the printers for a consignment of 'Mise en bouteille au Domaine' labels. In short, we can expect to see more of the individual wines that good UK wine merchants are now seeking out.

In this situation it is easy to brand the négociant as the only villain of the piece. This is patently not so. The crisis has been as much the growers' fault as the négociants'. As we gain the courage to say that we are tired of being robbed of good money for bad wine, the growers and the négociants are going to have to face up to each other for the first time in many years. The good grower will survive, without doubt. The good négociant? Maybe.

The problem for the négociant is that he is an endangered species. As the world becomes increasingly aware of what good burgundy should taste like, he will become less able to provide it unless he owns vineyards himself. Instead of being able to dictate terms to the growers on the Côte, demanding their best *cuves* of wine, the négociant may be unable to secure the best parcels as the grower decides to control his own destiny. He will be pushed farther and farther to the edges of the appellations, making do with second-rate wine. So many négociants have spent so long proving to an infatuated and ignorant market that they can meet every requirement without further discussion that, in a new age which is beginning to prize specialization, they are like those great behemoths, the department stores of which London seems to lose another every year, trying to stock the lot, and failing to see the specialist competition creaming off the best customers until it is too late.

The specialist competition is the grower himself. That best *cuve* he once had to sell to a négociant he is now bottling himself. Although his costs may be higher he will get twice the price if he sells it himself in bottle. If he's not pleased with some of the wine, then the négociant can have that. In the last 10 years there has been a terrific expansion in domaine bottling on the Côte d'Or; from less than a fifth to over half in 1984. But this, although a move in the right direction, is not a universal cure. It is often the ambitious grower who bottles his own. This doesn't make him a good grower, and will not necessarily stop him overcropping his vines or sugaring his wine. We're the ones who'll stop that. As the opportunities of buying real burgundy gradually increase, we won't buy the rubbish. Burgundy is a great name and a great vineyard. The name has been badly tarnished. The vineyard's still there, pining to be returned to glory.

Price Guide

Red

1982

£3.75–£4.75

Côtes de Beaune Villages, Charles Drapier (LHV)

Côte de Nuits Villages, Grivot (C&B)

c. £5.15

Côte de Beaune Villages, Albert Morey (BWC, PIP)

c. £6.20

Nuits St-Georges, Jean Chauvenet (C&B)

1981

£5.75–£6.75

★Côte de Beaune Villages, les Maranges (C&B)

★St-Romain, René Gras-Boisson (HHC)

Chassagne-Montrachet, Albert Morey (PIP)

Savigny-les-Beaune, Vigne aux Puits, Philippe Bouchard (MACK)

£6.75–£8.00

Pernand Vergelesses, M. Rollin (BIB)

★Santenay Tasteviné, Bichot (UNW)

Chassagne-Montrachet Clos St Jean, Micl Niellon (OWL)

Beaune, Clos de Renard, Philippe Boucha (MACK)

Aloxe Corton, Tollot-Beaut (L&W)

c. £8.40

Volnay Santenots, Matrot (C&B)

c. £10.25

Chambolle-Musigny, Labouré-Roi (ESV)

£12.50–£13.50

Volnay Clos des Ducs, Marquis d'Angerville (OWL, C&B)

Beaune Clos des Avaux, Hospices de Beaune (MAL)

★Gevrey-Chambertin, Cave Roty (C&B)

1980

£4.50–£5.50

★Côte de Beaune Villages (JH)

Hautes Côtes de Nuits, Geisweiler (BAL)

St-Aubin, Thomas Père & Fils (DDIR)

St-Romain, René Thevenin-Monthélie (DDIR)

Savigny-les-Beaune 1er Cru les Lavières, Charles Drapier (LHV)

★Chorey-les-Beaune, Tollot-Beaut (L&W, BWC, ASHE, PIP, SR)

Meursault Rouge, Côte de Beaune (CHAP)

£6.00–£7.00

★Gevrey-Chambertin (JH)

★Côte de Beaune, la Grande Chatelaine, Chantal Lescure (YFW)

★Gevrey-Chambertin, Domaine des Varoilles, Nalgeon Chauveau (SF)

Auxey-Duresses, Guy Roulot (DDIR)

Monthélie, Château de Monthélie (L&W)

Beaune, Guy Roulot (DDIR)

Gevrey-Chambertin, Clos Prieur, Domaine des Varoilles (L&W)

Chassagne-Montrachet, Albert Morey (DOL)

£7.00–£8.00

Pernand-Vergelesses 1er Cru Ile des Vergelesses, Chandon de Briailles (DDIR)

Beaune Grèves, Albert Morey (BWC)

Beaune les Epenottes, Machard de Gramont (TAN)

£8.00–£9.00

Savigny, Champs-Chevrey, Tollot-Beaut (PIP)

Chassagne-Montrachet, Clos de la Boudriotte, Bachelet-Ramonet (C&B)

Santenay Grand Cru Rousseau, Albert Morey (PIP)
Nuits St-Georges Les Vaucrains, Robert Chevillon (WW, RH)
Morey-St-Denis Clos des Ormes, Lignier (BIB)
Chambolle-Musigny, Labouré-Roi (CHAP)
Nuits St-Georges, Labouré-Roi (CHAP)
Gevrey-Chambertin, Louis Trapet Père et Fils (C&B, PIP)
Beaune, Clos du Roi, Tollot-Beaut (BWC, PIP)
Chambolle-Musigny, Domaine G. Roumier (DDIR, TAN)

£9.50–£10.00

Nuits St-Georges 1er Cru les Vaucrains, Robert Chevillon (WW)
Morey St-Denis, Domaine Dujac (ADN, L&W, C&B, OWL, TAN, P&C, DDIR)
Aloxe-Corton, Tollot-Beaut (BWC)
Nuits St-Georges les Maladières, Cuvée Mignotte (WSOC)
Nuits St-Georges 1er Cru les Boudots, Jean Grivot (DDIR)
Beaune, Clos des Ursules, Louis Jadot (L&W)

£10.75–£12.00

Morey St-Denis 1er Cru, Domaine Dujac (DDIR)
Grands Echézeaux, Henri de Villamont (MART)
Volnay Caillerets, Clos des 60 Ouvrées, Domaine de la Pousse d'Or (BWC)
Pommard 1er Cru Bertins, Machard de Gramont (TAN)
Beaune, Cuvée Brunet, Hospices de Beaune, Patriarche (CUL)
Latricières-Chambertin, Louis Trapet Père et Fils (C&B)

Nuits St-Georges Les Pruliers, Henri Gouges (OWL)

£12.00–£12.75

Corton, Tollot-Beaut (BWC)
★Volnay 1er Cru Bousse d'Or, Domaine de la Pousse d'Or (L&W)
Nuits St-Georges Les Vaucrains, Henri Gouges (OWL)
★Nuits St-Georges les Hauts Pruliers, Machard de Gramont (STWC)
Beaune, Clos des Mouches, Joseph Drouhin (HHC, MWS)
Corton-Bressandes, Tollot-Beaut (BWC)
Volnay Champans, Marquis d'Angerville (C&B)

£13.00–£14.50

Morey St-Denis, Clos de la Roche, Armand Rousseau (DDIR, L&W, OWL)
Vosne-Romanée 1er Cru Suchots, Alain Hudelot-Noellat (BWC)
Gevrey-Chambertin aux Combottes, Dujac (C&B)
Gevrey-Chambertin, Clos des Ruchottes, Armand Rousseau (DDIR)
Charmes-Chambertin, Dujac (L&W)
Chambolle-Musigny 1er Cru, Domaine Dujac (OWL)

£15.00–£20.00

Gevrey-Chambertin 1er Cru Clos St-Jacques, Armand Rousseau (DDIR, L&W)
Corton, Bonneau du Martray (C&B)
Bonnes Mares, Domaine G. Roumier (DDIR, L&W, TAN)
Chambolle-Musigny les Amoureuses, Comte de Vogüé (DDIR)
Chapelle-Chambertin, Clair Daü (ODD)
Clos de Vougeot, Alain Hudelot-Noellat (BWC)
Morey St-Denis 1er Cru Clos St-Denis, Dujac (TAN)
Ruchottes-Chambertin, Clos des Ruchottes, Armand Rousseau (OWL)
Clos de la Roche, Dujac (C&B)
Echézeaux, Henri Jayer (WW)
Chambertin Clos de Bèze, Armand Rousseau (DDIR, OWL)

£20.00–£26.00

Echézeaux, Domaine Dujac (OWL)

Chambolle Musigny les Amoureuses, Georges Roumier (TAN)
Musigny, Comte de Vogüé (DDIR)
Chambertin, Armand Rousseau (OWL)
Bonnes Mares, Domaine Dujac (OWL)
c. £39.00
Richebourg, Domaine de la Romanée-Conti (VICT)

1979
£5.00–£6.00
Auxey-Duresses, Duc de Magenta (DDIR)
Chorley-les-Beaune, Tollot-Beaut (DDIR, BYR, DOL, OWL, LADV)
Bourgogne, Pinot de Marsannay, Clair Daü (DOL)
le Corton, Rodet (CHAP)
Monthélie, Charles Drapier (LHV)
Chassagne-Montrachet, Albert Morey (DDIR, HT, LADV)
Pernand-Vergelesses, Roland Rapet (DDIR)
Savigny-les-Beaune, Bouchard Père (PD)
£6.00–£7.00
Savigny-les-Beaune, A. Rodet (ESV)
Monthélie, Château de Monthélie, Robert de Suremain (DDIR)
Savigny-les-Beaune, Simon Bize (DDIR)
Savigny-les-Beaune les Guettes, Machard de Gramont (WHIT)
Savigny-les-Beaune 1er Cru les Lavières, Tollot-Beaut (DDIR)
Pernand-Vergelesses 1er Cru Vergelesses, Roland Rapet (DDIR)
Fixin, Clos Napoléon, Pierre Gelin (DDIR)
Santenay 1er Cru Clos Tavannes, Domaine de la Pousse d'Or (DDIR)
Savigny-les-Beaune 1er Cru les Marconnets, Simon Bize (DDIR)
£7.00–£7.50
Savigny-les-Beaune 1er Cru les Vergelesses, Dubreuil-Fontaine (DDIR)
Savigny-les-Beaune 1er Cru les Guettes, Simon Bize (DDIR)
Meursault Rouge, Coche-Debord (BIB)
Santenay 1er Cru Gravières, Philippe Mestre (DDIR)
Beaune Blanches-Fleurs, Tollot-Beaut (DDIR)
⋆Morey St-Denis, Domaine Dujac (DDIR, L&W, SR, BWC)
Beaune, Michel Gaunoux (DDIR)
⋆Savigny-les-Beaune, Louis Latour (SF, RACK, GH, DAV)
£7.50–£8.00
Pernand-Vergelesses, Joseph Drouhin (MAL)
Volnay Clos des Chênes, Bernard Glantenay (BWC)
Beaune 1er Cru Grèves, Tollot-Beaut (DDIR)
Blagny Rouge, Leflaive (C&B)

Volnay-Santenots, Comte Lafon (DDIR)
⋆Gevrey-Chambertin, Boisset (WAIT)
Vosne-Romanée, Mongeard-Mugneret (DDIR)
£8.25–£9.25
Beaune, les Chouacheux (J&B)
Gevrey-Chambertin 1er Cru, Armand Rousseau (BWC)
Gevrey-Chambertin 1er Cru Combe-aux-Moines, Clair-Daü (DDIR)
Beaune 1er Cru Chouacheux, Machard de Gramont (RACK)
⋆Chambolle-Musigny, Machard de Gramont (DAV)
Savigny-les-Beaune, Clos des Guettes (MWS)
Nuits St-Georges, Alain Michelot (DDIR)
Savigny-les-Beaune, les Vergelesses, Dubreuil-Fontaine (DOL)
Volnay Santenots-du-Milieu 1er Cru, Tête de Cuvée, Domaine des Comtes Lafon (ADN)
£9.50–£10.00
⋆Beaune, les Epenottes, Parent (H&D)
Volnay Champans, Marquis d'Angerville (FFW, OWL, SR)
Corton, Roland Rapet (DDIR)
Aloxe-Corton, Tollot-Beaut (PIP)
Beaune, Vignes Franches, François Germain (MAL)
Charmes-Chambertin, Armand Rousseau (BWC, BYR, PIP)
Gevrey-Chambertin, Louis Jadot (FFW, WGA)
Bonnes Mares, Clair Daü (BYR)

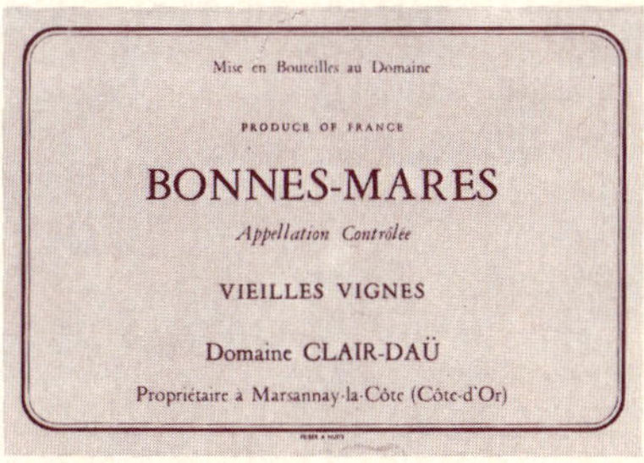

£10.00–£10.50
Chapelle-Chambertin, Clair Daü (BYR)

Pommard 1er Cru les Bertins, Chantal Lescure (LHV)
Volnay 1er Cru Clos de la Bousse d'Or, Domaine de la Pousse d'Or (DDIR)
Gevrey-Chambertin 1er Cru Aux Combottes, Domaine Dujac (DDIR, WW, TAN)
Beaune, Vignes Franches, Louis Latour (GH, SR, WHIT, VICT, YFW, RACK)
Nuits St-Georges 1er Cru les Vaucrains, Alain Michelot (DDIR)
⋆Volnay-Santenots, Ampeau (L&W)
Volnay 1er Cru Santenots, Jacques Prieur (TAN)
⋆Pommard, Clos Blanc, Machard de Gramont (J&B)

£10.50–£11.00

Pommard 1er Cru les Bertins, Machard de Gramont (WHIT, RACK)
Volnay 1er Cru Taillepieds, Domaine de Montille (DDIR)
Gevrey-Chambertin les Cazetiers, A Rousseau (SR, L&W)
Nuits St-Georges, Clos de la Maréchale, Faiveley (PG, CHAP)
Pommard, Parent (PIP)
Volnay, Clos des Ducs, Marquis d'Angerville (OWL)
Volnay 1er Cru Caillerets, Domains Pousse d'Or (L&W)
Clos de la Roche, Armand Rousseau (BWC)

£11.00–£12.00

Beaune, Clos du Roi, Tollot-Beaut (OWL)
Volnay Caillerets, Cuvée Carnot, Bouchard Père (WSOC)
⋆Aloxe-Corton, Louis Latour (GH, TAN, J&B)
Volnay Santenots, Jean Clerget (LADV)
Vosne-Romanée les Violettes, Clerget (DOL)
Vosne-Romanée, L. Jadot (BIB, GH)
Pommard 1er Cru Pezerolles, Domaine de Montille (DDIR)
Chambolle-Musigny, Louis Jadot (ASHE)

£12.00–£12.50

Volnay les Caillerets, Clos des 60 Ouvrées, Domaine de la Pousse d'Or (TAN)
Corton-Bressandes, Tollot-Beaut (BWC, OWL)

Gevrey-Chambertin, Armand Rousseau (PIP)
Corton, Tollot-Beaut (PIP, OWL)
Corton Renardes, Michel Gaunoux (DDIR)
Pommard 1er Cru Rugiens, Michel Gaunoux (DDIR)
Château Corton-Grancey Grand 1er Cru, Louis Latour (SF, WHIT)
Pommard, Clos de la Commaraine, Jaboulet-Vercherre (WGA)

£12.50–£13.50

Morey St-Denis, Clos de la Roche, Domaine Dujac (DDIR)
Chambertin, Clos de Bèze, Clair Daü (BYR)
Charmes-Chambertin, Dujac (L&W)
Clos de Vougeot, Mongeard-Mugneret (DDIR)
Latricières-Chambertin, Domaine Trapet (BWC, PIP)
Grands-Echézeaux, Mongeard-Mugneret (DDIR)
⋆Gevrey-Chambertin aux Combottes, Domaine Dujac (RH)
Chambolle-Musigny, les Charmes, Clerget (DOL)
Echézeaux, Clerget (DOL)
Corton Grand Cru, Tollot-Beaut (FFW)

£13.50–£14.50

Corton-Grancey, Louis Latour (GH, J&B)
Corton, Clos de la Vigne au Saint, Marcel Amance (MAL)
Volnay, Cuvée Général Muteau, Hospices de Beaune (L&W)
les Echézeaux, Bouchard Père (PD)
Nuits St-Georges les Vaucrains, Domaine Henri Gouges (HHC)
Morey St-Denis, Clos de Tart, Mommessin (BYR)
Clos Vougeot, Georges Roumier (L&W)
Pommard Rugiens, Clerget (ODD)

£14.75–£16.50

Corton, Clos de la Vigne au Saint, Louis Latour (TAN)
Morey St-Denis, Clos St Denis, Domaine Dujac (OWL, RH, VIGN)
Pommard Pezerolles, Domaine de Montille (OWL)

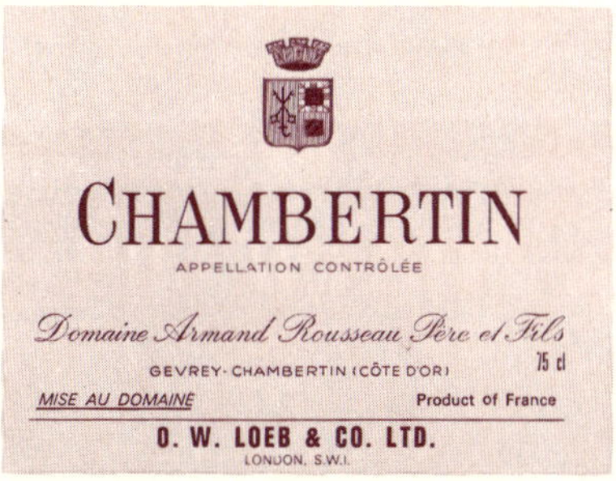

Chambertin, Armand Rousseau (L&W)
Gevrey-Chambertin, Clos St Jacques, Armand Rousseau (OWL, WNRY)
Clos de la Roche, Domaine Dujac (WW)

£16.75–£20.00

Clos Vougeot Grand Cru, Jacques Prieur (TAN)
Chambertin Clos de Bèze, Armand Rousseau (BWC, PIP)
Beaune, Hospices de Beaune, Cuvée Rousseau des Landes (J&B)
Chambertin, Domaine Trapet (BWC, C&B)

Gevrey-Chambertin Clos de Bèze, Armand Rousseau (P&C)
Chambertin Clos de Bèze, Roger d'Esgrigny (WHIT)
Pommard les Rugiens, Domaine de Montille (OWL)
Chambertin Grand Cru, Armand Rousseau (FFW)

c. £60.00

La Tâche, Domaine de la Romanée-Conti (J&B)

1978

£4.75–£5.75

★Hautes Côtes de Nuits, Caves des Hautes Côtes (HT, BWC)
Bourgogne de Marsannay, Clair Daü (HT)
Côte de Beaune-Villages, Chanson (CHAP)

£6.00–£7.00

Fixin, Pierre Gelin (DDIR)
Auxey-Duresses, Bouchard Père (PD)
Savigny-les-Beaune les Lavières, Remoissenet (L&W)
Santenay Maladière, G Prieur (VICT)
Pernand-Vergelesses, Ile de Vergelesses, Ponnelle (PG)

c. £7.35

Gevrey-Chambertin, Mommessin (ECD)

£8.25–£9.00

Volnay, Machard de Gramont (ADN)
Santenay le Passetemps, Prosper Maufoux (BOW)
Beaune 1er Cru, Patriarche (CUL)
Santenay 1er Cru les Gravières, Remoissenet (GH, MAL)
★Chassagne Montrachet, Raoul Clerget (YFW)

£9.00–£9.35

Corton-Bressandes, Jaboulet-Vercherre (WGA)
Beaune 1er Cru les Chouacheux, Machard de Gramont (ADN)
Gevrey-Chambertin, Moillard (ASHE)

£10.00–£11.00

Meursault, Clos de Mazaray, Jacques Prieur (HT)
Chambolle-Musigny, Louis Jadot (JH)
Nuits St-Georges 1er Cru Clos St Marc, Charles Vienot (TAN)
Morey St-Denis 1er Cru, Faiveley (BYR)
Volnay Santenots, Robert et Michel Ampeau (L&W)
Pommard 1er Cru Grands Epenots, Michel Gaunoux (DDIR)
Beaune Theurons, Louis Jadot (L&W)
Gevrey-Chambertin, Camille Giroud (L&W)

£11.00–£12.00

Nuits St-Georges, Boisset (PD)
★Gevrey-Chambertin, Clos du Meix des Ouches, Domaine des Varoilles, Tasteviné (L&W)
Nuits St-Georges 1er Cru les Damodes, Machard de Gramont (ADN)
Savigny-les-Beaune 1er Cru, Louis Latour (FINT)
Morey St-Denis, Clerget (P&C)
Beaune Vignes-Franches, Louis Latour (L&W, BOW, ODD)

£12.00–£13.00

Beaune 1er Cru, Remoissenet (MAL)
Beaune, Hughes et Louis Bétault, Hospices de Beaune, Emile Chandesais (WHIT)
Aloxe-Corton, Tollot-Beau (ADN)
Clos Vougeot, Remoissenet (L&W, MAL)
Corton Maréchaudes, Prince de Mérode (ADN)
Volnay Santenots, Louis Latour (WGA)

£13.00–£14.00

Aloxe Corton 1er Cru, Louis Latour (MAL)

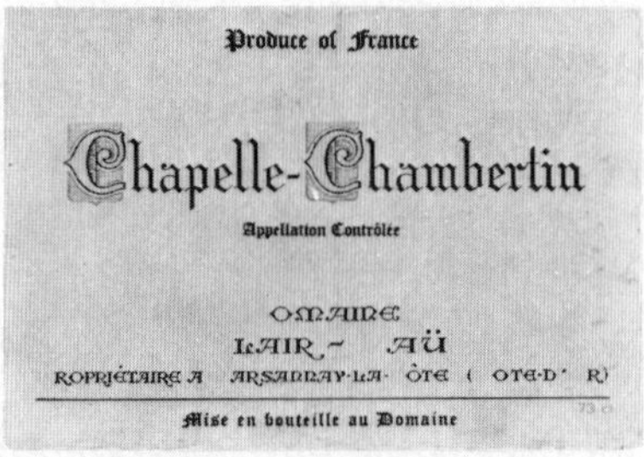

Volnay Santenots, Cuvée Jehan de Massol, Hospices de Beaune, Antonin Rodet (H&B)
Chapelle-Chambertin, Clair Daü (L&W)
Chambolle-Musigny 1er Cru, Joseph Drouhin (ADN)

£14.00–£15.00
★Gevrey-Chambertin les Varoilles, Tasteviné, Domaine des Varoilles (HHC)
Beaune, Clos des Mouches, Drouhin (WILL)
Corton, Tollet-Beaut (VICT, ADN)
Gevrey-Chambertin 1er Cru Clos des Varoilles, Domaine des Varoilles (TAN)
£15.50–£16.00
Chambolle-Musigny les Charmes, Remoissenet (MAL)
Gevrey-Chambertin, Joseph Drouhin (GH)
Mazis-Chambertin, Jean Velard (BOW)
£16.25–£17.25
★Gevrey-Chambertin 1er Cru, Clos St Jacques, Antonin Rodet (H&B)
Volnay Santenots, Cuvée Gauvain, Hospices de Beaune (L&W)
Corton, Bonneau de Martray (H&B)
Pommard, Château de Pommard (MACK)
Gevrey-Chambertin les Combottes, Remoissenet (MAL)
c. £18.00
Château Corton-Grancey, Louis Latour (MAL)
£19.75–£20.00
Chambertin, Clos de la Griotte, Thomas Bassot (BBR)
Latricières-Chambertin, Camus (VICT)
c. £23.00
Vosne Romanée, Louis Latour magnum (BIB)
c. £43.00
Echézeaux, Domaine de la Romanée-Conti (L&W)
c. £66.00
Richebourg, Domaine de la Romanée-Conti (L&W)
c. £68.50
La Tâche, Domaine de la Romanée-Conti (L&W)

1977
£6.75–£8.00
★Côtes de Nuits Villages, Maufoux (J&B)
Volnay 1er Cru En Caillerets, Domaine de la Pousse d'Or (DDIR)
Savigny-les-Beaune Les Guettes, Doudet Naudin (TW)
Savigny-les-Beaune la Dominode, Clair Daü (J&B)
£8.00–£8.50
Corton, Roland Rapet (DDIR)
Nuits St-Georges 1er Cru les Chaignots, Alain Michelot (DDIR)
Nuits St-Georges les Pruliers, Henri Gouges (J&B)
£9.25–£10.25
Gevrey-Chambertin Clos de Fonteny, Clair Daü (J&B)
★Nuits St-Georges, Doudet Naudin (TW)
Chambolle-Musigny, Comte Georges de Vogüé (GH)
c. £11.50
Corton, Bonneau du Martray (DDIR)
c. £17.25
★Musigny, Comte Georges de Vogüé (H&B)
c. £31.50
La Tâche, Domaine de la Romanée Conti (RSV)

1976
£6.50–£7.25
Morey St-Denis, Halgarten (WSOC)
Beaune, Clos des Marconnets, Chanson (JH)
Beaune 1er Cru, Chanson (BYR)
Santenay, Clos des Tavannes, Remoissenet (WSOC)
£8.00–£9.00
Savigny, les Lavières, Remoissenet (MAL)

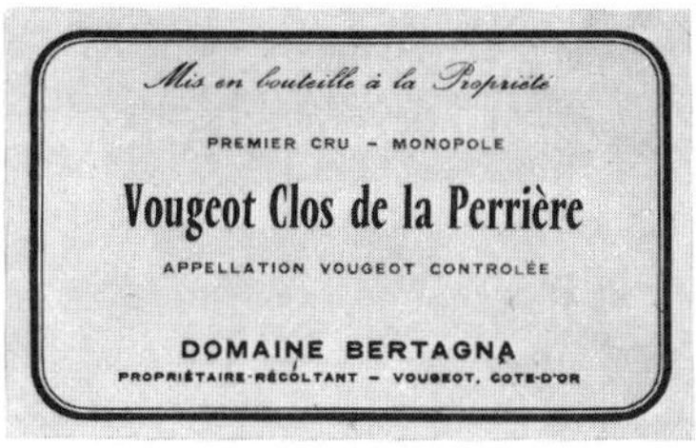

Volnay, Remoissenet (BYR)
Beaune Grèves, Chanson (WHIT)
St-Aubin Rouge, Raoul Clerget (YFW)
Volnay, Chanson (WILL)
Volnay Santenots, Remoissenet (WSOC)
*Volnay, H. Boillot (PG)

£9.25–£10.00

*Vougeot, Clos de la Perrière, Domaine Bertagna (PG, REID, ODD)
*Santenay, Raoul Clerget (YFW)
Fixin, Clos du Chapitre, Domaine Gelin (FINT)
Beaune Grèves, Remoissenet (MAL)
Vougeot 1er Cru, Bertagna (VIGN)
Vosne-Romanée, Genevrières, Charles Noellat (SF)

£10.25–£12.00

Beaune-Marconnets, Bouchard Père et Fils (LADV)
Pommard, Domaine Jean Michelot (JH)
Aloxe-Corton, Louis Latour (C&B)
Beaune, Vignes Franches, Louis Latour (PG)
Griotte-Chambertin, Thomas Bassot (MAL)
Pommard, Clos Micault, Domaine Parent (GH)
Corton-Bressandes, Chandon de Briailles (VIGN)
Nuits St-Geroges 1er Cru les Argillières, Tasteviné, Emile Chandesais (WHIT)
Nuits St-Georges, les Murgers, Prosper Maufoux (BBR)

£12.00–£14.00

Beaune Marconnets, Remoissenet (C&B)
Vougeot 1er Cru, Clerget (P&C)
Nuits St-Georges, les Boudots, Remoissenet (MAL)
Aloxe-Corton, Raoul Clerget (YFW)
Echézeaux, Mongeard-Mugneret (DDIR)
Morey St-Denis, Dujac (L&W, TAN)
Volnay, Clos d'Audignac, Domaine de la Pousse d'Or (DDIR)
Mazis-Chambertin, Armand Rousseau (L&W)

£15.00–£16.75

Gevrey-Chambertin, Clos St Jacques, Clair Daü (J&B)
Grands Echézeaux, Remoissenet (MAL)
Morey St-Denis, Leroy (BWC)
Clos de la Roche, Armand Rousseau (L&W, YFW)
Nuits St-Georges 1er Cru, Château Gris, Lupé-Cholet (FINT)
Gevrey-Chambertin, Clos St-Jacques, Armand Rousseau (L&W)

£19.00–£26.00

Pommard, Château de Pommard (MACK)
Chambertin, Clos de Bèze, Moillard (BBR)
Bonnes-Mares, Moillard (BBR)
Bonnes Mares, Comte Georges de Vogüé (VIGN, MAL)
Richebourg, Maufoux (HBV)

c. £27.50

Château Corton-Grancey Grand 1er Cru, Louis Latour (TAN)

c. £30.00

Echézeaux, Domaine de la Romanée-Conti (RSV, VICT, J&B)

c. £35.00

Romanée St-Vivant, Domaine de la Romanée-Conti (L&W, WILL, YFW)

c. £39.50

Grands Echézeaux, Domaine de la Romanée-Conti (WNRY, YFW)

c. £45.80

Romanée St-Vivant, Cuvée Marey Monge, Domaine de la Romanée-Conti (MWS)

c. £56.00

La Tâche, Domaine de la Romanée-Conti (VICT)

c. £88.00

Romanée-Conti, Domaine de la Romanée-Conti (WILL)

1975

c. £13.50

Corton, Bonneau du Martray (H&B)

1974

c. £7.00

Beaune, Clos de la Mousse, Bouchard Père (PD)

c. £15.00

Morey St-Denis Grand Cru Clos de Tart, Mommessin (TAN)

1973

£6.50–£9.75

Beaune, Clos du Roi, Chanson Père et Fils (TAN)

★Chorey-les-Beaune, Charles Vienot (HUN)
Pernand Ile des Vergelesses, Moillard (VICT)
Beaune, Cuvée Nicolas Rolin, Hospices de Beaune (BBR)
Volnay Taillepieds, Bouchard Père (WSOC)
Gevrey-Chambertin, Clair Daü (DOL)
£11.25–£13.50
Grands Echézeaux, Boisset (P&C)
Bonnes-Mares, Louis Jadot (L&W)
Beaune Perrières, Louis Latour (WGA)
Bonnes Mares, Ponnelle (WILL)
£16.00–£20.00
Chapelle-Chambertin, Louis Latour (WGA)
Beaune, Hospices de Beaune, Cuvée Maurice Drouhin magnum (WSOC)
Le Musigny, Pierre Ponnelle (MWS)

1972
c. £5.00
Pernand-Vergelesses les Vergelesses, Chanson (BAL)
£8.25–£9.75
Beaune, Clos des Mouches, Chanson (WILL)
Beaune Champimonts, Chanson Père et Fils (TAN)
★Beaune Bellisands, Bichot (UNW)
Clos Vougeot, Louis Jadot (RH)
Beaune Grèves, Heritiers Paul Chanson (REID)
Santenay, Clos du Haut Village, Lequin Roussot (BIB)
£10.25–£13.00
Clos de Vougeot Grand Cru, Louis Jadot (CV)
Chambertin, Clos de Bèze, Charles Deroy (MAL)
Corton, Chanson (J&B)
Nuits St-Georges 1er Cru, Pierre Bourée (WNRY)
c. £15.30
Charmes-Chambertin, Joseph Drouhin (ADN)
Clos de Tart, Mommessin (YFW)
c. £18.00
Bonnes Mares, Louis Jadot (HUN)
c. £31.00
Bonnes Mares, Drouhin Laroze (GH)
La Tâche, Domaine de la Romanée-Conti (GH)

1971
c. £12.00
Corton, Charles Vienot (H&D)
£15.50–£22.50
Chambolle-Musigny 1er Cru, Tasteviné, Faiveley (WGA)
Chambolle-Musigny, Charles Vienot (HUN)
★Nuits St-Georges 1er Cru Les Didiers, Cuvée Cabet, Hospices de Nuits (BIB)
Morey St-Denis, Clos de la Roche, Faiveley (WGA)
Grands Echézeaux, Chanson (WILL)
c. £50.60
Echézeaux, Domaine de la Romanée-Conti (GH)
c. £85.00
La Tâche, Domaine de la Romanée-Conti (VIGN)

1970
c. £13.50
Musigny Grand Cru, Jules Regnier (TAN)
c. £16.75
Bonnes Mares, Drouhin Laroze (REID)
Morey St-Denis, Clos de Tart (MWS)

1969
c. £16.50
Beaune, Clos des Fèves, Chanson (WILL)
£25.00–£26.00
Corton-Grancey, Louis Latour (RSV)
Chambolle-Musigny, Pierre Ponnelle (YFW)
Clos de Vougeot, Louis Latour (REID)

1967
c. £31.30
Charmes-Chambertin, Pierre Ponnelle (YFW)
c. £65.00
La Tâche, Domaine de la Romanée-Conti (RSV)

1966
£15.00–£20.00
Beaune Grèves, Remoissenet (REID)

Nuits St-Georges 1er Cru, Tête de Cuvée les St-Georges (BIB)
Nuits St-Georges, Raoul Clerget (YFW)
c. £25.00
Corton-Grancey, Louis Latour (RSV)

1965
c. £25.50
Richebourg, Domaine de la Romanée-Conti (RSV)

1961
£16.00–£18.00
Beaune, Doudet Naudin (VIGN)
Beaune, Clos du Roy, Doudet Naudin (BBR)

1959
c. £38.00
Morey St-Denis, Clos St-Denis, Pierre Ponnelle (YFW)

1955
c. £44.25
Latricières-Chambertin, Pierre Ponnelle (MWS)

1919
c. £450.00
La Romanée-Conti, Domaine de la Romanée-Conti (RSV)

White

1982
£5.50–£7.50
★Meursault, Moreau (JH)
Pernand-Vergelesses Blanc, M. Rollin (BIB)
Meursault, Louis Jadot (BYR, CV, VICT)
Meursault, Bouchard Père (PD)
St-Aubin, Bernard Morey (BWC)
Clos du Cromin, Javillier (ESV)
★Puligny-Montrachet, Clos de la Garenne, Duc de Magenta (HHC)
£7.50–£8.75
★Meursault, J. Germain (H&B)
Chassagne-Montrachet les Caillerets, Jean-Marc Morey (BWC)
Chassagne-Montrachet, J. N. Gagnard (J&B)
£21.00–£23.00
Bâtard-Montrachet, Albert Morey (PIP)
Chevalier-Montrachet Grand Cru les Demoiselles, Louis Jadot (FFW)
c. £29.50
Le Montrachet Grand Cru, Louis Jadot (FFW)

1981
£4.25–£5.25
Hautes Côtes de Beaune Blanc, Guillemard-Dupont (HUN)
St-Aubin 1er Cru, Thomas Père & Fils (DDIR)
★Mâcon-Villages Clessé, Thevenet-Wicart (HHC)
£6.25–£7.00
★St-Aubin, Albert Morey (HT)
Meursault, Pierre Olivier (ASHE)
Meursault, Jean Germain (DAV)
Pernand-Vergelesses, Laleur-Piot (DDIR)
£7.00–£8.00
Puligny Montrachet, Mommessin (ECD)
Chassagne-Montrachet, Blain-Gagnard (DDIR)
Meursault, Domaine Pouhin-Seurre (MAL)
Meursault, Michelot-Buisson (BWC, PIP)
£8.00–£9.00
Chassagne-Montrachet les Ruchottes, Bachelet Ramonet Père et Fils (C&B)
Chassagne-Montrachet, Michel Niellon (OWL)
★Chassagne-Montrachet, la Grande Montagne, Bachelet Ramonet Père et Fils (C&B)
Chassagne-Montrachet, Ramonet-Prudhon (LADV)
£9.00–£9.50
Puligny-Montrachet 1er Cru les Folatières, René Monnier (DDIR)
Puligny-Montrachet, Labouré-Roi (ESV)
Chassagne-Montrachet, Etienne Sauzet (L&W)
Meursault la Pièce sous le Bois, Ampeau (L&W)
Puligny-Montrachet, Etienne Sauzet (L&W, OWL)
Chassagne-Montrachet les Caillerets, Albert Morey (PIP)
£9.50–£10.00
Chassagne-Montrachet les Grandes Ruchottes, Pillot (J&B)
Chassagne-Montrachet les Baudines, Bernard Morey (DOL)
★Puligny-Montrachet, Leflaive (ADN, L&W, TAN)
Puligny-Montrachet les Referts, Louis Jadot (JH)

£10.25–£11.25
Puligny-Montrachet Truffières, Etienne Sauzet (WW, WSOC, TAN)
Chassagne-Montrachet la Romanée, Moillard (VICT)
Puligny-Montrachet, Bouchard Père (PD)
Puligny-Montrachet les Folatières, Robert Boisson-Morey (BWC)
Puligny-Montrachet Champ-Canet, Etienne Sauzet (WSOC)
Chassagne-Montrachet les Embrazées, Albert Morey (HT)

£11.25–£11.75
Puligny-Montrachet les Referts, Etienne Sauzet (OWL, TAN)
Puligny-Montrachet Combettes, Etienne Sauzet (L&W, TAN)
Beaune, Clos des Mouches, Joseph Drouhin (ADN, GH)
Puligny-Montrachet Clavoillon, Leflaive (ADN)
Bienvenues-Bâtard-Montrachet, Bachelet Ramonet Père et Fils (C&B)
Puligny-Montrachet, les Folatières, Louis Latour (HT, J&B)
£13.25–£15.00
Puligny-Montrachet Combettes, Leflaive (ADN)
Puligny-Montrachet Pucelles, Leflaive (C&B)
Bienvenues-Bâtard-Montrachet, Leflaive (ADN, TAN, C&B)
Corton-Charlemagne, Marquis de Laguiche (BIB)
£15.00–£17.50
Chevalier-Montrachet, Michel Niellon (OWL)
Bâtard-Montrachet, Leflaive (L&W, ADN, C&B)
Bienvenues-Bâtard-Montrachet, Louis Latour (WGA)
Corton-Charlemagne, Ancient Domaine des Comtes de Grancey (HT)
Chevalier-Montrachet, Leflaive (L&W)
£18.00–£21.25
Corton-Charlemagne, Louis Latour (BWC, REID)
Chevalier-Montrachet, Joseph Drouhin (YFW)

Webster's is an annual publication. We welcome suggestions for next year's edition.

Bâtard-Montrachet, Albert Morey (WNRY)
Bâtard-Montrachet, Joseph Drouhin (MAL)
c. £30.00
Le Montrachet, Domaine Jacques Prieur (MAL)
c. £36.00
Le Montrachet, Marquis de Laguiche, Joseph Drouhin (YFW)

1980
£4.50–£5.00
Auxey-Duresses, Duc de Magenta (DDIR, HHC)
St-Aubin, Thomas Père & Fils (DDIR)
St-Romain, René Thévenin-Monthélie (DDIR)
£6.25–£8.25
Chassagne-Montrachet, Albert Morey (DDIR)
Puligny-Montrachet 1er Cru Clos de la Garenne, Duc de Magenta (DDIR)
Chassagne-Montrachet, Javillier (L&W, DOL)
Puligny-Montrachet, Etienne Sauzet (BWC, P&C)
★Meursault, Henri Germain (TAN)
Chassagne-Montrachet 1er Cru Caillerets, Delagrange-Bachelet (DDIR)
Santenay Blanc, Marcel Amance (MAL)
£9.00–£10.00
Meursault Charmes, Abel Garnier (OWL)
★Chassagne-Montrachet La Boudriotte, Gagnard-Delagrange (HHC)
Chassagne-Montrachet, Etienne Sauzet (TAN)
Puligny-Montrachet, Leflaive (BIB, VIGN)
Chassagne-Montrachet, Duc de Magenta (ODD)
£10.25–£12.50
Meursault Santenots, Marquis d'Angerville (C&B)
Chassagne-Montrachet, Marquis de Laguiche (MAL)
Puligny-Montrachet les Folatières, Bouchard Père & Fils (WGA)

Puligny-Montrachet 1er Cru Clavoillons, Domaine Leflaive (C&B, GH)
Puligny-Montrachet les Combettes, Etienne Sauzet (PIP, OWL)
Puligny-Montrachet la Truffière, Etienne Sauzet (OWL)
Puligny-Montrachet, Clos de la Garenne, Duc de Magenta (BAL)

£13.50–£15.25

Puligny-Montrachet les Combettes, Leflaive (C&B)
Corton-Charlemagne, Tollot-Beaut (OWL, SF)
Criots-Bâtard-Montrachet, Blain-Gagnard (DDIR)
Corton-Charlemagne, Ancien Domaine des Comtes de Grancey, Louis Latour (SF)

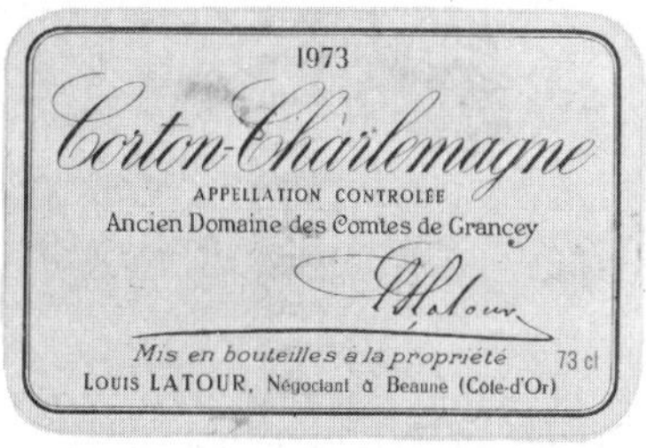

Corton-Charlemagne, Domaine Maurice Chapuis (MAL)

£15.75–£17.50

Bâtard-Montrachet, Albert Morey (DOL)
Corton-Charlemagne, Bonneau du Martray (H&B)
Puligny-Montrachet Pucelles, Leflaive (BBR)
Bâtard-Montrachet, Etienne Sauzet (OWL)

£20.00–£22.00

Bienvenues-Bâtard-Montrachet, Leflaive (GH)
Bâtard-Montrachet, Leflaive (BBR)

1979

£6.25–£7.25

Meursault, Jean Germain (LHV)
★St-Aubin, M. Amance (J&B)
★Côte de Beaune la Grande Chatelaine, Machard de Gramont (STWC)
★Meursault Clos du Château, Domaine du Château de Meursault, Patriarche (WAIT, CUL)
Meursault Meix Chavaux, Guy Roulot (DDIR)
Meursault les Luchets, Guy Roulot (DDIR)
Chassagne-Montrachet, Delagrange-Bachelet (DDIR)

£7.25–£8.00

Meursault 1er Cru, Jean Germain (BYR)
Meursault, Clos du Cromin, Domaine Michelot (DDIR)

Meursault, Clos de la Barre, Comte Lafon (DDIR)
Meursault, Cuvée Loppin, Hospices de Beaune (P&C)
Meursault 1er Cru Goutte d'Or, Comte Lafon (DDIR)
Meursault les Tessons, Clos de Mon Plaisir, Guy Roulot (DDIR)
Meursault les Casse Têtes, Jean Germain (BYR)

£8.25–£9.25

Puligny-Montrachet, Etienne Sauzet (SF)
Santenay, Clos des Gravières, Prosper Maufoux (BOW)
Meursault, Sous le Dos d'Ane, Bouchard Père et Fils (J&B)
Chassagne-Montrachet, Clos de Chapelle, Duc de Magenta (BYR)
Chassagne-Montrachet, Domaine Roland Thévenin (MAL)
Meursault 1er Cru Perrières, Guy Roulot (DDIR)
Meursault, Louis Latour (H&D, HT, RACK)
Meursault Charmes 1er Cru, Domaine des Comtes Lafon (ADN)

£9.75–£11.00

Meursault Goutte d'Or, Abel Garnier (OWL)
Meursault Blagny, Louis Latour (DAV, WSOC, TW)
Puligny-Montrachet 1er Cru, Clos de la Mouchère, H Boillot (SF)
★Meursault Charmes, Ampeau (L&W)
★Chassagne-Montrachet, Louis Latour (H&D)
Meursault Charmes, Domaine des Comtes Lafon (TAN)

⋆Chassagne Montrachet Blanc, Raoul Clerget (YFW)
Puligny-Montrachet, Champ Canet, Etienne Sauzet (OWL, SR)
Puligny-Montrachet, Clos de la Garenne, Duc de Magenta (VIGN)

£11.25–£12.50

Meursault Genevrières, Michelot-Buisson (PIP)
Puligny-Montrachet les Folatières, Thévenin (ODD)
Meursault, Cuvée Humblot, Hospices de Beaune, James Battault (MAL)
⋆Puligny-Montrachet Cavoillons, Leflaive (L&W, C&B)
Meursault Genevrières, Louis Latour (MAL, OWL)

Corton-Charlemagne, Domaine du Château de Beaune, Bouchard Père & Fils (WGA)
⋆Corton-Charlemagne, Bonneau du Martray (DDIR, C&B, VIGN)
Puligny-Montrachet les Folatières, Domaine du Château de Puligny-Montrachet, Thévenin (TAN)

£13.75–£15.25

⋆Puligny-Montrachet Pucelles, Leflaive (L&W)
Bâtard-Montrachet, Blain-Gagnard (DDIR)
Puligny-Montrachet Pucelles, Joseph Drouhin (L&W)
Corton-Charlemagne, Tollot Beaut (GH)
Corton-Charlemagne, Louis Latour (BYR, WGA, TAN)
Château Corton-Grancey Grand 1er Cru, Louis Latour (RACK)

£16.50–£18.25

Corton-Charlemagne, Louis Jadot (L&W)
Bâtard-Montrachet, Louis Latour (MAL, J&B, FINT)
Chevalier-Montrachet, Leflaive (L&W)

c. £42.30

Le Montrachet, Gagnard-Delagrange (HHC)

1978

£6.50–£9.00

Meursault les Forges, G Prieur (VICT)
⋆Meursault, Bouchard Père et Fils (J&B)
St-Aubin les Frionnes, Jean Velard (BOW)

⋆Auxey-Duresses, Louis Latour (MAL, REID)
Chassagne-Montrachet, Jean Germain (VIGN)
Meursault les Tillets, P Javillier (VIGN)

£9.00–£11.00

Meursault Charmes 1er Cru, Domaine des Comtes Lafon (ADN)
Meursault, Clos de Mazeray, J. Prieur (J&B)
Clos du Château, Domaine du Château de Meursault (QR)
Meursault, Remoissenet (MAL)
Chassagne-Montrachet, les Champs Gains, Albert Morey (HT)

£11.00–£13.25

Puligny-Montrachet, les Folatières, Remoissenet (MAL)
Meursault, Louis Latour (BBR)
Puligny-Montrachet, Clos de la Garenne, Domaine du Château de Puligny-Montrachet (SR)
Puligny-Montrachet, Domaine du Château de Puligny-Montrachet (VIGN)
Meursault-Blagny, Louis Latour (HT, TAN)
Puligny-Montrachet les Perrières, Etienne Sauzet (BWC)
Chassagne-Montrachet, Marquis de Laguiche (MWS)

£14.50–£17.75

Meursault Charmes 1er Cru, Cuvée de Bahèzre de Lanlay, Hospices de Beaune (L&W)
Corton-Charlemagne, Remoissenet (WSOC, MAL)
Corton-Charlemagne, Bonneau du Martray (QR)

c. £38.00

Montrachet, Domaine des Comtes Lafon (ADN, TAN)

1977

c. £7.40

Meursault 1er Cru Goutte d'Or, Comte Lafon (DDIR)

£13.50–£15.50

Corton-Charlemagne, Jules Belin (FINT)
Corton-Charlemagne, Louis Latour (ADN)

1975
£11.50–£12.75
Meursault Genevrières, Hospices de Beaune, Patriarche (CUL)
Corton-Charlemagne, Bonneau du Martray (H&B)
Chevalier-Montrachet, Bouchard Père (PD)
1976
c. £13.50
Meursault Perrières, Ampeau (L&W)
£16.00–£18.50
Corton-Charlemagne, Remoissenet (MAL)
Bâtard-Montrachet, Raoul Clerget (YFW)
Corton-Charlemagne, Bonneau du Martray (ADN)
c. £27.00
Le Montrachet, Domaine du Baron Thénard (MAL)
1974
c. £7.70
Meursault, Pontinet-Ampeau (BIB)
1973
c. £5.85
Santenay, les Gravières, Charles Deroy (MAL)
£10.25–£12.25
Puligny-Montrachet, Chanson (ADN)
Puligny-Montrachet les Folatières, Remoissenet (MAL)
c. £19.65
Chevalier-Montrachet, Remoissenet (MAL)
1972
£11.75–£13.75
Meursault Genevrières, Remoissenet (MAL)
Meursault Charmes, Domaine de Bahèzre de Lanlay, Hospices de Beaune (YFW)
1945
c. £35.00
Meursault Charmes, Hospices de Beaune (VIGN)

Rosé

1979
c. £3.90
Rosé de Marsannay, Clair-Daü (DDIR, DOL, CV)

Troubled Brilliance

The Côte d'Or is terribly confused right now, and the short-term prospect is wretched for some growers and merchants. The years of greed and disinterest have taken their toll both in the vineyard and the counting-house. Yet burgundy is tailor-made for success in a modern market thirsty for the hand-crafted, the individual, and the particular.

Burgundy must re-examine very carefully its objective as a wine region. Is it to produce a large amount of adequate red wine, sporting famous names, yet giving precious little in terms of personality? If so, fine; the growers should plant the new high-cropping Pinot Noir strains, and perhaps try to re-introduce the Gamay. But it shouldn't be expected that anyone will pay a higher price than they would for Beaujolais Villages. And cast an eye further north, to the Yonne, another tricky northern vineyard area, which used to have 10 times the acreage it has now. Except for Chablis, which established a reputation for first class dry whites, they made cheap, dull wine. They did OK, but only until people discovered that the south of France and the Rhône could do it cheaper and better. There are sheep grazing on the vineyards now.

No, what Burgundy *has* to do is to fcllow the lead of an increasing number of growers, and head back up the quality path. They have a desirable product which many have tried, and failed to duplicate, and while they produce some of the world's greatest white wines from the Chardonnay grape, the flame of great red burgundy is still alight, despite its annual drenching in the flood of mediocrity. Vine types must be chosen for quality, the right root stocks and fertilizers must be more carefully used, pruning must be honest and quality-orientated, sugaring and acidifying of musts should only be used when necessary, not out of habit, new oak barrels, or at least clean ones, must be re-introduced, and bottling should be sterile and at the wine's rather than the grower's convenience. Burgundy has so much to offer, it is painful to see how little of its potential is being realised. One more thing. When that quality returns, we'll pay the asking price.

CÔTE CHALONNAISE

THE COST OF A BOTTLE

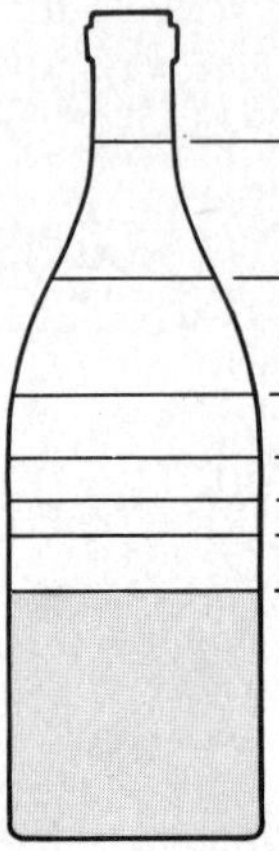

1983 Rully	**£4.90**
VAT	0.64
Merchant mark-up	0.84
Duty	0.68
Distribution	0.16
Shipping	0.08
Bottling	0.30
Wine	2.20

The Côte Chalonnaise has got a real identity problem. Where is it, for a start? Is it next door to Santenay, just south of the Côte d'Or? Or is it the northern tip of the Mâconnais? Is it the Côte Chalonnaise, or is it the Région de Mercurey? And is all this confusion the reason we hardly ever see it over here? That, and various other reasons.

If the Chalonnaise is an extension to any region it is to the Côte de Beaune, since the Côte de Beaune stops opposite Chagny and the Côte Chalonnaise starts there. But as the ordered vineyards of Beaune swing away and dwindle to the west, the higgledy-piggledy vineyards of the Chalonnaise hiccough and splutter into life as a patchwork of south- and east-facing outcrops, with no overall symmetry. This is the feeling in the region too; rather than a 'je suis bourguignon' identification, they give you a feeling of 'je suis de Rully', or 'je suis de Mercurey'. An attempt was made last year to get a promotional body going, but it immediately foundered on the ingrained suspicion and envy of one grower against another, one village against the next. And all growers against a quasi-official body.

Yet one can give a generalized overview on Chalonnaise wines. The reds in general are a little paler than the proper Côte de Beaune reds (note the word 'proper'). In cooler years they may lack a little of the dry, closed depth which many good Côte d'Or wine makers can create to give class to their 'off' vintages, but in anything approaching a warm year, the wines have a light, lingering, cherry Pinot flavour, quite high acidity and fairly low tannin. There are a few growers, particularly Baron Thénard in Givry, and de Suremain and Juillot in Mercurey who make deeper wines, but this lighter Rully-style red is more typical of the region.

The whites have one star which cannot be overshadowed by the famous Côte d'Or to the north. The village of Bouzeron makes the finest Aligoté in all France, and now has its own appellation to show for its pains. The vines are frequently old – more crucial for Aligoté than for most other whites – and the characteristic buttermilk soap nose is followed by a very dry, slightly lemony, pepper-sharp wine, too good to mix with cassis. However, it's Chardonnay which predominates, and usually it is particularly light and clean-tasting. This is most marked in Montagny, where the wine is so dry and stony that one longs for a little oak influence to fatten out the wine. Sadly, small oak-barrels are very much the exception for Chalonnaise whites, but, as one grower said, 'It's me who is the traditionalist, my father the modernist. He always vinified in (concrete) *cuves,* I use wood. He's 50, I'm 25. It should be the other way round. One must go towards oak, yet oak is the traditional method.'

Finally, the sparkling Bourgogne whites of the Chalonnaise are Burgundy's best, basing their style on slightly green Chardonnay and Aligoté grapes, and producing simple, slightly tart fizz – which is excellent for mixing with cassis.

Comparison of prices for Côte Chalonnaise and Côte d'Or				
	Côte Chalonnaise		Côte d'Or	
	Rully	Mercurey	Volnay	Nuits St-Georges
1970	—	—	21/5	22/3
1973	£1.98	£1.62	£1.81	£2.05
1974/75	£2.04	£1.85	£1.88	£1.85
1980	£3.50	£4.75	£5.95	£8.50
1982	£4.50	£5.25	£7.50	£9.50
1984	£4.69	£5.50	£8.00	£10.00

Source: Peter Dominic

Côte Chalonnaise reds are still holding out as pretty good-value burgundy, since their names aren't familiar enough to compete with the Côte d'Or. But it wasn't always so. On Peter Dominic's 1973 list Rully cost £1.98, while Volnay cost £1.81 and Nuits St-Georges was £2.05. By 1975, while the Rully had risen to £2.04, Volnay was at £1.88 and Nuits St-Georges was £1.85. The reason is that in 1975 the trade was still clearing its stocks of pre-EEC, non-appellation wine. By 1980 the true prices were biting. Rully was £3.50, while Volnay had climbed to £5.95 and Nuits St-Georges had rocketed to £8.50. The 1984 figures show this general ratio of Chalonnaise to Côte d'Or is being maintained.

Webster's is an annual publication. We welcome suggestions for next year's edition.

PRICE GUIDE

Red

1983
c. £4.70
Montagny 1er Cru, Caves des Vignerons de Buxy (IMB)

1982
c. £6.50
Rully, Clos de Bellecroix (CDM)

1981
£4.50–£5.00
★Rully, Tasteviné (JH)
★Rully, Domaine de la Renarde, Délorme (SF, HT)
Rully, Andre Délorme (WNRY)

1980
£4.00–£4.50
Bourgogne la Digoine, A. et P. de Villaine (DDIR)
Givry, Jean Chofflet (DDIR)
£5.25–£6.50
Rully 1er Cru les Clouds, H&P Jacqueson (DDIR)
Mercurey, Sazenay, Hugues de Suremain (DDIR)
Mercurey, Clos des Barraults, Michel Juillot (DDIR)
c. £8.00
Mercurey, Clos des Barraults, Michel Juillot (WW)

1979
£3.50–£4.50
★Rully, Domaine de la Renarde, Délorme (GH, VIGN, HBV, TAN)
Rully, Varot Rouge, Délorme (PD, H&D)
Givry, Clos du Cellier aux Moines, Délorme (HBV, WNRY)
£5.00–£6.00
★Mercurey, A. Rodet (PG, CHAP)
Mercurey, Michel Juillot (DDIR)
Mercurey, Clos l'Evêque, Michel Juillot (DDIR)
Mercurey Rouge, Domaine de la Renarde (P&C)

Mercurey, Château Philippe le Hardi, Compagnie des Vins d'Autrefois (LADV)

c. £7.00

Santenay 1er Cru, Grand Clos Rousseau, Albert Morey (HT)

c. £8.50

Mercurey, Louis Latour (TAN)

1978

c. £3.50

Bourgogne Passe-Touts-Grains, Vignerons de Buxy (CV)

£5.50–£6.50

★Rully, Clos de Bellecroix, Domaine de la Folie (RH, CV)

Rully, Domaine de la Renarde, Délorme (L&W, WSOC, ADN)

Givry, Roland Dagneau (PIP)

Mercurey, Domaine de la Renarde, Délorme (L&W)

Givry, Baron Thénard (WSOC)

c. £7.00

Rully Rouge, Pierre Cogny (TAN)

Mercurey Myglands, Domaine Faiveley (GH)

c. £9.50

Santenay, Gravières (WSOC)

1976

c. £5.75

Givrey, le Préferé du Roi Henry IV, Baron Thénard (H&D)

1972

c. £5.20

Rully, Domaine de la Renarde, Délorme (ADN)

White

1982

£4.25–£5.25

Bourgogne Aligoté, Cave Co-operative de Buxy (CDM)

Montagny 1er Cru, Cave de Buxy (BIB)

★Bourgogne Blanc, les Clous, Bouzeron, de Villaine (L&W)

Mercurey Blanc, Michel Juillot (DDIR)

Rully, Clos Saint Jacques, Domaine de la Folie (DDIR, CDM)

Montagny, Louis Latour (SF)

Bourgogne Aligoté de Bouzeron, A. et P. de Villaine (C&B)

1981

£3.75–£4.50

Bourgogne Aligoté Bouzeron, A. et P. de Villaine (DDIR, BWC)

Montagny 1er Cru, Cave du Buxy (DAV, ASHE, LADV)

£4.75–£5.75

Givry Blanc, Domaine Baron Thénard (H&D)

Bourgogne Blanc, les Clous, Bouzeron, de Villaine (MAL)

Rully Varot, Domaine de la Renarde, Délorme (WSOC, SF)

Rully 1er Cru, Robert de Suremain (DDIR)

Montagny, Louis Latour (BIB, QR, HT, BWC)

Montagny, Bernard Michel (CDM)

Mercurey Blanc, Michel Juillot (DDIR)

£6.25–£6.75

Rully 1er Cru, Château Monthélie (L&W)

Montagny, Tête de Cuvée, Louis Latour (WGA)

Rully, Domaine de la Folie, Clos St-Jacques, Noël-Bouton (FFW)

1980

c. £3.80

Montagny 1er Cru, les Coeres, Bernard Michel (DDIR)

c. £5.00

★Rully Varot, Domaine de la Renarde, Délorme (HBV)

Montagny, Louis Latour (CHAP)

1979

c. £3.90

Rully Varot, Domaine de la Rénarde, Délorme (GH, H&D)

£4.75–£5.50

Montagny 1er Cru, Cave de Buxy (SR)

Givry Blanc, Roland Dagneau (PIP)

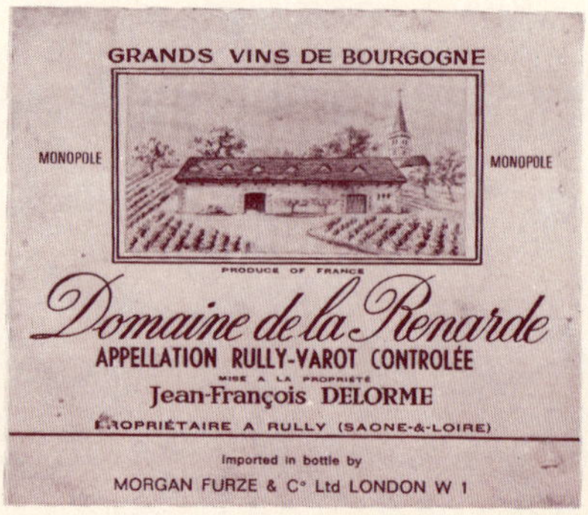

Montagny, Louis Latour (RACK)
Rully 1er Cru Margote, René Brelière (DDIR)
Montagny, Giroud, Tasteviné (L&W)
£6.25–£6.75
⋆Rully Blanc, P. Cogny (ADN, TAN)
Montagny, Louis Latour (FINT)
Montagny, Château de Davenay (FINT)

1978
c. £5.80
Rully Blanc, Meulien Pigneret (PD)
c. £6.60
⋆Rully, Pierre Cogny (L&W)

1977
c. £5.30
Montagny, Château de Davenay, Moillard (C&B)

Rare but Red

There is an air of optimism in a good deal of the Côte Chalonnaise, but by no means everywhere. The Chalonnaise reds and whites, in a time of frantic demand and high prices for the wines of the Côte d'Or, have been projecting themselves as the poor man's burgundy – real Pinot Noir and Chardonnay flavours for a good deal less than the going price in Puligny or Nuits. Well, they were certainly a good deal cheaper than the big guns of the famous villages, but by the time one got to Monthélie, St-Aubin, or Côte de Beaune-Villages, there wasn't a lot in it, and, quite rightly, they were more expensive than the Hautes-Côtes or the regional appellations. So they should have been; they were better wines. Now, the rush for burgundy has slowed to a casual amble, prices have tumbled accordingly. Though it may not show on négociants' lists, it shows from the growers' receipts, and many 1982 Côte d'Or prices in 1984 are as much as 50 per cent down, which means that Côte Chalonnaise wines no longer have a price advantage.

As with the rest of Burgundy, there is very real concern at the basic level, but good reason for optimism at the level of the committed grower and the wine maker who intends to produce personalized wines of quality. The village of Mercurey has increased its production by 666,000 bottles in the last 15 years, and all around Rully there is considerable evidence of undergrowth and trees being beaten back and replaced by vineyards on the well-exposed sites. Take note. The expansion is on hillslopes, not the flatlands. Find a red wine vineyard in the Chalonnaise and you will find a hillslope.

The quality of Rully white is particularly good, and the world demand for good light Chardonnay ought to keep the dollars rolling in. Givry isn't finding it easy because the town of Chalon-sur-Saône is a little too close for comfort and rather likes the idea of the vineyards as building plots. At the prices offered, a good few have disappeared, but the reaction of some quality-first growers is to plant more in defiance. Since Givry is fine wine, it may start to increase in price, but if we don't pay that price, they'll build semis.

MÂCONNAIS

If you're a Burgundian wine grower, this is where you want to live. Not in the crowded Grand Cru acres of Chambertin and Musigny, not even in the white wine meccas of Puligny and Meursault. No, you want to up sticks and use your life savings to bid for any land you can lay your hands on in the villages of Chaintré, Vergisson, Solutré - and Fuissé. Because it's here that you can start producing liquid gold rather than wine.

This is the home of Poolly Foos. Well, I know that sounds a bit like the name of a mid-Europen dress designer, but go into any marginally swish restaurant from Cape Cod to San Francisco Bay, and if you want to buy instant sophistication and an obsequious bow from the wine waiter, you must steel yourself to perpetrate one of the more bizarre mispronunciations which afflicts the French vineyards - and say 'I'll have the Poolly Foos.' You could say 'I'll have the Pwee Fweesay' (that looks even sillier), but it wouldn't have nearly the effect, and you'd end up having to order by the number on the wine list.

THE COST OF A BOTTLE

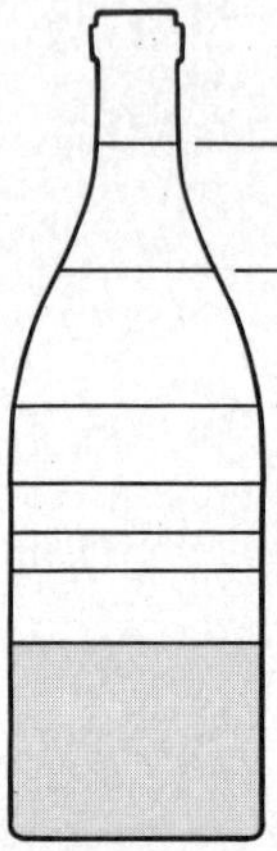

Mâcon-Prissé	**£3.70**
VAT	0.48
Merchant mark-up	0.64
Duty	0.68
Distribution	0.16
Shipping	0.08
Bottling	0.30
Wine	1.36

Pouilly-Fuissé (for it is he), and its dramatic success in America has quite distorted the Mâconnais scene, but at least it has brought a central core of prosperity to an area which is frequently struggling to find a market for its wines. For this is not an area of world famous names and lines of drinkers on bended knee - except, of course, for Pouilly-Fuissé. It is an area of large swathes of producers of fairly average red and white,

Vintage Table

All the good Mâconnais wines are delicious young, through top Pouilly-Fuissé can take several years' age. There is a wide variation between good and bad producers in Mâcon, and the cheapest bottle on the high street shelf is rarely a bargain.

***1983** Brilliant or horrid. The good Pouilly wines (Fuissé, Vinzelles, Loché and Saint Veran) are tremendous; balanced, exciting, creamy Chardonnay. But a hot autumn unbalanced many producers' wines.

1982 Some very attractive soft, rather fat wines, but too often the fat got the better of the balance. Again a hot autumn meant fermentation and volatile acidity problems. Drink up, don't keep.

***1981** A tiny harvest, but the wines which did appear are much better balanced than the Côte d'Or whites, and had good fruit to back up the quite intense flavour. Worth trying if you see a bottle.

with the co-ops and the négociants largely controlling the trade. Curiously, although the wine growers are dealing with the most magic name in white wine, Chardonnay, and though they have every right to proclaim proudly that their wine is 'white burgundy', that wine is not selling. At the moment Mâcon Blanc is suffering from the same *déclassé* reputation as Bordeaux Blanc on the other side of France.

There was a record-breaking amount of white wine made in 1982 - over 400 per cent up on the small 1981 crop - and 1983 produced three times the 1981, but the market still shows a price differential of 1:3 between basic Mâcon and Pouilly-Fuissé, even at négociant blend level. At the level of the top estates, the ratio is more like 1:5. Sadly, the quality of a lot of basic Mâcon is particularly dull; dirty, sulphurous, unbalanced wines give the area an understandable, but quite unnecessary bad name.

This is a pity, because the Mâconnais is one of the few areas where the co-operative movement sets a high tone for production standards, and all the major co-ops, led by villages like Prissé and Viré, are capable of high quality, characterful Chardonnay. One can only presume that the basic Mâcon Blanc and 'Villages' wines have become a traded commodity where price is all. But they possess an invaluable asset - the Chardonnay grape in a Chardonnay-mad world. They shouldn't waste it. In the meantime, the best value is in the middle-ranking ACs: wines like Mâcon-Viré/Lugny/Clessé, and the sub-Pouilly-Fuissé style of St-Véran, preferably from a single grower, but since these are hard to find, from the top co-ops, or from a négociant like Georges Duboeuf who specialises in the area. These will only be a few francs more than the basic Mâcon, but have far more flavour and style. One more thing. Despite all this talk of white, half of Mâcon is red! It's not expensive, but then, with Beaujolais setting the pace just to the south, these Gamay-based wines always seem a little stringy and raw and short on perfume.

PRICE GUIDE

White

Non-vintage
£3.75–£5.00
Mâcon Blanc (VICT)
*St-Véran, Cave de Charnay (STWC)
Le Piat de Mâcon-Viré (UNW)

1983
£5.50–£7.25
St-Véran, Corsin (IMB)
Pouilly-Fuissé, Domaine de l'Arillière (IMB)

1982
£3.00–£4.00
*Mâcon Blanc Villages, Mignot (WAIT)
Mâcon-Prissé, Georges Duboeuf (BWC)
Mâcon Villages, Georges Duboeuf (PIP)
*Mâcon Villages (JH)
St-Véran, Domaine St-Martin, Georges Duboeuf (BWC, PIP)
£4.00–£4.50
*Mâcon Villages Blanc, les Donzelles, Cave Co-operative de Viré (L&W)
Mâcon-Viré, Andre Bonhomme (DDIR)
Mâcon-Lugny les Genièvres, Louis Latour (PG, SF, DAV, SR, ASHE, GH, CUL, P&C, TAN, TW, YFW)
Mâcon-Clessé, Jean Thevenet (WW)
Mâcon Villages, Pierre Ferraud (CDM)
*Mâcon-Viré, Louis Jadot (RH)
£4.50–£5.25
*Mâcon-Lugny les Genièvres, Louis Latour (H&D, HT)
*St-Véran, Joseph Corsin (RH, CHAP, CDM, MART)

Pouilly-Fuissé, Loron (CHAP, PG)
Le Piat de Mâcon-Viré, Piat (PD)
Mâcon-Viré, Clos du Chapitre, Dépagneux (WSOC)
Pouilly-Fuissé, Georges Duboeuf (BWC, DAV)
★Mâcon Villages Blanc, Louis Latour (WGA)
★Mâcon-Clessé, Thevenet-Wicart (J&B)
★Pouilly-Fuissé (JH)

c. £7.25

Pouilly-Fuissé, Corsin (CDM, MART)

c. £10.30

Pouilly-Fuissé, Vieilles Vignes, Château Fuissé (L&W)

1981

£4.00–£4.75

Mâcon-Lugny les Genièvres, Louis Latour (BBR, BAL, FINT)
St-Véran, Georges Duboeuf (BYR)
★Mâcon Villages Chardonnay, Talmard (TAN)
★Mâcon Villages, Domaine de la Bon Gran, J. Thevenet (ADN)
Mâcon-Lugny les Genièvres, Louis Latour (RACK)

c. £8.50

★Pouilly-Fuissé, Château Fuissé (L&W)
Pouilly-Fuissé, Château Fuissé, Marcel Vincent (DOL)

1980

c. £3.25

Mâcon-Uchizy, P. et P. Talmard (DDIR)

£6.25–£7.50

Pouilly-Fuissé, Château Fuissé, Marcel Vincent (DDIR)
Pouilly-Fuissé, Château Fuissé, Vieilles Vignes, Marcel Vincent (DDIR)

1979

c. £6.00

Mâcon-Viré, Clos du Chapitre, Jacques Dépagneux (OWL)

c. £8.00

Pouilly-Fuissé, Château Fuissé (ADN)

1978

£5.75–£6.50

Pouilly-Fuissé, Duchamp Gravier (ADN)
Mâcon-Lugny les Genièvres, Louis Latour (BBR)
Pouilly-Fuissé, Domaine de l'Arillière (DDIR, RH, L&W, HUN)

UNFULFILLED PROMISE

The future for the Mâconnais is distorted by the continuing American love affair with Pouilly-Fuissé. The US, with a Herculean dollar, has swooped down on its favourite honeypot once more. The 1982 vintage of Pouilly-Fuissé sold fast and went up by 50 per cent in price during the year. The 1983 vintage opened at this increased price, and within a couple of months prices had gone up another 33 per cent – and there wasn't a bottle to be had.

Happily, many growers are now benefitting from this, whereas it was traditionally the négociants who used to take 75 per cent of the crop. New wood is appearing in the cellars of the better growers, and when you tap the casks and say 'your négociant will be happy to see you investing in new wood', the grower will snort and point at the tanks – *that's* the négoce wine; the new wooden barrels are for the wine going under *his* label from now on. Although we won't be drinking much Pouilly-Fuissé here, we should see more of the lesser appellations, and St-Véran in particular is worth trying. One only has to try the 1982 from the Prissé Co-op or the 1983 from Duboeuf to see the delicious soft honey style at its best. And prices are very good. In basic Mâcon there is a trend for growers to switch to red (just as in Bordeaux) because it's easier to sell red. This seems insane with the world swing to whites, led by local hero Chardonnay. But unless they improve the basic quality, the consumer can't be blamed for not buying, and you can't really blame the grower for switching to red.

Beaujolais

'The commerce of Beaujolais has changed. It is no longer the commerce of the giant tanker or the railway wagon, but that of the bottle.' Fighting talk, and a standpoint we heartily endorse. That's Mr. Beaujolais himself, Georges Duboeuf, standing up for the original and honest in Beaujolais, and we would add a rider. The commerce of Beaujolais is now the commerce of the proprietor and his vineyard. We don't even have to ask Duboeuf if he agrees. His list shows that he wholeheartedly supports the right of a man to harvest his crop in the knowledge that it will keep its identity, and not be lost in the blending vats of Villefranche or Mâcon. Duboeuf is the man who brought commercial awareness to Beaujolais, but he also brought a gleam of pride back into the wine maker's eyes, and he now reckons to have between 110 and 120 single vineyards on offer from any given vintage.

This is all the more refreshing when one remembers that Duboeuf is a négociant, and it points up the difference in attitudes prevailing in Beaujolais and Burgundy. However, in his case you can see the reason for this attitude; Duboeuf started out as a wine grower in the Mâconnais. He expects to get his shoes muddy, and luckily there are others in Beaujolais who are not worried about their shiny leather brogues. They are willing to venture forth and seek out their wines, rather than sitting back and waiting for them to appear. But there seems no doubt that the relationship between négociant and grower is healthier in Beaujolais than it is in Burgundy. One leading grower said that he felt the difference between Burgundy and Beaujolais was that in Beaujolais only 10 per cent of the négociants are bad, whereas in Burgundy only 10 per cent of them are good.

That's oversimplifying the position. At its most fundamental one could say that Beaujolais *is* simple. Gamay is a simple grape, and most people's expectation of Beaujolais is one particular taste; satisfy that and the job is done. The Pinot of Burgundy, on the other hand, is an immensely complicated grape, the Burgundy vineyards are fascinatingly different, and the commercial pressures to deliver a regular style over a wide range far more dramatic. The majority of Beaujolais négociants, even if they make good enough Beaujolais *tout court,* are not yet willing to seek out and promote single vineyard names and proprietors' personal styles, whereas most Burgundy négociants have at least some individual wines on their lists. Yet, as a perusal of any vineyard area (excepting Champagne) shows, if you blend the produce of various vineyards and wine makers, you are likely to lose the identity of all of them.

THE COST OF A BOTTLE

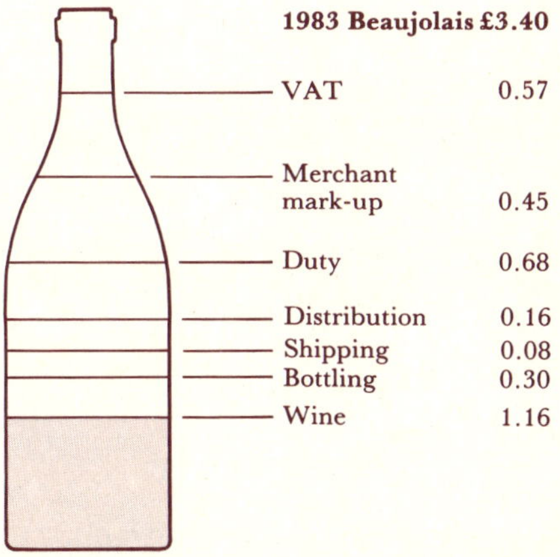

Until recently, we in the UK suffered more than most. Beaujolais is a good name. It reeks of La France, garlic and onions, big-bellied men with berets and striped vests, slim winking girls with short swishing skirts and fishnet stockings. Simple, clichéd images, and the gurgling name of Beaujolais fitted the fantasies to a tee. If the wine was suitably cheap, the taste didn't seem that important. It can't have done, because there was very rarely any Beaujolais at all in the heavy, thick sludge which was being offered for sale. In those days a good wine maker wasn't necessary, just a good graphic designer to create an evocative label. Things got so bad that a Sunday Times team took a random score of Beaujolais bottles off our High Street shelves, and drove them to Beaujolais, where the local growers' committee couldn't recognize a single mouthful as Beaujolais. Not surprising. They weren't.

If there's one thing we must thank the EEC for, it is that we can now get our throats round one of France's most simply enjoyable red wines in a reasonably pure form. But we can only do this in two ways. The first is to dive into the Nouveau millstream every November. A lot of people knock Nouveau instead of knocking it back. But the UK is such an important market that merchants are now sending us their best *cuves* as Nouveau, not merely the light and feeble, to try to get it drunk before it dies of galloping adolescence somewhere round New Year. And good Nouveau gets as close as we can get to the heart of Beaujolais – a foam-fresh jug of mountain wine.

The trouble is, after Nouveau there is a hefty gap before the next good mouthful. In the UK there is a woeful lack of a decent year-round supply of basic Beaujolais. While the standard of our Nouveau gets higher, the standard of our High Street commercial Beaujolais stays as gloomily low as ever.

But let's look at the Nouveau figures – it's eating the basic Beaujolais market alive. A few years ago, people reckoned that perhaps 30 per cent of appellation Beaujolais and 15 per cent of Beaujolais Villages were vinified as Nouveau. In 1983, 47 per cent of all Beaujolais and Beaujolais Villages was released as Nouveau. This year it'll be even higher.

Georges Duboeuf calls it 'le locomotive' of the Beaujolais wine region. In French, the word has two meanings. Engine, yes, but also pacemaker. There is an increasing danger that 'le locomotive' will outrun the field, and this explains why, for ten months out of twelve, we can't buy a decent bottle of straight Beaujolais over here.

So we have to skip to the top Beaujolais Villages wines, although there aren't many of those, and then the nine Cru communes which are considerably more

Maturity Chart

1983 BEAUJOLAIS CRU

This applies to a good proprieter wine from a good *Cru* Village.

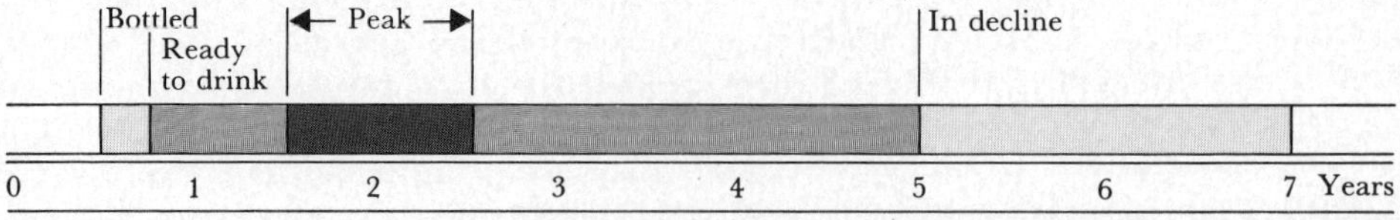

1983, BEAUJOLAIS NOUVEAU

Good Nouveau is actually better after a couple of months and even poor Nouveau can improve for a month or two.

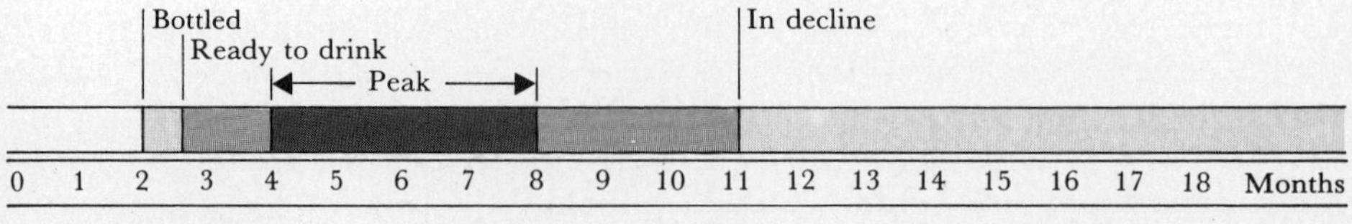

Vintage Table

With most Beaujolais the rule is drink it as young as possible, and any trademark Beaujolais should be the most recent vintage. Only the top wines from the best villages will benefit much by ageing, although much Nouveau can benefit from a month or two's rest.

***1983** Excellent stuff. Sometimes a bit big, but it has the fruit too. The proper Crus Beaujolais are the best since 1978, combining tannin and acidity with a delicious juicy fruit. Buy and drink.

1982 The classic Nouveau year – light, fresh, quick-drinking stuff. However, the Villages and the Crus have not shown a great deal of character, and though always pleasant, they're mostly losing their fruit.

1981 This looked so promising, yet didn't deliver the goods. After a good fruit/tannin balance to start with, the fruit has suddenly vanished to leave hard, dull wines. Don't buy, but if you have any, keep to see if they come round again.

1979 A good, light year, never very special, but enjoyable soft wines, now almost certain to be going toffee-ish at best and brown at worst.

1978 Lovely balance, good when young with their strong peppery fruit. The best single domaines are still very good mostly having gone soft and chocolatey and sweet.

1976 This was hardly ever like Beaujolais and still isn't. The really big Crus, like Moulin à Vent and Chénas made wines which have become tremendously dark and meaty. Nearly-but-not-quite-burgundies.

expensive, and *should* show a greater complexity, more character, more interest. Well, some of them do, but the Gamay grape is not much given to high-falutin' ideas like complexity and subtlety. It's best at giving a splashy, juicy taste, and it is only in the hands of the best proprietors, sought out by the best merchants, that it is actually worth paying the extra. Otherwise, after the rush of Nouveau has slowed to a trickle, if you want the straight gulping taste of new fruit you must switch to the fresh bright styles of the Côtes du Rhône or northern Italy.

However, in a year like 1983, the good guys have made delicious wines, from the light, cherry-soft styles of Brouilly and Chiroubles to the sweet perfumey flavours of Fleurie and St-Amour, and the weighty, rich, dark plum tasting wines of Morgon and Moulin à Vent. The good guys. Sadly, most of these producers do rather follow the mode, and the current mode is for light, quick consumption wines. Which is OK. If they'll accept light, quick consumption prices. But they won't, of course. They feel that they should receive about three times the price of a basic Beaujolais: 30 francs for a Moulin à Vent against 10 francs for a bulk Beaujolais. Quite right, if the wine shows the character and style of the village. But the price of the basic is rising, and the top Cru prices are wavering, because there are no stocks of the basic and there is too much of the Crus. The best true wines, preferably with vineyard or proprietor name displayed, from such companies as Thomas la Chevalière, Sarrau, Pierre Ferraud, Trenel and Duboeuf, are worth the full price, especially in the 1983 vintage. But if a wine just states 'Morgon' or 'Fleurie' in non-specific terms, be wary of paying that price. Order more Nouveau or switch to the Côtes du Rhône. Otherwise you may find yourself paying a 'serious' price for a wine neither exciting enough to be serious nor fragrant enough to be frivolous.

Beaujolais Nouveau

Beaujolais Nouveau is 158 years old this year. In England, that is; they've had it over there for rather longer. Now, admit Nouveau only caught on rather more recently, but the first shipment of Beaujolais Nouveau was from Jean de Salles of Beaujeu in 1826, when he popped over to London on a visit to his mate the French Ambassador, and brought two barrels of his 'new wine from Beaujeu' with him. As far as we can tell, his friend the Ambassador scoffed the lot by Christmas, and Beaujolais Nouveau slipped into an ill-earned obscurity for another 150 years. which brings us to the other anniversary.

'Modern' Beaujolais Nouveau is 10 years old this year. The phenomenon, that is. The razzamatazz, the jokes, the escapades and the fleeting fame afforded to the perpetrator of the most ludicrous way of getting this half-finished wine into our laps in the fastest possible time on the grey dawn of November 15th. But don't mock. Who else provides a much-needed party at the onset of the great British winter?

It all started so innocuously. Alan Hall was writing the Atticus column for *The Sunday Times,* and on November 10th, 1974 he devoted two and a half inches to a passing fancy. He wrote that if anyone felt interested, he'd be in his office on the morning of November 15th, and were this person to turn up bearing a bottle of the brand-new Beaujolais, he'd swap it for a bottle of champagne. Sounded like a good bargain. And to that tiny Atticus gag can be traced the hysteria which now accompanies Beaujolais Nouveau. Instantly it was a race. There's nothing the far-flung breed of eccentric Brits loves more than a genuine race with a ludicrous objective. They flocked to the starting line in Beaune, all boiling with lunatic schemes to beat the clock. Beaune to London is about 500 miles. Three hours after the off, the winner panted up the back stairs at Gray's Inn Road. Hall hadn't even had time to chill the champagne.

It's astonishing. In just a decade, a pleasant gluggy country wine from the dream-time hills of the Beaujolais had become the most famous, the most thirstily guzzled wine in Britain. In 10 years, from a standing start, we've become the most important importers of Nouveau wine. Whereas in 1981 a major shipping company languidly organised 15 container trucks of the wine, within 12 months they organizing 150. In 1983 Dover was so choked with traffic that the rush hour on the M2 seemed to last from 3 a.m. to midday. What's it all about?

Well, it certainly couldn't have been more opportune. Come the time, come the wine. In 1974 we had just joined the Common Market, but our experience of Bordeaux and Burgundy was a joke. Not one wine drinker in a hundred had tasted the real thing. Suddenly, here *was* the real thing. That light tangy taste was so pure many people thought there must be something with it. But it was just what the new generation of wine drinkers needed. The '60s had made their presence felt; wine no longer had to be approached with dumb reverence and an old school tie. Conventions and rules were there to be broken, and Beaujolais Nouveau did it brilliantly.

They said you had to drink red wine at room temperature and out of Paris goblets. Rubbish. Nouveau's better for an hour in the ice box, and it tastes the same out of a paper cup, a beer mug or a football boot. They said certain wines only went with certain foods. Nouveau goes with everything. And in particular its gurgling, fizzing fresh fruit goes with the restless food of the '80s; pizzas, kebabs, hamburgers, wine bar and take-away food - this purple-proud wine with its swoosh of fresh fruit goes with the lot. But it blows its cork at Christmas and is only fit for salad dressing by Whit Monday.

Again I say nonsense! any decent Nouveau will probably be even better at Easter than it was in November, by which time the left-over stock will be your only chance of catching the true taste of good basic Beauj. Well then, it's still an overpriced gimmick. Is it? In 1976 it was £2.40 or £2.50 in the shops. Last year it was about £2.40 or £2.50. This year? About £2.40 or £2.50. It may have been expensive in 1976. It isn't now.

Price Guide

Red

Non-vintage
c. £3.50
Le Piat de Beaujolais (SAIN, UNW)

1983
£3.75–£4.50
★Beaujolais, Domaine Joubert (BOW)
★Fleurie, Château de Fleurie, Loron (WGA)
★Juliénas, Domaine Joubert (BOW)

1982
£2.50–£3.00
Beaujolais, Jean Paul Bartier (ASHE)
★Waitrose Beaujolais (WAIT)
★Beaujolais, Loron (CHAP, PG)
Beaujolais, Quinson Fils (SF)
£3.00–£3.50
★Beaujolais Villages, Château du Basty (RH)
Beaujolais (BAL)
★Beaujolais Villages, Château de la Roche, Loron (CHAP, BAL)
★Beaujolais, Château de Tanay (RG, HR)
Beaujolais, Georges Duboeuf (BWC)
Beaujolais, Château Gaillard, Piat (PD)
★Beaujolais Villages, Paul Fortune (HBV)
Beaujolais, Château de la Plume, Georges Duboeuf (PIP)
Beaujolais, Pierre Ponnelle (RGA)
Beaujolais Villages, Pasquier-Desvignes (DOL, RGA)
★Beaujolais Lantignié, Château du Basty, Maurice Perroud (CV)
Le Piat de Beaujolais (VICT, ASHE)
£3.50–£4.00
Beaujolais, Château du Colombier (LADV)
Chénas, Domaine de la Combe Remont, Georges Duboeuf (BWC)
★Beaujolais, Mommessin (YFW)
Beaujolais Villages, Piat (PD, J&B)
★Beaujolais Villages, Château de Grand Vernay (L&W, RGHR)
★Côtes de Brouilly, l'Ecluse (HBV)
Brouilly (LHV)
Chénas, Château de Chénas, Sélection Eventail (SF)
Beaujolais Supérieur, Cave Beaujolais du Bois d'Oingt (RGHR)
★Beaujolais Villages, Château du Bluizard (C&B)
Brouilly, Pasquier-Desvignes (DOL)
Beaujolais Villages, Cuvée Grange Charton, Hospices de Beaujeu, Sarrau (ESV, YFW)
Beaujolais Villages, Hospices de Beaujeu (RGHR, HHC)
Beaujolais Villages, Georges Duboeuf (BYR)

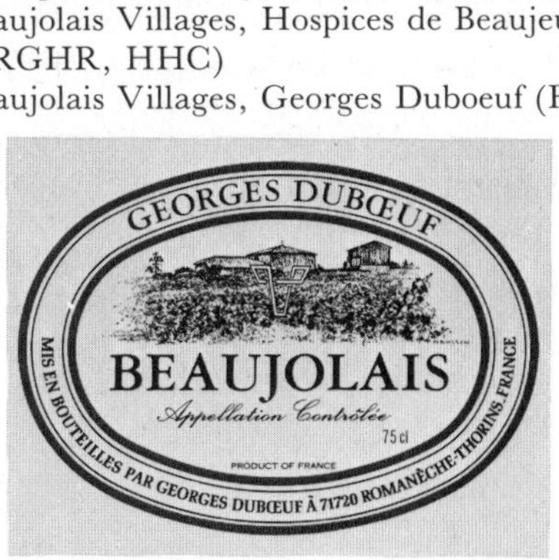

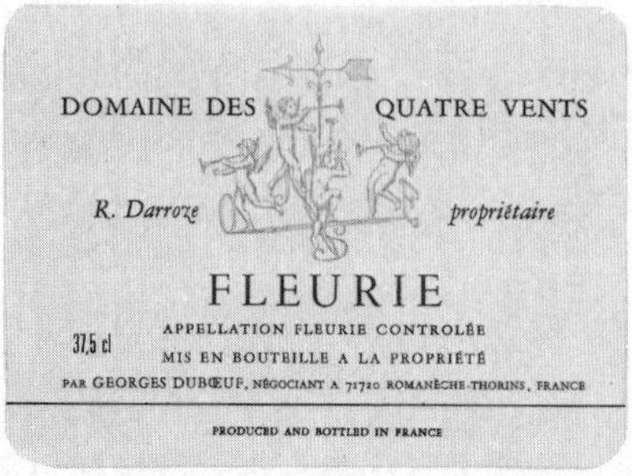

★Brouilly, Château de la Chaize, Marquis de Roussy de Sales (SF)
Chiroubles, Georges Duboeuf (BWC, LADV)
★Fleurie, Jacques Charlet (H&B)
Morgon, Château de Bellevue (RGHR)
Morgon, Pasquier-Desvignes (DOL)
Beaujolais, Domaine de Rochbonne (RGHR)
Juliénas, les Envaux, André Pelletier (SF)
★Brouilly, Château des Tours (BIB, SR, H&D)
Côte de Brouilly, Domaine la Taillebard, Georges Duboeuf (PIP)

£4.00–£4.25

Fleurie, Domaine de Montgénas, Sélection Eventail (SF)
Beaujolais, Pierre Charmet (RGHR)
Beaujolais, Jean Garlon (RGHR)
Beaujolais, Blaise Carron (RGHR)
Beaujolais, Albert and Rene Poyet (RGHR)
Chénas, Domaine de Chassignol, Favre (WSOC)
Morgon Charmes, Domaine Princesse Lieven, Georges Duboeuf (PIP)
Beaujolais Villages, Domaine de Ruyère (RGHR)
Beaujolais Villages, Georges Roux (RGHR)
Brouilly, Georges Duboeuf (BYR)
Fleurie Château de l'Abbaye, Quinson Fils (SF)
Juliénas, Domaine de la Seigneurie, Georges Duboeuf (BWC)
St-Amour (LHV)
Fleurie (LHV)

£4.25–£4.75

Fleurie, Domaine des Quatre Vents, Georges Duboeuf (BWC, C&B)
Côte de Brouilly, Château Thivin (L&W, RGHR)
Fleurie, Sélection Eventail (HBV)
★Moulin à Vent, Heritiers Finanz Devillaine (HBV)
Brouilly, Domaine Rolland (CDM)
Fleurie, Château de Poncie (SAIN)
Fleurie, Pasquier-Desvignes (DOL)
Juliénas, Pasquier-Desvignes (DOL)
Chénas, Château de Jean Loron, Beaudet (FFW)
Morgon, Château de Raousset (C&B)
Morgon, Domaine de l'Evêque (CDM)
Brouilly, Jean Lathuilière (RGHR)
Brouilly, Domaine de Garanches (RGHR)
Chiroubles, la Maison des Vignerons (RGHR)
Côte de Brouilly, Château de Grand Vernay (RGHR)
Fleurie, Château des Labourons, Comte de l'Escure (JH)
Beaujolais Villages Berengère, Pasquier Desvignes (MWS)
Morgon, Domaine de Ruyère, Paul Collonge (RGHR)
★Fleurie, Cave Co-operative Fleurie (RGHR)
Beaujolais Villages, Louis Latour (WGA)

£4.75–£5.00

Chiroubles, Gerard-Roger Mezait (RGHR)
Morgon, Domaine Aucoeur, Noel (RGHR)
Morgon, Domaine des Souchons (RGHR)
Brouilly, Domaine des Niveaudières, Mommessin (WGA)
Juliénas, Domaine de la Vieille Eglise, Loron (WGA)
Chénas, Henri Lespinasse (RGHR)
Moulin-à-Vent, Tour de Bief, Duboeuf (ASHE, PIP)
St-Amour, Elie Mongénie (RGHR)
Moulin-à-Vent, Georges Duboeuf (BYR)
Chiroubles, la Grosse Pierre, Dessalle (WSOC)
Fleurie, Château de Grand Pré (CDM)
Moulin-à-Vent, Domaine Lemanon, Loron (J&B)

£5.00–£5.75

Chiroubles, Robert Sarrau (YFW)
Brouilly, Château de Fouilloux, Pasquier Desvignes (MWS)
Morgon, Château Gaillard, Gutty (IMB)
Fleurie, Château Portier (RGHR)
Fleurie, Michel Chignard (RGHR)
St-Amour, André Poitevin (RGHR)
★Juliénas, Château des Capitans, Robert Sarrau (YFW)
Moulin-à-Vent, Château Portier (RGHR)
Moulin-à-Vent, Jean Picolet (RGHR)

Webster's has been compiled from the latest merchants' catalogues available at the time of going to press but neither we nor the merchants listed can guarantee that all the wines mentioned will be available by the time you read the book. Equally, other wines and new vintages will become available.

1981

£3.00–£4.00

Beaujolais, Loron (HUN)

Please don't blame ***Webster's*** *or the merchants listed if a wine is sold out or if the vintage you want is no longer available. Wine is a living entity and a limited commodity – continuity of supply cannot, alas, be guaranteed.*

Beaujolais Villages, Château de la Roche, Loron (L&W)
Morgon, Domaine des Vieux Cèdres, Loron (BAL)
St-Amour, Domaine des Billards, Loron (L&W)
Chénas, Sapin (PG)
Beaujolais, Blaise Carron (RGHR)
Beaujolais Villages, Geny de Flammerécourt (RGHR)
£4.25–£4.75
Juliénas, Clos des Poulettes (HUN)
Morgon, Domaine de Ruyère (L&W)
Fleurie, Sélection Eventail (WNRY)
★Morgon, Domaine Brisson (JH)
Brouilly, Château de Fouilloux (RGA)
Juliénas, Domaine de Beauvernay, Piat (PD)
Juliénas, Cave des Producteurs Juliénas (RGHR)
★Chénas, Jean Benon (RGHR, L&W)
Fleurie, Cave Co-operative Fleurie (RGHR)
Chénas, Cave du Château de Chénas (RGHR, TAN)
Moulin-à-Vent, Georges Duboeuf (BWC, PIP)
Chiroubles, Gerard-Roger Mezait (RGHR)
Juliénas, Jean Benon (RGHR)
£4.75–£5.00
Juliénas, Ernest Aujas (L&W)
Juliénas, François Condemine (RGHR)
Moulin-à-Vent, la Rochelle, Jacques Dépagneux (WSOC, OWL)
Brouilly, Château Thivin (ADN)
Juliénas, Château de Julienas, Sarrau (BAL)
£5.00–£6.00
Fleurie, Piat (PD)
Côte de Brouilly, Jacques Dépagneux (OWL)
Chénas, Domaine de Chassignol, Jacques Dépagneux (OWL)
Fleurie, Cave Colin, Jacques Dépagneux (OWL)
Juliénas, Georges Duboeuf (MAL)
Moulin-à-Vent, Georges Duboeuf (MAL)
Moulin-à-Vent, Château du Moulin-à-Vent (RGHR)

1980
c. £4.25
★St-Amour, les Bonnets (HBV)

1979
c. £5.50
Moulin-à-Vent, Domaine de la Rochelle, Mommessin (TAN)

1978
£4.25–£4.50
Morgon, le Clachet, Georges Brun (J&B)

Morgon, Jean Descombes (VIGN, CV)
St-Amour, Georges Duboeuf (VIGN)
Juliénas, Domaine de la Seigneurie, Georges Duboeuf (CV)
Morgon, Domaine les Vieux Cèdres (HUN)
Juliénas, Domaine de Beauvernay, Piat (J&B)
£4.50–£5.00
Fleurie, Château de Fleurie (WW)
Chénas, Cave du Château de Chénas (ADN)
Fleurie, Cave Co-operative de Fleurie (ADN)
Morgon, Charles Meras (MAL)
Morgon, Domaine Savoye à la Côte de Py (RGHR)
Juliénas, Clos des Poulettes, Loron (L&W, RGHR)
St-Amour, Clos des Billards (HUN)
£6.00–£6.75
Moulin-à-Vent, Château des Jacques (BYR, FINT)
Moulin-à-Vent, Clos du Grand Carquelin, Château des Jacques (CV)
Moulin-à-Vent, Grand Clos de Rochegrès, Château des Jacques (CV)

White

1982
c. £4.00
Beaujolais Villages, Château de Chatelard, Quinson (SF)

Webster's *is an annual publication. We welcome suggestions for next year's edition.*

c. £4.30
Beaujolais Blanc, Château des Tours, Georges Duboeuf (PIP)

1981
£4.00–£4.50
Beaujolais Blanc, Domaine de la Guinchule, Cellier de St-Jean (L&W)
Beaujolais Blanc, Domaine de la Guinchule, Producteurs Réunis Quincié (TAN)

1978
c. £5.00
★Beaujolais Blanc, Château de Chaintre, Georges Duboeuf (HT, MAL)
c. £6.25
Beaujolais Blanc, Château de Loyse, Thorin (FINT)

Rosé

1982
c. £3.50
★Beaujolais Supérieur Rosé, Cave Beaujolais du Bois d'Oingt (L&W)

Price Guide – Notes

There is a great deal of good Beaujolais Nouveau in this country, probably more good *wines than anywhere else in the world. Although it is sometimes fashionable to sneer at Nouveau, don't. British merchants are making considerable efforts to ensure the qualty of our Nouveau. However, ordinary Beaujolais is not special, so look for some evidence of vineyard or Domaine on the label.*

IMAGE UPTURN

Beaujolais is looking forward to a continuing expansion of its rôle in providing Nouveau to the world. Why not? If ever there was a wine which was in the right place at the right time, Beaujolais Nouveau is that wine. It caught the bright mood of the 60s, and kept the door ajar through the sicker 70s. Now with the 80s lifestyle becoming more positive and less traditional, more demanding in terms of instant pleasure and value for money, Beaujolais Nouveau is the perfect wine.

It's the perfect wine for the growers, too, but not necessarily for the merchants. The grower gets his wine made, paid and off his hands in record time. As one Beaujolais producer said, "Beaujolais Nouveau est bu, payé et pissé en un temps record." He can laugh all the way to his Christmas holiday in the Canaries.

The merchants find it more difficult. They're all cashing in on the Nouveau boom, but as our UK price stability shows, margins are continually shaved in this desperately competitive market. So they may not make much money on Nouveau, and then they've got another 10 months of the year to try to sustain an interest in basic Beaujolais which has been exhausted by the mad Nouveau fling. Not only that, even the fashion leadership of Beaujolais Nouveau is being threatened. Other French regions, even other countries, notably Italy, and more recently Spain, New Zealand and Australia, are showing that anything Beauj can do they can do better. And often cheaper. We're going to continue to lap up the Beaujolais version, but in Beaujolais itself, sooner or later the financial crunch is going to cause some broken heads and tears before bedtime.

Which is why the Beaujolais merchants are beginning to promote the nine 'Crus'. For several years now, as characterful burgundy became increasingly difficult to buy at an affordable price, English merchants have begun to use the Beaujolais Crus as alternatives. But some Beaujolais merchants began to play the burgundy game – classy name, feeble wine. So, just as the burgundy market is crawling back towards single domaine wines, the best Beaujolais merchants are beginning to offer single vineyard wines – individuality at a sensible price. That way lies an increasing share of the British classy red market.

CHAMPAGNE

For £5.99 you can buy one of the world's most potent symbols of luxury and extravagance – no, not a diamond ring, a mink coat, or a dinner at the Ritz, but – a bottle of champagne! Flash open the bottle, and for an hour you're touching fingers with the world of Rolls Royces in the drive and yachts at Monte Carlo. Champagne is the most fleeting, but also the most affordable of these potent symbols. And after an hour of dreaming and the laughter gurgling in your throat, you can always return to real life – if you wish. Even so, as a 75cl bottle of fermented grape juice, it's expensive. Why?

Champagne, though often regarded as a name for any sparkling wine, is legally only applicable to the sparkling wine, made by re-fermentation in the bottle, of a defined region east of Paris, which is France's most northerly vineyard area. The champagne method is complex and expensive, involving far more procedures than normal wine-making.

THE COST OF A BOTTLE

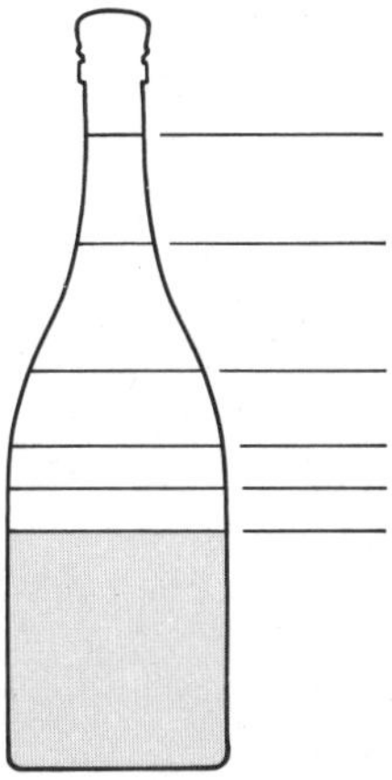

NV Grande Marque	**£10.50**
VAT	1.38
Merchant mark-up	2.38
Duty	1.12
Distribution	0.10
Shipping	0.09
Champagne/ Bottling	5.43

Méthode champenoise

The fermented grape juices, the produce of numerous different vineyards, are blended to produce a 'house style', then bottled with a dash of *liqueur de tirage* – a sugar and champagne concoction – to make it re-ferment. Re-fermentation in the bottle produces carbon dioxide which, since it can't get out, dissolves in the wine and creates the fizz – and ugly yeast deposits. As the wine matures, these deposits must be shaken down to the cork, usually by hand; the bottles are stored on their heads for anything from one year to six or seven, depending on the quality of the wine; and finally the little pellet of sediment is frozen and shot out.

But we're not finished yet. This champagne will now be totally dry, the fermentation having eaten up all the sugar, so it will be 'dosed' with a bit more to a desired level of sweetness or dryness. Then comes another cork – the most expensive, three-level cork in use for wine today – then the gold foil and the labelling, using the strongest glue available (to stop the label floating off in the ice bucket, they say). And it's finally ready.

So, as you can see, champagne is a 'creation'. The still, light wine of the area, by dint of a lot of skill, a lot of special equipment, unnecessary for normal wine, and far more time-consuming, interest charge-accruing maturation, is transformed into the world's greatest sparkling wine.

The growers, the merchants, the prices

So, what about these basic wines? Champagne is made from the black Pinot Noir and Pino Meunier grapes, quick-pressed to avoid the skins colouring the juice, and the white Chardonnay. Because of the investment and skill required in making champagne, the merchant houses increasingly took over the role of making the end product, demoting the growers to mere producers of grapes. So a 'them and us' situation, unusual in a wine area, developed.

Thus the merchants became more powerful than the growers, but as sales increased in the sixties and seventies it became apparent that there was not enough vineyard land. This, allied to several small vintages, gave the growers more power. They could dictate terms to the merchants, and the merchants had to buy, at the growers' prices, to preserve their increased sales.

The official price is set each year by committee, and villages are rated by a percentage system, from 100% for the best, to 77% for the least good. The grape price per kilo is for a 100% village, and the other villages each get their set percentage per kilo weight. Between 1975 and 1981 the price rose from 6.10 francs to 20 francs per kilo as demand outstripped supply. Only following the two biggest vintages ever recorded has the price slipped back, to 19.03 francs in 1982 and 15.33 francs in 1983. Since you need about one and a half kilos of grapes to make a bottle of champagne, in 1981 the grapes alone would have cost nearly £3 a

Vintage Table

A vintage table for champagne is not straightforward since so much champagne is blended without vintage designation. Also, vintage wines released and sold very young, while good for laying down, are unlikely to give any more pleasure than good non-vintage for immediate consumption. Most champagne can do with ageing; vintage champagne demands it. Historically, a vintage was 'declared' by champagne houses after an exceptional year, and then released at perhaps 6-7 years old when reasonably mature. Recently there has been a trend for some vintage wine to appear almost every year, and at only 4-5 years old. With luck the very small vintages of 1980 and 1981 have put a temporary stop to this.

1983-1980 Both 1983 and 1982 produced record-breaking crops of ripe grapes. One or other will probably be declared a vintage, and should produce attractive well-balanced wine in the style of 1973. 1981 & 1980 were tiny vintages, not over-ripe, unlikely to be much seen.

1979 Some examples have appeared. They are far too young. Even so, it was a massive vintage, and will eventually turn out mid-weight but soft and balanced. 1979 will be 'current' vintage for two to three years.

1978 Tiny vintage, and high in acidity. Again, don't buy it for pleasure now. But the present rather stringy acidity should soften and make a drier, deeper style than 1979.

1976 Too hot – remember? The champagne grapes were busting a gut when they got to the vat house. Mostly it shows. They lack the crisp bite which should go along with the fruit. And they're already getting old.

***1975** Not much about now. A pity, because this vintage really did mix the acid freshness with a perfumed, honeyed fruit. Good for now and it'll still improve.

***1973** A wonderful year. Initially criticised as being a bit fat and blowsy. Nonsense. Creamy is more like it. Honeyed, soft, delicious for now.

bottle. Though there are some restrictions on vineyard practice – for instance, no mechanical harvesting is allowed – the yields per acre are normally fairly good, and it's quite simply supply and demand. You can make a good living off a vineyard in Champagne with less land than almost anywhere else in the world. However, the huge cost of transforming these grapes into champagne is reflected by the fact that grape costs are only about 40% of the total cost of a bottle.

Laying Down

There is a rumour going round Epernay and Rheims that one should not age champagne. This is, quite simply, nonsense. It is obviously extremely attractive to the PR boys of a multi-million pound business to find a way to increase rapid turnover of stock, but the very thing which puts champagne in a different league to other sparkling wines is its ability to age, thereby transforming its flavours.

Most champagne is now offered for sale as a young, very fizzy, rather apple-fresh wine, marvellous for making a party sparkle, but without much complexity of taste. Excepting the very cheapest brands, a couple of years of cool, dark storage will transform the wine. If this storage is done for you in the cellars in France, so long as the wine is left lying in bottle on its own yeast deposits, it can age almost indefinitely. Bollinger have a Vintage RD, or 'Recently Disgorged', which has lain for two or three times the normal period, and is the nearest thing to ready-to-drink vintage champagne now being offered. One Chalons-based house will allow favoured customers to buy wine young and will mature it for them, on the yeast deposits, in their cellars. However, after two enormous harvests in 1983 and 1982, prices will be stable, as indeed they have been since 1982. So this year, laying down champagne is tremendously worthwhile for enjoyment, but not likely to bring any great financial gain.

Maturity Chart

Because of economic pressures, most champagne nowadays is put on the market when it is too young; even a cheap supermarket champagne may benefit from six months' ageing. However, it is a matter of taste, because although champagne loses some of its fresh sparkle as it ages, it also loses its biting acidity, becoming softer and more honeyed. Champagne stored hot, or in bright light will age and decay much more rapidly.

Maturity Chart

NON-VINTAGE CHAMPAGNE

Non-vintage is usually offered too young. Six months extra age can transform it.

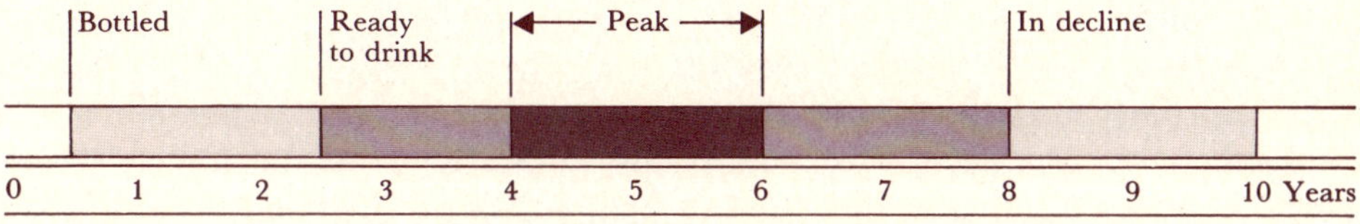

1978 CHAMPAGNE

People usually drink vintage champagne far too young. Pointless. Age it or don't drink it.

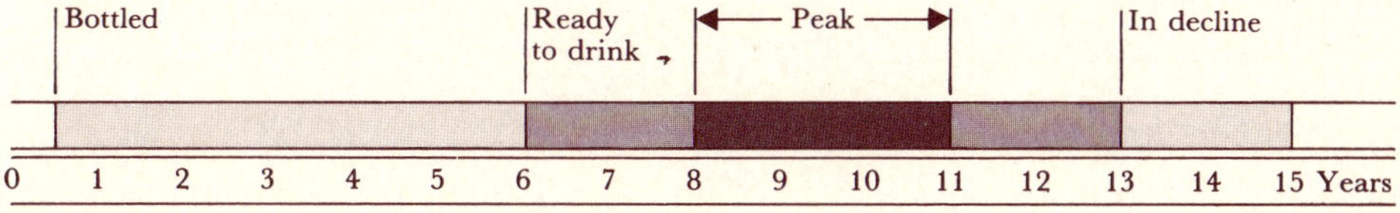

Champagne Price Survey

The term 'Grande Marque' is ambiguous, meaning literally a great brand. It is a self-styled grouping of, at last count, 28 champagne houses, including the 15 or so best known. They should be synonymous with quality, using more expensive grapes, older wines, and more rigid eventual selection of cuvées. Veuve Clicquot is one of the top three or four Grandes Marques.

Buyer's Own Brand (BOB) appears on the label of a wine blended to a buyer's specifications. The grapes are of lesser quality, the wines are usually younger, and they should be notably cheaper. We have chosen Duc De Marne, an English own label established in 1876, and a supermarket own-label champagne.

These figures show that the relationship between a Grande Marque and a traditional BOB is remarkable, with both accurately reflecting the tremendous sensitivity of the champagne industry to vintage shortage and glut. Short vintages are always followed by a big price hike, because of champagne's position as a 'necessary commodity' in many trading areas. The supermarket wine shows far more volatility in its reaction to shortage and glut, since separate deals can hurriedly be made between supermarket buyers and large own-label suppliers of champagne. The pre-Christmas 1983 price of £5.99 is directly attributable to this. Reacting to a massive 1983 harvest, within one week three supermarkets lopped a pound off their price. And still profitable, no doubt. Makes you think.

	Veuve Clicquot Vintage	**Veuve Clicquot NV**	**Findlater's house champagne Duc de Marne NV**	***Supermarket Own Brand (combined figures)**
1984	£14.62 (1976)	£12.35	(Jan) £8.68	£6.35–£5.99
1983	£14.62 (1976)	£11.88	£8.68	£7.50–£5.99
1982	(Apr) £13.95 (1975)	£12.67	£8.59	£6.99–£7.50
	(Feb) £13.77 (1973)			
1981	£12.72 (1973)	£10.43	£8.05	£5.75–£6.99
1980	£11.41 (1973)	£8.97	(Oct) £7.98	£5.75
			(Feb) £7.26	
1979	(Oct) £10.12 (1970)	£7.82	(May) £6.01	£4.50–£5.00
	(Jan) £9.05 (1970)		(Mar) £5.56	
1978	£7.77 (1969)	£6.35	£4.80	
1977	(Sep) £7.02 (1969)	£5.89	(Jul) £4.64	
	(Feb) £6.59		(Jan) £4.27	
1976	(Nov) £6.25 (1966)	£4.49	£3.39	
	(Feb) £5.51 (1966)			
1975	£5.42 (1966)	£4.41	(Sep) £3.30	
			(Apr) £3.73	
1974	£5.10 (1966)	£4.08	£3.40	
1973	£4.63 (1966)	£3.74	£2.67	

N.B. All prices include VAT at following rates: April 1973–July 1974, 10%; July 1974–June 1979, 8%; from June 1979, 15%.

*Own brand champagnes were not available from Supermarkets before 1979.

Price Guide

Non-vintage

£5.50 – £6.00

d'Arconnay Brut (LHV)
★Waitrose Champagne (WAIT)
★Tesco Champagne Brut (TES)

£6.00 – £6.50

Metayer (BIB)
★Comte de Beauvin Brut (ECD)
★Sainsbury's Champagne Extra Dry (SAIN)

£6.50 – £7.00

Chiquet, Blanc de Blancs (LHV)
★Chantal Brut (SF)
★Lambert Extra Dry (PD)
St Michael Champagne (M&S)

£7.00 – £7.50

Granger Private Cuvée (RGA)
Cuvée Malmaison Brut, Albert Larive (MAL)
★Duchatel (UNW)

£7.50 – £8.00

★Delamotte Brut (C&B)
Vicomte d'Almon (BAL)
Ayala, Extra Dry (WGA)
Baron de Beaupré Brut (L&W, ADN, TAN)
★Bauget Jouette Carte Blanche Brut (HBV)
★G. Brenner Carte Blanche (HUN)
★Billecart-Salmon Brut (SR, WW)
★Bruno Paillard Brut (WNRY, HT)
Charles Heidsieck Brut (WAIT, PD, DAV, THRE, BYR, CUL, PG, VICT, MACK, ASHE *& others*)
The Society's Champagne Brut (WSOC)
★Jules Mignon, La Reserve House Champagne (RSV)
Les Amis du Vin Réserve Privée Brut (LADV)

Mercier Brut Réserve (ODD, PD, VICT, CDM, THRE, UNW)
★Philipponat Royal Reserve (ODD)
★Pierre Vaudon Brut Premier Cru (HHC)
★Prieur Napoléon (PG)

£8.00 – £8.50

★G. Brenner Rosé Brut (HUN)
★Our Own Special Selection, Charles Benoit (CHAP)
★Maison Gérard Brut (GH)
Lanson Black Label Brut (ODD, CHAP, UNW, BIB, DAV, BYR, L&W, CUL, MWS, MACK *& others*)
★Camuset Brut Réserve (YFW)
★Boizel Brut or Rich (H&B)
★Joseph Perrier (BIB, H&D, L&W, TAN, GH, LADV)
Dagonet Cuvée Exceptionnelle (ESV)
Delande Frères Private Cuvée (DOL)
Louis Kremer Cuvée La Vigneronne Brut (VIGN)

£8.50 – £9.00

Canard Duchêne (ASHE, REID, WNRY)
de Venoge Cordon Bleu Extra Dry (WHIT)
★Besserat de Bellefon Crémant (PG, MACK, RSV)
★Duc de Marne Special Cuvée Extra Dry (FINT)

Taittinger Brut Réserve (RGA, L&W, PD, TAN)
Jacquesson Perfection Brut (YAPP)
★Sarcey Extra Dry, Justerini & Brooks (J&B)
Laurent-Perrier (ODD, QR, C&B)
★Avery's Special Cuvée (AV)
★Moët & Chandon Première Cuvée (TES, ODD, PD, L&W, CHAP, PG, WAIT, VICT, JH, SAIN *& others*)
Laurent-Perrier Brut (L&W, THRE, YFW)
★Bollinger Special Cuvée (RGA, ODD, MART, WAIT, BIB, HT, PG, REID, JH, THRE *& others*)
Bruno Paillard Brut Zéro (WNRY)
★Alfred Gratien Cuvée de Réserve Brut (RACK, MART, RH, LADV, VIGN)
Mumm Cordon Rouge Brut (ODD, THRE, FINT, UNW)

Perrier-Jouët Grand Brut (PG, HUN, MWS, WNRY, J&B)
★René Florancy 1er Cru de Champagne Blanc de Blancs Brut (CV)

£9.00 – £9.50

Berry Bros United Kingdom Cuvée (BBR)
Deutz Brut (MAL)
★Gilbert Bertrand Brut (TW)
Louis Roederer Extra Quality Brut (MART, ODD, BYR, BIB, HT, L&W, JH, CUL, HBV, TAN *& others*)
★Bruno Paillard Crémant Blanc de Blancs (HT)
Henriot (QR)
Lanson Rosé (RGA, BYR, CUL, L&W, CV, ASHE, BBR)
Besserat de Bellefon (CDM)
George Goulet Extra Quality Brut (PIP, YFW, ESV, TAN)

Piper Heidsieck Brut (ADN, REID, UNW, MACK, QR)
Veuve Clicquot Yellow Label Brut (ODD, WAIT, SAIN, BIB, PG, JH, BYR, REID, SR, DOL *& others*)
Wine Club's Champagne Premier Cru Blanc de Blancs (STWC)
★Pol Roger White Foil Brut (PG, ODD, DOL, BYR, H&D, WNRY, MWS, YFW, HHC, C&B *& others*)

£9.50 – £10.00

Heidsieck Dry Monopole Brut (HUN, J&B)
Moët & Chandon Brut (SAIN)
Taittinger (ODD, QR, J&B)
Pommery & Greno (BYR, J&B)

£10.00 – £10.50

★George Lilbert Blanc de Blancs Brut (TW)
Jean Paul Arvois Brut (TW)
Veuve Clicquot White Label Rich (L&W, TAN, VICT, J&B, BBR)

£10.50 – £11.00

St-Marceaux Brut (OWL)
Michel Labbé Premier Cru Brut (TW)
Deutz (WNRY)
Taittinger Brut (CUL, BWC, MACK, VIGN, UNW)

£11.00 – £12.00

Ruinart Brut Tradition RD (ESV)

Laurent-Perrier Ultra Brut (L&W)

£12.00 – £13.00

Pommery Brut (UNW)
Piper Heidsieck Brut Sauvage (ADN, MWS)
Laurent-Perrier Cuvée Rosé Brut (YFW, GH, MWS)
Mumm Crémant de Cramant (MAL, FINT)

c. £15.00

Krug Grande Cuvée (RGA, JH, CUL, DOL, PG, GH, ADN, MAL, L&W, BYR, PD *& others*)

c. £19.00

Laurent-Perrier Cuvée Grand Siècle (GH, L&W, MWS, C&B, FINT)
Bollinger Tradition RD (BIB)

£20.00 – £25.00

Moët & Chandon Première Cuvée magnum (TAN)
★Bollinger Special Cuvée magnum (TAN)

c. £25.00

★Michel Labbé Premier Cru magnum (TW)

£45.00 – £55.00

Taittinger Blanc de Blancs (UNW)
★Alfred Gratien Crémant jeroboam (RACK)
Veuve Clicquot Yellow Label Brut jeroboam (YFW)

c. £75.00
Pol Roger methuselah (ODD)
£100.00 – £130.00
Veuve Cliquot Yellow Label Brut methuselah (YFW)
★Alfred Gratien Crémant jeroboam (RACK)
Pol Roger salmanazar (ODD)
c. £165.00
Veuve Clicquot Yellow Label Brut salmanazar (YFW)

1980
c. £20.00
Perrier-Jouët Belle Epoque (MWS)

Stars (★) indicate wines selected by the merchants themselves as particularly good value in their class.

1979
c. £8.50
★Billecart-Salmon Blanc de Blancs (WW)

1978
£10.50 – £11.50
★Moët & Chandon Dry Imperial (ODD, L&W, MWS, CUL, ESV, ASHE, AV, VICT, DAV, YFW *& others*)
£11.50 – £13.00
Veuve Clicquot Gold Label (BIB)
Louis Roederer (MACK, TAN, MAL)
c. £14.00
Veuve Clicquot Rosé (BIB)
c. £16.00
Moët & Chandon Rosé (J&B)
c. £22.00
Louis Roederer Cristal Brut (ODD, BIB, HBV, HHC, GH, VIGN, MAL, WNRY, HUN, MACK, MWS *& others*)

1977
c. £9.00
★Bauget Jouette Carte Blanche Brut (HBV)
£11.00 – £13.00
George Goulet Extra Quality Brut (PIP)
Louis Roederer Extra Dry (HBV)
c. £17.50
Louis Roederer Cristal (RGA, L&W)

c. £70.00
★George Goulet Extra Quality Brut jeroboam (TAN)
c. £90.00
Lanson Black Label methuselah (TAN)
c. £195.00
★George Goulet Extra Quality Brut salmanazar (TAN)

1976
£8.00 – £10.00
Marquis de Conflans (SR)
Philipponat (ODD)
Ayala (WGA)
Billecart-Salmon Cuvée N.F. Billecart (SR)
★Charles Heidsieck Rosé (PD)
£10.00 – £12.00
Lanson (ODD, L&W, MACK)
Perrier-Jouët (PG, MWS, H&D)
Veuve Clicquot Gold Label Brut (ODD, WAIT, PG, SR, CHAP, REID, CUL, AV, JH, H&D *& others*)
Lanson Red Label (MWS, GH, BYR, CV)
Moët & Chandon (PD, ASHE)
Alfred Gratien (MART)
Pol Roger (PG, WNRY, BBR, J&B)
★Jean Paul Arvois Brut (TW)
Charles Heidsieck (MACK, BYR, FINT)
£12.00 – £14.00
Piper Heidsieck (REID)
Clos des Goisses (ODD)
Joseph Perrier (LADV)
★Alfred Gratien Grémant Brut (RACK)
Heidsieck Dry Monopole Brut (HUN)
Laurent-Perrier (YFW)

Bollinger Brut (ODD, PG, BIB, CHAP, REID, BYR, L&W, AV, CDM *& others*)
Maxim's Brut Salon le Mesnil Blanc de Blancs (BWC)

£14.00 - £17.50
Taittinger (TAN, MACK)
Louis Roederer Extra Dry (BBR)
Perrier-Jouët Belle Epoque (PG, HUN, TAN, MAL, VIGN, WNRY)
£17.50 - £20.00
Veuve Clicquot La Grande Dame (PG, VICT, L&W)
Salon le Mesnil (MACK)
£20.00 - £25.00
Dom Pérignon (ODD, L&W, ESV, DOL, PG, THRE, PD, HHC, CUL, TAN *& others*)

Krug (WSOC, ODD, PG, L&W, ESV)
c. £70.00
St-Marceaux Brut jeroboam (OWL)

1975
£7.50 - £10.00
★Pirrot (JH)
Besserat de Bellefon (CDM)
£10.00 - £12.00
de Venoge Brut (WHIT)
Joseph Perrier Cuvée Royale Brut (H&D)
Besserat de Bellefon Crémant Blanc (MACK)
Bruno Paillard Brut Blanc de Blancs (STWC)

Dom Ruinart Blanc de Blancs (ODD, ESV, TAN, YFW)
Lassalle Blanc de Blancs 1er Cru Chigny (VIGN)
Pol Roger (PG)
£12.00 - £15.00
Jacquesson Signature Brut Cuvée de Prestige (YAPP)
Laurent-Perrier Royal Wedding Cuvée (C&B)
Veuve Clicquot Royal Celebration Cuvée Brut (ADN)
Pol Roger Blanc de Chardonnay (WNRY)
£15.00 - £20.00
Bollinger Extra Brut (ADN)
★Pol Roger Réserve Special (PG)

Merchants stocking each wine are listed after each entry in ascending order of price or in alphabetical order if they offer the wine at the same price. However, prices do fluctuate (there are special offers and discounts as well as price increases) so remember to use ***Webster's*** *as a price* GUIDE *not a price* LIST.

£20.00 - £22.50
Perrier-Jouët Belle Epoque (HHC, GH)
Bollinger Tradition RD (CHAP)
★Krug (H&D, CDM, DOL, ADN, CHAP, J&B, BBR, C&B)
Taittinger Comtes de Champagne Blanc de Blancs (RGA, L&W, PD, TAN, GH, YFW, MWS)
Dom Pérignon (BIB, AV, VICT, CHAP, BYR, CDM)
c. £45.00
Bollinger Vieilles Vignes Françaises Blanc de Noirs (L&W)

1974
c. £18.00
George Goulet Cuvée du Centenaire (TAN)
c. £26.00
Alfred Gratien Crémant magnum (VIGN)

1975
£7.50 - £10.00
Bruno Paillard Rosé (LHV)
★Bruno Paillard (LHV, HT)
£10.00 - £12.00
★Alfred Gratien Crémant Brut (WSOC, RH, HT, VIGN, LADV, RACK)
Moët & Chandon Dry Imperial (ADN)
£13.50 - £15.00
Pol Roger (C&B)
Dom Ruinart Blanc de Blancs (HHC, VICT)
Taittinger (REID)
£16.50 - £20.00

★Bollinger Tradition RD (RGA, ODD, PG, ADN, L&W, GH, CDM, WSOC, HHC, C&B *& others*)

Champagne oblige
CHAMPAGNE
Lanson
Depuis 1760
LANSON
CHAMPAGNE
Lanson
BRUT
REIMS FRANCE
BLACK
LABEL

£20.00 – £25.00
★Salon le Mesnil (REID)
Krug (MAL, C&B, VIGN)

1971
c. £13.50
Lanson Red Label (J&B)
c. £25.00
Dom Pérignon (HT)

1970
c. £17.50
Bollinger Tradition RD (MAL, ADN, J&B, VIGN)
c. £30.00
★Alfred Gratien Crémant (RACK)
c. £50.00
Bollinger Vieilles Vignes Françaises (HT)

1969
c. £32.50
★Alfred Gratien Crémant (RACK)

1966
£17.50 – £20.00
Pol Roger (VIGN)
★Bollinger Extra Dry (J&B)
Louis Roederer Crémant (VIGN)
c. £40.00
★Alfred Gratien Crémant (RACK)

1964
c. £25.00
Taittinger Comtes de Champagne Blanc de Blancs (VIGN)
c. £42.00
★Alfred Gratien Crémant (RACK)

1961
£17.50 – £20.00
Gosset (VIGN)
Mumm Cordon Rouge (VIGN)
c. £47.50
★Alfred Gratien Crémant (RACK)

1955
c. £26.50
Pommery & Greno (VIGN)

Merchants stocking each wine are listed after each entry in ascending order of price or in alphabetical order if they offer the wine at the same price. However, prices do fluctuate (there are special offers and discounts as well as price increases) so remember to use ***Webster's*** *as a price GUIDE not a price LIST.*

Still White

Non-vintage
£6.00 – £7.00
Pol Roger Coteaux Champenois (MWS)
Bollinger Vin Nature Coteaux Champenois (MAL)
Ruinart Chardonnay (L&W, VICT, CV, YFW, ESV)
Laurent-Perrier Coteaux Champenois Blanc de Blancs de Chardonnay (YFW)
c. £10.00
Moët & Chandon Saran Nature (L&W, ESV)

Still Red

1980
c. £7.50
Bouzy Rouge (PG)

1979
c. £13.00
★Ay Rouge, La Côte aux Enfants, Coteaux Champenois, Bollinger (BOW)

Price Guide – Notes

Prices are remarkably stable and quality remains high. Splendid. Let's open a bottle to celebrate! The lesser known brands have probably never been better than they are now for spontaneous cork-popping. The ony caution is that there is a dangerous rumour being put about that champagne shouldn't, or can't age. Not true.

CHAMPAGNE FORECAST

April 1984 was a black month for British champagne drinkers. The United States took a definite lead in the export market for champagne for the first time since they had briefly nosed ahead of us in 1981. In the first quarter of 1984, the USA imported 220,000 more bottles of champagne than we did. But our intake was up 17 per cent and, given the astonishing strength of the US dollar, one might have expected their imports to be even higher.

Champagne really does swing backwards and forwards like a pendulum. A couple of years ago we were all being rationed. Now the market is bursting with the stuff. The Champenois, however, have at last taken steps to try to stabilise things. Although frosts and freak weather can still decimate a harvest, the chances of a shortfall are lessening because the official champagne body has authorised a planting programme to increase the vineyard area by 500 hectares a year over 10 years. Most of this land is in the Marne Valley and of pretty good quality. Production will increase by over three million bottles a year.

This expansion comes on top of the 1982 and 1983 harvests which were the biggest ever recorded, when the quality of the wine was far above what one might expect from such quantity, and caused a rash of cheap champagne 'special offers' on the British market. Most of this wine, although not vintage-dated, is of the 1982 vintage, released at the earliest possible legal date, in this case just before Christmas 1983. Because the 1982 wines are so balanced, these wines are good apple-fresh fizz, not having all the expected attributes of champagne but still managing to outperform their non-champagne rivals. They will continue to appear on the market because of the size of the 1983 harvest.

These two vintages will also promote the rarely seen but keenly priced single vineyard champagnes. Champagne usually relies on blending and so single domaine wines are not always a success. Based on the 1982 vintages, they can be. Grandes Marques, too, should gradually improve in quality during the year, as less green unripe wine is utilised, and the 1979 vintage, as it appears, will be delicious, classy drinking, particularly in the Blanc de Blancs sector.

Rhône

The Rhône valley owes a lot to Beaujolais Nouveau. A strange statement, but true, because with the realisation that the café wine of Lyons and Paris looked like developing into the most modern, most popular – and most classless – red wine that France could produce, the great grape bowl of the Rhône valley felt a distinct chill around the withers. For years the Côtes du Rhône had unconcernedly produced fairly strong, beefy reds, high in alcohol, tannic, not all that fruity, with that big, stark taste which hits you fair and square, but actually leaves no memorable characteristics whatsoever. And they'd found a ready market in a world which considered that a good red wine should be rather brawny, and shouldn't be attempted if you were wearing stiletto heels or had a history of vertigo.

So the sudden whooping success of Beaujolais Nouveau, spreading throughout the sixties and seventies into a worldwide phenomenon, made the Rhône growers take a careful look at what this upstart had that they hadn't. They didn't have to look far. Fruit. Freshness. Lightness. Gulpability. And luckily there were enough men in the Rhône with their wits about them to change radically the methods of vinification which had churned out the heavyweights for so many years. Shorter fermentation periods, much less violent pressings of the grapes, removal of skins and stalks, replacement of big wooden vats with cement or stainless steel, earlier bottling. And it quickly became apparent that the Côtes du Rhône could offer the freshness and fruit of Beaujolais, but in a richer, stronger style. As Beaujolais grew lighter and less tasty, with more and more marginal vineyards being pulled into production to meet the insatiable demand, the only thing the Rhône wines lacked was a magic name like Beaujolais Nouveau.

THE COST OF A BOTTLE

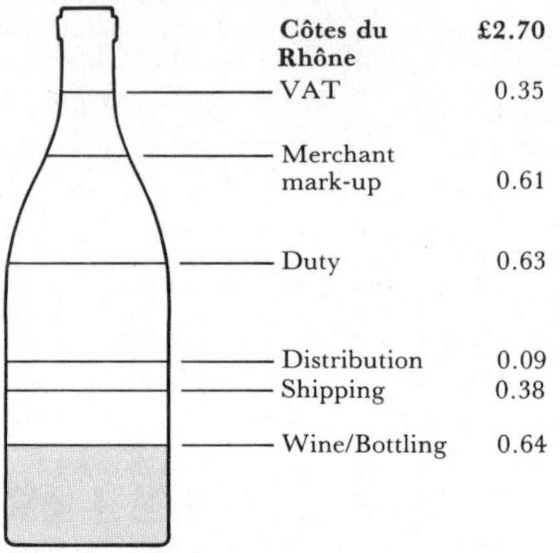

What the Côtes du Rhône has developed is an ability to provide all-year-round quality and value, while for much of the year the supply of basic Beaujolais leaves a lot to be desired. The export figures show how the Rhône valley has rapidly adapted to a modern market. In 1963, 122,278 hls were exported (1 hectolitre = 100 litres, or about 133 bottles). In 1975 this had risen to 418,025 hls, while by 1983 the figure was 584,293, of which the UK took 58,665 hls. The Rhône now exports more than the whole of Burgundy and Beaujolais, and only Bordeaux sells more abroad.

Even so, there is still a strange anonymity about the Rhône wines. They number at least one of the world's most famous wines – Châteauneuf-du-Pape – and at least two, perhaps three of the world's greatest: the red Hermitage and Côte Rôtie, and the white Condrieu. Yet incredibly few people have tasted or even heard of these last three. The problem is that the Rhône had been used for too long as the understudy and helpmate of Burgundy further north. Rhône wines were usually included in the Burgundy section on restaurant wine lists, and, for that matter, Rhône wines were usually included in Burgundy and Beaujolais bottles. Illegally, yes, but in poor years it did no end of good, even if the wine didn't much resemble what the label shyly announced. Two hundred years ago, Hermitage was regularly added to claret and the resulting blend highly prized (some great classed growths up to the 1860s were definitely Hermitagé). So it's nothing new. It's only now that the Rhône and its very varied wines are coming out proudly under their own names. But then, you could say the same for Beaujolais and Burgundy.

THE FASHION FOR HERMITAGE

In 1973, I could buy a bottle of Jaboulet's Hermitage La Chapelle 1970 (along with Chave's Hermitage, the greatest northern Rhône red) for £1.92 a bottle. A great wine, a classic year, and it was costing less than twice the price of a bottle of Liebfraumilch or Valpolicella. At the same time, if I'd decided to buy a top Burgundy, the Loeb wine list offered me several excellent examples of Chambertin, the wine Hermitage is most frequently compared with. Rousseau is a top grower, and his 1969 Chambertin would have cost £4.52, his 1970 £4.54. More than four times the cost of a basic hock. Anyone comparing Jaboulet's 1970 with Rousseau's 1969 would have been unable to justify this price difference on taste alone. No, it's simply fashion, and the immutable laws of supply and demand. Jaboulet was making one of the world's great reds in the narrow river valley below Lyons and no one was beating a path to his door. Rousseau was making great wine, and the clamour at his door could be heard right up the autoroutes to Paris and Switzerland, and, more importantly, in the newly awakened American market.

By 1976, the 1972 vintages were being offered, and for once, both Hermitage and Burgundy suffered the same slings and arrows of fashion. Bordeaux largely creates the reputation of a great vintage year, nationwide. 1972 claret was thin, mean, and quite disgracefully overpriced. By 1976, the 1972 bubble had burst and the vintage was openly derided. But Hermitage and Chambertin made excellent wines. One might have expected a switch of quality buyers to Burgundy and the Rhône. No. 1972 burgundies weren't popular – it took Loeb four years to shift the 1972 Chambertins – but that didn't stop the Chambertin opening at £9.78, more than doubling in three years. Hermitage just about doubled too, to £3.83, but the actual disparity between Chambertin and Hermitage widened more than two and a half times.

It took the great 1978 vintage to make Hermitage prices surge up to £7.38 when it opened in 1980. Loeb didn't have a 1978 Chambertin, but the somewhat comparable 1976 was at £14.44 – less than twice. Were things evening out? I'm afraid not. The 1979 Hermitage was actually cheaper in 1983, at £7.25. Such humbleness didn't affect 1979 Chambertin, piling in at £21.02, and as 1984 came in, Hermitage was further away than ever from catching up. The delicious 1980 stood at £9.56, while the good Chambertin 1980 was £24.36. The rays of hope for Jaboulet were that his famous 1978 was now being offered – and finding buyers – at £44.55 a magnum, and at least his hand-crafted wine was now worth nearly five times the price of a Liebfraumilch or Valpolicella. At £7.75 per bottle inclusive of duty and VAT, the 1982 Jaboulet Hermitage La Chapelle (offered by Loeb at that price up to 31st December 1983) represents tremendous value for money, since Rhône experts are unanimous in placing it close to the great 1978 vintage in quality and staying power. If you've got any, you had better keep your hands off it until at least 1990. Sorry!

(Prices from O.W. Loeb's retail list.)

Comparison of prices for Hermitage and Chambertin

On sale	Chambertin/Chambertin Clos de Bèze	Hermitage
1972/3	£4.54 (1970)	£1.92 (1970)
	£4.52 (1969)	
1973/4	£4.64 (1970)	
1974/5	£6.92 (1971 Clos de Bèze)	£3.49 (1972)
		£3.34 (1971)
1975/6	£8.57 (1971 Clos de Bèze)	£3.77 (1972)
		£3.61 (1971)
1976/7	£9.78 (1972 Clos de Bèze)	£3.02 (1974)
	£9.78 (1972)	£3.83 (1972)
	£8.77 (1971 Clos de Bèze)	£3.91 (1971)
1977/8	£9.95 (1972) Clos de Bèze)	£3.72 (1976)
	£9.95 (1972)	£5.50 (1971)
	£9.01 (1971 Clos de Bèze)	
1978/9	£10.50 (1972)	£4.41 (1976)
	£10.50 (1970 Clos de Bèze)	£5.38 (1975)
		£11.20 (1964)
		£17.95 (1961)
1979/80	£11.31 (1972 Clos de Bèze)	£7.38 (1978)
	£14.00 (1970 Clos de Bèze)	£5.07 (1977)
		£5.59 (1974)
		£14.79 (1962)
		£18.68 (1961)
1980/1	£14.16 (1977)	£6.65 (1979)
	£14.44 (1976 Clos de Bèze)	£7.98 (1978)
	£10.55 (1975)	£5.45 (1977)
		£19.04 (1961)
1981/2	£13.09 (1977)	£6.77 (1979)
	£10.68 (1975)	£7.65 (1975)
		£10.48 (1969)
1982/3	£16.88 (1979)	£7.55 (1980)
	£13.29 (1977)	£7.25 (1979)
	£15.51 (1977 Clos de Bèze)	£8.73 (1975)
1983/4	£12.68 (1980 Clos de Bèze)	£9.56 (1980)
	£21.02 (1979)	£9.92 (1979)
	£15.51 (1977 Clos de Bèze)	£22.23 (1978)
		£20.97 (1975)
		£19.27 (1974)

Prices, supplied by O.W.Loeb & Co., are retail excluding VAT

Laying Down Offers

Proof that the Rhône valley is finally being taken seriously comes with the spate of 'opening' (en primeur) offers for young Rhône wines from top-notch wine merchants to members of the public. The customer won't see his wine for some considerable time - certainly 6 months, maybe more - and he will be paying a price based on an unseen commodity lying unproven in a cellar in the Rhône valley. But it does mean that for as little as £9.20 you can purchase a case of good Rhône wine. Yes, I know you'd have to pay duty and shipping and VAT when it arrives, but somehow the thing that lingers in your mind most, and which gives you most pleasure to repeat endlessly at dinner, is that each bottle, initially, only cost you 76.66 pence. With the great Hermitages and Côte Rôties, you are buying some of the best pleasure investments French wine has to offer. So far this investment is primarily one of anticipation and pleasure, since the monetary gain from such wines is uncertain. What *is* certain is that they'd be extremely difficult to purchase mature, as most have disappeared down throats far too young, and, being some of the world's greatest wines, they're distinctly underpriced. Equally, I should warn you that the Jaboulet Hermitage La Chapelle - which the list below shows that you could have bought for around £69.00 lying in France in 1983 - was offered by all the merchants who made '82 Rhône opening offers (a limited group in itself) on a very strictly rationed basis, and even some of their very best customers were not able to secure a case.

1981 and 1982 Rhône Offers for Laying Down		**Price***
1982	Costières du Gard, Domaine de St. Benezet (H&D)	£27.80
1982	Vin de Pays de Vaucluse, Domaine de Grange Blanche, Jacques Mousset (H&D)	£28.70
1982	Côtes du Rhône, Domaine Bel-Air, Yves Ryckwaert (RH)	£33.00
1981	Côtes du Rhône Baronnie de Sabran (H&D)	£34.85
1981	Coteaux du Tricastin, Domaine du Vieux Micocoulier (H&D)	£36.90
1982	Côtes du Rhône, Jean Claude Assemat (H&D)	£37.26
1982	Côtes du Rhône, La Serre du Prieur, M. Chambovet (H&D)	£39.50
1982	Côtes du Rhône, Domaine la Garrigue (H&D)	£40.00
1981	Vacqueyras, Domaine la Garrigue (H&D)	£42.80
1982	Vacqueyras, Domaine la Garrigue (H&D)	£44.20
1981	Lirac, Domaine de Château St Roch (H&D)	£44.35
1982	Crozes Hermitage, Domaine de Thalabert, Paul Jaboulet Aîné (H&D, LADV, OWL, RH)	£48.00
1982	St Joseph, Le Grand Pompée (OWL, L&W, RH)	£48.00
1981	Gigondas, A. Bernard & Fils (H&D)	£52.55
1982	Cornas, Paul Jaboulet Aîné (H&D, OWL)	£57.60
1982	Châteauneuf-du-Pape, Roger Sabon (H&D)	£58.70
1981	Châteauneuf-du-Pape, Cuvée Reservée, Roger Sabon (H&D)	£64.50
1982	Côte Rôtie, Chapoutier (L&W)	£73.85
1982	Côte Rôtie, Les Jumelles, Paul Jaboulet Aîné (H&D, LADV, OWL, L&W)	£83.35
1982	Hermitage, La Chapelle, Paul Jaboulet Aîné, (H&D, LADV, OWL, RH, L&W)	£96.00

**Prices quoted – based on merchants' offers in November 1983 or thereabouts – are either the merchants' actual prices for wine 'available in the UK inclusive of VAT' or their ex-cellars price grossed up to include their own best estimates of duty, freight etc. – plus VAT.*

NORTHERN RHÔNE

People have been saying this for so long that I'll say it again, eternally optimistic that the message may eventually get across. Ready? The northern Rhône contains some of the greatest wine bargains in the world today. Sounds familiar? So it should. Serious wine merchants have been pleading with their customers for years to take notice of Hermitage, Côte Rôtie, Cornas, St-Joseph and Condrieu, and at long last we're beginning to see 'sold out' notices appearing in some of the windows. It's strange that the Rhône Valley, which is such a well-known area of France, has inspired none but a handful of wine lovers to delve below the surface of good old Côtes du Rhône and see whether there are any nuggets of gold lurking. There certainly are, and it was the 1978 vintage which finally hauled them to the surface.

This was when the northern Rhône growers at last took up their trumpets and blared 'Vintage of the Century' to the heavens. Well, they'd seen their colleagues in Burgundy and Bordeaux do it so often, it was only a matter of time before they caught on. And it worked! The 1978 Hermitage from Jaboulet or Chave, the 1978 Côte Rôtie from Jasmin or Guigal were suddenly star wines; people grappled for their allocation of a couple of cases or less, and talked confidently of the fine investment they'd made. And probably for the first time this century they were right; an investment market is just beginning to peek out in Rhône wines – but the position isn't secure yet. It took a good deal more than five years of stardom for Bordeaux to reach its present eminence. It takes decade after decade of relentlessly high quality, and a sensible pricing system which allows profit-earning for each part of the chain, from grower to eventual owner. And we're dealing with tiny areas: Hermitage is just 303 acres, Côte Rôtie 252 acres, and the wonderful white Condrieu comes from just 35 acres – one fair-sized apple orchard's worth to service world demand. Compare that with Bordeaux's top village of Pauillac which has 2,336 acres to play

Vintage Table

1983	Looks to be exciting in Hermitage and Côte Rôtie. Hard, deep wines. Loads of colour; they'll need lots of time.
***1982**	Brilliant wines. Right from the start they've had a deep, rich fruit, with masses of colour and enough tannin to age them.
1981	Very disappointing. Mostly they lack fruit, and the tannin and fruit stand out rather raw and harsh. No need to buy, so don't.
***1980**	A lovely middleweight year, with the Syrah in one of its light and fragrant moods. Already drinkable, but they'll keep well.
1979	Slightly disappointing, because many of the wines seem a little hot and jammy. They're OK soft drinking, but slightly flat.
***1978**	Sensational wines. All the power and the beauty of the Syrah, the best wines make you gasp with awe and pleasure. Can drink, but keep, keep, keep!

with, and one can see a dangerous situation developing.

If the great wines do take off in price, there are many other lesser growers who will wish to share in the gold-rush. They will plant less fine vines, they will prune less severely, they will begin to push and shove both politically and viticulturally for extensions to the vineyard area, or replanting of sections inside the allowed area which are historically less good. As yet there are probably no more than a dozen top wine makers in these appellations, whose wine one can take on trust as one does with so many Bordeaux châteaux. All the growers would do well to look north to Burgundy and see what chaos can ensue when the blind pursuit of instant extra profit supersedes the desire to earn it through superlative wine making.

To get a taste of the brilliant Syrah styles of wines, both St-Joseph and Cornas have remarkable individual flavours, at about half the price of Hermitage, while Crozes-Hermitage is big, gutsy and almost always excellent value for money.

Maturity Chart

1978 HERMITAGE

1982 has a similar ageing potential. 1980 and 1976 will reach peaks and decline approximately twice as fast.

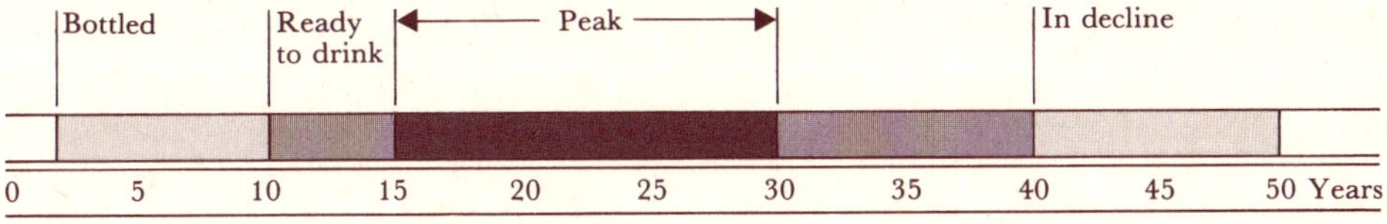

Price Guide

Red

Non-vintage
c. £2.50
★Sainsbury's Crozes-Hermitage (SAIN)
£8.50
★Hermitage, Cuvée Marquise de la Tourette, Delas (H&B)

1982
£10.50
Hermitage, la Chapelle, Paul Jaboulet Ainé (RSV)

1981
c. £4.00
St-Joseph, le Grand Pompée, Paul Jaboulet Ainé (L&W, HUN, TAN)
St-Joseph, Domaine Bernard Gripa (STWC)
Cornas, Paul Jaboulet Ainé (VICT)
£7.00–£9.00
Cornas, Auguste Clape (YAPP)

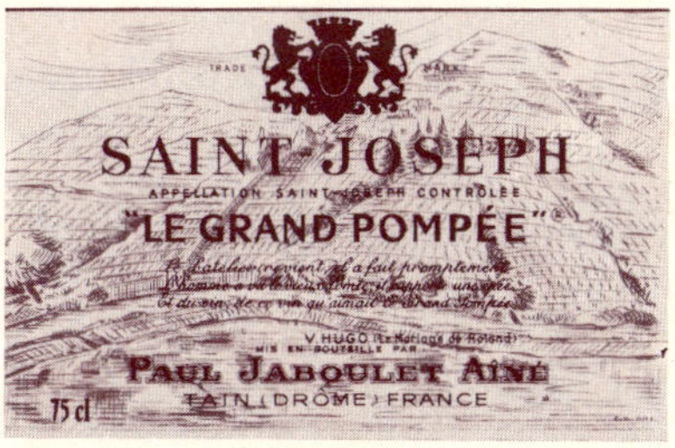

Côte Rôtie, la Chevalière d'Ampuis, Robert Jasmin (YAPP, VIGN, RSV)
Hermitage, Gérard Chave (YAPP)
Côte Rôtie, Emile Champet (VIGN)

1980
£3.00–£4.00
★Crozes-Hermitage, Pascal Frères (CHAP)
★Crozes-Hermitage, Vidal Fleury (PG)
★Hermitage, la Chapelle, Paul Jaboulet Ainé (CUL, REID, RH, MAL, L&W, WSOC, BWC, VICT *& others*)

Crozes-Hermitage, Domaine de Thalabert, Paul Jaboulet Ainé (RH, P&C, L&W, BOW, MAL, WSOC, TAN, OWL)
St-Joseph, Cave Cooperative Agricole de Saint Désirat-Champagne (YAPP)

£4.00–£5.00

★Crozes-Hermitage, Cave des Clairmonts (HHC)
Crozes-Hermitage, Domaine des Clairmonts, Vieilles Vignes, la Famille Barja (YAPP)
St-Joseph le Grand Pompée, Paul Jaboulet Ainé (WSOC, OWL, WW, PG, SR)
Crozes-Hermitage, les Meysonniers, Chapoutier (RACK)

£5.50–£6.50

Cornas, Paul Jaboulet Ainé (HUN)
★Hermitage, Paul Jaboulet Ainé (L&W, BAL)
Cornas, M. Voges (J&B)

£6.50–£8.00

Côte Rôtie, de Vallouit (L&W)
★Côte Rôtie, les Jumelles, Paul Jaboulet Ainé (L&W, HUN, LADV, TAN, OWL, SR)
Côte Rôtie, la Chevalière d'Ampuis, Robert Jasmin (L&W)
Hermitage, Gérard Chave (L&W, YAPP)

1979

£4.00–£5.00

★St-Joseph de Vallouit (L&W)
★Crozes-Hermitage, Paul Jaboulet Ainé (WW, SR, ASHE, ADN, MAL)
Crozes-Hermitage, Pascal Frères (VIGN)

£5.00–£7.00

Hermitage, la Chapelle, Paul Jaboulet Ainé (REID, L&W, BIB, LADV, ADN, MAL, WNRY, PG, RSV, J&B)

Cornas, Paul Jaboulet Ainé (SR, VIGN)
Côte Rôtie, Albert Dervieux-Thaize (BWC, PIP, FINT)

£8.00–£8.50

Hermitage, Gérard Chave (WSOC, YAPP, VIGN, RSV)
Côte Rôtie, Chapoutier (RACK)
Cornas, Auguste Clape (YFW)
Côte Rôtie, Brune et Blonde, Guigal (RH, L&W, BAL, BYR, MART, HHC, LV, REID)
★Côte Rôtie, Guigal (MAL, J&B, TAN)

c. £9.75

Côte Rôtie, Robert Jasmin (L&W)

£14.25–£15.00

Côte Rôtie, la Mouline, Guigal (L&W, TAN, CDM, J&B, REID)
Côte Rôtie, la Landonne, Guigal (CDM, J&B, REID)

1978

£4.50–£5.75

St-Joseph le Grand Pompée, Paul Jaboulet Ainé (MAL, GH)
Crozes-Hermitage, les Meysonniers, Chapoutier (J&B)

£8.50–£9.00

Côte Rôtie, Guigal (TAN)
Côte Rôtie, Brune et Blonde, Guigal (H&D, MACK)
Côte Rôtie, Chapoutier (L&W)

£9.50–£10.00

★Hermitage, de la Sizeranne, Chapoutier (J&B)
Hermitage, Guigal (VIGN)
Côte Rôtie, les Jumelles, Paul Jaboulet Ainé (PG)

£13.25–£14.00

Côte Rôtie la Landonne, Côte Brune, Guigal (ADN, H&D)
Côte Rôtie, la Mouline, Côte Blonde, Guigal (H&D)
Hermitage, Gérard Chave (ADN, REID)

1977

£6.75–£7.75

Hermitage, de la Sizeranne, Chapoutier (BIB, WHIT, RACK)

Côte Rôtie, Brune et Blonde, Guigal (BOW)
c. £11.55
Côte Rôtie, la Mouline, Côte Blonde, Guigal (WHIT)

1976
£10.00–£11.00
Côte Rôtie, Guigal (FINT)
Côte Rôtie, Brune et Blonde, Guigal (VIGN, GH, L&W)
c. £11.95
Hermitage, la Chapelle, Paul Jaboulet Ainé (VIGN)
c. £16.20
Côte Rôtie, la Mouline, Côte Blonde, Guigal (ADN)

1975
c. £8.50
Hermitage, la Chapelle, Paul Jaboulet Ainé (HT)

1972
£9.75–£10.75
Hermitage, Paul Jaboulet Ainé (L&W)
Côte Rôtie, Chapoutier (YAPP)

1971
c. £14.75
Côte Rôtie, Brune et Blonde, Vidal Fleury (REID)

1962
c. £21.00
Hermitage la Chapelle, Paul Jaboulet Ainé (MAL)

> *Merchants stocking each wine are listed after each entry in ascending order of price or in alphabetical order if they offer the wine at the same price. However, prices do fluctuate (there are special offers and discounts as well as price increases) so remember to use* ***Webster's*** *as a price GUIDE not a price LIST.*

1961
c. £51.60
Hermitage la Chapelle, Paul Jaboulet Ainé (OWL)

White

Non-vintage
£3.75–£4.25
Crozes-Hermitage, Mule Blanche, Paul Jaboulet Ainé (CUL)

1983
c. £9.60
Condrieu, Georges Vernay (LADV)

1982
c. £4.25
Crozes-Hermitage, Mule Blanche, Paul Jaboulet Ainé (HUN, L&W, HT, BOW, TAN, LADV)
c.£8.60
★Condrieu, Georges Vernay (L&W, BWC, RH, REID, BYR, PIP)
c. £11.50
Condrieu, Château du Rozay (HUN, WSOC)

1981
c. £4.20
★Crozes-Hermitage, Mule Blanche, Paul Jaboulet Ainé (RH, ODD, BAL, MAL, OWL, PG)
£6.50–£7.00
St-Joseph le Grand Pompée, Paul Jaboulet Ainé (OWL)
Hermitage, le Chevalier de Stérimberg, Paul Jaboulet Ainé (MAL, HUN, OWL, PG, L&W)
£7.75–£8.75
Hermitage, Gérard Chave (YAPP)
Hermitage, Chante Alouette Grande Cuvée, Chapoutier (HT, YFW)
c. £9.40
Condrieu, Château du Rozay (BIB, MAL, ADN, CV, YAPP, VIGN)

1980

£4.25–£5.25

★St-Peray, Cuvée Marquise de la Tourette, Delas (H&B)

★Crozes-Hermitage, Domaine des Clairmonts (YAPP)

St-Joseph, Jean-Louis Grippat (YAPP)

c. £6.65

Hermitage, le Chevalier de Stérimbourg, Paul Jaboulet Ainé (WSOC, BYR)

c. £8.55

Hermitage, Chave (VIGN)

c. £10.60

Condrieu, Château du Rozay (FINT, REID)

1979

c. £5.50

Crozes-Hermitage, Mule Blanche, Paul Jaboulet Ainé (MAL)

c. £8.00

Hermitage, Chante Alouette, Chapoutier (ADN, YAPP)

c. £23.75

Château Grillet (VIGN, YFW)

1978

c. £3.90

★St-Peray, Noyer (PG)

1976

c. £8.95

Hermitage, Chevalier de Stérimbourg, Paul Jaboulet Ainé (VIGN)

Sparkling

Non-vintage

c. £5.00

St-Peray Mousseux, Brut, Auguste Clape (YAPP)

Price Guide – Notes

An increasing number of merchants are getting the message about the Northern Rhône and beginning to list examples. Even so the selection looks a little thin until one sees that the quality of the producers listed is usually of the highest. Appellations like Crozes Hermitage should be seen more and more as suppliers of high class chewy reds, but in the meantime we should take advantage of the price/quality ratio of top producers like Jaboulet, Chave, De Vallouit, Guigal and Vidal Fleury.

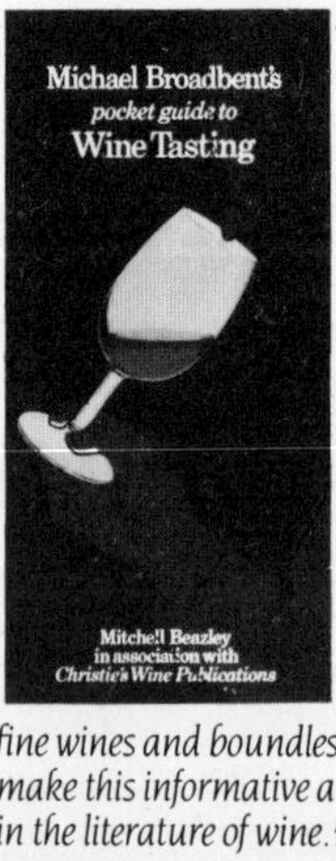

__Webster's__ has been compiled from the latest merchants' catalogues available at the time of going to press but neither we nor the merchants listed can guarantee that all the wines mentioned will be available by the time you read the book. Equally, other wines and new vintages will become available.

Mixed Prospects

The northern Rhône is an exciting area to be involved with at the moment. 1982 has produced wines of a sweetness and depth which nearly come up to 1978 in quality, while 1983 has produced dark, intense reds and apple-fresh whites which are also not far away from 1978 in potential. Three great vintages in six years, and the delicious 1980 is also weighing in there. It does seem as through this run of exceptional wines is spurring the British trade to try and market the stuff. There are, however, plus and minus points.

Côte Rôtie is suffering badly from undisciplined expansion of the vineyard area. It has always been one of the most difficult vineyards in France to work, clinging precariously to the steep Rhône Valley cliffs, but the authorities have now authorized a quadrupling of the vineyard area on the plateau land away from the river. First impressions indicate that this is a disaster, and if Côte Rôtie is to maintain its position something must be done to differentiate between 'côtes' and 'plateau'.

Hermitage, however, looks set fair to increase its reputation, with even the lesser growers producing a string of fine wines, while Crozes-Hermitage shows considerable possibilities. The general standard is of the 'excellent basic' level, but with many highspots, and the potential production of strong, sturdy reds has hardly been tapped. In 1970, Crozes produced 13,000 hls, in 1980 43,000 hls, but production can eventually reach 400,000 hls. St-Joseph is expanding too, but less happily, suffering from a touch of the 'Côte Rôties', while both Cornas and the white St-Péray need a bit of confidence-boosting just now.

Southern Rhône

The problems of the southern Rhône are very different from those of the north. Although the greatest appellation, Châteauneuf-du-Pape, is a bizarre amalgam of the good, the great and the ugly, there aren't really any other magic names with tiny hillside production areas, which can fall prey to the worst excesses of money grabbing. Unfortunately, over the last 15 years the Rhône valley has been used too often as an alternative supply following price explosions in Bordeaux and Burgundy, rather than always being able to work out a sensible price pattern for itself. Châteauneuf-du-Pape and Gigondas were hungrily snapped up by export buyers eager to replace the claret and burgundy they could no longer buy, and instead of seeing the chance to develop a permanent market demand, prices soared and quality sagged. The casual loyalty of the wine buyer to these new names was quickly demonstrated. From healthy sales in 1972, the market was shunning these price-mad parvenues by 1974, and stocks of unsold Châteauneuf and Gigondas doubled in just two years.

It still happens. Inside the healthy average export figures for the Rhône, there is still a surge of over-reaction whenever the price of Beaujolais or Bordeaux increases too sharply, and the red wine buyers turn once more to the basic Côtes du Rhônes. Prices rose steeply in 1981, and sales dropped 17 per cent over the next two years. 1982 produced masses of wine, and 1983 a fair amount, and of good quality, but 1984 still sees the prices 50 per cent above their 1981 level, and the stock of unsold Côtes du Rhône has increased from 14 months to 20 months' requirements.

This inability to get the price/quality ratio quite right is a pity, because the standards of wine-making, and the styles of wine coming out of the southern Rhône, are getting better and better. The big battalions in the reds are led by Châteauneuf-du-Pape and Gigondas.

Vintage Table

1983 Looks very promising for the best wines of Châteauneuf, Gigondas and Lirac, though Côtes du Rhône may lack a little fruit.

1982 Mostly pretty feeble. Too much Grenache, not enough Syrah, too many grapes, too hot, you name it, they got it.

1981 As with much of this side of France this is a rather pale, fruitless vintage, and even where there is some depth and colour, not inspiring.

***1980** Good Côtes du Rhône wines, mostly ready to drink. Châteauneuf and Gigondas are already good, but can happily use another couple of years. Some terrific Lirac.

1979 Some extremely good full, soft wines, mostly from the hillside vineyards. The flatter valley-floor wines are past it.

***1978** Excellent. Not quite so wild as in the northern Rhône but nearly all the wines will still be good, and Châteauneuf and Gigondas can sit in the broom cupboard for a few years yet.

Gigondas, while not the most attractive of reds when it's young, is nonetheless a remarkably consistent, big, plummy, rather solid wine, which always looks as though it will mature into something very special, but rarely gets the chance. Châteauneuf can be a quite delicious, deep, dusty red, almost sweet and fat, low in acidity, but kept appetising by just enough back-room tannin. *Can* be. It can also be fruit-pastilley and pointless, or dark, tough and stringy. Although it fulfils the original *appellation controlée* regulations, the name Châteauneuf-du-Pape has proved to be just too tempting. Experts reckon that perhaps one-third of the growers make good wine, and that as much as two-thirds of the wine sold on the world market exceeds the *appellation controlée* yields.

The Côtes du Rhône Villages and Lirac are probably the best areas to search for good, full reds which can also age, while well-made basic Côtes du Rhône is quite delicious when young. This isn't really white or rosé land; Tavel rosé is one of the most famous, but save yourself some money and buy Lirac rosé from next door. Dry whites are improving, but the best white is the ultra-fashionable sweet Muscat de Beaumes de Venise; not cheap, but worth it.

Maturity Chart

1980 CHATEAUNEUF-DU-PAPE

Years like 1978 and 1983 may even exceed this time-scale. Otherwise it is best to err on the young side.

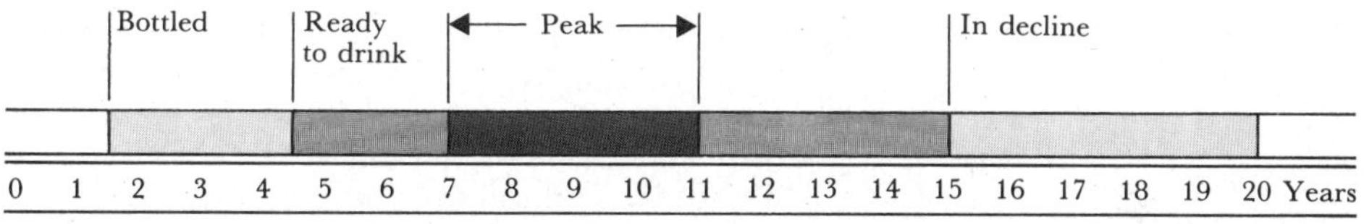

PRICE GUIDE

Red

Non-vintage
£1.75–£2.25
Vin de Pays des Bouches du Rhône (BIB)
Sainsbury's Coteaux du Tricastin (SAIN)
⋆Vin de Pays de la Principauté d'Orange (ECD, YAPP)
Tesco Côtes-du-Rhône (TES)
⋆Vin de Pays des Coteaux de l'Ardèche Syrah (CUL, SF)
Waitrose Côtes-du-Rhône (WAIT)
£2.25–£3.00
⋆Vin de Pays des Coteaux de l'Ardèche Cabernet Sauvignon (ECD, SF)
⋆Côtes du Vivrais (SF)
⋆Vin de Pays des Coteaux de l'Ardèche Gamay (SF)
Vin de Pays des Bouches du Rhône,

Domaine du Temps Perdu (BBR)
⋆Côtes du Ventoux, Domaine des Anges (L&W, ADN)
⋆Vin de Pays des Coteaux de l'Ardèche (YAPP)
⋆Vin de Pays de Vaucluse, Domaine Vieux Chêne (J&B)
⋆Côtes du Rhône, Château Domazon (TES)

£3.00–£4.00

⋆Châteauneuf-du-Pape, Pascal (CHAP)
⋆Châteauneuf-du-Pape les Arnevals (TES)

c. £4.75

St Michael Châteauneuf-du-Pape, Château Belgrave (M&S)

1982

£2.00–£3.00

⋆Côtes du Ventoux, Bernard Pical (ASHE)
Côtes du Luberon, Cellier de Marrenon (SF, CV)
⋆Vin de Pays des Coteaux de l'Ardèche Gamay (BIB, LADV, VIGN, SR, YAPP, PG)
Vin de Pays de Vaucluse, les Producteurs Associés à Vacqueyras (BWC)
Côtes du Rhône, Domaine Maby (LHV)
⋆Vin de Pays des Coteaux de l'Ardèche Syrah (SR, PG)
⋆Côtes du Ventoux, Domaine des Anges (MART, TAN, ESV)
⋆Côtes du Rhône, Domaine Bel-Air (RH, SR, VIGN)
Vin de Pays des Coteaux de l'Ardèche Syrah, Producteurs de St-Desirat-Champagne (CV)
Vin de Pays des Coteaux de l'Ardèche Gamay, Producteurs de St-Desirat-Champagne (CV)
⋆Côtes du Rhône, Château du Grand Moulas (L&W, ADN, BAL, TAN)
⋆Côtes du Rhône, André Brusset (HHC)

£3.00–£3.50

Côtes du Ventoux la Vieille Ferme (MAL)
⋆Côtes du Rhône, Caves des Vignerons de Vacqueyras (TAN)

*Merchants stocking each wine are listed after each entry in ascending order of price or in alphabetical order if they offer the wine at the same price. However, prices do fluctuate (there are special offers and discounts as well as price increases) so remember to use **Webster's** as a price GUIDE not a price LIST.*

⋆Côtes du Rhône, Domaine de la Bégude (FINT)
Côtes du Ventoux, Paul Jaboulet Ainé (HUN)
⋆Côtes du Rhône Valréas, Bouchard (BOW)

1981

£2.50–£3.00

Côtes du Ventoux, la Vieille Ferme (BIB)
Coteaux du Tricastin, Domaine de la Tour d'Elyssas, Cru du Devoy (BIB)
⋆Côtes du Rhône, Domaine des Trois Oratoires, Testut (HBV, HT)
Coteaux du Tricastin, Domaine de la Tour d'Elyssas, Cru de Meynas (BIB, FINT)
⋆Vin de Pays des Coteaux de l'Ardèche, Syrah (VIGN)
⋆Côtes du Rhône, Domaine de Bel Air, Bellicard (PD)
⋆Côtes du Rhône, Dudet (C&B)
Coteaux du Tricastin, Domaine de la Tour d'Elyssas, Vin de Syrah (BIB, BOW)
⋆Côtes de Luberon Blanc Cellier de Marrenon (AV)
⋆Côtes du Rhône Villages, Domaine de Verquière, Bernard Chamfort (WW)
⋆Vin de Pays des Coteaux de l'Ardèche, Cuvée de Lussas, Syrah (H&D)

£3.00–£4.00

⋆Côtes du Rhône, St-Vincent, de Vallouit (L&W)
⋆Coteaux du Tricastin, Domaine de Grangeneuve (HHC, CDM, YAPP)
⋆Côtes du Rhône, Domaine de Tout Vent, J. Mousset (BAL)
Côtes du Rhône, Coopérative Vinicole Comadine-Dauphinoise (YAPP)

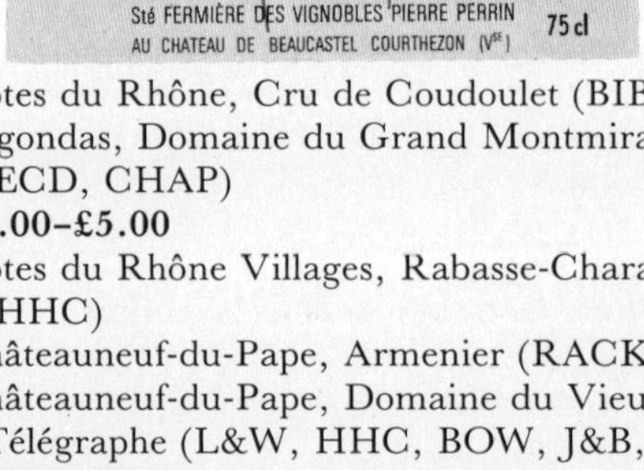

⋆Côtes du Rhône, Cru de Coudoulet (BIB)
⋆Gigondas, Domaine du Grand Montmirail (ECD, CHAP)

£4.00–£5.00

⋆Côtes du Rhône Villages, Rabasse-Charavin (HHC)
⋆Châteauneuf-du-Pape, Armenier (RACK)
⋆Châteauneuf-du-Pape, Domaine du Vieux Télégraphe (L&W, HHC, BOW, J&B, BYR, RH)

c. £6.25

Châteauneuf-du-Pape, Domaine de Nalys (VIGN)

Please don't blame ***Webster's*** *or the merchants listed if a wine is sold out or if the vintage you want is no longer available. Wine is a living entity and a limited commodity – continuity of supply cannot, alas, be guaranteed.*

1980

£2.50–£3.50

Vin de Pays des Coteaux de l'Ardèche, Gamay (DOL)

Vin de Pays des Coteaux de l'Ardèche, Syrah (DOL, YAPP)

⋆Côtes du Rhône, Vacqueyras, Pascal (CHAP, LHV, J&B)

⋆Lirac Testut (GH, ODD, SF, HT)

Côtes du Rhône, Domaine Saint Gayan (YAPP)

Lirac, Domaine de la Tour, Charles Pons-Mure (BOW)

£3.50–£4.00

Lirac, Domaine de la Genestière, Georges Bernard (L&W)

Vacqueyras, Caves des Vignerons des Vacqueyras (L&W)

⋆Lirac Rouge, Domaine les Garrigues (AV)

⋆Châteauneuf de Gadagne, Domaine de la Chapelle (HBV)

£4.00–£5.00

⋆Côtes du Rhône, Guigal (HT)

Gigondas, l'Oustau Fauquet Domaine de la Fourmone (L&W)

Gigondas, Domaine des Bosquets, Gabriel Meffre (SF)

£5.00–£6.00

⋆Châteauneuf-du-Pape, Domaine du Vieux Télégraphe (L&W, ADN, BAL, TAN, LADV)

Châteauneuf-du-Pape, Château de Beaucastel (BIB, CDM)

Châteauneuf-du-Pape, Domaine du Vieux Lazaret (WSOC)

Gigondas, Domaine Saint Gayan, Roger Meffre (YAPP)

Châteauneuf-du-Pape, les Cèdres, Paul Jaboulet Ainé (L&W, HUN, OWL)

Châteauneuf-du-Pape, Domaine Font de Michelle (YAPP)

c. £6.20

Châteauneuf-du-Pape, Domaine de la Nerte (ODD)

Châteauneuf-du-Pape, Château Fortia (ODD)

1979

£3.00–£3.50

⋆Coteaux du Tricastin, Domaine de Grangeneuve, Mme Bour (H&D, GH)

Côtes du Rhône, Jaume (WSOC)

⋆Lirac, Domaine Maby (LHV, WSOC)

Coteaux du Tricastin, Domaine du Devoy (STWC)

Cairanne, Caves des Coteaux Cairanne (L&W)

Vacqueyras, Pascal (ESV)

Lirac, la Fermade (YAPP)

£3.50–£4.00

Lirac, Philippe Testut (HBV)

⋆Côtes du Rhône, la Haie aux Grives, Domaine Vieux Chêne (J&B)

Lirac, Domaine de Castel Oualou (PG, VIGN)

⋆Châteauneuf de Gadagne, Domaine de la Chapelle (HBV)

£4.25–£5.00

⋆Lirac, Domaine du Château St-Roch (CDM)

Vacqueyras, Paul Jaboulet Ainé (HUN, PG)

⋆Gigondas, l'Oustau Fauquet (TAN, ADN)

⋆Châteauneuf de Gadagne, Domaine de la Chapelle, Réserve (HBV)

⋆Gigondas, Domaine des Bosquets, Gabriel Meffre (H&D)

Gigondas, Pascal Frères (VIGN)

£5.25–£6.00

Châteauneuf-du-Pape, Domaine du Vieux Télégraphe, Brunier (ADN, J&B)

Gigondas, Paul Jaboulet Ainé (ODD, HUN)

Châteauneuf-du-Pape, Domaine de Mont Redon (BAL, MAL)

Châteauneuf-du-Pape, Vignoble Abeille, Domaine de Mont Redon (WGA)

Châteauneuf-du-Pape les Cèdres, Paul Jaboulet Ainé (HUN, WSOC, TAN, OWL, SR)

£6.00–£7.00

⋆Châteauneuf-du-Pape, Château de Beaucastel (BIB, BWC, LADV, PIP, YFW)

Châteauneuf-du-Pape, Clos de l'Oratoire des Papes (PIP)
Gigondas, Domaine Saint Gayan, Roger Meffre (YFW)
Châteauneuf-du-Pape, Château Fortia (CUL)

1978
£2.50–£3.50
Côtes du Rhône, Domaine de la Seraphine (LHV, SR)
⋆Côtes du Rhône, Cuvée Personnelle, Pascal (ECD, CHAP, LHV, ESV, J&B, YAPP)

⋆Côtes du Rhône, Château de Boussarges (AV)
Côtes du Rhône, Réserve Personnelle, Charles Pax (BIB)
Vacqueyras, Cuvée Spéciale, Pascal (WW)
£3.75–£4.75
Lirac, Domaine de Castel Oualou, Marie Pons Mure (BYR)
Châteauneuf-du-Pape (VICT)
Vacqueyras, Pascal (YAPP)
⋆Gigondas, Domaine de la Chapelle, Meffre (PG)
£6.00–£6.50
Châteauneuf-du-Pape, Château Fortia (BIB)
Châteauneuf-du-Pape, Château de Beaucastel (TAN, ADN)
Châteauneuf-du-Pape, Clos de l'Oratoire (BYR)
£7.50–£8.50
Châteauneuf-du-Pape, Domaine de Mont Redon (GH)
Côtes du Rhône, Château de Fonsalette, Reynaud (WW, PG, OWL)

Châteauneuf-du-Pape, la Bernadine, Chapoutier (RACK)
c. £14.10
⋆Châteauneuf-du-Pape, Château Rayas, Reynaud (FFW, PG, OWL, VIGN)

1977
c. £6.20
Châteauneuf-du-Pape, les Cailloux (H&D)

1976
c. £3.20
Lirac Rouge, Marie Pons Mure (P&C)
c. £5.95
Châteauneuf-du-Pape, Domaine de Mont Redon (MAL, HT, WSOC, REID)
c. £7.50
Châteauneuf-du-Pape, Vignoble Abeille, Domaine de Mont Redon (WSOC)
c. £9.00
Côtes du Rhône, Château de Fonsalette, Reynaud (PG)
c. £12.15
Châteauneuf-du-Pape, Château Rayas (ADN, GH)

1974
c. £11.25
Châteauneuf-du-Pape, Château Rayas (ADN)

1973
c. £4.95
⋆Châteauneuf de Gadagne, Domaine de la Chapelle, Réserve (HBV)
c. £12.20
⋆Châteauneuf-du-Pape, Château Rayas, Reynaud (GH)

1972
c. £8.75
Châteauneuf-du-Pape, Château de Beaucastel (ADN, YFW)

1970
c. £15.05
Châteauneuf-du-Pape les Cèdres (OWL)

1969
c. £7.95
Châteauneuf-du-Pape, de Vallouit (L&W)
c. £15.90
Châteauneuf-du-Pape les Cèdres (OWL)

Stars (⋆) indicate wines selected by the merchants themselves as particularly good value in their class.

1967
c. £12.60
Châteauneuf-du-Pape les Cèdres, Paul Jaboulet Ainé (HT, GH)

1962
c. £24.40
Châteauneuf-du-Pape les Cèdres (OWL)

White

Non-vintage
£2.75–£3.50
Vin de Pays de Vaucluse, Domaine Vieux Chêne (J&B)
Côtes du Rhône, Domaine de la Présidente (YAPP)
Coteaux de l'Ardèche Chardonnay Louis Latour (L&W)
£3.75–£5.00
Vin doux Naturel de Rasteau, Jean Liautaud (YAPP)
⋆Muscat de Beaumes de Venise, Cave des Vignerons de Beaumes de Venise (YAPP, LADV, HHC, FINT, TAN)
Muscat de Beaumes de Venise, Cave Cooperative (WW, PIP, YFW)
Muscat de Beaumes de Venise, Domaine de Durban (YAPP, VICT, BOW, RH, CV, ODD)
c. £6.45
Muscat de Beaumes de Venise, Vidal Fleury (BIB, CDM, WSOC, YFW)

1982
£3.00–£4.00
Côtes du Luberon Blanc, la Vieille Ferme, Perrin (MAL)
⋆Côtes du Rhône Blanc (UNW)
⋆Lirac, la Fermade (YAPP)
Chardonnay de Pays des Coteaux de l'Ardèche, Louis Latour (CV)
£5.25–£6.50
⋆Châteauneuf-du-Pape, de Vallouit (L&W)
Châteauneuf-du-Pape, Domaine de Mont Redon (PG)
Châteauneuf-du-Pape, Domaine Font de Michelle (YAPP)
Châteauneuf-du-Pape, Domaine du Vieux Télégraphe (J&B)
c. £8.35
Châteauneuf-du-Pape, les Cèdres Blanc, Paul Jaboulet Ainé (LADV)

1981
c. £3.50
⋆Côtes du Rhône Blanc, Serre de Bernon, les Vignerons de Quatre Chemins (HT)
£6.00–£7.50
Châteauneuf-du-Pape Blanc, Mont-Redon (WSOC)
Châteauneuf-du-Pape Blanc, Domaine de Nalys (VIGN)
Châteauneuf-du-Pape Blanc, Château de Beaucastel, Perrin (YFW)

> *Merchants stocking each wine are listed after each entry in ascending order of price or in alphabetical order if they offer the wine at the same price. However, prices do fluctuate (there are special offers and discounts as well as price increases) so remember to use* ***Webster's*** *as a price GUIDE not a price LIST.*

1980
c. £5.40
Châteauneuf-du-Pape Blanc, Vignoble Abeille, Domaine de Mont Redon (MAL)
c. £10.80
Châteauneuf-du-Pape Blanc, Château Rayas (OWL)

1978
c. £2.90
Côtes du Rhône, Pascal (C&B)
Châteauneuf-du-Pape les Cèdres Blanc, Paul Jaboulet Ainé (OWL)
c. £7.70
Châteauneuf-du-Pape, Château Rayas (ADN)

1976
c. £11.50
Châteauneuf-du-Pape, Château Rayas (ADN)

1973
c. £12.10
Châteauneuf-du-Pape, Château Rayas (ADN)

1957
c. £16.70
Châteauneuf-du-Pape, Château Rayas (ADN, VIGN)

Rosé

Non-vintage
£3.50–£4.00
Tavel Rosé, Domaine de Trinquevedel (WW)
Tavel Rosé, Domaine de la Genestière (L&W)

1982
£3.50–£4.00
Tavel Rosé, Château d'Aquéria (LADV)
Tavel, la Forcadière, Domaine Maby (YAPP, RH)

1981
£3.00–£4.00
Tavel Rosé, Domaine Maby (WNRY)
Tavel Rosé, Domaine de la Genestière (TAN, PIP)
c. £4.20
Tavel Rosé, Domaine du Vieux Moulin, Gabriel Roudil (CV)

1980
c. £3.30
⋆Tavel Rosé, Bernard (ODD)
c. £4.45
Tavel Rosé, Domaine de la la Genestière, Bernard (ADN)

Sparkling

Non-vintage
c. £4.75
Clairette de Die Mousseux, Brut, Archard-Vincent (YAPP)
Clairette de Die Tradition, demi-sec, Archard-Vincent (YAPP)

1981
c. £4.50
⋆Clairette de Die Brut, Cave Coopérative (RSV)
⋆Clairette de Die Tradition, Cave Coopérative (RSV)

Price Guide – Notes

The Southern Rhône is beginning to burst at the seams or, at very least, bulge out of its traditional areas. This has been accelerated by the meteoric quality rise in vin de pays *areas like the Ardèche, remarkable low-price quality consistency of Côtes du Ventoux and the revival of self confidence in Lirac. It's difficult to say where the Southern Rhône area stops, and single domaine wines are now appearing from as far down as the River mouth at the Mediterranean. In the traditional heartland of the Rhône, around Châteaneuf-du-Pape and the Côtes du Rhône Villages, modern wine-making techniques and an increasing awareness of market needs are producing very attractive fruity wines which still preserve their Rhône character as well as maintaining a fair price. On British lists, it is particularly worth seeking out Ardèche, Tricastin, Ventoux for high quality cheap reds. For something bigger and more stylish, there are a lot of particularly good Côtes du Rhône Villages from co-ops or growers, and Gigondas, Lirac and Châteauneuf-du-Pape from growers. And prices are still very reasonable.*

SOUTHERN PROSPECTS

As demand for basic 'gros rouge' (French slang for red plonk) drops, and demand for *appellation controlée* wines increases, the southern Côtes du Rhône is well placed to take advantage, as long as it can do something to curb the current see-saw of prices. The south is far less prone to vintage variation, if only because the heights its wines achieve are not as exciting as the Syrah wines from the north. Also, most of its wines, even the best, are made up of a combination of grapes which, skilfully handled, can turn out a fairly similar product year by year.

The future is particularly bright for the better placed Côtes du Rhône-Villages, most of whom have a mixture of good individual growers and an effective co-operative, and for the 'fringe' areas of Côtes du Ventoux, Côtes du Luberon, and Costières du Gard, which are producing increasing quantities of fresh, fruity wine at not much more than *vin de table* prices. Of the single-village appellations, Lirac still looks good and cheap for both red and rosé, while Tavel looks just as expensive as usual, and its wines taste just as heavy. Five years ago, Châteauneuf seemed grossly overpriced, and the reputation obviously lingers on because, despite stable prices, people are still thinking of the wine as pricey. Good single-domaine Châteauneuf is *not* expensive. Rhône whites are slowly becoming drinkable, particularly from modern co-ops like Chusclan, and one can only see Muscat de Beaumes de Venise going from strength to strength. But producer's will have to be very self-critical if standards are to be maintained.

ALSACE

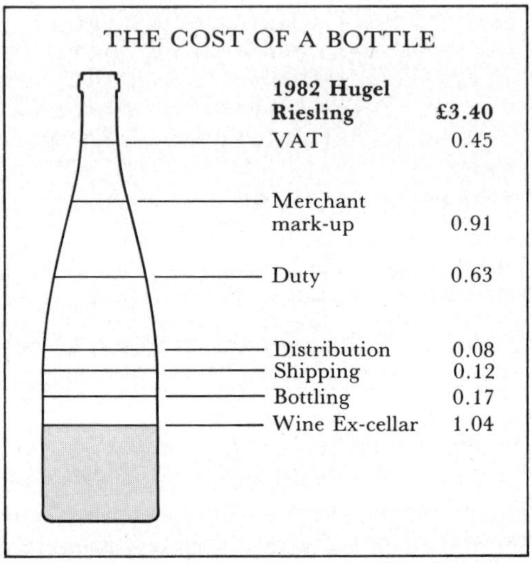

Alsace always seems to be about to catch the boat to worldwide popularity, but then gets caught in a traffic jam half-way to the docks, and rushes gasping to the quayside just as the last hawser is thrown ashore. For years people have been saying – you know the most underrated, the best value for money, the most reliable wine in France? Alsace. But they've been whispering it, and there's the rub. Alsace has never had anyone to trumpet its wares; the Alsace people seem cut off in their frontier valley, away from the other great areas of France. There's never been one wine – like 'champagne', 'claret' or 'burgundy', which in fact hides a hundred different styles but they always seem to be that one wine. Alsace wines always seem to be the separate units rather than a mass-marketable whole. You say Alsace Riesling, Tokay d'Alsace, Alsace Gewürztraminer, but you don't say 'Let's have some Alsace', as you would say 'Let's have some burgundy'.

This is all rather unfair, because Alsace wines are generally of a high quality. They *do* deserve to be better known, and they are among the most suitable French wines to drink on their own, nearly always preserving something flowery or spicy from their predominantly German vine varieties. Also, they have made more effort than any other modern vineyard area to ensure quality, not just cosy tradition, in their appellation laws. The reason was that from 1870 to 1918, Alsace was German, and used as a highly efficient producer of plonk to beef up the lighter German wines. Riesling and Traminer were actually forbidden, so as not to provide competition for the conqueror's home-brews.

Once Alsace was French again in 1918, there was obviously no future in making boring, characterless wines at a latitude which might be pretty far south for Germany, but was pretty far north for France. It could only survive through a quality-first approach, and so the ravaged vineyards were laboriously replanted with the noble grapes, led by Traminer and Riesling. Until 1940, when the pendulum of fate was wrenched back by another brutish war-machine, and the vineyards were again chiefly used for target practice. The result was that, bang on the nail in 1945, Alsace registered a single *appellation contrôlée,* that of Alsace, and once again set its cap at quality. It worked. By 1972, Alsace became the first appellation to enforce 100 per cent original-bottling and now even the quite classy lesser grapes like Sylvaner are in steep decline being replaced by Pinot Blanc, Pinot Gris, Muscat, Gewürztraminer and Riesling.

What is produced is a wine unique in France's enormous range. Although German grapes are used, the sweetness of German wines is dismissed curtly as baby-talk. The Alsace growers ferment their wines to complete dryness. With the Riesling this makes for one of the driest wines in France, in no way resembling the flowery, grapey Riesling of the German Rhine. With Gewürztraminer it makes the astonishing bone-dry, but soaked in spicy fruit, wine which has now

Vintage Table

***1983** Great wine at every level. Tremendous ripeness and acid balance. Buy the best Rieslings, Pinot Gris and Gewürztraminers to keep, and even the lesser wines could age a while.

1982 The Big One. A massive vintage of soft, easy wines. Properly made they have a gentle, fruity style, though less good producers may offer flabby wine.

***1981** Dryer, more concentrated than 1982, more exciting, with the individual grape flavours very strongly marked. Good to drink or keep a bit.

***1979** A big crop. The wines started a bit soft, but they're now beautiful, gentle Alsace wines. Don't keep. Drink!

***1976** Brilliant, deep, late-picked wines bursting with flavour and richness, but still dry. An experience, if you can find an example.

Off-vintages such as 1980 and 1977 can produce very steely, dry Rieslings which by now will be reeking of petrol and delicious for old Riesling freaks.

Maturity Chart

1979 RIESLING AND GEWURZTRAMINER

Years like 1976 and 1983 (especially the richer wines) will mature more slowly and last longer. Less good years can give very good dry Rieslings for 5–8 years.

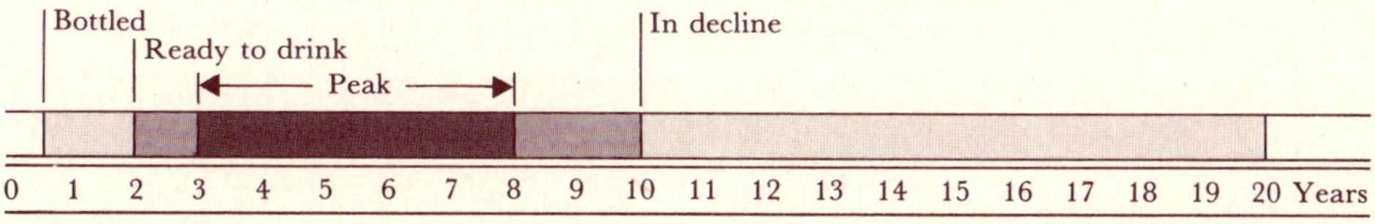

led to an explosion of Gewürz production across the world. With Muscat, it makes a wine so dry it should be tart, and yet so fragrant it should be succulent sweet, and with the Pinot Gris, it draws out all the honey and grapey sweetness – and yet the wine remains dry.

They are remarkable wines, and it's difficult to see why they don't get the success they deserve. Perhaps they are indeed highly successful, and it's just that the UK market is merely a steady rather than an obsessive buyer of the wines, because Alsace, with 20 per cent of the total French white *appellation contrôlée* production, has around 45 per cent of French domestic sales of white AC. We Brits do hear endless pleas to drink more Alsace; maybe there's not that much available to increase our consumption with.

To try to improve their image, which is often of the attractive and reliable, but not world-beater sort, they have begun to late-gather their grapes in the German way, but still aiming for a dry wine, though the odd gram of sugar may remain. These late-gathered wines are called Vendange Tardive and the really special ones, made in a grape-by-grape way as with the great German Beerenauslesen, are called Sélection des Grains Nobles. These aren't possible every year - 1976 and 1983 are the two best recent examples - and some of them are even beginning to show a slight investment potential.

Vendange Tardive wines do not normally appear until about three years after the vintage. The 1976s first appeared in 1979. The Hugel Gewürztraminer was then £85.50 per case, the Hugel Riesling was £91.77, and the Hugel Pinot Gris, or Tokay, was only £77.28. By 1984 the Gewürz had moved slightly to £95.50, the Riesling had made a healthy increase to £140.30, while the Tokay had rocketed from lowest to highest - up to £147.94. In any other classic wine, an increase of 100 per cent in five years would not be regarded as unusual, but it only occurred here because of the tiny amount of this grape available. Yet an increase of only £10 over five years as with the Gewürz would be regarded as appalling. But then the idea of Vendange Tardive only began in 1959, and only got going with the 1976 vintage. It takes longer than that to persuade investors they have a classic on their hands.

CRÉMANT

Potential alternatives to champagne continue to flow thick and fast, and one of the creations with the greatest quality potential has to be Crémant d'Alsace. The Dopff company has been making this all century, but in 1976 an appellation Crémant d'Alsace was granted, and things have taken off since. In five years the number of registered makers has grown from eight to 200, and the Crémant industry is now sucking up around five per cent of the total Alsace harvest, but they certainly intend to top that. The three biggest producers have formed the Société des Crémants d'Alsace to give themselves an identity. They expect to sell 1.2 million bottles in 1984 but 5 million in 1987.

As yet, 80 per cent is drunk in Alsace itself, and that market seems secure. However, the rise in popularity elsewhere has been greatly aided by recent tiny vintages in Champagne, with the consequent shortages of stock and massive hikes in price. This gave Alsace, already sporting a quality image, a tailor-made chance to offer a class champagne-method alternative. But 1982 and 1983 have produced massive champagne harvests; the prices have tumbled, and the cellars are suddenly bulging with stock. Alsace's fairly pricey alternative suddenly looks less good value. Add to that the fact that the best base wine is Pinot Blanc, which is rapidly becoming Alsace's new star in the still wine sky. It makes light, fresh, young whites with just a hint of honey, which are spearheading export sales, particularly to the UK. Will Crémant have to turn to other grape varieties? Will the price gap with champagne become too narrow for comfort? Watch this space!

Price Guide

White

Non-vintage
c. £3.00
Alsace, Grants of St James's (VICT)
Tesco Gewürztraminer (TES)
Waitrose Alsace Gewürztraminer (WAIT)
★Pinot Blanc, Hugel (PD)
The Society's Vin d'Alsace, Hugel (WSOC)

£3.75–£4.50
Flambeau d'Alsace, Hugel (YFW, TAN)
Riesling d'Alsace, Hugel (PD)
Sylvaner, Trimbach (UNW)
Gewürztraminer d'Alsace, Hugel (PD)

£4.75–£5.25
Muscat, Hugel (WGA)
Gewürztraminer, Trimbach (UNW)
c. £6.30
Crémant d'Alsace Brut, Louis Gisselbrecht (PIP)

1983
c. £3.65
★Muscat, Lucien Tempé (BOW)

1982
£2.50–£3.00
Sylvaner d'Alsace, Weissenburger (MART)
Sylvaner, Louis Gisselbrecht (BIB, H&D, PIP)
★Pinot Blanc, Louis Gisselbrecht (CUL, BIB, ASHE, RH, H&D, PIP)

Edelzwicker, Pichet d'Alsace, Michel Laugel (SF, VIGN)
Sylvaner, Michel Laugel (SF)
£3.00–£3.50
★Edelzwicker, Rolly-Gassmann (RH)
Riesling, Heim (SR)
Gewürztraminer d'Alsace, Weissenburger (MART)
Pinot Blanc, Preiss Henny (BWC)
Tokay, Louis Gisselbrecht (BIB, PIP)
Sylvaner Cuvée Tradition, Kuentz-Bas (DOL)
Muscat, Louis Gisselbrecht (BYR, BIB, H&D)
★Pinot d'Alsace Réserve, Blanck (L&W)
Riesling, Louis Gisselbrecht (CUL, H&D)
Riesling Réserve, Victor Lorang (LHV)
Edelzwicker d'Alsace, Cave de Kientzheim (STWC)
Riesling, Preiss Henny (BWC)
Sylvaner, Lucien Tempé (BOW)
Vin d'Alsace, Zind Humbrecht (MAL)
Pinot Blanc Cuvée Tradition, Kuentz-Bas (DOL)
Pinot Blanc, Lucien Tempé (BOW)
★Pinot Blanc Réserve, René Schmidt (HHC)
Riesling Cuvée Tradition, Kuentz-Bas (DOL)
Sylvaner, Preiss-Zimmer (VICT)
£3.50–£4.00
Gewürztraminer Réserve, Victor Lorang (LHV)
★Riesling, Henri Wiederhirn (HBV)

Pinot Blanc, Hugel (WGA)
Pinot Blanc, Preiss-Zimmer (VICT)
⋆Tokay Pinot Gris, Henri Wiederhirn (HBV)
Gewürztraminer, Preiss Henny (BWC)
Riesling, Trimbach (ODD)
Riesling d'Alsace Réserve, René Schmidt (HHC)
Riesling, Hugel (SF, DAV, CV, YFW)
⋆Tokay d'Alsace Cuvée Particulière, Victor Lorang (LHV)
Gewürztraminer, Michel Laugel (SF)

Tokay, Preiss-Zimmer (RH, VICT)
Gewürztraminer Réserve Spéciale, Blanck (L&W)
⋆Gewürztraminer, Louis Gisselbrecht (ASHE, H&D, CUL, PIP, RH, RSV)

⋆Gewürztraminer, Henri Wiederhirn (HBV)
Gewürztraminer, Cuvée Tradition, Kuentz-Bas (DOL, MWS)
Tokay Réserve, Trimbach (ODD)

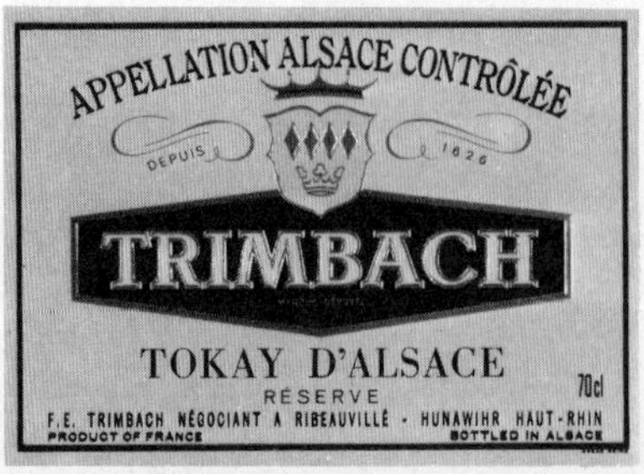

£4.00–£4.25
⋆Muscat, Henri Wiederhirn (HBV)
⋆Gewürztraminer Réserve, René Schmidt (HHC)
Muscat Réserve, Trimbach (ODD, YFW)
Gewürztraminer, Trimbach (ODD)

£4.50–£5.00
Gewürztraminer, Hugel (PG, CUL, DAV, MWS, YFW)
⋆Riesling Réserve, Henri Wiederhirn (HBV)
⋆Gewürztraminer Réserve, Henri Wiederhirn (HBV)

£5.75–£6.50
Gewürztraminer Réserve, Faller Frères (OWL)
Muscat, Faller Frères (OWL)
Riesling Réserve Personnelle, Faller Frères (OWL)
Gewürztraminer Réserve Personnelle, Faller Frères (OWL)

£7.25–£8.00
Riesling Schlossberg Grand Cru, Faller Fréres (OWL)
Tokay d'Alsace Réserve Particulière, Faller Frères (OWL)

c. £11.50
Gewürztraminer Vendanges Tardives, Faller Frères (OWL)
Tokay d'Alsace Vendanges Tardives, Faller Frères (OWL)

__Webster's__ is an independent guide. We have received an enormous amount of information and assistance from the wine trade but responsibility for editorial content is the editors' and publishers' alone.

1981

£2.50–£3.00
Sainsbury's Sylvaner d'Alsace (SAIN)
Pinot Blanc, Gaschy (ODD)
Sylvaner, Gaschy (ODD)
Edelzwicker Royal d'Alsace, Heim (SR)
Riesling, Gaschy (ODD)
⋆Sylvaner Réserve, Heim (WW, SR)

★Sylvaner, Dopff & Irion (PG)

£3.00–£3.50

Alsace, Les Amis du Vin (LADV)
Tokay d'Alsace, Heim (SR)
Tokay d'Alsace, Louis Sipp (WHIT)
★Muscat d'Alsace, Heim (WW)
★Riesling, Louis Gisselbrecht (BIB, ASHE, BYR, RH, HT, PIP, LADV, RSV)
Gewürztraminer, Gaschy (ODD)

★Pinot Blanc, Clos de Strangenberg, Heim (SR, WW)
★Sainsbury's Gewürztraminer (SAIN)
★Gewürztraminer, Heim (SR, WW)
Riesling d'Alsace, Domaine d'Engelgarten (WAIT)
Riesling, Gustave Lorentz (THRE)

£3.50–£4.00

Sylvaner, Hugel (WSOC, CV, MWS)
★Tokay d'Alsace, Louis Gisselbrecht (FFW)
Pinot Blanc Réserve, Ziegler (CDM)
Riesling d'Alsace, Cave de Kientzheim (STWC)
Sylvaner, Trimbach (CHAP, YFW)
★Gewürztraminer, Dopff au Moulin (PG)
Gewürztraminer, Louis Gisselbrecht (BIB, HT)
Pinot Blanc, Trimbach (HT, RACK)
Pinot Blanc, Hugel (WSOC, BIB, WNRY, MWS, BBR, MAL, TAN, P&C)
Riesling, Ziegler (CDM)
Sylvaner, Kuehn (TAN)
Pinot Blanc, Domaine Schlumberger (MACK)

Riesling, Preiss-Zimmer (VICT)
Riesling, Heydt (C&B)
★Gewürztraminer Réserve, Heim (SR, PG)
Riesling Réserve, Les Eglantiers, Heim (SR)
Tokay d'Alsace, Ziegler (CDM)
★Muscat, Louis Gisselbrecht (HT, BYR, PIP, LADV)
Gewürztraminer, Gustave Lorentz (THRE)

£4.00–£4.50

Riesling, Trimbach (CHAP, RACK)
Tokay Cuvée Tradition, Hugel (SF, MWS)
★Riesling, Réserve Spéciale, Schlumberger (L&W)

Muscat Réserve Personnelle, Kuentz-Bas (DOL)
★Gewürztraminer, Henri Wiederhirn (HBV)
★Riesling, Kuehn (TAN)
Gewürztraminer, Ziegler (CDM)
Muscat d'Alsace, Charles Schleret (YAPP)
Tokay d'Alsace, Charles Schleret (YAPP)
Riesling, Cuvée Saint Barnabé, Lucien Tempé (BOW)
Muscat Réserve, Rolly-Gassmann (RH)
★Gewürztraminer Zinnkoepflé, Heim (SR)
Riesling, Hugel (WSOC, CUL, BIB, JH, MWS)
Riesling, Jos Meyer (MACK)
★Pinot Blanc des Blancs, Cuvée les Amours, Hugel (AV, FINT)
Gewürztraminer, Preiss-Zimmer (VICT, HUN)

£4.50–£5.00

Gewürztraminer, Trimbach (CHAP, HT, CV, RACK)

Riesling, Clos Hauserer, Zind-Humbrecht (MAL)
Riesling Grande Réserve, Schlumberger (MACK)
Gewürztraminer Réserve, Cuvée Selectionnée, Schmidt (ESV)
Riesling Cuvée Tradition, Hugel (GH, WSOC, J&B, AV, TAN)
★Gewürztraminer, Fleur de Guebwiller, Schlumberger (L&W)
Gewürztraminer, Hugel (BYR, WSOC, JH, P&C)
★Gewürztraminer, Heydt (C&B)
Riesling Herrenweg Turckheim, Zind-Humbrecht (MAL)
Gewürztraminer Bollenberg Médaille d'Or, Théo Cattin (C&B)
Pinot Gris Réserve Spéciale, Schlumberger (L&W)
Gewürztraminer, Cuvée des Evêques, Hugel (J&B)
★Gewürztraminer Réserve, Henri Wiederhirn (HBV)
Muscat Réserve, Trimbach (CV, BAL)
Muscat Cuvée Réserve, Jos Meyer (MACK)
Gewürztraminer, Kuehn (TAN)
£5.00–£5.50
★Gewürztraminer Réserve Personnelle, Blanck (L&W)
Riesling Grand Cru, Schlossberg, Blanck (L&W)
Gewürztraminer, Cuvée Baron Symon de Blonay, Lucien Tempé (BOW)
Tokay Réserve, Trimbach (YFW)
Gewürztraminer, Beyer (GH)

Muscat Cuvée Tradition, Hugel (MWS, AV, MAL)
Gewürztraminer, Jos Meyer (MACK)
Gewürztraminer Cuvée Tradition, Hugel (WSOC)
Gewürztraminer Herrenweg Turckheim, Zind-Humbrecht (MAL)
c. £5.65
Gewürztraminer, Seigneurs de Ribeaupierre, Trimbach (PG)
£7.50–£8.00
Riesling Schoenenberg Réserve Spéciale, Dopff au Moulin (YFW)
Gewürztraminer Réserve Personnelle, Hugel (WSOC)
£8.00–£9.00
Gewürztraminer Mambourg, Vendange Tardive, Sparr (CDM)
Gewürztraminer Hengst, Vendange Tardive, Zind-Humbrecht (MAL)

1980
£3.25–£4.00
★Edelzwicker, Rolly Gassmann (FFW)
Sylvaner, Jos Meyer (H&B)
Riesling, Hugel, (PG, WNRY)
Riesling, Charles Schleret (YAPP)
£4.00–£5.00
Muscat Cuvée Tradition, Hugel (BYR)
Pinot Noir, Hugel (BYR)
Tokay Réserve, Trimbach (BAL)
Riesling d'Alsace, Beyer (GH)
Gewürztraminer, Hugel (WNRY, FINT)

1979
£2.75–£3.25
Sylvaner, Louis Sipp (WHIT)
★Muscat d'Alsace, Heim (SR)
£3.25–£4.00
★Riesling Réserve, Heim (SR, BIB)
★Riesling Réserve, Les Eglantiers, Heim (WW)

£4.00–£4.50
Gewürztraminer, Charles Schleret (YAPP)
Gewürztraminer, Louis Sipp (WHIT)
Tokay Cuvée Tradition, Hugel (BYR, WNRY)
Muscat, Schmidt (ESV)
★Sylvaner, Hugel (P&C)
Gewürztraminer, Michel Laugel (LADV)
Muscat d'Alsace, Ziegler (CDM)

Tokay d'Alsace Cuvée Particulière, Schmidt (ESV)
Riesling, Schoenenberg (ESV)

£4.50–£5.00
Riesling, Les Pierrets, Jos Meyer (H&B)
Tokay d'Alsace, Trimbach (HHC)
Gewürztraminer Réserve Personnelle, Kuentz-Bas (DOL, PG, BOW)
Gewürztraminer Réserve, Trimbach (MART, MAL)
Muscat Cuvée Tradition, Hugel (H&D)
Gewürztraminer Réserve, Zinkoepflé, Heim (WW)
Muscat Réserve, Trimbach (GH, HHC)

£5.00–£5.50
Gewürztraminer Cuvée Tradition, Hugel (SF, WSOC, J&B, GH, BBR)
Muscat Réserve Personnelle, Hugel (SF, HUN)
Riesling, Cuvée Frédéric Emile, Trimbach (PG, L&W, BOW, VIGN, LADV)
Pinot Gris, Preiss Henny (BWC)
Muscat, Les Amandiers, Dopff & Irion (PG)
★Gewürztraminer, Les Archenets, Jos Meyer (H&B)

£5.50–£6.00
Gewürztraminer Réserve Personnelle, Hugel (SF, PD, WSOC, J&B, TAN, MWS, WNRY)
★Riesling Kitterlé, Schlumberger (L&W)
Riesling Réserve Personnelle, Hugel (SF, J&B, H&D, MWS, TAN, WNRY)
Riesling Altenbourg, Sparr (CDM)
Muscat, Léon Beyer (WNRY)
Gewürztraminer, Seigneurs de Ribeaupierre, Trimbach (ODD, LADV, MAL)

£6.00–£6.50
Gewürztraminer Réserve Personnelle, Heydt (C&B)
Gewürztraminer Mambourg, Sparr (CDM)
Riesling, Clos St Hune, Trimbach (PG)
Eichberg Gewürztraminer Réserve Spéciale, Dopff au Moulin (YFW)

£8.25–£9.50
★Gewürztraminer Grand Cru, Vendange Tardive, Heim (SR)

Gewürztraminer Vendange Tardive, Dopff & Irion (PG)

1978

c. £5.25
Tokay d'Alsace Cuvée Tradition, Hugel (AV)

c. £6.50
Riesling Schoenenburg Réserve Spéciale, Dopff au Moulin (WHIT)

c. £7.50
Gewürztraminer Vendange Tardive, Wolfberger (PG)
Eichberg Gewürztraminer Réserve Spéciale, Dopff au Moulin (WHIT)

c. £9.00
Riesling, Clos St Hune, Trimbach (VIGN, WNRY, TAN)

1977

c. £8.75
Riesling, Clos St Hune, Trimbach (VIGN)

1976

£4.00–£4.50
Gewürztraminer, Louis Sipp (WHIT)
Riesling Kirchberg Sélection Particulière, Louis Sipp (WHIT)

£5.50–£6.50
Gewürztraminer, Preiss Henny (BWC)
Riesling Cuvée Tradition, Hugel (BBR)

£7.00–£8.00
Gewürztraminer Vendange Tardive, Schmidt (AV)
Gewürztraminer Réserve Personnelle, Hugel (L&W, H&D, REID)

£8.00–£9.00
★Gewürztraminer Vendange Tardive, Hugel (SF, WSOC, H&D, PG, GH, REID, J&B)
Gewürztraminer Sélection Personnelle, Hugel (HT)
★Gewürztraminer, Cuvée Christine Schlumberger (L&W)
Riesling Vendange Tardive, Dopff & Irion (MAL)

£12.00–£13.50
★Riesling Vendange Tardive, Hugel (REID, WSOC, MWS, L&W, FFW, VIGN, LAV, YFW)

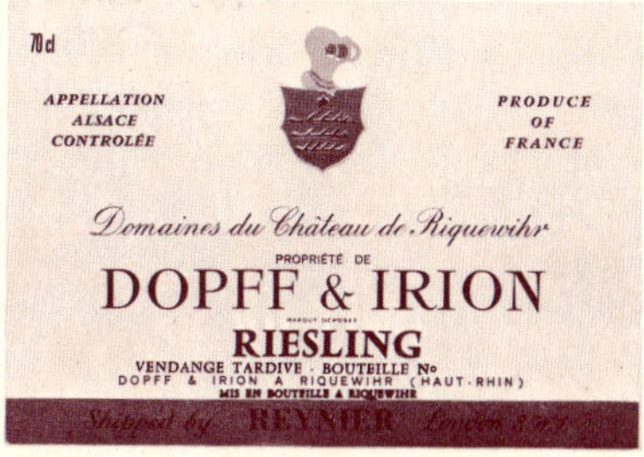

Gewürztraminer Christine Schlumberger Vendange Tardive (REID, VIGN)
⋆Tokay Vendange Tardive, Hugel (WSOC, L&W, FFW, VIGN)
Gewürztraminer Vendange Tardive, Léon Beyer (L&W)
c. £16.00
Gewürztraminer, Cuvée Anne Schlumberger (L&W)
c. £19.00
⋆Gewürztraminer Sélection de Grains Nobles, Hugel (L&W, J&B, WGA, FFW, MWS, REID, VIGN, ADN, YFW, LADV, WNRY)
£20.00–£25.00
Gewürztraminer Anne Schlumberger Vendange Tardive (REID)
Riesling, Sélection des Grains Nobles, Hugel (ADN, L&W, MWS)
c. £30.00
Tokay Sélection des Grains Nobles, Hugel (L&W, REID, MWS)

> ***Webster's*** *has been compiled from the latest merchants' catalogues available at the time of going to press but neither we nor the merchants listed can guarantee that all the wines mentioned will be available by the time you read the book. Equally, other wines and new vintages will become available.*

1975
c. £5.30
⋆Muscat, Les Amandiers, Dopff & Irion (PG)

1973
c. £5.00
Riesling Cuvée Tradition, Hugel (REID)
c. £10.00
Gewürztraminer, Cuvée Seigneurs de Ribeaupiere, Trimbach (REID)

1971
£9.00–£10.00
Riesling Réserve, Boeckel (VIGN)
Riesling Spätlese, Hugel (VIGN)
c. £20.00
Riesling, Clos St Hune, Trimbach (VIGN)

1967
c. £8.00
Gewürztraminer Réserve, Trimbach (L&W)
c. £45.00
Gewürztraminer Beerenauslese, Hugel (REID)

1966
c. £7.00
Muscat Grande Réserve, Trimbach (HUN)

1959
c. £27.00
Traminer Réserve Exceptionelle Auslese, Hugel (VIGN)

Red

1982
c. £3.50
Pinot Noir, Victor Lorang (LHV)
c. £4.75
Pinot Noir d'Alsace, Ziegler (CDM)

1981
c. £3.30
Pinot Noir, Louis Gisselbrecht (BIB, PIP, FFW)
£4.50–£5.00
Pinot Noir, Beyer (GH)
Pinot Noir Hugel (YFW, MWS)

1980
c. £4.25
Pinot Noir, Charles Schleret (YAPP)

1979
c. £3.20
Pinot Noir, Louis Sipp (WHIT)

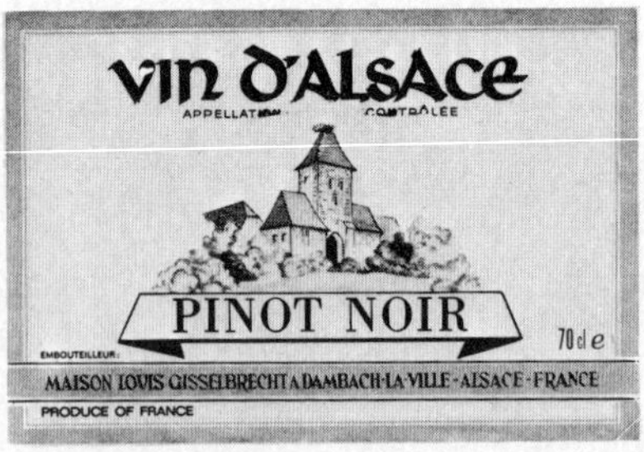

Sparkling

Non-vintage
c. £4.75
⋆Crémant d'Alsace Imperial Brut, Heim (SR)
c. £5.25
Crémant d'Alsace, Cuvée Julien, Dopff au Moulin (L&W)
c. £6.00
Crémant d'Alsace Brut, Michel Laugel (VIGN)

Price Guide – Notes

It is one of the commonest cries in the British wine trade that Alsace wines are so wonderful but no one ever buys them. Someone must do, because import figures keep rising, and it can't just be wine merchants drowning their sorrows in Gewürztraminer. In fact virtually every wine merchant has some Alsace wines on his list, but the actual variety is relatively small, being dominated by very few wines from very few shippers. Luckily the quality of these is usually good, but even so, encourage the others by searching out lesser known growers, and also try moving on from Riesling and Gewürztraminer to Pinot Blanc, Pinot Gris and Muscat.

FINE FORECAST

Alsace should have a bright future for two reasons. The move to promote a unique and specialist image has been given a great boost by the happenings of 1983. Two dozen of the traditionally best vineyard sites were designated 'Grand Crus', the first move towards a hierarchy of Alsace wines which will, with any luck, create and foster an interest in single vineyard, vintage wines, without which the individuality and exclusivity the collector/investor demands is lacking. And 1983 was without question the year to get down to this in earnest. It's just possible that it is the finest vintage this century. Of the other great vintages only 1976 has made a lot of top wines, but in 1983 there was not only masses of wine, but the incredibly high sugar readings were spread across the board, with the exception of Muscat. Growers believe they have another 1921, the *annus mirabilis* for all the great sweet wines of Europe. Since they have chosen this year to promote Alsace as an 'extra-quality' wine area, they couldn't have wished for a better start.

The other bright spark of hope is that Alsace may have found itself the flag-waver it has so far lacked, and from a most unlikely quarter – the erstwhile lowly Pinot Blanc. It is fast becoming the perfect wine-bar wine. In the UK market, this is crucially important, since we are one of the few markets to take strongly to the idea of regular wine-drinking without food. Pinot Blanc is soft, fresh, very slightly spicy, and the name is good, pronounceable, vaguely glossy. They'll need to keep planting this one.

LOIRE

When I see people describe the Loire as the most varied and exciting wine area of France I reach nervously for my tasting notes and thumb back through the months. I always come to the same conclusion: there *are* lots of wines, often with encouragingly different names, but the tastes are startlingly similar in a very few, basic styles. And when I see Loire wines being described as soft, meadow-fresh, charming, and easy to enjoy, I scoot back to those same notes, and come across endless repetition of 'harsh', 'unripe' and 'acid', punctuated by 'fresh', 'grassy' and other 'green' adjectives.

It's difficult to know why everyone began to describe these Loire wines as soft and gentle, because the great characteristic of all good Loire wines – red, white, and, dare we say it, rosé – is acidity. This is far-north wine-growing, and the grapes they've planted, the white Chenin and Sauvignon, the red Cabernet and Gamay, are all varieties prized for their fairly acid and raw qualities. Curiously, the wine everyone has come to presume to be the driest, tartest wine of all France – Muscadet – is made from a grape which used to be called the Melon de Bourgogne, but is now known as Muscadet except sometimes in Burgundy itself, which has so little natural acidity that even on the vineyards sprawled out past the estuary flats round Nantes they have to harvest it incredibly early, simply to preserve some semblance of acidity in the finished product.

It's not difficult to see why the Loire has been described as France's most varied wine river. It does flow on for an awfully long way, starting almost in the Rhône valley south of Lyons. By the time it has executed a great, wide-flung arc north and west, it has spawned as many as a hundred different wines. However, because of the major grapes which are planted, a lot of variation in style isn't possible. With Muscadet, the essentially neutral taste of the Melon grape is the whole point. With the Chenin, which by some unhappy quirk of fate is the principal Loire white grape, the incredibly late-ripening fruit gives you stabbing acidity and not a lot else which can be talked of in polite company (the exception here is the occasional great sweet wines some producers make, see *Loire Sweet Wines*. The Sauvignon may have only one taste, but at least it's a good one, being green and smokey and slightly sharp, but also, usually, with enough body to get away with it.

The reds are dominated in quality by Cabernet Franc, which this far north can normally only manage a fairly piercing, but muddy, blackcurranty fruit, and the Gamay, still generally marked by rather tough acid and tannin, but slowly being dragged out of its pit by modern methods, to produce – a simple, fresh red. Simple tastes all the way. There are also pockets of Pinot Noir, Chardonnay, and various other tolerated, but not cooed-over, varieties. None of these varieties give wine of great complexity. Which is OK, because the Loire wines are pretty cheap. With the exception of Sancerre, and Pouilly-Fumé (suddenly world-famous and relentlessly copied), these light, simple tastes command a light, simple price – and those 'sweet stickies' are a proper bargain. It's encouraging to see that a region which has had more than its fair share of 'mode' wines, has mostly managed to keep prices fairly attractive.

Dry White Wines

The Loire has two of the most famous dry whites in the world, at diametrically opposite ends of the river. Muscadet sprawls across the salty lowland country at the river's mouth, while Sancerre is coaxed from the chalky hillsides high up half-way across France. Their notoriety has developed in equally opposite ways.

Muscadet built its reputation in jugs on the café tables of Paris, becoming the white half-sister of Beaujolais Nouveau in their double-headed surge from local thirst-quencher to international star. But Muscadet never had a very sophisticated air. Her yields were high, her vineyards easily expandable, her wine renowned, if anything, for its relative lack of flavour and acidity, plainly offering something fresh and simple and new. Graduating from jug to bottle didn't mean that she had suddenly learned to curtsey and recite Shakespeare. No, that simple, undemanding taste is precisely why Muscadet is popular.

Sancerre's rise to fame wasn't a bit like that. Sancerre had loads of taste, of a green, smoky, tangy sort that was so refreshing and so memorable that it didn't take many journalists extolling its virtues for it to be slung into a slot as the expense-account diner's most fashionable white. It had never had a 'café' image to overcome; it went straight into the flashy world of media men and *terrine de légumes.* The price progress illustrates that point very clearly. In London in 1975, a good Muscadet at £1.62 was more expensive than a Sancerre at £1.42. By 1979 the Muscadet was £2.60, but the Sancerre was £4.10, while by 1983 Sancerre had climbed to £4.95, while Muscadet had crept to £3.02. Sancerre growers have prospered and been imitated all round the world, while Muscadet growers are at this moment engaged in a desperate power struggle for survival. When Chablis prices shot up in the mid-seventies, Muscadet was seen as an effective substitute, and its prices rose accordingly.

THE COST OF A BOTTLE

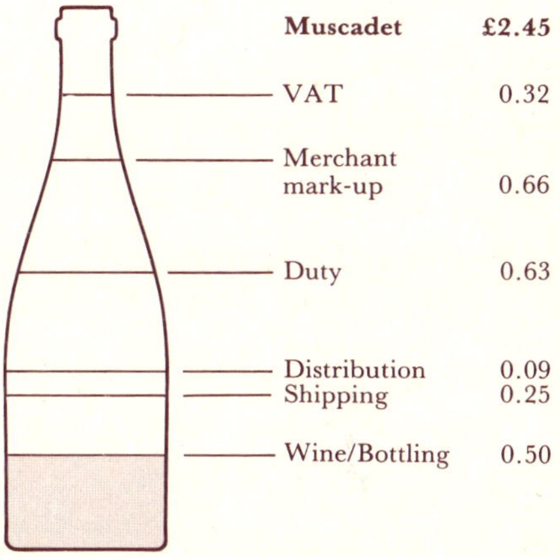

1979 produced loads of Chablis and the price plummeted. Muscadet tumbled after, and despite its popularity, is so lumbered with the 'cheap' tag that many growers cannot get a decent price, and have refused to sell for less than 1,200 francs a barrel (215 litres). Trouble is, there's loads of '82 and '83, so the merchants are humming and twiddling their thumbs while the growers go down the Swannee, under the sheer weight of their unsold wine.

This seems insane for a popular wine, but those growers who take the trouble *can* get a better price by producing their wine *sur lie,* which means that it's bottled off its own yeast sediment, and the resultant wine has a roundness and nutty softness, and possibly a very slight spritz which certainly makes the best of the rather dull fruit. There were rumours last year that *mise sur lie* had become a meaningless term, but our researches show that it's very definitely still meaningful, and a sign of higher quality.

The Sauvignon taste, up-river, is the one that everyone is gasping for, and the promotion of Touraine Sauvignon, and more recently Vin de Pays du Jardin de la France, has allowed people to drink Sancerre look-alikes at a far lower price.

And in America, South Africa, New Zealand and Australia, people are squinting with concentration to try to recreate what seems to be the essence of the Sauvignon flavour, as perfected by Sancerre and Pouilly-Fumé. No one's been crawling round trying to clone Muscadet. Maybe that price differential is fair after all.

In between these extremes we have Vouvray, which is certainly one of the best Loire wines – dry, medium, sweet or sparkling – but perhaps suffers from its multiplicity of talents, since good 'commercial' Vouvray is largely a pipe-dream. But a pipe-dream made more bearable by the fact that the fine, rare, single-domaine Vouvrays are in slight demand, and therefore cheap.

And we have Anjou. If that just means rosé to you, you're being unfair, because this is the most important producer of the whole Loire valley. The problem is that Anjou has never felt the need to strike out for quality, and has suddenly found itself left behind by the more sophisticated areas nearby. The dreaded Chenin grape must take a lot of the blame. In a modern world which prizes freshness, cleanness, reliability, we stumble across the dirty, hard-tasting Chenin, which ripens (if at all), at least a fortnight after its neighbours. Despite being Anjou's leading white variety, it's sufficiently unpopular for the authorities to judge a grape type's right to get a 'premium' rating by how soon *before* the Chenin it ripens. Basic Anjou table wine can command a higher price than the *appellation controlée* wine, and a sense of disorganisation and demoralisation is prevalent.

There are two remedies. The most constructive is shown by those growers who have planted extra varieties like Chardonnay, and are creating, with or without the Authorities' help, a style where the Chardonnay fruit is maximised, and the Chenin dullness is minimised. These wines will be some of France's best bargains when production increases. Secondly, a grower can produce large yields of high-acid Chenin to be processed into sparkling wine. The centre for this is Saumur, where the chalk hills, familiar from Champagne, also dominate the landscape. Saumur can be an excellent champagne method sparkler, but will never equal champagne, if only because the Chenin taste is so one-dimensional: fresh, tart, 'white', rather raw. While still Chenin wines can at length achieve a fascinating 'mature' taste, there's not much evidence the sparklers can. But even here the wretched Chenin is under attack, and the good producers now blend in Chardonnay and Cabernet Franc,

Vintage Table

Loire vintages are *very* important, and can be radically different along the river length. In poor vintages, Muscadet is most likely to be OK, while in hot vintages Sauvignon goes dull, and the Chenin finally ripens.

***1983** Marvellous right along the river. Exciting, tangy Sauvignons from Sancerre and Touraine, good Anjou Chenins, and excellent Muscadets. Drink, or keep up to two years old.

1982 Tricky. Too much sun, far too much wine, led to disappointingly flat Sancerres and Sauvignons, fair Anjous, and good Muscadets. Buy 1983 for preference.

1981 Some lovely wine, with a delicious balance of fruit and acidity. Heresy, maybe, but the best Muscadets and Sancerres can still improve.

which makes the champagne-Saumur price-gap less believable, and a lot more inviting.

Saumur vs Champagne
The Loire's various sparkling wines will never achieve the astonishing quality-level of champagne, but they are good, fresh wines, and this price comparison for the new Crémant de Loire appellation with a top champagne shows what good value they can be.

Saumur and Champagne Prices Compared

	Crémant de Loire (1)	**Veuve Clicquot NV (2)**	**Crémant as a % of champagne**
1984	£4.45	£10.74	41
1983	£4.45	£10.33	43
1982	£4.40	£10.14	43
1981	£4.40	£ 9.07	48
1980	£3.96	£ 7.80	50
1979	£3.68	£ 6.80	54
	(1) Wine Society	(2) Findlater's	

Price Guide

Dry White

Non-vintage
£1.75–£2.50
- ⋆Sainsbury's Blanc de Blancs du Val du Loire, Saumur (SAIN)
- Sainsbury's Blanc Anjou (SAIN)
- Sainsbury's Muscadet de Sèvre et Maine (SAIN)
- Vin de Pays du Jardin de la France Blanc de Blancs (VICT)
- ⋆Waitrose Muscadet (WAIT)
- Anjou Blanc (UNW, TAN)
- ⋆Sainsbury's Sauvignon Vin de Pays du Loir et Cher (SAIN)
- Tesco Touraine Sauvignon (TES)
- Vin de Pays du Loir et Cher, Celliers de St George (BAL)

£2.50–£3.00
- Vin de Pays du Loir et Cher, Blanc de Blancs (STWC)
- Vin de Pays du Jardin de la France Chenin Blanc (LADV)
- Vin de Pays du Jardin de la France Pinot Blanc Château de la Roche (L&W)
- Vin de Pays du Jardin de la France Sauvignon Château de la Roche (L&W)
- ⋆Muscadet sur lie (WAIT)
- ⋆Muscadet sur lie, Domaine du Hercy (CUL)
- Vin de Pays du Jardin de la France Chardonnay, Château de la Roche (L&W)
- Vin de Pays du Jardin de la France Chardonnay, le Chouan (ASHE)
- ⋆Saumur Blanc Sec, Château de Parnay (CHAP)
- ⋆Touraine Sauvignon, Boucher (PD)
- Vin de Pays du Loir et Cher Sauvignon, Caves St Vincent (TAN)

£3.00–£3.50
★St-Pourcain-sur-Sioule (YAPP)
★Savennières, Clos des Fougeraies (YAPP)
★Muscadet de Sèvre et Maine sur lie, Domaine du Logis du Moulin (LADV)
c. £6.10
★Sancerre, Château de Thauvenay (TAN)

1983
£1.75–£3.25
Vin de Pays du Jardin de la France, Domaine de Poche, Chanier (RACK)
★Sauvignon du Haut Poitou, Cave Coop (SF)
★Chardonnay du Haut Poitou, Cave Coop (SF)
★Sauvignon Touraine, Oisly & Thésée (WW)
£4.00–£4.75
Savennières, Château de Chamboureau, Soulez (BOW)
Pouilly Fumé, André Dezat (RACK)
Sancerre, Michel Thomas (LADV)

1982
£2.00–£2.50
Anjou, Domaine des Rochettes, Chauvin (RACK)
★Muscadet, Jean Paul Bartier (ASHE)
Muscadet de Sèvre et Maine, Cuvée du Cardinal (ECD)
Vin de Pays du Jardin de la France Chenin (RGA)
Muscadet, Sauvion (DOL)
£2.50–£3.00
★Anjou Blanc (JH)
St-Pourçain (ESV, PIP)
★Muscadet de Sèvre et Maine, Sautejeau (THRE)
Muscadet, Metaireau (PG)
★Sauvignon de Touraine, Cave Coop. Onzain (PG)
★Auvernat, Corifruit (YAPP)
Gros Plant du Pays Nantais, Auguste Bonhomme (BWC)
★Muscadet de Sèvre et Maine, Philippe Moreau (HHC)
★Muscadet, Domaine des Pierres Noires sur lie (HBV)
★Sauvignon du Haut Poitou (BIB, MART, L&W, BOW, ADN, FFW, CDM)
Gros Plant, Château de la Gallissonière, Pierre Lusseaud (SF)
★Montlouis, Domaine de St. Martin (L&W)
Touraine Sauvignon, Guillaume Charron (LADV)
Vin de Pays du Jardin de la France Pinot Blanc, Château du Breuil (CV)
★Muscadet, Château de la Gallissonnière, Pierre Lusseaud (PD, J&B)

Muscadet de Sèvre et Maine sur lie (THRE)
★Muscadet sur lie, Château de la Jannière, Pierre Lusseaud (DAV)
£3.00–£3.25
Muscadet de Sèvre et Maine sur lie, Château de la Jannière, Pierre Lusseaud (SF)
★Anjou Blanc Sec, Domaine de Bellevue (HBV)
★Muscadet de Sèvre et Maine sur lie, Robert Bossard (RH)
★Muscadet de Sèvre et Maine, Domaine de la Roche (JH)
★Saumur, Cave Coop (YAPP)
Vin de Pays des Marches de Bretagne, Chardonnay, P. Lusseaud (HT)
Saumur Blanc, Cave de St Cyr en Bourg (STWC)
Pinot Chardonnay du Haut Poitou (L&W, CDM)
★Sauvignon de Touraine, J. Moreau (J&B)
★Muscadet de Sèvre et Maine sur lie, Domaine de la Jousselinière (HUN)
★Muscadet sur lie, Henri et Vincent Chéreau (YAPP)
£3.25–£3.50
★Muscadet de Sèvre et Maine sur lie, Clos de Barillères, Bouchereau (CV)
★Vouvray, Clos Meslèrie (L&W)
Sauvignon de Touraine, Domaine Guy Mardon (SR)
Muscadet de Sèvre et Maine, Château de la Cassemichère (VICT)
★Muscadet de Sèvre et Maine, Fief de la Brie, A. Bonhomme (ADN, BAL, TAN)
Azay-le-Rideau, Pavy (WSOC)
Chardonnay, Haut Poitou Co-op (ADN)
★Muscadet de Sèvre et Maine sur lie (SR)
★St-Pourçain Blanc, Domaine de Bellevue (CDM)

⋆Vouvray, Château des Bidaudières (SAIN)
Cheverny, Jean Gueritte (CDM)
⋆Muscadet de Sèvre et Maine sur lie, Moulin de la Gravelle (LHV)
⋆Muscadet de Sèvre et Maine sur lie, Domaine des Dorices (CDM)

£3.50–£4.00

Muscadet de Sèvre et Maine, Domaine de l'Aurière, Sauvion (DOL)
⋆Savennières, Domaine de la Bizolière (SAIN)
Azay-le-Rideau, La Basse Chevrière, Sec (YAPP)
Sauvignon de Touraine, Domaine de la Croix de la Touche, Oisly et Thésée (C&B)
Sauvignon de Touraine, Oisly et Thésée (HHC, BWC, OWL)
Saumur Blanc, Château de Parnay, Collé (WSOC)
⋆Quincy, Pierre Mardon (BOW, HUN, CDM)
Touraine Blanc, Château de Quincay, Oisly et Thésée (BWC, PIP)
Cheverny, Domaine Gaudronnière, Raymond Dorléans (YAPP)
⋆Muscadet de Sèvre et Maine sur lie, Grand Fief de la Cormeraie (LHV)
Pouilly-Fumé, les Griottes, Maurice Bailly (WAIT, RH, WSOC, CDM)
⋆Ménétou Salon, Jean Teiller (YAPP)

£4.00–£4.50

⋆Savennières, Château de Chamboureau, Soulez (L&W, YAPP, H&D, ADN, WSOC)
⋆Ménétou Salon, Coeur (PG)
Bourgeuil, Auguste Bonhomme (PIP)

★Quincy, Raymond Piper (YAPP)
Reuilly Henri Beurdin (BIB, VICT, CDM)
Pouilly Fumé, Gérard Coulbois (JH, SR)
★Sancerre Domaine de la Garenne, Reverdy (BIB, RH)
Ménétou-Salon, Pellé (WSOC, HHC)
★Pouilly Fumé, les Pechignolles (HBV)
★Sancerre, les Creux (HBV)
Vouvray, Marc Brédif (BOW)
Sancerre, Clos des Roches, Vacheron (L&W)
★Sancerre, Pal Prieur (JH)

£4.50–£5.00
Sancerre, Cuvée les Baronnes, Bourgeois (ECD)
★Sancerre, les Carroy Maréchaux (HBV)
Anjou Blanc, Château de Fesles, type Chardonnay (TW, VIGN)
Sancerre, Roger Raimbault-Barrier (L&W, PG)
★Pouilly Fumé, la Loge aux Moines, Moreux (C&B)
★Sancerre, Château de Thauvenay (CHAP)
★Sancerre, les Belles Dames, Pascal Gitton (WW)
★Sancerre, Clos Paradis, Vacheron (H&B)
★Pouilly Fumé, Château de Tracy (L&W, PG, CV, LHV, CDM, MAL)
★Sancerre, Domaine de Marcigoi, Pierre and Gérard Thirot (CV)
Jasnières, Caves aux Tuffières, Jean-Baptiste Pinon (YAPP)
Muscadet de Sèvre et Maine sur lie, Château du Cleray (HUN)

★Pouilly Fumé, Château de la Roche (H&B)
Pouilly Fumé, Domaine St Michel (MAL)
Sancerre, les Monts Damnés, J. Delaporte (BAL)
Sancerre, le Cloux Sallebeuf, Gitton (BWC)
★Pouilly Fumé, les Loges, Saget (TAN, ESV, BAL)
★Sancerre, Domaine du Nozay, Philippe de Benoist (C&B)
★Sancerre, les Crilles, Gitton (ASHE)
Sancerre, Vacheron (WSOC, CDM, BYR)

£5.00–£6.00
★Savennières, Roche aux Moines, Soulez (HBV)
Pouilly Fumé, les Loges, Jean-Claude Guyot (YAPP)
★Sancerre, Clos les Perriers, Jean Vatan (YAPP)
Sancerre, Comte Lafond de Ladoucette, Château du Nozet (PG, BYR, YFW)
Sancerre, Côte des Monts-Damnés, H. Bourgeois (HHC)
Pouilly-Fumé de Ladoucette, Château du Nozet (PG, H&D, HHC, VICT, YFW, J&B)
Sancerre, Clos du Chêne Marchand, L. Crochet (J&B)

1981
£3.25–£4.00
Gros Plant, Le Douivet, Mme Baffreau (YAPP)
★Muscadet de Sèvre et Maine, Château du Poyet, A. Subileau (LHV)

Gros Plant du Pays Nantais, Martin-Jarry (H&D)
Sauvignon de Touraine, Domaine du Bouc, Oisly et Thésée (H&D)
Sauvignon du Haut Poitou, Cave Coop (H&D)
Muscadet de Sèvre et Maine, Château la Noë (MACK, RSV)
Muscadet, Château de Guerches, Drouet (MAL)
★Muscadet de Sèvre et Maine sur lie, Château de Chasseloir (LHV)

£4.25–£5.25
★Reuilly, Robert and Gérard Cordier (YAPP)
★Sancerre, Domaine du Fort (WAIT)
Savennières, Château de Chamboureau (L&W)
Savennières Clos du Papillon, Baumard (PG, CDM, TAN)
★Sancerre, Domaine des Garennes (LHV)
Vouvray, le Mont demi-sec, Huet (WSOC)
Pouilly-Fumé, les Griottes, Maurice Bailly (FFW, GH)
Pouilly-Fumé, Château de Tracy (L&W, ADN)
£5.50–£6.50
Muscadet de Sèvre et Maine, Métaireau (STWC)
Savennières, la Roche aux Moines, Marc Brincard (YAPP)
Pouilly-Fumé de Ladoucette (SAIN, BIB, RSV, WNRY, TAN)
Sancerre, Comte Lafond (MAL, TAN)

c. £9.60
Pouilly-Fumé, Baron de L, Château du Nozet de Ladoucette (BIB, YFW)
Coulée de Serrant, Château de la Roche aux Moines (TAN)

1980
c. £2.90
Anjou Blanc, Touchais (DOL)
£4.00–£5.00
★Montlouis, demi-sec, Domaine des Liards, Jean and Michel Berger (YAPP)
Ménétou-Salon, Henri Pelle (P&C, BYR, H&D)
Savennières, Clos du Papillon, Domaine de Baumard (VICT, YAPP)
Vouvray Sec, Clos de Bourg Huet (AV)
★Savennières, Clos St Yves (AV)
Pouilly Fumé, les Foltières, Pascal Gitton (WW)
Pouilly-Fumé, Les Loges, G. Saget (ADN)

c. £6.00
Pouilly-Fumé, Château du Nozet de Ladoucette (BYR, FINT)
1979
£3.50–£4.50
★Muscadet, Domaine des Mouline (AV)
Muscadet, Château la Noë (BYR)
Quincy, Mardon (PG)
Vouvray sec, Foreau (BYR)
Muscadet, Domaine de Cleray (BYR)
c. £8.05
Savennières, Coulée de Serrant, Mme Joly (YAPP, GH, BYR, LADV, TAN)
c. £11.00
Pouilly Fumé de Ladoucette, Baron de L. (VICT, WNRY)

1978
£3.75–£5.50
Muscadet Château l'Oislinière sur lie (TW)
Vouvray demi-sec, Marc Bredif (MAL)
Jasnières, Caves aux Tuffières, Pinon (VIGN)
c. £9.25
Savennières, Coulée de Serrant (HUN)

1976
c. £4.30
Vouvray sec (YAPP)
c. £7.30
Vouvray, Clos Naudin demi-sec (OWL)

1975
c. £6.00
Vouvray, Clos Naudin demi-sec (GH)

1947
£23.50
Vouvray, demi-sec, Marc Brédif (ADN)

__Webster's__ has been compiled from the latest merchants' catalogues available at the time of going to press but neither we nor the merchants listed can guarantee that all the wines mentioned will be available by the time you read the book. Equally, other wines and new vintages will become available.

Price Guide – Notes

Dry Loires are comprehensively covered in the UK and all merchants have some selection of Muscadet, Anjou and Upper Loire wines. However, the best wines are from single estates, and often less well known villages, and these, though not expensive, are still comparatively rare. They're worth seeking out, especially in the 1983 vintage.

Sparkling

Non-vintage
£3.25–£4.25
Touraine Blanc de Blancs, Bron (ODD)
★Sainsbury's Saumur, Méthode Champenoise (SAIN)

Tesco Sparkling Saumur (TES)
Saumur, la Grande Marque, sec (ADN, L&W, TAN)
★Saumur 1811, Ackerman (CHAP, CV, H&D)
★Saumur Veuve Amiot (THRE)
Saumur Soleil, Gratien Meyer (ECD, RH, WSOC, HT)
Crémant de Saumur, Gratien et Meyer (MART)
★Saumur, Langlois-Château (ODD, PG, BIB, GH, AV)
£4.25–£5.75
Blanc Foussy, Vin Vif de Touraine Brut, Blanc de Blancs (VICT)
Saumur de Neuville, Méthode Champenoise (SR)
★Crémant de Loire, Cuvée Princes de Loire, Ackerman (CHAP)
Saumur, Langlois-Château, Blanc de Blancs (HT, L&W, CV)
★Crémant de Loire Brut, Gratien Meyer (WSOC, RH, MART, RACK, ASHE, LADV)
Vouvray, Aimé Boucher (PD)
Saumur Brut, Bouvet-Ladubay (DAV, DOL, WNRY, MWS)
★Saumur Brut, Gratien Meyer (PD, LADV, VICT, THRE, J&B)

Vouvray Brut, Marc Brédif (ODD, BOW)
Touraine, Domaine des Echardières, Méthode Champenoise (MWS)
Vouvray Pétillant sec, Marc Brédif (BOW)
Saumur, Langlois-Château Brut France (AV)

1982
c. £4.15
Saumur, La Grande Marque (BAL)

1980
c. £5.30
Saphir Brut Excellence, Bouvet-Ladubay (DOL)

1975
c. £7.45
Vouvray Pétillant demi-sec, A. Foreau (WNRY)

Price Guide – Notes

The champagne method wines of the Loire are by far the most common champagne-substitute sparklers. They are usually fairly sharp although they are gradually being made softer. However, if champagne prices stay low, it is important that the Loire price doesn't rise too high because, refreshing and bitingly tasty though they may be, they still lack that something which makes champagne so exciting.

CREATIVE TROUBLESHOOTING

The Loire dry whites have the potential to fit the modern world's wine demands like a glove. There is a general swing (outside France) to whites, and in particular to fairly-priced, fruity, clean wines. While Sancerre and Pouilly Fumé sit contented with their rather startling fame way up-river, the Touraine area and parts of the Upper Loire are beginning to turn out high-quality Sauvignon wine at a far lower price than Sancerre or Pouilly would want to accept. This is now backed up by the enormous Vin de Pays du Jardin de la France – one of the most successful *vin de pays* creations.

Muscadet is in trouble at the moment, because people have thought of it for too long solely in terms of price. They buy, nonetheless, but that's no way to run a railroad, when your producers can't make a decent living. One of the UK's most conscientious wine shippers uses 'excess' (declassified) Muscadet as his basic house white, because it's cheaper – and better – than plonk from the Midi. He's happy for his customers, but he's very concerned that a fair price/quality ratio should be returned to. So we shall probably see more *sur lie* domaine bottlings as growers try to get a fair return.

Anjou remains a problem. Figures show that the increase in earnings for the basic growers has been only 10 per cent of the rate of inflation. Certainly the Chenin is a deservedly unpopular grape with consumers and growers, but it's there, and it takes commitment, effort and money to replant a vineyard. The ray of hope is that when the modern blends of Chenin with Chardonnay and Sauvignon become available, they'll be some of France's best bargains.

SWEET WINES

The sweet wines of the Loire have one great publicist: Monsieur Touchais, who seems able to flick his fingers and reveal to the astounded hordes endless serried ranks of old, sweet Moulin Touchais wine. No one's ever quite got to the bottom of the why and the wherefore of these wines, but there's no doubt that the newspaper articles and the TV programmes spawned by him and his cellar full of golden oldies have been a shot in the arm for a largely neglected species - the sweet, Chenin-based wines of the Loire.

Moulin Touchais itself is only appellation Anjou, and although Vouvray makes a certain number of vaguely-to-genuinely sweet wines, the most specialized and best production is centred on the two appellations of Bonnezeaux and Quarts de Chaume, in the Layon valley. With hot, south-facing slopes, a river to provide dampening autumn mists, and the susceptible Chenin grape, noble rot strikes with enough frequency to make it worthwhile going through all the pain and passion of producing great sweet wine. Because of the irrepressibly high acidity of the Chenin these wines can seem curiously disappointing when they're young; the sweetness is more of a biscuity softness, with a touch of honey and a rather ripe-apple fruit. But the Chenin manages to put on weight and become sweeter and sweeter for perhaps 20 years before bursting out into a richness as exciting as all but the very best of German or Bordeaux sweet whites.

THE COST OF A BOTTLE

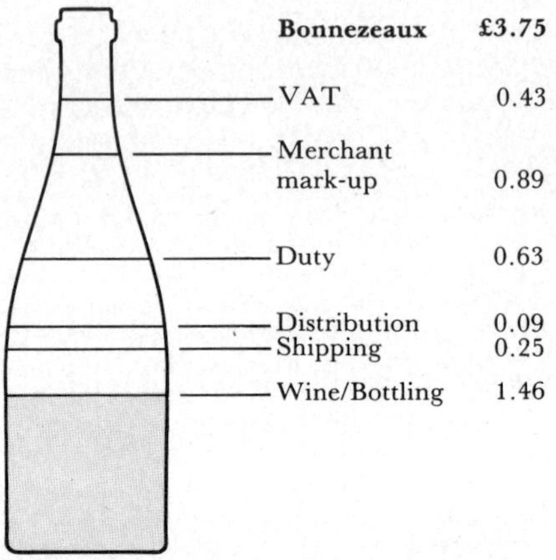

And it'll stay there indefinitely. I don't think I've yet managed to find a great sweet Loire wine which was definitely too old, but then I've only gone back to 1870, so perhaps I haven't researched the subject hard enough. The wonderful thing is that while I couldn't afford to research mature German sweet wines at all, and mature Sauternes would make my wallet whimper a fair bit, these old sweet Loire wines are available in the UK at between 15 and 30 years old from a starting price of just over a fiver a bottle. Great for us, but just think: how many of the already tiny band of sweet wine makers will continue to make this rare, difficult wine if we're so busy crowing over our bargains that we won't consider paying a proper price.

Maturity Chart

1983, 1969, 1947 SWEET WHITES

Chart only applies to top estate wines from good years.

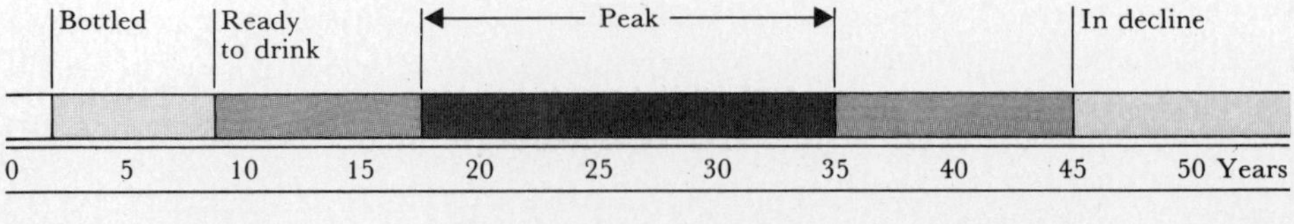

Bonnezeaux.
René Renou says he has only one ambition — to own 10 hectares of good Bonnezeaux, and exist solely by making his golden sweet wine. As things stand now, however, the President of the Bonnezeaux growers is probably grateful for one or two ways to supplement his income; he manages a large nearby estate and he's the surveyor always consulted on any vineyard problems in the area. So if hail strikes, at least he can earn a bit by assessing the damage.

Without his other activities, it's difficult to see how he could make ends meet. With four and a half hectares of Bonnezeaux and a yield limited to 25 hectolitres per hectare (hls/ha), his settling price is around 20 francs a bottle. A leading Sauternes château with a yield of 16 hls/ha could expect to receive nearer 60 francs, and the Bonnezeaux costs of making a noble rot wine are broadly similar, except for two crucial differences.

These sweet Loire wines don't get new-barrel ageing, and they're released for sale much younger. A new barrel holds 300 bottles and costs 1,700 francs; with the cost of financing over two or three years, 8-10 francs per bottle may be added to the Sauternes grower's costs, but still leaves a fairly large price differential.

Next, the Bonnezeaux grower is unlikely to pick through his vineyards, looking for noble-rotted grapes as frequently. Renou might make three 'tries', as against six or more for a top Sauternes, and reckons his vintaging costs at 3,600 francs a hectare as against up to 10,000 francs a hectare in Sauternes. This compromise on noble rot, picking as many rotted grapes as possible and making up the rest with merely ripe ones, means that his vintaging costs will work out at about 1.50 francs a bottle, as against about 7 francs a bottle for Sauternes.

But all his other costs — chemical treatments, tractors, bottle costs — are no different. There's still a gap of at least 20 francs a bottle in the price he can get, yet the Sauternais complain that *they* can't make a living off *their* prices.

Next time we pick up a Bonnezeaux or a Quarts de Chaume for the incredibly low prices at which we can still find them, it might be worth sparing a thought for René Renou's ambition — that one day he'll actually be able to make a living out of his beloved sweet wine.

Splendid Value among the Great Sweet Wines
The Chenin, either sweet or dry, demands to be aged. In the sweet wines of Vouvray, Bonnezeaux, Quarts de Chaume and Coteaux du Layon, it is quite simply too boring when it is young. The top dry wines of Vouvray, Montlouis and Savennières are so dry and hard when they're young that they just don't give any pleasure. Age sweetens the sweet, and deepens the dry. Since the price remains low, they're tremendously worthwhile to seek out. Wines nearly thirty years old may cost under £10, and even older vintages cost little alongside their counterparts in Bordeaux. Wine merchants listing such old vintages include Lay & Wheeler, Avery, Yapp Bros, Adnams and O.W. Loeb.

1976	Vouvray, Jacques Chevreau (L&W)	£7.13
1976	Coteaux du Layon, Château du Breuil (L&W)	£5.87
1976	Vouvray moelleux, Clos Naudin (OWL)	£8.56
1973	Coteaux du Layon, Château du Breuil (L&W)	£5.46
1973	Vouvray moelleux, Clos Naudin (OWL)	£6.61
1969	Vouvray, Jacques Chevreau (L&W)	£8.28
1969	Coteaux du Layon, Château du Breuil (L&W)	£5.87
1959	Coteaux du Layon, Château du Breuil (L&W)	£10.24
1959	Anjou Blanc, Moulin Touchais (ADN)	£6.44
1959	Bonnezeaux, Château des Gauliers (YAPP)	£13.80
1955	Anjou Blanc, Moulin Touchais (L&W)	£7.48

Price Guide

1982
£3.00–£4.50
Bonnezeaux, H. Chouteau (ESV)
⋆Chaume, M. Tijou (HBV)
⋆Bonnezeaux, René Renou (L&W)
Coteaux du Layon, Clos de Ste Catherine, Domaine de Baumard (VICT)

1981
£2.75–£3.75
Coteaux du Layon, Luc Béranger (BAL)
Bonnezeaux, René Renou (AV, YAPP)
Coteaux du Layon, Château de la Roche (L&W)

1980
£2.75–£3.00
Coteaux du Layon, Luc Béranger (ADN)
Coteaux du Layon, Château de Beaulieu (SAIN)
Coteaux du Layon (ESV)
c. £5.25
Bonnezeaux, Château de Fesles (VIGN)
c. £8.30
Quarts de Chaume, Jean Baumard (BOW)

1979
£3.50–£5.00
⋆Chaume, M. Tijou (HBV)
Coteaux du Layon, Château du Breuil (CV)
Vouvray moelleux, Daniel Jarry (YAPP)
c. £8.10
Bonnezeaux, Château de Fesles (GH)

1978
c. £7.00
Quarts de Chaume, Château de l'Echarderie (YAPP)

1976
c. £4.10
Coteaux du Layon, Château des Rochettes (MAL)
c. £5.90
Coteaux du Layon, Château du Breuil (L&W)
£7.00–£9.00
Vouvray, Jacques Chevreau (L&W)

Please don't blame ***Webster's*** *or the merchants listed if a wine is sold out or if the vintage you want is no longer available. Wine is a living entity and a limited commodity – continuity of supply cannot, alas, be guaranteed.*

Vouvray, l'Aigle Blanc, Prince Poniatowski (DOL, CDM)
Vouvray moelleux, Clos Naudin (OWL)

1975
c. £6.50
Quarts de Chaume, Jean Baumard (MAL, PIP)

1974
c. £4.10
⋆Chaume, M. Tijou (HBV)

1973
c. £4.00
⋆Chaume, M. Tijou (HBV)

1972
c. £7.90
Vouvray, Jacques Chevreau (L&W)

1971
c. £4.75
Bonnezeaux (WSOC)
£7.00–£7.75
Vouvray moelleux, Foreau (BYR, OWL, GH)
Coteaux du Layon Chaume, Château de la Guimonière (MACK)

1969
c. £5.90
⋆Coteaux du Layon, Château du Breuil (L&W, CV, MACK)
c. £8.00
Coteaux du Layon, Clos de Ste Catherine, Baumard (GH)
Vouvray, Jacques Chevreau (L&W)

1967
c. £5.50
Vouvray moelleux, Le Mont, Gaston Huet (WW)

1964
c. £5.60
Coteaux du Layon, Clos l'Aiglérie, demi-sec, Gousset (WSOC)
c. £8.40
Bonnezeaux, Château des Gauliers, Mme Fourlinnie (YAPP)

1959
c. £5.25
★Anjou Moulin Touchais (RGA, ADN, RH, GH, MAL, AV)
£10.00–£14.50
★Coteaux du Layon, Château du Breuil (L&W)
Bonnezeaux, Château des Gauliers, Mme Fourlinnie (YAPP)
Vouvray, les Clos, Caves de la Maison Prunier (BWC, WNRY)
c. £18.70
Vouvray doux, Marc Brédif (MAL)

1955
c. £7.50
Anjou Moulin Touchais (L&W, VIGN)

1947
c. £25.00
Bonnezeaux, Château des Gauliers, Mme Fourlinnie (YAPP)
Vouvray moelleux (YAPP, BOW)

1945
c. £13.00
Anjou Moulin Touchais (MAL)
c. £17.30
Vouvray doux, Foreau (MAL)

1929
c. £21.50
Anjou Moulin Touchais (ADN)

1928
£17.00–£18.00
Anjou Rablay, Caves de la Maison Prunier (ADN)
★Anjou, M. Prunier (BOW, VIGN)
1921
c. £55.50
Vouvray moelleux, Marc Brédif (YAPP, VIGN)
£78.20–£81.00
Vouvray liquoreux, Marc Brédif (ADN)
Vouvray doux, Marc Brédif (MAL)

Sweet and Well-made

The general trend in white wine is away from the sweet, away from the heavy, away from the old and hoary, which would seem to count out the great sweet Loire wines on a technical knock-out before they even set foot in the ring. But the trend is also towards the special, the rare, the unique, the hand-crafted. This trend may involve only a minority of wine drinkers, but probably encompasses most of the serious ones.

If wines such as Bonnezeaux and Quarts de Chaume are going to survive, there has to be an increase of interest from the consumer. At the moment they offer the best value by a street in French sweet wines, but since their sweetness is primarily brought on by noble rot, a highly risky and yield-shrivelling method of sweetening up your daily bottle, and since there is little sign of an Australian or Californian whizz-kid appearing in the valleys and injecting noble rot into the long-suffering Chenin by new-fangled transatlantic methods, the future is still precarious. Luckily 1983 is both big and good.

LOIRE ROSÉS

It's typical of the topsy-turvy world of fashionable eating and drinking, that, while the demand for basic rosé wine seems to be dropping in favour of the more sophisticated reds and whites worldwide, at that altar of up-country trend-setting, Sancerre, they've managed to buck the trends as usual, and demand is rising for what is surely one of the most over-priced and esoteric drinks around: Sancerre Rosé. It's those Paris restaurants again. But you can see why: the colour's pretty, the flavour, if hardly memorable, is dry and clean, and the name is fashionable. Fashion hits rosé more than most wines. It's becoming obvious that cheap rosés are *déclassé,* while pink champagne is back in vogue for the first time since Edward VII.

Some efforts have been made to make the ever-present Anjou rosé a better drink, in particular by vinifying from Cabernet, but it suffers from the same ills as Anjou Blanc. Dullness, over-sulphured fruit, and a 'neither one thing nor the other' sweetness. Also they're caught in the cleft stick of having been too cheap for too long. When we complain about prices for basic wines rising, we customers should remember that if we keep them artificially low for too long, the producer's only recourse is to reduce the quality of his wine – *or plant turnips.*

Non-vintage
£2.00–£3.00
Sainsbury's Rosé Anjou (SAIN)
Cabernet d'Anjou Rosé (CUL)
Tesco Anjou Rosé (TES)
*Waitrose Rosé d'Anjou (WAIT)
Anjou Rosé, Cellier de la Loire (L&W)
Anjou Rosé (VICT)
Rosé d'Anjou, Union Viticole (ADN)
Vin de Pays du Jardin de la France, Gris Fumé (ADN)

1983
c. £5.40
Sancerre, Michel Thomas (LADV)

1982
£2.25–£3.00
Anjou Rosé, Métaireau (PG)
Cabernet d'Anjou Rosé, Sautejeau (VIGN)
Cabernet Anjou Rosé, Charron (LADV)
Cabernet d'Anjou, Château de Beaulieu, Gérard Chauvin (CV)

£3.00–£4.00
*Cabernet d'Anjou, Domaine de Bellevue (HBV)
Rosé de Cabernet du Haut Poitou (BOW)
Pineau d'Aunis, Domaine des Echardières (HUN)
£4.25–£5.25
Sancerre Rosé, Balland-Chapuis (DOL)
Sancerre, Domaine de la Garenne, Reverdy (BIB)
Sancerre Rosé, Vacheron (CDM, BYR)

1981
£2.00–4£.00
Cabernet d'Anjou, Château de Beaulieu, Chauvin (RACK)
*Anjou Rosé, Henri Chouteau (CHAP)
Cabernet Anjou Rosé, Château de la Roche, Marc Morgat (H&D)
*Coteaux d'Ancenis, Jacques Guindon (YAPP)
Anjou Cabernet Rosé, Château de Tigné (YAPP)

1979
c. £3.90
Vin de Pays du Jardin de la France, Gris Fumé (TAN)

1959
c. £7.90
Anjou Moulin Touchais (BYR)

Loire Red Wines

THE COST OF A BOTTLE

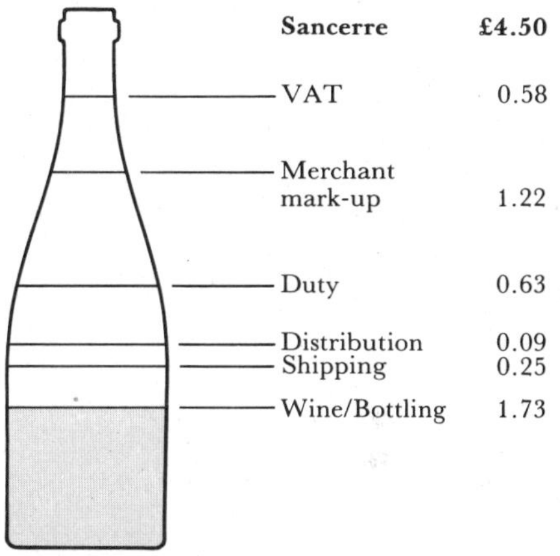

If you find the new vogue for Sancerre Rosé a bit difficult to stomach, especially at the price, here's another slap in the eye for good sense – Sancerre Rouge. It seems that those of us who go for the bright, tangy pleasures of white Sancerre are very much the parvenus, because in the nineteenth century there was more red Sancerre produced from the Pinot Noir than white from the Sauvignon. Which is about the only saving grace for those eternally predictable Paris sommeliers who, instead of being leaders of fashion, are slaves to it; if one is unwise enough to request their advice about what to drink with the fish, they are certain to spring forward and slop a half-frozen Sancerre rouge into your shivering glass. Two things wrong here. Firstly, there are much better and cheaper Loire reds, as well as much better Pinot Noirs from Burgundy. Secondly, this idea of red with the fish has really gone a bit far. Although Sancerre Rouge, except from a real boiler-house year like 1976, often seems closer to white than red in style, there are large numbers of white wines willing to do battle with the turbot far more effectively and far more cheaply. Even so, hats off to the Sancerre publicity boys; I sometimes think that if they decided to market a Sancerre square wheel, it'd sell.

It's the red wines from further down the Loire which hold more interest, and in particular the wines made from Cabernet Franc and Gamay. Whether they are enjoyable or not in this fairly cool vineyard area relies to a greater extent upon the vintage than with the whites, but also upon whether the wine-maker has the know-how and determination to coax the fruit and flavour out of his rather raw grapes.

Cabernet is certainly the superior grape, and in Touraine, especially in the villages of Chinon and Bourgeuil, it can give quite delicious wine, so long as you're the kind of person who takes kindly to cold showers and no sugar in your tea. Because these wines are dry, tart, maybe slightly earthy, but when good they have such an astonishing nettles and blackcurrant clarity that you want to jump and shout. They don't have a lot of body, except in years like 1976, but the top vintages are well worth ageing for some time, and 10 years in the bottle will give you a very cheap, and highly individual substitute for a good Médoc. Although it is cooler down the river in Anjou, there is a group of growers who are working hard to produce good Cabernet, and, again in hot years, these are good, dry, slightly earthy reds. At Saumur Champigny, we're even back in the world of juicy, raw blackcurrants, and the only word of warning is – don't ever buy the off-years, because you'll need to re-enamel your teeth.

The Gamay can produce a hard, harsh wine, completely devoid of fruit, with as much charm as a traffic warden outside a registry office. But with the advent of modern, 'no wood', sterile wine-making methods, such as *maceration carbonique,* Anjou and Touraine Gamay, bottled young and drunk young, can be a lighter and *fresher* example of Beaujolais' often rather ''sweet'' efforts – and cheaper.

PRICE GUIDE

Non-vintage
£2.50–£3.25
★Saumur Rouge, Cave Coop. (PD)
St-Pourçain-sur-Sioule, Union des Vignerons (YAPP)
Gamay de Touraine, Domaine de la Charmoise (BIB)
★Cabernet de Pays des Marches de Bretague, Bouchereau (CV)

1983
£2.75–£4.75
★Cabernet du Haut Poitou, Cave Coop (SF)
★Gamay du Haut Poitou, Cave Coop (SF)
★Côtes Roannaises, Vignoble du Picatier, Vagneur-Tachon (BOW)
Sancerre Rouge, Michel Thomas (LADV)

*Merchants stocking each wine are listed after each entry in ascending order of price or in alphabetical order if they offer the wine at the same price. However, prices do fluctuate (there are special offers and discounts as well as price increases) so remember to use **Webster's** as a price GUIDE not a price LIST.*

1982
£2.50–£3.50
Anjou Rouge, Domaine de Flines (VICT)
Gamay de Touraine, Coop. Onzain (PG)
Gamay du Haut Poitou (L&W)
★Cabernet, Oisly & Thésée (WW)
St-Pourçain Rouge, Domaine de Bellevue (CDM)
★Côtes Roannaises, Robert Serol (LADV, YAPP)
★St-Nicolas de Bourgeuil, Domaine de la Rodaie (LHV)
£3.50–£5.00
Chinon, Charron (LADV)
Anjou Cabernet, Clos de Coulaine (BIB)
Chinon, l'Arpenty, Raymond Desbourdes (YAPP)
St-Nicolas de Bourgeuil, Clos de la Contrie, Claude Ammeux (YAPP)
Saumur Champigny, Cuvée Jeunes Vignes, Domaine Filliatreau (VICT)
Sancerre Rouge, Balland-Chapuis (DOL)
★Sancerre Rouge, Domaine de Marcigoi, Pierre et Gérard Thirot (CV)
★Sancerre Rouge, Jean Vacheron (CDM)

1981
£3.00–£4.00
Anjou Rouge, J.P. Tijou (HBV)
Touraine Cabernet (AV)
★Saumur Champigny, Cave Coop (YAPP)
Gamay de Touraine, Domaine des Echardières (HUN)
£4.00–£5.00
Anjou Rouge Cabernet, Château de Chamboureau (YAPP, WSOC)
Saumur-Champigny, Château de Parnay (BYR)
Sancerre Rouge, Clos les Romains Vacheron (BIB)
Sancerre Rouge, Roger Raimbault-Barrier (L&W)
Bourgueil, Caslot Jamet (WSOC)
Chinon, Olga Rafault (WSOC, BOW)
Chinon Rouge, Jamet (YFW)
Bourgueil, Cuvée Grandmont, Pierre-Jacques Druet (YAPP)
Chinon, Couly-Dutheil (PG)

1980
c. £4.85
Bourgueil, la Hurolaie, Caslot-Galbrun (CDM)
Sancerre Rouge, Vacheron (WSOC)

1979
£4.50–£6.50
Bourgueil, Domaine des Raguenières (SR)
Chinon, Olga Raffault (VICT)
Chinon, Cuvée des Varennes du Grand Clos Charles Joguet (OWL)
Chinon, Couly-Dutheil (TAN)

1978
£4.00–£5.00
Bourgueil, la Hurolaie, Caslot-Galbrun (BYR, RH, BIB, MAL, CV, CHAP, PIP)
Cabernet de Touraine, Oisly et Thésée (OWL)
Bourgueil, Domaine des Raguenières, Paul Maitre (HT, OWL)
Chinon, Olga Raffault (H&D)
Sancere, les Romains, Vacheron (RH, BYR, MAL, VIGN)

1976
c. £5.00
Bourgueil, Domaine du Grand Clos, Audebert (BBR)
c. £7.75
Bourgueil, Lamé-Delille-Boucard (VIGN)

1975
c. £5.20
Anjou Rouge, Château de la Roche aux Moines (L&W)

Price Guide – Notes

Hopefully, as wine-making techniques improve, the slightly unripe grapes of the Loire will increasingly supply a need for light, low alcohol reds with simple fresh fruit and not too much tannin or acid. There are signs that they may, but it will take time, since modernizing red wine-making techniques does require investment and a re-think of objectives. Most Cabernets and Gamays are still a little tough, but the quality wines of Chinon and Bourgeuil can provide delicious, sharp red flavours. Red Sancerre is very trendy, and sometimes rather good.

*Please remember that **Webster's** is a price GUIDE and not a price LIST. It is not meant to replace up-to-date merchants' lists.*

NEW RÉGIME

If it wasn't that Anjou is at present so concerned with stemming the decline in rosé's popularity, and the public's quite understandable indifference to the majority of her Chenin whites, she would realise that both her Cabernets and Gamays are just right for a market increasingly interested in light, fresh reds, and 'varietal' or 'single grape' wine styles when possible. We're slowly seeing more Anjou reds on the shelves, and they're *cheap*. Indeed, if consistency can be achieved, the British wine market *needs* these tangy young reds. Chinon and Bourgeuil have a steady market, but although prices are fair they're no longer a give-away. In 1976 a good Chinon or Bourgeuil cost much the same as a good Muscadet, while in 1984 the Chinon is nearer £4.50 and the Muscadet around £3.00. At least the Chinon growers can afford to have meat on the table. Sancerre Rouge? Well, surely we won't go as batty about it as the French, whose current obsession with the stuff is put down by the obsessed to health reasons – red does not 'excite' the stomach nor cause 'crisis' in the liver to the same extent as white – and by some more reflective and analytical restaurateurs to President Mitterand who has turned his compatriots from four-course-plus-two-bottle-types into plat-du-jour-and-cheese-with-one-bottle-only pragmatists. I wish I thought the price of that Corton-Charlemagne I cannot nowadays afford would come tumbling down in response. We can but live in hope!

FRENCH COUNTRY WINES

Visions of lazy meadow picnics, jugs of frothy, fresh *réserve du patron* on a hundred leafy-lane café tables, something simple, unashamed, absurdly attractive *en route* south, desperately wistful *en route* back to Calais, and, though you'd never admit it, just faintly disappointing as you pop the cork over the bangers and mash in deepest Decembered suburbia.

French country wines deserve all that on the spot, holiday-induced enthusiasm, but increasingly they *can* stand up to scrutiny when they're brought back home, and figures show they're one of the fastest rising sectors of wine imports. If we leave country wines simply as ill-defined holiday memories, without enquiring more deeply into what makes them special and different, we're dismissing out of hand some of France's most traditional and respected wines, as well as belittling the recent efforts to improve much of France's plonk. The term 'country wines' really means wines which are not in the mainstream, wines of a merely local fame, and the official designation of *vin de pays,* (which translates as country wine) is the latest attempt to give regional character and distinction – and higher prices – to the nation's mass producers.

The wines fall into three categories.

Appellation Contrôlée

Some of the minor appellations have such weird names, it's no surprise they're still minor! Have you ever heard of Châtillon en Diois? Nor had I until I tried a marvellous Aligoté this year, sought it out on the map, and found it tucked into a valley off the Côtes du Rhône – with a fully fledged AC. What about Rosette? Doesn't quite sound serious, does it? But it's a real AC, although it only makes 20,000 bottles a year, and it's a lovely sweetish wine from Bergerac. Trouble is, no one's buying it, and production is dwindling. Hurry, hurry!

While you're in the region, give a thought to Pacherenc de Vic Bihl. Yes, another AC, not half as terrifying as it sounds; it means 'posts in a line from the Vic Bihl hills', presumably a comment on viticultural practice rather than a particularly obfuscating tasting note. There are loads more like this. Unfamiliar names, often hiding a considerable tradition, as in Jurançon or Pécharmant, although sometimes relatively recent promotions from the next rank below AC, which is VDQS.

Vin Délimité de Qualité Supérieure

Or, more simply – VDQS. They're the Avis of French wine. They try harder. They have to, because VDQS is the halfway house between *vin de pays* and *appellation contrôlée,* and they all want not only to keep ahead of *vin de pays* but also be promoted to full AC. Every year another one squeezes into the top rank, but there is often a fair amount of criticism of such promotions, and an ominous mutter of politics may be heard over the café tables – usually, it must be said, over the café tables of the neighbouring village, whose wines are still stuck with the middling VDQS label.

There are some quite well known names here – Minervois, Coteaux d'Aix en Provence – which hope to follow Corbières and Faugères to full AC soon, while others like Sauvignon de St Bris are kept down because they produce the wrong grape in the wrong place – in this case Sauvignon in Chardonnay's homeland of Burgundy (similarly, Chardonnay is denied AC in Sauvignon's territory of the Loire), and these remain just below top rank despite their qualities.

Vin de pays

Country wine. That's what it says, that's what it means. This ancient-sounding title is in fact the newest of them all, coined in 1973, but is already one of the most important parts of French viticulture. Indeed in 1983 it was the only sector of French wine declarations which posted an increase.

	1983	1982
AC	17,175,715 hls	19,841,583 hls
VDQS	2,331,873 hls	2,513,403 hls
Vin de pays	7,794,746 hls	7,634,353 hls
Vin de table	30,089,944 hls	36,690,677 hls

While the overall harvest of French wines was understandably smaller than the giant 1982 vintage the most interesting figures are for *vin de pays* and *vin de table.* It's *vin de table,* the basic unnamed, unloved plonk, produce of so much of France, which showed the biggest fall, down more than six million hectolitres (hls). Some of that is certainly due to 1983's climatic conditions, but more is a result of the farmers being persuaded to turn to other crops rather than relentlessly flooding the Wine Lake, and to the increasing success of *vin de pays* – up 160,000 hls. Because *vin de pays* is, in simplest terms, *vin de table* with a name on it.

These wines used to be loosely defined as 'wines of simple origin', but that never really got going (it sounded too much like a comment on the wine-maker's lack of grey matter) and it wasn't until 1973 that the 'table wine' producers were approached with the idea that if they limited their yields, cut out some of their worst grapes, like Aramon and Alicante Bouchet which give good colour but not much taste, and followed some fundamental rules in vinification, ageing and bottling, they could climb out of the rut, put their own name on the label, and develop the personal incentive to improve quality.

So *vin de pays* is like a more lax *appellation contrôlée.* The yields allowed will be higher, between 80 and 90 hls to the hectare, and the alcoholic degree required will be fairly low, between 9 and 10 degrees, although this will usually be surpassed. The geographical definition can be pretty broad; the Vin de pays du Jardin de la France covers the entire Loire valley, the Vin de pays d'Oc covers all of Languedoc Roussillon. The grape varieties must be those 'recommended', but grapes like the Carignan, officially discouraged for much AC wine, are the backbone of most southern country wines.

In some ways *vin de pays* has potentially tighter controls than many ACs. The wine must be approved by an 'official' tasting panel to get its label; and the levels of sulphur and volatile acidity are closely controlled. Also, in areas where the appellation enshrines some rather dull grapes, like Chenin in the Loire, or Ugni and Clairette in the south, *vin de pays* frequently allows for the planting of more attractive grape varieties like Sauvignon, Chardonnay, Cabernet or Merlot, which the AC doesn't allow. So sometimes we get a position, slightly similar to Italy's, where many supposedly inferior *vins de pays* are in fact better than their local ACs.

A Round up of What's What

East and South East

In the Jura mountains and up towards Switzerland, there are a fair number of wines, mostly light and white. But Arbois (AC) in the Jura produces surprisingly dark, full-tasting reds, whites and rosés, and it does have two great rarities: Vin de Paille, intensely sweet, and Vin Jaune, a wine of breathtaking flavour – so long as you like the unbearably powerful flavour of fino sherry times about three.

The Rhône Valley is skirted by various wines, usually red, but with one or two particularly fine whites. Clairette de Die is a dull, still white, from the Clairette grape, but Clairette de Die Tradition is a superb sparkling wine based on Muscat, made by the *méthode dioise,* a sort of semi-champagne method.

Vin de Pays de l'Ardèche and Coteaux de l'Ardèche (VdP) are producing high quality Chardonnay as well as excellent Syrah and Cabernet and even passable Gamay.

Coteaux du Tricastin (AC), Côtes du Ventoux (AC), Côtes du Vivarais and Côtes du Lubéron (both VDQS) and Principauté d'Orange (Vdp) are all good sources of cheap fruity red wine when vinified in a modern way.

Provence in the south is certainly one of the most lovely vineyard areas of France, but on the whole the wines are dull and disappointing. When one thinks of the massive captive and, largely, undiscriminating audience the local wines have every summer, it's easy to see why few producers bother to perk up their quality. However, there are pockets! Coteaux d'Aix en Provence and Coteaux de Baux en Provence (VDQS) provide some of the best reds in the south of France, often using Syrah and Cabernet to supplement the normal grapes. Rosés are good too. In Côtes de Provence (AC), rosés are normally the best and can be lovely dry wines if drunk young enough – and that means *really* young. On the coast, Bandol and Cassis (AC) make particularly good reds and whites respectively, but they're not cheap. Mont-Caume is the best *vin de pays,* and may even include some Cabernet.

The South

The Gard doesn't have anything stunning, but Costières du Gard (VDQS), and Vin de Pays du Gard can be fairly good meaty reds. The most interesting production is of Vin de Pays des Sables du Golfe du Lion, vines planted in the sand dunes stretching across the Gulf of Lion. The biggest vineyard owner in France is here – the Salins du Midi, who harvest salt but also have mile upon mile of vines, and are, amongst other things, the largest growers of Cabernet in France! Their Listel trademark is good for red, white, rosé and sparkling.

The Hérault is the Midi at its deepest and, potentially, most depressing. The carpet of vines which crawls across the landscape rarely seems to have any distinguishing mark. But it's here, in the heart of plonk production, that modern vinification is having most effect. Where there was hardly an AC before, there are now several good ones, as well as *vins de pays* of all shapes and sizes. Faugères and St-Chinian are very good sturdy ACs, while La Clape, St-Georges-d'Orques and St-Saturnin are good red VDQS. But *vins de pays* is where the Hérault goes to town, and in 1982 it produced over 200 million bottles. Rosés are good, reds may well contain Cabernet, Merlot or Syrah, and can be excellent, while even some good whites are emerging. And they're cheap.

The Aude is the next wine well and, with the Hérault, is providing most of the exciting discoveries in cheap French wine. Blanquette de Limoux (AC) is a remarkably good fizz, St-Jean-de-Minervois makes a lovely sweet Muscat, and Corbières (AC) and Minervois (VDQS) are bywords for big rough-and-tumble reds. As with the Hérault, there is a flood of *vins de pays* – over 150 million bottles in 1982.

The Pyrenées area is chiefly famous for the dusty, chunky Côtes du Roussillon reds and the big sweet Muscats of Frontignan and Rivesaltes, but Vin de Pays des Pyrenées Orientales and Vin de Pays Catalan are very good understudies to the red Roussillons.

Corsica, out in the ocean, has still not shown much sign of reacting to the modern market, and so the last major country wine area is the **South West.** Most of the names are unfamiliar, but some of the wines have considerable reputations.

Jurançon (AC) in the far south can be as sweet as Sauternes from a single domaine, but usually we see the unimpressive co-op wines over here. Round Toulouse, the Côtes du Frontonnais (AC) makes some sensational, silky, strawberry red wine, while both Madiran and Cahors are at their best when dark and strong. Gaillac (AC) produces good, rather big whites, and lighter reds, as well as some fizz, but is still struggling to recover past glories, while near Bordeaux, Côtes de Duras and Côtes de Buzet (AC), and Côtes du Marmandais (VDQS) produce a sort of mini-claret and good Sauvignon.

Bergerac is often thought of as a staging post between the Loire and Bordeaux in style, but increasingly its most exciting wines are Cabernets, made fresh and racy, and bursting with raw fruit. They *can* age, but there's no reason for them to do so. The dry whites should be sharp and tangy, but have been a little disappointing of late, except from such modern set-ups as Domaine de la Jaubertie. Pécharmant is a tiny, distinguished (AC) making very high-class Cabernet, while Monbazillac *can* rival Sauternes as a sweet white. But it rarely does, since people won't pay Sauternes prices for a true noble rot wine. So the wines are usually only semi-sweet, and not special, though cheap.

The Loire also has some gems hiding behind the big names. Gros Plant (VDQS) is a sharp, acid seaside white, Haut-Poitou (VDQS) makes extremely good Sauvignon and good Chardonnay, while Reuilly, Quincy, and Ménétou-Salon (AC) give Sancerre style at a much lower price. Côtes Roannaises and Côtes du Forez (VDQS) give a passable imitation of Beaujolais, and the catch-all Vin de Pays du Jardin de la France is as good a bet for cheap dry white wine as France offers.

Ardèche If there's one wine that France has no trouble selling, it's white burgundy. And the reason is that in a wine drinking world which is switching to white in a rush (except in France, strangely enough), white burgundy is made from the Chardonnay grape. Simple as that. The Chardonnay grape has become so popular that it's virtually a brand name in itself, like Blue Nun or Hirondelle. In California they're so desperate to produce more of this golden wine that they're cutting off perfectly healthy red grape vines at the roots, and grafting on Chardonnay. With a few rogue exceptions, it works! What may have produced a perfectly good Cabernet for 20 years is, overnight, producing a perfectly good Chardonnay.

Louis Latour, one of Burgundy's largest purveyors of white Chardonnay wine whose Mâcon Lugny is one of the best known up-market brands in the UK, spotted the trend, and realised that there was no room (literally) for expansion in Burgundy. So, if he was to cash in on the Chardonnay craze, he had to look elsewhere. Several companies were investing in California, but he took the far more practical long-term view of looking on his own doorstep and investing in France itself. He chose a high, lonely, upland area, totally unexploited, yet with prime vineyard possibilities – the Ardèche.

The vineyard tradition was ancient here, but recent achievements minimal. However, the soil was chalky (ideal for Chardonnay), and the climate, though hot, was cooled by continual breezes. He now has a presshouse, a local bottling plant and 60 local growers who have planted Chardonnay and been contracted to Latour for five years. Things certainly look hopeful. The 1982 vintage began on August 25th – France's earliest – and yielded 12 hectolitres per hectare (hls/ha) of fat, but very typical Chardonnay wine. In 1983 it yielded 28 hls/ha and 1984 may have produced as much as 45 hls/ha. And he's sold it. At 25 per cent less per bottle than his Mâcon-Lugny, there's certainly a market, and the first releases seem to show just how good the classic grapes can be in the unclassic areas of France.

Cahors. Cahors has been discovered by the French. Is this a cause for celebration? Well, according to Nick Belfrage MW, one of Cahors' greatest supporters over here, what that means is that we must get in sharpish, because whenever France 'discovers' a wine, the first thing that happens is the price shoots up.

Cahors has been discovered before. About 200 years ago it was one of France's most famous wines and the 'Black Wine' of Cahors is still held up as an example of how it used to be done. It isn't done like that anymore. Not even in Cahors. The wine was made black by the simple expedient of giving the grapes a quick crushing, and then, literally, boiling the must! Just as boiling gets the stain out of a shirt, so it gets the tannin and colour out of a grape skin. Fruit? Er, no. But strength and stability and massive ageing potential - yes. Without fruit it's difficult to know what it was expected to age to, and the old Cahors wines I've had have certainly been dark, but they've also been thick and hefty and tannic and certainly haven't given me any fun.

However, the evidence suggests that the Paris restaurants have taken up Cahors in a big way, and that's a sure sign of a rising star. If so, it says a lot for the determination of the local winegrowers. Their vines were killed off in 1880 by phylloxera with unparalleled efficiency, and all the vineyards on the steep limestone escarpments high above the river Lot, which were supposed to give the best wine, disappeared. After that it wasn't until 1971 that Cahors got its AC, following a well-publicized struggle, and now some of those vineyards are back in production. But the majority are still from the valley floor, and over 50 per cent of the wine comes from the co-op. These wines are light and uninspiring, and in no way likely to spark off riots in a Paris bistro. However, there is an increasing number of dark, tannic, but sweet-fruited reds beginning to appear from private producers, and there's no doubt that these *have* got the whiff of fine wine about them.

PRICE GUIDE

Bergerac Red

Non-vintage
c. £2.00
★Tesco Bergerac Rouge (TES)
c. £4.50
Pécharmant Château de Tiregand (TAN)

1982
£2.25–£3.25
Bergerac Château Viel Orme (MART)
★Bergerac Château la Briat Rouge (ODD)
Bergerac Château la Jaubertie Rouge (BIB, L&W)
★Bergerac (STWC)

1981
£2.75–£3.25
Côtes de Bergerac Château de Fayolle (ECD)
Bergerac Château la Jaubertie Rouge (SF, LADV)

1980
£2.75–£3.50
Bergerac Château la Croix Blanche (ESV)
Bergerac Château la Jaubertie (BYR)

1979
£2.75–£3.00
Bergerac Château la Grange Neuve Rouge (HUN)
Bergerac Château Bellevue (WHIT)
c. £4.00
Pécharmant Domaine du Haut Pécharmant (BIB)

Bergerac White

Non-vintage
£2.75–£3.00
Sainsbury's Monbazillac (SAIN)
★Monbazillac, Delaunay Frères (THRE)

1983
c. £2.25
Côtes de Bergerac, Yvon Mau (ODD)

1982
£2.50–£3.00
Côtes de Bergerac Château de Fayolle (ECD)
Bergerac Château la Jaubertie (BIB, HBV)

1981
c. £3.00
Bergerac Domaine de Grandchamps (SF)

1980
£3.25–£3.50
Bergerac Château la Jaubertie (BYR)
Monbazillac Château le Reyssac (WSOC)

1979
c. £4.25
★Monbazillac Château la Brie (PD)

1978
c. £4.50
★Monbazillac Château la Jaubertie (HBV)

1976
£4.50–£5.25
Monbazillac Château Pion (ESV)
Monbazillac Château la Brie (LADV)

Cahors Red

1982
£3.00–£4.00
★Cahors Carte Noir, Rigal (MART)
Cahors Clos la Coutale (SF)
★Cahors Domaine des Grauzils (CDM)

1981
£3.75–£4.25
★Cahors Domaine de Meriguet (LADV)
Cahors Château de Cayrou (CDM)

1980
c. £3.50
★Cahors Domaine de Quattre (ESV)

1979
£2.75–£4.00
Cahors les Côtes d'Olt (SW)
Cahors Château de Haute-Serre, Vigouroux (WSOC)

1978
c. £4.00
Cahors les Côtes d'Olt (MAL)
Cahors Domaine de la Souque (H&D)

1977
£2.75–£3.00
Cahors les Côtes d'Olt (WHIT)
Cahors Co-op d'Olt (ODD)

Corbières Red

Non-vintage
£2.25–£2.75
Corbières Château de Montrabech (L&W)
Corbières The Society's French Country Red (WSOC)
Corbières Château les Palais (VICT)
Corbières, Chantovent (ADN)

1982
c. £2.75
Corbières Château de Fabrezan (LADV)

1981
c. £2.50
★Corbières Château de Montrabech (BAL, TAN)

1980
c. £2.45
★Corbières Château de Carpendu (LHV)

1979
c. £3.00
Corbières Château de Carpendu (AV)

Corsica Red

Non-vintage
c. £2.75
★San Giusto (YAPP)

1979
c. £2.65
Vin de Corse Domaine de Torraccia (PG)

1978
c. £3.00
Vin de Corse Domaine de Torraccia (TAN)

Gaillac/Tarn Red

1978
c. £2.50
Gaillac Rouge (WHIT)

Gaillac/Tarn White

Non-vintage
£2.25–£3.25
Gaillac Sec (WHIT)

Gaillac Sec Perle (WHIT)
Vin de Pays des Côtes du Tarn, Albert Decunnac (ADN)
Gaillac Perle Cave Labastide de Levis (BAL)
Gaillac Blanc Cordes sur Ciel Cave de la Labastide de Levis (H&D)
Gaillac Moëlleux (WHIT)

1980
c. £3.00
Vin de Pays du Tarn Domaine de Saurs, Yves Pages (H&D)

Jura Red

Non-vintage
c. £3.00
Bonchalaz, Henri Maire (SW)
c. £7.00
Côtes du Jura Château d'Arlay Rouge (MWS)

1978
c. £5.00
Côtes du Jura Arlay Rouge, Jean Bourdy (OWL)
1969
c. £9.25
Côtes du Jura Arlay Rouge, Jean Bourdy (OWL)

Jura White

Non-vintage
c. £7.85
La Grangière Vieux Paille, Henri Maire (VIGN)

1978
c. £5.50
Côtes du Jura Arlay Blanc, Jean Bourdy (OWL)

1976
c. £6.30
Côtes du Jura Arlay Blanc, Jean Bourdy (OWL)

1975
c. £17.00
Vin Jaune Château d'Arlay (TAN)

1973
c. £14.25
Château-Chalon Vin Jaune, Jean Bourdy (OWL, GH)
1972
c. £12.00
Vin Jaune, Jean Bourdy (OWL)

1971
c. £12.75
Vin Jaune Château d'Arlay, Comte de Laguiche (VIGN)

1969
c. £9.50
Côtes du Jura Arlay Blanc, Jean Bourdy (OWL)
Château-Chalon Vin Jaune, Jean Bourdy (OWL)

1964
c. £16.20
Vin Jaune, Jean Bourdy (OWL)

1961
c. £18.90
Château-Chalon, Henri Maire (VIGN)

Limoux

Non-vintage
£3.25–£4.25
Blanc Nature de Limoux Cuvée Aimery (ESV)
Tesco Blanquette de Limoux (TES)
Blanquette de Limoux (AV, WAIT, PG, CUL, HUN, BWC, ESV)

Loire

see Loire Price Guides for Vin de Pays du Jardin de la France

Midi Red

Non-vintage
£1.75–£2.00
Sainsbury's Minervois (SAIN)

Tesco Côtes Catalanes (TES)
★Vin de Pays de l'Hérault Domaine de St Macaire (WHIT)
★Vin de Pays des Sables du Golfe du Lion Domaine du Petit Chaumont (ECD, LADV, H&D)
★Vin de Pays des Pyrenées Orientales Castel Frères (PG)
Sainsbury's Vin de Pays de l'Hérault (SAIN)
★Vin de Pays du Mont Baudile (ASHE)
★Vin de Pays d'Oc Chantovent Prestige Cépage Cabernet Sauvignon (RACK)

£2.00–£2.50

★Vin de Pays des Coteaux du Salavès (PD)
★Vin de Pays des Coteaux Varois Domaine St Estève Gassier (L&W)
★Costières du Gard Château de Nages (WAIT)
Vin de Pays du Gard Domaine des Corrèges (ASHE)
Vin de Pays de l'Uzège (VICT)
★Vin de Pays d'Oc Cépage Merlot Domaine de Vaisserie (RACK)
★Vin de Pays d'Oc Cépage Syrah Domaine de Gourgazaud (RACK)
Vin de Pays de l'Hérault Domaine de Bosc Cépages Cinsault/Syrah (VICT)
★Vin de Pays des Pyrenées Atlantiques Vin de Fleur (RH)
Coteaux du Languedoc Domaine de Grangeneuve (L&W)

£2.50–£3.00

Fitou Rouge Chantovent (L&W, TAN)
Minervois Cuvée Jean d'Alibert (L&W)
Côtes du Roussillon Gallaire (BAL)
★Côtes du Roussillon Villages (THRE)
★Vin de Pays du Vaucluse Rouge, Peter Dominic (PD)
Vin de Pays d'Oc Listel Cabernet Sauvignon (ASHE, MAL)
Vin de Pays des Sables du Golf du Lion, Cuvée de Sables, Domaine de l'Espiguette, Sicarex (TAN)
Chinian Chantovent (MAL)
★Vin de Pays des Sables du Golfe du Lion, Domaine du Bosquet (ESV)

1983

c. £2.75

★Vin de Pays de la Valée du Paradis, Cave Embres et Castelmaure (STWC)

1982

£2.00–£3.00

★Minervois Château St Léon (ECD)
★Vin de Pays de l'Hérault Cante-Cigale Cinsault/Syrah (WAIT)
★Coteaux de Carcassonne Domaine de Paretlongue (PG)
★Costières du Gard Domaine des Beaux-Bois (JH)
★Minervois Château de Gourgazaud (RACK)
★Vin de Pays des Coteaux de Laurens Cave de Laurens Sélection Epervier (STWC)
Costières du Gard Château Roubaud (FINT)
★Faugères (JH)

c. £3.60

Faugères, Gilbert Alquier (DOL)

1981

£2.00–£3.00

Vin de Pays de l'Aude Merlot (VICT)
★Vin de Pays de l'Aude Foncalieu Cabernet Sauvignon (WAIT)
Vin de Pays de l'Hérault Domaine de la Grange Blanc de Blancs (DOL)
★Côtes du Roussillon Château de Corneilla (PD)
Costières du Gard Domaine des Consuls (GH)
Minervois Château de Pouzols (BBR)
Vin de Pays d'Oc Domaine d'Ormesson (PIP)

c. £3.50

Côtes du Roussillon Château St Martin (TAN)

Côtes du Roussillon Caramany (TAN)
Coteaux du Languedoc Prieuré de St Jean de Bebian (BOW)

c. £4.80

Vin de Pays de l'Hérault Mas de Daumas Gassac (BIB, BOW)

1980

£2.25–£3.00

Minervois Château de Millegrand (BAL)
⋆Minervois Château de Paraza (ESV)
Minervois Château de Gourgazaud (TAN)
Vin de Pays d'Oc Domaine d'Ormesson (CDM)

c. £3.65

Côtes du Roussillon Château de Canuet (SR)

£4.25–£5.00

⋆Côtes du Roussillon Château Cap de Fouste (MART)
Vin de Pays de l'Hérault Mas de Daumas Gassac (VIGN)

1979

£2.75–£3.00

⋆Fitou Rouanet (HBV)
Minervois Cuvée Jean d'Alibert (WSOC, MAL)

1978

£3.00–£3.25

Minervois Cuvée Jean d'Alibert (TAN, AV)
Fitou Caves de Mont Tauch (H&D, MAL)

Midi White

Non-vintage

£2.00–£2.50

Vin de Pays de l'Aude Blanc de Blancs (CUL)
⋆Vin de Pays des Pyrenées Atlantiques (RH)
Vin de Pays des Sables du Golfe du Lion Listel Villeroy Dry (VICT, MAL, ESV, LADV)

£2.50–£3.25

Vin de Pays de l'Aude Domaine de Contenson (BBR)
⋆Vin de Pays du Vaucluse Blanc, Peter Dominic (PD)
Costières du Gard SICAREX (ADN, TAN)
Vin de Pays d'Oc Listel Sauvignon Blanc (MAL, BBR)

1982

£2.15–£3.00

⋆Vin de Pays de l'Hérault Cante-Cigale (WAIT)
Costières du Gard Château Roubaud (FINT)
Minervois Château de Gourgazaud (TAN)
Costières du Gard Domaine St Louis la Perdrix (BBR)

1981

c. £3.20

Costières du Gard Domaine la Perdrix Blanc (TAN)

Provence Red

Non-vintage

£2.25–£3.00

Vin de Pays des Coteaux Varois Domaine St Estève (TAN)
Coteaux d'Aix en Provence Château de Fonscolombe (L&W, ADN, BAL, TAN)
⋆Coteaux d'Aix-en-Provence Château de Calavon (ESV)
Coteaux d'Aix-en-Provence Château la Coste Cuvée Lisa Rouge (CV)

1982

£3.00–£4.15

Côtes de Provence Rouge Domaine de Vieux Lazaret (WSOC)
Coteaux d'Aix-en-Provence Domaine de la Crémade (GH)

Côtes de Provence Château de Pampelonne, les Maîtres Vignerons de St Tropez (BWC, PIP)
Côtes de Provence Domaine des Hauts de St Jean, Cuvée Speciale Pawlowski (YAPP)

1981
£2.75–£3.25
⋆Vin de Pays des Coteaux Varois Domaine des Chaberts (HBV)
Coteaux d'Aix en Provence Commanderie de la Bargemone (SF)
Côtes de Provence Château Montaud Rouge (FINT)
⋆Vin de Pays des Coteaux Varois Domaine de St Jean, Cuvée de l'Heritier (ESV)

1980
£2.75–£3.50
Vin de Pays des Coteaux Varois Domaine des Chaberts (ADN)
Coteaux des Baux en Provence Terres Blanches Rouge (SF)
£4.15–£5.00
⋆Coteaux des Baux en Provence, Domaine de Trévallon, Dürbach (YAPP)
⋆Bandol, Domaine Tempier (WW, BWC, PIP)
c. £7.75
Côtes de Provence Château de Selle Rouge, Domaines Ott (YFW)

1979
£4.50–£5.00
Bandol Domaine la Bastide Blanche (LADV)
Bandol Château Vannières (YFW)
Bandol Mas de la Rouvière (YAPP)
c. £6.15
Palette Château Simone Rouge (MAL)

1978
c. £5.30
Côtes de Provence Domaine Richeaume, Hoesch (OWL)

1977
c. £6.45
Coteaux d'Aix en Provence Château Vignelaure (VIGN)

1975
c. £8.25
Coteaux d'Aix en Provence Château Vignelaure (VIGN)

1974
c. £6.10
Bandol Domaine Tempier Grande Réserve, Peyraud (MAL)

Provence White

Non-vintage
£2.50–£3.00
Coteaux d'Aix en Provence Château de Fonscolombe (L&W, ADN, BAL, TAN)
Vin de Pays des Maures Domaine St Julien (SR)
⋆Coteaux d'Aix en Provence Château la Coste Blanc de Blancs (CV)
c. £6.85
Côtes de Provence Clos Mireille Blanc de Blancs, Domaines Ott (L&W)

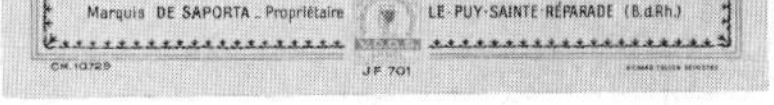

1982
£2.50–£3.00
Vin de Pays des Coteaux de Varois Domaine des Maurels (PIP)
Coteaux d'Aix en Provence Domaine de Paradis (BBR)
Côtes de Provence Château Montaud Blanc (FINT)
c. £8.90
Bellet Château de Crémat Blanc (MAL)

1981
c. £2.80
Vin de Pays des Coteaux Varois Domaine des Chaberts (HBV)

c. £4.60
Cassis Clos St-Magdeleine, François Sack (YAPP)
c. £8.00
Côtes de Provence Clos Mireille Blanc de Blancs, Domaines Ott (YFW)

1980
c. £4.70
Bandol Mas de la Rouvière, P. P. Bunan (YAPP)
c. £7.50
Côtes de Provence Clos Mireille, Domaines Ott (BIB, GH)

Rhône

see Rhône Price Guides for Coteaux de l'Ardèche, Coteaux du Tricastin and Vin de Pays de Vaucluse

Savoie White

Non-vintage
c. £3.75
Vin de Savoie Château de Ripaille (MAL)

1982
c. £3.90
Apremont, Pierre Boniface (ODD)
Vin du Bugey Chardonnay (SR, P&C)

1980
c. £4.70
Crepy Creyptant (MAL)

Southwest Red

Non-vintage
£2.25–£3.30
⋆Côtes du Frontonnais (ASHE)
Madiran Cave Co-op de Courseilles (ADN)
Madiran Cuvée de la Confrerie (FINT)
Irouleguy (BIB)

> ***Webster's** has been compiled from the latest merchants' catalogues available at the time of going to press but neither we nor the merchants listed can guarantee that all the wines mentioned will be available by the time you read the book. Equally, other wines and new vintages will become available.*

1982
£2.75–£3.25
Côtes du Marmandais Rouge (SF)
Côtes du Frontonnais Château Bellevue la Fôret (LADV, ESV)

1981
£2.25–£3.00
⋆Côtes de Duras, Seigneuret (WAIT)
Côtes du Frontonnais Château Bellevue la Fôret (BWC, ESV)
c. £3.25
Madiran Domaine Bouscasse, Alain Brumont (BIB)
c. £4.25
Côtes de Buzet Château de Padère (GH)

1980
c. £2.75
Côtes de Buzet (BIB)
c. £4.00
Côtes de Buzet Cuvée Napoléon (RACK)

1979
£3.00–£3.75
Madiran Domaine de Fitère (CV)
Côtes de Buzet Les Vignerons Réunis (ADN)
Côtes de Buzet Cuvée Napoléon (LADV, VIGN)
c. £4.50
Madiran Château de Peyros (CDM)

1978
c. £3.25
Fitou Caves de Mont Tauch (H&D)
c. £4.25
Côtes de Buzet Cuvée Napoléon (TAN)

1976
c. £3.50
Madiran Cave de Crouseilles (WHIT)

1973
c. £3.10
Côtes de Buzet Vignerons Réunis (WHIT)

Southwest White

Non-vintage
£2.25–£3.00
Vin de Pays des Côtes de Gascogne, Colombard (ASHE, ADN)
⋆Vin de Pays Pyrenées Atlantiques Grand Large Caves Vinicole de Gan Jurançon (L&W, BAL)
Vin de Pays de la Dordogne, Henri de Dietrich (LADV)
Jurançon Sec Blanc de Blancs, Caves Vinicole de Gan Jurançon (L&W)
Côtes de Duras Sauvignon Blanc (PD)
£3.00–£4.00
Jurançon Blanc de Blancs Sec (ESV)

Jurançon Moelleux Quadri Centenaire, Caves Vinicole de Gan Jurançon (L&W, TAN)
Jurançon Château Jolys Sec (MAL)

1982
c. £2.00
★Vin de Pays Charentais (WAIT)
★Vin de Pays des Côtes de Gascogne, Colombard (PG, WAIT, ECD)
£2.75–£3.50
Côtes du Marmandais Blanc (SF)
Côtes du Duras Sauvignon Seigneuret (ESV)
Côtes de Duras Sauvignon, les Vignerons des Coteaux de Duras (BAL, BWC)
Côtes de Duras Sauvignon, UNIDOR (AV)

1981
c. £4.35
★Jurançon Cru Lamouroux Non Moelleux, Jean Chigé (RH)

Other French Country Wines

Fortified Wine

Non-vintage
c. £3.00
Rasteau Cave des Vignerons de Rasteau (VIGN)
c. £4.00
Muscat de Rivesaltes Aphrodis (CUL, ESV)

1973
c. £5.00
Banyuls Grand Cru Ancestral Dry (VIGN)

Rosé

Non-vintage
£2.50–£3.00
Coteaux d'Aix en Provence Château de Fonscolombe Rosé (L&W, ADN, BAL, TAN)
Listel Gris de Gris (BIB)
Jules Reuss Rosé (WAIT)
Coteaux d'Aix en Provence Château de la Gaude, Baron de Vitrolles (YAPP)
Cendre Vin Gris, Maire (GH)
Coteaux d'Aix en Provence Château de Calavon (ESV)
Vin de Pays des Sables du Golfe du Lion, Domaine de Jarras, Gris-de-Gris (ESV)
c. £3.50
Coteaux d'Aix en Provence Château de Fonscolombe Cuvée Speciale (TAN)

1982
c. £3.50
Vin de Pays des Coteaux Varois Rosé du Domaine de St Jean (SR)
Côtes de Provence Domaine des Feraud (CDM)

1981
£2.75–£3.25
Bergerac Château la Jaubertie Rosé (L&W, SF, LADV)
Vin de Pays des Coteaux Varois Domaine des Chaberts (HBV)
La Clape Château de Pech Redon Rosé (STWC)
Vin de Pays des Coteaux Varois Vin Rosé de St Jean (ESV)
c. £6.90
Côtes de Provence Château de Selle, Domaines Ott (BIB, YFW)

1980
c. £4.30
Côtes de Provence Domaine Malherbe Rosé, Domaines Ott (YFW)
c. £7.00
Côtes de Provence Château de Selle, Domaines Ott (GH, TAN)

Sparkling

Non-vintage
c. £2.00
★Duc d'Ordy Belgian Fruit Wine (WAIT)
£2.65–£3.00
Duc de Paris Brut (CHAP)
★Jules Reuss Brut (WAIT)
★Jules Reuss Demi Sec (WAIT)
★Lorne House Cuvée Brut (LHV)
★Duc de Monteronne Cordier (PG)
Chanterelle Cordon d'Argent (PD)
★Bouquet d'Or Brut (RGA)
St Michael French Sparkling (M&S)
Veuve du Vernay Brut (ODD, CUL, VICT, ASHE, AV, UNW, TAN)
£3.25–£4.00
Comte de Jouvance Méthode Champenoise Brut (ECD)

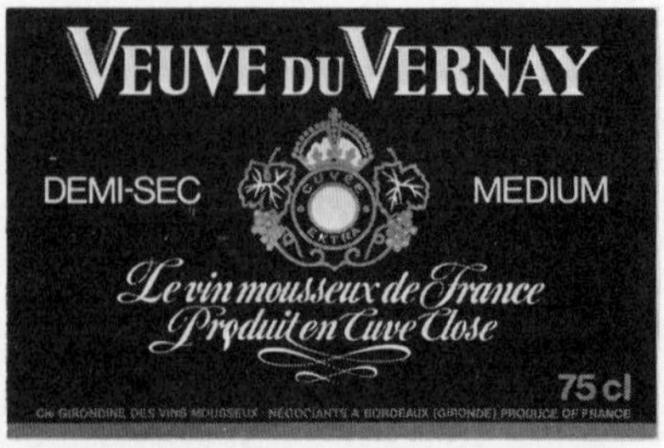

★Veuve du Vernay Demi-Sec (CUL, YFW)
Terenger Brut (UNW)
Gaillac Brut (SF)
Le Piat Crystal Brut (PD, THRE, UNW)
Brut de Listel Blanc de Blancs (ESV)
Vinfou, Henri Maire (MAL)
£4.25–£5.00
Kriter Brut (UNW, ASHE, TAN)
Kriter Demi Sec (TAN)
Bergerac Blanc de Blancs Brut Méthode Champenoise Nicholas Ryman (HBV)
Seyssel Blanc de Blancs, Varichon & Clerc (HT, WSOC, MAL)

1980
c. £3.90
★Café de Paris Brut Blanc de Blancs (HHC)

UNDISCOVERED JEWELS

The future has to be bright for the majority of lesser known French wines, but not right across the board. There are various small appellations which have not established a sufficiently loyal following or sufficiently strong characteristics to survive. Appellations like Rosette, and country wines like Vin de Pays de Moselle, which only produces about 4,000 bottles of wine, will probably disappear; and in areas like the Aude and the Hérault, there is such a multiplicity of *vin de pays* names, without any rhyme or reason, that many of them are sure to sink into the wider regional *vin de pays* designation with few tears shed.

Otherwise, however, there is a considerable surge in the demand for French country wine in all categories, but the most encouraging is in the *vin de pays*. Whereas some producers only see *vin de pays* classification as the first step towards full AC, the French government is much keener that it should be seen as a particular style, and, maybe, a particular price range. It certainly seems to be working over here. Last year's figures showed an increase of 60 per cent in import value and the reason is evident – they are tasty, individual wines which are now frequently under £2 a bottle.

France still has the highest quality image of any wine-producing country, and these comparatively simple wines get a good rub-off from the overall sophistication. For that matter, so do ordinary French *vins de table* (up by a quarter last year) which probably don't deserve it, but *vins de pays do* deserve it, not only enshrining local practice where it seems constructive to do so, but also allowing a framework within which to experiment. The work being done on Chardonnay in the Loire, on Cabernet in the Hérault and Aude, and on Syrah in Roussillon, is almost entirely inside the *vin de pays* package.

French Table Wine

Red

Non-vintage
£1.85–£2.50
★Cachet Rouge Bouchard Père (CUL)
★le Vin Rouge du Patron (CHAP)
Maison Calvet (HBV)
★Chanut Rouge Chanut Frères (FFW)
Bonne Vigne Rouge Loron (L&W)
Menotte Rouge (ESV)
★Cuvée Charlet (CHAP, ESV)
★The Club's French Red (STWC)
★Cuvée Maison Dulong Frères et Fils (HHC)
Baton (H&B)
Nicolas (ASHE)
★Costevin Rouge Pierre Coste (L&W)
Père Patriarche (CUL, UNW)
Chantarel Red (TAN)
Le Piat d'Or (WAIT, TES, SAIN, PD, ASHE, UNW)
Waitrose Vin Rouge (WAIT)
£2.50–£3.00
Dominic's Vin de Table rouge, litre (PD)
Sainsbury's Vin Rouge de France, litre (SAIN)
★Marcilly Red (ODD, CDM)
★Tesco Vin Rouge Medium (TES)
Cuvée des Gaulois Les Vignerons de la Meridionale (ADN)
Toujours Rouge, litre (THRE)
Hicks & Don Vin de Table Rouge No. 1 (H&D)
Hicks & Don Vin de Table Rouge No. 2 (H&D)
Les Chais Rouge (PD)
Solitaire Red, litre (WGA)
£3.00–£4.00
★Le Fleurion Vin Rouge de Table (CV)
Nicolas Red Vieux Ceps, litre (SAIN, VICT, THRE)
★Pavion Rouge Magnum (ODD)
Selection Tanners E. Loron, litre (TAN)
La Villageoise, 1.5 litres (ASHE, THRE)

White

Non-vintage
£1.85–£2.50
★Cachet Blanc Bouchard Père (CUL)
Marquis de Grandefont Blanc de Blancs Sec (ECD)
Victoria Wine French Medium Dry White (VICT)
Sainsbury's Bergerac Blanc Dry (SAIN)
★le Fleurion Vin Blanc de Table (CV)
★Vin des Caves (CDM)
★Chanut Blanc Chanut Frères (FFW)
Calvet Blanc (HBV)
Bonne Vigne Blanc Loron (L&W)
Baton (H&D)
Menotte Blanc (ESV)
Nicolas Medium Dry (ASHE)
Nicolas Sweet (ASHE)
★Cler Blanc Sauvion (HUN)
Père Patriarche (CUL)
Cuvée Charlet (ESV)
Chantarel Dry White (TAN)
Chantarel Sweet White (TAN)
★Blanc de Mer Blanc de Blancs (PD)
Le Piat d'Or (WAIT, TES, THRE, SAIN, VICT, ASHE, PD, UNW)
Waitrose Vin Blanc, litre (WAIT)
£2.50–£2.75
Dominic's Vin de Table Blanc-Sec, litre (PD)
Dominic's Vin de Table Blanc Demi-Sec, litre (PD)
Dominic's Vin de Table Blanc Doux, litre (PD)
Sainsbury's Vin de France Medium Dry, litre (SAIN)
Sainsbury's Vin de France Dry, litre (SAIN)
Sainsbury's Vin de France Sweet, litre (SAIN)
Tesco Vin Blanc Medium Dry (TES)
Blanc de Blancs 11° Henri Simondin (MAL)
Toujours Dry White, litre (THRE)
Saget Blanc de Blancs (HHC)
£2.85–£3.75
Les Chais Blanc (PD)
Nicolas Dry (ASHE, VICT)
Solitaire White, litre (WGA)
Solitaire Rich, litre (WGA)
Nicolas Medium White Chassepré, litre (SAIN)
Selection Tanners E. Loron, litre (TAN)
c. £4.00
La Villageoise, magnum (ASHE)

Rosé

Non-vintage
£2.50–£3.25
Baton (H&B)
★Marcilly Rosé (ODD)
Solitaire Rosé, litre (WGA)
Nicolas Vin Rosé (VICT)

GERMANY

Thank goodness for the 1983 vintage in Germany. I was beginning to wonder whether I would ever write about German wines again. In fact, one German wine-shipping friend has recently written to me saying that he had only just realised that I *was* a wine writer, since his UK agent only sends him press cuttings relevant to Germany.

This is a terrible admission, given that Germany is one of the oldest and greatest wine nations of the world, but, sadly, it reflects to a great extent the state of the German wine market in the UK today. German wine is now synonymous with Liebfraumilch, Niersteiner Domtal etc; and whilst I do not have anything against (and have even from time to time written about them with some enthusiasm) these simple, sweetened inoffensive types – which account for the huge annual growth in German imports, and provide the simplest and most accessible means for the newcomer to wine to get started without much strain on the taste buds (for these wines consciously suppress the complex subtleties of greater wine in favour of a uniform and facile consistency) – I grieve over our general ignorance as a wine-drinking nation of the wonderful individual German vineyard wines which *are* available, but too rarely tried.

And now there is yet a further reason to fear for our rediscovery of the treasures of Germany; a development which, it must be said, is roundly condemned by all serious and honourable German wine growers and shippers, be they purveyors of fine wines or the marketeers of reliable brands: I speak of the so-called EEC Tafelweins. Their labels, which sport frolicking Rhine maidens, fairy castles clinging to crags above the Lorelei rock and Gutenburg-bible script, are designed to imply that they are the product of Germany. Not so! These truly horrible concoctions are for the most part Germanised versions of pretty low-quality plonk trucked north from some of southern Europe's least distinguished vats.

This base (in both senses) wine is sweetened with a slurp of grape juice, sulphured to an intolerable degree and pushed out into the unsuspecting marketplace dressed for all the world like a good, honest, German citizen. The fact that they are not German is usually stated on the label in very small print, and not always in English. I am pleased to report that there is a growing lobby – not least in Germany – to put an end to what can scarcely be described as an honest practice, but it will take time, and so the business of helping the public to discover the more sophisticated pleasures of Germany's diverse wine culture is yet further retarded.

But what was that about the 1983 vintage? Yes indeed – just in time, up rolls 1983 to give this guide and its editor, and all lovers of fine German wines, a real opportunity to demonstrate exactly what so many of us are missing.

Germany probably has fewer good vintages than any other European wine growing nation with the exception of the UK, and the last time we had anything to get excited about was 1976 when the incredibly hot summer baked the German river valleys, and the grapes surged to massive ripeness. It might have happened again in 1982, but the hopes of quality were wrecked at the last minute by the sweeping storm clouds to which any northern region is prey in the autumn. What was left was the biggest vintage ever – of dilute wines. Nowhere to store it, no one to buy; the going price for Liebfraumilch slumped 50 per cent almost overnight, as the sorry grape musts were dumped on the market, and eventually the government had to move in with an emergency distillation purchasing programme to restore equilibrium. Three hundred million litres of wine were pulled out of the bullring, and burned off in the distilleries. Luckily, in 1983 the weather held, and fine wine was made all over Germany.

Since the vast majority of German wine drunk in Britain is of the medium-sweet, grapey, blended sort, the consistency of which is a remarkable (and usually honourable) tribute to chemists and blenders, do vintages in Germany really matter? Yes they do! We may primarily be a market for the mass-produced blends, but Germany also produces some of the most sublime wines in the world, and it is unfortunate that, in a period of unprecedented growth in UK wine consumption, and particularly of white wine consumption, there has been no exceptional vintage to demonstrate the astonishing quality of German wine at its best, until 1983.

'Quality'. In German wine that is a much vexed word. Quality implies specialness, uniqueness, something memorable and particular. But not in German wine law. Whereas the rest of Europe would readily admit that most of its wine was of the pretty basic sort, and classify it accordingly, Germany has managed to produce a system whereby, *in any year,* 90–95 per cent of her produce will reach the quality or Qualitätswein level. All that this means is that it reaches the most modest semi-ripe sugar level in the grape, and the slack can then be taken up with a good dosing of sugar. Certainly there *is* a *real* quality level, the Qualitätswein mit Prädikat, or quality-wine-with-special-attributes level. Here the grape must will not be sugared, and certain vineyard definitions will be observed. Although that doesn't sound too impressive, the best wines will, in theory, be made from a single vineyard, usually well exposed to the sun, and often from the greatest German grape – the Riesling. They can be quite dry in the Kabinett class, but at Spätlese, Auslese, Beerenauslese and Trockenbeerenauslese level, they get sweeter and sweeter to become some of the most astonishing noble rot-affected sweet wines the world has to offer. What marks them out is the running edge of exciting acidity, which keeps the fruit strong and interesting while the sweetness builds up. In a word: balance. Which is why a TBA, for all its sweetness never cloys.

These wines, with the vineyard names, grapes, and classifications clearly marked on the label, are the wines which we seem to have lost sight of in the UK. And the reason is not difficult to find. Whereas 10 years ago it was reasonably sophisticated to proffer a glass of Kabinett or Auslese to your guests, any such niceties have been stifled by a new snobbery which regards anything German as *déclassé* sugar water.

The prices of the excellent wines have been held down – in 10 years the price of a good Rheingau Kabinett has risen only 50 per cent – yet the market has dwindled. The sugar-water image of Liebfraumilch is undoubtedly partly to blame, since the balancing acidity so crucial to successful German wines is here swamped by the addition of sugar and unfermented grape juice to meet the mass-market taste requirements. But the dilution of Prädikat standards by all but the very best growers is also to blame; as is the replacement of Riesling by other highly aromatic, but far less exciting grape varieties, and the overly clever antics of some German wine-makers, too keen to create a style, albeit unnatural, to suit what they see as the market, rather than making the kind of wine that a particular year's vintage will allow.

Which is why 1983 is so important. They call it the Year of the Riesling. Lovely, fragrant wines, stung with acidity and rich in taste have been made on the Mosel and the Rhine. For the first time in seven years, the quality inherent in Germany again has the chance to lift its wine above the morass of innocuous baby-juice, and everyone should try at least one 1983 Kabinett or Spätlese, if only to be fair to one of the world's great, but battered, wine cultures.

German Sweeties

There's a rule of thumb about German wine; the more unpronounceable the label is, the better the wine inside the bottle is likely to be. Germany has built its trade on easily pronounceable names – Piesport, Bernkastel, Nierstein, and the ever present Liebfraumilch. But it has made its reputation as one of the truly great wine areas by producing this little bundle of indecipherable letters Trockenbeerenauslese – which means, approximately, shrivelled berries, gathered late. That's a very pedestrian, if accurate translation of what is one of the world's great taste sensations. There are two fellow-travellers of Trockenbeerenauslese (or TBA for short) – the straightforward Beerenauslese, meaning that the berries were picked singly, but not quite so over-ripe, and Eiswein, which is just that; 'ice wine', picked at dawn in the depths of winter when the grapes are actually frozen.

All three of these will probably be infected by noble rot, a fungus which feeds on the water in the grapes rather than the sugar. As autumn turns to winter, the grape begins to shrivel and to look quite disgusting, but the acid and the sugar just get stronger and stronger in relation to the liquid. To qualify for the TBA description they have to reach a ripeness of 21.5 degrees potential alcohol, and some of the great wines reach an astonishing 30 degrees. Anything much over 15 degrees in strength begins to stifle the yeasts involved in fermentation, so, frequently, the fermentation virtually doesn't get going at all, and a year later the liquid may have five – six degrees of actual alcohol but 15–20 degrees of unconverted (i.e. unfermented to alcohol) sweetness. A top Sauternes might be picked at round 22 degrees potential alcohol, but would end up with about 11 degrees alcohol and 11 degrees sugar in the finished wine. Which explains my assertion that TBAs are the sweetest wines in the world!

Few growers even try to make them because of the risk and the cost. They have to pay pickers to spend several days plucking single grapes off the vines to produce perhaps 200 bottles. The vines are producing a glass of wine each instead of a bottle. That's why the TBAs are expensive – usually starting at £30–£40 ex-cellars, but even at those prices a grower won't make any money on them. It's pride that makes him do it.

Beerenauslese from new, non-Riesling grapes can be a little disappointing and one-dimensional; the Huxelrebe grape, for instance, takes to rot so easily that you can make a beerenauslese Huxelrebe before you've begun to pluck any of your Riesling. But any Riesling BA or TBA, and many Scheurebes and Sylvaners, will be truly astonishing experiences, which, if you ever decide to buy a bottle, you can age for as long as most of us will last.

Eisweins (picked, as I said, during winter at dawn from frozen grapes), have even higher acidity, because the grapes are likely to be a little less over-ripe. What happens is that the water in the grapes is frozen into a pellet of ice, leaving a sludgey fruit concentrate. The frozen fruit is dashed to the presshouse by the frozen pickers, quickly and carefully pressed so that only the slimey sweet concentrate is removed, and the water stays separate and removable in its icy state. More Eiswein was produced in 1983 than ever before, because of a sudden drop of temperature in November which had the growers scuttling for their snowshoes. But Eiswein is very hard to make in quantity, so the eventual quality of the 1983s is still a little uncertain.

Rhine

The Rhine is by far the most famous area of German wine growing, but having said that, what exactly does 'the Rhine' encompass? After all, it's a very long river. Well, if we stick to the letter of the law, it includes at least three areas we almost never see in the UK.

The Ahr valley, which ironically contrives to celebrate its northernmost German position by being famous for red wines.

The Mittelrhein is the Rhine gorge at its most beautiful, providing all the label ideas for castles clinging to the cliffs high above the steam boats and river-front cafés. It really is like that, and the tourists sensibly flock there in enormous numbers, and just as sensibly drink almost all of its wine. If you do see a bottle, try it, because it's almost all Riesling grape on those slatey slopes. Difficult to grow, and almost impossible to fake.

Running off the Mittelrhein, and surrounded by it, is the third area: the Hessische Bergstrasse – a tiny side valley running down to Heidelberg, where, presumably, all its wine is drunk, because it never gets over here. The central town of Bensheim has one of the highest average temperatures of any wine region of Germany, so, like the rest of the Mittelrhein, it's worth seeking out.

The other side valley – which *is* found in the UK – is the Nahe, snaking south

THE COST OF A BOTTLE

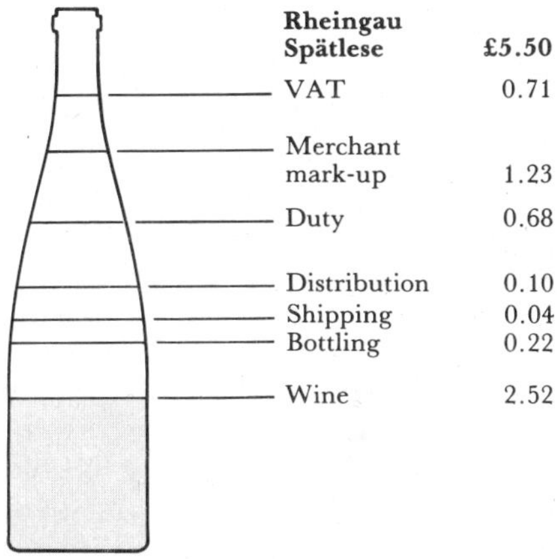

Maturity Chart

1976 AUSLESE

Lesser vintages will produce Auslese in name only, lacking the real noble rot concentration. They'll peak quicker and fade sooner.

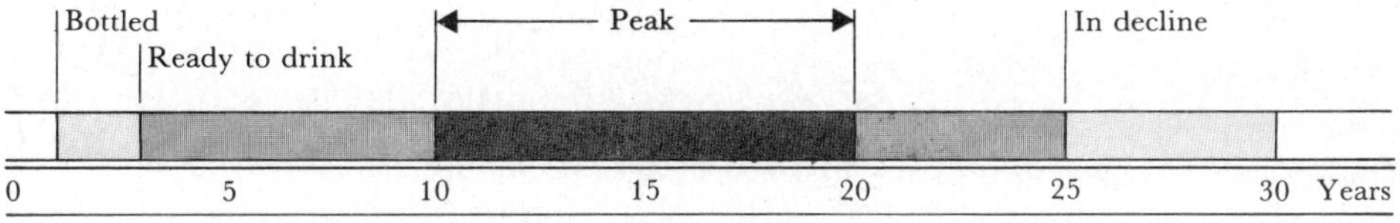

1983 LIEBFRAUMILCH

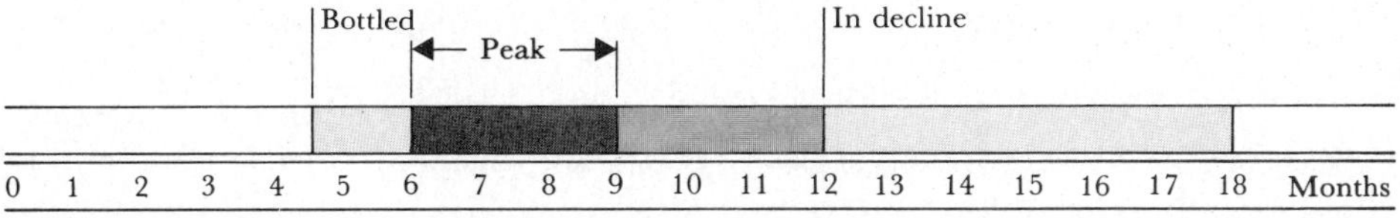

Vintage Table

There is no point in buying a Bereich Nierstein or Liebfraumilch of anything but the latest vintage. Some of them are dead on their feet within the year. Riesling wines age much better than the other varieties. These notes therefore refer to QmP wines only.

***1983** Exciting year. Desperately needed, this is a Riesling year, since only the Riesling could cope easily with the torrid summer. Wonderful Rheingau Kabinett and Spätlese, good Rheinhesse Spätlese, and even some exciting Auslese in the Palatinate.

1982 Massive. Germany nearly sank with this vintage, her biggest ever. It shows, in that most of the wines are just too light, and are already beginning to fade. Buy 1983 instead.

1981 Not bad; some lovely, gentle Rheingau and Nahe Kabinetts, which are now ready. The Riesling wines should still be good, but the vintage was light, so don't keep.

1979 A little disappointing. It promised to be a good Kabinett year, but by now, their lack of acidity, and relatively dilute state has left most of them a bit stranded.

1976 Brilliant. Even the Kabinett wines could taste of noble rot! This is a year for big sweet wines from all the Rhine areas particularly Rheinhesse and Palatinate, where the concentration is remarkable. Still worth buying and keeping, if you see them.

from Bingen. An important valley, because many of Germany's best Kabinetts and Spätleses come from its middle slopes, wines with a grapey taste balanced by quite high acidity, and something slightly mineral too. Away from this centre of quality the wines are sadly, less reliable.

North and west of Bingen (and staying now with what we can find in the UK), spreads the greatest of the main areas, the Rheingau. When the hillside vineyard is right, the ripening period long and warm, and the wine maker caring, this is where the Riesling makes its most remarkale wines. It's not the place to look for a little 'off the beaten track' bargain, because the Rheingau contains more world-famous villages than any other German vineyard area, and even its lesser villages are well aware of their area's prestige. Riesling is its great grape, and it may well have first been cultivated here. It almost seems a shame to grow the lesser grapes at all here, since the Riesling picks up the slatey dryness, the tangy acidity, and a delicious grapey fruitiness, varying from apple-fresh in a good Kabinett, to almost unbearably honeyed in a great Trockenbeerenauslese.

The Rhine turns south at Wiesbaden into the Rheinhesse, and this, despite having one village as famous as any in the world – Nierstein – is packed with unknown backwoods names. Single vineyard wines from Nierstein and its unsung neighbours, Nackenheim, Oppenheim and Bodenheim, can be superb, softer than Rheingaus, but still beautifully balanced and grapey. Otherwise, we're in the land of Liebfraumilch and Bereich Nierstein. Bereich means area, and poor old Nierstein has had to lend its name to a mass of flabby upcountry wines which have nothing to do with the riverfront specials of the village itself. Part of this is due to the favourite hobby of the wine growers, which seems to be to plant as many unlikely different varieties as possible. The Rheinhesse's general reputation was built on light, flowery wines, notably from Müller-Thurgau and Sylvaner. Yet since 1964, the percentage of these vines planted has been halved to around 40 per cent of the whole area. I can't even pronounce all the names of the ones which have taken their place.

The Rheinpfalz, or Palatinate, has two very different halves. The northern half is clustered round some extremely good villages, in particular Forst, Wachenheim and Ruppertsberg. There's lots of Riesling and the wine has a spicey, fiery fruit, rather exotic in a tropical-fruit-salad way, but with the lovely clear Riesling bite.

In the south, the Südliche Weinstrasse ('southern wine road') is a massive grape bowl of flat, high-producing vineyards, now also losing its Müller-Thurgau and Sylvaner like the Rheinhesse, and going into overdrive in terms of mechanizing the vineyards, reaping enormous quantities of the new perfumey grape inventions, and at the same time opening the throttle in the marketing department. Much Liebfraumilch comes from here, and is normally a bit tastier than the Rheinhessen equivalent.

LIEBRAUMILCH

Last year a leading analyst of the wine and spirits market in the UK concluded that there was a drift away from Liebfraumilch in the public taste. Makes you wonder where they get all their data from. Ask the wine buyer for Tesco, for Sainsbury, for Waitrose – indeed *any* group involved in mass-marketing wine to the public, and such an analysis will get very short shrift. *Every* supermarket group we talked to reported Liebfraumilch as its top seller – by a street. And frequently its second best seller was a Niersteiner. In the top six there was probably also a Piesporter or a Bernkasteler. Which seems to imply that, far from a drift away from Liebfraumilch, there's a positive obsession with the stuff.

It seems a rather innocuous liquid to get obsessed with, but that very harmlessness is what has made it such a runaway success. Many people are convinced that wine is harsh and bitter, and consequently have always avoided taking the plunge. Liebfraumilch and its sugary cohorts offer you the chance to start paddling in the shallows of wine drinking, rather then going head-first off the high board into something like claret, or Côtes du Rhône, or Chianti. It hardly tastes like wine at all, and indeed when the name became so popular that some kind of protective definition had to be given to it, the laws simply said they'd prefer the wine to come from somewhere on the Rhine, and be 'mild', or of 'pleasant character', and that it should have at least 18 grams of sugar in it.

And that was it. Since Liebfraumilch is now purely a commodity, and is bought and sold as such (except for the leading brands with some kind of consumer loyalty), this gave the producers the chance to blend 'to a price'. And blend to a price they do, since the actual name 'Liebfraumilch' has become a brand in itself. In an attempt to smarten its image, the wine now has to come from one single stated area – usually Rheinhesse or Rheinpfalz – but in fact that is likely to reduce quality rather than increase it for the good blender. For the poor blender there's not much reduction possible.

It wasn't always like that. One random wine list of 50 years ago shows Liebfraumilch as being more expensive than

Mouton Rothschild or Brane-Cantenac, but in those days Liebfraumilch might have been the real stuff – 'Our Lady's Milk' from the vineyards of Our Lady's Church at Worms, which is where the idea for this astonishing marketing phenomenon came from. And I've had 1921 Blue Nun Auslese (honestly!) which at 60 years old was absolutely superb.

However, you could walk across that vineyard in five minutes. If you tried to walk through all the vineyards it takes to satisfy our annual Liebfraumilch thirst, you'd need to take a year's sabbatical, because 60 per cent of all German wine exports are this single wine – Liebfraumilch, and the most conservative estimates are that 44 per cent of all *our* German wine imports are Liebfraumilch. Others reckon it's nearer 50 per cent. If 70 per cent of all our wine drinking is now white (and that's what the statistics say), and Germany's white wine import figures leapt 37.7 per cent in 1983, accounting for nearly a quarter of our table wine imports, then I don't need a pocket calculator to suggest that one bottle in every ten bought in the UK is – Liebfraumilch.

Comparative prices for Liebfraumilch

On Sale	Blue Nun	Findlater's Liebfraumilch
1970	£1.02	£1.05
1971	£1.06	£1.10
1972	£1.13	£1.21
1973	£1.16	£1.14
1974	£1.40	£1.25
1975	£1.61	£1.55
1976	£1.90	£1.71
1977	£2.11	£2.14
1978	£2.20	£2.19
1979	£2.37	£2.33
1980	£2.79	£2.44
1981	£2.93	£2.62
1982	£3.32	£2.64
1983	£3.33	£2.72
1984	£3.10	£2.51

PRICE GUIDE

White

Non-vintage
£1.85–£2.25
★Tesco Morio Muscat Tetra Pack (TES)
★Tesco Hock (TES)
Tesco Niersteiner Gutes Domtal (TES)
Sainsbury's Liebfraumilch (SAIN)
Liebfraumilch St Dominic (PD)
Thresher Liebfraumilch (THRE)
★Tesco St Johanner Abtei Kabinett (TES)
£2.25–£2.75
Deinhock, Deinhard (PG, HBV, UNW)
Liebfraumilch, Drathen Crock (ASHE)
★Niersteiner Gütes Domtal, von Furstenberg (CHAP)
★Liebfraumilch St Catherine (ASHE)
Niersteiner Gütes Domtal, Zentralkellerei Rheinischer Weingenossenschaft (PD)
★Tesco Liebfraumilch Brik Pak 1 litre (TES)
Liebfraumilch Blue Nun (WAIT, SAIN, PD, VICT, ASHE, QR, THRE, UNW, AV)
Liebfraumilch Rhine Bear (PD)
Merchant Vintners Hock (ADN)
£3.00–£4.00
Liebfraumilch Hirondelle (UNW, PD)
Liebfraumilch Wedding Veil (ASHE)
Liebfraumilch Golden Oktober (VICT, ASHE, PD, UNW)
Morio Muskat litre (VICT)
Liebfraumilch Crown of Crowns (VICT, PD, ASHE, UNW, QR)
Liebfraumilch Black Tower (VICT, PD, ASHE, THRE, QR)
Hanns Christof Kabinett (VICT, UNW)
The Society's Rhine Wine litre (WSOC)

1982

£2.00–£2.50

Niersteiner Spiegelberg, Rudolf Müller (RACK)
★Waitrose Liebfraumilch (WAIT)
Liebfraumilch (VICT)
★Niersteiner Gütes Domtal (SR)
★Westhofener Bergkloster, Müller (ODD, ESV)
Sainsbury's Oppenheimer Krötenbrunnen Kabinett (SAIN)
★Hainfelder Ordensgut Kabinett, Drathen (ODD)
★Oppenheimer Krötenbrunnen (PD, ASHE)
★Harveys Rheinpfalzwein (JH)

£2.75–£3.00

★Bereich Schloss Böckelheim, Zentral Kellerei (J&B)
★Mainzer Domherr Kabinett, Hallgarten (PG)
Liebfraumilch, Rudolf Müller (C&B)
★Bereich Bingen Kabinett, Schmitt Söhne 'Kabinett' (CV)
★Pfalzer Landwein Halbtrocken litre (LHV)
★Armsheimer Adelberg (STWC)
★Kreuznacher Breitenweg Riesling, Finkenauer (L&W)
Liebfraumilch Blue Nun (DAV, ODD, MWS, YFW, CUL, TAN)
Liebfraumilch Crown of Crowns (THRE, MWS, YFW, TAN)
Niersteiner Gütes Domtal, Langenbach (THRE)

£3.25–£4.25

Rüdesheimer Rosengarten, Rudolf Müller (TAN)
Dexheimer Doktor Spätlese (WAIT)
Schloss Böckelheimer Burgweg, St Ursula (VICT)
Sylvaner litre (WAIT)
★Alsheimer Rheinblick Spätlese, Ernst Jungkenn (ASHE)
Dexheimer Doktor Silvaner Kabinett, Peter Louis Guntrum (BBR)
Liebfraumilch Black Tower (DAV)
Rüdesheimer Burgweg, Schloss Groenesteyn (JH)
Hanns Christof Kabinett, Deinhard (MWS, YFW)
★Kaiserstuhl Tuniberg litre (ODD)
Oppenheimer Schloss Müller-Thurgau Trocken, Guntrum (MWS)
Forster Mariengarten Kabinett, Bürklin-Wolf (SF)
★Traiser Rotenfels Riesling, Weingut Crusius (STWC)
Johannisberger Klaus Riesling, Schönborn (ASHE)
★Deidesheimer Herrgottsäcker Riesling Kabinett, von Buhl (ASHE, CV)

£4.50–£5.00

Kiedricher Grafenberg Riesling Kabinett, Weil (CV)
★Schloss Böckelheimer Kupfergrube Riesling Kabinett, Staatliche Weinbaudomäne (HT)
Niersteiner Rehbach Riesling Kabinett, Guntrum (MWS)
Wachenheimer Gerümpel Riesling Kabinett, Bürklin-Wolf (VICT)
★Niederhäuser Hermannshöhle Riesling Spätlese, Staatliche Weinbaudomäne (HT)
Forster Jesuitengarten Riesling Kabinett, Bürklin-Wolf (P&C)
Steinberger, Staatsweingut Eltville (MAL)

£5.00–£6.00

Schloss Böckelheimer Königsfels Riesling, August Anheuser (YFW)
Forster Ungeheuer Kabinett, von Buhl (L&W)
Kreuznacher Narrenkappe Optima Spätlese, von Plettenberg (MAL)
Ruppertsberger Hoheburg Riesling Kabinett, von Buhl (OWL)
Schloss Vollrads Blue-Silver, Matuschka-Greiffenclau (QR, YFW)

c. £9.50

Erbacher Marcobrunn Riesling Spätlese, Langwerth von Simmern (OWL)

1981

£2.75–£3.75

Halbtrocken Südliche Weinstrasse, Sichel (HT)
Liebfraumilch, von Furstenberg (CHAP)

Bereich Nierstein, Rudolf Müller (HHC)
Niersteiner Rosenberg Riesling, Anton Balbach (JH, J&B)
Rüdesheimer Rosengarten, Rudolf Müller (H&D)
Liebfraumilch Crown of Crowns (CHAP)
Liebfraumilch Blue Nun (CHAP, HHC)
Niersteiner Spiegelberg Riesling Kabinett, Rudolf Müller (H&D, J&B)
★Dexheimer Doktor Silvaner, Baron von Kaulbars (PIP)
Kreuznacher Kahlenberg Riesling, von Plettenberg (PIP)
Hanns Christof Kabinett, Deinhard (HBV, RGA, GH)
Wormser Liebfrauenmorgen Kerner Kabinett, Winzergenossenschaft Wonnegau (PIP)
Niersteiner Bildstock Riesling Kabinett, J. Strub (WW)
Winzenheimer Rosenheck Riesling Kabinett, von Plettenberg (PD, OWL)
★Niersteiner Klostergarten Trocken Kabinett, Guntrum (PG)
Rüdesheimer Magdalenerkreuz Riesling Kabinett, Schloss Groenesteyn (PD)

£4.00–£4.50
Binger St Rochuskapelle Spätlese, Guntrum (MAL)
Deidesheimer Hergottsacker Riesling Kabinett, von Buhl (BWC, L&W)
Steinberger Riesling, Staat Domäne (JH)
Liebfraumilch Hanns Christof (TAN)
Kiedricher Heiligenstock Kabinett, Schloss Groenesteyn (JH)
Schloss Böckelheimer Kupfergrube Riesling, Staatliche Weinbaudomäne (HT)
Steinberger Riesling, Staatsweingut Eltville (PIP)
Kiedricher Grafenberg Riesling, Dr. Weil (L&W)
Niersteiner Rosenberg Riesling Spätlese, Gessert (WSOC)
Schloss Vollrads Riesling, Matuschka-Greiffenclau (WGA)
Forster Mariengarten Riesling Kabinett, Bürklin-Wolf (WW)

★Dürkheimer Feuerberg Gewürztraminer Spätlese, Winzergenossenschaft Bad Dürkheim (PG)
Kreuznacher Narrenkappe Scheurebe Kabinett, Paul Anheuser (MAL)
Steinberger Kabinett Halbtrocken, Staatsweingut Eltville (H&B)
Schloss Vollrads Greencap (L&W)
Dürkheimer Feuerberg Gewürztraminer Spätlese, Vier Jahreszeiten (HT)

£4.50–£5.00
Winzenheimer Rosenheck Riesling Spätlese, von Plettenberg (PIP)
Kreuznacher Kahlenberg Riesling Spätlese, Paul Anheuser (L&W)
★Forster Schnepfenflug Gewürztraminer Spätlese, Winzerverein Forst (CV)
Forster Pechstein Riesling Spätlese, von Buhl (HT)
Niersteiner Oelberg Riesling Spätlese, Hermann Franz Schmitt (H&D)

£5.25–£5.50
Hochheimer Hölle Riesling Kabinett, Schönborn (L&W)
Johannisberger Erntebringer Riesling, Schönborn (C&B)
Wachenheimer Gerumpel Riesling Kabinett, Bürklin-Wolf (L&W)
Niederhäuser Steinberg Kabinett, Staatliche Weinbaudomäne (OWL)
Niersteiner Auflangen Riesling Kabinett, Gustav Gessert (OWL)
Oestricher Lenchen Riesling Kabinett, Deinhard (HBV)
Forster Jesuitengarten Riesling Kabinett, Bassermann Jordan (L&W)
Erbacher Marcobrunn Riesling Kabinett, Langwerth von Simmern (L&W)
Forster Freundstück Riesling Spätlese, von Buhl (BIB)
Hochheimer Königin Victoria Berg Riesling Kabinett, Deinhard (HBV, WHIT, MWS)

£5.75–£7.00
Gewürztraminer Spätlese, Winzer Bad Dürkheim (C&B)
Hochheimer Domdeschaney Riesling Kabinett, Aschrott'sche Gutsverwaltung (OWL)

Niersteiner Oelberg Riesling Auslese, Anton Balbach (SF)
Forster Ungeheuer Riesling Spätlese, Deinhard (TAN)

1980
c. £2.75
*Johannisberger Erntebringer (LHV)
£4.25–£4.75
Schloss Böckelheimer Königsfels Riesling, Anheuser & Fehrs (HHC)
Kreuznacher Brückes Riesling Kabinett, Anheuser (DOL)
Deidesheimer Herrgottsacker Riesling Kabinett, Deinhard (GH)

1979
£3.50–£4.50
Schloss Böckelheim Riesling Spätlese, von Plettenberg (QR)
*Kreuznacher Breitenweg Riesling Kabinett-Halbtrocken, Finkenauer (L&W)
Kiedricher Sandgrube, Schloss Eltz (AV)
Schloss Vollrads Riesling Trocken (WILL)
Ruppertsberger Reiterpfad Riesling Kabinett, Bassermann Jordan (GH)
Hattenheimer Nussbrunnen Riesling, Schloss Reinhartshausen (PIP)
Kreuznacher St Martin Riesling Kabinett, August Anheuser (WHIT)
Binger Scharlachberg Riesling Kabinett, Villa Sachsen (VICT)
*Deidesheimer Herrgottsacker Riesling Kabinett, Bürklin-Wolf (PG, WHIT)

Oestricher Lenchen Riesling Kabinett, Nägler (WHIT)
Kreuznacher Mollenbrunnen Scheurebe Spätlese, Finkenauer (L&W)
£4.50–£5.00
*Kreuznacher Narenkappe Riesling Spätlese, Anheuser (ASHE)
*Rauenthaler Langenstück Riesling Spätlese, Diefenhardt (PG)
Oestricher Doosberg Riesling Kabinett, Schönborn (MAL)
Niersteiner Pettenthal Riesling Spätlese, Louis Guntrum (FINT)

Erbacher Marcobrunn Riesling Kabinett, Staatsweingut (PD, SR, VIGN)
*Deidesheimer Hergottsacker Riesling Spätlese, von Buhl (J&B, BIB)
Rauenthaler Steinmacher Spätlese, Staatsweingut (ODD, L&W)
Kreuznacher Hofgarten Müller-Thurgau Spätlese, von Plettenberg (GH)
Winzenheimer Berg Riesling Kabinett, von Plettenberg (OWL)
Forster Mariengarten Riesling, Bürklin-Wolf (P&C)
£5.00–£5.75
Niersteiner Pettenthal Riesling Spätlese, Anton Balbach (SF, JH, J&B)
Rüdesheimer Berg Schlossberg Riesling Spätlese, Schönborn (PD)
Hattenheimer Nussbrunnen Kabinett, Langwerth von Simmern (AV)
Rauenthaler Baiken Riesling Kabinett, Staatsweingut Eltville (PIP)
Forster Jesuitengarten Riesling Spätlese, von Buhl (FINT)
Hattenheimer Nussbrunen Riesling Kabinett, Georg Müller Stiftung (OWL)
Herxheimer Honigsacker Gewürztraminer Spätlese, Johann Schenk (MAL)
Steinberger Spätlese, Staatsweingut (VIGN)
Oppenheimer Sackträger Ruländer Auslese, Ernst Jungkenn (ASHE)
Steinberger Riesling Kabinett, Staatsweingut Eltville (GH, MAL)
Oestricher Doosberg Spätlese, Schönborn (AV)
Wachenheimer Goldbächel Spätlese, Bürklin-Wolf (WSOC)
Johannisberger Klaus Riesling, Landgraf von Hessische (FINT)
Hallgartener Hendelberg Riesling Kabinett blau, Fürst Loewenstein (OWL)
£6.00–£6.50
Eltviller Sonnenburg Riesling Kabinett, Schloss Eltz (FINT)
Winkeler Jesuitengarten Riesling Spätlese, H. H. Eser (OWL)
Rüdesheimer Berg Rottland Riesling Spätlese, Heinrich Nägler (OWL)
Oppenheimer Sackträger Riesling Auslese, Guntrum (MAL)

Kreuznacher Narrenkappe Scheuerebe Auslese, Paul Anheuser (CV)
Schloss Böckelheimer Felsenberg Riesling Spätlese, Crusius (WHIT)
Schloss Vollrads Riesling Kabinett Blaugold, Matuschka-Greiffenclau (PG, OWL, DOL)
Forster Ungeheuer Riesling Spätlese, Deinhard (J&B)
Kiedricher Sandgrub Riesling Spätlese, Fischer (WSOC)
Rauenthaler Baiken Riesling Kabinett, Langwerth von Simmern (WHIT)
Schloss Johannisberg Riesling Kabinett Red Seal (WILL, L&W)
Wachenheimer Gerumpel Riesling Spätlese, Bürklin-Wolf (MAL)
Forster Ungeheuer Scheurebe Auslese, Forster Winzerverein (VICT)
Niederhäuser Hermannsberg Riesling Spätlese, Staatliche Weinbaudomäne (OWL)
Hochheimer Hölle Riesling Spätlese, Sichel (WILL)
Forster Ungeheuer Riesling Spätlese Trocken, von Buhl (WNRY)

£6.75–£7.75

Rudesheimer Berg Rottland Riesling Spätlese, Deinhard (GH)
Schloss Böckelheimer Kupfergrube Riesling Spätlese, Staatliche Weinbaudomäne (OWL)
Eltviller Sonnenberg Riesling Spätlese, Schloss Eltz (GH)

Rudesheimer Berg Rottland Riesling Spätlese, Schloss Groenesteyn (VICT)
Kiedricher Sandgrub Riesling Spätlese, Anheuser & Fehrs (HHC)
Hattenheimer Nussbrunnen Riesling Spätlese, Schönborn (L&W)
Niersteiner Oelberg Riesling Auslese, Senfter (YFW)

c. £8.00

Hochheimer Königin Victoria Berg Riesling Spätlese, Deinhard (GH, TAN)

1978

£3.75–£4.75

Schloss Böckelheimer Kupfergrube Riesling, Staatliche Weinbaudomäne (PIP)
Rauenthaler Steinmacher Kabinett, Staatsweingut (MAL)
Wormser Liebfrauenstift Scheurebe, Langenbach (QR)

c. £5.00

Schloss Johannisberger Gelblack Riesling (PIP)

c. £11.00

Weinheimer Kirchenstuck Kerner Auslese Eiswein, Guntrum (MAL)

1977

Forster Freundstück Riesling Spätlese, von Buhl (GH)

1976

£4.50–£6.00

★Ruppertsberger Hoheburg Riesling Spätlese, von Buhl (SF, QR)
Oestricher Lenchen Riesling Kabinett, A. Eser (WSOC)
★Ruppertsberger Linsenbusch Riesling Auslese, von Buhl (HT, BIB, ODD)
Kiedricher Gräfenberg Riesling Spätlese, Weil (PG)
Kreuznacher Steinberg Riesling Spätlese, Anheuser (BBR)
Erbacher Schlossberg Riesling Spätlese, Schloss Reinhartshausen (PD)

£6.25–£6.50

Wachenheimer Luginsland Riesling Auslese, Bürklin-Wolf (GH, WGA)
Kreuznacher Kronenberg Riesling Spätlese, Anheuser (DOL)
Kreuznacher Monchberg Riesling Auslese, von Plettenberg (GH)
★Rauenthaler Rothenberg Riesling Auslese, Diefenhardt (PG, H&D)
Wachenheimer Böhlig Riesling Spätlese, Bürklin-Wolf (OWL)
Kiedricher Sandgrub Riesling Spätlese, Dr Weil (BBR)
Kiedricher Sandgrub Riesling Spätlese, J. Fischer Erben (WGA)
Niersteiner Rehbach Riesling Auslese, Guntrum (MWS)
Kreuznacher St Martin Riesling Spätlese, A. Anheuser (MAL)
Rüdesheimer Berg Schlossberg Riesling Spätlese, Schönborn (DOL)

£6.50–£7.25

Erbacher Honigberg Riesling Spätlese, Schloss Reinhartshausen (BBR)
Wachenheimer Goldbachel Riesling Spätlese, Bürklin-Wolf (MAL)
Schloss Böckelheim Königsfels Auslese, Anheuser (J&B)
Binger Rosengarten Scheurebe Auslese, Villa Sachsen (VICT)
Kreuznacher Brückes Riesling Spätlese, A. Anheuser (ADN)

Winkeler Hasensprung Riesling Spätlese, Deinhard (WILL)
Kiedricher Gräfenberg Riesling Spätlese, Schloss Groenesteyn (BBR)
Forster Ungeheuer Riesling Auslese, Bassermann-Jordan (JH)
Wachenheimer Rehbachel Riesling Spätlese, Bürklin-Wolf (MAL)
Wormser Liebfrauenmorgen Huxelrebe Beerenauslese (BIB)

£7.50–£8.50

Eltviller Sonnenberg Riesling Auslese, Jacob Fischer Erben (PIP)
Kreuznacher Krotenpfuhl Auslese, Paul Anheuser (ODD)
Kreuznacher Monchberg Riesling Auslese, von Plettenberg (OWL)
Winzenheimer Rosenheck Riesling Auslese, von Plettenberg (OWL)
Wachenheimer Mandelgarten Scheurebe Auslese, Bürklin-Wolf (H&D, WSOC)
Erbacher Siegelsberg Riesling Spätlese, Schloss Reinhartshausen (BBR)
⋆Niederhäuser Hermannshöhle Riesling Auslese, Staatliche Weinbaudomäne (HT)

£8.75–£9.75

Rüdesheimer Berg Roseneck Riesling Auslese, Heinrich Nägler (OWL)
Erbacher Siegelsberg Riesling Auslese, Schloss Reinhartshausen (PIP, GH)
Niersteiner Oelberg Riesling Beerenauslese Senfter (PD)

£9.75–£10.25

Johannisberger Hölle Riesling Auslese, Deinhard (BBR)
Eltviller Sonnenberg Riesling Auslese, von Simmern (L&W)
Steinberger Riesling Auslese, Staatsweingut (L&W)
Niersteiner Kranzberg Riesling Beerenauslese, Gustav Gessert (OWL)
Harxheimer Schlossberg Silvaner Beerenauslese, Sichel (WILL)
Binger Schlosssberg-Schwätzerchen Ruländer Beerenauslese, Staatliche Weinbaudomäne (HT, OWL, L&W)

£15.50–£16.25

Schloss Johannisberg Pink Seal Auslese, Furst von Metternich (L&W)
Binger Scharlachberg Riesling Beerenauslese, Staatliche Weinbaudomäne (ADN)
Kiedricher Gräfenberg Beerenauslese, Dr. Weil (H&D)
Schloss Johannisberg Riesling Rosalack Auslese, Metternich (C&B)

£18.00–£20.00

Erbacher Marcobrunn Riesling Beerenauslese, Schönborn (WGA)
Hattenheimer Nussbrunnen Riesling Auslese, Langwerth von Simmern (OWL)

Niersteiner Oelberg Riesling u Ruländer Trockenbeerenauslese, Senfter (WHIT, PG, MWS)
Deidesheimer Herrgottsacker Riesling Beerenauslese, Deinhard (BBR)

£23.00–£25.00

Geisenheimer Schlossgarten Riesling Beerenauslese, Schönborn (VICT)
Winkeler Hasenprung Riesling Beerenauslese, Deinhard (HBV, GH)
Niersteiner Orbel Sylvaner Trockenbeerenauslese, Guntrum (MAL)

£25.75–£28.75

Wachenheimer-Gerümpel Riesling Beerenauslese, Bürklin-Wolf (OWL)
Geisenheimer Kläuserweg Riesling Beerenauslese, Deinhard (TAN)
Niersteiner Oelberg Scheurebe Trockenbeerenauslese, Senfter (C&B)

c. £32.00

Wachenheimer Altenberg Riesling Trockenbeerenauslese, Winzergenossenschaft Wachenheim (VICT)

c. £48.75

Winzenheimer Rosenheck Riesling Trockenbeerenauslese, von Plettenberg (OWL)

c. £80.00

Niederhäuser Hermannshöhle Riesling Trockenbeerenauslese, Staatliche Weinbaudomäne (OWL)

1975

£4.75–£6.00

Winzenheimer Rosenheck Riesling Spätlese, von Plettenberg (MAL)

Erbacher Schlossberg Riesling Kabinett, Schloss Reinhartshäusen (HUN)
Niersteiner Auflangen Riesling Spätlese, Senfter (WHIT)
Niersteiner Oelberg Riesling Spätlese, Senfter (WHIT)
Johannisberger Hölle Riesling Kabinett, Zerbe (ADN)

c. £8.75

Steinberger Auslese, Staatsweingut Eltville (L&W)

c. £16.25

Hochheimer Hölle Riesling Auslese Eiswein, Geh'rat Aschrott (BBR)

c. £17.75

Oestricher Lenchen Riesling Auslese Eiswein, Deinhard (ADN)

1973

c. £6.25

Niederhäuser Hermannsberg Riesling Spätlese, Staatliche Weinbaudomäne (OWL)

c. £24.50

Johannisberger Hölle Riesling Beerenauslese Eiswein, Zerbe (PG)

1971

£5.75–£6.75

Wachenheimer Luginsland Riesling Spätlese, Bürklin-Wolf (MAL)
Rauenthaler Wulfen Riesling Spätlese, Schloss Rheinhartshäusen (WNRY)
Wachenheimer Gerumpel Riesling Spätlese, Bürklin-Wolf (MAL)
Hattenheimer Wisselbrunnen Riesling Spätlese, Schloss Reinhartshäusen (GH)
Kreuznacher Kahlenberg Riesling Auslese, von Plettenberg (QR)
Winkeler Jesuitsgarten Riesling Spätlese, Hessisches Weingut (VIGN)
Schloss Johannisberg Kabinett (VIGN)

£7.00–£8.50

Hattenheimer Wisselbrunnen Riesling Auslese, Schloss Rheinhartshäusen (WNRY)
Wörmser Liebfrauenmorgen Ruländer Auslese, Wissmann (WHIT)
Steinberger Riesling Spätlese, Staatsweingut (VIGN)
Kreuznacher Gutenthal Riesling Auslese, Finkenauer (L&W)
Forster Pechstein Traminer Auslese, Bürklin-Wolf (ADN)

c. £9.50

Johannisberger Klaus Riesling Auslese, Schönborn (ADN)

c. £11.00

Wachenheimer Gerümpel Riesling Auslese, Bürklin-Wolf (ADN)

£18.75–£20.75

Kreuznacher Forst Riesling Trockenbeerenauslese, Finkenauer ½ bottle (L&W)
Rüdesheimer Berg Roseneck Riesling Beerenauslese, Deinhard (BBR)
Niersteiner Spiegelberg Riesling & Gewürztraminer Beerenauslese, Senfter (C&B)

c. £23.85

Wachenheimer Gerümpel Riesling Trockenbeerenauslese, Deinhard ½ bottle (MWS)

c. £33.75

Erbacher Marcobrunn Riesling Beerenauslese, Schönborn (OWL)

c. £72.75

Oestricher Lenchen Riesling Trockenbeerenauslese, Deinhard (TAN)

1969

c. £11.75

Hochheimer Königin Victoria Berg Riesling Auslese, Deinhard (MWS)

1959

c. £23.50

Erbacher Honigberg Riesling Cabinet Feine Spätlese, Schloss Reinhartshäusen (HUN)

1949

c. £25.00

Marcobrunner Auslese, Schönborn (VIGN)

Red

1982

£3.25–£4.00

Ingelheimer Kaiserpfalz Portugieser (MWS)
Ruppertsberger Linsenbusch Portugieser, Winzerverein Ruppertsberg (PG)

1981

c. £3.75

Wickerer Nonnenberg Spatburgunder, Frankhof Kellerei (PIP)

MOSEL

If your only experience of Mosel wine is Bereich Bernakastel or Piesporter Michelsberg, Zeller Schwarze Katz or Kröver Nacktarsch, I make a heartfelt plea. *Don't* judge the Mosel by these. It's like judging the Rhine by Liebfraumilch, or the Loire by Anjou Rosé. Quite simply, these are the names which have caught the imagination of the holidaymaking public as they've ambled up and down one of the most lovely valleys wine growing has to offer.

Take Kröver Nacktarsch. Kröv's a nice enough village on one of the wider bends of the river. The café tables spread out in the sun along the street, the river lapping coolly at its banks. But what's this? Every time the waiter asks this busload of tourists what they want to drink, the ladies all titter and go pink, and the more jocular of their gentlemen friends jump up and begin striking the seat of their pants, amidst loud guffaws and hooting. The waiter yawns indulgently and brings another tray of 'bare bum'. Yes, that's what Nacktarsch means – bare bum. It's Kröv's most famous vineyard and all the Kröver Nacktarsch labels carry pictures of boys being spanked by a variety of adults. Frankly, no one cares what goes in the bottle, because they'll all be giggling so much while they drink it, they'll probably choke anyway.

Good, clean (?) fun, but nothing to do with the real glories of the Mosel, which can make Rieslings of such racy style, sourness balancing honey, apple freshness spiced up even further by the slatey dry edge so many of the wines have, that very few wine makers elsewhere have even tried to copy them. The bottle, yes; they'll copy that, because it's the most alluring of bottles, tall and thin, cool and green, matching the light, green-flecked wine which should gurgle out of its neck. Whenever wine growers want to imply that their wine is light and cool and thirstquenching, you'll find the Mosel bottle cropping up.

THE COST OF A BOTTLE

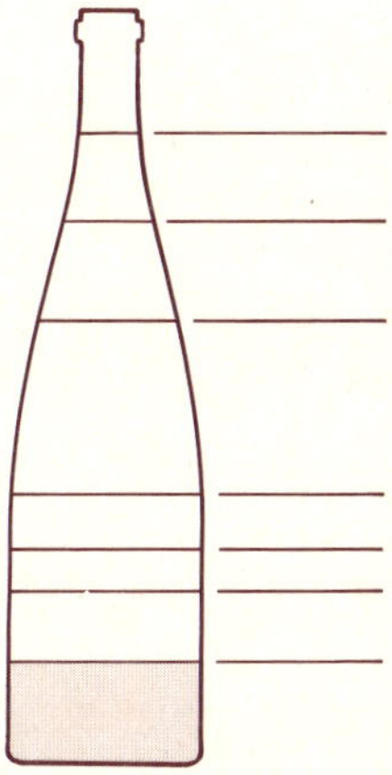

Mosel	**£2.00**
VAT	0.25
Merchant mark-up	0.41
Duty	0.68
Distribution	0.10
Shipping	0.04
Bottling	0.22
Wine	0.30

But they can't duplicate the Mosel style. Frequently the wine is so light, the fruit is so direct, and the acidity so cooking-apple-fresh, that it seems difficult to believe that it's wine at all. Just as on the Rheingau the Kabinett (i.e. drier) style shows the beauty of the Riesling to best advantage, so it is on the Mosel. Which is just as well, because it's very difficult to ripen the grapes on this steep-sided twisting valley, resembling the swathe a giant Loch Ness monster might have threshed through the Highlands. The vineyards are insanely steep, and all the best ones are covered with slate and stone. In a village like Bernkastel, the vineyards are so steep behind the clustered houses, you wonder why they don't have safety nets to catch the workers who drink too deep at lunch, and fall off when they bend over to do a bit of post-prandial pruning.

This mixture of slate, Riesling and cool summers gives wines which seem a whole category below Rhine wines in sweetness, a Spätlese often feeling only as full as a Rheingau Kabinett. This impression is pretty accurate, because the Mosel

Vintage Table

If a Mosel wine is from a single vineyard and a Riesling, it *can* be surprisingly good from off years like 1977 and 1980, and age well in a dry, steely way. There is no point whatsoever in ageing Bereich Bernkastel and the like.

***1983** A wonderful Riesling year, and all the Mosel areas are superb. The fruit is sweet and ripe, but balanced as yet by a piercing acidity, and some thrilling slatey bite. Buy, drink, *and* age.

1982 Not up to much. They looked as though they would provide light, fruity drinking for a year or two, but the enormous crop dilution has caught up with most of them. Buy 1983s.

1981 A 'nearly' vintage. The quite high acidity suited the Mosel, but those steely dry styles we expected didn't get over here much. Kabinetts should still be OK. I'd still buy '83.

1979 The softness you can get away with on the Rhine is a killer on the Mosel. Wines up to Auslese were made, but they never tasted real, and the wines that are left are fairly lifeless.

***1976** This sort of year really suits the Rhine best, but the Mosel had a good go, and has produced remarkable, high acid, deep, honeyed wines. Interestingly, they've often aged rather fast, but if you see Spätlese wines upwards, try them.

Maturity Chart

1983 MOSEL KABINETT

1983 has excellent acidity. Softer vintages will mature much faster.

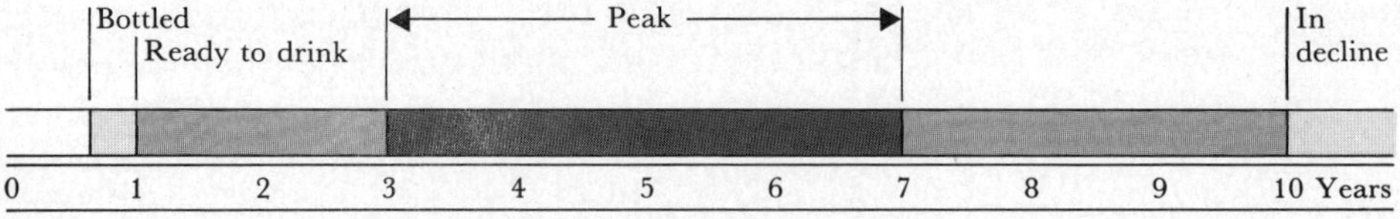

ripeness levels are lower all round, and while a Rheingau Spätlese will have to make 11.4 degrees of potential alcohol ripeness to qualify, a Mosel will only have to make 10 degrees of alcohol

Which makes a lot of the sweetened commercial concoctions we have to put up with all the more difficult to bear. But, as with the bare bums up the river, if the wine has a name or an image which sells, an awful lot of growers are going to take the easy way out and go for the quick buck. Nothing illustrates this more than the worrying decline of the Riesling, the only grape to make really fine Mosel. In 1910 it was 88 per cent. Even in 1964 it was 80 per cent, but in 1984 it's hovering at a little over 50 per cent. That Bereich Bernkastel or Piesporter Michelsberg may very well contain no Riesling *at all*.

Use 1983 as an excuse to seek out single vineyard Riesling Kabinetts and Spätleses from the Mosel, and its side valleys, the Saar and the Ruwer.

PRICE GUIDE

Non-vintage

£2.00–£3.00

Sainsbury's Moselle Deutscher Tafelwein (SAIN)

Deinmoselle (PG, GH, UNW, MWS)

The Merchant Vintners Moselle (ADN, TAN)

Goldener Oktober Mosel-Saar-Ruwer, St Ursula (VICT)

Goldener Oktober Riesling, St Ursula (VICT)

£3.00–£4.00

Mosel Spezial litre (PD)

Bereich Bernkastel Green Label, Deinhard (WILL, VICT, PD, QR)

The Society's Moselle litre (WSOC)

1982

£2.25–£3.00

⋆Riesling Mosel-Saar-Ruwer (SR)

⋆Bereich Bernkastel Riesling, von Furstenberg (CHAP)

Waitrose Bereich Bernkastel (WAIT)

Waitrose Piesporter Michelsberg (WAIT)

⋆Piesporter Michelsberg, von Furstenberg (CHAP)

Bereich Bernkastel, Zentralkellerei (PD)

⋆Urziger Schwarzlay Halbtrocken (LHV)

⋆Bernkasteler Kurfurstlay Kabinett, Müller (ODD)

⋆Wiltinger Scharzberg Riesling, Brueckenkellerei (PG)

⋆Schloss Böckelheimer Burgweg Riesling, von Furstenberg (CHAP)

⋆Piesporter Michelsberg, Zentralkellerei Moselle (J&B)

⋆Zeller Grafschaft, Hegemann (H&D)

Piesporter Michelsberg, Rudolf Müller (C&B, TAN)

£3.00–£4.00

Piesporter Michelsberg Riesling, Max. Ferdinand Richter (DOL)

Bernkastel Kueser Kardinalsberg Riesling Kabinett, Zentralkellerei (TAN)

Bereich Bernkastel Green Label, Deinhard (DAV, MWS, YFW, CUL, ASHE)

⋆Ockfener Geisberg Riesling Kabinett, Friedrich-Wilhelm Gymnasium (HT)

£4.25–£5.25

Wehlener Sonnenuhr Riesling Kabinett, Max. Ferdinand Richter (DOL)

Scharzhofberger Riesling Kabinett, von Kesselstatt (HT)

Scharzhofberger Riesling Kabinett, von Hovel (CV)

Ayler Kupp Riesling Kabinett, Bischöfliches Konvikt (L&W)

Piesporter Goldtröpfchen Kabinett, Reuscher-Haart-Schwang (WSOC)

Trittenheimer Apotheke Riesling Spätlese, Friedrich-Wilhelm Gymnasium (ASHE)

£5.75–£6.50

Trittenheimer Apotheke Spätlese, Josef Schmitt (OWL)

Maximin Grünhäuser Abtsberg Riesling Kabinett, von Schubert (ASHE, OWL)

Brauneberger Juffer Sonnenuhr Riesling Spätlese, von Schorlemer (L&W)

Piesporter Goldtropfchen Kabinett Riesling, Vereinigte Hospitien (P&C)

Piesporter Domherr Spätlese, von Kesselstatt (OWL)

c. £9.75

Wehlener Sonnenuhr Auslese, J. J. Prüm (OWL)

c. £10.00
Scharzhofberger Spätlese, Egon Müller (OWL)

1981
£2.50–£3.25
Bernkasteler Kurfürstlay Trocken, Michel Schneider (WHIT)
Zeller Schwarze Katz, Zentralkellerei (PD)
⋆Trierer Roemerlay, Vogt & Rendenbach (PG)
Zeltinger Münzlay, Sichel (HT)
⋆Zeltinger Himmelreich Riesling Kabinett, Koppelkamm (L&W)
£3.75–£4.50
Ockfener Herrenberg Riesling, Gebert (CHAP)
Lieserer Schlossberg Riesling, von Schorlemer (PIP)
⋆Zeltinger Himmelreich Riesling Kabinett, von Kunsberg (PIP)
⋆Piesporter Treppchen Kabinett (JH)
Ockfener Geisberg Riesling, Friedrich-Wilhelm Gymnasium (HT)
Urziger Würzgarten Riesling Spätlese, Rudolf Müller (L&W)
Graacher Himmelreich Kabinett, Pfeiffer (MWS)
Bernkasteler Badstube Riesling, von Schorlemer (PG)
Bereich Bernkastel Green Label, Deinhard (TAN)
Ockfener Bockstein Riesling Kabinett, Rudolf Müller (L&W, CHAP, ESV)

Wehlener Sonnenuhr Riesling Kabinett, Erben (C&B)
Bernkasteler Badstube Riesling, Friedrich-Wilhelm Gymnasium (WSOC, CV)
£4.75–£5.75
⋆Trittenheimer Apotheke Riesling Spätlese, Friedrich-Wilhelm Gymnasium (HT, L&W, OWL)
Graacher Domprobst Riesling Kabinett, Licht-Berweiler (J&B)
Piesporter Goldtröpfchen Riesling Kabinett, von Kesselstatt (PIP)
Bernkasteler Badstube Riesling Kabinett, Deinhard (HBV)

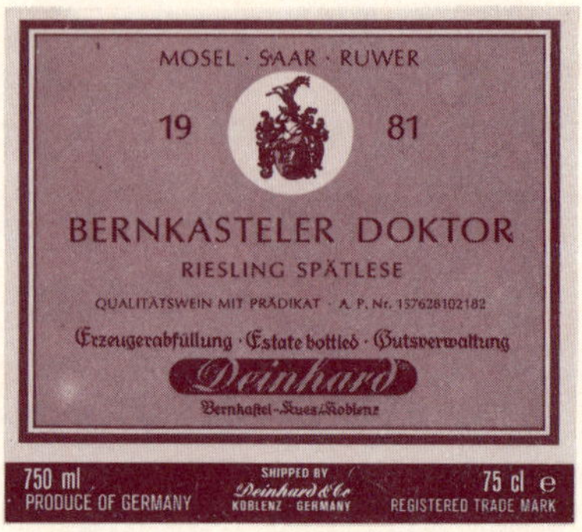

Maximin Grünhäuser Herrenberg Riesling Kabinett, von Schubert (HT)
Piesporter Grafenberg Riesling Spätlese, von Kesselstatt (HT)
Wehlener Sonnenuhr Kabinett, von Schorlemer (YFW)
Erdener Treppchen Riesling Kabinett, Bischöfliches Priesterseminar (L&W)
Trittenheimer Altärchen Riesling Kabinett, Bischöfliches Priesterseminar (ADN)
Graacher Himmelreich Kabinett, J. J. Prüm (L&W, OWL)
£6.00–£7.00
Zeltinger Sonnenuhr Spätlese, Friedrich-Wilhelm Gymnasium (WSOC)
Urziger Würzgarten Spätlese, Bischöfliches Priesterseminar (WSOC)
Scharzhofberger Riesling Spätlese, von Kesselstatt (PIP)
Kaseler Herrenberg Riesling Spätlese, von Kesselstatt (J&B)
Zeltinger Sonnenuhr Riesling Spätlese, von Kesselstatt (L&W)
Dhron-Hofberger Spätlese, Bischöfliches Priesterseminar (OWL)
c. £9.25
Bernkasteler Doktor Riesling Kabinett, Deinhard (WHIT)

1980
c. £3.85
Bereich Bernkastel Green Label, Deinhard (HHC)

1979
£3.50–£4.50
Merler Adler Riesling Spätlese, Schneider (H&B)
Zeltinger Himmelreich Riesling Kabinett, Adolph Huesgen (BBR)
⋆Reiler Mullay Hofberg Riesling Spätlese, Rudolf Müller (L&W)
Bernkasteler-Kueser Kardinalsberg Spätlese, Drathen (ODD)
Brauneberger Mandelgraben Riesling Spätlese, Max. Ferdinand Richter (DOL)

Graacher Himmelreich Kabinett, Thanisch (L&W)

£4.75–£5.75

Brauneberger Juffer-Sonnenuhr Riesling Kabinett, Thanisch (L&W, ADN)

⋆Burg-Layer Schlosskapelle Beerenauslese, Optima (CHAP)

Bernkasteler Badstube Riesling Kabinett, Friedrich-Wilhelm Gymnasium (L&W, ADN)

⋆Bernkasteler Badstube Riesling, Pfarrkirche Bernkastel (PG)

⋆Wehlener Sonnenuhr, Bergweiler-Prüm (PG)

Ayler Kupp Riesling Kabinett, Winzerverein Ayl (FINT)

Schloss Böckelheimer Königsfels Kabinett, A. Anheuser (WSOC)

Serriger Vogelsang Kabinett, Weinbaudomäne Trier (WSOC)

Waldracher Krone Riesling Spätlese, Peter Scherf (HT, BOW)

Ockfener Bockstein Riesling Spätlese, Dr Fischer (CV)

⋆Ockfener Bockstein Riesling, Rheinart Erben (PG)

Leiwener Klostergarten Riesling Kabinett, Weingut Josefinengrund (FINT)

Ockfener Geisberg Riesling Kabinett, Friedrich-Wilhelm Gymnasium (MAL)

⋆Trittenheimer Altärchen Kabinett, Steinlein-Schmitt (FFW)

Piesporter Goldtröpfchen Kabinett, von Kesselstatt (OWL)

Kaseler Nies'chen Kabinett, Erben, von Beulwitz (OWL)

£6.00–£7.00

Ayler Herrenberg Spätlese, Bischöfliches Konvikt (WSOC)

Scharzhofberger Riesling Kabinett, Egon Müller (WHIT, OWL, GH, WNRY)

Erdener Treppchen Kabinett, Bischöpfliches Priesterseminar (OWL)

Bernkasteler Badstube Kabinett, J. J. Prüm (OWL, WNRY)

Wiltinger Braunfels Spätlese, von Kesselstatt (SR)

Waldracher Krone Riesling Spätlese, Sichel Söhne (TAN)

Wehlener Sonnenuhr Riesling Spätlese, Peter Prüm (VICT)

Maximin Grünhäuser Abtsberg Kabinett, von Schubert (WSOC)

Wehlener Sonnenuhr Riesling Auslese, Max. Ferdinand Richter (DOL)

Wiltinger Sandberg Riesling Auslese, Ernst Faust (PD)

£7.25–£8.50

Eitelsbacher Karthäuserhofberger Sang Spätlese, Werner Tyrell (L&W)

Trittenheimer Apotheke Riesling Auslese, Friedrich-Wilhelm Gymnasium (MAL)

Bernkasteler Gräben Riesling Spätlese, Deinhard (GH)

Maximin Grünhäuser Abtsberg Spätlese, von Schubert (SR, L&W)

£9.00–£9.50

Eitelsbacher Karthäuserhofberg Riesling Auslese, Werner Tyrell (WNRY)

Wehlener Sonnenuhr Auslese, J. J. Prüm (L&W)

c. £17.50

Bernkasteler Doktor Riesling Spätlese, Deinhard (TAN)

c. £22.75

Bernkasteler Doktor Riesling Auslese, Deinhard (HBV)

1978

c. £4.50

Brauneberger-Juffer Riesling Kabinett, Thanisch (L&W)

c. £6.50
Wehlener Sonnenuhr Kabinett, J. J. Prüm (WSOC)

1977
c. £5.25
Brauneberger-Juffer Sonnenuhr Riesling Kabinett, Thanisch (C&B)
c. £14.00
Graacher Himmelreich Riesling Spätlese, Bergweiler-Prüm (PG)

1976
£5.50–£6.50
★Piesporter Treppchen Riesling Auslese, von Schorlemer (PG, SF, H&D, WHIT)
★Wintricher Ohligsberg Riesling, von Schorlemer (PG)
Ayler Kupp Auslese, R. Langguth (WGA)
Wiltinger Schlangengraben Riesling Spätlese, von Schorlemer (BBR)
★Dhroner Hofberger Riesling, Schmitt Schenk (PG)
★Ockfener Bockstein Riesling, Rheinart Erben (PG)
Ockfener Geisberg Riesling Spätlese, Friedrich-Wilhelm Gymnasium (MAL, GH)
Graacher Himelreich Riesling Auslese, Deinhard (WILL)
Falkensteiner Hofberg Riesling Auslese, Friedrich-Wilhelm Gymnasium (HT, AV, JH)
Graacher Himmelreich Auslese, Winzergenossenschaft (WSOC)
Urzier Würzgarten Riesling Auslese, Paul Müller (BBR)
Eitelsbacher Karthaüserhofberg Burgberg Spätlese, von Rautenstrauch (WSOC)
£6.75–£7.75
Eitelsbacher Marienholz Riesling Spätlese, Bischöfliches Konvikt (MAL)
Maximin Grünhäuser Abtsberg Spätlese, von Schubert (JH)
★Kaseler Nies'chen Riesling Auslese, Bischöfliches Priesterseminar (ASHE)

Graacher Himmelreich Riesling Auslese, Friedrich-Wilhelm Gymnasium (GH, WGA)
Eitelsbacher Karthäuserhofberger Kronenberg Auslese, Werner Tyrell (L&W)
Kaseler Kehrnagel Auslese, Erben von Beulwitz (OWL)
Wiltinger Kupp Riesling Auslese, Bischöfliches Priesterseminar (JH)

£8.00–£9.50
Urziger Würzgarten Riesling Auslese, Bischöfliches Priesterseminar (JH)
Brauneberger Juffer-Sonnenuhr Riesling Auslese, Thanisch (C&B)
Ayler Kupp Riesling Auslese, Bischöfliches Konvikt (ADN)
Scharzhofberger Riesling Auslese, Hohe Domkirche (BBR)
Maximin Grünhäuser Herrenberg Riesling Auslese, von Schubert (HT, GH, OWL)
Maximin Grünhäuser Herrenberg Auslese, von Schorlemer (H&D)
Trittenheimer Apotheke Riesling Auslese, Friedrich-Wilhelm Gymnasium (P&C)
£9.75–£10.50
Ayler Herrenberger Auslese, Bischöfliches Konvikt (WSOC)
Bernkasteler Graben Riesling Auslese, Deinhard (ADN)
Maximin Grünhäuser Abtsberg Auslese, von Schubert (L&W)
£12.00–£14.50
Erdener Treppchen Riesling Beerenauslese, Pfeiffer (MWS)
Zeltinger Himmelreich Riesling Beerenauslese, Zentralkellerei Mosel (ADN)
Lieserer Schlossberg Ortega Beerenauslese, Thanisch (C&B)
Neumagener Rosengärtchen Beerenauslese, Josef Schmitt (OWL)
c. £24.25
Scharzhofberger Riesling Beerenauslese, Koch (C&B)
c. £29.25
Piesporter Goldtröpfchen Beerenauslese, von Kesselstatt (OWL)

c. £35.75
Wehlener Sonnenenuhr Auslese lange Goldkapsel, J. J. Prüm (OWL)
c. £60.50
Piesporter Goldtröpfchen Trockenbeerenauslese, von Kesselstatt (OWL)
c. £64.00
Wehlener Sonnuhr Beerenauslese, J. J. Prüm (OWL)
c. £169.50
Graacher Himmelreich Trockenbeerenauslese, J. J. Prüm (OWL)

1975
£4.50–£5.50
Zeltinger Himmelreich Spätlese, Studert (C&B)
Ockfener Bockstein Riesling Auslese, von Schorlemer (HUN)
★Zeltinger Sonnenuhr Riesling Auslese, von Schorlemer (CV)
Trittenheimer Altärchen Riesling Auslese, Friedrich-Wilhelm Gymnasium (WW)
£6.00–£7.00
Piesporter Treppchen Auslese, von Schorlemer (P&C)
Urziger Würzgarten Riesling Auslese, Berres (WGA)
Scharzhofberger Riesling Spätlese, von Hovel (MAL)
Serriger Heiligenborn Spätlese (WSOC)
Kanzemer Altenberg Auslese, Bischöfliches Priesterseminar (WSOC)
Brauneberger Juffer Sonnenuhr Riesling Auslese, H. Erben (P&C)
Wintricher Ohligsberg Riesling Auslese, von Schorlemer (P&C)

£7.25–£8.25
Wiltinger Kupp Riesling Auslese, Bischöfliches Priesterseminar (GH)
Kaseler Nies'chen Riesling Auslese, Bischöfliches Priesterseminar (YFW)
Graacher Himmelreich Riesling Auslese, Prüm (ADN)
c. £16.25
Bernkasteler Doktor Riesling Auslese, Thanisch (L&W, C&B)

c. £42.50
Bernkasteler Bratenhöfchen Riesling Beerenauslese Eiswein, Deinhard (MWS, TAN)

1971
c. £5.25
Niedermenninger Herrenberg Riesling Auslese, von Kesselstatt (HT)
Wehlener Sonnenuhr Riesling Spätlese, Bergweiler (C&B)
c. £11.00
Maximin Grünhäuser Abtsberg Auslese, von Schubert (OWL)

Price Guide – Notes

Single vineyard wines are reasonably available in the UK, but actual 'grower produced and bottled' wines are few and far between. It is sadly true that the surge in cheap German wine has been accompanied by a loss of interest in the finest wines. Although the listings may look impressive, very few of these top wines have more than a single, specialized supplier. Estate bottled wines are not expensive, and readers should use the 1983 vintage as an excuse to try some of them.

FRANKEN

The British have never really got into Franken wines. Lucky for our German friends, because they need every bottle they can get. Franken, or Franconia, has always made the driest German wines, and even Spätleses and Ausleses, while being fairly big and beefy, are still basically dry. So, given the fairly sweet nature of most of Germany's wines, they have achieved a considerable snob following among the Germans who drink wine with meals. (By no means everybody. Beer is more often seen at mealtimes). The consequence is that these slightly earthy, slightly vegetal, dryish wines can charge prices of up to double what an equivalent Rhine or Mosel might cost.

Well, that might wash with the Germans, but not with us. We have such a wide array of dry white wines available in Britain, and at prices to meet every purse, that these rather overpriced oddities seem unlikely to catch on over here. And not just because they come in a Mateus Rosé look-alike bottle. More than ever the British taste (in German wines at least) is for the slightly sweetened styles, and, sadly, more than ever for the cheaper and cheaper styles. The Franken wines, based on the solid Sylvaner or the slightly raw Müller-Thurgau are, therefore, (a) the wrong style and (b) never cheap enough to build a market.

Their market in Germany, however, is also under threat. The Germans are drinking more and more imported wines, much of it dry and white, and, instead of Franken having the 'dry' world to itself, the other wine regions of Germany have rushed into producing *trocken,* or 'dry' wines to try to meet the demand. To be honest, the Franken wines, even if you don't go a bundle on the style, are mostly far better than these new *trockens,* which are frequently so tart and painful to the teeth that you have to put all your food through a liquidizer for 48 hours after drinking them. Franken has had two big crops, in '82 and '83, so prices may have to fall. If so, it might be worth trying them, but right now, they haven't a lot of chance in the UK market.

PRICE GUIDE

White

Non-vintage
£4.25–£4.75

Eibelstadter Kappellenberg Traminer Trocken, Winzergenossenschaft Eibelstadt (BOW)

Franken Sylvaner St Ursula (VICT)

1982
£4.50–£6.50

Iphöfer Kronsberg Scheurebe, Hans Wirsching (SF)

Würzburger Stein Müller-Thurgau, Juliusspital (PG)

Iphöfer Kalb Silvaner Kabinett, Shulz & Wagner (PIP)

Würzburger Stein Riesling Kabinett, Juliusspital (OWL)

1981

c. £5.00

Iphöfer Kronsberg Müller-Thurgau Kabinett, Hans Wirsching (BWC)

c. £6.85

Escherndorfer Lump Silvaner Kabinett, Cristoph Herpfer (L&W)

1980

c. £6.25

Escherndorfer Lump Riesling, Gebietswinzergenossenschaft (WHIT)

1979

c. £8.50

Iphöfer Julius Echter Berg Silvaner Spätlese, Juliusspital (OWL)

c. £49.50

Würzburger Stein Rieslaner Trockenbeerenauslese, Juliusspital (OWL)

1977

c. £7.25

Iphöfer Julius Echter Berg Riesling Kabinett, Juliusspital (OWL, GH)

1976

c. £7.75

Prichsenstadter Krone Ortega Auslese, Cristoph Herpfer (L&W)

c. £10.25

Würzburger Abtsleite Silvaner Auslese, Bürgerspital Zum Heiligen Geist Würzburg (PIP)

*Please don't blame **Webster's** or the merchants listed if a wine is sold out or if the vintage you want is no longer available. Wine is a living entity and a limited commodity – continuity of supply cannot, alas, be guaranteed.*

BADEN-WÜRTTEMBERG

Did you know that the richest (sweetest) German wine ever recorded was made in Württemberg in 1983?

Did you know that Germany's only Sauvignon Blanc is made in Baden?

Did you know that about one bottle in four of German wine comes from Baden-Württemberg?

In fact, did you know anything at all about Baden-Württemberg?

Don't worry if you didn't, because the UK market has hardly been touched by these giants of the south. One of the reasons is the usual one – yes, the locals drink it all! The Badeners drink on average twice as much wine as the rest of Germany, and the Württembergers aren't far behind with Stuttgart (the capital) not only growing a fair amount of wine inside the city boundaries, but also putting away about 44 litres per head per year, against a national average of about 25 litres. Württemberg wines are unlikely to hit the UK market very hard, but if you have to visit Stuttgart it is worth seeking out the Württemberg Rieslings, and bypassing the infuriatingly sweetened Trollinger reds in favour of the Schillerwein rosés.

Quite the best rosé, however, is over the hills in Freiburg, where Baden's greatest grape, the Ruländer, is mixed with Pinot Noir to produce a spectacular pink wine. Ruländer is the Pinot Gris or Tokay of Alsace, which is anyway only an hour's drive away across the Rhine. In Baden, even in normal years, it produces a quite absurdly good honeyed wine, not at all in the modern vogue of dry, light, and tart, nor of the sugary and feeble persuasion. The German Food Centre in London usually has one, and it's well worth seeking out.

Otherwise, Baden is still trying to make an impression over here. It should manage it in the end, because the big spicey grapes like Gewürztraminer and Ruländer ripen regularly and well in this (Germany's warmest) wine area, and the organisation of the region is the best in Germany.

There are 100 co-operatives, handling 90 per cent of the grapes, and the Central Co-op at Breisach really is spectacular. It was founded as a marketing operation in 1952, but is now intimately involved in making some 400–500 different wines each year from the production of 25,000 growers. It pioneered low temperature fermentation, is ruthless in its selection of grapes according to quality, and is one of the few co-ops worth seeking out for its quality rather than just its price.

White

Non-vintage
c. £2.50
Grants of St James Baden (SAIN)
Baden Dry (VICT)

1981
£3.50–£4.50
Breisgau Ringsheimer Kaiserberg Müller-Thurgau Kabinett (VICT)
Neuweierer Mauerberg Riesling, Winzergenossenschaft Neuweier (PIP)

1979
£3.75–£5.00
Oberbergener Bassgeige Rülander Kabinett, Winzergenossenschaft Oberbergen (PIP)
Steinbacher Yburgberg Riesling Kabinett, Winzergenossenschaft Steinbach und Umweg (L&W)

> ***Webster's*** *prices are per bottle, including VAT. If you buy a case or more, this may affect the price per bottle.*

OTHER WINES OF GERMANY

Table Wine

Non-vintage
£2.00–£2.50
★Tafelwein von Furstenberg (CHAP)
Merchant Vintners Hock, Bauer (L&W)
Thresher Hock (THRE)
Thresher Mosel (THRE)
Merchant Vintners Mosel (L&W)
★Rieslingperle, Winzerverein (PD)

1982
c. £2.75
★Pfälzer Landwein, Morio Muskat und Müller-Thurgau, Deutsche Tafelwein (STWC)
★Halbtrocken Pfalzer Landwein (ASHE)

1981
c. £2.85
★Rheinfest Deutscher Tafelwein, Rudolf Müller (H&D)

Sparkling

Non-vintage
£2.50–£4.00
Waitrose Sekt German (WAIT)
Schloss Rheingarten (YFW)
Henkell Trocken (CUL, PG, THRE, VICT, UNW, YFW, ASHE, MWS, H&D)
Fiscarl Trocken (FINT)
£4.50–£5.50
Blue Nun Sekt (PD)
Sparkling Moselle Deinhard (GH, TAN)
Deinhard Lila Imperial Riesling (RGA)

EEC TAFELWEIN

Almost one bottle in four of the German table wine we imported last year wasn't German at all. Shock! Horror!! Sensation!!! Too damn right. We're on the receiving end of some thoroughly questionable footwork over there in Germany, with the purveying as 'German type' of large amounts of nasty anonymous wine with labels which can only be taken as a deliberate attempt to mislead the public and cash in on the German wine boom built by Liebfraumilch and other brand marketeers.

This dread liquid – I find it difficult to grace it with such a noble name as wine, it is the so-called EEC Tafelwein. It comes primarily from Italy, and represents the very sludge of their Trebbiano juice lake. It gets shunted up to Gemany, and as soon as it's over the border it can be re-exported under the general heading of German Wine Exports.

Before the German 1971 Wine Law there was a fairly loose attitude towards blending wine from one German district with another, and an awful lot of southern German Palatinate wine used to end up softening the edges of the frequently sour produce of the Mosel. Yet it was absolutely forbidden to blend non-German white wine with German white wine. That's all out the window now, and these 'Euroblends' now account for 25–30 per cent of all Germany's wine exports. There is *some* hope, because the USA has refused to recognize the Euroblends as German wine exports, and has insisted that the ingredients be clearly stated on the label. This would be a cause of considerable embarassment to some shippers, since analysis would show that there was *no German wine at all* in many of these German look-alikes. But already they represent the majority of the German wine exports to some countries, Japan, for instance; and indeed the Italians are hoist with their own petard – over half of the German wine exports to Italy are Euroblends.

It's a situation which is worrying the serious German growers and shippers a good deal. Despite tremendous efficiency and high yields, Germany's wine is grown so far north and in such a highly paid economy, that it can never be as cheap as Italy's. This Euroblend nonsense is merely a further twist in the downward spiral of cause and effect, triggered by the runaway success of Liebfraumilch. Highly popular, it has had to become cheaper and cheaper. As it gets increasingly difficult to make a decent profit out of Liebfraumilch, shippers have tried to reduce costs by buying rock-bottom South European grape musts, doctoring them a bit, and re-exporting them as Euroblends. It can only end in disaster, and will make the task of those concerned to improve the sales of Germany's fine wines even more difficult.

For obvious reasons we have decided not to list the prices of any EEC 'tafelweins'.

IMPECCABLE TIMING

Forecasting the future for German wines ought simply to be the blowing of a great trumpet call of success. The light white wine style is gaining ground, even given the general surge in wine drinking. White consumption is now 70 per cent of all consumption, and if we look at the sales figures for the important supermarket groups, they *all* report Liebfraumilch as their top seller, and most of them state that Bereich Nierstein is close on its heels. A good way behind, but still doing very well, comes Bereich Bernkastel.

Without doubt, Liebfraumilch was in the right place at the right time, providing the perfect, approachable taste for millions of first-timers eager to see what all this wine fuss was about. But basic German wines are now virtually traded as a commodity, and they're far too price-sensitive for shippers to base their sales strategy on them alone. Except for the top half-dozen brands, expensively supported by advertising, Liebfraumilch, Nierstein and Bernkastel are bought by the consumer primarily on price.

Even so, with the massive 1982 vintage still going through the system, prices are unlikely to rise much, and the 1984 budget has brought some so-called Liebfraumilches back into the under £1.50 a bottle range. No one's going to be making much money on that. Where the future profitability lies is in the creation of premium brands – although there's very little room for another big one as yet – and the fostering of an interest in the higher quality wine styles.

At last the 1983 gives shippers a chance to do this, and it is interesting to note that what was previously one of the important Liebfraumilch brands – Deinhard's Hanns Christoff – has pulled out of the rat race, and re-launched itself as a Kabinett. Since Deinhard's Green Label Bernkastel is already sold on a 'quality' image basis, it became very apparent that the only road to building a fellow brand would be to get rid of the name Liebfraumilch altogether, and offer a less price-sensitive quality wine.

Langguth Erben is another group which has decided to offer a 'brand' in the higher quality ranges, and they do an Erben Kabinett, Spätlese, and even Auslese with the brand name Erben very big on the label and the name of the village and vineyard very small.

But creating a brand is big business and expensive. The 1983 vintage is important because there is an enormous amount of high quality wine to follow 1982's even bigger quantity of fairly basic stuff. All British traders see the German miracle as likely to continue, and many of them are hoping to persuade customers to trade up from basic Liebfraumilch to Kabinett or Spätlese. However, this fine wine end of the German market has been in decline for some years, as the image of German wines has cheapened, and it now accounts for only five per cent of the UK market. In 1983, many areas of Germany actually made a majority of Prädikat, or 'special quality' wines. The Rheingau made 71 per cent special wines, and even the northerly Mosel made 51.9 per cent. The national average ripeness level was that suitable for a good Kabinett. 1983 Rhines and Mosels offer the best chance since 1971 to taste German wines at their delicate, fragrant best.

ITALY

It's very difficult to remain non-committal about a country like Italy. Everything she does seems to be done with style and bravado, from her architecture to her inflation rate, from her food to her football. Wine is no exception. She's more involved with wine than any other nation on earth. She produces more, and drinks it more enthusiastically. She is more chauvinistic and proud. Which is why I find her so infuriating!

Any Italian will tell you that not only do *most* of the world's greatest wines come from Italy – they *all* do. Then why is it that my taste buds so regularly tell me that if this is really the best they can offer, I'll head back north over the Alps. It's all very well to say that the best wines stay at home – maybe they do, but you'll never build an international reputation by offering travellers a few bonnes bouches in your vine-clad cantina, and then a string of disappointments when they get back to Blighty.

France and Germany have built their reputation on their export trade, and Italy is only now beginning to wonder if she's taken the wrong route in her drive into foreign lands. She took the low road. She still takes the low road, but particularly in the UK market she's just beginning to feel her way towards abandoning the quantity above all else approach, and having a go at the quality field.

But if you're the biggest producer of wine in the world, and 88–90 per cent of that wine is unclassified *vino da tavola* (as against Germany which somehow contrives to give well over 90 per cent of her wine a 'quality wine' rating), you can't just turn off the taps of plonk. You'd drown.

Italy is producing about 7.5 billion litres a year – nearly 8 billion in 1983 – that's nearly a quarter of the world's wine! And to make things worse, the Italians are beginning to drink less of it. In 1961 they produced 5.25 billion litres and drank 108.2 litres per head. 1968 showed that the drinkers were manfully keeping abreast of production: there were 6.5 billion litres produced and the Italians were up to 116 litres a head. That was the high spot, though. It's been downhill ever since – for the drinkers, that is. By 1981 they'd dropped to 74 litres a head, and areas like Sicily, bulging with excess blending wine, were down to less than 50 litres a head. Meanwhile methods had been modernised, and produce peaked at 8.4 billion litres in 1980.

Certainly there is a market for Italy's excess production. She's the chief supplier of wine to Germany, mostly to create those wretched Euroblends, to France, to help beef up the thin dismal wines which France herself overproduces way down south, to Canada and the USA. The USA wine drinking habit was fuelled by the great exodus of Italians, usually from the parched south. They drink masses of wine, but they base their wine loyalties on innocuousness, reliability and cheapness. For the majority of Italians, at home and abroad, wine is like bread – something they consume more or less of, but don't waste much time thinking about. However, all the major wine producing countries except Portugal are now showing a general decline in wine drinking, and in particular a decline in the consumption of faceless, nondescript plonk.

So it becomes imperative to attack more sophisticated markets. As Angelo Gaja said to Joseph Berkmann, when he began to import Gaja Barbaresco, 'Whatever you do, don't try to sell my wine to Italians. They'll say it's too expensive.' Berkmann says he spent five years getting a bloody nose trying to sell top Barbaresco to Italian restaurants at £70 a case. For restaurateurs, 'Barbaresco e Barbaresco. One's at £70, one's at £40. We take the £40. Unless maybe you got one at £35?' Ten years ago 95 per cent of all sales of Italian wine in bottle were to restaurants. Now the figure is closer to 80 per cent – an improvement, but still dangerously high. One only has to go to a random selection of Italian restaurants to find that purchasing is (all too obviously) still done on price.

The important development areas for Italian wine in the UK are the sales in bulk or bottle to the large chains, particularly the supermarkets, and the increasing number of specialist merchants who are prepared to take a wine on considerations of quality and individuality. The next problem is to get those merchants to persuade us to buy the wines, when we already have such a wide range of the rest of the world's wines. A clean, well-made Soave seems fairly priced at £1.99, but what about a Chianti Classico at £6, or a Barbaresco at £10? The consumers are not yet persuaded.

Even so, the message must be starting to get across. In the generally booming UK scene, Italy is up with the market in the important quality categories. In red quality wines, the 1983 figure is up 7.11% on 1982, while in white quality wines, Italy reflects the general swing to white with a 24 per cent increase. Lambrusco (fizzy) styles are way up, to 65.89 per cent, and sparkling wines show a healthy increase of 13.24 per cent. Only white 'non classified', up 3.11 per cent, and red/rosé basics, down 5.04 per cent, are sluggish.

By quality wines we mean wines with the *Denominazione di Origine Controllata,* or DOC. Certainly the famous names are there – Chianti, Valpolicella, Soave, Frascati and the like. But *not* all of Italy's best wines figure, because when the DOC system finally got on the road in 1963, it set about enshrining existing practices rather than allowing innovation and modernization their say. Many of Italy's top wine makers are forced to make their wines outside the DOC system and declare them as *vino da tavola,* because they believe they can make better wines that way. But the authorities say – there's the law: shape up or ship out! If the law's a bad one, as in Chianti, or Valpolicella, or Bardolino, that's tough luck, because the regulations are certain to reflect the local political and social pressures at the time they were set down.

If you're a modernist, much Italian wine is not for you. But Italians are proving that they *can* make some of the world's greatest Cabernets and Merlots, some of the finest Chardonnays and the purest Pinot Biancos and Pinot Grigios. And the modernists are also taking the old grapes – Sangiovese, Nebbiolo, Barbera, Montepulciano, Verduzzo – taking them by the scruff of the neck and dragging them squealing into the '80s. So don't just stick to the time-worn names. Don't always buy simply on price. Italy's got the bit between her teeth, and we'll be one of the first markets offered the chance to see what she can do.

NORTHWEST ITALY

The Italian north-west is the mountain home of those fearsome black beasts – Barolo and Barbaresco. For years they have been supremely unconcerned about the winds of fashion, proud of their dark, inhospitable wines, and, for us in the UK at least, rarely letting anyone get much of a sighting of why they were supposed to be so special. Well, they are going to have to make it a bit more obvious from now on, because the Italians have suddeny deserted their most fabled red wines in a big way.

It used to be suggested in Italy that we Brits were in some way deficient because so few of us could get to grips with the black, tarry harshness of a big Barolo, and that 50 million Italians couldn't be wrong. Well, just as a few thousand of us were beginning to see what all the fuss was about, it seems that the 50 million Italians have realised that we weren't quite so silly after all, and have stopped buying Barolo – in droves. Barbaresco – usually the more elegant and reliable – is still selling, but Barolo faces a problem.

For years the producers have been complaining that the export market refuses to pay a fair price, and that Barolo should be at least as expensive as a fine claret or burgundy. Overnight, the bargaining position has been hopelessly weakened by the loss of the domestic market. It doesn't seem fair, but the trouble is that the Nebbiolo grape, which makes these wines, is astonishingly tannic and harsh, and although the mature flavours can – in the best wines – finally get a very exciting sweet-plum-and-smoke richness, they rarely overcome the acid and the tannin, produced by the mixture of the Nebbiolo grape and excessively long ageing in big old wooden casks. Indeed, there have been some Barolos from 'off' years available in the UK at ridiculously low prices; ridiculous, that is, until you taste them, when you realise they are dear at any price.

THE COST OF A BOTTLE

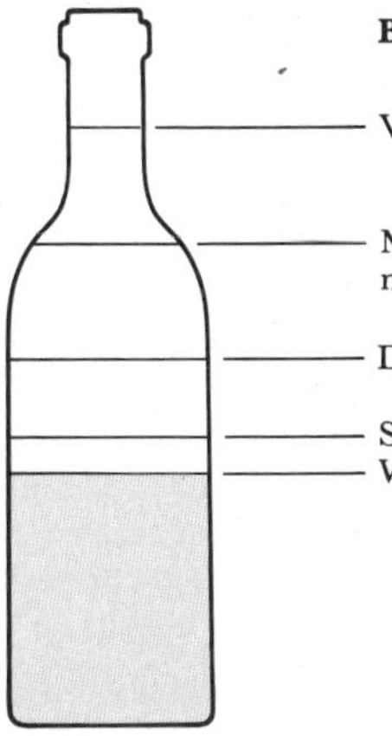

Barolo	**£4.10**
VAT	0.53
Merchant mark-up	0.72
Duty	0.68
Shipping	0.10
Wine/Bottling	2.07

It's those DOC laws again, and, as in Chianti, many producers are discreetly trying to bend the laws on the use of wood and the length of ageing. Stainless steel is more and more evident, and, though the laws stipulate wood ageing, some producers are doing the whole thing in stainless steel to try to preserve the fruit.

Others, like Angelo Gaja of Barbaresco, having tasted the best that France can do, and watched with excitement rather than horror the rise of Californian expertise in the far west, are now piling in the small oak barrels, and modernising their operations with open reference to the most up-to-date Californian ideas. Gaja has even got a computerised control in each vat so that he can achieve a perfect fermentation pattern for each vat, every vintage.

One can only hope the wind of change succeeds, preserving traditional flavours, but cutting out the dreadful tannic fruit loss of careless over-ageing. It *can* be done – the Nebbiolo (often known locally in non-DOC forms as Spanna) is already making lovely raisin-and-chocolate wines in the Novara hills. Look out for names like Gattinara, Ghemme and Carema.

Interestingly Piedmont also possesses,

Vintage Table

North-west vintages are difficult to generalise about because it isn't always easy to catch them at their best. Often good basic fruit is spoilt by too much rather haphazard wood ageing.

1980 These may turn out pretty well from a remarkably late vintage, if not aged too long.

1979 Not a big hefty year, but some of the wines are pleasantly soft and fruity, and should be enjoyed for that.

1978 This has the chance of being absolutely stunning. Loads of fruit and lots of deep, dark structure. Needs keeping – in bottle, not barrel.

1976 Rather good. Not tannic in Piedmont terms, but with attractive rather sweet fruit.

1974 A classic, hard, ripe vintage, but many of the wines have wasted their potential by too much wood ageing.

1971 Those that have preserved their fruit are lovely browning wines with loads of class.

in the Barbera and the Dolcetto, two thoroughly modern grapes capable of tangy deep purple reds to drink young, and certainly not to think to weightily about. Indeed, some 1981 Dolcetto's are already too old, whilst the best of the 82s are eminently quaffable.

Piedmont has one white, Gavi, which is perfectly good, but for which the home market will pay almost any price. It must make a Barolo producer weep.

Another superb wine, almost invariably dismissed by pundits in the UK, is Asti Spumante. This is one of the best examples of the delicious fresh fruit of the Muscat grape, and there's now quite a lot of Piedmont Muscat being made sweet and just slightly *pétillant* – even better.

Both Piedmont and Lombardy are making increasing quantities of very good dry sparklers, from Pinot Bianco and Chardonnay, often by the champagne method, for which, again, the Italians will pay loony prices. You can't help feeling a slight twinge of sympathy for those so quickly out of fashion heavy reds from the hills. Let's hope and pray that the Gaja's of this world win the day and produce enough good modern wine fast enough to back up the assertion that Piedmont can stand shoulder to shoulder with Bordeaux and Burgundy.

Maturity Chart

1978 BAROLO RISERVA

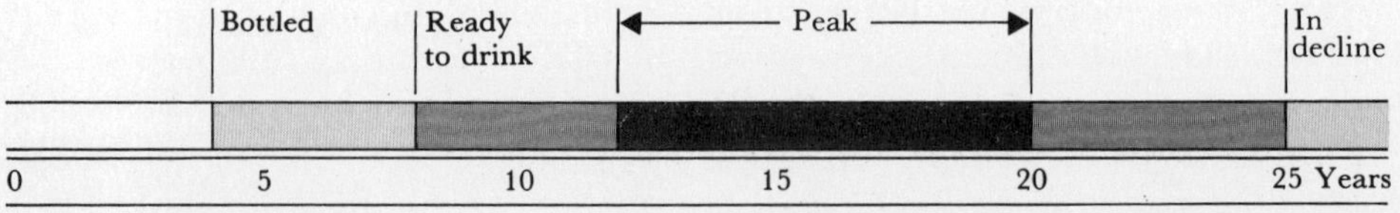

PRICE GUIDE

Red

Non-vintage
£2.25–£2.85
Sainsbury's Barbera del Monferrato (SAIN)
Barbera del Monferrato, Graziola (CHAP)
Barbera d'Alba, Fontanafredda (PD, J&B)
c. £4.00
Barolo, Fontanafredda (J&B)

1982
c. £2.85
★Bardone Langhe, Fontanafredda (PD)
c. £4.85
Dolcetto d'Ovada, Vigna Trionzo, Giuseppe Poggio (ADN)
c. £6.25
Dolcetto d'Alba, Vignabajla, Gaja (ADN)

1981
£3.50–£3.75
Barbera Oltrepo Pavese, Fugazza (WGA)
Bonarda Oltrepo Pavese, Fugazza (WGA)
Barbera d'Alba, Pio Cesare (RACK)
c. £8.25
Nebbiolo d'Alba, Vignaveja, Gaja (BWC)

1980
£3.00–£3.50
Dolcetto d'Alba Treiso, Vietti (CB)
Barbera d'Asti, Nicolello (PG)
Inferno Valtellina Superiore, Negri (PG)

Barbera d'Alba, Giacomo Borgogno (WGA)
Franciacorta Rosso, Longhi-de-Carli (WGA)
Dolcetto d'Alba, Giacomo Borgogno (WGA)
£3.75–£4.25
Nebbiolo d'Alba, Giacomo Borgogno (WGA)
Franciacorta (WW)
Barbera d'Alba, Vigneto Pian Polvere Soprana, Ceretto (VICT)
Dolcetto d'Alba, Pio Cesare (FINT)
Grignolino del Piemonte, Pio Cesare (FINT)

1979
£3.00–£3.50
Dolcetto d'Alba, Cantina Terre del Barolo (WHIT)
Sassella, Nera (CHAP)
Inferno, Nera (ODD, L&W)
Barbera d'Alba, Pio Cesare (MART, ASHE, BIB, FINT, VIGN)
Dolcetto d'Alba, Fontanafredda (VIGN)
Nebbiolo d'Alba, Fontanafredda (VIGN)
Grumello Valtellina Superiore, Negri (VIGN)
Inferno Valtellina Superiore, Negri (VIGN)
£3.50–£4.00
★Grumello, Casa Vinicola Enologica Valtellinese (STON)
Barolo, Fontanafredda (PG, WAIT, VICT, CV, MART, ASHE, VIGN)
Barbaresco, Fontanafredda (PG, VIGN)
Grumello, Nino Negri (MACK)
Sassella, Nino Negri (MACK)
£4.50–£5.50
Barolo, Fratelli Oddero (STON, PIP)
Franciacorta Rosso, Ca del Bosco (H&D)
Nebbiolo d'Alba, Franco-Fiorina (PIP)
★Sfursat, Casa Vinicola Enologica Valtellinese (STON)
★Bricco Manzoni, Podere Rocche dei Manzoni (STWC)
£5.75–£6.25
Barbaresco, Messoniano di Neive, Accademia Torregiorgi (ADN)
Barbaresco Vigneto Asili, Ceretto (L&W, PIP)
Sfursat Valtellina Superiore, Negri (VIGN)
Barbaresco, Gaja (WW, BWC)
★Barolo, Bel Colle (STON)

Barolo, Franco-Fiorina (ODD)
£6.50–£6.75
⋆Barbaresco, Bel Colle (STON)
Barolo Brunate Zonchetta, Ceretto (ODD, L&W)
c. £8.25
Barolo Bricco Bussia, Poderi Aldo Conterno (BWC)

1978
£2.85–£3.75
Spanna, Villadoria (STON)
⋆Gutturnio dei Colli Piacentini (H&B)

⋆Barbera d'Asti Superiore, Pavese (STON)
Ghemme, Brugo (WGA)
£4.25–£5.00
⋆Nebbiolo d'Alba, Pio Cesare (MART)
Gattinara, Brugo (WGA)
⋆Antica Rhaetia Riserva, Casa Vinicola Enologica Valtellinese (STON)
Barbaresco, Luigi Cauda (SR)
⋆Inferno Riserva, Casa Vinicola Enologica Valtellinese (STON)
⋆Sassella Riserva, Casa Vinicola Enologica Valtellinese (STON)
⋆Paradiso Riserva, Casa Vinicola Enologica Valtellinese (STON)
Barolo, Fontanafredda (PG, CV, MACK)
£5.75–£6.50
Barolo Rocche di Castiglione, Vietti (CB)
⋆Barbaresco Riserva Speciale, Feyles (STON)
Barbaresco, Vietti (CB)
Barbaresco d'Alba, Nicolello (TAN)
⋆Barolo Riserva, Feyles (STON)
Barolo d'Alba, Nicolello (TAN)
£7.00–£7.75
⋆Barbaresco, Bel Colle (STON)
⋆Barolo, Bel Colle (STON)
Barolo, Pio Cesare (MART, ADN)
Barolo, Giacosa Bruno (GH)

Barolo, Vigneto Villero, Ceretto (ADN)
Barolo, Ceretto (WSOC)
c. £10.25
Barolo Brunate Bricco Rocche, Ceretto (RSV)
c. £13.85
Barbaresco, Gaja (ADN)
c. £25.50
Barbaresco, Costa Russi, Gaja (ADN)

1977
£3.25–£3.85
Barolo, Scavino (H&B)
Barolo, Fontanafredda (PD)
Barbaresco, Cantina del Barbaresco (WHIT)
Barbaresco, La Brenta d'Oro (WGA)
Barolo, La Brenta d'Oro (WGA)
c. £4.75
Barolo, Cantina Terre del Barolo (H&D)
Gattinara, Antoniolo (VIGN)
c. £7.25
Barolo, Pio Cesare (FINT)

Please don't blame ***Webster's*** *or the merchants listed if a wine is sold out or if the vintage you want is no longer available. Wine is a living entity and a limited commodity – continuity of supply cannot, alas, be guaranteed.*

1976
£3.75–£4.50
Ghemme, Brugo (WSOC)
Gattinara, Francoli (L&W, CV)
Gattinara, Brugo (WSOC)
Gattinara, Antoniolo (PG)

Gattinara Riserva, Nervi (STON, TAN)

£4.50–£5.25

Barolo Riserva, Giacomo Borgogno (P&C, WGA)

★Barolo, Kiola (H&B)

Barolo Riserva del Centenario, Contratto (SR, WSOC, BAL, TAN, MWS)

Carema, Ferrando (L&W, STON)

c. £5.75

Barolo, Vigneto Zonchetta, Ceretto (ADN)

1975

c. £3.50

Gattinara, Borgo Cav Ercole (WHIT)

Gattinara, Francoli (CHAP, ESV)

c. £6.25

Barolo Marcanesco, Abbazia dell'Annunziata, Ratti (VIGN)

1974

£5.00–£6.00

Nebbiolo d'Alva, Pio Cesare (FINT)

Barolo Riserva Speciale, Borgogno (WGA, RH)

Barolo Riserva, Borgogno (VIGN)

Barolo Grignore, Ceretto (MAL)

Barbaresco Riserva Speciale, La Brenta d'Oro (WGA)

c. £6.50

Barbaresco, Pio Cesare (FINT, VIGN)

★Barbaresco Riserva Speciale, Pavese (STON)

£8.00–£9.50

Barolo Riserva, Pio Cesare (FINT)

Barolo, Contratto (LADV)

Barbaresco, Gaja (VIGN)

1971

c. £4.50

★Barolo, Berteletti (PG)

c. £7.00

Barbaresco Riserva Speciale, La Brenta d'Oro (WGA)

1970

c. £6.25

Barbaresco Riserva, Franco-Fiorina (ODD, WSOC)

£8.00–£8.50

Barbaresco Riserva Speciale, Franco-Fiorina (CV)

Barolo Riserva, Franco-Fiorina (WSOC)

1969

c. £5.75

Spanna, Antonio Vallana (VIGN)

1968

c. £7.75

Barbaresco Riserva Speciale, La Brenta d'Oro (WGA)

1967

c. £8.75

★Barolo Riserva, Borgogno (WGA)

1964

c. £10.00

★Barolo Riserva, Borgogno (WGA)

1961

c. £10.50

Barolo Riserva, Borgogno (WGA, WNRY)

1958

c. £11.00

Barolo Riserva, Borgogno (WGA, VIGN, WNRY)

c. £12.85

Barolo Riserva Speciale, Borgogno (L&W)

White

1982

£3.25–£4.00

Pinot Bianco, Fontanafredda (VIGN)

★Malvasia, Pavese (STON)

★Cortese di Gavi, Pavese (STON)

1981

c. £3.25

Cortese d'Alba, La Brenta d'Oro (WGA)

c. £4.50

Arneis dei Roeri, La Brenta d'Oro (WGA)

c. £5.50

Gavi, Tenuta San Pietro (WGA)

1980

£3.00–£3.50

★Vino Fiore, Fontanafredda (PG)

Erbaluce di Caluso, Casina Variselle (CB)

c. £5.75

Gavi, Tenuta San Pietro (RH)

1978

c. £2.50

Erbaluce di Caluso, Mattia Thione Sartori (WHIT)

Sparkling

Non-vintage

£3.00–£3.50

Asti Spumante, Aliberti (ODD, WHIT)

Asti Spumante, Calamandrana (WGA)

Asti Spumante, Giovanni Bosca (CB)

£3.50–£4.00

Asti Spumante, Zoppa (L&W, ADN)

Asti Spumante, Martini (WAIT, CHAP, CUL, MWS, THRE, YFW, WHIT, VICT, GH, ASHE *& others*)

Asti Spumante, Cinzano (THRE, UNW)

★Gancia Pinot di Pinot (H&B)

Asti Spumante, Fontanafredda (SR, VIGN)

Spumante, Gancia (PD)

Riccadonna President Reserve (PD)

c. £9.85

Franciacorta Pinot Brut Metodo Champenois, Ca del Bosco (H&D)

1980

c. £6.75

★Frescobaldi Brut (HUN)

PROLIFIC PROMISES

Piedmont is in danger of getting itself awfully confused. It is famous, or notorious, for making Europe's, possibly the world's, most massive, and often unapproachable red wine – Barolo. The Nebbiolo, seemingly the pride of generations of fog-bound hillsmen, is a brute of a grape to deal with, and the trend in modern wine is moving sharply away from brutes. The big, over-oaky Cabernets of Australia and California were massive – but they were basically sweet-oaked, rich, jammy in their grossness. But the Nebbiolo is thunderingly dry and harsh. Opinion veered away from the transatlantic monsters, and it's not taking too kindly to the old-wood-and-cold-tea Nebbiolos from Piedmont. So some producers are now vinifying in stainless steel, some are using small *barriques* to age, twisting and turning to try to find a way to preserve their giant and yet popularize it.

Dolcetto and Barbera, however, are increasingly making the sort of sturdy but soft-edged young reds which *can* be in demand, and although there's an excess of Barbera, it can make good cheap red.

The whites show considerable promise, and the Cortese grape, which produces Gavi, seems to be going through a bit of a vogue just now. When it gets over that, and can re-assume a sensible price, it is one of Italy's best native whites. As is the *frizzante* or sparkling Moscato wine. Moscato plantings have increased, and hopefully, now that it's a relatively expensive wine, we'll begin to take some notice of its delicious flavour rather than just making fun of it.

NORTHEAST ITALY

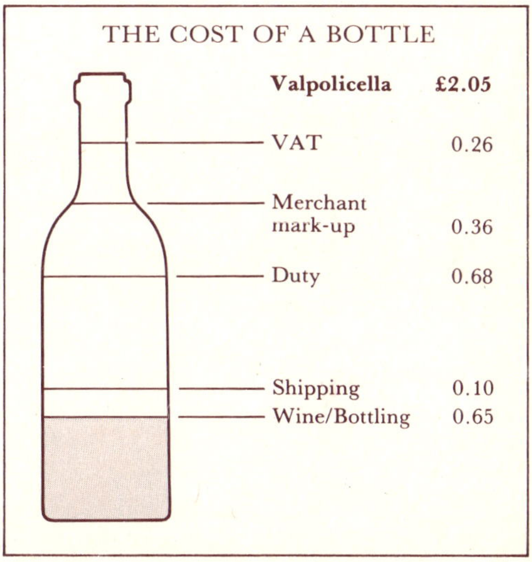

'Buon giorno, Herr Tiefenbrunner'. I'd done it again. Here I was, two hours up the valley from Verona, in the part of Italy that has a higher percentage of DOCs than any other, and I couldn't decide whether to speak German or Italian. With my somewhat hazy command of both languages, I felt safer mixing them, but I would probably have been better off sticking to German, because the Alto Adige region of Italy is really the Südtirol. Except for the main town of Bozen, where there are a fair number of pure Italians, you could be in Austria, Which, of course, is what they want you to think, since Südtirol is only Italian because of deals done in 1919, and its wine-making styles look steadfastly north.

In reds this may not be such a good thing because it has produced an over-emphasis on the Vernatsch grape, which makes massive amounts of light red wine. Sweetened up a bit, it's very popular from Innsbruck to Aachen, and is probably the same grape which makes the undistinguished Trollinger (Tirolinger? Geddit?) wines in Germany. However, for the UK market, good Vernatsch, particularly from Santa Maddalena, is excellent – soft, fruity, with a rather smokey strawberry taste. As a red to wean the hordes off Liebfraumilch, you couldn't find better. And the more serious wines of Cabernet, Pinot and the indigenous Lagrein can be superb.

The whites are some of Italy's finest, but again the cultural divide is evident, since these Rieslings, Müller-Thurgaus and Sylvaners are dry, fruity, and Germanically balanced. Gewürztraminer often seems rather unperfumed, simply because the 'gewürz' type of Traminer grape is grown less frequently than the duller 'red' Traminer. The big potential for growth is in the Pinot Bianco, and, as ever, the Chardonnay. Till recently these have largely been grown for shipping south to be turned into fizz and thus have often been from flatter sites, picked early to preserve acidity. However, the Vernatsch, which has occupied so many of the classic hillside sites, is slowly being infiltrated by all these top white varieties. The Südtirol is brilliantly suited to high-quality reds and whites, and is sure to be one of Italy's most successful areas, so long as quality comes first.

The Trentino is only one hour further down the valley towards Verona, but is straightaway completely Italian. The vineyards are far more valley floor, and the wines are broader and softer. Even so, there's a lot of good wine about, but it's less likely to come from the Riesling-type whites, and the red Vernatsch, or Schiava, as it is called here. Softness and sweetness can go a bit far, and Schiava di Lago di Caldaro is likely to test the goodwill of even this equable grape. Best to go for Pinot Bianco, Chardonnay and Cabernet from single producers like Pojer & Sandri, and the Istituto di San Michele.

Another hour back down the valley brings us to Verona itself – bang in the middle of the terrible trio of north Italian wine. Bardolino, Valpolicella, Soave. Three famous names, three evocative names, but three wines which are highly unlikely to bear much resemblance to the local original when bought in your average UK wineshop.

Bardolino is one of the most delicious fresh, light, nearly-rosé reds Europe has to offer. It is almost cherry-tasting and has a bitter twist in its tail. It should be drunk as young as possible, yet many UK outlets still offer a 1981.

Valpolicella is this, plus a bit extra; a little more weight, a slight tobacco spice, and the bitter twist slightly more marked. It should *not* taste of hot, over-pressed grape skins and raisins, but often does. This is hardly surprising, since it is permissible to supplant 15 per cent of the real light Valpolicella fruit with heavy southern muck.

Soave too should be very fresh, rather nutty, clean, slightly sharp, and *young.* It shouldn't be yellow, sulphured and dead; or harsh and reminiscent of nail varnish remover. It often is.

Along with Chianti, these names have carried the burden of spreading the gospel of Italian wines abroad. It is a pity that they have now become equated with cheapness to such an extent that it will be difficult to restore their former simple pleasures, because, absurdly, it would cost more to do so. Valpolicella, incidentally, almost makes up for the dullness of her normal reds with some quite superb wines called Recioto and Recioto Amarone – brilliant, almost shocking sweet and sour reds. Strong, unique, and superb.

The Veneto does produce a great deal of basic plonk, but it can do it pretty well, and there are encouraging signs of grapes like the red Raboso and the white Verduzzo beginning to make their own cheap and cheerful mark. And as in all the Italian regions, exciting new properties making really special, if unconventional wines, are breaking out, led here by the uncompromising excellence of Venegazzù.

Up by the Yugoslav border, some of Italy's juiciest and softest Merlots are made in Friuli, as well as the tough smokey Refosco, and an increasing number of strongly-flavoured modern dry whites to match the best in Italy. In all these areas there's room for improvement; in most, it's already under way.

Price Guide

Red

Non-vintage
c. £2.00
⋆Waitrose Valpolicella Classico (WAIT)
Sainsbury's Raboso del Veneto (SAIN)
Sainsbury's Valpolicella (SAIN)
⋆Tesco Bardolino (TES)
Tesco Valpolicella (TES)
⋆Valpolicella (THRE)
£2.00–£2.50
Sainsbury's Bardolino (SAIN)
Valpolicella Victoria Wine (VICT)
Merlot, Cesari (BAL)
Bardolino, Zonin (DAV)
Valpolicella, Zonin (DAV)
Bardolino, Boscaini (WGA)
⋆Cabernet Vinicola del Piave (SR)
Valpolicella, Boscaini (WGA)

£2.85–£3.50
⋆Merlot, Ricordi litre (SR)
⋆Pinot Nero, Pedrotti (PD)

> ***Webster's** prices are per bottle, including VAT. If you buy a case or more, this may affect the price per bottle.*

Cabernet Franc di Aquileia, Ca'Bolani (ASHE)
Bardolino Bolla (H&B)
Valpolicella Classico, Bolla (H&B, UNW)
Cabernet Grave del Friuli, Collavini (L&W)
c. £5.00
⋆Caldaro Classico, Kettmeir magnum (HT)

1982
£2.25–£3.00
Valpolicella, Ambra (PG)
Casteller, Cavit (ADN)
Cabernet Grave del Friuli, Collavini (WGA, ADN)
Merlot Grave del Friuli, Collavini (WGA)
£3.25–£4.50
⋆Refosco, Butussi (STON)
Lagrein Dunkel, Tiefenbrunner Schlosskellerei Turnhoff (ADN)
Teroldego Rotaliano, Zeni (WGA)
c. £4.75
Teroldego Rotaliano, Conte Martini (ADN)

1981
£2.75–£3.25
Bardolino Classico Superiore, Masi (CHAP, STON)
Bardolino Classico Superiore, Rizzardi (CDM)
Cabernet Franc di Aquileia, Tenuta Ca'Bolani (SF, MACK)
Lagrein Dunkel, Tiefenbrunner (HT)
Pinot Noir, Tiefenbrunner (HT, ADN)
£3.25–£3.50
Merlot Grave del Friuli, Collavini (VIGN)
Valpolicella Classico Superiore, Bolla (YFW)
⋆Collio Merlot, Attems (STON)
Marzemino del Trentino, Letrari (WSOC)
Merlot di Pramaggiore Selva Maggiore, St Margherita (RACK)
£3.50–£4.50
⋆Cabernet Franc Collio, Attems (STON)
Sudtiroler Cabernet Sauvignon, Hofstätter (WSOC)
Marzemino Trentino, de Tarczal (WGA)
Teroldego Rotaliano Vigneto Pini, Zeni (ADN)

1980
£2.00–£2.75
Bardolino Classico, Campagnola (MART)
⋆Cabernet del Piave (LHV)
Valpolicella Classico Superiore, Masi (CHAP, STON, MART, PIP)
Bardolino Classico Superiore, Sartori (WHIT)
Valpolicella Classico Superiore, Sartori (WHIT, MAL)
£2.75–£3.00
Bardolino Classico, Tedeschi (WGA)
Valpolicella Classico Superiore, Tedeschi (WGA, RH)
Valpolicella Classico Superiore, Bolla (MART, TAN)
Merlot del Piave (VICT)
Valpolicella Classico Superiore, Rizzardi (CDM)
Cabernet Colli, Berici, Castello di Belvedere (CB)
⋆Marzemino Trentino, Fedrigotti (PG, STON)
Cabernet Franc di Aquileia, Tenuta Ca'Bolani (WHIT)
Cabernet Sauvignon, Kettmeir (CUL)
⋆Teroldego, Delana (STON)
£3.00–£3.85
⋆Cabernet Isonzo, Attems (STON)
Bardolino Classico Superiore, Bolla (YFW)
Cabernet Grave del Friuli, Colavini (RH, BAL)
Merlot di Pramaggiore, Santa Margherita (FINT)
Venegazzu Cabernet Sauvignon (VIGN, WSOC)
Refosco Grave del Friuli, Collavini (WGA)
Bardolino Classico Superiore, Bertani (TAN)
c. £4.25
Cabernet Franc Collio Conti, Formentini (FINT)
c. £4.85
Valpolicella Classico Superiore, Serègo Alighieri, Masi (ADN)
c. £5.85
Cabernet del Trentino, Cavit 1.5 litres (WSOC)

1979
£2.50–£3.00
★Pinot Nero della Marca Trevigiana (LHV)
Valpolicella Classico, Masi (ODD)
Valpolicella Classico Superiore, Bolla (PG, HHC)
Refosco dal Peduncolo Rosso di Aquileia, Tenuta Ca'Bolani (WHIT)
£3.00–£3.50
Valpolicella Classico, Tedeschi (L&W, ADN)
Raboso di Annone, La Fornarina (CV)
★Foianeghe, Fedrigotti (PG, STON)
Quattro Vicariati, Cavit (WSOC)
Valpolicella Valpantena Secco, Bertani (WSOC)
£3.75–£4.25
Refosco del Peduncolo Rosso Grave del Friuli, Santa Margherita (FINT)
Venegazzu, Loredan (MART, STON, VICT)
★Teroldego, Donati (STON)
Merlot Collio Conti, Formentini (FINT)
c. £5.25
Castel San Michele, Istituto Agrario Provinciale (L&W)
c. £6.00
Recioto Amarone della Valpolicella, Bolla (H&B)

1978
£3.25–£4.00
Campo Fiorin, Masi (ODD, MART)
★Venegazzu (PG, WAIT, BIB, CUL, ASHE)
Valpolicella Valpantena, Bertani (TAN)
c. £4.25
Capitel San Rocco Rosso delle Lucchine (WGA)

c. £5.00
Recioto Amarone della Valpolicella, Masi (ODD)

1977
c. £2.75
Raboso di Annone, La Fornarina (CHAP)
c. £3.50
Campo Fiorin, Masi (L&W, STON)
£4.50–£5.00
Recioto Amarone della Valpolicella Classico Superiore, Sartori (WHIT)
Recioto Amarone della Valpolicella Riserva, Tommasi (CHAP)
★Recioto Amarone della Valpolicella Classico, Montresor (PG)
c. £5.50
Recioto Amarone della Valpolicella Classico, Bolla (PG)
Recioto Amarone della Valpolicella, Masi (STON, HHC)

1976
c. £5.00
Recioto Amarone della Valpolicella, Tedeschi (WGA)

1975
c. £7.50
Recioto Amabile della Valpolicella, Masi (MAL)

1972
c. £7.50
Recioto Amarone della Valpolicella Classico, Bertani (WSOC)
c. £8.50
Recioto Amarone della Valpolicella Classico Superiore, Bertani (TAN)

1971
c. £7.50
Recioto Amarone della Valpolicella, Boscaini (WNRY)
Recioto Amarone della Valpolicella Classico, Masi (VIGN)

White

Non-vintage
£2.00–£2.50
★Waitrose Soave (WAIT)
Sainsbury's Verduzzo del Piave Dry (SAIN)
Sainsbury's Soave (SAIN)
★Soave (THRE)
Tesco Soave (TES)
Soave Victoria Wine (VICT)
Soave, Zonin (DAV)

★Soave Classico, Lamberti (PD)
★Soave Classico, Fabiano (ASHE)
Soave, Boscaini (WGA)
£2.75–£3.00
Tocai Friulano di Aquileia (SAIN)
★Tocai del Veneto litre (SR)
Soave Classico Superiore, Masi (BIB)
Soave, Bolla (H&B, UNW)
c. £3.50
Pinot Grigio Grave del Friuli, Collavini (L&W)
Chardonnay, Atesino (VICT)
Pinot Grigio, Santa Margherita (ASHE)
c. £5.00
★Valdadige Bianco, Kettmeir magnum (HT)

1982
£2.00–£2.75
Soave Ambra (PG, VIGN)
Soave Classico, Masi (ODD, STON)
Sauvignon Colli Berici, Castello di Belvedere (CB)
Soave Classico, Tedeschi (ODD, WGA, ADN)
Valadige Bianco, Cavit (ADN)
£2.85–£3.00
Verduzzo del Piave Bianchi, Kunkler (VICT)
Pinot Bianco di Aquileia Tenuta, Ca'Bolani (SF)
Tocai Friulano di Aquileia Tenuta, Ca'Bolani (SF)
★Casa Bianca Chardonnay del Veneto (WAIT)
Pinot Blanc, Tiefenbrunner (MART)
Chardonnay, Kettmeir (CUL, HT)
Pinot Grigio Grave del Friuli, Collavini (WGA, RH, ADN)
Tocai Grave del Friuli (WGA)
£3.25–£3.50
Tocai Enofriulia (BIB)
Venegazzu Pinot Grigio (PG, VIGN, VICT)
Chardonnay, Kupelwieser (CB)
★Chardonnay Atesino, Delana (STON)
Gewürztraminer, Tiefenbrunner (MART, ADN)
★Tocai Collio, Attems (STON)
Tocai Friulano di Aquileia (MACK)
Riesling Renano, Kupelwieser (CB)
Pinot Grigio, Kupelwieser (CB)
★Gewürztraminer, Walch (ASHE)
Sudtiroler Gewürztraminer, Hofstätter (WSOC)
£3.75–£4.00
★Pinot Grigio Collio, Attems (STON)
★Sauvignon Collio, Attems (STON)
★Goldmuskateller, Tiefenbrunner (MART)
Soave Classico, Bertani (BBR)
Chardonnay, Enofriulia (BIB)

⋆Pinot Bianco Collio, Formentini (STON)
Pino Grigio Alto Adige, Santa Margherita (MACK)
⋆Soave Classico Superiore, Pieropan (WNRY, MART, RH, LADV, STON, STWC, RSV)

£4.25–£4.75
Capitel San Rocco Bianco Vino da Tavola, Tedeschi (WGA)
⋆Pinot Bianco, Donati (STON)
Chardonnay di San Michele, Zeni (WGA, ADN, RH)

1981
£2.75–£3.00
Saove Classico Superiore, Sartori (WHIT)
Soave Classico Superiore, Bolla (PG, MART, HHC, TAN)
Soave Classico Superiore, Masi (PIP)
Pinot Blanc, Tiefenbrunner (HT, WW, ADN, MWS)
Chardonnay Mezzocorona, Kettmeir (WSOC)
Pinot Bianco di Aquileia, Tenuta Ca'Bolani (WHIT)
Tocai Friulano di Aquileia, Tenuta Ca'Bolani (WHIT)

£3.25–£3.85
Soave Classico Superiore, Villa Girardi (YFW)
Rheinriesling, Tiefenbrunner (HT, MWS)
Soave Classico Superiore, Bertani (WSOC, TAN)
Gewürztraminer, Tiefenbrunner (HT, WW, MWS)
Masianco, Masi (L&W)
Pinot Grigio, Enofriulia (BIB)
Pinot Grigio Grave dei Friuli, Collavini (HHC)
Chardonnay, Santa Margherita (FINT)
Pinot Grigio, Santa Margherita (FINT)

c. £4.50
Pinot Grigio Collio, Formentini (FINT)

c. £10.75
Torcolato, Vino Liquoroso, Maculan (ADN)

1980
£2.75–£3.85
Soave Classico Superiore, Masi (CHAP)
⋆Traminer Aromatico, Walch (STON)
Soave Classico Superiore, Sartori (MAL)

1979
c. £3.25
Pinot Grigio Grave del Friuli, Collavini (ADN)

1977
c. £17.00
Picolit, Collavini (MAL)

Rosé

Non-vintage
c. £2.00
Sainsbury's Chiaretto di Bardolino dry (SAIN)
⋆Tesco Chiaretto di Bardolino (TES)

1982
c. £2.85
Lagrein Kretzer, Tiefenbrunner (MART)

c. £3.50
⋆Rosato di Lucinico, Attems (STON)

1981
c. £3.00
Lagrein Kretzer, Tiefenbrunner (HT)

Sparkling

Non-vintage
£3.00–£3.75
Prosecco del Veneto Spumante, Peccolo (CB)
Prosecco Brut, Venegazzu (MACK)
Prosecco di Conegliano Valdobbiadene Spumante, Peccolo (CB)

c. £6.00
Gran Spumante Brut Metodo Champenois (WGA)

1979
c. £7.50
Gran Spumante Brut de Brut, Ferrari (WGA)

MIXED RESULTS

There's no question the future is bright-to-brilliant for many parts of north-east Italy. However, in other parts it is bleak-to-black. Where something has got to be done fast is in the quality pits of Valpolicella, Bardolino and Soave.

These wines have been sold in the UK for so long on a price-first, quality-last basis that it will be extremely difficult to make them an important and profitable part of the future here. But good Bardolino and Valpolicella can be delicious, light, softly fruity wines, ideally suited to the emerging British taste. They may have left it too late, since various other north-east wines are itching for their share of the market.

The market researchers who found that the perfect red wine would be Blue Nun Liebfraumilch with a slug of cochineal should take a look at the Südtirol where Kalterersee already makes it! Light and soft, it's got enormous potential as a delicious, almost sweet red, and it's cheap.

The big reds and fragrant Germanic whites from good producers are some of Italy's finest and least known wines. Trentino wines often try to steal the image of the Südtirol, but are rarely as good, and their version of Kalterersee, in particular, must be avoided.

The hill areas of Friuli, near Yugoslavia, are also producing very good modern wines, particularly Cabernet and Merlot, which combine loads of flavour with hardly any tannin or acidity. Even the plains of the Veneto can make lovely, low-priced wines, when the producers can be persuaded to follow the simple British requests for clean fresh tastes – and no messing.

Central Italy

Central Italy has more than its fair share of the famous names of Italy, and so ought to be in a fairly chipper state when it comes to resisting the whims of the fickle wine-drinking public. Trouble is, it just doesn't work like that. If your fame is in white wine, preferably light and fresh, then there's a chance you can swoop in on the current white wine boom and shove a healthy wad of million lire notes under the mattress.

If your fame is in red, particularly in red which requires some ageing, and which is difficult to adjust to the 'nouveau' fad which is sweeping Italy later than most other countries, then your fame is not going to be to your advantage at all, as consumers turn against your particular wine regarding it as a classic example of something suddenly *déclassé*.

The danger for the whites is that they may bite the hand that feeds them, push their prices and their production too high, and be rewarded for trying to regard the drinking public as dumbos by seeing the consumption shift to other areas eager to fill the gap. Frascati, flushed by new-found fame on the export market, is in danger of this, as is Orvieto, while Verdicchio has managed to tread the difficult line between profitability and exploitation with more success.

The hope for the reds is that come the hour, come the man. Chianti – on which we must concentrate because it is *the* central Italian name as far as the UK is concerned – has been deep in crisis because the makers seemed to have lost sight of what their markets demanded and how much they were likely to pay. When the general feeling is that a grower needs to take home at least 3,000 lire a bottle to scrape a profit, Chianti is available ex-cellars for as little as 1,000 lire. Many producers will go to the wall, but the boom-bust 70s *have* thrown to the fore producers who are prepared to blend the ancient with the modern and find new markets for the ones Chianti has lost.

Some, like Riecine or Fonterutoli, have nailed their colours to Chianti's more traditional virtues, but pursued to the highest level; others take the view that in a time when the wine world is being swamped by the enthusiastic experimentation and innovation of the New World (in particular California and Australia), they are ideally placed to fight back endowed as they are with one of the world's most natural vineyards.

The weapons so far are exclusion of white grapes from the wine; the planting of Cabernet Sauvignon, from which a series of non-Chianti blends, led by Tignanello and inspired by the splendid DOC of Carmignano which pointed the way with its 6–10 per cent Cabernet mix, are appearing; and the re-thinking of one of the main struts in Italian wine philosophy, and as such often inflexibly enshrined in the law – that of ageing. Much of the criticism of Chianti from Anglo-Saxon markets has been that it is harsh and fruitless. Exclusion of white grapes will aid depth and fruit, while the use of smaller, newer barrels for a much shorter time than before will preserve that fruit and add softer and more exciting oak flavours. For these wines, the Tuscan innovators believe high prices can be charged, and so far they are being proved right. The only thing is, it's probably not the traditional Chianti drinker who's paying, but the traditional claret and burgundy enthusiast.

Tuscany already has one brilliant wine which certainly appeals to the claret drinker: the 100 per cent Cabernet Sassicaia, grown on the coast near Livorno – it's as close as a Cabernet freak is ever likely to get to his perfect wine. Further inland there are another couple of reds – Vino Nobile di Montepulciano and Brunello di Montalcino – which are rather more Burgundian in their ideas. You know – up the price, see what the market will bear, then push a bit more. Well, the names may be famous, but the cellars are full of expensive, unsold wine. Just like Burgundy.

Emilia Romagna has never suffered much from expensive, unsold wine, since it's the home of that frothy, purple-red happy-juice everyone loves to hate – Lambrusco. She has got some better wines in the hills nearby, and so far has shown all the flexibility that Tuscany has lacked, with some delicious Chardonnays and Cabernets, as well as the silky sweet sparkling Malvasias from the Bologna hills.

Otherwise it's the whites all the way. Tuscany is having a good go at using up her excess of white grapes with wines like the new Galestro (Antinori's excellent bianco is reasonably available in the UK), which has a *maximum* strength of 10.5 degrees to try to achieve freshness, and a flood of sparkling wines to try to snatch a few crumbs from the fizz craze. But it isn't quite working yet, which leaves Vernaccia di San Gimignano as very much the leading white from the Sienese hills.

Orvieto and Est! Est!! Est!!! are famous (and we plan to be notorious as the first publication *not* to tell the Est! Est!! Est!!! story), and Orvieto in particular used to be known for an off-dry golden wine, honeyed and nutty. Well, Orvieto *(secco)* sales are doing well, but the wine is now frequently indistinguishable from Rome's mouthwash down the road – Frascati.

Frascati used to be very fresh, almost spritzy, with a weird and wonderful nuts-and-sour-cream taste. But now it's frequently indistinguishable from . . . and so on. Yes. Modern Italian white wine making has veered so sharply away from the full and strong, to the neutral and clean and empty, that many of her whites are losing whatever character they had in the name of modernity.

Vintage Table

Unless you are absolutely sure of your 'property', our advice, regrettably, has to be to drink Chianti as young as possible – regardless of the vintage, since too much wood ageing, and too much white grape inclusion are death to a wine's ageing potential. Also, *Riserva* all too rarely means a more enjoyable wine, merely a more mature one by the time it reaches you.

***1982** A tremendous year. And one in which the modern Tuscan methods are beginning to show. So expect some deep 'fruity' wines on the market within the year.

1981 Some quite attractive light wines, but mostly they're ready now and won't improve. Carmignano is particularly good, and this vintage marks the watershed between crisis and cure in Tuscany.

1980 Drink these up. They're usually a bit lean and dry, which isn't a good sign for Chianti, even though it's all too common.

***1979** A big vintage of fairly ripe wines. Some even have a softness and sweetness which is now very attractive, so don't hang around – drink them. Tignanello drinking well now.

1978 High reputation, not always justified, but excellent for the interlopers like Tignanello and Sassicaia.

CHIANTI IN CRISIS

THE COST OF A BOTTLE

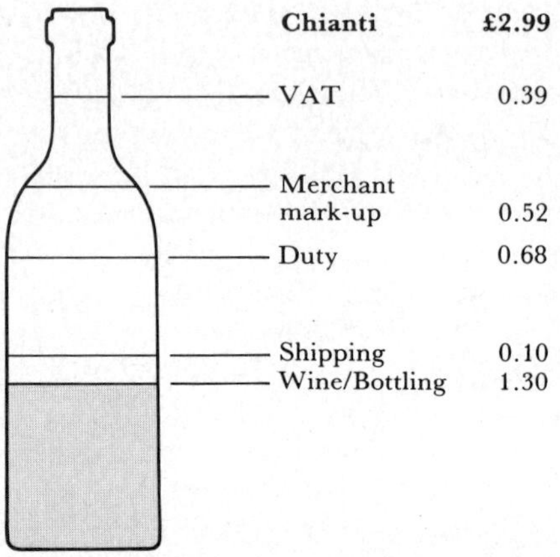

In 1983 the consumption of wine in Italy fell by an amount equal to the entire annual consumption of the United Kingdom. At the same time exports were going into a state of crisis, at the six-month mark being 37 per cent down on 1982. Sure, the UK showed a net increase of Italian imports, up 11.6 per cent on 1982, but since Italy registered an uncomfortably large harvest of around 7.9 billion litres in 1983, how would you feel if you were a producer in Chianti, Italy's largest DOC zone?

In the last 10 years Chianti production has stoically risen while no one has evinced any particular interest in buying the extra wine. With 1983 bursting the vats, the going rate for an ordinary Chianti now *has* to be below the cost of production. Chianti can be bought from the cellar door for about 1,000 lire a bottle. Opinions vary as to what it costs simply to buy a labelled, capsuled, corked empty bottle, but it's between 500 and 700 lire, depending on the quality. So you could be facing a gross profit of 300–500 lire on your wine-filled bottle. In any other currency than Italian that might do for starters, but there are about 2,250 lire to the pound, so we're talking of perhaps 14–22p profit per bottle.

Well, if you do all the work by yourself, never spray, never need new barrels, have paid for the tractor and all the equipment and don't owe the bank anything on your house, you might be able to eke out a living. The trouble is you *have* to employ people, even on quite a small estate, you've never paid off the bank, your tractor always needs repairing. So what can you do? You can cheapen production as far as possible. White grapes are allowed in Chianti, and the white Trebbiano grows like a weed, so you use the maximum allowed, 30 per cent, and come up with a pale insipid wine no one wants.

You *could* make this work by modernizing your equipment, and bringing a fresh, pink, 'nouveau' touch to it – but that costs money, so you stick with your old barrels which quickly leach out whatever colour and flavour the wine might have had, and in pretty short time it's unsaleable and undrinkable.

Or you *could* get your colour back by adding 15 per cent of cheap but dark south Italian red wine. That can't be legal. Yes, it is. You'll have saved a few pence, and your wine will taste less like Chianti than ever. So you try to sell it in bulk, without the cost of bottles, labels, and corks. But even here you're fighting a losing battle; the price of Chianti sold in bulk declined from 500 lire per litre in 1978 to 450 lire per litre in 1983. Add to that an annual inflation rate of 17.5 per cent and you've got a drop in real earnings from a litre of Chianti of over 50 per cent in five years.

As one Chianti producer said 'Frankly, it's not worth carrying on at this level. Our only hope is that a lot of people will go out of business, soon.'

How on earth did this state of affairs grip Italy's most famous wine, with a name as familiar as champagne or Beaujolais? While these last two have been expert players of world opinion, Chianti never managed to learn the rules. In the

60s and 70s the world wine boom brought a flood of investment in Chianti – which meant a swift expansion of production in expectation of a surge in demand. But it also brought the planting of inferior grape types, in the wrong sort of vineyard sites, absentee, or, at best, weekend landlords, and a complete upset of the traditional balance of the area.

Tuscany does have many large estates, but traditionally they maintained a balance with the numerous peasant proprietors, both able to make a living. Much of the influx during the 70s was of people with wealth derived from other businesses. They might *like* to sell their wine for a high price but if they couldn't, well, Tuscany was a lovely place to have an estate and they could bear the loss of offloading the wine. It didn't matter that much to them; it did to the farmer. One grower says the saddest sight now is that of northern industrialists buying up the land of bankrupt farmers for weekend cottages.

But the turbulence of the 70s may eventually help restore Chianti to its traditional renown. Yet it will be a very different wine which re-injects both profitability and reliability into Tuscan wine making. Some will be cheap, light, fresh, ready to drink almost at once. As such it will actually be much closer to the ideal of Baron Ricasoli who invented Chianti's particular style over 100 years ago when he was trying to create a young fresh wine for the Florentine market from his rather harsh red grapes. He added white Malvasia grapes, and also a litte extra grape must to freshen the wine up, and it was a whopping success.

As frequently happens, the growers began to aspire to higher things, and the idea of 'reserve' – *riserva* – wines for ageing caught hold; the image nosed its way up market. To be fair, it seemed a good idea at the time, since the raffia flask Chianti had been so mercilessly copied elsewhere that it had lost all credibility as 'the true Chianti'. So they began to make their wines for ageing. But the local market still wanted the wine young and simple, fresh, pink-red, gushing with fruit. And the export market was well supplied with 'reserve' style wines without having to consider Chianti.

The future lies in two directions. The young table-wine market can best be met by giving up the use of wood, investing in stainless steel, keeping some Malvasia and Trebbiano, which are murder for a wine's keeping qualities, but which do soften the hard edges of young red wine, and using quick, short macerations for the red grapes. That'll keep the Tuscan throats lubricated, and, once financed, will be cheap to produce and cheap to sell. For those who wish to keep out of the bulk market, the only way to get the higher price necessary to stay in business is to convince the world that Chianti possesses a higher quality worth paying for.

There are two key words – Cabernet, and *barrique.* Cabernet, because this Bordeaux grape has shown a brilliant aptitude for the Tuscan hills, and can give a purer, sweeter fruit here then almost anywhere in Europe. Blended in gently with the predominant Sangiovese grape, it can make a wine of stunning quality.

Barriques are the small 225-litre oak barrels used in Bordeaux. Chianti's wood

Maturity Chart

1982, 1978 CHIANTI RISERVA

Because of differing techniques many will fade more quickly, though a few will last better.

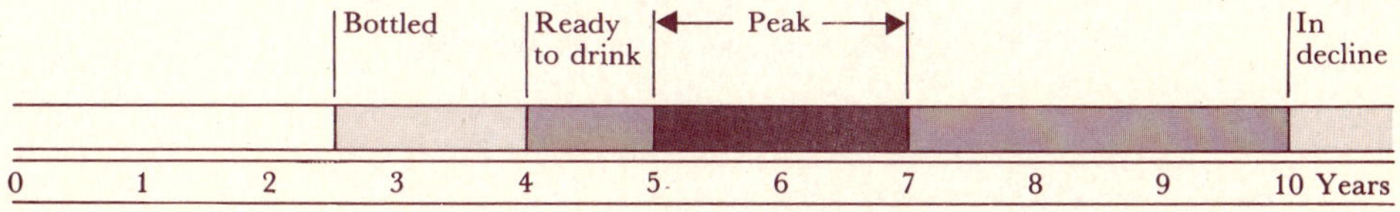

has traditionally been big and old. Make it newer and small, and you totally change the taste of the wine. 'That's just it!' cry the traditionalists, 'we don't want to make second class Bordeaux, we want to make first class Chianti.' Fair enough; stick to your old ways. But men like Counts Antinori and Bonacossi, and Sig. Castelli of Volpaia and Badia a Coltibuono have shown that it is perfectly possible to embrace the new, and produce wine definably, excitingly Tuscan, yet also excitingly profitable and saleable.

PRICE GUIDE

Red

Non-vintage
£2.00–£2.25
★Chianti (THRE)
Chianti, Victoria Wine (VICT)
★Tesco's Chianti Classico (TES)
Chianti Ambra (ASHE)
Finatello Sangiovese di Forli (FINT)
£2.50–£3.00
Sainsbury's Chianti Classico (SAIN)
Chianti Sante Dame (UNW)
Chianti Melini (CHAP)

Chianti Ruffino (H&B)
Chianti Classico Riserva, Villa Cerna Cecchi (WHIT)

1982

£2.00–£2.50

Rosso della Maremma Toscana, Montepescali (ODD, CV)
Chianti Artimino (MART)
Chianti Ambra (VIGN)
Chianti Rufina, Villa di Vetrice (MART, ADN)

1981

£2.25–£2.75

Chianti Luigi Cecchi (P&C, WHIT)
Chianti Classico, Rocca delle Macie (PG, CV, BIB)
⋆Chianti Colli Fiorentini, Poggio Romita (STON)
⋆Vino del Poggio dei Vigneti di Brunello (H&D)
Chianti Colli Aretini, Cignano (WGA)
⋆Chianti Classico, Viticcio (LHV)

£3.00–£3.50

Chianti Putto Colli Fiorentini, Poppiano Guicciardini (CB)
Chianti Classico, Isole e Olena (ESV)
⋆Gutturnio dei Colli Piacentini, Fugazza (WGA)

1980

£2.75–£3.00

⋆Chianti Putto Colli Fiorentini, Castello di Coiano (CV)
Chianti Cecchi (ADN)
Chianti Classico, Melini (BIB)
The Society's Chianti Classico (WSOC)

£3.50–£4.50

⋆Carmignano Capezzana (PD)
Chianti Classico, Castello di Volpaia (CDM)
⋆Chianti Classico Riserva, Pagliarese (WGA)
Chianti Classico Santa Christina, Marchesi Antinori (TAN)

c. £5.25

Brusco dei Barbi, Colombini (STON)

c. £9.50

Sassicaia (CV, STON, VIGN, TAN, CDM)

1979

£2.25–£3.00

⋆Waitrose Chianti (WAIT)
Rosso Cònero, Garofoli (WHIT)
⋆Chianti Classico, Castelli dei Rampolla, Napoli Rampolla (SF)
⋆Chianti Montalbano, Capezzana (STON)
⋆Chianti Classico, Villa Cerna (THRE)
Rosso Piceno Superiore, Villa Pigna (STON)

£3.00–£3.50

Chianti Classico, Pigiatello (ADN)
⋆Chianti Classico Riserva, Rocca delle Macie (ASHE, LADV)
⋆Chianti Classico, Vicchiomaggio (GH, RACK, BAL, MAL, TAN, MWS)
Vino Nobile di Montepulciano Riserva, Cantine Baiocchi (CHAP)

£3.75–£4.00

Chianti Classico Riserva Ducale, Ruffino (PG)
Ghiaie della Furba, Capezzana (ESV, STON)
Vino Nobile di Montepulciano, Cecchi (WHIT)
Tignanello, Antinori (SR, STON, VIGN, HHC)

c. £4.30

Chianti Classico Riserva, Villa Antinori (CDM, CV)
⋆Chianti Classico Riserva, Castello di Volpaia (STON, CDM)

c. £5.00

Carmignano Riserva, Villa di Capezzana (MART, STON, ADN, J&B)

c. £9.00

Sassicaia (L&W, SR, GH, ADN, MAL, MWS, AV)

1978
£2.85–£4.00
Chianti Classico Riserva, Rocca delle Macie (PG, VIGN)
Torgiano, Lungarotti (MART, STON, WSOC, HHC)
Vino Nobile di Montepulciano, Cerro (WGA)
Chianti Montalbano Riserva, Villa di Capezzana (MART)
Chianti Classico Riserva, Villa Antinori (BIB, SOC, STON, SR, VIGN, H&D, TAN)
£4.00–£4.75
Chianti Classico, Castello di S Polo in Rosso (CDM)
Carmignano, Capezzana (ESV, PG)
Chianti Classico Riserva, Badia a Coltibuono (GH)
Chianti Classico Riserva, Vicchiomaggio (VIGN)
£6.00–£7.50
⋆Tenuta di Pomino, Il Benefizio, Frescobaldi (HUN)

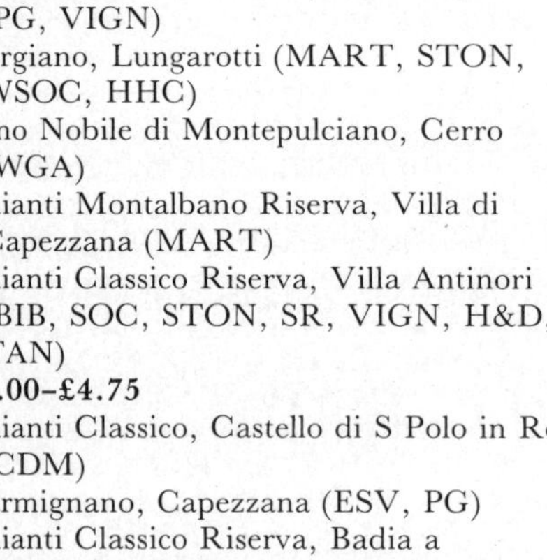

Lungarotti Cabernet Sauvignon (VIGN)
Brunello di Montalcino, Caparzo (CB)
Brunello di Montalcino, Colombini (VIGN)
c. £8.85
Sassicaia (ESV, AV)

1977
£3.25–£4.00
⋆Chianti Rufina Riserva, Villa di Vetrice (MART)
⋆Chianti Colli Fiorentini Riserva, Poggio Romita (STON)
⋆Selvapiana Riserva (STON)
£4.25–£4.50
Chianti Classico, Badia a Coltibuono (L&W)
Chianti Classico Riserva, Vicchiomaggio (BIB)
Chianti Riserva Ducale, Ruffino (PD)
⋆Chianti Classico Le Lodoline Riserva (STON)
£6.25–£6.50
Brunello di Montalcino, Tenuta Argiano (WGA)
Brunello di Montalcino, Poggione (BIB, WNRY, TAN)
Tignanello, Antinori (BIB, VICT, WSOC, PG, WNRY, H&D, VIGN)
c. £7.50
Brunello di Montalcino Colombini, Fattoria dei Barbi (VIGN)
c. £8.75
Sassicaia (RH, VICT, AV)
c. £9.50
Chianti Classico Primavigna, Vicchiomaggio (VIGN)

1976
c. £5.85
⋆Brunello Riserva, Camigliano (STON)

1975
c. £2.85
⋆Chianti Classico Riserva, Bertolli (PG, ODD)
£4.25–£4.85
Vino Nobile di Montepulciano, Fassati (WSOC, TAN)
Chianti Classico, Fattoria Poggiarello (L&W)
Carmignano Riserva, Capezzana (WW, STON)
⋆Chianti Classico Riserva, Le Lodoline (STON)
c. £6.25
Brunello di Montalcino, Poggio alle Mura (CHAP, L&W, WSOC)
£7.25–£8.25
Rubesco Torgiano Riserva, Vigna Monticchio, Lungarotti (ADN, WSOC)

1974
c. £4.50
Carmignano Riserva, Capezzana (ESV)
c. £6.25
Chianti Classico Riserva, Villa Antinori (LADV)
£7.85–£8.50
Brunello di Montalcino Il Greppo, Biondi Santi (RSV)
Barolo Riserva, Pio Cesare (BIB)
Rubesco Riserva, Vigna Monticchio, Lungarotti (BIB)

1973
£6.00–£7.00
Brunello di Montalcino, Poggio alle Mura (CV)
Brunello di Montalcino, Il Poggione (MAL)

1971
c. £25.50
Brunello di Montalcino, Il Greppo, Biondi Santi (MAL)

1970
c. £4.50
★Selvapiana Riserva (STON)
c. £25.75
Brunello di Montalcino, Il Greppo, Biondi Santi (MAL)

1969
c. £9.00
Chianti Classico Riserva, Badia a Coltibuono (LADV, GH)
c. £22.00
Brunello di Montalcino, Il Greppo, Biondi Santi (MAL)

1968
c. £15.50
Rubesco Torgiano Riserva, Lungarotti magnum (VIGN)
c. £17.00
Brunello di Montalcino, Fattoria dei Barbi (VIGN)
c. £30.25
Brunello di Montalcino, Il Greppo, Biondi Santi (MAL)

1966
c. £7.00
Chianti Classico Riserva, Pagliarese (STON)

White

Non-vintage
£1.85–£2.25
Trebbiano di Forli, Finatello (PG, FINT)
Tesco Riesling Italico (TES)
St Michael Frascati (M&S)
£2.25–£2.50
★Frascati (THRE)
★Tesco Frascati (TES)
Orvieto Abboccato, Cecchi (CHAP, WHIT)
Orvieto Secco, Cecchi (CHAP, WHIT)
Sainsbury's Orvieto Secco (SAIN)
£2.50–£3.00
Frascati Ambra (ASHE)
Trebbiano di Romagna, Cantinecorrado (MAL)
Marino Superiore, Gotto d'Oro (ASHE)
★Orvieto Classico Abboccato, Bigi (ASHE)
Orvieto Classico Secco, Bigi (ASHE)

Orvieto Secco, Ruffino (H&B)
Frascati Superiore, Fontana Candida (ASHE, UNW)
Verdicchio Classico, Umani Ronchi (H&B)
£3.00–£3.50
Verdicchio dei Castelli di Jesi Classico, Staphilus (FINT)
Verdicchio dei Castelli di Jesi Classico, Fazi-Battaglia (WSOC, BAL, VIGN, BBR, H&D, MAL, YFW, HHC)
Orvieto Abboccato, Antinori (UNW)
Orvieto Secco, Antinori (UNW)

1982
£2.00–£2.75
Bianco della Maremma Toscana, Montepescali (ODD)

★Frascati Superiore, Monteporzio (PG)
Orvieto Classico Abboccato, Bigi (PG, CDM, FINT)
Bianco Eburneo, Cignano (WGA, RH)
Est! Est!! Est!!! Secco, Cantina Sociale di Montefiascone (WGA)

£2.75–£3.00

Marino Superiore, Gotto d'Oro (VIGN)
Orvieto Secco Classico, Bigi (CDM, VIGN, FINT)
Verdicchio dei Castelli di Jesi, Castelfiora (STON)
Verdicchio dei Castelli di Jesi Classico, Garofoli (WHIT)
Est! Est!! Est!!! de Montefiascone, Bigi (VIGN)
Frascati Colli di Catone (ODD)
Frascati Superiore, Fontana Candida (BIB, VIGN, MACK)
Frascati Superiore, Villa Catone (WGA, RH)
Orvieto Classico Secco, Antinori (VICT, STON, BAL, WSOC, YFW, TAN)

£3.00–£3.85

★Capezzana Bianco (STON)
Frascati, Fontana Candida (CDM)
Frascati Superiore, Cantine Colli di Catone (CHAP, LADV, WNRY)
Orvieto Classico Abboccato, Antinori (STON, TAN)
Vernaccia di San Gimignano, Terruzzi e Puthod (MART)
Galestro, Antinori (WNRY, VIGN, SR, TAN, MWS)
Montecarlo Bianco, Fattoria Buonamico (ADN)
Tenuta di Pomino, Frescobaldi (HUN)

1981

£2.75–£3.00

Vernaccia di San Gimignano, Conti Serristori (ODD, PIP, CV)
Orvieto Classico Secco, Antinori (BIB, MAL)
Orvieto Classico Abboccato, Antinori (VICT, BAL, MAL)

£3.00–£3.75

Orvieto Secco, Vincenzo Cotti (L&W)
Galestro, Antinori (VICT)
Vernaccia di San Gimignano, Bruni (WSOC)
★Vernaccia di San Gimignano, Frigeni (STON)
Frascati Superiore Colli di Çatone (L&W, PIP)
Est! Est!! Est!!! di Monte Fiascone, Antinori (MAL)

1980

c. £2.50

Vernaccia di San Gimignano, Cecchi (WHIT)

c. £3.75

★Villa Antinori Bianco (H&D)

c. £4.75

Torre di Giano Bianco Riserva, Vigna il Pino, Lungarotti (ADN)

1979

c. £4.25

★Montecarlo Bianco, Mazzini (STON)

Rosé

1981

c. £3.00

Rosé di Bolgheri, Antinori (VICT)

Webster's is an independent guide. We have received an enormous amount of information and assistance from the wine trade but responsibility for editorial content is the editors' and publishers' alone.

Sparkling

Non-vintage
£2.00–£2.50
★Lambrusco (THRE)
Lambrusco, Giacobazzi (MART)
Sainsbury's Lambrusco Grasparossa di Castelvetro (SAIN)
Lambrusco Grasparossa di Castelvetro, Giacobazzi (CHAP)
£2.50–£3.00
Lambrusco di Sorbara, Cavicchioli (L&W)
★Lambrusco Amabile, Cavicchioli (STON)
Lambrusco di Sorbara Secco (MWS)
Lambrusco di Sorbara Amabile, Cesari (WGA)
Lambrusco, Gavioli (YFW)

Fortified

1978
c. £4.50
Vin Santo Rocco delle Macie (PG, VIGN)

Price Guide – Notes

Chianti prices are low, but still not necessarily good value. Many of the most exciting Tuscan reds have some Cabernet grape in them, and some have small barrel ageing. Other central reds go from the ultra-serious Brunellos and Vino Nobiles to the ultra-frivolous Lambruscos. So far we see more of the latter! Whites cover the famous names Orvieto, Est! Est!! Est!!!, Frascati etc. which can be good and are easy to find, but the more interesting wines are some of the 'new' Tuscan whites, the Torgiano whites, the varietals from Romagna, and Rome's 'other' wines – Marino and Montecómpatri.

TUSCAN TRAILBLAZERS

Vinattieri Rosso is dark purple, stinking of sweet coconutty spice, and tasting as exciting as any top quality new world Cabernet. But it's 100 per cent Sangiovese, made by Maurizio Castelli of Castello di Volpaia, using all his modern knowhow – and small oak barrels. It's brilliant. It's expensive. And he could sell every bottle twice over before it's even released. That's one side of the new Tuscany: high quality, high prices, new methods. Often new grapes too, because the Cabernet-influenced blends have won acclaim wherever they've been shown. We're certain to see more of them as the rigid and irrational Chianti DOC laws are bent further and further in the name of quality, though for the time being most of them will not have that word Chianti appearing on the label.

Burton Anderson, author of *Vino* and the English-speaking world's leading expert on fine Italian wine, has referred to Tignanello as a sort of prototype for what a good modern Chianti ought to be. I see it rather as the prototype for a kind of Chianti 'Cru Classé'.

Lower down the scale, Tuscany holds such a centre-stage position in Italian life that it is sure to find a way out of its present troubles. But it looks like being a painful road. Chianti just hasn't got the class image it so desperately desires, and the majority of wines coming over here certainly haven't deserved it. How else can one explain the rash of Chiantis in the shops at well under £2.00? It's quite simply the going rate. But the chorus of discontent with over-ageing poor wines in poor wood is growing, and the growers themselves are beginning to realise that they can't go on shovelling second-rate white grapes and third-rate hefty southern reds into their venerable vats, and hope to get away with it.

Elsewhere Verdicchio ought to maintain its position as one of Italy's most reliable dry whites, while Frascati, though currently doing very well in the UK, is looking a bit peaky on the quality front, which may let in two cheaper look-alikes – Marino, and Montecompatri. And, while the demand for Lambrusco falters in the US, last year's import figures show that we could be next for the fizzy red tide.

SOUTHERN ITALY

Two per cent of Apulia's annual production of nearly one billion litres is DOC. Sicily, with a similar production, manages 3.5 per cent as DOC. Campania, centred on Naples, has so little regard for the legalistic approach to wine making that it declares exactly 0.4 per cent as DOC. But at least the Falernum of Naples, the most famous wine of Roman times will be classified. Won't it? Well, it's a bit difficult to know on what you'd base your classification.

They found a couple of hundred amphorae of wine from near Falernum last year, stuck on the bottom of the Mediterranean. If it's anything like one Jacques Cousteau discovered a few years back, they won't provide any further clues. Baron le Roy of Châteauneuf du Pape, and the writer Alexis Lichine opened his amphora and poured out the liquid. They eyed the colour – nothing, crystal clear. They smelt it. Nothing. They tasted this 2,000-year-old wonder. Nothing. Simply the water the grapes had first sucked up from the ground, and at the bottom of the vase, a few crystals of minerals. Even so, the Baron thought he recognised it. 'Some bad Burgundian shipper, no doubt' he sighed.

Actually Falernum might have started out quite tasty, but by the time the Romans had played their normal tricks of adding resin, spices, honey – and sea water – we're probably not missing much. Even so, the whole of southern Italy was an area of considerable settlement and civilization from the Greeks' day to the nineteenth century. Since when it has been used almost exclusively for the production of large amounts of blending plonk. The Primitivo grape (possibly a relative of Zinfandel) from Apulia in the heel is Europe's earliest ripener, often getting to 14 degrees of alcohol by August. Vinified quickly and shoved into a waiting tanker, the hefty purple brew speedily arrives at all kinds of back doors from Rome to Vosne Romanée, ready (for a consideration) to help out the paler northern brews.

Basilicata, Apulia's neighbour, has the Aglianico, which is probably Europe's latest ripening grape, and as Aglianico del Vulture is one of Italy's best reds.

That's the paradox of the south; there is a great sea of blending wine from the flat areas, white for vermouth, red for, well, whatever needs it. But up in the hills and valleys, and out on the islands, there are some exciting wines.

Sardinia, and, more especially, Sicily, are beginning to produce some of Italy's best light, cheap table wine, and Sicily is also exporting some markedly tasty, big wines, such as Regaleali, Rapitalà and Libecchio, as well as the wine which made her famous – Marsala. It is at last becoming fashionable again, and not all ends up at the bottom of the zabaglione pen. Add to this some delicious Moscatos and Sicily is clearly more than the plonk bucket her reputation implies.

We don't see much of Calabria, but Cirò, and Greco di Bianco are building a reputation, and we don't see much of Basilicata, but the aforementioned Aglianico del Vulture, whose best producer is Fratelli d'Angelo, has now arrived in England, and is a really fine red.

Campania is where all those endless bottles of Lacryma Christi spring from; the fact that they've been offered DOC, and yet they still can't get it together shows how disorganised it all is. However, Greco di Tufo is good, and any wine from the Mastroberardino estate is a safe bet. Molise you don't see even in Italy – it has only just got its first DOC!

Abruzzi has at least got the good gutsy red Montepulciano di Abruzzo, while Apulia, always named as the blending source *par excellence,* has now begun to make some of these hefty Primitivos and Negroamaros (bitter blacks!) for their own sake, as well as some pretty good rosés and a fair supply of those light, neutral clean whites the Italians lap up. There's a long way to go, but it's a start, and at least they've seen that the market for plonk is irreversibly on the wane.

Price Guide

Red

Non-vintage
c. £2.75
⋆Montepulciano del Molise, Masseria di Majo Norante (STWC)
c. £3.25
Corvo Rosso, Duca di Salaparuta (H&B, UNW)
c. £5.50
Sansovino Rosso 2 litres (VICT)

1981
£2.50–£3.25
Monica di Sardegna (STON)
Montepulciano d'Abruzzo Riserva Numerata, Casal Thaulero (LADV)
Rapitalà Rosso (PIP, STON)
Regaleali Rosso (WGA, ADN, STON, VICT)

1980
£3.00–£3.50
Montepulciano d'Abruzzo, Illuminati (PG)
Corvo, Duca di Salaparuta (VIGN, TAN)

1979
£3.00–£3.85
Corvo, Duca di Salaparuta (PG, FINT)
Montepulciano d'Abruzzo, Illuminati (WW, VIGN)
Cannonau, Sella & Mosca (STON)
Ravello Rosso Gran Caruso (FINT)
Lacrima Christi del Vesuvio Rosso, Scala (FINT)
Cannonau di Alghero (MWS)

1978
c. £3.00
⋆Montepulciano d'Abruzzo, Tollo (ODD)
Copertino Riserva, Barone Bacile di Castiglione (ESV)
c. £5.50
Taurasi, Mastroberardino (WSOC)

1977
c. £6.50
Taurasi Riserva, Mastroberadino (RH)

White

Non-vintage
c. £1.85
⋆Bianco di Alcomo (TES)
c. £3.00
Corvo Bianco di Salaparuta (CHAP, H&B, FINT, UNW)
c. £3.50
Rapitalà (H&D)
Ravello Bianco Gran Caruso (FINT)
⋆Corvo Colomba Platino (H&B)

1982
£2.50–£3.50
Nuragus, Dolianova (STON)
Rapitalà Bianco di Alcamo (PG, ODD, STON)
Regaleali Bianco (WGA, STON, VICT, ADN)
Torbato di Alghero, Sella & Mosca (STON, WSOC, GH)
Corvo, Duca di Salaparuta (VIGN)

1981
£2.85–£3.85
Rapitalà Bianco di Alcamo (PG)
Torbato di Alghero, Sella & Mosca (TAN, MWS)
c. £4.75
Greco di Tufo, Mastroberardino (WSOC)

1980
£3.25–£3.85
Torbato di Alghero, Sella & Mosca (WNRY)
Lacryma Christi del Vesuvio Bianco, Scala (FINT)
c. £5.25
Lacryma Christi del Vesuvio, Mastroberardino (TAN)

Fortified

Non-vintage
£4.00–£4.85
Marsala Garibaldi Dolce (VIGN, WSOC)
Marsala Secco SOM (VIGN)
Tanit Moscato Passito di Pantelleria (WGA)
c. £6.00
Marsala Vecchia Riserva 1880, Pellegrino (STON)

DOC or die

The forte of this region in the past has been the easy, careless production of immense quantities of big reds and whites, no name, no style, no pride. They were given a tremendous fillip when France withdrew from North Africa, and, appalled by the sourness of her own Midi plonk, cast longing eyes south to the heady potent reds of deepest Italy.

The most hopeful direction for the south now is a pretty smart about-turn: light, fresh whites, big but fruity rosés, and some big but digestible reds. By picking early and vinifying cool, the wines of Sicily and Sardinia can be amazingly good. And they're beginning to take the DOC system seriously too, even taking pride in it (!), which should give some of the beefier reds a chance to make a name for themselves.

OTHER WINES OF ITALY

Red

Non-vintage
£1.75–£2.50
St Michael Italian Full Red (M&S)
Hirondelle (H&B, ASHE, UNW)
Sainsbury's Vino d'Italia Medium Dry litre (SAIN)
c. £3.85
Pedrotti Rosso 1.5 litres (PD)
c. £4.00
Caldorino Rosso 2 litres (CHAP, CDM)

White

Non-vintage
£2.35–£3.85
Hirondelle (H&B, ASHE, UNW)
Sainsbury's Vino d'Italia Medium Dry White litre (SAIN)
Pedrotti Bianco 1.5 litres (PD)
£4.25–£5.00
Gambellara 1.5 litres (WHIT)
⋆Caldorino Bianco 2 litres (CHAP, ESV)
Sansovino Bianco 2 litres (VICT)

Rosé

Non-vintage
c. £2.35
Hirondelle (H&B, ASHE, UNW)
c. £3.85
Pedrotti Rosato 1.5 litres (PD)

Sparkling

Non-vintage
£2.00–£2.25
⋆Carino Spumante Italian (WAIT)
⋆Gran Moscato Spumante Riviera (ASHE)

SPAIN

The thing that strikes one most about Spain is not that there are so many wines but that there aren't more. There she is, sitting on the world's biggest acreage of vineyards, and not only are there very few famous names, but if we delve down into those endless fields of vines there doesn't even seem to be the local identity, supposed or otherwise, which makes France and Italy so perpelexing yet also so rewarding.

This is made even more difficult to understand when you consider that over half of her 1.6 million hectares are accorded the *Denominación de Origen* seal, implying both a geographical and a traditional 'specialness' in the style of wine, vaguely recognizable in the flavours wafting up from your glass. Italy, which one might regard as a reasonable parallel, has only 10 per cent of her vines covered by *Denominazione di Origine Controllata,* and in those areas not covered by it, there is a positive burst of estates and enterprises deciding to upgrade their quality and improve their status.

But if we look at some figures, two things become apparent. First, taking 1980 as a fairly typical year, Italy, with the smaller vineyard area of 1.2 million hectares produced 8.4 billion litres of wine, while Spain produced only 4.5 billion litres. Second, in 1980 Italians drank 80 litres per head despite falling consumption – a drop of 20 litres in five years, while the Spaniards only drank 64.7 litres, a drop of 11 litres in the same period. While 1974 was the all-time peak of Spanish wine drinking, at 77 litres per head, the Italian peak in 1968 was 116 litres. The daily *porón* (jug) of *tinto,* though important, is less so than one would expect. This helps to explain the historical divide in Spain, not between localities but between the carafe wine and Rioja.

Until the recent rise of Catalonia as an exciting table wine producer, every hotel and restaurant wine list nationwide carried the wines from the high Rioja valley in northeast Spain, and below that was the local carafe. With a few exceptions like the cider-sharp northern wines of Chacolít, and the rasping *vinho verde* of Galicia, these were made with very little concern for the palate; they were simply typical hot country wines of the 'mañana' school of wine making. Mañana means that if the grapes are already getting too ripe, we pick them – tomorrow; if the fermentation's going too hot or too long, we cool it or stop it – tomorrow; if the wine needs bottling or selling now, while it's still fresh, we do it – tomorrow.

The international view of Spain was even more polarized. The one wine which gave her global fame was the fortified wine sherry. Traders from northern Europe, using Cadiz as their port, would take on wines as barter or ballast. The one thing this early sherry *was* good at was building up a formidable alcohol ripeness, and then quickly oxidizing to a heavy, sweetish grog which went down a treat in the damp foggy haunts of England and the Low Countries.

By the eighteenth century the sherry town of Jerez was peopled with English and Irish merchants making every style of wine from achingly dry to intensely sweet, and sherry was on its way to becoming one of the world's most famous, most individual, and, eventually, most copied styles of wine. But the complete export orientation of the sherry trade is shown by the fact that, even now, it is very difficult to get a decent glass of sherry in Spain, outside the production area of Andalusia.

For the rest? Spain's reputation until less than 20 years ago relied solely on her ability to provide very cheap, very strong, ribsticker blending wines, virtually to order. The light-coloured but alcoholic reds of the La Mancha plain, mixed with the fierce reds of the Levante slipped down a lot of contented British throats under the title of Spanish Burgundy. Even this year, when Grants of St James revamped their Don Cortez range, introducing cold-fermented, fresh fruity whites and rosés, they left the red as it had been for the last 20 years because 'people like it like that'! Spanish Chablis, Spanish Graves and Spanish Sauternes always seemed to represent the most basic forms of dry, medium and sweet wines respectively on offer in the off-licence. Rioja and Penedès were unheard of as quality wine areas, and except by a few stalwarts like Dolamore in the UK, they were probably regarded as unsaleable and presumably undrinkable.

That is the legacy Spain has now set about overcoming. She has a long way to go, but all the signs are encouraging. Maybe it is because there is so much to do that the eventual results could be so exciting. That relatively low per capita consumption reflects an astonishingly low yield in the vineyards. The regions of Yecla, Manchuela and Alicante, all big bulk producers, only manage 11–13 hectolitres per hectare of vineyard. The bulk producers of Italy and France would be working on a really short rein to manage less than a hundred, and could easily do double. The average national wine crop in Spain represents a yield of just 20 hectolitres per hectare. That's tiny. The most quality-conscious First Growth claret would be worried by that yield, and yet it's the bulk areas which are the chief offenders. Rioja and Penedès produce more than double that, sherry yields are four times as much.

These yields are the result of very conservative, old-style methods being employed on pretty barren vineyard land, but they could be increased four- or five-fold in many areas, and, with up-to-date vinification, make a better, more modern wine as a result.

However, even if that is achieved, there is still the problem of declining domestic consumption. In the Mediterranean countries, an increase in sophistication means a move away from the wine-drinking habits of the older generation, towards beer, spirits and cocktails. A far cry from northern Europe, where increased sophistication is shown by a move *towards* wine, and away from beer and spirits.

So an increase in yields *must* be accompanied by an increase in exports, and the market for Spanish plonk is a declining one.

But Spain is now up and running, led by the surprisingly recent revelation of Rioja as a quality wine and followed by Catalonia's sparkling Cava wines, and the reds and whites of Torres. From every area of Spain we're seeing the beginnings of the move towards cold-fermentation modern whites, and reds with varietal definition and wood only being used for positive flavours. Despite those yields, prices remain low, and Spain has the chance to offer some of Europe's best wine bargains over the next decade, EEC or no.

RIOJA

Rioja hit the UK with a bang in 1978 – suddenly it was everywhere. I tried a bottle of Montecillo 1971 from a shop on Wandsworth Common and that was it. I was hooked. Within months I was buying the stuff by the case, amazed at the soft, sweet taste, so unlike anything I'd ever had before. 'It's like claret!' some people cried. 'It's like burgundy!' cried others. But it wasn't like either really. The creamy, vanilla flavour pervaded everything, the tannin and the acidity were pretty low, the fruit not all that obtrusive, and the butter-sweet taste from the oak casks totally, seductively in charge. People said I'd get tired of the taste, that it was too one-dimensional. It's six years now, and I'm not tired yet.

THE COST OF A BOTTLE

Rioja	**£2.50**
VAT	0.33
Merchant mark-up	0.72
Duty	0.68
Distribution	0.09
Shipping	0.10
Bottling	0.20
Wine	0.38

Nor are Rioja's sales in the UK. 1978 *was* a highspot, with half the merchants in London crowding onto the Iberia Airlines boneshaker to Bilbao to try to procure an agency agreement. Predictably, 1979 figures of Rioja went into a steep decline. There was simply too much wine trying to percolate through the system. We weren't drinking less, just taking our time to lap up the over-enthusiasm from 1978.

Recent figures show that Rioja is back on an even keel, and succeeding in getting its message across. In 1981, out of total Rioja export figures of 19,681,611 litres, we took 2,114,578 litres, or 10.74 per cent of all her exports. 1982 saw our share rise to 11.2 per cent of all exports at 2,449,165 litres out of 21,876,865 litres while 1983 showed us with 14 per cent of all exports – taking 3,110, 815 litres out of a 22,129,032 litre total.

But that's enough of figures. Incidentally, I often wonder with these statistics who it is who counts that last bottle. Anyway, we're firmly in second place, behind Denmark and ahead of Holland. All three countries, with their cold climates, are partial to wine with a soft, warming flavour. Markets not so concerned with the need for their reds to quench their thirst, and more eager, with stern wine duty levels, to get a reassuring feeling of high quality for low cost.

That is exactly what was so shocking and exciting about Rioja when it hit Britain in the 1970s – brilliant flavour, unbeatable price. The early 70s had seen the hype and hysteria of massive price rises firstly for good wines, then for second rate ones, from Bordeaux and Burgundy. The prices rose to their towering crest and, just as the wave faltered and crashed, canny merchants nipped out from its path, and headed where the Bordeaux merchants had headed a hundred years ago, in the face of phylloxera ravaging their own vineyards – to the high river valley of Rioja in Northern Spain. Their intention was to recreate Bordeaux at a bargain basement price, but what they did was to create an entirely new market with a taste which had been waiting a hundred years for its day.

That exodus from Bordeaux 100 years ago provides the key to red Rioja's present popularity, because when the French set up residence in Rioja they were in no mood to sit back and start making Spanish wines. They had seen their livelihood and their pride devoured by a plague no one understood, and they'd headed south to build Bordeaux below the Pyrenees, with their wine-making techniques and expectations honed over the centuries. Of all the ideas they brought, one was to transform Rioja wine; the concept of using small new oak barrels to age the wine. But they didn't find a docile, compliant population – Rioja has a wine history possibly even longer than Bordeaux's, and some sources say that the Romans selected from Rioja the grape which was to become the glory of Bordeaux – the Cabernet. However, Marqués de Murrieta and Marqués de Riscal had already begun to use Bordelais methods, and soon their ideas became the norm for the area.

As phylloxera was defeated in France, the French returned home, but they had succeeded in replacing the old 'lagar' open vat method of vinification, where everything is done in what looks like an extended horse trough, with what is now the hallmark of Rioja – that scented, rich vanilla flavour of wine aged in 225-litre oak barrels. And until the 1970s, Rioja was left in a time warp. As Bordeaux

Vintage Table

There was a time when vintages in Rioja were held to be at best a vague indication of age, and at worst an endless regurgitation of some particularly successful long-past harvest. There were even suggestions that one merchant had tried to register 'Vintage 1929' as a trade mark. Things are better now! Wines labelled *crianza* shouldn't be aged too long. *Reservas* are usually at their best at between six and eight years, and *gran reservas* at about 10, though the best will last for 20 years or more.

1983/ 1982 Very good years in the offing. Tiny, expensive crops, but try Vina Faustino to see the quality potential – and those new-style whites.

1981 Just coming on stream. The reds look good. Not too deep, but they *do* have fruit and the bigger *reservas* should eventually age well.

1978 At their peak now. *Reservas* with some vanilla-ey wood will age, but why wait?

1976 Not as super-ripe as the rest of Europe, these are well balanced, soft, slightly strawberry-tasting reds and should be drunk.

1973 The best *gran reservas* are marvellous, deep, sweet-fruited reds which you could age – but again, why? They won't improve. Straight *reservas* need drinking.

Maturity Chart

1978 RIOJA RESERVA TINTO

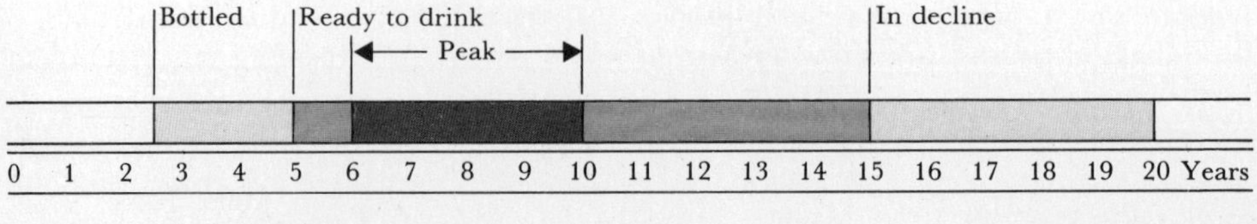

modernized its methods and reduced its reliance on oak ageing for reds and whites, Rioja continued to age her wines for anything from two to 20 years in oak. The result was often a wine which more resembled a mouthful of woodshavings than a happy blend of vanilla and fruit.

That was when the British merchants became so important. They persuaded the wine makers to cut back on their wood ageing, often to a mere couple of years, and not more than four years even for the best wines. The result? Soft elegant flavours that didn't leave a hole in your wallet. The burgundy effect without the burgundy price. And in whites they persuaded wine makers that, though the very finest might resemble an old Meursault if kept for aeons in oak, most of them were terminally ill with oxidation before they reached our shores. So the pendulum swung back with unnerving force, and now Rioja is Spain's leading exponent of very dry, very fresh, cold-fermentation white wines. Some modern Spanish whites lack a bit of personality, but not Rioja. If anything they have too much, often of a scarey, grapefruity kind. But softened out, they've taken their place in less than 10 years as truly modern wines.

Rioja as a Claret Understudy

It's easy to see why Rioja got its 'claret understudy' tag. In England in the early 1970s, when the Bordeaux growers had finally decided to earn some real money by doubling and tripling their prices, and Rioja tentatively offered itself as the saviour of the Englishman's divine right to down a pint of something good and red and affordable with his cold mutton, it was a good deal nicer than any of the other alternatives. But if the Bordelais hadn't tried so greedily to force the singularly unpleasant 1972s down our throats, they might have got away with it. But then we might never have developed a partiality to Rioja.

The reason it was dubbed the 'claret understudy' was because of the soft oaky vanilla flavour, combining with a gentle and extremely reliable ripeness of good fruit. But is Bordeaux famous for that? Isn't it famous for wines of high acidity and tannin, tough when young, unfolding to a lovely soft yet cedary maturity? Ah, that's the key. That cedary perfume also had a sweetness imparted by the new oak barrels in which the best Bordeaux classed growths had spent a couple of years while ageing.

Suddenly it all becomes plainer. Rioja had one very important taste facet of the best classed growth clarets; the sweetness of oak, and the ability to oxidise gently, with its fruit drying but staying perfumed and not going stringy. Rioja wasn't so much a substitute for basic claret as for the high quality classed growths. And people who'd never tasted a classed growth were quickly talking about their new-found claret substitute. It reached this taste peak very much more quickly than a Bordeaux classed growth, because its grapes were less austere, and the wine spent much longer in cask. Casks age wine far faster than bottles. Claret was spending two to three years maximum in cask, while Rioja *riservas* might have six to eight years of wood. After that long in wood, it's at least as mature as a 20-year-old claret, and since the English have always liked their claret when it's reached middle age at the very least, Rioja could give you a taste of portly middle age for a teeny bopper price. But Rioja as claret? I've always thought it tasted more like burgundy.

Even so, there's no doubt that Rioja still gives you the soft and mature taste cheaper than any other wine, and it can give you the deep, old, hoary, taste, if you like that sort of thing, at way below the price a claret or burgundy would fetch by the time it reached that state.

Dolamore, one of the original British Rioja importers, as well as a strong claret firm, showed us their price lists of the last 15 years. What was interesting was that, while in the period of crisis in the early and mid 1970s Rioja had indeed filled a very important gap, Rioja is now under far greater strain to hold its prices down than all but the top clarets.

Between 1973 and 1975, the price of Château Patache d'Aux 1970, a good, typical Bourgeois claret rose from £1.27 to £2.85. Rioja price changes were as follows:

	1973	1975
Ederra (basic)	£0.78	£1.20
Vina Zaco (good)	£1.17	£1.60
Vendimia Especial (top quality)	£2.30	£2.80

Obviously Rioja was taking some advantage, but not much. In 1973 a good straight claret had matched a good straight Rioja for price. Within two years the middling claret was topping the best traditional Rioja on show.

These dramatic price rises continued until 1979, with Rioja notching up enthusiastic price progress in its new-found popularity.

1979 figures	
Patache d'Aux 1973	£4.30
Ederra	£2.02
Vina Zaco	£2.75
Vendimia Especial	£4.10

The 1983 figures illustrate the way that, although Rioja may still be providing the best 'old wine' prices, claret has fought back to the kind of price stability for its middle range wines which has made it the perennial favourite red of the British.

1983 figures	
Patache d'Aux 1979	£4.30
Ederra	£2.79
Vina Zaco	£3.85
Vendimia Especial	£5.75

PRICE GUIDE

Red

Non-vintage
£2.25–£3.25
⋆la Rioja Viticola (PD)
⋆Lagunilla Valle (PD)
Paternina Banda Azul (PD)
St Michael Marqués del Romeral-Rioja (M&S)
Viña Alberdi, Rioja Alta (A&K)
£3.50–£5.25
⋆Viña Cumbrero Tinto, Bodegas Montecillo (JMW)
⋆Viña Ardanza, Rioja Alta (PD)
Reserva 904, Rioja Alta (CDM)

1982
c. £2.50
⋆Cumbrero (ASHE)

1981
c. £2.75
Solar de Samaniego Blanco, Alavesas (A&K)

1980
£2.25–£2.75
Utrero Red, José Palacios (ECD)
Paternina Banda Azul (VICT, CUL)
Olarra (CUL, SW, WAIT, BOW)
⋆Cumbrero (ASHE)
Beron Tinto (JMW)
£2.75–£3.75
Viña Alberdi, Rioja Alta (PG, L&S)
Rioja Tinto, CUNE (WNRY)
CUNE Monopole (VIGN)

1979
£2.50–£4.00
Carta de Plata, Berberana (PG, SW)
Campo Viejo (SW)
Siglo Saco (SW)
Marqués de Riscal (A&K, PG, CUL, SW, TAN)
Viña Pomal, Bilbainas (PG)

1978
£2.50–£3.00
Paternina Banda Azul (CHAP)

Viña Berceo (L&W)
⋆Marqués de Cáceres Tinto (JMW, ODD, RACK, CDM, BIB, L&W, A&K, ASHE, WSOC, TAN *& others*)
Olarra (JMW)
Faustino V Tinto (PG, FINT)
Viña Alberdi, Rioja Alta (WW)

£3.00–£4.00

Cumbrero (SW, L&S)
Viña Real, CUNE (ESV, L&S, SW, TAN)
Don Sebastian Tinto (STWC)
Viña Pomal, Bilbainas (DOL, L&S)
Lancorta (MAL)
Muga (L&S)
Viña Magdala, Torres (CUL)
Marqués de Riscal (L&S, VICT, HHC)
Marqués de Murrieta (PG, L&S, A&K, TAN)

1977

£3.50–£4.00

Viña Bosconia 5th year, López de Heredia (L&S)
Viña Pomal Tinto, Bilbainas (JMW)

1976

£2.25–£3.00

⋆Rioja Reserva, Goikoa (WAIT)
⋆Marqués de Cáceres (PG, WW, J&B, SW, WNRY)
Faustino V Tinto (JMW)
Carta de Oro, Berberana (PG, SW)
⋆Domecq Domain (PG, VICT, CUL, SW)
Solar de Samaniego Tinto, Alavesas (A&K)

£3.00–£3.50

⋆Viña Lanciano (JH)
Muga (SW, A&K)
Viña Albina Reserva, Bodegas Riojanas (LADV)
Faustino I Gran Reserva (CDM, PG, FINT)
Monte Real Reserva, Bodegas Riojanas (LADV)

£3.50–£4.00

⋆Bosconia Tinto, López de Heredia (JMW)
Viña Pomal (A&K)
⋆Viña Ardanza Tinto, Rioja Alta (JMW, L&S, PG, CDM, BIB, VIGN, SW, A&K, VICT)
Cerro Anon Reserva, Olarra (SW)
Marqués de Riscal (ASHE)
Carta de Oro, Berberana (A&K, MAL)
Tondonia, López de Heredia (A&K, L&S, SW, MAL)
Viña Zaco, Bilbainas (DOL, PG, SW, L&S)
Faustino I Tinto (JMW)

£4.00–£6.50

Viña Arana, Rioja Alta (WSOC)
Lancorta Reserva (MAL)
Marqués de Murrieta (L&W)
Muga Prado Enea Reserva (L&S)

1975

£3.00–£4.00

Olarra Tinto (JMW)
⋆Viña Berceo Reserva (L&W)
Utrero Divisa Oro Gran Reserva, Jose Palacios (ECD)
Carta de Oro, Berberana (WSOC)
Viña Zaco, Bilbainas (A&K)
⋆Tondonia, López de Heredia (CHAP, JMW)
Monte Real Reserva, Bodegas Riojanas (SW, L&S)

£4.00–£4.50

Viña Albina 6th year, Bodegas Riojanas (L&S)
Viña Real Reserva, CUNE (SW)
Imperial Reserva, CUNE (A&K, L&S, ASHE, WNRY, C&B)
Cerro Anon Gran Reserva, Olarra (SW)

1974
c. £4.00
Faustino I Reserva (A&K)

1973
£3.25–£4.00
Solar de Samaniego Tinto, Alavesas (A&K)
Marqués de Cáceres Reserva (ODD, A&K, SW, L&S, BOW)
Gran Reserva, Berberana (PG, SW)
£4.00–£5.00
Beronia Tinto Reserva (JMW)
Viña Albina Gran Reserva, Bodegas Riojanas (LADV)
⋆Montecillo Viña Monte Gran Reserva, Bodegas Montecillo (JMW)
Monte Real Gran Reserva Bodegas Riojanas (SW, LADV, JMW)
⋆Viña Lanciano Reserva (JH)
Reserva Berberana (A&K)
Paternina Gran Reserva (VICT)
Viña Real Gran Reserva, CUNE (L&W, L&S, SW)
£5.00–£7.00
Imperial Gran Reserva, CUNE (L&W, L&S)
Lancorta Reserva (MAL)
Tondonia Gran Reserva, López Heredia (SW)
Imperial Rioja Tinto, CUNE (WNRY)

1970
£4.00–£5.00
Solar de Samaniego Reserva, Alavesas (A&K)
Campo Viejo Reserva (SW)
Gran Reserva, Berberana (PG, WSOC, SW)
Reserva 904, Rioja Alta (PG, JMW, WW, L&S, A&K, VIGN, BIB, CUL, MAL, SW *& others*)
£5.00–£6.00
Reserva Berberana (A&K)
Olarra Gran Reserva Tinto (JMW)

Viña Real Reserva, CUNE (C&B)
Paternina Gran Reserva Especial Tinto (JMW)
Viña Albina Gran Reserva, Bodegas Riojanas (JMW, LADV, L&S)
Vendimia Especial Gran Reserva, Bilbainas (DOL, JMW)
Viña Pomal Gran Reserva, Bilbainas (DOL, PG, SW, L&S)
Tondonia Reserva (MAL, CHAP, JMW)
£6.00–£7.00
Monte Real Gran Reserva, Bodegas Riojanas (L&S, SW, LADV)
Vendimia Especial Tinto Reserva, Bilbainas (JMW)
Tondonia Gran Reserva, López de Heredia (SW)

1968
£5.25–£6.75
Reserva 904, Rioja Alta (JMW)
Faustino I Rioja Gran Reserva (FINT)
Paternina Gran Reserva Especial Tinto (JMW)

1967
c. £7.00
Paternina Gran Reserva Especial Tinto (JMW)

1966
£5.50–£6.00
Campo Viejo Reserva (SW)
Gran Reserva, Berberana (PG)
c. £8.00
Vendimia Especial Tinto Reserva, Bilbainas (JMW)

1964
£6.50–£8.00
★Gran Reserva, Berberana (PG)
Reserva, Berberana (A&K)
Reserva 904, Gran Reserva, Rioja Alta (VIGN)

1952
c. £10.00
Gran Reserva, Berberana (PG)

White

Non-vintage
£2.25–£3.75
★Olarra (WAIT)
Paternina Banda Dorada (VICT)
Metropol Extra Blanco Seco, Rioja Alta (JMW)
★Gravonia Fine Dry, López de Heredia (CHAP)

1982
£2.25–£3.50
Sainsbury's Rioja Seco, Viña Castil Dry (SAIN)
★Marqués de Cáceres (PG, ASHE, BIB, WW, RACK, WSOC, CDM, BOW, SW, HHC *& others*)
Siglo (SW)
Canchales, Bodegas Riojanas (SW)
Faustino V Rioja (FINT)
★Don Sebastian Blanco (STWC)

1981
c. £3.00
Marqués de Cáceres Blanco (A&K, JMW, L&W, J&B, L&S)

1980
£2.50–£3.50
Olarra Blanco Seco (CUL, SW)
Cumbrero, Bodegas Montecillo (SW)

Rioja Blanco, CUNE (WNRY)
★CUNE Monopole (ASHE, SW, L&S)

1979
£3.50–£4.00
CUNE Monopole (L&W)
Marqués de Murrieta (PG, SW)

1978
£3.00–£4.00
Olarra Blanco (JMW)
CUNE Monopole (A&K, WNRY)
Marqués de Murrieta (L&W, A&K, L&S, LADV, TAN)

1977
c. £3.00
Medieval (BIB)

1976
c. £4.00
Tondonia (A&K, L&S, SW)

1975
£3.25–£4.00
Medieval Blanco Extra Seco, Bodegas Riojanas (JMW)
★Viña Tondonia Blanco Seco, López de Heredia (JMW)

1973
c. £3.50
Muga (SW)

Rosé

1982
£2.75–£3.50
Rivarey (SW)
Faustino V Rioja Rosada (FINT)

1980
c. £2.80
Rivarey Marqués de Cáceres (A&K)

Price Guide – Notes

We don't have quite such a flood of Rioja as we used to a few years ago, and some of the less reliable producers are not seen any more, but the variety is still good. Merchants' lists are dominated by such professional outfits as Marqués de Cáceres, CUNE, Rioja Alta, Olarra and Marqués de Riscal, but it's also worth seeking out such bodegas as Montecillo, Berceo, Bilbainas, Lancorta and Campo Viejo. Rioja rosés are particularly good but no one seems to buy them, which is a pity and Rioja whites can be first class, both in the very fresh, dry style of Rivarey, Cáceres and Montecillo, or the fuller richer style of Murrieta, CUNE Monopole and Muga.

Flexible Future

Rioja's future may well rest on its flexibility. As recently as 10 years ago, it was known solely for those big, rich, heavily oaked and variously oxidised reds and, for a few brave cognoscenti, for deep, intensely strong whites, fat, dark and murky with oak. Well, both of these styles still exist, though the flavour of oxidation is increasingly one which finds little favour with modern drinkers. But then the flavour of raw rough red isn't too popular either – and much of Rioja's red would be harsh and raw without help from oak.

So the future lies in a careful use of good, newish oak, imparting the vanilla flavours, but not leading into that tired, brown oxidised state, and also, surprisingly, in a revival of the old 'lagar' style. Faustino have produced a remarkably successful young red based on the Tempranillo grape which is virtually vinified in the old oakless way, and resembles a particularly good Beaujolais Nouveau.

The one serious danger is price increases. With EEC membership coming in 1986, there will be a flood of cheap wine into Spain. She will need to keep her exports healthy to avoid chaos. The 1983 vintage was small; grape prices rose 80 per cent, wine prices rose 40 per cent. Dangerous, because once Rioja moves up a bracket in price, it may find the going rather tougher against established French classics. The new-wave whites seem to have more price stability, and we can expect to see a lot more of them, because when they get the acid fruit balance right, they're remarkably tasty, super-fresh wines. Super-modern too. One even has a 'best before' date. Just like Sainsbury's grapefruit juice!

OTHER WINES OF SPAIN

When one of the UK's leading supermarket buyers first started out 15 years ago, his biggest seller was medium sweet Spanish white. Now his company's entire Spanish range has dropped to only eight per cent of total wine sales, and his biggest Spanish seller is *medium* white. But even that he sees as fading out, in favour of Rioja, Penedès, Vallformosa, Jumilla, Cava . . . new names? Maybe. Rioja has become a household word, but Spain is much more than that, and these names will become increasingly important in the next few years.

The highest profile belongs to Catalonia, and, in particular, to Penedès. Not only does it contain the world's largest *méthode champenoise* cellars – those of Codorníu, bigger even than the giant Moet & Chandon *in* Champagne – but it is also the province of one of Europe's most brilliant winemakers, Miguel Torres, and a host of others eager to emulate him. These sparkling wines are called *cavas* when made by the champagne method, but are still hiccoughing in their attempts to establish themselves over here. This has been caused by a certain lack of marketing identity, a slightly peppery, earthy taste far removed from any champagne prototype, and a loss of their initial price advantage over, say, Saumur or Touraine in recent years, but in the USA they're a tremendous success, and are spearheading Spain's attack on that market.

That is, if Miguel's sister, the redoubtable Marimar Torres, isn't already doing it almost singlehanded with the Torres North America operation, which must rank as one of Spain's most successful marketing ventures since the Costa Brava. The Torres family are the most innovative and internationally aware wine makers in Spain. Far from being satisfied with the traditional Catalan grape varieties, Miguel has imported most of the top French varieties, as well as Gewürztraminer and Riesling of more Germanic origin, and is the leading Spanish exponent of cold-fermentation and early bottling for whites, and new small oak-barrel ageing for reds. The León estate nearby is producing fine Chardonnay and Cabernet, and a lot more will happen in Penedès. Elsewhere in Catalonia, Raimat, an estate created out of long-forgotten vineyards by the Codorníu sparkler firm is producing delicious Cabernet-influenced reds, while Alella, off-dry, fruity and soft, could be the Liebfraumilch drinker's intro to Spanish wine – if only there were enough of it to go round.

Otherwise the north contains some pretty fair rosés from Navarra and León as well as some blackstrap blending monsters in Cariñena and Campo de Borja. We may have drunk these, but almost certainly under another name! More interesting are the very modern whites of Rueda, an area primarily famed for a pretty death-defying sherry-type wine, and an even more hair-raising red – Vega Sicilia, which may count as Spain's most fabled grand wine, but certainly doesn't count as her most enjoyable. Valdeorras isn't upfront on easy, soft flavours either, but is a good gutsy halfway house to the harsh cold-shower-before-breakfast pleasures of Galician 'green' wines.

Central Spain, after years of unconcernedly pumping out curiously light, yet bucklingly strong reds for the carafe market is just beginning to realise that the gentle, almost mild reds of La Mancha and Valdepeñas could make their mark in a British market keen on softer tastes, while the Levante in the east of Spain, as well as producing excellent Muscat and rosé in Valencia, has begun to tame some of her reds.

Further south, Malaga is trying to make a deserved come-back as a high class dessert wine, and Montilla is fighting to maintain its position as a low cost sherry alternative. The sherry producers have enough trouble on their hands without Montilla's success, and their latest venture is to market a white table wine from the Palomino grape – soaking up the surplus capacity while sherry sales remain depressed.

TORRES GRAN CORONAS BLACK LABEL

In 1979, Spain strode up to the gates of Paris and walloped the best that France had to offer. It was the occasion of the much trumpeted Gault-Millau Wine Olympics. Don Miguel Torres entered his 1970 Gran Coronas Black Label in the top Cabernet class, and watched as a panel of 27 Frenchmen and just two Spaniards voted it first against such competition as La Mission Haut Brion 1961 and Latour 1970.

It was the summit of achievement for Torres, who, ever since setting to work in the family business in 1962, has seemed consumed with a desire to produce wines of world-beater class. That it took him less than 20 years to deliver this *coup de grâce* is a remarkable achievement. But, characteristically, he feels that the latest releases of Black Label will be even better than the 1970, as the vines mature and the proportion of Cabernet Sauvignon climbs higher. The 1975 vintage is the first one where the local grape varieties have been completely excluded; the mix is 90 per cent Cabernet Sauvignon and 10 per cent Cabernet Franc. Going against the Spanish blending tradition, the grapes come from a single 32-acre vineyard on the top of a hill at Pachs del Penedès. Torres has moved further and further up the hillsides to plant his vines, and is now also reaping the rewards of Chardonnay, Riesling and Gewürztraminer planted high up in some of Spain's coolest vineyards.

Also against Spanish tradition, Black Label is fermented in stainless steel, and then given six months ageing in new small American oak barrels, followed by up to two years in one- and two-year-old barrels, and then it's bottled; again, very early for a big Spanish red. If all this sounds familiar from the trail-blazers of Australia, California and New Zealand – the predominance of cool-grown Cabernet Sauvignon, the pure, controlled fermentation, the Bordeaux-style small-barrel ageing, the early bottling – you're right. That's the path the New World iconoclasts have taken towards glory, copying then developing the claret model, and it's in precisely this major league that Miguel Torres has chosen to battle it out.

Maturity Chart

1975 TORRES GRAN CORONAS BLACK LABEL

1970 was the first vintage of this 'new classic'. It is still superb, though just beginning to tire.

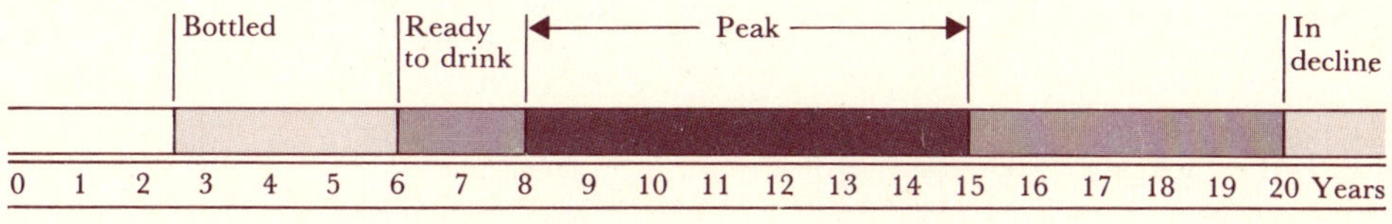

***Webster's** is an annual publication. We welcome suggestions for next year's edition.*

Price Guide

Red

Non-vintage
£1.75–£2.00
Sainsbury's Viña de España Tinto (SAIN)
Tesco Spanish Mellow Red Wine (TES)
⋆Condestable Tinto Jumilla (JMW, L&S)
Waitrose Spanish Red Wine (WAIT)
⋆Ashes (ASHE)
£2.00–£3.00
Corrida (THRE)
Dominic's Spanish Red (PD)
Don Cortez litre (VICT)
Palacio de León 4 año (JMW, HUN, SF)
Viña Coyanza Tinto (A&K)
Valdeorras Tinto, Cooperativa El Barco (L&S)
Viña Montana Tinto, Yecla (L&S)
£3.00–£3.50
Viña Ecoyen Señorio de Sarría (L&S)
Coronas Dry Red, Torres (PD)
Ribera Duero 2nd year (L&S)
⋆Don Suero Reserva Tinto 6 ano, Vinos de León (JMW)
£4.00–£5.00
Masía Tinto, Masía Bach (L&S)
Gran Vino del Señorio de Sarría (A&K)
Peñafiel 5th year, Ribera Duero (A&K, MAL, L&S)
£7.00–£7.50
Valbuena 3rd year, Vega Sicilia (L&S)
Protos Gran Reserva (SW)
c. £10.00
Valbuena 5th year, Vega Sicilia (L&S)

1982
c. £3.50
⋆Viña Esmeralda, Torres (ASHE)

1980
c. £3.00
Coronas Torres (CUL, SW, ASHE)
c. £5.00
Castel de Fornos, Bodegas Chaves (VIGN)
c. £6.50
Chardonnay Penedès, Jean León (CDM)

1979
£2.00–£3.25
Castillo de Manza (SW)
Conde de Caralt Tinto (JMW, SW)
⋆Sangredetoro Tres Torres (CHAP, PG, SW, HT, L&S)
⋆Coronas Torres (PG, CHAP, JMW, A&K, HT, L&S, SF, L&W, BOW, TAN *& others*)
Tinto Reserva, Manual Sanche (A&K)
£3.50–£5.50
⋆Sangre Brava Tinto, Torres (STWC)
Gran Coronas Torres (TAN)
Cabernet Sauvignon, Jean León (L&S, CDM)
c. £21.00
Vega Sicilia (MAL)

1978
£2.00–£3.00
Sainsbury's Jumilla (SAIN)
⋆Viña Albali Valdepeñas (ASHE)
René Barbier Tinto (L&S)
Sangredetoro Tres Torres (JMW)

£3.50–£5.00
Viña Alberdi, Rioja Alta (H&D)
Gran Sangredetoro Reserva (PG)
Masía Bach Tinto (JMW)
⋆Viña Magdala, Torres (HT)
Cabernet Sauvignon, Jean León (L&S, WW, BIB)

1977
£3.00–£3.50
Vall Fort, Masía Vallformose (L&S)
Coronas Torres (MAL)
⋆Gran Sangredetoro Torres (CHAP, HT, L&S)
£3.50–£4.75
Masía Bach Cordoníu (PG)
⋆Gran Coronos Torres (CHAP, WAIT, PG, A&K, SW, L&S, HT, SF, L&W)
Viña Magdala Penedès, Torres (ESV, JMW, L&S, L&W)
Cabernet Sauvignon, Jean León (L&S)

1976
c. £3.75
Gran Sangredetoro Torres (A&K, JMW, VICT)
c. £4.00
⋆Magdala, Torres (A&K, CHAP, PG)
c. £9.50
Gran Coronas Reserva Black Label (L&S, L&W, JMW, PG)

1975
£3.50–£4.00
Vall Reserva, Masía Vallformosa (L&S)
⋆Viña del Perdón Tinto (JMW, ESV, L&S, WSOC, MAL)
Gran Coronas Reserva Tinto, Torres (JMW)
c. £9.50
Gran Coronas Reserva Black Label (L&S, A&K)

1974
c. £4.50
Viña Santa Digna Tinto, Torres (JMW)
c. £5.75
Gran Vino del Señorio de Sarría Reserva (TAN)
c. £6.75
Protos, Ribera Duero (L&S, MAL)

1973
£3.00–£4.50
Conde de Caralt Reserva (JMW, SW)
René Barbier Reserva (L&S)
⋆Señorio de Sarría Tinto Reserva (JMW)
Viña Arana, Rioja Alta (H&D)
Gran Vino del Señorio de Sarría (VIGN, L&S)
c. £7.25
Protos (VIGN)
c. £9.50
⋆Gran Coronas Reserva Black Label, Torres (CHAP, HHC)

1972
c. £4.00
Reserva, Masía Bach (A&K)

1971
c. £5.00
Viña Santa Digna Tinto, Torres (JMW)

1970
c. £3.00
Yecla (PG)
c. £5.00
Reserva 904, Rioja Alta (H&D, HT)

1969
c. £19.00
Vega Sicilia (PG, L&S, VIGN, SW)

1966
c. £17.00
⋆Vega Sicilia (JMW)

White

Non-vintage
£1.75–£2.00
Sainsbury's Vino de España Seco (SAIN)
Sainsbury's Vino de España Dulce (SAIN)
Tesco Spanish Sweet White (TES)
⋆Tesco Spanish Dry White (TES)
Waitrose Spanish Dry White (WAIT)
Waitrose Spanish Sweet White (WAIT)
£2.00–£2.25
Corrida (THRE)
Sainsbury's Moscatel de Valencia (SAIN)
Dominic's Spanish Medium Dry White (PD)
Dominic's Spanish Sweet White (PD)

Don Cortez Dry litre (VICT)
Don Cortez Sweet litre (VICT)
★Palacio de León Blanco Seco (JMW)
Palacio de León Blanco Dulce (JMW)
£2.25–£3.00
Moscatel de Valencia (VICT)
Viña Coyanza Blanco (A&K)
Valdeorras Blanco, Cooperativa El Barco (L&S)
Marqués de Riscal Blanco, Rueda (A&K, VICT)
Marqués de Monistrol Blanc de Blancs (CUL)
Marqués de Monistrol, Viña Artal (CUL)
£3.00–£4.00
Viña Esmeralda, Torres (VICT, PD)
Masía Bach Extrisimo Reserva (A&K)
Masía Bach Seco (L&S)
Masía Bach Extrisimo Blanco Seco (JMW)

1982
£2.25–£3.00
Castillo de Manza (SW)
Conde de Caralt (SW)
★Viña Sol Blanco Seco Torres (JMW, SW, PG, HT, SF, CHAP, ASHE, TAN)
Blanco Anada Manuel Sanche (A&K)
★Gran Viña Sol Torres (CUL, HT, SW, TAN)

★Viña Esmeralda Torres (CUL, CHAP, PG, JMW, SW, HT, ESV, A&K, TAN)

1981
£3.00–£3.50
Gran Blanc Sec, Masía Vallformosa (L&S)
Viña Sol, Torres (A&K,L&S, L&W)
San Valentin (L&S)
Gran Viña Sol Reserva Blanco Seco, Torres (JMW, PG, L&S, A&K, L&W, BOW, VIGN)
Viña Esmeralda (L&S)
Marqués de Riscal, Rueda (ASHE)

1980
£2.50–£3.50
Ochoa Marca (SW)
Ochoa Seco (SW)
Señorio de Sarría Seco (L&S)
Viña Sol, Torres (MAL)
Marqués de Riscal (SW)
c. £4.50
★Gran Viña Sol Green Label, Torres (HT, CHAP)
c. £5.75
Chardonnay, Jean León (L&S, WW, A&K, VIGN)

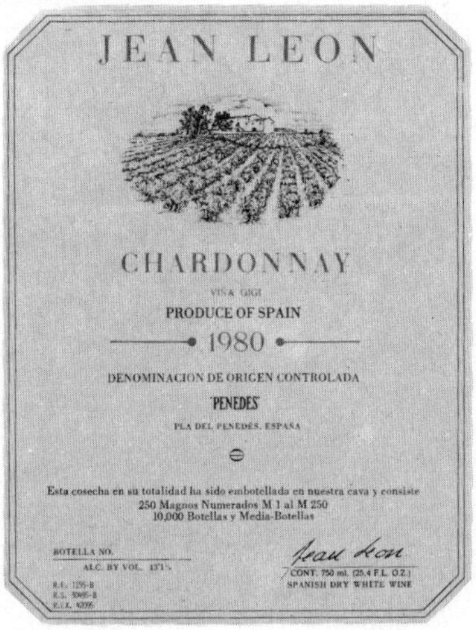

1979
c. £2.75
★Castello de San Diego, Barbadillo (H&D)
c. £4.25
Gran Viña Sol Green Label, Torres (A&K, VIGN, PG, L&S, JMW, TAN)
c. £6.00
Cabernet Sauvignon, Jean León (VIGN)

1978
c. £6.00
Cabernet Sauvignon, Jean León (VIGN)

1977
£3.75–£4.75
Mont Marcal Blanco Reserva (VIGN, MAL)
Gran Sangredetoro, Torres (VIGN)
Gran Coronas, Torres (VIGN)
c. £6.25
Cabernet Sauvignon, Jean León (VIGN)

1976
c. £4.50
Viña Magdala, Torres (VIGN)

1975
c. £10.00
Gran Coronas Black Label, Torres (VIGN)

1964
c. £16.50
Gran Coronas Black Label, Torres (VIGN)

Rosé

Non-vintage
£2.00–£2.50
Corrida (THRE)
Don Cortez litre (VICT)
Palacio de León Rosado (JMW)

1981
c. £2.75
De Casta Rosado Torres (JMW, L&S)

Sparkling Wine

Non-vintage
£3.00–£4.00
Sainsbury's Cava Spanish Sparkling Wine (SAIN)
Segura Viudas Brut (CUL, JMW)
Conde de Caralt Brut (SW)
Marqués de Monistrol Seco Gran Crémant (JMW)
Jean Perico Brut (JMW)
Marqués de Monistrol Brut (JMW)
Castellblanch Brut Zero (VIGN, JMW, WNRY, SW)
£4.00–£5.00
★Private Cuvée Brut Méthode Champenoise, Hicks & Don (H&D)
Freixenet Carta Nevada Brut (MWS)
Freixenet Cordon Negro (L&W, ASHE, A&K, YFW)
Cordoníu Grand Corday Brut (VICT, UNW, WNRY, SW, JMW)
Mont Marcal Cava Méthode Champenoise (RACK)
Codorníu Non Plus Ultra (HT, JMW, SW)

1980
c. £4.00
Mont Marcal Seco (A&K)

1979
£3.75–£4.75
★Freixenet Brut Nature (LHV, JMW, L&S, ESV, FFW)
★Freixenet Cordon Negro Brut (JMW, L&S, FFW, MWS)
Mont Marcal Brut (A&K)

1978
£4.00–£4.50
★Freixenet Cordon Negro (LHV, SW, HHC, TAN)
★Segura Viudas Brut (JMW, WAIT)
Freixenet Brut Nature (JMW, L&S, ESV)
Freixenet Brut Rosé (WNRY)

1975
£4.00–£4.50
Conde de Caralt Brut Nature (JMW)
Marqués de Monistrol Brut Nature (JMW)

Fortified Wine

Non-vintage
£2.00–£3.00
Montilla Monte Cristo Medium Dry (CHAP)
Montilla Los Palcos Extra Dry (SW)
Montilla Los Palcos Cream (SW)
Montilla Cream, Bodegas Alvear (TAN)
Montilla Medium Dry, Bodegas Alvear (TAN)
Montilla Pale Dry, Bodegas Alvear (TAN)
Montilla Palest Dry, Hicks & Don (H&D)
Montilla Finest Medium-Dry, Hicks & Don (H&D)
c. £4.00
Málaga Solera Scholtz 1885 (L&S, PG, SW)

Showing Some Promise

The future has to be bright for many of these wines, if only because any decent oenologist combining with an enthusiastic local Consejo has almost virgin material to deal with in so many areas. Valdepeñas is a classic example, where the appointment of a new and dynamic oenologist as president of the local Consejois is dragging one of Spain's most traditional areas into export awareness and a new saleability.

The same can't be said for La Mancha, a far larger area which engulfs Valdepeñas. Here most of the wine is dull, flat, lifeless white, high in alcohol, low in acid, low in taste. Too much of Spain's white is like this, and in the centre and south it will take a number of years before something halfway decent can be squeezed from this unpromising base. But there is an increasing number of good fresh whites – often a little neutral, but refreshing – like the Rueda wines; sometimes rather soft and fruity, like the wine bar delight Alella; and just occasionally, stunningly good, fresh and deep, etched with character, like the Penedès wines of Torres and Leon.

Despite big efforts with the whites, it is still the reds which are most promising in the short term. Penedès reds would be more popular if the prices were slightly lower, since they usually are just that bit more than an equivalent Rioja. The mini-Rioja styles of Navarra, the sturdy, but not too sturdy Jumillas and the dark, sharp Valdeorras wines could all make headway here.

SHERRY

Sherry isn't a Spanish drink. Perhaps I should re-phrase that. Sherry isn't a drink the Spaniards drink. The Andalusians, yes; they make it, and in fact seem to drink little else. Though the dry *manzanilla* or *fino* sherry, ice-cold in its dumpy little half-bottle never tastes better and more refreshing than it does in dark bar-room boltholes from the fierce Andalusian sun, there are times when you long for a glass of Rioja or even a Coca Cola – (separately or together depending on whether you're with the head of the bodega, or some of the lads from the bottling line). It is estimated that about seven per cent of all sherry is drunk in the Jerez region. Some figures reckon that the rest of Spain only accounts for three or four per cent of the total. The rest is export. And in the export market the UK is undisputed leader, and has been virtually since Falstaff snuffed it from drinking an intolerable deal too much of sherris-sack.

It's a rather worrying responsibility for the British sherry drinker to shoulder, because in a period when wine drinking has been proceeding at an unprecedented rate, and, despite recession, the UK is notching up more consumers and greater per capita consumption every year, sherry has something of the image of a yesterday's man.

It wasn't always thus. In the 1970s sherry drinking in the UK registered an average annual increase of 7.5 per cent. Strange beasts such as the pale cream sherries became instant successes and, although only invented in the 1960s, reached an estimated 20 per cent of a growing market by the end of the 1970s. The outlook seemed so bright that although most of the best Jerez Superior land was already planted, massive new plantations on marginal soils were effected to provide for a confidently predicted surge in sherry drinking.

It didn't happen. The growth in UK sherry drinking had been fuelled by the short-term profiteering of lower and lower prices and less and less quality control. Sherry shippers who piously maintain that all sherry shipped was, naturally, of good quality, checked by the Consejo and so forth, obviously hadn't been sniffing round the rash of cheaper brands which were flooding the market till last year, many bearing as much resemblance to 'real' sherry as Liebfraumilch does to an estate-bottled Rheingau.

With the 1980s the expansion shuddered to a halt. The new decade was ushered in with the realisation that those rosy 70s had turned into these gloomy 80s, with an immediate reversal of about eight per cent in sherry-drinking growth. It all came as something of a shock to the chaps in Jerez. But it shouldn't have done. Sherry has been described as 'middle-class and middle-aged'. It had become a byword for uninspired home entertainment – 'Will you have a glass of sherry?', meaning, have a drink of anything, since it was usually followed by 'Or would you prefer . . . ?'

In pub and club, sherry was still being served lukewarm, in tiny measures, in those absurd wasp-waisted Elgin glasses, which hardly held one decent mouthful of something which seemed increasingly over-priced and out of date. In a period when cocktails began to boom, and light, soft white wines became runaway successes as fresh, easy undemanding drinks, a thimbleful of rather alcoholic, heavy brown liquid wasn't going to raise the pulse rate much past bath-chair level. And despite an opinion poll which managed to persuade itself that sherry was still the 'Top People's Favourite Drink', the world of these Top People wasn't where everything was buzzing commercially. It was all happening down in the basement, in the CD socio-economic groups and with the under-25s and the 25–35s. And the last thing most of those people wanted was a drink which seemed in the least fuddy-duddy.

Things had to change, and they did – with a crash. The collapse of the gigantic Rumasa empire last year meant that the company which had done more price-cutting and quality-stretching than any other was suddenly in the hands of the Spanish government. They would find it very much in their interests to stop the dumping of inferior wine at low prices and build up a long-term strategy of selling sherry as a quality drink, and promoting it in an entirely different way. It's not certain yet how quickly success will come, but the first signs are encouraging. Of those vineyards planted in the 1970s, swelling the Jerez area to 50,000 acres, 5,000 had already been uprooted by 1983 and another 7,000 acres should revert to tomatoes and grain by 1986.

Although the changes may be difficult to implement, the Rumasa shock has united the shippers, albeit temporarily, into proposing a minimum price for export which *must* be adhered to. It is still incredibly low, around 43p per litre for bulk shipment, but it will allow a small profit to be made by everybody, and it serves to illustrate just how much the price had been forced down with the in-fighting of a couple of years ago. And the shippers have begun to re-think exactly what they want their target market to be. Without doubt they have to try to capture a younger audience, whose stated wine preferences are predominantly white and easy-tasting, whose beer preferences are for the chilled and neutral, and whose spirits preferences are for something white and tasteless, to give a hidden kick to long cold drinks.

In the next four years £28 million will be spent on UK advertising, mostly by the already very successful brands, but also with a £4 million drive into generic sherry promotion. It began with the exhortation to take it on the rocks, and although that didn't quite get its message right (with some unkind wits remarking that sherry was on the rocks already, so why rub it in?), the latest campaign has the now familiar grouping of fresh-faced, fun-loving, clean-living 20–30 year olds all laying into their *copitas*. Couple that with the attempt to produce a sherry 'mixer', and the attempt to wean barmen off the dreaded Elgin glass, and on to a decent measure of sherry poured over ice, and it may work.

One encouraging sign already evident is that this affluent young target market is unimpressed by sherry as a cheap drink, but *is* interested in it for quality and individuality. If this trend continues, sherry is on the way back, and you won't have to wear a tie and grey flannel suit to the sherry parties of the 1980s.

Sherry prices over the years

In a decade when the prices of many traditional wines in Britain have been careering about like Yo-Yos, and only now seem to be returning to a period of stability, sherry prices have shown little volatility, and, with the exception of the brand leaders like Tio Pepe and Harvey's Bristol Cream, have found it difficult to charge a high price for their product. In fact we know from specialist wine merchants that some of the best sherries are being sold at prices which mean that the shipper *cannot* be making money.

In the period from 1972 to 1983, Cockburn's Special Reserve Port climbed from £1.39 to £4.06, while Dry Fly, an important sherry brand, went from £1.41 to £3.02. The costs of production aren't that different, and the financial difficulties which the sherry houses have landed in are highlighted by that pound a bottle price difference.

A maturity chart as such for sherry is impossible since the solera system does not permit any precise definition of age. Once sherry is bottled it is ready to drink, and in the case of fino or manzanilla sherry should be drunk within six or nine months of bottling, otherwise it loses its freshness. To ensure that your sherry is freshly bottled, buy it from a wine merchant with a fast turnover.

Price Guide

Dry

£2.25–£3.00

Waitrose Fino Sherry (WAIT)
⋆Fino, Tio Carlos (CHAP)
⋆Manzanilla, Tio Carlos (CHAP)
⋆la Gitana Manzanilla, Hidalgo (ODD, BOW)
⋆Fino de Balbaina, Barbadillo (ODD, H&D, L&S)
Lolita Fino, Diez (SF)
Zuleta Fino (CV)
Zuleta Manzanilla (CV)
Manzanilla, Maria Ruiz Berdejo (ESV)
Ostra Manzanilla (L&W)
The Society's Fino (WSOC)
Harveys Luncheon Dry (CHAP, MWS, JH, GH, SF, UNW)

£3.00–£3.50

Double Century Fino (UNW)
Fino, Hidalgo (BOW)
San Patricio Fino, Garvey (ODD, SF, DOL, VICT, WSOC, A&K, HT, HHC, MWS, L&S *& others*)
Fino, Lustau (A&K)
⋆Gran Manzeda Manzanilla (BAL)
Les Amis Fino (LADV)
Fiesta Fino, Domecq (WGA)
⋆Manzanilla de Sanlucar, Barbadillo (H&D, C&B, L&S, GH)
⋆Palo Cortado de Jerez, Hijos de Julio Covenas (CHAP, ESV)
Tanners Dry Sherry, O'Neale (TAN)
Amontillado Viejo, Lustau (ODD)
La Luna Manzanilla, Findlater (FINT)
⋆La Goya Manzanilla Pasada, Zuleta (HT)
La Lidia Manzanilla, Garvey (SF, GH, L&S)
Tia Lola Fino, Findlater (FINT)
Harveys Manzanilla (JH)
Mariscal Fino, O'Neale (TAN)

Mariscal Manzanilla, Hidalgo (TAN)
Palo Cortado, Lustau (ODD)
Harveys Bristol Dry (ODD, GH, CHAP)

£3.50–£4.00

Manzanilla Pasada de Sanlucar, Colon (ESV)
Tio Pepe, Gonzalez Byass (ODD, WAIT, CHAP, MWS, SF, HHC, SW, UNW, CV, J&B)
⋆Manzanilla Pasada de Sanlucar, Hidalgo (CHAP)
⋆Solear Manzanilla Pasada, Barbadillo (H&D, L&S)
La Ina, Domecq (UNW, CHAP, SW, HHC, GH, CV, J&B, C&B)
Inocente Fino (WSOC)
Tio Guillermo Amontillado, Garvey (MWS, SF, HT, GH, L&S, A&K, LADV)
La Guita Manzanilla Pasada, Pérez Marín (L&S, HBV, SW)

£4.00–£4.50

⋆Palo Cortado, Cuvillo (L&S, CV)
⋆Berisford Manzanilla Pasada 1914 Solera (TW)
⋆Berisford Rare Fino 1914 Solera (TW)
Tio Diego Amontillado (WSOC)
⋆Oloroso Seco, Barbadillo (H&D)
⋆Principe Amontillado, Barbadillo (H&D, L&S, BOW)
Oloroso Especial, Hidalgo (L&W)

£4.50–£5.50

Fino Especial, Hidalgo (L&W)
⋆Jerez Cortado, Hidalgo (L&W)
Oloroso Very Dry approx. 19 years, Sandeman (ADN)
⋆Harveys Palo Cortado (JH, VICT)
⋆Manzanilla Pasada, Hidalgo (L&W)
⋆Alfonso, Gonzalez Byass (CV)
Don Zoilo Dry Oloroso, Ruiz-Mateos (BOW)

£5.50–£6.00
- ⋆Apostoles Oloroso, Gonzalez Byass (L&S, CV)
- ⋆Del Duque Amontillado, Gonzalez Byass (L&S, CV)
- Don Zoilo Very Old Amontillado (GH)
- Don Zoilo Very Old Fino (GH)

c. £12.50
- Oloroso Extra Solera 70 years, Blazquez (ADN)

c. £13.25
- Palo Cortado Solera 100 years, Blazquez (ADN)

Medium

£2.25–£3.00
- Waitrose Amontillado Sherry (WAIT)
- ⋆Amontillado, Tio Carlos (CHAP)
- ⋆Golden Oloroso, Tio Carlos (CHAP)
- Double Century Oloroso (CHAP, WAIT, UNW)
- Dry Fly, Findlaters (ODD, CHAP, UNW, FINT)
- Zuleta Amontillado (CV)
- Harveys Club Amontillado (WAIT, ODD, MWS, CHAP, JH, GH, HHC)

£3.00–£3.50
- San Sebastian Fine Amontillado, Maria Ruiz Berdejo (ESV)

- Double Century Amontillado (UNW)
- Double Century Pale Cream (UNW)
- San Angelo Amontillado, Garvey (A&K, MWS)
- ⋆Gran Finito Amontillado (BAL)
- Les Amis Amontillado (LADV)
- Fiesta Amontillado, Domecq (WGA)
- ⋆Amontillado de Sanlucar, Barbadillo (H&D, L&S)
- ⋆Oloroso de Jerez, Rosario Farfante Rodriguez (CHAP)
- The Society's Medium Dry (WSOC)
- Tanners Medium Dry Sherry, Hidalgo (TAN)
- Dry Sack, Williams & Humbert (CHAP, UNW)

- Amontillado Napoleon (BOW)
- Mariscal Amontillado, O'Neale (TAN)
- Oloroso Viejo, Lustau (ODD)

£3.50–£4.00
- Amontillado de Sanlucar, Barbadillo (L&S)
- Cecilia Amontillado, Findlater (FINT)
- Pemartin Solera 1914 Amontillado, Jose Pemartin (SF)
- ⋆Rio Seco Fino Amontillado, Justerini & Brooks (J&B)
- Very Fine Old San Lucar Amontillado, Hidalgo (TAN)

£4.00–£5.00
- Mariscal Oloroso Sec, Hidalgo (TAN)
- Berry Bros Finest Amontillado Pasado (BBR)
- ⋆Berisford Amontillado 1914 Solera (TW)
- ⋆Berisford Amoroso 1914 Solera (TW)
- Harveys Reina Victoria Amontillado (VICT)
- Jerez Cortado, Hidalgo (TAN)
- Fifty Plus Old Oloroso (DOL)
- Solera 1847 Oloroso, Gonzalez Byass (SF, CV)
- ⋆Harveys Fine Old Amontillado (JH, VICT)

£5.75–£7.50
- ⋆Bicentenary Amontillado (C&B)
- Almacenista Oloroso Muy Viejo, Lustau (LADV)
- Berry Bros Dos Palmas (BBR)
- Berry Bros Alonso el Savio Solera 1973 (BBR)

Sweet

£2.25–£3.00
- ⋆Pale Cream, Tio Carlos (CHAP)
- ⋆Rich Cream, Tio Carlos (CHAP)
- Cream Sherry, Domecq (WAIT)
- Pale Cream Sherry, Domecq (WAIT)
- Zuleta Cream (CV)
- Zuleta Pale Cream (CV)

£3.00–£3.50
- Double Century Cream (UNW)
- Croft Original Pale Cream Sherry (WAIT, CHAP, MWS, ODD, J&B, GH)
- Fiesta Cream, Domecq (WGA)
- Harveys Bristol Cream (CHAP, WAIT, MWS, ODD, UNW, JH, GH, HHC)

Tanners Cream Sherry, Hidalgo (TAN)
Mariscal Cream, Hidalgo (TAN)
The Society's Cream (WSOC)

£3.50–£4.00

Findlater's Cream (FINT)
Oloroso de Jerez, Rodriguez (ESV)
Harveys Bristol Milk (JH, CHAP, UNW)

Pemartin Solera 1914 Cream, José Pemartin (SF)
Harveys Bristol Cream (UNW)
Berry Bros Finest Old Brown (BBR)

£4.00–£6.25

*Sanlucar Cream, Barbadillo (H&D)
Matusalem Oloroso, Gonzalez Byass (L&S, CV)
Don Zoilo Very Old Cream (GH)
Harveys Bristol Milk Bottled 1973 (JH)
Harveys Bristol Cream Bottled 1973 (JH)

__Webster's__ is an independent guide. We have received an enormous amount of information and assistance from the wine trade but responsibility for editorial content is the editors' and publishers' alone.

SHERRY, THE NEW SOPHISTICATE

My most abiding image of sherry from last year is of an extremely bronzed young lady sitting on a diving board with her feet encased in concrete. She was also leaning fairly far backwards, as if to avoid the tall, ice-filled tumbler which was being proferred. What was a nice girl like that doing with her feet encased in concrete? What was the terrible icy potion she was so keen to avoid?

Well, the answer is that the torrid sun-baked concrete round her ankles was in fact supposed to be ice. And that tumbler contained a generous measure of sherry – on the rocks – and the bronzed beauty was supposed to be going quite weak at the knees, or in this case, the ankles, at the thought of it. Yes, this was part of the first generic campaign to try to reverse the decline in sherry drinking in this country.

Hmmm. It was certainly a controversial path for sherry to tread, breaking right away from its traditional mould, sensibly trying to banish our memories of liverish Sunday afternoons following a couple of pre-lunch glasses of Dad's South African or Cyprus 'medium', but it looks as though it just might be bearing fruit. People do seem to be more aware of sherry as more than just a convenient gift at Christmas. And figures show that, although the heavy sweet sherries are in decline, the 'think dry, drink sweet' pale creams are building up strength, as are the drier sherries. Dry is where the experts see most growth potential following the general boom in white wine drinking, as that endlessly elusive 'typical' customer becomes more sophisticated and starts drinking dry.

The most notable development in the UK has been the interest shown in speciality sherries. Sainsbury's now do the rare *palo cortado* style under their own label, and companies like Hicks & Don and Lustau are offering special *almacenistas,* i.e. individually chosen, separately aged lots of fascinating mature sherries, which are being snapped up.

If sherry can build a connoisseur following, and also, through its generic advertising, catch the 20 to 35-year-old age group, then that 'middle-aged, middle-class' epithet won't stick anymore.

And certainly, despite the difficulty of seeing what the lady in the concrete slippers was up to, middle-class and middle-aged she ain't.

PORTUGAL

TABLE WINES

There seems to be a pretty good reason why we don't know more about Portuguese table wine – they drink most of it themselves. But this isn't just the usual old-chestnut excuse made for the absence of some obscure regional wine from the supermarket shelves by blaming it on the astonishing intoxication of the natives. No, with Portugal we are in the major league. It's the seventh biggest producer, usually slotting in behind the USA, while keeping comfortably ahead of South Africa. But it reguarly trades second and third positions with Italy in the table of major consumers, and while France and Italy are finding their consumption dropping annually, Portugal is the only leading wine-producing country which is actually gulping down more. They like it. They cheerfully drink three-quarters of their production, and until recently the general view has been that if any foreigners wanted to buy Portuguese wines, well, this is how the Portuguese like to drink it – so take it or leave it.

The trouble is, that's not good enough for us Brits. We have the widest choice of wines anywhere in the world. Why should we say 'But of course! Send us those strange Atlantic potions we were just beginning to get used to at Estoril, and we'll put aside our habitual French/Italian/German tipple.' But then the Portuguese are a proud and very conservative race. With an evidently keen domestic thirst, they are not the kind of people to touch their forelocks and beg to know our pleasure. I mean, they got down to an *appellation contrôlée* system a good generation before the French; but, as often happens, it doesn't always help to be the first. The kind of regions and traditional practices enshrined in the laws have not helped Portugal modernise her wine industry or promote her wares, and it is interesting to note that many of Portugal's best wines now have no geographical definition at all, but just a trade name on the label, and frequently *garrafeira,* implying a special selection.

This situation applies largely to what are called 'mature' wines; they are whacked into their vats and barrels and left until the reds will tan the hide of an ox and the whites will provide a good marinade for the carcass. Dão is the most commonly seen of these, and despite its rather solid style, it is indeed a fair mouthful for a fair price. The most hopeful sign in 'mature' reds is the area of Bairrada, whence in fact, nudge nudge, wink wink, the big companies have been drawing base wines for their top blends for ages. After several years of Brit travellers returning home with tales of having 'discovered' Bairrada, the authorities are at last exporting them here. They have the sturdy strength of Dão, but with much more fruit and ripeness, and they could catch on in a big way.

Portugal's other table-wine style is *vinho verde,* or 'green wine'. 'Green' here means youthful-green, immature-green, un-aged, rather than implying that the liquid is the colour of a croquet lawn. In fact, it's normally a definite yellow colour, only saved by the little haze of fizz which flares briefly in the glass. These 'young' green wines are sharp and tart in their natural white – and red! – state, and we seem to get them here slightly sweetened, but they are low in alcohol, very refreshing and perfectly suited to the modern crisp 'don't make me think too hard' wine styles which people seem to want.

Dão, *vinho verde* and rosé are the three basic styles we import, and the following figures show that, while Dão is only slowly finding a place in the UK market, *vinho verde* is definitely catching the mood, while poor old rosé has come a terrible cropper as it stumbles up against a general, and not entirely explicable, consumer resistance to 'the Pink One' (figures are totals - bulk and bottled - in thousand litres):

	1981	1982	1983 (Jan-Sep)
Red (mostly Dão)	356	318	346
Rosé	3,898	3,031	1,337
Vinho verde	757	964	1,162

Ten-year-old wines
A 10-year-old wine for under £2.50; a 16-year-old wine for under £3.00: it makes that 14-year-old wine for under £3.50 seem almost over-priced. But there's only one country in the world which can now offer you these kinds of bargains, and that is Portugal. If you've got an anniversary coming up and want to celebrate with something firm and red made on the day you first clasped hands under the silvery moon, but don't quite feel up to shelling out the readies for vintage champagne or old claret, you have to go to Portugal, which offers you more genuine antiquity per penny than any other country. Only trouble is, you're going to have to like a certain style of wine for your celebration to be a success. Whereas we've got used to wines with an obvious fruit, not too much bite and something fairly fresh about them, the Portuguese like to keep their reds in great, big, old wooden barrels until the bank manager threatens to foreclose, and then they bottle them with all the tannins and acidities in fine fettle, but the fruit distinctly past its first flush. Even so, at these prices you must have a go. Dão is the most widely available, but unlikely to be as good as either a *garrafeira* - a non-geographical term implying 'special selection' - or one of the recently-introduced Bairradas.

Mateus
My father finally got back from the Far East after the war with a brand-new wife, not too many thoughts of a brand-new son and a desire to push the boat out. For a belated celebration he took my mother to one of the smart, smart clubs. You know, The Blue Train, The Bag o'Nails, Ciro's (no, I'm not showing my age, just remembering the words of a song I once sang), and ordered their most chic, most expensive wine. Mateus Rosé!! Honest! It was more expensive and smarter than champagne.

Ten years before he couldn't have ordered it - because it didn't exist. They didn't have Portuguese sparkling rosé until Fernando Guedes invented it in 1942. It now sells a million bottles a week, and until the dramatic slump in sales of all rosés in 1983, accounted for up to 85 per cent of Portuguese table-wine sales here. Before we knock it, just try to think of any other wine which started out so exclusive and within 40 years ended up as the answer to every maiden aunt's prayer. And one more thing. It's still the most reliable light, fizzy, Portuguese rosé, despite all the attempts to mimic it.

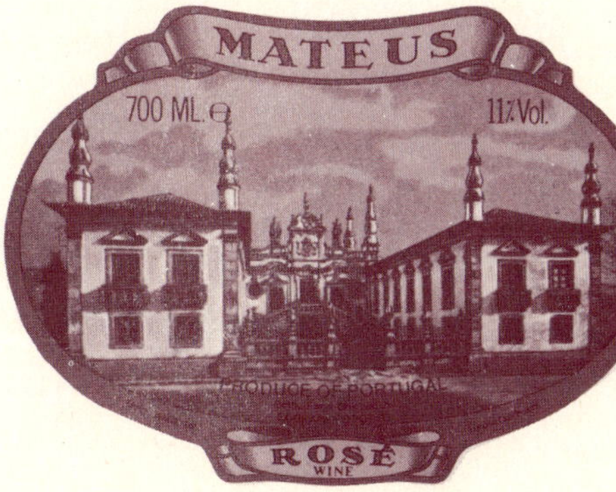

Price Guide

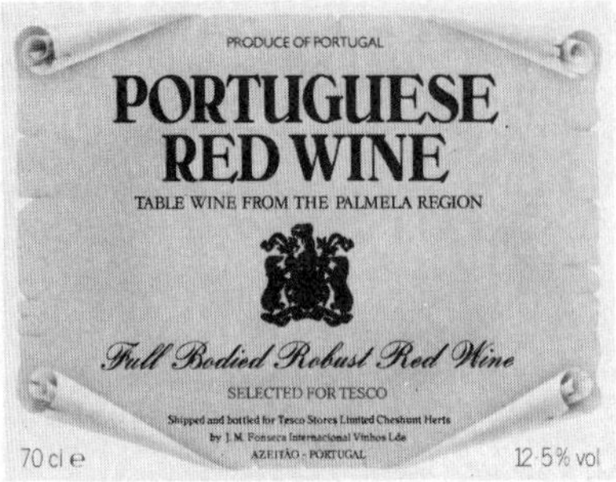

Red

Non-vintage
c. £2.00
Sanguinhal A. P. da Fonseca (ODD)
⋆Tesco Portuguese (TES)
c. £3.25
Tinto da Anfora, João Pires (BIB)

1979
£2.50–£3.00
⋆Dão, Caves Velhas (THRE, ODD)
⋆Dão Terras Altas, Fonseca (PG)
Pasmados, Fonseca (BYR)

1978
£2.50–£3.00
Dão Imperial (DAV)
⋆Tinto da Anfora, Fonseca (WAIT)
£3.00–£4.00
Dão, Grão Vasco (ASHE, H&B)
Perequita, Fonseca (ASHE, TAN)
Dão Terras Altas (TAN)

1977
c. £2.50
Dão, Catedral (WAIT)

1976
£2.50–£3.50
Dão, Grão Vasco (BYR)

⋆Dão, Ribalonga (ESV)
Colares Reserva, Companhia Real Vinicola (L&W)

1975
£3.00–£4.00
⋆Dão Garrafeira (BYR, H&B)
Dão Reserva (BYR)
Dão, Grão Vasco (DOL)

1974
£2.25–£3.25
⋆Sainsbury's Dão (SAIN)
⋆Dão Dom Ferraz (MART, WAIT)
⋆Pasmados, Fonseca (PG, CHAP)
c. £4.50
Dão Reserva, Caves Dom Teodosio (MWS)
c. £5.50
Periquita, Fonseca (BYR)

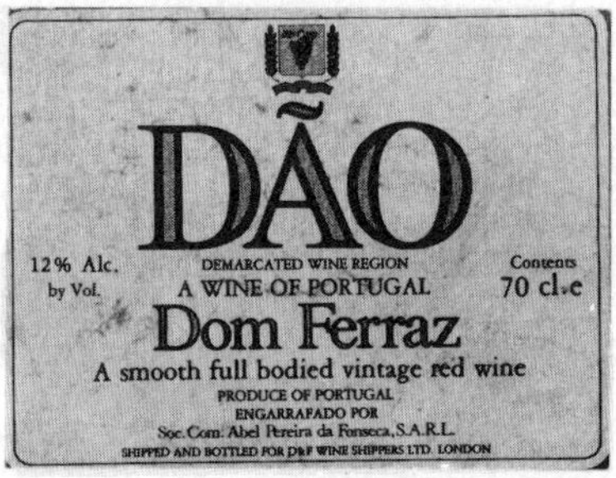

1971
c. £4.25
Pasmados, Fonseca (ODD, CUL, MAL)
Periquita, Fonseca (PG)
Dão Reserva, Aliança (MAL)

1970
c. £3.85
Dão, Udaca Reserva (GH)
Dão Reserva, Barrocão (BBR)

1968
c. £3.00
Garrafeira, Caves Velhas (ODD)

1963
c. £4.00
⋆Cavenal Reserva, Caves Nacionais (PG)

White

Non-vintage
£2.00–£2.50
St Michael Vinho Verde (SAIN)

★Vinho Verde, Verdegar (WAIT, ODD, THRE)
Vinho Verde, Caves Alianca (P&C)
£2.50–£3.00
Vinho Verde, Dom Silvano (BIB)
Vinho Verde Aveleda (PG, CUL, DAV, H&B, MWS, TAN, AV)
★Vinho Verde, Casalinho (L&W, GH, PG, MAL)

£3.00–£4.00
Dão Terras Altas Reserva Fonseca (L&W)
Mateus white (H&B, THRE)
Bucelas Velho, Cavas Velhas (TAN)

1980
c. £3.20
Dão, Grão Vasco (H&B)

1979
c. £2.95
Dão Terras Altas, Fonseca (PG)

1978
c. £2.95
Bucelas, Cavas Velhas (PG)

Rosé

Non-vintage
c. £3.00
Mateus Rosé (ODD, BYR, GH, ASHE, SAIN, THRE, CUL, DAV, H&B *& others*)

Fortified

Non-vintage
c. £4.00
★Moscatel de Setubal, Fonseca (PG, WSOC)
1978
c. £4.75
Moscatel de Setubal, Fonseca (ESV, CUL)

1934
c. £24.00
Moscatel de Setubal, Fonseca (PG)

BRIGHT FUTURE FOR WHITES

Mr Dias of F&D Wines, one of Britain's tiny band of specialist Portuguese shippers, says he's been waiting since the fifties for UK recognition and acceptance of Portuguese wines as a quality product, and he's still waiting! It seems that awareness of Portugal as a wine-producing country has been dominated by port, and more recently Mateus and its imitators. Its other wines uneasily straddle French and Spanish wines in both quality and price.

Things are on the move, though. I've tasted Bairrada back to the 1960 vintage, and it's stunning stuff. There seem to be some good companies, and they are at last being helped to export. In whites, so long as they can keep the sulphur levels down and the stock rotation quick, we're sure to see a big leap in *vinho verde* sales as one of summertime's best whites, since they've now expanded to TV advertising. Dão whites could also begin to make a mark as modern vinification techniques slowly take hold in the uplands.

Port

Port isn't natural. Not port *drinking*. Port itself. Port comes from way up the Douro valley in northern Portugal; if you'd been around in the early eighteenth century, when the Methuen Treaty of 1703 made it exceedingly difficult to get a decent glass of French claret or burgundy in England, while offering the Portuguese *carte blanche* to show us their all, you'd have been offered Finest Red Douro Wine by your merchant. Which would have been quite enough to persuade you that "port" drinking certainly wasn't natural either.

These basic Douro wines were harsh, coarse, and close to indigestible for a nation brought up on the pale red wines of Bordeaux. A solution was found for their delicate English clientèle by the merchants, who paddled through the Bay of Biscay to make their fortune by inventing an entirely new style of wine.

They took this fierce, coarse, raw red wine, and instead of allowing it to ferment right out, and thus make an alcoholic, dry wine, they stopped its fermentation about half-way (usually with about 6 degrees alcohol produced, and about another 6 degrees-worth of sugar still unconverted in the wine) by pouring in a massive slug of brandy. To about 440 litres of half-fermented red wine they added 110 litres of this fire-water. That's what the Portuguese still call it: *aguardente.* Not surprising. It's 77 degrees alcohol. Whisky's only 40 degrees! It had the effect of killing the yeasts; well, not exactly killing – just rendering legless and unfit for further employment – and so the fermentation stopped, with at least half the natural grape sugar left in the wine.

This was about 250 years ago, and the methods haven't changed very much. Port still has a duty to be red (though there is a little white), and it still has a duty to be sweet. The wood-aged tawnies, however, will be less red, inclining to tawny, and less sumptuously sweet, since ageing for anything from five to fifty years in barrel will reduce all the most assertive elements (tannins, sugar and that fire-water) to a mellow softness, which may be the reason why tawny has never been terribly popular in the UK – we've always wanted a bit of bite and wallop to our ports.

This need for a port which seems to do you a bit of good is more evident than ever in the 1983 market. Shippers have tried white port, without success, and with localised success in tawnies, but it wasn't till 1983 that they saw a way to stem the decline in our port consumption, which had fallen from 10.8 million litres in 1979 to 6.5 million litres in 1982. Their solution was a brilliant one. Combine the mystique and kudos of a vintage port with the handiness of a straight ruby; package it well, stick the words 'vintage', 'vintage character', 'special reserve', in prominent positions on the label and pitch its price between ordinary and vintage, *et voilá!* A nice smooth, 'no rough edges' port, with no sediment, which gives everyone the impression of being a vintage wine. The idea has been a whopping success with everyone except traditional port drinkers who find it rather bland and sugar-sweet. They shouldn't carp too much. It's the success of this clever marketing device which will keep their favourite vintage brands in business, and their opening vintage prices affordable by the faithful band who still wish to lay them down.

To get a peek at what vintage port can be like, don't buy late-bottled vintage. There's not a lot of similarity, to put it bluntly. Buy Crusted Port or Single Quinta vintage dated port. Single Quintas (or farms) are usually from the best vineyards in the less brilliant years, but instead of bottling and shipping them after only two years or so to the cold slow maturing cellars of GB, they're bottled

Vintage Table

Vintage port takes a very long time to reach the smooth, mellow peak that induces leather-chaired slumber in the face of a guest's homily on the necessity of a good gun-dog. But young vintage port, despite the disapproval of the pundits, can be a brilliant, fiery, intensely sweet, show-stopper of a wine. If you hanker for that pepper, cough-mixture and plum brandy full-frontal attack, go ahead and down a 1977 or a 1970 – but cancel any early appointments the next morning.

1980 A good vintage, rather grumpily reviewed initially because of its high price. This is really too young even to treat to the 'hit 'em while they're young' policy. It should begin to soften about 1990 and reach a peak about 1995.

***1977** Brilliant wine. At seven years it hasn't even begun to mature, and the flavour is a marvellous mixture of great fruit sweetness and intense spice and herb fragrances. When 1980's on the way down, this'll still be on the way up.

1975 Rather feeble. People are already drinking these light, sugar-sweet wines. Why not? There's not a lot to wait for. I don't suppose a revolution does much for the style of a vintage, and these really don't have the guts and stuffing a vintage needs.

***1970** Lovely stuff. Curiously, this vintage has often been only cautiously praised. Fainthearts, take up your corkscrews! This is an exceptional, balanced port, already good to drink, very sweet, with a fascinating citrus flash of freshness running through it.

1966 They didn't rate this to start with, but they do now. It's gained body and oomph and is still improving. Trouble is, it's rocketed in price, so it might be best to cut your losses and buy some more 1970.

1963 They call it the 'classic' year, and one can see why. It's like 1977; having finally got a bump start and moved into third gear, there's another two gears and overdrive yet to come. It's big, deep, and spicy, but getting a gorgeous mellow sweetness to the fruit. It's so good, the best ones may also pass 1980 as it retires gracefully in 20 years' time.

1960 This started out rather raisin and brown-sugar sweet, but since then has become lovely midweight port. At its peak for the past five years, it'll still hold a bit longer.

after two years, but frequently stored for up to 10 years in Portugal's warmer climate, and are shipped mature and ready to drink. They'll cost several pounds a bottle less than similarly mature vintage port.

Laying down

Vintage port is back in fashion. And if vintage port is back in style, then there's no question – to get the best out of the wine, and out of your money, you've got to get back into the laying-down game.

Of all the famous wines vintage port is the one which takes longest to reach its peak. Madeira may live longer, but fine madeira is so rare a commodity, you'd be hard put to find two people who could tell you what its peak might taste like, so that you had some vague idea about whether you'd caught it or missed it. But vintage port has been the staple after-dinner drink of so many generations of Englishmen that there's no shortage of opinions being offered as to when it's ready. But don't wait *too* long.

I believe that there is a lot of pleasure to be had in drinking it supposedly too young, and I won't surrender to the horrified wails of 'Infanticide!' which rise from behind spreadeagled copies of the Daily Telegraph when someone suggests they crack open a bottle of 1970. Too much is made of 'peaks of maturity', and 'the pefect age' for drinking a port. In simple terms, a port reaches its peak when it won't get any better. Certainly there is a plateau along which a vintage port *may* roll contentedly for a number of years. On the other hand it might only stay at that peak for a matter of weeks. The only certain thing you will ever know about the peak of maturity of a port, is that you've missed it, and then you'll kick yourself for not having drunk it younger. There's an enormous pleasure to be got from saying 'This is good, and will get better.' Far more pleasure than saying 'This is fine, but was finer a couple of years ago.'

There has always been money to be made out of buying the top ports in the top years – those 'declared' by the majority of houses (this usually happens every three or four years, e.g. 1960, 1963, 1966, 1970). The wonderful thing about laying fine wine down is that once the money has been spent on an opening offer of the most recent vintage, you get one further nasty shock when the wine is shipped here, since duty and VAT become payable, but after that, there's only a small annual storage charge or, if you've got a cellar, no charges at all, while the wine becomes more and more drinkable, and more and more valuable. Accountants among you may fret about interest rates and return on capital, but I just heave a sigh of relief as the bank passes the first big cheque. Then for years I can bask in the knowledge that I own it, and one day my wine is going to give me and my friends such a treat as none of us could readily afford at that far-off day's prevailing prices.

Port used to be particularly cheap to buy young; the price would go into a stagnant coma until it became the 'current' vintage for hotels and restaurants, when it would shoot up. Many a gentleman's private cellar has been paid for on this principle. Nowadays, with Portuguese inflation running at an annual 25 per cent or more, and with the Americans, amazingly late, suddenly taking an interest in vintage port, it begins to increase in value much sooner. In 1981 the young 1975s could be bought in Sotheby's auction rooms for £40 a dozen. They were in the usual young port doldrums, and a bottle of Cockburn's Ruby in a shop would have cost much the same at £3.45. By 1983, those 1975s had doubled to £80 a case. The 1966s had leapt from around £70 to £160 a dozen in

Maturity Chart

1970 PORT

Lesser Ports may be ready within 10 years and last less long.

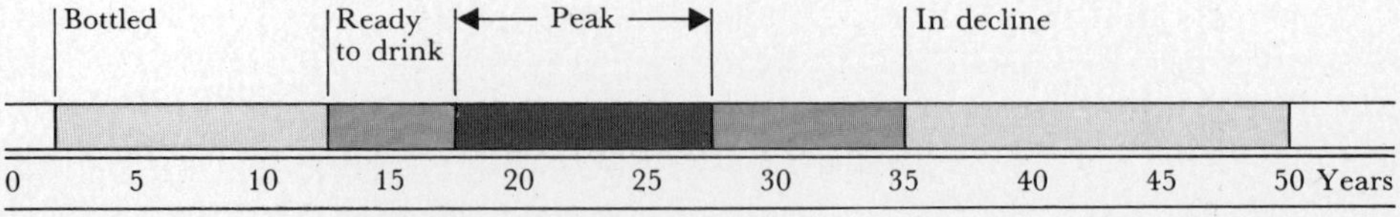

just a year, and in *The Decanter* Auction Price Index for vintage port, having strolled along quite sedately from 100 in August 1978 to 144.4 in January 1983, had reached 235.83 by March 1984. The splendid but young 1977s, which entered the Index at 100 in September 1983, had reached 253.8 in only 6 months! Those price-leaps bear all the marks of investors rushing into the port market, and the only advice possible for the port buyer not interested in boom-bust is to buy 1970 (although that's getting popular too), or those unfashionable 1975s and 1980s while you wait for the next 'classic' to be declared.

The extent to which vintage port is becoming a highly mobile investment market again is shown by comparing the typical retail price of Cockburn's Ruby Port, the UK market leader, with a leading vintage from a leading house, in this instance Taylor 1970.

	Cockburn	Taylor
1978	£2.40	£5.75
1980	£2.92	£6.99
1982	£3.74	£11.62
1983	£4.07	£13.02

By the end of 1984, the Taylor will be selling for about £18 a bottle, and as 1970 succeeds 1966 as the next current vintage, it will probably double in value in the next two years. All this for a wine which only got to the shops in 1975 – at £3.45 a bottle, compared to Cockburn's Ruby at £2.29.

Port: a historical price survey

	Year of sale 1966	1968	1972	1975	1977	1978	1979	1981	1982	1983
1960 Vintage										
Dow	26/6	32/-	£2.16	£3.74	£5.42	—	£10.44	—	—	—
Graham	—	—	£2.62	—	—	—	—	—	£16.34	—
Quinta do Noval	—	—	£2.55	£3.61	£5.00	£7.50	—	£11.68	£15.71	—
Taylor	—	—	£2.62	£4.60	—	£8.64	—	—	—	—
1963 Vintage										
Dow	24/6	29/-	£1.90	—	—	£6.80	£9.92	—	£14.63	—
Graham	25/-	—	£2.44	—	£5.67	—	—	—	—	—
Quinta do Noval	24/6	29/-	£2.10	—	£4.91	—	—	£11.66	—	—
Taylor	25/-	—	£2.44	—	£6.25	—	—	—	—	—
1966 Vintage										
Dow	—	26/6	£1.98	£3.16	—	—	£7.90	£9.46	—	—
Graham	—	26/6	—	—	—	—	—	—	£11.99	£16.10
Quinta do Noval	—	26/6	—	—	—	—	—	£9.37	£11.52	£15.89
Taylor	—	26/6	—	£3.30	£5.00	—	—	£9.60	£13.48	£17.94
1970 Vintage										
Dow	—	—	—	—	—	£5.35	£5.80	—	—	—
Graham	—	—	—	—	£4.27	£5.34	£5.80	—	—	—
Quinta do Noval	—	—	—	—	—	—	—	—	—	£10.81
Taylor	—	—	—	£3.45	—	£5.75	£6.40	—	£11.62	£13.02
1977 Vintage										
Dow	—	—	—	—	—	—	£47.00*	—	—	£8.36
Graham	—	—	—	—	—	—	£48.00*	£7.50	£8.76	£18.26†
Quinta do Noval	—	—	—	—	—	£4.72	£4.77	—	—	—
Taylor	—	—	—	—	£4.83	—	—	£8.00	—	—

*Price per case ex Oporto †magnum

Port Classification

If you think that Burgundy and Bordeaux make a meal out of classifying their vineyards, just take a look at how rigidly port is controlled. Various factors of soil, altitude, gradient, age of vine are implicit in the French classifications, but once they have decided where the best wines *can* be made, they rather leave the rest to a gentleman's agreement that the vigneron will do his best.

Not so port. Nothing is left to chance. The age of the vines is classified on a scale from 0 to 60 points. The level of upkeep of the vines is ruthlessly marked from – 500 to + 100 points. The objective is to score as many points as possible, because the authorities allow the top scorers to turn a larger proportion of their crop into port. The highest possible score for the school swot would be + 1,680 points, while the bottom score possible would be a massively embarrassing – 3,430. They'd have to be very bad indeed to get anywhere near that.

The classification, based on points scored, is from A to F, and controls how many litres of juice per 1,000 vines can be turned into port. The rest has to go as table wine, which gives a smaller return, so there is considerable incentive for the growers to score highly.

The vineyard elements

Productivity
(Ranging from about 500 litres per 1,000 vines to about 2,000 litres; the lower the yield the better.)

Low: – 900 points High: + 120 points

Altitude
(Ranging from a highest allowable altitude of 650 metres to a lowest of 150 metres.)

Low: – 900 points High: + 150 points

Soil
(Scored according to type. Schist scores best, granite worst.)

Low: – 350 points High: + 100 points

Geographical position
(Predetermined locations score different marks.)

Low: – 50 points High: + 600 points

Upkeep of vineyard
(Good house-keeping awards for various factors.)

Low: – 500 points High: + 100 points

Variety and quality of grapes

Low: – 300 points High: + 150 points

Gradient
(From 1-in-6 to 1-in-30 – the steeper the better.)

Low: – 100 points High: + 100 points

Shelter

Low: 0 High: + 60 points

Age of vines
(With 5-year-olds scoring 30; up to 25-year-olds scoring 60.)

Low: 0 High: + 60 points

Distance root to root
(The distance from the end of one vine's root to the start of the next root – too close is frowned upon.)

Low: – 50 points High: + 50 points

The experts then add up all these points and classify the vineyards according to score as follows:

A	1,200 points or more:	Allowed to make up to 600 litres of wine per 1,000 vines
B	1,000–1,199:	600 litres allowed
C	800–999:	590 litres allowed
D	600–799:	580 litres allowed
E	400–599:	580 litres allowed
F	Below 400 points:	260 litres allowed

Price Guide

Non-vintage

£3.50–£4.00

Waitrose Fine Ruby (WAIT)
Waitrose Fine Tawny (WAIT)
Smith Woodhouse Ruby (DAV, WW, SR)
Cockburn's Ruby (WILL, WAIT, PG, YFW, GH *& others*)
Sandeman Ruby (MWS, UNW)
Cockburn's Tawny (WAIT, GH, UNW, DAV)
Warre's Ruby (SF)
Warre's Tawny (SF)
⋆Chaplin's Fine Old Wood Matured (CHAP)
Graham Ruby (PG)
Sandeman White (PG, UNW, TAN)

£4.00–£5.00

Cockburn's White Port (UNW, DAV, YFW)
Cockburn's Fine Old Ruby (JH, UNW)
Cockburn's Fine Old Tawny (JH)
Cockburn's Fine Old White (JH)
⋆The Major's Ruby (BAL)
Sandeman Tawny (UNW)
Taylor's Special Ruby (HHC, L&W, MWS)
Taylor's Special Tawny (HHC, L&W)
The Society's Port (WSOC)
⋆No. 4 Selected Old Vintages (C&B)
Croft Fine Tawny (J&B)
Croft Fine Ruby (J&B)
Taylor's Ruby Port (CDM, VIGN)
Taylor's Tawny Port (CDM, VIGN)
Smith Woodhouse Fine Old Tawny (H&D)
Fonseca Bin 27 (WAIT, PG, WILL, DOL, L&W, GH, YFW, HHC, MWS, PIP *& others*)
Graham Late Bottled 1978 (PG, SF, L&W, BWC, TAN)
Cockburn's Special Reserve (WAIT, GH, CHAP, JH, UNW)
Cockburn's Ruby, Special Reserve (PG, CHAP, UNW)
Director's Bottle, Vintage Character, Justerini & Brooks (J&B)
⋆After Dinner Port, Hicks & Don (H&D)
Taylor Late Bottled 1976 (PG, CDM, HBV, PD, TAN)

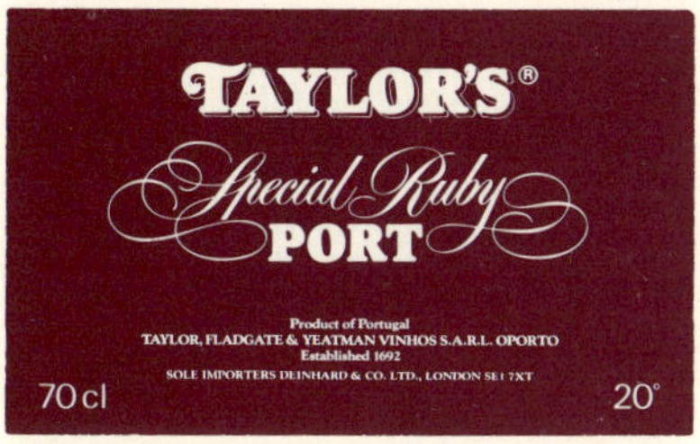

£5.00–£6.00

The Society's Vintage Character (WSOC)
The Society's Crusted Port (WSOC)
Noval Late Bottled (PG, WILL, SF, CHAP, HT, H&D, MWS, YWF, PD, TAN)
Warre's Warrior, Vintage Character (GH, WNRY)
Old Priory, Vintage Character, Smith Woodhouse (WW)
Taylor Late Bottled (HT)
Smith Woodhouse Vintage Character Port (MAL)
Taylor Late Bottled 1978 (WILL, L&W, MWS, VIGN, HHC, BOW, BAL, CV, DAV, WNRY, FINT)
Taylor's Chip Dry White Port (VIGN, CDM, WNRY, TAN, GH)
Croft Late Bottled 1978 (PD)
Old Lodge, Finest Old Tawny, Smith Woodhouse (WW)
Smith Woodhouse Late Bottled 1974 (SF, CHAP)

£6.00–£8.00

⋆Quinta Gold Cap Very Fine Old Tawny (BAL)
Cockburn Crusting, Bottled 1978 (JH)
Cockburn's Crusted, Bottled 1974 (WSOC)
⋆Warre Late Bottled 1974 (SR, RH, HHC, CV)
⋆Graham Tawny, 10 year old (PG, MACK)
Investiture Finest Vintage Reserve (AV)
Taylor Crusted (PG)
Old Chandos Tawny (WSOC)
⋆Warre's Nimrod Tawny (GH, HHC, H&B, WSOC, MAL, WNRY)
Fonseca 10 year old Tawny (HT, CDM, REID, VIGN)
Warre Late Bottled 1979 (SF)
Taylor Crusted Port, Bottled 1978 (L&W, C&B)

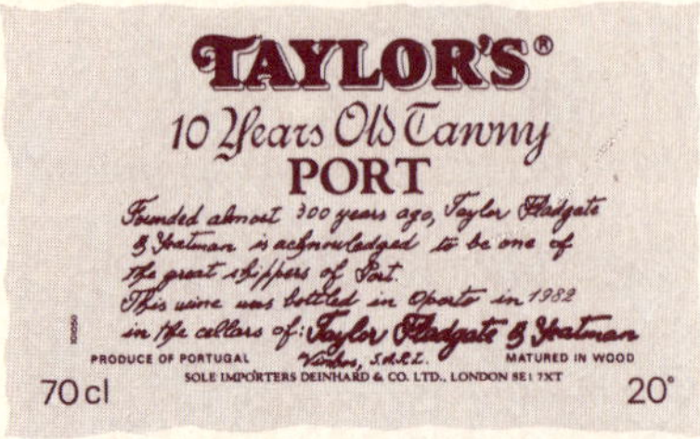

Noval Tawny 10 year old (MACK)
Dow Crusted Port, Bottled 1978 (TAN)
⋆Taylor Tawny, 10 year old (PG, MWS, TAN)
Taylor Crusted Port, Bottled 1973 (BBR)
⋆Warre Late Bottled 1969 (SR, CHAP, FFW, CV, C&B, H&D)
Smith Woodhouse Late Bottled 1974 (BBR)

£8.00–£10.00
Fonseca Guimaraens (BIB)
⋆Quarles Harris Crusted Port (TW)

£11.00–£13.50
⋆Graham Quinta dos Malvedos 1965 (BWC)
⋆Graham Malvedos Port 1967 (UNW)
⋆Graham Tawny, 20 year old (PG, TAN)
Quinta do Noval, 20 year old Tawny (HT)
⋆Taylor Tawny, 20 year old (PG, GH)
Fonseca 20 year old Tawny (MAL)

c. £30.00
⋆Taylor Tawny, 40 year old (PG, TAN)

1980

£8.00–£9.00
Delaforce, Quinta da Corte (C&B)
Taylor (MAL, L&W, YFW, MWS, WHIT, PG, HHC, TAN, J&B, BBR)
Warre (L&W, WSOC, J&B, TAN, BBR)
Fonseca (SF, L&W, C&B, BAL, J&B, BBR)
Graham (L&W, BAL, J&B, TAN, BBR)

£9.00–£10.50
Quarles Harris (HHC)
Dow (BAL, HHC, J&B, TAN, BBR, C&B)
Berry's Own Selection (BBR)
Sandeman (TAN, J&B)
Croft, Quinta da Roêda (C&B, J&B)
Gould Campbell (J&B, BBR)

1978

£7.50–£10.00
Taylor Quinta de Vargellas (BOW)
Quinta do Noval (SF, MWS, ESV, WILL, J&B)
⋆Croft, Quinta da Roêda (C&B)

1977

£7.25–£9.00
Gould Campbell (WHIT, MAL, WSOC, OWL, TAN, MACK, BBR, WILL)
Smith Woodhouse (MAL, SR)
Quarles Harris (VIGN, BBR)
Warre (SR, L&W, BIB, CHAP, TAN, BOW, ESV, FINT, UNW, WILL . . .)
Graham (SR, BIB, GH, ODD, L&W, ESV, FINT, WHIT, UNW, WILL *& others*)
Dow (SR, L&W, CHAP, GH, BAL, HHC, ESV, UNW, TAN, YFW *& others*)
Offley (WILL)
Croft (TAN, MAL, L&W, UNW, J&B, BBR, C&B)
Fonseca (SR, SF, L&W, CHAP, ADN, FINT, ESV, WILL, BYR, TAN *& others*)
Sandeman (TAN, ODD, BAL, FINT, UNW, PD, JH, J&B, BBR)
Offley Boa Vista (TAN)
Taylor (MWS, L&W, UNW, BYR, PG, VIGN, WHIT, YFW, WILL, J&B *& others*)
Warre, Smith Woodhouse (WW)

£10.00–£11.00
Delaforce (PD, J&B, OWL)
Berry's Own Selection (BBR)
⋆Justerini & Brooks (J&B)

1975

£6.00–£7.00
Offley Boa Vista (ADN)
⋆Croft (SR, MAL, L&W, WHIT, REID, BBR, HUN, J&B, OWL, C&B, YFW *& others*)
Dow (SR, BIB, ADN, C&B, ESV, BYR, J&B, HHC, BBR, UNW *& others*)
Delaforce (ADN, BBR, J&B, DOL, PD)
Gould Campbell (WHIT, J&B, BBR)
Graham (REID, ODD, MAL, L&W, AV, WHIT, BYR, JH, GH, PD *& others*)
Rebello Valente (REID, ESV)
⋆Smith Woodhouse (VIGN, WHIT, WSOC, J&B, UNW)

£7.00–£8.50
Quinta do Noval (BIB, L&W, WHIT, MAL, BBR, J&B, WILL)
Cockburn (ADN, L&W, MAL, BYR, JH, BBR, J&B, UNW, C&B, WILL)

Sandeman (ADN, AV, BYR, BBR, H&B, FINT)
★Corney and Barrow's Special Quinta (C&B)
Warre (L&W, WHIT, ODD, BAL, ESV, REID, SF, BYR, C&B, WILL *& others*)
Fonseca (MAL, AV, L&W, BYR, GH, BBR, J&B)
Taylor (L&W, BYR, UNW, VIGN, BBR, WHIT, TAN, WILL, YFW)
Berry's Own Selection (BBR)
Martinex (JH)
Offley (WILL)

1974
£6.00–£7.00
Dow Reserve (HUN)
Smith Woodhouse (SR)
Taylor Quinta de Vargellas (BOW)

1972
£7.00–£8.00
Offley (BAL)
Dow (DAV)
Taylor Quinta de Vargellas (ODD, L&W, SR, WAIT, HHC, CV, PG, BOW, MAL)
c. £9.00
Offley Boa Vista (WGA)

1970
£8.00–£10.00
Sandeman (ADN, REID, UNW, BYR, WILL, BBR, WNRY)
Offley Boa Vista (L&W, C&B, PD, J&B, TAN)
Gould Campbell (WHIT, TW)
Martinez (CHAP, REID, BIB, JH)
Fonseca (AV, SR, HT, BAL, C&B, CDM, ODD, BYR, L&W, PD *& others*)
Dow (ADN, UNW, PG, ESV, WILL, C&F, REID, HHC, BYR *& others*)
Quinta do Noval (BIB, C&B, PD, WHIT, WILL, FINT, TW, TAN, BBR, J&B, H&B)
Warre (UNW, L&W, ESV, C&B, GH, WILL, BIB, BYR, WHIT, J&B)
Smith Woodhouse (TAN, PG, UNW)
Cockburn (ADN, PG, BIB, HHC, BYR, JH, FINT, WILL, TW, J&B *& others*)
Croft (ADN, HT, C&B, WGA, J&B, WNRY)

£10.00–£12.00
Offley (WILL)
Graham (HT, GH, WHIT, L&W, PG, HUN, DOL, BBR, WGA, J&B, WILL)
★Delaforce (PD, J&B, BBR)
£11.00–£12.00
Fonseca, Smith Woodhouse (WW)
Taylor (BYR, L&W, HT, WAIT, ODD, PG, WHIT, VIGN, BIB, J&B *& others*)
Rebello Valente (BBR)

1969
£8.50–£10.00
Warre, Smith Woodhouse (WW)
Taylor Quinta de Vargellas (DOL)

1968
c. £8.00
Fonseca Guimaraens (SF, ODD, L&W, HT, SR, GH, VIGN, CV, BOW, YFW)
c. £11.00
Taylor Quinta de Vargellas (YFW)

1967
£11.00–£13.00
Taylor Quinta de Vargellas (SR, HT, ADN, REID, RH, CV, VIGN, TAN, BBR)
Cockburn (REID, BAL, L&W, ODD, DAV, JH, BYR, TAN, WILL, MACK, WHIT . . .)
Sandeman (DOL, H&B, BYR, WHIT, UNW) UNW)
Martinez (TW, WHIT)
Croft (HT)

1966
£10.00–£12.00
Offley (WILL)
Gould Campell (WSOC, BBR)
Sandeman (AV, HHC, WHIT, BIB, J&B)
£12.50–£14.00
Croft (HT, VIGN, BBR, J&B, HUN)
Berry's Own Selection (BBR)
Taylor (HT, AV, JH, WHIT, C&B, TW, J&B, TAN, GH, YFW)
£14.00–£16.00
Rebello Valente (CHAP)

Quinta do Noval (WW, HHC, L&W, MACK, WHIT, SR, C&B, BBR, J&B, TAN, WGA)
Warre (HHC, TW, C&B, MACK, WHIT, TAN, HUN, WILL, H&B)
Dow (DAV, HHC, BBR, J&B, WILL, WHIT, MACK, RH, YFW)
Delaforce (BBR)
Offley Boa Vista (BBR)
Fonseca (HHC, C&B, BBR, J&B, WGA, YFW, GH)
Graham (BBR, GH, MACK, C&B, TAN, WILL)
c. £20.00
Cockburn (HUN)

1965
£8.50–£10.00
Fonseca Guimaraens (WAIT, TAN)
Guimaraens (L&W, DOL, CV, UNW)
Graham Quinta dos Malvedos (WILL, H&D, PG, HT, L&W, DOL, YFW, LADV, TAN)
c. £13.00
Taylor Quinta de Vargellas (BBR)

1964
c. £9.50
Guimaraens (WSOC, PG, BAL, HT)

1963
c. £11.00
Offley Boa Vista (L&W, WSOC, C&B, TAN)
Rebello Valente (MACK, CHAP, VIGN, BBR)
£15.00–£17.50
Offley (WILL)
Quinta do Noval (WHIT, BAL, ESV, L&W, REID, J&B, WGA, WNRY, C&B)
Delaforce (BBR)
Martinez (WHIT, JH)
Croft (ADN, MAL, BAL, REID, HT, TAN, C&B, BIB, BOW)
Fonseca (ADN, WHIT, HT, L&W, J&B, C&B, YFW)

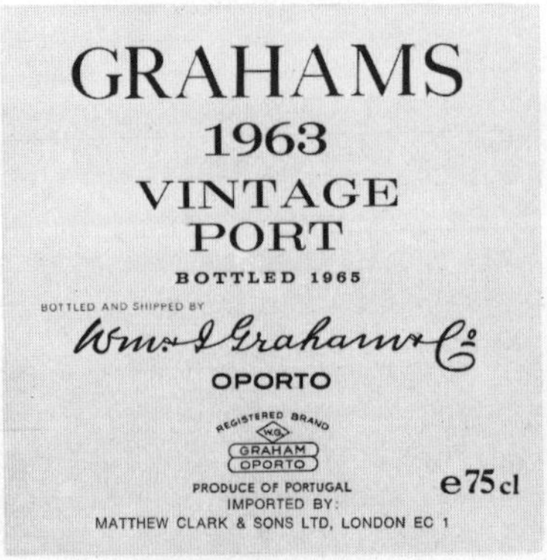

Graham (ADN, HHC, HT, L&W, WHIT, BIB, C&B, WILL)
Warre (ADN, L&W, REID, C&B, HUN, BIB, H&B, WILL)
Sandeman (REID, SR, ODD, HUN, WHIT)
Cockburn (MAL, HHC, VIGN, L&W, JH, J&B, WGA, C&B, HUN, BIB, YFW)
£17.50–£20.00
Gould Campbell (J&B)
Graham, Smith Woodhouse (WW)
£20.00–£25.00
Dow (FINT, HUN, WILL, C&B, BIB, YFW)
Taylor (GH, J&B, L&W, BOW, BIB, C&B, TW, YFW)

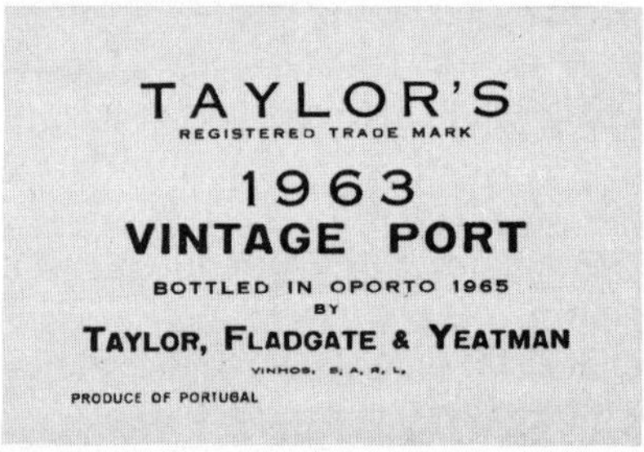

1961
c. £12.00
Graham Malvedos (HT)

1960
£12.00–£15.00
Sandeman (AV, VIGN, H&B, J&B, BIB)
Martinez (L&W, REID, TAN, FINT)
Cockburn (WHIT, REID, TAN, WILL)
Fonseca (WHIT, REID)
Dow (REID, L&W, HHC, J&B, WHIT, WILL)
Quinta do Noval (VIGN, REID, C&B)
Graham (L&W, HHC, REID, HT, HUN, BOW, WILL, C&B)
Warre (L&W, REID, GH, HUN, WHIT, BIB, C&B)
£17.50–£25.00
Croft (WHIT, HUN, WILL, TAN, BIB, C&B, YFW)
Offley Boa Vista (TAN)
Taylor (WILL)

1958
£10.00–£12.50
Quarles Harris (BIB)
Quinta do Noval (AV, REID, CHAP)
£13.00–£16.00
Sandeman (REID, VIGN)
Taylor Quinta de Vargellas (SR, BOW)

1957
c. £11.50
Sandeman (AV)

1955
£20.00–£30.00
Gould Campbell (MAL)
Martinez (WHIT, L&W, TAN)
Graham (HHC)
Warre (CHAP)
Quinta do Noval (L&W)
Dow (L&W)
£30.00–£35.00
Sandeman (REID)
Cockburn (WHIT, MACK, TAN, YFW, REID)
Croft (REID)
£40.00–£45.00
Fonseca (REID)
Taylor (J&B, L&W, BIB, YFW)

1950
c. £17.50
Sandeman (REID, MACK)
£20.00–£25.00
Cockburn (REID)
Taylor (VIGN)

1948
£35.00–£45.00
Fonseca (MAL)
Taylor (WHIT, BIB)
Sandeman (VIGN)
c. £60.00
Graham (BIB)

1947
£25.00–£30.00
Warre (MAL)
Cockburn (MAL, VIGN)
c. £40.00
Tuke Holdsworth (J&B)

1946
c. £35.00
Sandeman (VIGN)

1945
c. £40.00
Croft (MAL)
c. £75.00
Sandeman (REID)
Graham (BIB)
c. £100.00
Taylor (YFW)

1935
c. £40.00
Sandeman (BIB)
c. £56.00
Taylor (MAL)

1927
c. £45.00
Feuerheerd (VIGN)
c. £65.00
Fonseca (REID)

GOOD PROSPECTS FOR PORT

1984 is seeing port shippers looking happy and excited for the first time in years. Although the UK is a much smaller export market than France, we have traditionally been the strongest market for the top wines – the vintage ports – as well as taking a fair chunk of ordinary ruby and tawny. These latter were usually bottled here, but the basic wines are beginning to lose out to the Oporto-bottled 'speciality' ports. There's no question that this is the growth area which most excites the port shippers. They have been searching for the middle ground for some time to fill the gap between the spit and sawdust, port 'n' lemon image at one end, and the silent, dignified stuffiness of old-fashioned vintage at the other.

The Late-Bottled Vintage port style fills that bill beautifully, and all the companies who promoted one in 1983 reported an upsurge in sales. Come the time, come the port. Actually LB, as they call it, has been around for ages. Quinta do Noval LB, Taylor's LB, Cockburn's Special Reserve. The masterstroke was to promote the vintage word and not charge the vintage price. You don't get the vintage flavour either, because these ports have spent five years in big vats softening up, while real vintage is bottled hard and violent after only two years in the wood.

You can also feel that the shippers are itching to get their hands on another declared vintage, with the current boom in value of these top wines and recently some shippers did declare a 1982. In the meantime, we should see more effort going into promoting the high-quality, single-quinta vintage wines from undeclared years, which give you a taste of vintage at a (just) affordable price.

MADEIRA

THE COST OF A BOTTLE

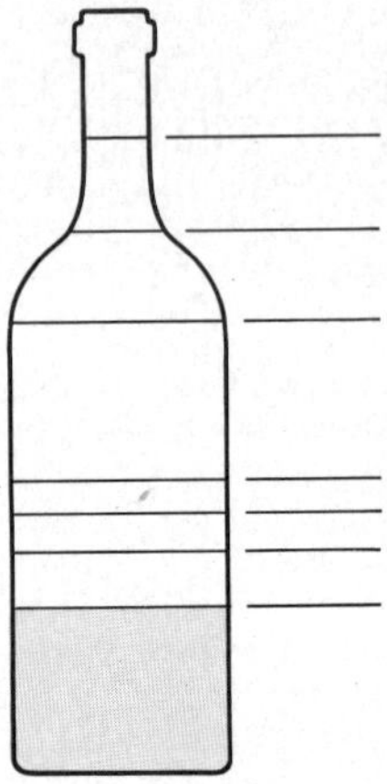

Good Company Sercial	£4.50
VAT	0.58
Merchant mark-up	0.89
Duty	1.16
Distribution	0.20
Shipping	0.15
Bottling	0.26
Wine	1.26

Madeira has an inescapably brown image: the brown of old wallpaper, of deep leather chairs, of well-cut country suits from a bygone age, and, just occasionally, of the deep amber candle-glint against a mahogany dining-table, or the matching tones of a rich fruit-cake. If that sounds a bit fanciful, just think – when did you last taste madeira? Have you ever? If you have, was it as a pick-me-up on the way to the disco, or was it as a welcome conversation-loosener with a rarely visited and distinctly elderly distant relative? While other fortified wines like port and sherry have made some attempt to brighten up their act, and, as the Portuguese officials so tantalisingly put it, 'educate and seduce a younger audience', madeira has stayed firmly behind the lace curtains, wedged between last season's copies of *Country Life* and the doilies. You can almost see the dust raise its voice in protest as the cork is eased out.

And I'm talking about one of the world's greatest wines – yes, I mean it! Madeira *is* one of the great wines of the world, and in the nineteenth century our forebears would have had as good a time drooling over their choicest madeiras as over clarets and vintage ports. But the Victorian vine plagues of oidium and phylloxera hit the tiny island off the African coast far harder than they hit the European mainland, and when the Madeirans got round to replanting, most of them used the kind of hybrid vines which had been banned throughout all of Europe's fine wine areas for generations.

Madeira is a fortified wine, like port, but gets much of its uniqueness from being 'cooked', very gently, in or above warm storerooms (at around 45°C) for a period of months after the brandy has been added. It used to get a free cruise to the East Indies and back to get baked by the tropical sun, but aeroplanes and containerisation put a stop to that perk. It should be made from one of four 'noble' grapes; the Sercial, a type of Riesling, which makes a superbly biting, smokey, dry wine; the Verdelho, softer and slightly sweeter; the Bual, making a big sweet wine; and the Malmsey or Malvasia, whose wine, smokey, acid and treacly all at once, is one of the truly great rich wines.

That *should* be it. But there's a fifth grape, ominously titled Negra Tinta Mole, which actually accounts for 80 per cent of the plantation, and which is simply bashed about in different ways to produce wines in the above four styles. If it wasn't for *sauce madère* providing a regular income for this, 'no questions asked' Tinta Mole madeira the whole island might have gone over to banana production – which it's rather good at, and which commands a pretty good year-in, year-out price.

But luckily the good guys held on, and, with the prospect of strict labelling laws when Portugal joins the EEC, the Instituto do Vinho da Madeira was formed in 1979 to bring back quality and credibility to the island's wine. Just in time. Those Sercials will now have to be at least 85 per cent Sercial grapes rather than early-picked Negra Tinta Mole.

Since the plantations of Sercial have dropped to just one and a half per cent of the island's noble grape quota, the Institute's crash programme of replanting has come none too soon.

The Institute certainly took the bull by the horns. It simply made it illegal for any madeira maker to produce wine from the non-noble hybrid grapes. End of argument. And it created a 5:1 differential between noble and non-noble grape prices. It also realised that if Madeira were to have any chance in the modern world, it had to do what it was best at – making fabled fortified wines of high quality and capable of almost limitless ageing. Stuck in the middle of the Atlantic, with half the vineyards steep enough to practise the Cresta Run on, there was absolutely no point in allowing the production of young undistinguished wines to go a step further. So the Institute enforced a reduction on exports until the production of noble grape wines could be seen to surpass the volume of sales. Exports dropped by 30 per cent, but companies began once again to build up stocks, taking care to mature the wine gently, blend it skilfully, and having the confidence to wait for it to blossom. Madeira will now become more expensive, but 1983 saw the first signs of the UK market beginning to take it seriously again. Sainsbury's have introduced an own label, and the Sunday Times Wine Club launched their Malmsey and Sercial in October 1983 – and sold out in six weeks. If madeira really is making a comeback, breathe a sigh of relief. The world of wine can't afford to lose one of its great originals.

PRICE GUIDE

Non-vintage
£4.00–£5.00
Bual, Henriques & Henriques (PG)
Malmsey, Henriques & Henriques (PG)
Sercial, Henriques & Henriques (PG)
Verdelho, Henriques & Henriques (PG)
Bual Old Trinity House, Rutherford & Miles (BIB, HT, HBV, HHC, H&D, CV, UNW, LADV)
Sercial Extra Pale, Rutherford & Miles (BIB, CV, YFW)
La Reina Verdelho, Rutherford & Miles (BIB, HBV, HT, BOW, H&D, YFW)
Bual Old Trinity, Rutherford & Miles (BOW, YFW, TAN)
Fine Old Malmsey, Rutherford & Miles (HT, H&D, CV, YFW, TAN)
Moscatel de Setubal 5 year old (ODD)
Sercial, Rutherford & Miles (HBV, BOW, LADV)
Malmsey, Rutherford & Miles (HBV, BOW)
Good Company Sercial, Cossart Gordon (CHAP, ESV, MACK, MAL)
Good Company Rainwater, Cossart Gordon (CHAP, SR, ESV, WSOC, VIGN, MACK)
Good Company Bual, Cossart Gordon (CHAP, ESV, MACK)
Good Company Malmsey, Cossart Gordon (CHAP, SR, HHC, ESV, MACK, MAL)
Duke of Clarence Malmsey (GH, DAV, UNW)
Good Company Sercial Dry, Cossart Gordon (HHC)
La Reina East India Verdelho, Rutherford & Miles (CV, TAN)
Fine Old Malmsey (WSOC)
⋆Finest Old Sercial, Cossart Gordon (SR, ESV, VIGN)
⋆Finest Old Bual, Cossart Gordon (SR, VIGN)
Finest Malmsey, Cossart Gordon (ESV, SR, VIGN)
⋆Leacock's Sercial (STWC)
£5.00–£7.50
Old East India Madeira (ESV)

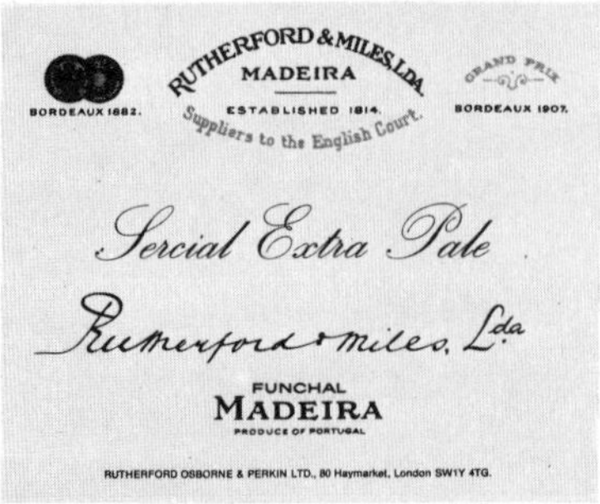

Sercial (WSOC)
Reserve Malmsey, Bottled 1981 (BBR)
Reserve Bual, Bottled 1981 (BBR)
£7.50–£10.00
Moscatel de Setubal 25 year old (ODD)
★Blandy's 10 year old, Malmsey (H&B)
£10.00–£12.50
Reserve Malmsey, Rutherford & Miles (BOW)
Duo Centenary Celebration, Very Old Bual, Cossart Gordon (ADN, L&W, S&R, CHAP, TAN, HHC, ESV, LADV, AV, REID)
Very Old Duo-Century Medium Rich, Cossart Gordon (WSOC)
c. £20.00
Malmsey 1863 Solera (TAN)
Bual 1845 Solera, Cossart Gordon (VIGN)
£21.00–£25.00
Finest Old Verdelho 1851 Solera, Bottled 1973 (BBR)
Verdelho 1880 Solera, Blandy (H&B)
Malmsey 1863 Solera, Blandy (H&B)
£30.00–£30.00
Sercial 1835 Solera, Blandy (VIGN)
Bual 1820 Solera, Lomelino (VIGN)
Bual 1845 Solera, Cossart Gordon (SR)
Bual 1815 Solera, Cossart Gordon (VIGN)
Sercial Extra Pale, Rutherford & Miles (TAN, H&D)

1954
c. £16.50
Bual, Henriques & Henriques (PG)
c. £43.00
Malmsey, Cossart Gordon (SR)

1952
c. £21.00
Verdelho Vintage, Leacocks (TAN)

1950
£12.50–£13.50
Sercial, Rutherford & Miles (PG)
c. £25.00
Sercial Vintage, Rutherford & Miles (VIGN)

1940
c. £29.00
Sercial, Bottled 1961 (BBR)

1934
£19.50–£21.00
Bual, Rutherford & Miles (PG)
Verdelho, Henriques & Henriques (PG)
£30.00–£40.00
Verdelho, Cossart Gordon (L&W)
Verdelho Vintage (MAL)
Bual Vintage (MAL)
Verdelho Vintage, Cossart Gordon (ESV, SR)
Bual Vintage, Cossart Gordon (SR)
c. £42.50
Bual Vintage, Rutherford & Miles (VIGN)
1920
£32.50–£37.50
Malmsey, Cossart Gordon (L&W)
Malmsey Vintage (MAL)
Bual, Bottled 1964 (BBR)
Malmsey, Bottled 1964 (BBR)
Malmsey Vintage, Cossart's (ESV)
£37.50–£42.50
Bual, Cossart Gordon (J&B)
Malmsey Vintage, Cossart Gordon (VIGN)
1916
£42.00–£47.50
Malmsey Vintange, Cossart's (ESV)
Malmsey Vintage (MAL)
Malmsey, Cossart Gordon (LADV)
1915
c. £39.50
Bual, Cossart Gordon (L&W, LADV)
1914
c. £40.50
Bual, Bottled 1961 (BBR)
1910
c. £37.00
Sercial, Cossart Gordon (L&W)
1907
£35.00–£40.00
Bual Vintage, Blandy (H&B)
Bual Vintage, Blandy (VIGN)
1905
c. £46.50
Sercial, Bottled 1961 (BBR)
1895
£45.00–£47.50
Bual, Cossart Gordon (L&W)
Malmsey Vintage (MAL)
c. £58.00
1895 Bual Vintage, Cossart (ESV)
1880
c. £60.00
Malmsey Vintage, Blandy (H&B)
1875
c. £60.00
1875 Sercial Vintage, Blandy (VIGN)

CALIFORNIA

AND THE PACIFIC NORTHWEST

California wines are down in price. How, you may ask, with a dollar riding arrogantly high and our pound seemingly languishing in awe of it? Common sense is the simple answer to that. Geoffrey Roberts, the UK's most influential importer of a wide range of California wines, has gone over there and done some straight talking. If you want to keep your expanding UK market, he's told them, you've got to stay competitive.

The whole world wants a slice of the UK action. Everyone sees northern Europe as prime target for their wines, and the following here for California wine is far too fragile to cope with mindless price hikes. Link that to a sudden surplus of production in the Golden State, while European wines flood into the US on that same strength of the dollar versus their feeble currencies and, luckily, the California producers could see the present slight surplus developing into an industry-strangling glut if they didn't act immediately.

So they not only kept prices stable, they reduced them. Vintage on vintage, prices *dropped* by up to £24 a case (yes, £2 per bottle) for the Edna Valley 1982 Chardonnay as against the 1981, and £26 a case for Mondavi's 81 against his 80 Chardonnay. And this means, as French prices for claret and white burgundy climb ever higher, that for the first time California wine can not only compete on quality terms, but can be better value than the French equivalent.

But, you may say, I don't like the California style; it's too big, it's too fat, it's too greasy and top-heavy with taste. Then you haven't tasted the latest releases. Acidity is there, the oak sweetness has turned to the more exciting smokey, savoury oak of Côte d'Or burgundy, and the alcohol levels now keep your head clear enough to be able to enunciate phrases like 'Another bottle, please', without having to repeat yourself and pretend that slurred s's run in the family.

And it's not just Chardonnays. Sauvignon Blanc, the new fad grape closely following Chardonnay's success, has been fat, blowsy and dull for all its years in California soil. Not anymore. The 1982 vintage shows for the first time a burst of varietal definition. Some of them are sporting the sharp gooseberry greenness of Upper Loire Sauvignons, some of them are showing the moist honey richness of the great white Bordeaux, but, either way, they're showing character. The Chenin Blanc, for so long in California a rather soft and seedy workhorse grape, sweetish, biscuity, and far from refreshing is going back to its high-acid French roots, but taking a honeyed ripeness with it.

In reds, the same thing is happening. At last, natural fruit flavours, balanced by oak and tannin, are taking over the California style. And it's long overdue. Since about 1976, when the idea of France versus California tastings was first mooted, we've seen hairy great hulks piling across the Atlantic looking for trouble. Comparison, comparison was what they were itching for. American Cabernet makers were full of boasts that no Bordeaux classed growth stood a chance against their wholesome all-American product. The white Chardonnays were wheeled out for the same purpose, and even the volatile, fickle Pinot Noir wines were held aloft as being Burgundy's peers.

I remember those wines. And I remember those tastings. They were usually set up as 'Old World vs. New World' battles, and the objective was always to *prove* that California was better than Europe. And that's usually how it turned out. But what is better? Richer? Stronger? More mind-blowing? I frequently felt rather sorry for the French wines, since their more subtle virtues were literally blasted aside by the bruisers from the West. Which proved two things. First, that the tastings were normally loaded in favour of the strong, brash flavours of the California valleys. Second, that comparison must be like with like, and, in the late 1970s, the styles of French and California wine weren't even similar, let alone comparable.

But it was flattery, in a curious way. California aspired to the great wines of Europe. These were the models the ambitious winemaker had to beat. But a thousand years of trial and error, perfecting your product, is surely going to weather a few full-frontal setbacks from California's rising stars. The exciting thing about California now is that the European lessons of subtlety, balance, perfume and even beauty in a wine seem to have been taken to heart so quickly. After all, 10 years ago California wine was virtually a domestic phenomenon. Now it can command more column inches per release than any other wine in the world.

Common sense again. Faced with a crisis of production in California, and a surge of imported wines, the good wineries and wine makers are starting to offer the markets the flavours they want at an affordable price. It is most immediately obvious in the whites, but the reds, too, are beginning to lose that hot, raisin and berry taste, which became such a clear California marker that it often concealed any further flavours the wine might possess. This change of heart has come just in time, because, although US wine exports to the UK show a massive rise from 1978 to 1983, this was from a tiny base. There was even a *drop* in 1983, and the success of the Paul Masson carafe range distorts the figures. The simple fact was that California wines were becoming too expensive here, and better value was apparent, not only from Europe itself, but from Australia, New Zealand, Chile and elsewhere in America – the Pacific Northwest, in particular, and now even New York State. There's no doubt that California can make some of the world's great wines, and as the period of bashing Europe over the head recedes, we'll now have a chance to see just how good those Chardonnays, Sauvignons, Cabernets, Zinfandels and Pinot Noirs can be.

But California will be facing stiff competition from up the road in Oregon and Washington, as well as some gentle ribbing from the unlikely bounds of New York State, whence the Sauvignons, Rieslings and Chardonnays so far released from such outfits as Vinifera Vineyards, Gold Seal, and Hargrave out on Long Island, show all the cool, acid-sharp flavours that the Californians crave, as well as enough ripeness to let the varietal taste blossom. However, Pacific Northwest is more than just a nudge in the ribs. Mark Savage of Windrush Wines, who is the leading importer of Oregon and Washington wines in the UK, believes that in terms of style and cost, the Northwest is about to hit a winning streak. He reckons that a Pacific Northwest wine will only be half to three-quarters of the cost of a California equivalent, citing Oregon Chardonnays at £48 a case versus Napa equivalents at £70–£80, and Pinot Noirs where the difference is easily £15 or £20 a case. Admittedly there is as yet less demand for Washington and Oregon wines, but then there is a far lower level of investment, and far less pressure to recoup large amounts to combat high interest rates.

There are, as yet, fewer than 50 producers in the Northwest, and Oregon, in particular, has no 'jug wine' producers to cheapen its overall image, and no big wineries of any sort. Knudsen Erath, probably the state's most important outfit, produces 80,000 cases, very middle-range in California terms. Most of the wineries are of the small family type, and with Pinot Noir much in evidence, comparisons with single domaine burgundies are inevitably being made in the press.

While California is now struggling to

reduce alcohol levels and preserve fruit, the Northwest's natural style of wine achieves that without breaking sweat. The wines usually come in with two degrees less alcohol, and the difference is most marked in precisely those varietals that California finds most difficult – Riesling, Sauvignon and Pinot Noir. The slower-ripened fruit brings exactly that refreshing, northern European feel to the whites which meet modern market needs, and that same balance is drawing rave reviews for the Pinot Noirs. Me? I'm reserving judgement, because, although burgundian in style, they're on Côte de Beaune Villages level not Premier Cru.

Price Guide

Reds

Non-vintage
£2.50–£3.00
Delicato Vineyards Mountain Red (SR)
Geoffrey Roberts California Reserve (CUL, STUD, BIB, CDM)
Paul Masson Californian Red litre (WAIT, THRE, PD, ASHE, CUL)
Sainsbury's Zinfandel (SAIN)
£3.25–£4.50
California Red, les Amis du Vin (LADV)
★Round Hill House Cabernet (WW)
Paul Masson Cabernet Sauvignon (PD)
Christian Brothers Zinfandel (J&B)
£5.00–£6.00
★Inglenook Cabernet Sauvignon (ASHE)
Trefethen Eshcol Table (CDM, LADV, WNRY)
Fetzer Premium Red (STUD)

1981
£3.00–£3.50
Paul Masson Zinfandel (PG)
Paul Masson Cabernet Sauvignon (STUD)
c. £9.50
Chateau Chevalier Pinot Noir (STUD)

c. £15.50
Diamond Creek Cabernet Sauvignon Volcanic Hill (WW)

1980
c. £3.75
★Louis Martini Zinfandel (SR)
£7.00–£8.50
Simi Chardonnay (C&B)
Trefethen Pinot Noir (L&W, STUD)
Ridge Zinfandel Paso Robles (HT, LADV, CDM, STUD)
St Clement Cabernet Sauvignon (WW)
£9.25–£9.75
Ridge Zinfandel Geyserville (ADN)
Matanzas Creek Merlot (WW)
Chateau Chevalier Cabernet Sauvignon (STUD)
Robert Mondavi Reserve Pinot Noir (STUD)
Sterling Merlot (CDM)
£10.75–£11.75
Iron Horse Cabernet Sauvignon (STUD)
Ridge Cabernet Sauvignon (STUD)
Matanzas Creek Cabernet Sauvignon (WW)
Carneros Creek Pinot Noir (STUD)

__Webster's__ is an annual publication. We welcome suggestions for next year's edition.

1979
£3.00–£3.75
Paul Masson Cabernet Sauvignon (PG)

Paul Masson Pinot Noir (PG)
Concannon Zinfandel (STUD)
Almaden Cabernet Sauvignon (PG, CV)

£4.25–£5.50

Inglenook Zinfandel (JH)
Inglenook Cabernet Sauvignon (JH)
Pedroncelli Cabernet Sauvignon (C&B)
Firestone Merlot (STUD)
Parducci Wine Cellars Cabernet Sauvignon (LADV)

£6.00–£7.00

Firestone Pinot Noir (VIGN)
Lytton Springs Zinfandel (VIGN)
Clos du Val Zinfandel (REID)
Firestone Cabernet Sauvignon (CDM)

£7.50–£8.50

Clos du Val Cabernet Sauvignon (REID)
Clos du Val Merlot (AV, STUD)
Chateau Montelena Zinfandel (STUD)
Joseph Phelps Syrah (STUD)
Trefethen Cabernet Sauvignon (GH, BIB)
Ridge Zinfandel Paso Robles (ADN, HHC, TAN)
Jekel Pinot Noir (STUD)

£9.00–£10.50

Conn Creek Cabernet Sauvignon (WW)
Clos du Bois Merlot (HUN)

Jekel Cabernet Sauvignon (STUD)
Stag's Leap Cabernet Sauvignon (CDM, STUD, C&B, VIGN)
Chalone Pinot Noir (ADN)
⋆Sterling Cabernet Sauvignon (LADV, CDM)

c. £12.75

Stag's Leap Chardonnay (C&B)

1978

£3.25–£4.75

Almaden Zinfandel (CHAP, MART, CV)
Wente Bros Cabernet Sauvignon (HT, STUD)
Louis Martini Zinfandel (H&D)
⋆Papagni Zinfandel (PG)
⋆Louis Martini Cabernet Sauvignon (SR, BIB, H&D, WSOC, STUD)

£5.00–£6.50

Simi Zinfandel (C&B)
⋆Firestone Ambassador's Vineyard Merlot (LADV, HT, MAL)
Heitz Grignolino (VIGN)
Conn Creek Zinfandel (L&W, STUD)
Firestone Santa Ynez Merlot (HUN)
Firestone Pinot Noir (HT, LADV)

£6.75–£7.25

Clos du Val Zinfandel (REID)
Dry Creek Zinfandel (MAL)
Firestone Cabernet Sauvignon (HT, STUD)
Joseph Phelps Zinfandel (GH, LADV)
Trefethen Pinot Noir (BIB)
Dry Creek Cabernet Sauvignon(WNRY)
Spring Mountain Cabernet Sauvignon (VIGN)
⋆Clos du Val Merlot (REID)

__Webster's__ has been compiled from the latest merchants' catalogues available at the time of going to press but neither we nor the merchants listed can guarantee that all the wines mentioned will be available by the time you read the book. Equally, other wines and new vintages will become available.

£8.00–£9.00
★St Clement Cabernet Sauvignon (L&W)
Clos du Val Cabernet Sauvignon (REID, STUD)
Trefethen Cabernet Sauvignon (WSOC, TAN)
★Robert Mondavi Cabernet Sauvignon (STUD, CDM, LADV, TAN)

Joseph Phelps Syrah (WNRY, LADV)
£9.25–£10.00
Joseph Phelps Cabernet Sauvignon (WSOC, CDM, STUD, TAN)
Freemark Abbey Cabernet Sauvignon (STUD)
Mount Veeder Cabernet Sauvignon (STUD)
Jekel Cabernet Sauvignon Private Reserve (L&W)
£10.50–£12.50
Robert Mondavi Pinot Noir Reserve (MAL)
Carneros Creek Pinot Noir (MWS)
Stag's Leap Merlot (C&B, STUD)
Ridge Cabernet Sauvignon York Creek (ADN, L&W)
Heitz Cabernet Sauvignon (STUD)
c. £16.25
Chateau Montelena Cabernet Sauvignon (STUD)
c. £21.00
Robert Mondavi Cabernet Sauvignon Reserve (LADV)
c. £25.50
Heitz Martha's Vineyard Cabernet Sauvignon (STUD)

1977
£5.00–£6.00
Cuvaison Zinfandel (L&W)
Zaca Mesa Cabernet Sauvignon (L&W)
Veedercrest Cabernet Sauvignon (VIGN)
Firestone Cabernet Sauvignon (BIB, MAL)
Simi Cabernet Sauvignon (C&B)
Rutherford Vintners Cabernet Sauvignon (STUD)
£6.25–£8.00
Robert Mondavi Pinot Noir (WSOC, HHC)
Chateau Montelena Zinfandel (ADN)
Conn Creek Cabernet Sauvignon (L&W)
Rutherford Hill Cabernet Sauvignon (LADV)
Clos du Val Cabernet Sauvignon (REID, AV)

£8.50–£10.00
Chappellet Cabernet Sauvignon (VIGN)
Cuvaison Cabernet Sauvignon (STUD)
Trefethen Cabernet Sauvignon (WNRY)
Jordan Cabernet Sauvignon (L&W, FINT)
£10.75–£13.50
Joseph Phelps Cabernet Sauvignon (STUD)
Beaulieu Vineyards George de Latour Cabernet Sauvignon Private Reserve (AV)
Chateau Montelena Cabernet Sauvignon (STUD)
c. £27.00
Heitz Bella Oaks Cabernet Sauvignon (LADV)

1976
c. £3.50
★Inverness Zinfandel (RSV, GH)
£7.25–£9.50
Cuvaison Cabernet Sauvignon (WW)
Chateau Montelena Cabernet Sauvignon (ADN)
Freemark Abbey Cabernet Sauvignon (VIGN)
£10.00–£12.50
Jordan Cabernet Sauvignon (L&W)
Mayacamas Cabernet Sauvignon (VIGN)
c. £15.50
Heitz Fay Vineyard Cabernet Sauvignon (ADN)
c. £26.75
Heitz Martha's Vineyard Cabernet Sauvignon (ADN, TAN)
c. £28.75
Heitz Bella Oaks Cabernet Sauvignon (STUD, TAN)

1975
£8.50–£9.75
Phelps Syrah (VIGN)
Freemark Abbey Cabernet Sauvignon (STUD, VIGN)
c. £13.00
Chateau Montelena Cabernet Sauvignon (VIGN)

c. £25.00
Robert Mondavi Cabernet Sauvignon Reserve (H&D)

1974
c. £10.75
Louis Martini Special Selection Cabernet Sauvignon (STUD, VIGN)
£15.50–£18.00
Chateau Montelena Cabernet Sauvignon (ADN)
Mayacamas Zinfandel Late Harvest (VIGN)
Sterling Cabernet Sauvignon (VIGN)
c. £18.50
Mayacamas Cabernet Sauvignon (VIGN)
c. £45.00
Heitz Martha's Vineyard Cabernet Sauvignon (VIGN)

1973
£10.00–£13.50
Heitz Cabernet Sauvignon (GH, WNRY, ADN, VIGN)
Freemark Abbey Cabernet Sauvignon (VIGN)
c. £17.00
Chateau Montelena Cabernet Sauvignon (VIGN)

1971
c. £29.00
Mayacamas Cabernet Sauvignon (VIGN)

White

Non-vintage
£2.50–£3.25
★Delicato Vineyards Mountain White (SR)
Geoffrey Roberts California Reserve CUL, CDM)
Paul Masson Californian White litre (WAIT, PD, ASHE, CUL)
Sainsbury's Pinot Chardonnay (SAIN)
California White, les Amis du Vin (LADV)
£3.25–£4.00
Christian Brothers Chateau la Salle (PD)

Almaden Chardonnay (CHAP)
Paul Masson Medium litre (ASHE)
Christian Brothers Chenin Blanc (PD, J&B)
c. £6.25
Trefethen Eshcol Table (CDM, LADV, GH)
c. £7.50
Beaulieu Sauvignon Blanc (AV)

1982
£3.50–£5.00
Paul Masson Chardonnay (STUD)
Conn Creek Chateau Maja Chardonnay (WW)
c. £8.50
Firestone Chardonnay (STUD)

1981
£3.25–£4.50
Paul Masson Chardonnay (PG)
River Oaks Vineyard (STWC, LADV)
Pedroncelli French Colombard (H&D)
★Felton Empire White Riesling (SR)
£5.00–£6.50
★Louis Martini Chardonnay (SR)

Inglenook Chardonnay (JH)
Dry Creek Chenin Blanc (GH, MAL)
St Clement Sauvignon Blanc (WW)
Joseph Phelps Gewurztraminer (ODD, LADV)

£6.75–£7.50

Carneros Creek Sauvignon Blanc (STUD)
Robert Mondavi Fume Blanc (STUD, L&W, CDM, TAN)
Felton Empire Selected Late Harvest White Riesling (BIB, H&D)
Dry Creek Sauvignon Blanc (LADV)

£8.25–£9.00

Felton Empire Tepusquet Vineyards Johannisberg Riesling Selected Late Harvest (VIGN)
Firestone Sauvignon Blanc (HUN)

St Clement Chardonnay (WW)
Robert Mondavi Moscato d'Oro (LADV)
Sterling Sauvignon Blanc (LADV)
Beaulieu Chardonnay (AV)

£9.50–£10.50

Firestone Select Late Harvest ½ bottle (STUD)
Jekel Chardonnay (STUD)
Iron Horse Chardonnay (HT)
Edna Valley Chardonnay (HT, MAL)

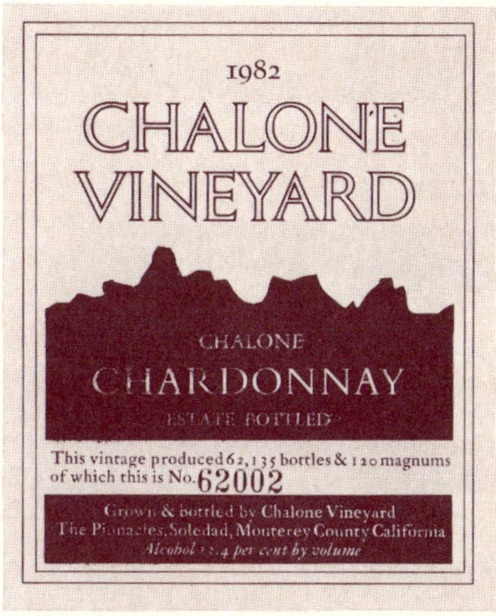

Robert Mondavi Chardonnay (LADV, CDM)

£10.75–£12.00

Carneros Creek Chardonnay (STUD)
Matanzas Creek Chardonnay (WW, STUD)
Chateau St Jean Chardonnay (STUD)
Chalone Pinot Blanc (ADN)

c. £15.00

Chalone Chardonnay (LADV, ADN, STUD)

1980

£3.25–£3.75

Almaden Chenin Blanc (CHAP, PG, MART, CV)
Almaden Chardonnay (PG)

£6.50–£7.50

Parducci Chardonnay (ADN)
Felton Empire Gewurztraminer ½ bottle (STUD, BIB, VIGN)
Joseph Phelps Riesling (LADV)
Dry Creek Fume Blanc (MAL)
★Mark West Chardonnay (LADV, STUD)

Cuvaison Chardonnay (WW)

£8.25–£10.00

Robert Mondavi Fume Blanc (WSOC, GH, HHC)
Firestone Chardonnay (HHC)
Chateau St Jean Chardonnay (BIB, WSOC, STUD)

£10.75–£11.50
Spring Mountain Chardonnay (AV)
Conn Creek Chardonnay (STUD)
Jordan Chardonnay (L&W)
Freemark Abbey Chardonnay (LADV, STUD)

1979
£3.50–£4.75
★Louis Martini Folle Blanche (SR)
Almaden Cabernet Sauvignon (CHAP)
Dry Creek Chardonnay (BIB)
Almaden Chardonnay (CV)
Wente Bros Chardonnay (STUD)
£7.00–£8.75
★Conn Creek Chardonnay (L&W)
Robert Mondavi Fume Blanc (ADN, HUN)
Clos du Bois Chardonnay (MAL)
Trefethen Chardonnay (ADN, L&W, STUD)
c. £10.00
Firestone's Ambassador Vineyard Johannisberg Riesling (TAN)
c. £12.50
Robert Mondavi Chardonnay (HUN)

c. £14.25
Chateau Montelena Chardonnay (STUD)

1978
c. £4.25
Paul Masson Gewurztraminer (PG)
c. £6.75
Carneros Creek Chardonnay (WW)

£8.75–£9.50
Firestone Johannisberg Riesling Selected Harvest (GH)
Joseph Phelps Chardonnay (H&D, HT, TAN)
Robert Mondavi Chardonnay (HHC, TAN)
£12.50–£12.75
Mayacamas Chardonnay (VIGN)
Grgich Hills Chardonnay (STUD)
c. £16.75
Robert Mondavi Sauvignon Blanc Botrytis ½ bottle (STUD)
c. £20.00
Chateau St Jean Belle Terre Vineyard Johannisberg Riesling Individual Dried Selected (VIGN)

1977
£9.50–£12.75
Cuvaison Chardonnay (STUD)
Stag's Leap Chardonnay (VIGN)
c. £27.00
Robert Mondavi Johannisberg Riesling Botrytis Affected (ADN)

1975
c. £11.50
Cuvaison Chardonnay (VIGN)
c. £16.50
Mayacamas Chardonnay (VIGN)

1974
c. £19.50
Robert Mondavi Reserve Chardonnay (VIGN)

Rosé

Non-vintage
c. £3.75
Paul Masson Califoirnia Carafe litre (PD, ASHE, CUL)

(*actual illustrations full-colour)

IRAN: Latter-day miracle. Turning Wine into Water

Sparkling

Non-vintage
c. £12.50
Domaine Chandon Brut (STUD, ADN)

1980
£10.50–£11.00
Schramsberg Cuvee de Pinot (BIB, STUD, LADV)
Schramsberg Blanc de Blancs (BIB, ADN, STUD, LADV)

1978
c. £12.75
Schramsberg Blanc de Noirs (BIB, LADV)

Northwest Red

1980
£4.75–£6.75
The Associated Vintners Cabernet Sauvignon (WW)
*Tualatin Pinot Noir (WW)
c. £9.00
Eyrie Pinot Noir (WW)

1979
c. £8.75
Knudsen Erath Pinot Noir (ADN)

1978
c. £6.25
Knudsen Erath Pinot Noir (L&W)

Northwest White

Non-vintage
c. £4.25
Associated Vintners Valley White (L&W)

1981
£3.75–£5.75
Associated Vintners Valley White (WW)
Knudsen Erath Chardonnay (WW)
Knudsen Erath Riesling (WW)
*Ste Chapelle Chardonnay (WW)

1980
£6.75–£8.25
*Tualatin Chardonnay (WW)
Ste Chapelle Chardonnay (HHC)

1979
c. £4.75
*Knudsen Erath Chardonnay (WW, ADN)

US Forecast

You only have to look a couple of California wine makers in the eye to be convinced that the future is rosy for them. So far they've faced up to every challenge thrown at them head on. And, like it or not, they've licked each one. They've done it with a mixture of passion, high tech know-how, and a back pocket stuffed full of 100-dollar bills. They've thought, bought and fought their way out of any crisis.

This latest crisis isn't quite so easy. They've made too much wine, they've made it too expensive, and consumers have shown that loyalty is only as firm as the price tag on the next bottle. The dollar has been too strong, and imports are very cheap. The fact that the Californians have characteristically reacted by reducing prices and realigning wine styles to the market needs, shows that the mixture of high idealism and hard-fisted business nous is still standing them in good stead. We can expect to see an increase in market presence for good quality California Cabernets, Chardonnays, Sauvignons, and even Pinot Noirs and Zinfandels. We'll also see some dumping – already California varietals can be seen here and there for as little as £1.79.

The Pacific Northwest is also aware that a wine surplus could occur as more vineyards come into production, and have set up a levy fund on sales to pay for future promotional efforts, as well as forming Washington and Oregon Wine Institutes. Our PNW expert at Windrush Wines feels that anyone who tastes Pacific Northwest wines will be converted, and reckons he'll soon be selling more Oregon than California. With promotional activity being set in motion, he won't be the only one who begins to feel the fresh breeze of the Pacific Northwest.

AUSTRALIA

We really must start taking the Australians more seriously. They're the biggest drinkers in the Anglo-Saxon world for a start. I'll just wait while the guffaws die down, and then explain that it isn't just a procession of ice-cold tubes of Fosters being shovelled down the parched outback throats. Their beer consumption is actually in decline! The brewers are complaining to the government about it! 1975 showed a peak consumption of 140.3 litres of beer per head of population. By 1983 it had slumped to only 124.6 litres.

So what is the mighty Okker doing with his right arm? I'll tell you what. He's shouldering a four-litre bladder pack of Fruity Gordo and sloping off to Bondi for the duration. Which in plain English means he is purchasing a four-litre wine box, full of slightly sweet, rather aromatic white wine based on the Muscat grape, for which he will pay about 50p a bottle, and taking the afternoon off in favour of outdoor pursuits. Beer costs about 75p a bottle! Now the Aussie's very sensitive to the amount of kick he gets for his dollar. Faced with a bargain like that, no wonder the right-thinking Down Under chunder artist is switching allegiances. In 1975 he was drinking 12.3 litres of wine per head. In 1983 he'd got to 19.9 litres. That's what *his* right arm is for nowadays.

This domestic wine boom has been based on the incredibly cheap and incredibly good basic wines Australia can produce in her over-hot, irrigated interior vineyards. But what has happened concurrently is that the rising tide of wine drinking – the fastest increase in the Anglo-Saxon world – has fuelled a great surge of high-quality 'boutique' wineries, as the wine-boom drinkers move up-market and demand more sophisticated products. The big companies have also recognised the trend towards individuality and superior varietal wines, and it is not at all naïve to say that in many areas it isn't California but Australia which now leads the field in modern winemaking techniques.

Certainly, in terms of the wines we see over here, the Aussies can frequently see off not only European but also Californian opposition, because Australian wine makers have come to grips with their torrid climes much more quickly than the Californians, and have moved sharply away from the hot valley-floor vineyards of 20 years ago to an assortment of cooler, more European microclimates, spread across the states of New South Wales, Victoria, South Australia and Western Australia.

Twenty years ago, we actually took more Australian wine than we do now – it was thick, tarry, ferruginous stuff, innaccurately dubbed burgundy, and somehow accorded a 'good for you' tag, largely, it seemed, for the more mature spinster. Aunt Mabels from Bournemouth to Belfast found it calmed the nerves, kept out the cold, and made them feel ever so slightly frisky. The EEC put an end to such Empire preferences, and it's only in the last couple of years that the Australians have taken another bash at the UK market. If the first offerings to arrive over here are anything to go by, it has the potential to produce some of the world's most exciting Cabernets and Chardonnays, some of its most distinctive Shiraz (alias Syrah), Semillon and Riesling, and some of its most startling double-sweet Muscats.

And they're cheap. Top varietal wines can be less than £5 a bottle, and some of her greatest glories, matching the best of America and Europe, can be had for less than a tenner.

The trouble is, they haven't yet persuaded the Poms to take them seriously. Max Lake, one of Australia's grandest wine men, who reintroduced Cabernet to the fabled Hunter Valley, has a motto – 'yer gotta have a go'. To prove it, this year he's harvesting Australia's only Petit Verdot, and he's noble-rotted some Chardonnay too. If we're not going to miss out on some sensational taste experiences, *we* gotta have a go. From a small base, exports to the UK were up 46 per cent last year, and they've now targeted us as their prime export market. Which is good news for us, because the wines deserve more of our attention.

Western Australia
Chiefly famous for the ultra-traditional Houghton reds and whites, but they're now winning medals for Chardonnay and Cabernet, and we'll see more of them.

South Australia
The biggest producer. Although some of the Barossa reds and whites may be a bit hefty and sluggish, there are loads of cooler areas producing very fine Cabernet – in particular the isolated Coonawarra valley – and also producers like Marienberg, Hill Smith, and Krondorf around the hot centre. Shiraz is also good, with Grange hermitage being Australia's most celebrated wine, while Rhine Riesling from high valleys like the Eden and Clare can be Australia's best.

Victoria
This is historically Australia's best vineyard area and was winning medals against European opposition 100 years ago. However phylloxera chose Victoria for its bullseye down under and almost killed the industry. It's now recovering and producing wonderful minty Cabernets and honeyed Chardonnays as good as any in California. Her Muscats from northeast Victoria are sensational deep fortified wines as good as all but the greatest ports and Madeiras.

New South Wales
The Hunter Valley is famous, mainly because Sydney is so close and Sydney is good at publicity. However, wineries like Lake's Folly, Brokenwood, Rothbury and Tyrrell do make superb reds and whites, with the irrigated Upper Hunter beginning to produce cheaper, but classy wines, especially dry whites.

PRICE GUIDE

Red

Non-vintage
c. £2.50
Willliam Jacob (PG, PD)
£3.50–£4.50
McWilliams Bin 35 Shiraz (AV)
Brown Bros Cabernet Sauvignon (L&W)

1982
c. £7.25
Hungerford Hill Pokolbin Chardonnay (C&B)

1981
£3.75–£5.00
Hill-Smith Red (MWS)
Arrowfield Shiraz (MAL)
Rosemount Coonawarra Cabernet Sauvignon (CUL)
£5.50–£7.50
Tyrrells Vat 7 Dry (AV)
Hungerford Hill Coonawarra Cabernet Sauvignon (C&B)
Brokenwood Cabernet Sauvignon/Hermitage (L&W)

1980
£3.00–£3.75
Hill-Smith Red (CV, DOL, YFW)
Mildara Shiraz (STWC)
*Tollana Cabernet Sauvignon Shiraz (PG)
£4.00–£5.00
Rosemount Shiraz (PG, CUL)
Brown Bros Muscat Blanc (BBR)
Rothbury Hermitage (BIB, PIP, LADV)
Wynn's Ovens Valley Shiraz (VICT, WNRY)
Rosemount Coonawarra Cabernet Sauvignon (ESV, MAL, WSOC)

£6.50–£7.50
Rothbury Hermitage-Cabernet (PIP)
Balgownie Cabernet Sauvignon (BOW)
Leasingham Bin 56 Cabernet Malbec (MAL)
Allandale Leonard Cabernet Sauvignon (L&W)
c. £8.00
Tyrrells Pinot Noir (AV)

1979
£4.00–£5.00
Brokenwood Shiraz/Cabernet Sauvignon (WNRY)
Rothbury Cabernet Sauvignon (BIB, LADV)
Rosemount Cabernet Sauvignon (BIB, VICT)
Houghtons Cabernet Sauvignon (VICT)
⋆Wynn's Coonawarra Cabernet Sauvignon (HT, CHAP, VICT)
£5.00–£5.50
Craigmoor Cabernet Sauvignon (ADN)
Krondorf Shiraz/Cabernet (J&B, WNRY)
Mildara Coonawarra Cabernet Sauvignon (MAL)
Brown Bros Koombahla Cabernet Sauvignon (BIB, PG, WSOC, HT, HUN, VIGN, MAL)
£5.50–£6.50
Hungerford Hill Coonawarra Cabernet Sauvignon (C&B)
Stanley Leasingham Cabernet Malbec Bin 56 (AV)
Krondorf Cabernet Sauvignon (WNRY)
c. £10.50
Petaluma Winery Hermitage-Cabernet (LADV)

1978
£3.50–£4.50
Berri Cabernet Sauvignon/Shiraz (RACK)
⋆Brown Bros Cabernet Sauvignon (CHAP, WNRY, HT, PG, J&B, RH)
Wynn's Coonawarra Shiraz (VICT)
Tulloch Wilkinson Cabernet Sauvignon (PD)
£4.50–£5.50
Chateau Tahbilk Cabernet Sauvignon (PG, RH)
Craigmoor Shiraz (ADN)
Brown Bros Koombahla Cabernet Sauvignon (CUL)
Wynn's Coonawarra Cabernet Sauvignon (H&D, TAN)
Tulloch McLaren Vale Cabernet Sauvignon (J&B)
⋆Baileys Bundarra Shiraz (STWC)
£5.50–£6.00
Leasingham Bin 56 Cabernet Sauvignon-Malbec (L&W)
Penfolds Shiraz Coonawarra Bin 128 (BBR, WNRY)
c. £7.75
Stanley Leasingham Cabernet Sauvignon Bin 49 (AV)

1977
£4.25–£5.00
McWilliams Cabernet Sauvignon (AV)
Chateau Tahbilk Shiraz (GH)
Brown Bros Meadow Creek Cabernet/Shiraz (HUN)
c. £7.00
Hill-Smith Cabernet Sauvignon (MWS)

1976
c. £4.00
Tulloch Glen Elgin Dry Red (PD)
Hill-Smith Shiraz (CV, CUL, YFW, MWS)
Brown Bros Shiraz (CUL)
£5.00–£6.00
Mildara Cabernet Sauvignon (J&B)
Hardy's Cabernet Sauvignon (WNRY)
Hardy's Keppoch Cabernet Sauvignon (HT)
Hill-Smith Cabernet Sauvignon (CV, CUL, YFW)

1975
£3.50–£4.50
Tyrrells Silver Medal Dry (AV)
Tulloch Wilkinson Shiraz (PD)
Brown Bros Shiraz (PG)
c. £15.50
Penfolds Grange Hermitage Bin 95 (ADN)

1961
c. £13.50
McWilliams Mount Pleasant Richard Hermitage (VIGN)

White

Non-vintage
£2.50–£4.00
William Jacob (PG, PD)
McWilliams Bin 77 Traminer Riesling (AV)
★Brown Bros Muscat Dry (ASHE)
£4.25–£4.75
Brown Bros Muscat Blanc Late Picked (L&W)
★Orlando Chardonnay (ASHE)
c. £6.00
Brown Bros Select Muscat (WNRY)
c. £8.25
Brown Bros Family Reserve Muscat (CUL)

1983
£3.00–£3.75
Hill-Smith Barossa Riesling (CUL, MWS)
★Hill-Smith Old Triangle Rhine Riesling (ASHE)
Hill-Smith White (MWS)

1982
£3.50–£4.50
Hill-Smith Barossa Valley Riesling (YFW)
Hill-Smith Old Triangle Rhine Riesling (DOL)
Brown Bros Dry Muscat Blanc (CHAP, BIB, CUL, HT, J&B, RH)
Rosemount Chardonnay (PG, BIB, ESV, CUL, MAL, WSOC, J&B)
Rosemount Fumé Blanc (PG)
£4.75–£5.75
Rosemount Traminer (CUL)
Wynn's Coonawarra Rhine Riesling (VICT)
Arrowfield Gewürztraminer (MAL)
Arrowfield Chardonnay (MAL)
Hardy's Siegersdorf Rhine Riesling (WNRY)
Rosemount Show Chardonnay (VICT)
£6.25–£6.50
Tyrrells Sauvignon Blanc (AV)
Brown Bros Chardonnay (CUL)
£7.75–£8.00
Balgownie Chardonnay (BOW)
Tyrrells Vat 47 Chardonnay (AV)
£8.50–£9.50
Allandale Sutherland Chardonnay (L&W)
Petaluma Rhine Riesling (LADV, WNRY)
Allandale Winery Chardonnay (HT)
1981
£3.00–£4.50
Hill-Smith White (CV)
★Houghton's Supreme (WAIT, WNRY)
Hill-Smith Riesling (YFW)
£5.00–£5.50
Brown Bros Semillon (BIB)
Brown Bros Sauvignon Blanc (CUL)
Craigmoor Semillon Chardonnay (ADN)
c. £7.25
Brown Bros Chardonnay (MAL)
1980
£3.75–£4.75
Hill-Smith Riesling (MAL, CV, BBR)
Brown Bros Dry Muscat (VIGN, HUN, GH, WSOC, ADN)
Brown Bros Muscat Blanc late picked (CHAP, H&D, WNRY, VIGN, RH, MAL)
Chateau Tahbilk Riesling (GH)
Brown Bros Semillon (H&D, CUL, HT)
£5.00–£6.50
Tyrrells Vat 1 Semillon (AV)
Milawa Semillon Special Limited Production (WSOC)
Brown Bros Chardonnay (BIB, HT, VIGN, WNRY)
1979
£3.85–£4.85
Leasingham Spring Gully Rhine Riesling (L&W)
Tulloch Semillon Glen Elgin (PD)
Brown Bros Muscat Blanc late picked (GH)
Craigmoor Chardonnay (ADN)
1978
£4.25–£5.50
Stanley Leasingham Rhine Riesling Bin 7 (AV)
Rothbury Estate Semillon (LADV, WNRY)
Rothbury Individual Paddock Semillon (VIGN)
1976
c. £5.25
Rothbury Individual Paddock Semillon (BIB, PIP, LADV, WNRY, VIGN)

New Zealand

New Zealand still gets lumped in with Australia in people's minds, but her fine wine industry is very much newer, and totally different in style. It's the nearest vineyard area to the South Pole, and so could be likened to Germany in northern Europe. Similarly, her whites are so far her best, and she has led the world in showing how good Müller-Thurgau can be. Not only that, her Gewürztraminers are world beaters, capturing all the oily, peppery spice of the grape, but keeping the wine light and acid-fresh. Only the very best from Alsace can compete. In Chardonnay, too, the cooler ripening period allows a lighter wine, but with intense, high-acid flavours, softened out by new oak barrels into the most successful burgundy look-alikes the New World has yet produced. Reds have tended to be a bit light and sharp, but this is also being overcome as the young vineyards mature. The Cabernets are certainly dry, but they show a piercing blackcurrant-and-nettles fruit about as pure as you can get.

The curious Pinotage – a Cinsault/Pinot Noir cross much loved in South Africa – here produces a deep strong purple-red wine, smokey in a toasted marshmallows way, and stinking of raspberries. And it also looks as if the world's great rogue grape, the Pinot Noir, may be finding its feet here. The 1983 vintage showed a South Island Pinot so good it could have walked out of any village in Burgundy.

Price Guide

1980
c. £3.50
Montana Pinotage (PG)

1979
£3.50–£3.75
Cooks Cabernet Sauvignon (CUL, AV)
Marlborough Cabernet Sauvignon (PG)

1978
c. £4.25
Montana Cabernet Sauvignon (J&B)

Red

Non-vintage £3.25–£3.75
Montana Pinotage (WILL)
Montana Cabernet Sauvignon (PD, WILL)
Cooks Pinot Noir (WILL)

1981
£3.50–£4.25
Cooks Pinot Noir (PG)
Cooks Te Kauwhata Cabernet Sauvignon (TAN)

White

Non-vintage
£2.50–£3.75
Cooks New Zealand White (WAIT)
Cooks Medium Dry White (PD, WILL)
Cooks Chenin Blanc (PD, WILL)
⋆Cooks Müller-Thurgau (PD)
Montana Marlborough Benmorven Riesling (WILL)
Montana Marlborough Riesling Sylvaner (WILL)

Cooks Pinot Gris (WILL)
Cooks Gewürztraminer (WILL)

1982
£3.25–£3.50
Cooks Müller-Thurgau (L&W, MAL)
Cooks Chenin Blanc (PG, CUL, MAL)
Cooks Te Kauwhata Chenin Blanc (CHAP)
★Cooks Gewürztraminer (PG, CUL, MAL)
£4.50–£5.25
Matawhero Gewürztraminer (AV)
Matawhero Traminer Riesling (AV)
c. £6.50
Cooks Chardonnay (MAL)

1981
£3.25–£4.25
Cooks Chenin Blanc (L&W, TAN)
Cooks Müller-Thurgau (CUL)
Cooks Te Kauwhata Müller-Thurgau (CHAP)
Cooks Te Kauwhata Pinot Gris (WSOC)
Cooks Gewürztraminer (L&W)
Cooks Te Kauwhata Chenin Blanc (ADN)
Cooks Te Kauwhata Gewürztraminer (ADN)

1980
£3.00–£4.00
★Montana Marlborough Müller-Thurgau (WAIT)
Montana Riesling Sylvaner (PD, PG, J&B)
Cooks Pinot Gris (L&W)
Cooks Müller-Thurgau (AV)
c. £6.50
Cooks Chardonnay (AV)

1978
c. £5.50
Nobilo Cabernet Sauvignon (AV)

Price Guide – Notes

The word is getting through about Australian and New Zealand wines, but all merchants report that it is hard work persuading the customers. Be persuaded. These are some of the best value wines in Britain today, and although never the cheapest wines on the list, they frequently offer more flavour for the price asked than European equivalents. But this flavour is not hefty and exhausting; the standard of wine making is so good that freshness and fruit are rarely overpowered by alcohol and strength. So we must encourage the merchants by trying the wines, otherwise they might stop stocking them.

South Africa

Table Wines

There's no question that things are happening inside South Africa's wine world, it's just that very little evidence of it is seeping northwards over the Sahara to the thirsty throats of northern Europe. Sometimes one is tempted to believe the South African who said quite bluntly that she only exports wine to offer 'tangible proof that we have an established wine culture, that we are a civilised people'. That seems an absurdly self-deprecating view, when many writers have said that South African vineyard conditions are difficult to better anywhere in the world. Hugh Johnson lists the advantages, and it sounds like a roll-call of all the desirable factors a wine-grower could wish for.

The Cape Province is the chief wine-growing area, and it has ideal slopes facing in every direction – important in a hot climate. To get light, fresh whites, for instance, the slopes need to face away from the sun; for a blockbuster red they need to square up sunwards from dawn to dusk. The vines have an extended eighth-month ripening period, and don't seem to be prone to any of the perennial torments of European vintners. Frost and hail, which between them have wrecked more European wine-growers' hopes of a Christmas bonus than any other blight, virtually don't occur – well, this is Africa, after all. The kind of autumn rain which can drastically dilute or even wreck a European vintage is again something of a rarity, leading to the assertion that all South African vintages are the same. Not true. There are considerable variations across the numerous microclimates – it's just that excess heat rather than excess rain is likely to influence the outcome.

One factor which might please the Californians, who regard soil as primarily a geological phenomenon (unlike the French who regard it as possessed of mystical powers), is the fertility of the soil. As in the Napa valley, where the soil has only been farmed, and thus weakened, for a couple of hundred years, as against a thousand or more in most European countries, the Cape soil is strong, and easily regenerates itself year after year, needing only 10 per cent of the fertilizer its European counterparts require. A European might say that this means the vine doesn't have to struggle and strain to survive and ripen its fruit, and therefore the wine cannot be of such high quality. And a dispassionate taster, faced with South Africa's finest reds, would respectfully agree.

Over-ripeness is the constant factor against which South Africa is fighting, paradoxically, not helped by her near-perfect climate, hot days and cool nights, which combine to increase remorselessly the vine's stock of ripening sugars.

Over-ripeness, leading to a dullness, a smokey lava flatness, even on the good Cabernets and Pinotages (there's a name to conjure with – it's a cross between Pinot and Cinsault, and produces a high-flavoured wine which tastes as though it's been rolled through a volcanic crater en route to the bottling line), is a problem which must be overcome, since the increasingly selective northern hemisphere markets are demanding lighter, fresher wines. Certainly, California and Australia, after a somewhat ham-fisted start, have responded enthusiastically to the challenge of producing light, acid-fresh wines in climates considerably more difficult to deal with than the Cape's.

Interestingly, while they've been getting their wires crossed about what the export market might want in reds, the South Africans have managed to transform their whites with considerable success. This breakthrough has obviously been prompted by the demands of the domestic market, because in the hot African sun the demand is for thirst-quenching whites. They have come up with a world-beater, which, again seemingly for lack of sustained effort, has made far less impact on the UK market than it deserves. This is their Chenin Blanc. The Loire valley is pretty unlucky to be lumbered with the Chenin as its basic white grape, because it's too far north for it to ripen well, but in sun-drenched South Africa, the uncharmingly high acidity of the grape is crucial, and provides South Africa with a very good basic white wine.

But if the Chenin can do so well, why not the Sauvignon, the Chardonnay, the Merlot, the Pinot Noir? Simply because there is a dreadful dearth of top quality vines in the country, as a result of resolute government blocking of attempts by the good growers to introduce the best varieties. Let it be known that you're visiting South Africa, and in no time the phone's buzzing with furtive calls, asking if you can bring a cutting from Sancerre, a cutting from Volnay, a cutting from Pomerol.

It must be that the export of individual and personalised wines is of almost negligible importance to the South African trade - London only has one merchant really making an effort with them.

South Africa's trade with us has traditionally been in fortified wines, not table wines: indeed her Wines of Origin appellation system was only brought into force in 1972. Australia and California, who shared the start of the wine boom, have now left South Africa far behind. But change is coming, however slowly, and a few estates are producing limited amounts of fine Cabernet, Sauvignon and Chardonnay. The only problem is, since the UK has such a wide range of other wines to choose from, is anyone going to seek them out?

Price Guide

Red

Non-vintage
£2.75 - £3.25
KWV Roodeberg (ASHE, VICT, THRE, DAV, P&C, UNW)
Drostdy Hof Rouge Select (COL, SW, VIGN)
KWV Cabernet Sauvignon (DAV, P&C, UNW)
c. £4.00
Nederburg Paarl Cabernet Sauvignon (L&W, JH, UNW)
c. £5.50
Meerlust Cabernet Sauvignon (HW)

1982
c. £2.50
Pinotage Culemborg Paarl (WAIT)

1980
£3.50 - £4.50
Fleur du Cap Shiraz (COL, CPW)
Meerendal Pinotage (PG, COL, CPW, CPW, ESV, VIGN, TAN)
Meerendal Shiraz (COL, CPW, TAN)
£5.00 - £6.00
Meerlust Cabernet Sauvignon (PG, HW, BYR, COL, CPW)
Meerlust Rubicon (PG, COL, CPW, VIGN)

1979
£2.50 - £3.00
KWV Roodeberg (HW, WAIT, CPW, PG, RGA, VIGN, MWS, FINT)
★KWV Cabernet Sauvignon (PG, CPW, RGA, CHAP, MAL, VIGN)

£3.00 – £3.75
⋆Fleur du Cap Roodebloem (COL, ESV)
Nederburg Pinotage (HW, CPW)
Fleur du Cap Pinotage (COL, CPW)
Nederburg Cabernet Sauvignon (HW, PG, DOL, CPW, MWS, TAN)
£3.75 – £4.50
⋆Fleur du Cap Cabernet Sauvignon (COL)
Zandvliet Shiraz (COL, CPW)

1978
£2.75 – £3.50
KWV Cabernet Sauvignon (HW, BIB)
KWV Pinotage (HW, PG, CPW, RGA, BIB, FINT)

KWV Roodeberg (BIB, H&D)
Fleur du Cap Pinotage (HW)
Fleur du Cap Shiraz (HW)
£3.50 – £4.00
Nederburg Paarl Cabernet Sauvignon (BYR)
Fleur du Cap Cabernet Sauvignon (HW, CPW)
£4.00 – £5.00
Goede Hoop (ESW)
⋆Meerendal Pinotage (HW, CHAP, MAL)
Uitkyk Carlonet (COL, CPW)
c. £6.25
Meerlust Cabernet Sauvignon (VIGN)

1977
c. £2.75
⋆Roodeberg (CHAP)
c. £4.75
Fleur du Cap Cabernet Sauvignon (AV)

1976
£4.00 – £5.00
Meerendal Shiraz (HW)
Fleur du Cap Pinotage (AV)
Meerendal Pinotage (VIGN)
Uitkyk Carlonet Cabernet Sauvignon (VIGN)
c. £7.00
Meerlust Cabernet Sauvignon (TAN)

1971
c. £16.00
Nederburg Cabernet Sauvignon (VIGN)

White

Non-vintage
£2.25 – £3.00
⋆Grunberger Stein (CHAP, BYR, CPW, COL, ESV, MWS, TAN, AV)
Vredenburg Chenin Blanc (PD)
⋆KWV Cape Bouquet (ASHE)
KWV Chenin Blanc (ASHE, DAV, P&C, UNW)
KWV Steen, Dry (DAV)
£3.00 – £3.50
KWV Riesling (RGA, UNW)
Nederburg Stein (CPW)
Nederburg Fonternel (L&W)
Fleur du Cap Brut (HW, COL)
£3.50 – £4.00
Nederburg Parl Riesling (L&W, UNW)
Twee Jongegezellen Schanderl (PD)
c. £5.00
Nederburg Première Cuvée Brut Close (MWS)

1983
£3.00 – £4.00
⋆Fleur du Cap Chenin Blanc (CPW, COL)
Koopmanskloof Blanc de Marbonne (COL)
de Wetshof Rhine Riesling (COL, CPW)
£4.00 – £4.50
de Wetshof Sauvignon Blanc (COL, CPW)
Nederburg Brut (HW)
de Wetshof Chardonnay (COL, CPW)

1982
£2.50 – £3.00
KWV Chenin Blanc (THRE, MWS)
Fleur du Cap Chenin Blanc (HW, WSOC)
⋆KWV Cape Foret (CUL)
£3.00 – £3.50
⋆Fleur du Cap Special Late Harvest (COL)
Fleur du Cap Riesling (COL, CPW)
£3.50 – £4.00
Nederburg Special Late Harvest (HW, CPW)
Koopmanskloof Blanc de Marbonne (ESV, MAL)
£4.00 – £5.00
de Westhof Chardonnay (BYR, VIGN)
Theuniskraal Gewürztraminer (COL)

1981
£2.50 – £3.00
⋆KWV Steen (CHAP, CPW, RGA, TAN)
KWV Chenin Blanc (RGA, BIB, H&D, MAL, FINT)
KWV Steen Special Late Harvest (RGA)
£3.00 – £3.50
KWV Riesling (CPW, VIGN, FINT)
Fleur du Cap Chenin Blanc (HHC)
Fleur du Cap Riesling (HW)
Nederburg Fonternel (DOL)
Fleur du Cap Special Late Harvest (CPW, WSOC)

c. £5.00
Theuniskraal Gewürztraminer (CPW)

1980
£3.00 – £3.50
Nederburg Fonternel (HW, CPW, JH, MWS, TAN)
Nederburg Paarl Riesling (HW, DOL, CPW, MWS)
£4.00 – £5.00
de Wetshof Riesling (VIGN, AV)
Nederburg Special Late Harvest (MWS)

1979
c. £2.75
KWV Steen (HW)
c. £4.50
Fleur du Cap Riesling (AV)

1978
£3.00 – £3.50
Nederburg Paarl Riesling (BYR)
KWV Roodeberg (H&D)

1975
c. £18.00
Nederburg Edelkeur (VIGN)

*Please remember that **Webster's** is a price GUIDE and not a price LIST. It is not meant to replace up-to-date merchants' lists.*

SHERRY

South African sherry used to be a common sight on the best sideboards, and almost had a certain inverted snob value. It is one of the few sherry imitators which enjoys the right conditions to have a bash at the real thing, but it has suffered a decline steeper than the generally sluggish sherry market. A look at the following figures shows the reason. It used to be a good wine with a distinct price advantage over Spanish sherry. The Spaniards decided they would squeeze their rivals out by blending their own sherries down to a price which would claw back trade from the imitators. Obviously, if the price difference is tiny, the consumer will buy the real thing – which is exactly what happened. Except that the ruthless price-cutting and quality deterioration means that now the customer is not too keen on the real thing; the Spanish sherry boys have nearly cut their own throats by concentrating on fixing their rivals rather than the quality of their own product.

These figures show UK retail prices for Landdrost South African Sherry and Dry Fly, a leading Spanish brand.

	Landdrost	**Dry Fly**
1967	16*s* 6*d* (£0.82½)	21*s* 8*d* (£1.08)
1969	19*s* 9*d* (£0.99½)	25*s* 9*d* (£1.29)
1975	£1.20	£1.92
1979	£1.85	£2.12
1981	£2.50	£2.75
1983	£2.90	£3.02

The South African price may be an honest reflection of value, but at only 12p difference in price, who'll buy it?

PRICE GUIDE

£2.00 – £2.50
Waitrose Cream South African Sherry (WAIT)
Waitrose South African Sherry (WAIT)
KWV, Onzerust, Medium Dry (HW, CHAP, HHC, GH, TAN)
£2.50 – £3.00
Medium Dry South African Sherry, Hicks & Don (H&D)
Cavendish Cape, Medium Dry (CPW, J&B)
Renasons, pale dry (TAN)
£3.00 – £3.50
Landdrost dry (FINT)
Landdrost medium (FINT)
Landdrost cream (FINT)
£3.50 – £4.00
Drostdy Full Cream (COL, CPW)
Drostdy Medium Cream (COL, CPW)
Drostdy Pale Dry (COL, CPW)

ARGENTINA

Which Spanish-speaking country has its chief wine critic writing in elegant English? Argentina. If that is initially surprising, it becomes less so when one remembers that Argentina and England have always been particularly close, which made the 1982 war all the more distressing. With an English-speaking population of some 100,000 or so, it has its own English schools and newspapers, and not that long ago the future Edward VIII had to be discreetly corrected when he said that he wouldn't mind if Britain lost the Empire just so long as she didn't lose Argentina.

With a frequently devalued currency which never shows the remotest sign of being a serious means of purchasing goods, and annual inflation rates of well over 100 per cent, Argentine wines were always cheap and would probably still be among the cheapest on the market if they were available. There certainly doesn't seem to be any prejudice against them, and several merchants are still selling pre-war (Falklands, that is) stocks at very low prices with no sign of adverse consumer reaction.

PRICE GUIDE

Red

Non-vintage
c. £2.75
Parral Red (WILL)

1975
c. £3.50
Andean Cabernet Sauvignon (CUL, WILL)

1974
c. £3.75
Andean Cabernet Sauvignon (VIGN)

White

Non-vintage
£2.00–£3.50
Franchette (CUL, UNW)
Parral White (WILL)
Andean Chardonnay (WILL)

1980
c. £3.50
Andean Chardonnay (CUL)

1975
c. £2.25
Andean Pinot Blanc (WILL)
Andean Riesling (WILL)

CHILE

Chile is altogether more serious, but is very slow at getting the message across. Whereas Argentina used to scoop the value-for-money award in the bargain basement tastings, Chile's wines are a much more sophisticated proposition. They won, and still win, tastings based on their out-and-out class and unique flavours. There is one overriding reason for this. Phylloxera, the dreaded vine louse, never made it to Chile. If you look on the map you can see that it isn't immediately obvious how human beings would get there in 1984, let alone a fairly dumb aphid a century ago. The Andes, the Pacific, the fierce deserts to the north, and the South Pole at the other end. All the kind of natural barriers the Phylloxera can't be bothered with. The result is red wines of tremendous style. Chile's Cabernet Sauvignon, from old, ungrafted natural vines, has got an astonishing blackcurrant fruit, sweet, jammy but pure, like no other country's efforts, and it also has a smokiness which is again unique, rather like the smoke of a good coal fire in mid-winter.

Pinot Noir is grown, with a fair amount of sweet, hot success, and the white Sémillon is quite common, making wonderfully obvious wine. Not nice to drink, mind you, being oily and petrolly in the same way as old Australian Sémillons, but obvious. However, there is a move to modernise wine-making techniques which can only be good. A younger style of Cabernet is developing which looks notable, and some Chardonnays and Sauvignons are getting a ripe but clean varietal taste. And the presence of one of Europe's greatest wine makers, Miguel Torres, shows that things are beginning to spark. He regards the Chilean vineyards as his most exciting prospect. Chile invited its first group of journalists out there this year. The buzz on their return was that the potential is massive and only just beginning to be realised.

PRICE GUIDE

Red

Non-vintage
£3.00–£3.25
Concha y Toro Vino Reservado (H&D)
Torres Viña Santa Digna Red (WILL)

1981
c. £2.85
★Concha y Toro Cabernet Merlot (CUL, ESV)

1980
£2.75–£3.25
Concha y Toro Cabernet-Merlot (HT)
Concha y Toro Cabernet Sauvignon (CUL)
Cabernet Sauvignon (SF)

1979
£2.75–£3.75
★Concha y Toro Cabernet Sauvignon (WAIT, HT, ODD, H&D, WSOC)
Viña Linderos Cabernet Sauvignon (CUL, P&C, TAN)

1978
c. £3.75
Concha y Toro Casillero del Diablo (SF)

1977
£3.00–£4.50
Torres Viña Santa Digna (PG, VIGN)
Concha y Toro Marqués de Casa (SF)
Cousiño Macul Cabernet Sauvignon (CUL)
Viña Undurraga Pinot Noir (CUL)

1976
c. £4.00
Concha y Toro Casillero del Diablo Cabernet Sauvignon (SW)
Cousiño Macul Antiguas Reservas Cabernet Sauvignon (HT, ASHE, MAL)

White

Non-vintage
c. £3.25
Torres Viña Santa Digna White (WILL)

1983
c. £2.85
Concha y Toro Sauvignon Semillon (CUL)

1982
c. £3.50
Concha y Toro Chardonnay (CUL)

1981
£2.85–£4.25
Concha y Toro Oro del Rhin (CUL)
★Concha y Toro Sauvignon Semillon (ESV)
Cousiño Macul Chardonnay (VIGN)

1980
c. £3.50
Torres Viña Santa Digna White (VIGN)

United Kingdom

Are we really giving English vineyards a decent break? Or do we regard them as the absurd figments of a few demented imaginations? Which poses the question: are any of us actually buying their wine? Almost without exception the wine-growing countries of the world are remarkable for their full-blooded chauvinism when it comes to the local produce. And frequently that chauvinism is a good deal less than nationalistic. Parochial, more like. Find me a Burgundian who will do more than grimace and spit at the thought of a claret. Find me a Bordelais who would regard Beaujolais as anything more than fruit juice fit for children and church fêtes. Find me a Rhône grower, favoured with sticky, dark Syrahs, and fleshy, alcoholic Grenaches who will give house room to the light, gentle wines of Burgundy's Côte d'Or. All of them, to a man, are branded with a fierce pride in their own wines. And all of the local inhabitants, not necessarily involved with the wine business, will be fanatical supporters of their local brews. Head further north, away from the easy-growing, sprawling vineyards of the south, and you may find a few enlightened souls prepared to compare claret with burgundy, but always French with French. In Italy, Italians may trade bulk wine with Germany, but they wouldn't drink her hocks and mosels in return. Spaniards would regard anything from north of the Pyrenees as watery and feeble, barely fit to wash in.

But when it comes to England, these natural laws of chauvinistic protectionism undergo a sea change. If we want to have the remotest family resemblance to the real world of wine-growing, we should already be the King Canutes of the wine-drinking world, turning back the waggonloads of foreign muck which threaten to pollute our British palates and decay our moral fibre.

But more than that! If the mainstream Europeans are anything to go by, with a man from Nuits Saint Georges swearing his wines are always better than the wines of Beaune, just down the road, or a man from Chianti refusing to discuss anything not grown within hailing distance of his own horizontal press, we should have the drinkers of Benenden defending to the death their Müller Thurgau against the Reichensteiner of Devil's Cauldron, the Siegerrebe of Lamberhurst and the Dusty Miller of Spots Farm (I thought I'd throw in an English name – I'm tired of all those umlauts. Actually, the Dusty Miller is the French Pinot Meunier, but the French wouldn't call their grapes by English names, so I'll put my oar in for honest Anglo-Saxon chauvinism and stick to Dusty Miller.) These are the names of some of the vineyards just a few miles from each other in Kent. How many of us have drunk even one of them?

We hardly even know our own vineyards exist, and there are precious few of us, who, faced with bottles of imported or domestic wines at similar prices, will not lunge for the French, or Italian, or German, and dismiss the home brew with a few disparaging remarks like: 'Oh, it couldn't be any good, look at our weather . . .' or 'I knew a friend of a friend who used to make wine in his potting shed; went crazy with it and shot the vicar . . .' 'Anyway, it's *far* too expensive, I could get 11 litres of that red plonk we get at Benidorm for the same price . . .'

Well, it's time to stop and think. 1983 produced what one pundit reckoned was the best vintage for two thousand years. Quite how he obtained details of the other 1,999 is uncertain, but we're not going to argue; inside that bold assertion lie the seeds of some healthy chauvinistic arrogance which the English and Welsh wine makers are going to need if they intend entering the big time of European wine-making, because we've got most of the dice loaded against us.

Wine in a cold climate

The weather is the most obvious problem. Vines like it hot, and vines like it pretty dry, too. In the heatwave summer of 1976, vineyards were almost the only splashes of green visible in the scorched English countryside, as they thrived in the arid conditions. But most years we have too little sun and too much rain. The French, understandably unwilling to approve of any non-Gallic vineyard area, have pronounced that the vine cannot ripen above the 50th parallel. A quick glance at my atlas shows that this gives the green light to the massed hordes of wine growers on the Scilly Isles and Lizard Point in Cornwall, but leaves the rest of our nation out in the cold. Out in the cold is about right, when we look at the mean temperatures a vine needs to ripen. Annual temperatures are measured by a unit called the 'degree day', and about a thousand of these units are needed to ripen the vine. Southern England gets an average of 762! Not a lot, but much of Germany gets less than a thousand, and we're one of their biggest importers. So it's a case of having to try twice as hard and take twice as many risks to achieve what the French normally manage standing on their heads.

It's not only our lack of sun – it is also the wind. Remarkably, a lot of the people who rushed into establishing vineyards in the 1970s (and there are now over 200 of them), didn't bother to research what kind of conditions would best suit the vines, and gaily planted on wide, windy stretches of land. Not wise. The presence of trees and other windbreaks dramatically increases vineyard temperature and the chance of the fruit ripening.

And then there's the rain. The vine doesn't care for anything more than an occasional drenching, and is unlikely to stay free of diseases with more than 30 inches of rain a year. Well, some of our quite warm acres get over 100 inches a year. East Anglia is luckiest with an average nearer 20, but East Anglia is wide open to those icy blasts from Siberia, so while vines there may not develop trench-foot or gangrene, they'll still be awfully prone to chilblains.

And the government could be more helpful. Although it allows a winery to keep a maximum of 240 gallons of wine for 'home consumption' (Some home! Some consumption!), the Inland Revenue nonetheless has not granted agricultural status to wine, and thus can assess buildings and outhouses, as if they were in industrial use. If a farmer just sold grapes, he'd qualify for the beneficial agricultural rating. Since the grapes he grows don't taste nice, have no value for a greengrocer, and only have a use when transformed into wine, we allow our puritan past to rear its ugly head, and despite EEC rulings, industrial ratings apply. Add to that the payment of duty by the producer (in Germany and Italy the producer pays nothing), the imposition of VAT, and the inability of our vineyards, as yet, to produce large yields, and you can see why English wine seems expensive.

But then look again. The Carr Taylor vineyard in Sussex will sell you a bottle of their Hastings wine for less than £2.80. Is it really *that* expensive? Not if you like the taste, it isn't, and with our very long ripening seasons, as with all British fruit, the flavours do become more refined and pointed. Indeed, our light white wines seem to be well-placed to take advantage of the move towards lighter, fresher, gourmet cooking, a point which David Carr Taylor amply proved last year, when he filled the boot of his car with bottles of Carr Taylor wine, and headed for the Paris Agricultural Show. For three days he endured the jokes and jibes, but by the end of it he'd sold 80 cases to top Paris restaurants who thought the wine was the perfect accompaniment to their Nouvelle Cuisine creations. So, doubting Thomases, get out and try a bottle, and stop knocking our newest national drink.

Webster's is an annual publication. We welcome suggestions for next year's edition.

Price Guide

White

Non-vintage
£3.25–£4.00
Carr Taylor Vineyards Hastings Table Wine (ESV)
Lamberhurst Priory Seyval Blanc (PD)
Carr Taylor Gutenborner (PD)
c. £5.30
Lamberhurst Priory Müller-Thurgau (J&B)
Adgestone (J&B)

1983
c. £3.65
★Wooton Müller-Thurgau (BOW)
★Wooton Schönburger (BOW)
★Elmham Park (H&D)
Ditchling Müller-Thurgau (RACK)

1982
£3.25–£4.00
Penshurst (SF)
Lamberhurst White (CUL)
Lamberhurst Priory Seyval Blanc (CUL)
Tenterden (RACK)
Lamberhurst Priory Reichensteiner (ODD, VICT)
Ditchling Müller-Thurgau Ortega (RACK)
Ditchling Reichensteiner (RACK)
Spots Dry Gutenborner (RACK)
Spots Farm Seyval Blanc (RACK)
Staple St James Huxelrebe (MART, RACK)
Staple St James Müller-Thurgau (RACK)
c. £5.50
Wooton Schönburger (VICT)

1981
£3.00–£4.00
New Hall Huxelrebe (L&W)
New Hall Müller-Thurgau (L&W)
Westbury Farm Reichensteiner (DOL)
Lamberhurst Priory Müller-Thurgau (DAV, H&D, GH)
Lamberhurst Seyval Blanc (WSOC, YFW)
£4.75–£5.50
Adgestone (GH, CUL, VICT, TAN)
Wraxall White (AV)
Pilton Manor Müller-Thurgau (AV)

1980
£4.00–£4.50
Chilford Hundred Schönburger/Ortega (P&C)
Wooton Schönburger (VIGN, WHIT)
Elham Park (GH)

*Please don't blame **Webster's** or the merchants listed if a wine is sold out or if the vintage you want is no longer available. Wine is a living entity and a limited commodity – continuity of supply cannot, alas, be guaranteed.*

Wooton Müller-Thurgau (WHIT)
c. £5.60
Cavendish Manor Müller-Thurgau (YFW)

1979
£3.75–£4.75
Chilford Hundred Müller-Thurgau/Schönburger (P&C)
Felstar Müller-Thurgau & Sieger (P&C)
Lamberhurst Priory Müller-Thurgau (HHC)
New Hall Huxelrebe (TAN)

Red

1978
c. £6.00
Westbury Pinot Noir

Rest of the World

Austria

Austria's lack of success on the British market is both puzzling and distressing. She produces what one might call Thinking Man's Liebfraumilches far better than anyone else. They have much more guts and 'vininess' than the German creation, and though the Bulgarian version is impressively clever, you might not want to spend all night drinking it. Yet from Austria, even the basic Schluck brand is undeniably good wine, having the softness and grapey fruit that this enormously important part of the market needs, as well as having a positively interesting flavour when compared to German equivalents.

But it is price that matters in this neck of the woods – price, or a big advertising budget. On the Victoria Wine list, Schluck's tricky 'twixt the devil and the deep blue wine lake' position is cruelly clear. Own-label Liebfraumilch is at the psychologically important threshold of £1.99. Blue Nun Liebfraumilch, the UK's leading brand, can command a premium price of £3.09. In between is the part-brand, part-value-for-money Schluck at £2.39 – stuck between the two. Just like Austria's wine image.

Somewhere between Germany and France in the consumer's perception of styles, Austria's very distinct wines have never got off the ground here. In 1983 Austria had less than one per cent of the British market, and Schluck accounted for 50 per cent of that. However, there *are* a couple of hopeful areas. Various companies are now turning to Austria to provide own-label Liebfraumilch alternatives. The Welschriesling is normally used for this, but the Grüner Veltliner makes an altogether more interesting wine, often dry, rather peppery, with a green streak of freshness, and is beginning to appear under own-label.

The other area of expansion is in big, rich, late-picked dessert wines. Several large companies have taken these on, and they provide the cheapest high quality dessert wines on the market today. A Beerenauslese can cost less than £5.00 for a slightly one-dimensional but undeniably luscious wine, sweet as sin, and about one-third the price of the German equivalent. Austria may not be able to match the Liebfraumilch boys, but move up a rung or two in quality and she's more than a match for Germany.

White

Non-vintage

£2.00–£2.75

Sainsbury's Grüner Veltliner (SAIN)
Grüner Veltliner (VICT)
Schluck, Lenz Moser (SAIN, WILL, WAIT, VICT, AV, THRE, CHAP, P&C, P&D, UNW *& others*)
Amadeus Welsch Riesling, Morandell (WILL)
★Harveys Grüner Veltliner (JH)
Vogelberg Welschriesling, Lenz Moser (HHC)

£3.75–£4.75

Gumpoldskirchner Herrenlese, Lenz Moser (VICT)
Riesling Sylvaner (DOL)

1982

c. £2.65

Schluck, Lenz Motor (DAV, CL, GH)

£4.00–£5.00

Grüner Veltliner Riede Hundschupfen Retz (VICT)

Gewürztraminer Spätlese, Lenz Moser (MAL)
Weissburgunder Beerenauslese, Lenz Moser (ODD)

1981
£3.15–£4.00
Ruster Welschriesling (DAV)
Ruster Weissburgunder Beerenauslese, Lenz Moser, ½ bottle (LADV)
★Gewürztraminer Kabinett (ODD, CUL)
Klosterneuberg Muskat Ottonel (ODD)
Kremser Sandgruber Grüner Veltliner (TAN)
c. £4.75
Ruster Weissburgunder Beerenauslese (CHAP)
Gumpoldskirchner Gold Zierfandler (TAN)
£5.00–£6.25
Ruster Gewürztraminer Trockenbeerenauslese, Lenz Moser, ½ bottle (LADV)
Ruster Beerenauslese, Lenz Moser (VICT)
★Pinot Blanc Trockenbeerenauslese (CUL)

1980
£2.25–£3.50
Falkensteiner Grüner Veltliner, Morandell (WILL)
Blue Danube (WHIT)
Schluck, Lenz Moser (WHIT)
Kremser Sandgrube Müller-Thurgau, Morandell (WILL, L&W)
Gumpoldskirchner Zierfandler, Morandell (WILL)
★Klosterdawn Grüner Veltliner (PG)
Steinerhund Rheinriesling, Morandell (WILL)
Ruster Spätlese Neuburger, Morandell (WILL)
c. £5.50
Eiswein Neusiedlersee, Morandell (WILL)
c. £9.10
Weissburgunder Trockenbeerenauslese, Lenz Moser (ODD)

1979
£3.00–£4.00
Gumpoldskirchner Herrenlese (GH)
Kremser Muskat Ottonel (GH)
Burgenland St Margarethener Auslese (VIGN)
Ruster Auslese Weissburgunder, Morandell (WILL)
Kremser Müller-Thurgau Spätlese, Metternich'sche Weinguter (PD)
£4.50–£5.75
Nussberger Hohenweg Traminer (BIB)
Ruländer Beerenauslese, Lenz Moser (PD)
Ruster Beerenauslese Weissburgunder, Morandell (WILL, GH)
Ruster Trockenbeerenauslese ½ bottle (WHIT)
Ruster Trockenbeerenauslese Fruhoter Veltliner (GH)

1978
c. £2.50
Krems Schmidt Grüner Veltliner (WILL)
c. £6.00
Traminer Eiswein (BIB)

1977
c. £2.50
Krems Weinzierl Grüner Veltliner (WILL)
c. £5.00
Ruster Beerenauslese (WHIT)
Klosterneuberg Weissburgunder Auslese (ODD)

1976
£9.50–£10.00
Donnerskirchner Welschriesling Trockenbeerenauslese, Lenz Moser (VICT)
Bouvier Trockenbeerenauslese (WSOC)

1973
c. £5.60
Welschriesling Trockenbeerenauslese (BIB)
c. £8.00
Ruster Trockenbeerenauslese, Morandell (L&W)

Red
Non-vintage
c. £2.40
Klosterkaiser Blau Portugieser (L&W)

1981
c. £3.00
Ruster Blaufrankisch Spätlese, Morandell (WILL, WHIT)

1979
c. £2.75
Krems St Laurent (WILL)
Ruster Blaufrankisch, Morandell (WILL, L&W)
c. £4.30
Ruster Blaufrankish Spätlese, A. Unger (TAN)

Bulgaria

Bulgaria's wine industry has pushed and shoved itself into a leading position in the world export market in a remarkably short time; it was virtually created from scratch after World War II. Up till then,

Muslim influence meant that wine wasn't exactly high in the list of priorities. But Bulgaria needed hard currency, and it was a very far-sighted politician in the dark days of the 1940s who saw wine as a currency earner par excellence. This aggressive but consumer-aware attitude still marks out the Bulgarian approach and, alone of all the Eastern bloc countries, Bulgaria seems eager to listen to what the UK wants and act on those wishes.

Her Cabernet Sauvignon was for a long time as cheap as any wine in the shop, and brilliantly blackcurranty in a simple, obvious way. The latest winner is a Liebfraumilchski – Italian Riesling minutely tailored to suit the British taste. Prices are extremely low, with (for once) central planning having a reasonably healthy effect on wine supplies and styles. The only worrying thing about Bulgaria at the moment is that the reds seem to be becoming more sophisticated. I wish they wouldn't. It doesn't suit them.

Red

Non-vintage

£1.75–£2.75

Bulgarian Red (WAIT, VICT)
*Mehana Red (CUL)
Ashe's Bulgarian Red (ASHE)
Bulgarian Cabernet Sauvignon (P&C, PD, CHAP, J&B)
Bulgarian Merlot (P&C)
Bulgarian Pinot Chardonnay (BIB)
Hirondelle Cabernet Sauvignon (H&B, BYR)
Mavrud Asenovgrad (PD)

1979

£2.25–£2.50

*Bulgarian Cabernet Sauvignon (WAIT, CUL, BIB, MART, ASHE)
Bulgarian Merlot (BYR, SW, MAL)
*Cabernet, Pavlikeni (STWC)

1978

c. £2.25

Bulgarian Cabernet Sauvignon (DOL, BYR, DAV, PG, SW, VIGN, TAN)

1977

£2.75–£3.50

Bulgarian Cabernet Sauvignon (AV)
Mavrud Asenovgrad (VIGN)

1976

Sakar Mountain Cabernet Sauvignon (SW, VIGN, VICT)

White

Non-vintage

£1.75–£2.00

Bulgarian White (WAIT, VICT)
Mehana White (CUL)
Ashe's Bulgarian White (ASHE)
Bulgarian Riesling (P&C, CUL, DOL)

£2.00–£3.00

*Bulgarian Pinot Chardonnay (PD, CHAP, PG, DOL, SW)
*The Club's House White (STWC)
Pinot Chardonnay (CUL, DAV)
*Tesco Bulgarian Welschriesling litre (TES)

1982

c. £2.40

*Chardonnay, Provadya (STWC)

1979

c. £2.15

Bulgarian Riesling (MART, BYR)
Bulgarian Chardonnay (MART, BYR)

Canada

Canada does try. When you've got a government still pursuing an antiquated protectionist policy which allows sales of alcohol only through government stores, and that kind of sullen disapproval that goes with it, as well as a climate which goes from Mediterranean broiling to Scandinavian frozen and back again, you wouldn't have very high hopes. Even so, she tries. Most Canadian wine is from the pretty ghastly Labrusca grape types (banned in European vineyards), but there are a couple of more normal wines. We'd love to say they're worth a go, but we can't. Being kind, we'll call them 'uninspiring'.

White
1981
c. £4.20
Inniskillin Riesling (AV)
1980
c. £4.20
Inniskillin Chardonnay (AV)

Red
1980
c. £4.20
Inniskillin Gamay Noir (AV)

Cyprus

Cyprus is struggling to overcome the trauma of the partition, and the increasing unfashionability of her chief product, Cyprus Sherry. With the aid of an excellent government research institute at Limassol, she is getting onto the right track, particularly with the attempt to break into the boom market of light white table wines. Most of the grapes are unfortunately of the non-aromatic, rather neutral southern sort, but there is some good Muscat, both sweet and dry, and she has produced a clever, medium, Germanic concoction, closely resembling the Bulgarian efforts with Italianski Riesling. Her best new wine, though, is red – a marvellous deep Syrah, all smoke and pepper and raspberries. But that's another of the research institute numbers. We'll have to wait a while before we get anything like that commercially.

Fortified
£2.25–£2.50
Mosaic Cream (CHAP)
Mosaic Dry (CHAP)
Mosaic Medium (CHAP)
⋆Emva Cream (CHAP, DAV, THRE)
Emva Dry (THRE)
⋆Emva Medium Dry (THRE, DAV)
Emva Pale Cream (THRE)

Red
c. £2.40
Othello Keo (VICT, BYR)

White
c. £2.50
Aphrodite Keo (VICT, BYR)
Hirondelle sweet white (H&B, THRE)
St Pancrass medium sweet, Keo (BYR)
St Panteleimon, Keo (VICT)
Bellapais Keo Pétillant (VICT)

Greece

As the newest member of the EEC, it may be hoping for rather too much to expect her to dash off a string of French or German inspired classics to please the wine buffs of northern Europe. I'm afraid that Greece is still the home of the tired, drying out oxidized red and the fat, oily, tired white – with a couple of glorious exceptions. The first is her most notorious wine – retsina. People are far too rude about it; if you tasted some of the other whites you'd see why they need to shove them into a resinated goatskin for a bit. But retsina is a unique wine, and we get some reasonably good ones over here.

There's also some fairly tasty Muscat, both sweet and dry, made on the island of Samos, but the ones we get are somewhat charmless and marmaladey, lacking perfume; adequate, not brilliant. And Château Carras is a new winery, advised by Professor Peynaud from Bordeaux, and injected with massive amounts of cash. The whites are rather raw, but the red Carras is excellent. It's French, though, not Greek!

Red
Non-vintage
c. £2.40
Demestica, Achaia Clauss (PD, VIGN, UNW)

Apollo Red (CUL)
Danielis, Achaia Clauss (PD)

1979
c. £4.50
★Château Carras, Cava Carras (H&D)

1978
c. £2.65
Castel Danielis, Achaia Clauss (PG)
c. £4.65
Château Carras, Côtes de Meliton (VIGN)

1975
c. £4.10
Château Carras, Côtes de Meliton (WILL, WSOC)

White
Non-vintage
£2.25–£3.50
Demestica, Achaia Clauss (PD, VIGN, UNW)
Retsina, Achaia Clauss (PD, CUL)
Apollo White (CUL)
★Metaxas Retsina (DAV, P&C)
Samos Muscat (ODD)
Domaine Port Carras Blanc de Blancs, Côtes de Meliton (WILL, VIGN)

Hungary

Hungary is a curious mixture. It has one of the UK's most successful wine brands – Bull's Blood. It has one of the world's most fabled sweet wines – Tokay. And it led the charge with the vaguely sweet, foggy-day reds and flabby innocuous own-label whites which now adorn every supermarket shelf but don't satisfy anybody's taste buds very much. This is a pity, because Hungary has as fine a wine tradition as any country in Europe.

There was a time when Bull's Blood was so good that you could take it to any wine buff's table and be applauded for your originality. Now, each bottle seems different from the last, and one wonders if the chaps over there have any interest at all in what the UK market wants.

Tokay is a different story because the taste that marks this out is oxidation. It's no longer a fashionable taste, but gutsy stuff, and is usually fairly priced and reasonable value for money. But don't expect the honey sweetness of Sauternes, or the grapey richness of a Muscatel. This is rasping, fiery wine, with its personality dragged out of a hectic Magyar past.

The one area where Hungary does seem to have taken note of some kind of UK need, is in the light, sweetish reds which quite a few supermarkets offer as a 'mellow' red. If you catch it young enough, it's quite good. The Olasz Riesling white is just plain dull as, sadly, are some of the most bewildering and bewitching wine names ever etched onto a label – Badacsonyi Szurkebarat, Keknyelú, Debroi Harslevelü – these wines used to spit their big loud flavours at you. Not any more.

White
Non-vintage
£2.00–£2.75
Pecs Olasz Riesling (ODD, UNW)
Hungarian Chardonnay Villany (WILL)
Tokay Szamarodni sweet ½ litre (CHAP, MAL)
Tokay Szamarodni dry ½ litre (CHAP)
c. £3.50
Tokay Aszu 3 Putts ½ litre (L&W, PD, P&C, MWS)
Tokay Aszu 5 Putts ½ litre (CHAP, L&W, LADV)

1980
c. £2.65
★Badacsonyi Szurkebaret (PG)
Debroi Harslevelu (PG)
1978
c. £3.00
Tokay Szamarodni sweet ½ litre (WHIT)
1977
c. £3.15
Tokay Szamarodni dry ½ litre (ADN, WILL)
1976
£2.75–£3.75
Tokay Szamarodni dry ½ litre (WHIT)
Tokay Szamarodni sweet ½ litre (WILL)
Tokay Aszu 5 Putts ½ litre (PG, WHIT, GH, VIGN, WSOC, ADN)
Tokay Aszu 3 Putts ½ litre (VIGN)
1975
£3.50–£4.50
Tokay Aszu 5 Putts ½ litre (WILL, BBR, MWS)
Tokay Aszu 4 Putts ½ litre (VIGN, BBR)
Tokay Aszu 4 Putts ½ litre (BBR)
1974
£3.50–£4.25
Tokay Aszu 3 Putts ½ litre (WILL)
Tokay Aszu 4 Putts ½ litre (WILL, WHIT)
Tokay Aszu 5 Putts ½ litre (BYR, HHC)
1973
c. £4.00
Tokay Aszu 3 Putts ½ litre (ADN)
1964
c. £26.75
Tokay Aszu Essencia ½ litre (ADN, PG, VIGN, WHIT)
c. £34.75
Tokay Essence ½ litre (HHC)
1959
c. £35.00
Tokay Aszu 6 Putts ½ litre (MAL)
1957
c. £35.00
Tokay Aszu 6 Putts ½ litre (MAL, ADN)
c. £39.10
Tokay Aszu Essencia (ADN)
1956
c. £33.00
Tokay Aszu 5 Putts ½ litre (ADN)

Red
Non-vintage
£2.00–£2.50
Hajos Cabernet (P&C)
Bulls Blood Egri Bikaver (WILL, PD, THRE, UNW, AV)
Hungarian Cabernet Sauvignon Villany (WILL)
1981
c. £3.15
Bulls Blood Egri Bikaver (MWS)
1980
c. £2.35
Bulls Blood Egri Bikaver (PG)
1979
c. £2.40
Bulls Blood Egri Bikaver (GH, WHIT)
1978
c. £3.30
Bulls Blood Egri Bikaver (HHC)
1977
c. £2.30
Bulls Blood Egri Bikaver (BYR)

Lebanon

If the Middle East is the cradle of the grape, we are only able to taste the modern day equivalent of those first wine efforts through the astonishing bravery of the Hochar family, and in particular Serge Hochar, who makes the wine of Château Musar. Much of the bitterest fighting between Lebanese factions has been in the Bekaa valley, precisely where Hochar has his 50-year-old vineyard which forms the basis for the Musar wine.

In 1982 the civil war established a front line between his vineyard and his winery and it was only due to the confusion following the Israeli invasion that his trucks could zigzag backwards and forwards across the lines with the precious harvest of grapes. In 1983 the American gunboats enforced a troubled truce lasting just long enough for Hochar to whip up his pickers, put all the truck drivers on a bonus, and bring in the vintage with all the daring and proud courage of a *Boy's Own* hero.

Red
1980
c. £2.75
Cuvée Musar (CUL)
1978
c. £3.50
Cuvée Musar (L&W)
1977
c. £3.00
Cuvée Musar (BYR, WILL)
c. £4.00
Château Musar (PG, BYR, RACK, WAIT, BIB, CHAP, L&W, UNW, CUL, ESV, *& others*)
1975
c. £4.20
Château Musar (WILL, PG, BYR, BIB, ESV)
1972
c. £4.75
Château Musar (WILL, ADN, BIB, VIGN)
1970
c. £5.60
Château Musar (BYR, AV, BIB, LADV, VIGN)
1969
c. £7.00
Château Musar (PG, BYR)
1967
c. £5.60
Château Musar (ADN)

1966
c. £7.75
Château Musar (L&W, VIGN)
1964
c. £10.00
Château Musar (LADV)
1961
c. £10.35
Château Musar (ADN)

White
1980
c. £3.00
Cuvée Musar (WILL)
1969
c. £5.50
Château Musar (VIGN)

North Africa

Algerian red, Moroccan red, Tunisian red. Every shop used to have one. They're much rarer birds nowadays. Tunisia is trying to respond to export needs, but so far can't get past the heavy, oxidizing curse of overripe grapes and uncontrolled fermentation and ageing. Algeria is making some good wine, but we hardly see it here. Only Morocco has any UK presence, and the Tarik and Sidi Brahim brands are worth their place. Dark purple-red wines with loads of fruit and oomph, they're not exactly modern, but when the winter evenings begin to set in I can think of worse fates than a mug of one of these two.

Red
1981
c. £2.35
Sidi Brahim (MACK)
1978
c. £2.10
⋆Tarik (ODD)

Romania

You could be forgiven for asking whether Romania makes wine at all, it's seen so little over here. One company tried for years, but got little help from the State and couldn't match the competitiveness of the Bulgarians and Hungarians. In 1984 another company was established to make a dent on the market. First signs are hopeful; Riesling and a Cabernet are both cheap and good, but at the moment the wines have to be bottled in Munich. The sweet Murfatlar whites available here a few years ago were of a remarkably high quality, and very cheap.

Red
1977
c. £2.90
Romanian Merlot (AV)

Switzerland

The Swiss Centre in London is an expensive place – just order a bottle of wine to get the full force of that argument. Swiss wine is expensive in Switzerland. It's *very* expensive here. Even so, the quality can be high, but in a way which we are not keen to pay for – light, snow-fresh whites, wines with gentle perfume and a spritzy acid bite.

The wines over here are usually of the ski resort brand-name Fendant type. But there are some good Grand Cru estates, making an interesting variety of whites and some reds. They're well worth seeking out *in situ,* but not over here.

Red
1982
c. £6.60
Dôle Romane, Orsat (PG)
1979
c. £6.60
Dôle Romane, Orsat (MWS)
1977
c. £5.40
Dôle Romane, Orsat (WILL)

White
Non-vintage
c. £6.50
Samuel Chatenay 1er Cru Neufchatel (WILL)
1982
c. £6.30
Johannisberg Vent d'Est, Orsat (PG)
1978
c. £6.30
Johannisberg Vent d'Est, Orsat (MWS)

Rosé
1976
c. £4.40
Eden Rosé, Orsat (WILL)

Yugoslavia

One can spend too much time in Eastern Europe churning out 'might have been' and 'one that got away' stories, but they do ask for it. Yugoslavia is a classic case. A few years ago Yugoslav Cabernet Sauvignon was the *first* of the varietal wines to make inroads into the UK market. It was excellent; big, rather soupy stuff, but with loads of fruit, the blackcurrant mixed up with a strong meaty roasted taste. But as soon as a few of the others like Bulgaria threatened to get in on the act, Yugoslavia seemed to give up the ghost. Her Cabernets now tend to be so coarse and raw, tasting of grapeskins and harsh, overpressed fruit, that in blind tastings the 'Yugoslav' harshness has become a shorthand description for the desperately tough concoctions poorly-made Cabernet Sauvignon can be.

Although we're sorry to see the mighty Cabernet sink so low, the Vranač grape is showing a bit more form, and has a distinct style: tough, but with lots of fruit. Let's hope it stays that way, although in UK market terms the Yugoslav red production could disappear and hardly anyone would notice, because 95 per cent of Yugoslav sales in the UK are white. And of that, 70 per cent is a single brand – the ubiquitous Lutomer Laski Riesling.

Although the wine has never been that brilliant, it became a household name, and in the 1970s was notching up annual sales increases of over 20 per cent. I don't know how it was doing in the 60s, but that was when I had my first mouthful of white wine. What was it? Daft question. Lutomer Riesling – what else? Yugoslav Riesling has become something of a cliché, but the Yugoslav slice of the British market is quite important! In 1978 it was over six per cent, but over the next four years it lost out to Germany in the battle for the light, fruity sector. Even so, 1983 showed that there was still a place for this originator of the boom in innocuous wine styles, and Yugoslav wines notched up a 14 per cent increase taking them back to a market share of 4.9 per cent. Nearly all of this is Laski Riesling, but the more interesting wines are the Traminers and Sauvignons; big, gutsy, but rather good with it.

White
Non-vintage
£1.95–£2.50
Sainsbury's Laski Riesling (SAIN)
Tesco Yugoslav Laski Riesling (TES)
Waitrose Yugoslav Laski Riesling (WAIT)
Lutomer Laski Riesling (SAIN, PD)
Lutomer Sauvignon (WILL)
Cloberg Laski Riesling (PD)
Fruska Gora Traminer (ASHE)
Peter Dominic Lutomer Gewürztraminer (PD)

1982
£2.25–£2.75
Milion Laski Riesling (SW)
Fruska Gora Dry Riesling (SW)
Fruska Gora Dry Sauvignon (SW)
Fruska Gora Medium Traminer (SW)

1981
£2.00–£2.50
Lutomer Laski Riesling (PG)
Beli Burgundec Pinot Blanc (PG)
Lutomer Gewürztraminer (PG)
Fruska Gora Sauvignon (VIGN)
Fruska Gora Traminer (VIGN)
c. £3.15
Yugoslav Traminer (WSOC)

1980
£2.15–£3.15
Ranina Lutomer Tiger Milk Spätlese (BYR)
Renski Rizling, Maloze (WSOC, VIGN)
Rumeni Muscat (WSOC)

> ***Webster's** prices are per bottle, including VAT. If you buy a case or more, this may affect the price per bottle.*

1979
£2.00–£2.50
Beli Burgundec Pinot Blanc (BYR)
Lutomer Gewürztraminer (BYR)

Red
Non-vintage
£1.95–£2.95
Pinot Noir Lutomer (WILL)
Lutomer Merlot (WILL)
Milion Merlot (ASHE)
Sainsbury's Cabernet Sauvignon, 4 × ¼ litre (SAIN)

1981
c. £2.40
Milion Cabernet Sauvignon (SW)
Milion Merlot (SW)

1980
c. £2.15
Modri Burgundec Pinot Noir (PG, WHIT)
Slovin Cabernet Sauvignon (WILL, WHIT)

1979
c. £2.15
Mordi Cabernet Sauvignon (BYR)
Mordi Pinot Noir (BYR)
c. £4.20
Dingac (VIGN)

Glossary

Amontillado Sherry term. It should imply a quite dry, nutty, style, but usually now equals medium.

Appellation Contrôlée The French system, abbreviated as AC, of categorising the country's top wines, chiefly by grape variety, yield, and geographical location.

Barrique A small oak barrel, usually of about 225 litres, important in the maturation of many fine red wines, especially claret, and crucial to impart a taste of oak to any wine.

Beerenauslese (literally 'berries selection') German term for wine made from late-picked single berries, now also adopted in the New World for very sweet styles.

Bianco, branco, blanco, blanc, weiss – white.

Chai Literally the building where wine making is done, and maturation is begun.

Classico As in Chianti, Valpolicella, Soave etc. The central, traditional area of vineyards for a particular wine.

Clarete A light red Spanish style, loosely based on claret style.

Classé Classified. Various areas use classifications of vineyard quality, but Bordeaux, and in particular the 1855 classification for Haut Médoc, is the most renowned.

Consorzio Consortium. Usually a growers' group formed to promote and defend a particular wine.

Côtes Slopes. Slopes usually make better wine. Plains make plain wine.

Crémant A champagne style implying slightly less fizz than usual. Also used in the Loire, Alsace and elsewhere.

Cru bourgeois Loose term covering good properties in the major Bordeaux areas which weren't included in the various original classifications of 1855. There is now even a 'Bourgeois' classification.

Cuve Vat. Normally this refers to large fermenting and maturing vessels, now often made out of cement or stainless steel rather than the traditional wood.

Cuve close Tank method sparkling wine. The fizz-giving second fermentation takes place in pressurized tanks, not in the bottle. Only one or two top German Sekts and the good Asti Spumantes produce exciting wine by this method.

Cuvée Also ***Tête de Cuvée, Cuvée de Prestige*** etc. Refers to a selection from the best vats.

Denominazione di Origine Controllata DOC The Italian appellation system. As with French AC it is geographically based, but has proved less affective so far. A new ***Garantita*** DOC is coming into effect for some top wines, as yet without noticeable effect.

Denominación de Origen The Spanish appellation system. Quite effective, though not yet always a guarantee of a characterful wine.

Département The French regional system, corresponding to our counties.

Enoteca Italian term for a centre displaying (and sometimes selling) a wide range of particular wines. Literally a 'wine library'.

En primeur Term for wines still in cask – and as offered for sale immediately after the vintage. The most effective way of buying top clarets, burgundies and Rhônes.

Fermentation The process of transforming grape juice by yeasts into wine – bluntly, turning sugar into alcohol. Many white wines are now 'cold fermented' to preserve their fresh fruit tastes. This means that the fermentation temperature is kept at less than 20°C. Most grape musts would naturally reach 30°C or so during fermentation.

Grand Cru In Burgundy, the very top vineyards. Elsewhere it may have some worth, as in St-Emilion, but is often simply a producer's whim.

Grande Marque Great Brand. The name given to the major champagne houses. Almost all the famous brands are 'Grandes Marques'.

Halbtrocken Half-dry. An attempt in Germany to create a dryer, more food-orientated wine style than their usual slightly sweet offerings.

Trocken Dry. Normally a bit too raw to enjoy.

Hectare Metric measurement of land. One hectare = 2.47 acres.

Hectolitre Equals 100 litres, approximately 22 gallons. Hectolitres per hectare, hls/ha, usual measurement of vineyard yield.

Maduro Mature. Portuguese term for wine which has undergone ageing, usually in wood, as against *vinho verde,* which means fresh, unaged wine.

Méthode champenoise Champagne Method. The second fermentation is induced inside the bottle, and the resulting carbon dioxide is dissolved in the wine, creating that whoosh of bubbles when the cork is released. All the best sparklers world-wide use this method.

Metodo classico Italian term for champagne method. **Modern style.** Generalisation implying light, fruity and fresh wines, produced by scrupulously clean, up-to-the-minute methods. *Maceration carbonique* reds and cold fermentation (cf. fermentation) whites are two examples.

Maceration carbonique Red wine fermentation method where fermentation is begun inside the uncrushed grapes, giving lots of colour and fruit, and low tannin levels. Used for Beaujolais and similar wines.

Mousseux Fizzy, but usually applied to non-champagne method wines.

Must Term for the grape juice before it is transformed into wine by fermentation.

Noble rot A form of fungus *(botrytis cinerea)* which, instead of wrecking the grapes, feeds on the water in the juice, thus concentrating the sugars and acids. All great sweet wines are made from noble rot affected.

Oenology The science of wine making.

Oloroso Big, heavy style of sherry, basically dry, but usually sweetened slightly for Amontillado and a good deal for cream.

Opening Price Many properties offer a proportion of each vintage for sale early on at the 'opening price', generally the lowest price ever available. In any good vintage the prices will rise substantially after these 'opening prices'.

Own Label Any wine labelled with the retailers logo rather than the producer's.

Parcel Usually implies a number of cases of wine offered as a unit, then broken up for sale by the retailer. Also applies to a small section of a vineyard holding.

Phylloxera A vine louse which almost destroyed European wine growing in the nineteenth century. Now prevented by grafting European vines onto American vine rootstocks.

Pétillant Very slightly sparkling. Usually on purpose with young fresh wines, but sometimes a result of unintended second fermentation in the bottle.

Quinta Farm. Portuguese term for a single property. Some 'single quinta' ports are good value.

Reserva Spanish term implying better quality wine and longer wood ageing.

Riserva Italian version of *Reserva.* Except with the top quality wines, it should not be taken to mean necessarily better wine. Careless wood ageing will lead to dried out, prematurely senile wines.

Vin doux naturel Term for spirit-fortified sweet wine in the south of France.

Vino novello Italian version of 'New Wine', i.e. wine expressly fermented for very early consumption, often within a couple of months, like Beaujolais Nouveau.

Vin de Garde A wine which has been expressly made for ageing and mature drinking. The opposite of Vin Nouveau.

Vin Ordinaire Ordinary wine. Usually basic French Vin de Table with no distinguishing features.

Vin de Primeur Basically the same as Vin Nouveau.

Vin de Table, Vino da Tavola, Tafelwein, Vino do mesa Table Wine. Implies the bottom grade, but in Italy it can also be applied to first rate but non-conformist wines.

Merchant Directory

This is a list of alphabetically coded wine merchants whose wines are included in the Guide. If the merchants do not have a code, we have not listed their wines but referred to them in some other context. A listing of merchants by region appears at the end of this directory.

Adnams **ADN**
Sole Bay Brewery, Southwold, Suffolk IP18 6JW (0502) 722424
Wine Shop, South Breen, Southwold (0502) 722138
Very go-ahead and comprehensive list, giving one of the widest selections in the country, as well as particularly reliable basic wines, all backed up by the highly readable and often controversial comments of wine director, Simon Loftus.

Les Amis du Vin **LADV**
7 Ariel Way, Wood Lane, Shepherd's Bush, London W12 7SN (01) 743 2066/740 0053
51 Chiltern Street, London W1M 1HQ (01) 847 3419
30 James Street, London WC2 (01) 836 4666
Traditional wine shop and warehouse. An interesting and varied list; California is strong through the close association with Geoffrey Roberts; Rioja too, and French country wines. Their regular list is supplemented by additional offers. Mail order.

Arriba Kettle & Co **A&K**
5 St Philips Place, Birmingham B3 2PY
(021) 236 8186
Small, specialist Spanish wine merchant with wines from all over the country. Mail order only.

T. F. Ashe & Nephew Ltd **ASHE**
Ellis Ashton Street, Huyton Industrial Estate, Liverpool L36 6JB (051) 480 5678
320 Shops mainly in Midlands and North. Familiar brands peppered with Bordeaux châteaux, Burgundian estates and domaine wines from around the world.

Averys **AV**
7 Park Street, Bristol BS1 5NG (0272) 214141
Traditional Bristol wine merchants, with a special interest in fine burgundy. John Avery was one of the pioneer importers of New World wines, so California, Australia and New Zealand feature in their list. Mail order, in-store shop at Debenhams, Oxford.

Cynthia Bacon **CB**
ffowlers' Bucke, South Harting, Petersfield, Hants GU31 5QB (073) 085 471
This is a merchant for Italophiles, with just one single wine (English) from outside Italy. Piedmont is particularly well covered, with a variety of different producers. Mail order, one mixed case minimum.

Balls Brothers **BAL**
313 Cambridge Heath Road, London E2 9LQ
(01) 739 6466/1642
A good all-round list at this wine centre, especially for Bordeaux, champagne, port and sherry. Mail order.

Augustus Barnett Wine Merchants
46 Beak Street, London W1 (01) 437 0366
A chain undergoing a revival under Bass Charrington's new ownership, offering an increasingly good selection of many Bass wines which were previously difficult to obtain.

Berkmann Wine Cellars **BWC**
12 Brewery Road, London N7 9NH (01) 609 4711
These are the people for Georges Duboeuf's Beaujolais and his white wines of the Mâconnais. Côtes d'Or burgundies and Chablis are also strong. Mail order; and a wine club, Le Nez Rouge.

—— Wine at Christie's ——

A 200 year history of wine sales and an informed and expert staff enable us to offer a wide range of services to buyers and sellers of fine wines.

Specialised sales of Claret and White Bordeaux and Fine Wines are held on alternate Thursdays throughout the season, and we are happy to advise on all aspects of buying and selling wine at auction.

We welcome parcels of wine, even single old or rare bottles, and our invaluable Price Index of Vintage Wines offers sound guidance on wine values. The Index lists over 5000 different wines/ vintages and their current auction prices.

For information on our terms and services and details of the Price Index, together with our current Wine book list, please contact us at the address below.

Christie's **Wine** Department.

8 King Street, St. James's, London SW1Y 6QT Telephone: (01) 839 9060

Antique Furniture, Rare Metalwork & Fine Arts
Regd. VAT No. 120 802 519

CHRISTOPHER SYKES

ANTIQUES
The Old Parsonage, WOBURN, Milton Keynes MK17 9QL
Bedfordshire, England
Tel. Woburn 259 & 467
(STD Code 052 525 259)

CORKSCREWS BY MAIL ORDER.

PLEASE SEND £3 OR $8 AIR MAIL, FOR CATALOGUE ILLUSTRATING OVER 250 ANTIQUE, VINTAGE AND UNUSUAL CORKSCREWS (PRICED FROM £5 to £350 EACH) AND WINE RELATED ANTIQUES. VISA OR ACCESS/MASTERCARD ACCEPTED.

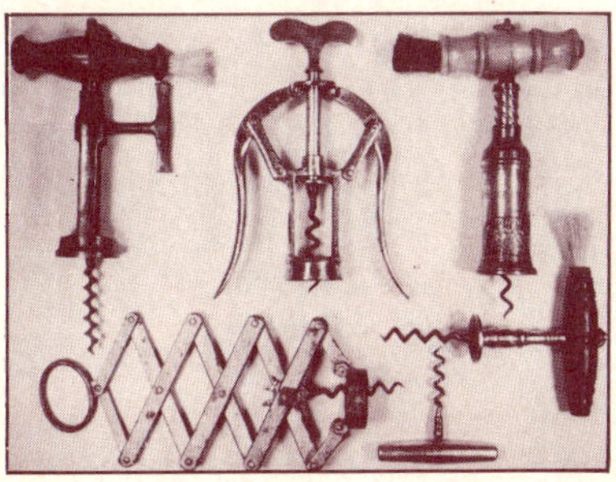

L. ROSENHEIM & SONS LTD.

Shippers of Fine Wines

EPERON

ESTABLISHED 1858

—PRESENT—

'The Hallgarten Rhône Collection'

Hallgarten were pioneers in the selection of fine individual Rhône wines and have been shipping an excellent range for over 30 years. Our price list has a comprehensive selection of these lovely wines which are available through your wine merchant.

Please send for our 1984 price list. For a complimentary copy of Peter Hallgartens Book "Guide to the wines of the Rhône" (Pitman series edited by Pamela Vandyke Price), please send 30p stamp ($2 overseas).

L. ROSENHEIM & SONS LTD.
53 Highgate Road, London NW5

Berry Bros & Rudd **BBR**
3 St James's Street, London SW1A 1EG
(01) 930 1888/5331
The Wine Shop, Houndmills, Basingstoke, Hampshire RG21 2YH (0256) 23566
Traditional wine merchants with the same address in St James's for two and half centuries. Claret and burgundy are their strong points, with a good selection of Rhine and Moselle too.

Bibendum **BIB**
113 Regents Park Road, London NW1 8UR
(01) 586 9761
A splendid wine emporium in NW1 with wooden claret boxes galore. Good on claret – petits châteaux and classed growths alike. French country wines feature prominently, and also California. Monthly wine festivals, and wines open daily for tasting. Mail order.

Bow Wine Vaults **BOW**
10 Bow Churchyard, London EC4M 9DQ
(01) 248 1121
City wine merchants with a strong French flavour, both classic and lesser known appellations. Sherry and madeira are also well represented. Mail order.

D. Byrne & Co **BYR**
12 King Street, Clitheroe, Lancashire BB7 2EP
(0200) 23152
A list with variety and bargains – all areas are well represented, but especially strong on claret, Germany and California. Mail order.

Cape Province Wine **CPW**
11 Clarence Street, Staines, Middlesex TW18 4SU
(0784) 51860/55244
All the great names in South Africa are on this list, from Edelkeur to Fleur du Cap.

Caves de la Madeleine **CDM**
301 Fulham Road, London SW10 9QH
(01) 351 1136/5863
As the name implies, the emphasis here is on France, with a good selection from all the traditional and less classic areas. California too has quite a substantial showing. Mail order.

Chaplin & Son **CHAP**
35 Rowlands Road, Worthing, Sussex BN11 3JJ
(0903) 35888
There's a bit of everything in this list – claret, burgundy, Australia, Italy and so on round the world. Mail order.

Chesterford Vintners **CV**
The Old Greyhound, Great Chesterford, Saffron Walden, Essex CB10 1NY (0799) 30088
A good variety. Strong on burgundy, a wide selection of clarets, as well as wines from the Bordeaux periphery; some German estate wines. Mail order.

Christopher & Co
4 Ormond Yard, London SW1 (01) 930 5557
Christopher's reputation is as a traditional St James's wine merchant, a role they fill well, but they are more inventive than that, and in particular have made a big effort with Chilean and Australian wines, as well as pioneering Blanquette de Limoux.

Henry C. Collison **COL**
7 Bury Street, St James's, London SW1Y 6AB
(01) 839 6406/6591
South African specialists. Fine estate wines that are some of best the Cape produces.

Corney & Barrow **C&B**
12 Helmet Row, London EC1V 3QJ (01) 251 4051
118 Moorgate, London EC2 (01) 628 2894
Traditional City wine merchants – an excellent claret list concentrating on Pomerols from Moueix. Some great names in burgundy too; good German list and a representation of the New World, Spain and Italy.

W. H. Cullen and Cullens Winemart **CUL**
142 Battersea Park Road, London SW11 4DX
(01) 622 4467
40 specialist off-licences, mainly in London and South-East. A splendidly eclectic list, with wines from all over the world, including Australia, Bulgaria and Chile. Mail order; warehouse in Weybridge; W. H. Cullen Wine Club £2 annual subscription, one mixed case minimum.

J. T. Davies & Sons Ltd **DAV**
7 Aberdeen Road, Croydon, Surrey CR0 1EQ
(01) 681 3222
Nearly 90 branches in London and the Home Counties. Strong on claret, petits châteaux as well as great names, and vintage ports.

Del Monico
64 Old Compton Street, London W1 (01) 437 2738
Bargain hunter's paradise. This cramped Soho establishment always has a variety of wines at prices which you think must be a mistake, as well as a good range of Europe's mainstream wines.

Dolamore **DOL**
15 Craven Road, London W2 (01) 723 8894
Wellington Street, Cambridge CB1 1HW
(0223) 350929
In Store at Joshua Taylor, Market Passage, Cambridge CB2 3JN (0223) 316455
106 Walton Street, Oxford OX2 6AJ (0865) 57734
College house range; good petits châteaux; some fine burgundies and Nederburg from South Africa.

Domaine Direct **DDIR**
29 Wilmington Square, London WC1 (01) 837 3521
Burgundy specialists with a selection of the best domaines in recent vintages. Mail order.

Peter Dominic **PD**
A High Street off-licence with about 500 branches scattered throughout the country; Cambridge, Southampton and Orange Street, London W1 have the widest choice. The French selection is strongest, and there is around-the-world coverage. The Wine Mine Club sends out a quarterly magazine and offers a discount on Club selections with no extra membership fee.

George Dutton & Son see **WILL**
Godstall Lane, St Werburgh Street, Chester CH1 1LJ (0244) 21488

Ebury Chatham & Dover **ECD**
178 Ebury Street, London SW1 (01) 730 8206/9
A small European selection. Mail order, one mixed case minimum.

Ehrmanns **EHR**
24–25 Scala Street, London W1P 1LU
(01) 637 0387
also own Old Chelsea Wine Stores at 56 Lamb's Conduit Street, London WC1N 3LW (01) 405 3106 and at 358 Kilburn High Road, London NW6
Three shops with a strong Iberian emphasis and a good range of French and Californian wines. Mail order.

REID WINES

We specialise in fine and rare wines and are pleased to buy or sell in small and large amounts. Our list of Claret goes back to the '20s and beyond and we have an extensive list of Burgundy, Rhone, Alsace, Champagne, Port, Madeira and German Wines as well as Fine Cognacs Armagnacs and Eaux de Vie

THE MILL, MARSH LANE, HALLATROW, BRISTOL BS18 5EB

telephone: 0761 52645 telex: 444565 (Reidwn)

UK AGENTS: MICHAEL DRUITT WINES
9 Deanery Street,
Park Lane,
London W1Y 5LF
Telephone: 01-493 5412/3

PALLANT WINES
Main Road, Birdham,
Chichester, W. Sussex.
(Adjoining Birdham Stores)
Tel: Chichester (0243) 512922

WINES BY THE CASE
at attractive prices.
Out wine selection includes the Louis Latour Burgundies, Theo Cattin Alsace, KWV South African and several of our own importing from the Loire.
Regular special offers, features and tastings.

Open 10 a.m. – 5 p.m. Mondays to Saturday
10 a.m. – 1 p.m. Sundays
Access and Barclaycard accepted.
Deliveries arranged.

GREATWINES

at palatable prices

Our wine list is drawn from all the major wine-producing countries at most quality levels.

Whatever your taste or price range you'll find a fine wine to enjoy. Send for a list or contact Mike Hall to discuss your special requirements

DON'T FORGET YOUR JAMES WHITE SUFFOLK CIDER! A pure delight – price list on request.

White-Hall Vintners (Anglia) Ltd.
Istana, Cratfield, Halesworth, Suffolk
Tel 098683-293 Telex 987703 CHACOM G "WHVIN"

Ellis Son & Vidler Ltd **ESV**
57 Cambridge Street, London SW1V 4PS
(01) 834 4101/4102
29 White Rock, Hastings, Sussex TN34 1JY
(0424) 420156
With David Cossart of the Madeira family Cossart Gordon as managing director, madeira has to be the strength of this company. However, also go to them for claret, and French country wines. Mail order.

Farthinghoe Fine Wine & Food **FFW**
Old Lane, Farthinghoe, Brackley,
Northamptonshire NN13 5NZ (0295) 710018
A strong French emphasis. Particularly good on Alsace, with wines from Hugel, Trimbach and Gisselbrecht, and also Rhône and burgundy. Less choice of claret. Mail order, one mixed case minimum.

Findlater Mackie Todd **FINT**
Findlater House, 92 Wigmore Street, London
W1H 0BB (01) 935 9264
A reliable, traditionalist, strong on claret and burgundy, but also good Rhônes and champagnes. Germany and Spain are fair, and Italy is much more imaginative than usual.

Richard Granger **RGA**
West Jesmond Station, Newcastle upon Tyne, NE2
3HH (0632) 815000
A small but well chosen selection. Mail order, one mixed case minimum.

Peter Green **PG**
37 A-B Warrender Park Road, Edinburgh
EH9 1HJ (031) 229 5925
An extensive and imaginative list of wines from all round the world, with some particularly good buys in France. Good selection of half bottles. Mail order.

Gerard Harris **GH**
2 Green End Street, Aston Clinton, Aylesbury,
Buckinghamshire HP22 5HP (0296) 631041
This village shop is owned by the famous Bell Inn restaurant. Strong points are Bordeaux and Germany, but other countries and regions are well covered. Mail order.

Roger Harris Wines **RGHR**
Loke Farm, Weston Longville, Norfolk NR9 5LG
(0603) 880171/2
The Beaujolais specialist par excellence *with over 60 different wines, including white and rosé, plus some white Mâconnais. Mail order, one case minimum.*

John Harvey & Sons **JH**
27 Pall Mall, London SW1 (01) 839 4695
Order Office: Harvey House, PO Box 55, Bristol
BS99 7JE (0272) 836161
12 Denmark Street, Bristol BS99 7JE Tel as for order office
16 The Hard, Portsmouth PO1 3DT (0705) 825567
Sherry (Harveys Bristol Cream), port (Cockburn's Special Reserve), and claret (close associations with Château Latour) are the strengths of their company. Mail order.

Richard Harvey Wines **RH**
The Auction House, East Street, Wimborne
Minster, Dorset BH21 1DX (0202) 881111
A one-man band with a bit of everything, all from reputable producers. Mail order, one mixed case minimum.

Haynes Hanson & Clark **HHC**
17 Lettice Street, London SW6 4EH (01) 736 7878
36 Kensington Church Street, London W8 4BX
(01) 937 4650
A wine warehouse at Lettice Street and a shop in Kensington Church Street. The list is dominated by France, plus some Californian, and vintage port. Mail order. Associated with John Arlott Wine Club.

Hedges & Butler **H&B**
153 Regent Street, London W1R 8HQ
(01) 734 4444
The fine-wine group of the brewers Bass Charrington. A good claret list, Jos Meyer Alsace wines, some Italian, vintage ports. Mail order, one case minimum.

Hicks & Don **H&D**
Order office: 4 The Market Place,
Westury,Wiltshire BA13 3EA (0373) 864723
Head Office: Park House, Elmham, Dereham,
Norfolk NR20 5AB (036) 281 571
Strong on opening offers of claret, port and the Rhône. Fine sherries from Barbadillo; a selection of lesser known French wines, as well as the classics. The rest of Europe and the New World are covered – not forgetting England, as Robin Don is a wine maker too. Mail order, one mixed case minimum.

High Breck Vintners **HBV**
Spats Lane, Headley, Hampshire GU35 8SX
(0428) 713689
Germans from Deinhard; Château de la Jaubertie in Bergerac; and a good range from other parts of France. Regular tastings for customers. Mail order, one mixed case minimum.

J. E. Hogg
61 Cumberland Street, Edinburgh EH3 6RA
(031) 556 4025
Claret buyer's delight. This little shop frequently has a queue outside of Edinburgh's most canny wine enthusiasts. Opening offers are good but mature claret and burgundy are excellent, as are malt whiskies.

The Hungerford Wine Co **HUN**
128 High Street, Hungerford, Berkshire RG17 0DL
(0488) 83238
An extensive claret list, plus sweet Bordeaux, Jaboulet from the Rhône, Hugel from Alsace. Opening claret offers whereby customers agree to a prior commitment scheme in order to save money. Mail order, one case minimum.

Imbibers Wines **IMB**
Lairg House, Brill Road, Oakley, Nr Thame, Bucks
HP18 9QH (0844) 237233/237861
Some good Austrians, Portuguese and New World. Mail order, one mixed case minimum.

Justerini & Brooks Ltd **J&B**
61 St James's Street, London SW1A 1LZ
(01) 493 8721
39 George Street, Edinburgh EH2 2HN
(031) 226 4202
Smart St James's wine merchants with a list to match – an impressive claret list with old vintages, a strong French emphasis, some good vintage port, and of course J&B whisky.

Lay & Wheeler **L&W**
6 Culver Street West, Colchester, Essex CO1 1JA
(0206) 67261
Gosbeck's Road, Shrub End, Colchester, Essex
CO2 9JT (0206) 71386
Also in Keddies.
These Colchester wine merchants have one of the most comprehensive lists in the country, with some of the best producers in each region. The claret is particularly good, but the others take a lot of beating. Mail order.

Laymont & Shaw **L&S**
The Old Chapel, Mill Pool, Truro, Cornwall
TR1 1EX (0872) 70545
Spanish specialists and pioneers – not just Rioja, but Penedès, La Mancha, Navarre and Malaga. Mail order, one case minimum.

O. W. Loeb & Co **OWL**
15 Jermyn Street, London SW1Y 6LT
(01) 734 5878
A list of superlatives – top Rhône, top Alsace, top burgundies, and top Germans. No shop, so they need prior warning of collection from Jermyn Street. Mail order.

Lorne House Vintners **LHV**
Unit 5, Hewitts Industrial Estate, Elmbridge Road,
Cranleigh, Surrey GU6 8LW (04866) 3542
These are the Muscadet specialists, but they have other wines as well; Loire, Rhône, Burgundy and Rioja. Mail order, one case minimum.

Mackie & Co **MACK**
4 Apothecary Street, London EC4V 6EU
(01) 236 7080
A mixture of everyday wines and some rare vintages, and Château Rieussec. Mail order.

Malmaison Wine Club **MAL**
28 Midland Road, London NW1 2AD
(01) 388 5086
A good all-round list. Has its home in Layton's wine cellars, so a shop as well as mail order, one mixed case minimum. Tastings for members.

Manor Wine Shop **MWS**
The Old Smithy, Raikes Road, Skipton (0756) 4175
No particular specialities, but a good all-round selection. Mail order.

The Market **MART**
700–702 Fulham Road, London SW6
(01) 736 4295/4834
A small London chain. Good range with an Italian emphasis, but strong on France too.

Marks & Spencer **M&S**
256 licensed stores all over the country. Not a comprehensive range, but a small selection of fast sellers. Full range carried by 25 stores in London and main provincial centres.

Milroy's
3 Greek Street, London, W1V 5LA
(01) 437 0893/2385/9311
Known as London's finest malt whiskey merchant, the wine side is just as serious and is one of London's best for Beaujolais, burgundy, champagne, mature port and claret, as well as such rarities as Bandol.

J. Moreno Wines **JMW**
2 Norfolk Place, London W2 1QN (01) 723 6897
11 Marylands Road, London W9 2DU
(01) 286 0678
The largest range of Spanish wines in the country. Riojas galore, Leon, La Mancha and Navarre and a fine selection of sherries.

Oddbins UK Ltd **ODD**
St John's Wharves, 73 Wapping High Street,
London E1 9PL (01) 488 9066
50 shops around London, Home Counties, West Country, East Midlands, Scotland and Paris. Their range is amongst the best of the High Street wine merchants. France is imaginatively covered, Italy too, and Portugal. Mail orders Oddbins by Post 34/36 The Highway, London E1 9BG.

Peatling & Cawdron **P&C**
Westgate House, Bury St Edmunds, Suffolk
IP33 1QS (0284) 5949
29 branches in East Anglia. A strong traditional French emphasis, some fine German estates and a smattering of wines from elsewhere.

Christopher Piper Wines **PIP**
1 Silver Street, Ottery St. Mary, Devon Ex11 1DB
(040 481) 4139
Any customer can purchase from the wholesale list, provided they buy at least three cases. A solid selection of respectable growers and négociants – Duboeuf's Beaujolais, some serious German estates, Bodegas Riojanas, and a good selection of half bottles. Mail order, one case minimum.

Quellyn Roberts **QR**
The Old Crypt, 11-23, Watergate Street, Chester
CH1 2JX (0244) 20515
A good claret list; some German estate wines and vintage port. Mail order.

Arthur Rackham's Wine Shops **RACK**
Winefare (Wholesale division), 5 High Road,
Byfleet, Surrey (09323) 51585
15 shops in the London area. Special features are English wines and Alfred Gratien champagne, but a selection from around the world.

Seymour Ramsay **SR**
Southmede Widmoor, Wooburn Green, High
Wycombe, Buckinghamshire HP10 0JG
(06285) 27210
A selection of reputable producers from all over the world, including Jaboulet from the Rhône, Heim in Alsace, Felton Empire and Louis Martini from California. Mail order/minimum one mixed case.

Reid Wines **REID**
The Mill, Marsh Lane, Hallatrow, Bristol BS18
5EB (0761) 52645
This is the place for fine old bottles – clarets go back to 1920. Also old madeira and vintage port. Mail order.

La Réserve **RSV**
56 Walton Street, London SW3 (01) 589 2020
47 Kendal Street, London W2 (01) 402 6920
Fine old and rare wines are the speciality, especially from Burgundy and Bordeaux. Mail order: associated with College Cellars.

Safeway
All 109 supermarkets stock wine. Over 40 stock fine wines.

Sainsbury's **SAIN**
Main Wine Branches: Nine Elms, London* Cromwell Road, London* Hornchurch, Leatherhead, Tottenham, Kempston, Bedfordshire, Coldhams Lane, Cambridge, Purley, Crystal Palace, London, Bath, Telford, Solihull, Burton-on-Trent.
Freezer Centres — Welwyn Garden City.
Off Licences attached to Supermarkets — Chester, Leeds, Archer Road, Sheffield, Golders Green.
*these two branches have exclusive wines.
Sainsbury's with 235 supermarkets is the country's largest wine retailer. A sound list enlivened by a vintage selection of fine wines available only from main stores.

Stapylton Fletcher **SF**
Woodfalls Farm, Laddingford, Yalding, Kent ME18 6DA (0622) 872304
Good sound selection of French wines with a smattering from elesewhere. Mail order, one mixed case minimum.

Sherston Wine Co. **SW**
1 Church Street, Sherston, Malmesbury, Wiltshire SN16 0LA (0666) 840644
Eight shops in the West Country. Spanish specialists who have expanded to include France, Italy and Portugal. Mail order (from Malmesbury) one mixed case minimum.

Stonehaven Wines **STON**
Grayshott Road, Headley Down, Bordon, Hampshire GU35 8JL (0428) 712700
Italian specialists par excellence, *representing a variety of some of the best producers from the Dolomites to Sicily. Mail order, one mixed case minimum.*

Sunday Times Wine Club **STWC**
The Wine Club, New Aquitaine House, Paddock Road, Reading, Berkshire RGA OBY
(0734) 481713
Mail order only. Its associate company is Bordeaux Direct. Britain's best known wine club. President is Hugh Johnson. Strong list. Wines from around the world, plus a quarterly journal and wine tours. Membership fee is £3 per annum.

T & W Wines **T&W**
51 King Street, Thetford, Norfolk IP24 2AU
(0842) 63855
Good people to hunt out old and rare wines, as well as wines for laying down, especially claret and port.

Tanners of Shrewsbury **TAN**
26 Wyle Cop, Shrewsbury, Shropshire SY1 1XD
(0743) 52421/61370
10 shops in Shropshire, Hereford and Mid-Wales. An old family firm with a varied selection of wines from all over the world. Good clarets, burgundies and California among others. Mail order, one mixed case minimum.

Tesco's Ltd **TES**
An ever-improving wine list; from basic Liebfraumilch and table wines they are expanding to include more imaginative wines from all over the world.

Threshers **THRE**
368, shops mainly in the south. A selection dominated by every day brand names.

Henry Townsend **HT**
Chalk Pit House, Coleshill, Amersham, Buckinghamshire HP7 0LW (024 03) 3823/22924
44 Hurlingham Road, London SW6
Superb on claret, with a special supplement to the main list. An enormous range of fine German estate wines. Mail order, one mixed case minimum.

Unwins Wine Merchants Ltd. **UNW**
279 shops throughout London and the Home Counties.
High street wine merchants with familiar brands and some finer estates from around the world.

Victoria Wine Company **VICT**
Over 900 branches throughout Great Britain. A wide range of wines for a High Street off-licence. France is well represented and Italy too. Spain is dominated by Don Cortez. A good New World spread.

La Vigneronne **VIGN**
105 Old Brompton Rd. London SW7 3LE
(01) 589 6113
Variety is the name of the game here; old clarets, a large range of Californians, and wines from Greece and Switzerland. Mail order.

The Vintner **see RACK**
66 Kensington Church Street, London W8
(01) 299 2629

Waitrose Ltd. **WAIT.**
70 licensed supermarkets.
There are few own-label wines, but an incredibly good range of wines from all round the world. As part of the John Lewis partnership they are 'never knowingly undersold'.

Whitesides of Clitheroe **WHIT**
Shawbridge Street, Clitheroe, Lancashire BB7 1NA
(0200) 22281
A varied list and a good allround selection. Mail order, one case minimum.

House of Wilkins **HW**
Bomarsund House, Fortis Green, London N2 9EW
(01) 883 2394
South African specialists, with K W V, Nederburg and Fleur du Cap, as well as fine estate wines. Mail order, six bottles minimum.

Willoughby's **WILL**
53 Cross Street, Manchester M2 4JB
(061) 834 6850/0641
100 Broadway, Chadderton, Oldham OL9 0AA
(061) 620 1374
A good varied worldwide selection including England and Hungary as well as more traditional areas. Mail order, one case minimum.

Windrush Wines **WW**
The Barracks, Cecily Hill, Cirencester, Gloucestershire GL7 2EF (0285) 67121
North-West Pacific and California are the specialities here. The rest of the world is covered by a selection of fine estates. Mail order, one mixed case minimum.

Wine Growers Association **WGA**
230 Great Portland Street, London W1N 5HG
(01) 451 0981/1135
Main Cellars: Willesden Bond, London NW10
Branches also at: No. 1, The Aldwych, London WC2
135 Western Road, Brighton
5 Castle Meadow, Norwich
An all-round European selection, with a special interest in Italy.

The Wine Society **WSOC**
53 Bolsover Street, London W1P 7HL
(01) 387 4681
Gunnels Wood Road, Stevenage, Hertfordshire SG1 2BG (0438) 314161
You have to be a member (£10 for life membership) to buy wines from this non-profit making cooperative. One of their aims is to seek out new wines, but they are good on classics too, especially claret. Mail order.

The Wine Studio **STUD**
9 Eccleston Street, London SW1W 9LX
(01) 730 7596
North American specialists with a superb range of California wines plus a few Australians. Mail order, one case minimum.

Wineland see **RACK**
200 Upper Richmond Road, London SW15
(01) 788 5641

The Winery **WNRY**
4 Clifton Road, London W9 (01) 286 6475
2 Charleville Road, London W14 (01) 385 3582
Two new shops with an imaginative and varied list. Australia is a speciality. Mail order, six bottles minimum.

Yapp Brothers **YAPP**
The Old Brewery, Mere, Wiltshire BA12 6DY
(0747) 860423
The Loire and Rhône specialists with some of the best producers of each river in their list. Mail order.

Yorkshire Fine Wines **YFW**
Nun Monkton, York YO5 8ES (0901) 30131
Champagnes in different sizes and a fine range of claret. Mail order, one case minimum.

Regional Directory

London

Les Amis du Vin	**LADV**
Cynthia Bacon	**CB**
Balls Brothers	**BAL**
Berkmann Wine Cellars	**BWC**
Berry Bros & Rudd	**BBR**
Bibendum	**BIB**
Bow Wine Vaults	**BOW**
Caves de la Madeleine	**CDM**
Henry C. Collison	**COL**
Corney & Barow	**C&B**
W. H. Cullen	**CUL**
J. T. Davies & Sons	**DAV**
Dolamore	**DOL**
Domaine Direct	**DDIR**
Peter Dominic	**PD**
Ebury Chatham & Dover	**ECD**
Ehrmanns	**EHR**
Ellis Son & Vidler	**ESV**
Findlater Mackie Todd	**FINT**
John Harvey & Sons	**JH**
Haynes Hanson & Clark	**HHC**
Hedges & Butler	**H&B**
Justerini & Brooks	**J&B**
O. W. Loeb & Co	**OWL**
Lorne House Vintners	**LHV**
Marks & Spencer	**M&S**
Mackie & Co	**MACK**
Malmaison Wine Club	**MAL**
The Market	**MART**
J. Moreno Wines	**JMW**
Oddbins	**ODD**
Arthur Rackham's Wine Shops	**RACK**
La Réserve	**RSV**
Sainsbury's	**SAIN**
Sunday Times Wine Club	**STWC**
Tesco's	**TES**
Threshers	**THRE**
Unwins	**UNW**
Victoria Wine Co	**VICT**
La Vigneronne	**VIGN**
The Vintner	see **RACK**
Waitrose	**WAIT**
House of Wilkins	**HW**
Wine Growers Association	**WGA**
The Wine Society	**WSOC**
Wine Studio	**STUD**
Wineland	see **RACK**
The Winery	**WNRY**

Southeast and Home Counties

Cynthia Bacon	**CB**
Chaplin & Son	**CHAP**
W. H. Cullen	**CUL**
Peter Dominic	**PD**
Gerard Harris	**GH**
High Breck Vintners	**HBV**
The Hungerford Wine Co	**HUN**
Imbibers Wines	**IMB**
Marks & Spencers	**M&S**
Oddbins	**ODD**
Arthur Rackham's Wine Shops	**RACK**
Seymour Ramsay	**SR**
Sainsbury's	**SAIN**
Stapylton Fletcher	**SF**
Stonehaven Wines	**STON**
Tesco's	**TES**
Threshers	**THRE**
Henry Townsend	**HT**
Unwins	**UNW**
Victoria Wine Co	**VICT**
Waitrose	**WAIT**
Wine Growers Association	**WGA**

Southwest

Averys	**AV**
Peter Dominic	**PD**
John Harvey & Sons	**JH**
Richard Harvey Wines	**RH**
Hicks & Don	**H&D**
Laymont & Shaw	**L&S**
Marks & Spencer	**M&S**
Oddbins	**ODD**
Christopher Piper Wines	**PIP**
Reid Wines	**REID**
Sainsbury's	**SAIN**
Sherston Wine Co	**SW**
Tesco's	**TES**
Threshers	**THRE**
Victoria Wine Co	**VICT**
Windrush Wines	**WW**
Yapp Brothers	**YAPP**

East Anglia

Adnams	**ADN**
Chesterford Vintners	**CV**
Dolamore	**DOL**
Peter Dominic	**PD**
Roger Harris	**RGHR**
Hicks & Don	**H&D**
Lay & Wheeler	**L&W**
Marks & Spencer	**M&S**
Oddbins	**ODD**
Peatling & Cawdron	**P&C**
Sainsbury's	**SAIN**
T&W Wines	**T&W**
Tesco's	**TES**
Threshers	**THRE**
Victoria Wine Co	**VICT**
Waitrose	**WAIT**
Wine Growers Association	**WGA**

Midlands

Arriba Kettle & Co	**A&K**
Dolamore	**DOL**
Peter Dominic	**PD**
Farthinghoe Fine Wines	**FFW**
Marks & Spencer	**M&S**
Oddbins	**ODD**
Sainsbury's	**SAIN**

Continued on p.412

Tanners of Shrewsbury	**TAN**
Tesco's	**TES**
Threshers	**THRE**
Victoria Wine Co	**VICT**
Waitrose	**WAIT**

North

T. F. Ashe & Nephew	**ASHE**
D. Byrne & Co	**BYR**
Peter Dominic	**PD**
George Dutton & Son **see**	**WILL**
Richard Granger	**RG**
Manor Wine Shpp	**MWS**
Marks & Spencer	**M&S**
Oddbins	**ODD**
Quellyn Roberts	**QR**
Sainsbury's	**SAIN**
Tesco's	**TES**
Threshers	**THRE**
Victoria Wine Co	**VICT**
Waitrose	**WAIT**
Willoughby's	**WILL**
Yorkshire Fine Wines	**YFW**

Scotland

Peter Dominic	**PD**
Peter Green	**PG**
Justerini & Brooks	**J&B**
Marks & Spencer	**M&S**
Oddbins	**ODD**
Tesco's	**TES**
Threshers	**THRE**

Wales

Peter Dominic	**PD**
Marks & Spencer	**M&S**
Oddbins	**ODD**
Sainsbury's	**SAIN**
Tanners	**TAN**
Tesco's	**TES**
Threshers	**THRE**
Victoria Wine Co	**VICT**

Notes

Notes

Notes

Notes

Notes